Practical Argument
A Text and Anthology

Laurie G. Kirszner
University of the Sciences

Stephen R. Mandell
Drexel University

Bedford/St. Martin's
Boston ■ New York

For Bedford/St. Martin's

Executive Editor: John E. Sullivan III
Production Editor: Peter Jacoby
Production Supervisor: Jennifer Peterson
Marketing Manager: Molly Parke
Editorial Assistants: Alicia Young, Shannon Walsh
Art Director: Lucy Krikorian
Text Design: Jerilyn Bockorick
Copy Editor: Rosemary Winfield
Indexer: Melanie Belkin
Photo Research: Rachel Youdelman
Cover Design: Billy Boardman
Cover Art: Comparison of a plastic water bottle and an alternative, a reusable stainless steel water bottle. © Valery Rizzo/Getty Images
Composition: Nesbitt Graphics, Inc.
Printing and Binding: RR Donnelley and Sons

President: Joan E. Feinberg
Editorial Director: Denise B. Wydra
Editor in Chief: Karen S. Henry
Director of Marketing: Karen R. Soeltz
Director of Production: Susan W. Brown
Associate Director, Editorial Production: Elise S. Kaiser
Managing Editor: Shuli Traub

Library of Congress Control Number: 2010928031

Manufactured in the United States of America.

5 4 3 2 1
f e d

For information, write: Bedford/St. Martin's, 75 Arlington Street,
Boston, MA 02116   (617-399-4000)

ISBN-10: 0-312-57092-9
ISBN-13: 978-0-312-57092-7

In recent years, more and more college composition programs have integrated the teaching of argumentation into their first-year writing sequence, and there are good reasons for this. Argumentation is central to academic as well as to public discourse, so students who are skilled at argumentation are able to participate in the dynamic, ongoing discussions that take place both in their classrooms and in their communities. Clearly, argumentation teaches valuable critical-thinking skills that are necessary for academic success as well as for survival in today's media-driven society.

What has both surprised and troubled us as teachers, however, is that college argument texts are simply too difficult. Frequently, a divide exists between the pedagogy of these texts and students' ability to understand it. In many cases, technical terminology and excessively abstract discussions create confusion instead of clarity. The result is that students' worst fears are realized: instead of feeling that they are part of a discourse community, they see themselves as outsiders who will never be able to understand, let alone use, the principles of argumentation.

Because we know that students struggle to master important principles of argumentative thinking and writing, we drew on our years of classroom experience to create a book that is both different and innovative. *Practical Argument: A Text and Anthology* is a straightforward, accessible, and visually stimulating introduction to argumentative writing that explains concepts in understandable, everyday language and illustrates them with examples that actually mean something to students. *Practical Argument* is meant to be an alternative for instructors who see currently available argument texts as too big, too complicated, and too intimidating for their students. Its goal is to demystify the study of argument. Thus, *Practical Argument* focuses on the things that students actually need to know, omitting the confusing, overly technical concepts they often struggle with. For example, *Practical Argument* emphasizes the basic principles of classical argument and downplays the more complex Toulmin logic, treating it as simply an alternative way of envisioning argument.

Practical Argument works because it is "practical"; it helps students to make connections between what they learn in the classroom and what they experience in their lives outside of it. As they do so, they become comfortable with the rhetorical skills that are central to effective argumentation. We believe there's no other book like it.

Organization

Practical Argument is both a text and a reader, and it includes in one book everything students and instructors need for an argument course.

- **Part 1, Understanding Argument,** discusses the role of argument in everyday life, explains the value of studying argument, presents definitions of what argument is not and is, the means of persuasion (appeals to logic, emotion, and authority), and explains the basic elements of argument (thesis, evidence, refutation, and concluding statement).

- **Part 2, Reading and Responding to Arguments,** explains and illustrates critical thinking and reading; visual argument; writing a rhetorical analysis; logic and fallacies; and Rogerian, Toulmin, and oral argument.

- **Part 3, Writing an Argumentative Essay,** discusses and illustrates the process of planning, drafting, and revising an argumentative essay.

- **Part 4, Using Sources to Support Your Argument,** covers evaluating print and Internet sources; summarizing, paraphrasing, quoting, and synthesizing sources; documenting sources in MLA style; and avoiding plagiarism.

- **Part 5, Patterns and Purposes,** explains and illustrates some of the most common kinds of arguments: argument by definition, causal argument, evaluation argument, proposal argument, argument by analogy, and ethical argument.

- **Part 6, Debates, Casebooks, and Classic Arguments,** includes both contemporary and classic arguments. The contemporary arguments are arranged in five pro-con debates and five in-depth casebooks on issues such as the rights of the homeless and the place of gays in the military. The nine classic arguments include well-known pieces by writers such as Jonathan Swift, Martin Luther King Jr., and Rachel Carson.

Finally, Appendix A provides instruction on writing literary arguments, and Appendix B covers APA documentation style.

Key Features

Concise in a Thoughtful Way

Practical Argument covers everything students need to know about argument but doesn't overwhelm them. It limits technical vocabulary to what students and instructors actually require to understand and discuss important concepts in argument and argumentative writing. In short, *Practical Argument* is argument made accessible.

Argument Step by Step, Supported by Helpful Apparatus

Practical Argument takes students through a step-by-step process of reading and responding to others' arguments and writing, revising, and editing their own arguments. The book uses a classroom-tested, exercise-driven approach that encourages students to participate actively in their own learning process. Chapters progress in a clear, easy-to-understand sequence: students are asked to read arguments, to identify their key elements, and to develop a response to an issue in the form of a complete, documented argumentative essay based on in-book focused research.

Exercises and writing assignments for each selection provide guidance for students as they work toward creating a finished piece of writing. Throughout the text, checklists, grammar-in-context and summary boxes, and source and gloss notes provide support. In addition, a dozen unique argument templates—located in the end-of-chapter exercises—provide structures students can use for guidance as they write arguments by definition, causal arguments, evaluation arguments, proposals, arguments by analogy, ethical arguments, and so on.

Thematically Focused Approach with Compelling Chapter Topics

Students learn best when they care about and are engaged in an issue. *Practical Argument* uses readings and assignments to help students learn argumentation in the context of one high-interest contemporary issue per chapter. These topics include "green" campuses, student credit cards, and campus safety—issues that have real meaning in students' lives.

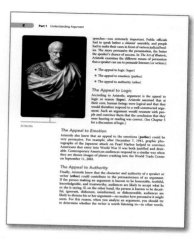

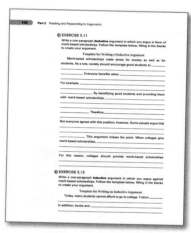

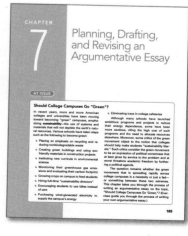

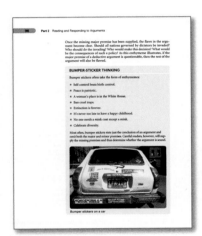

Readings on Relevant and Interesting Issues

Ninety-two accessible, professional readings—on issues that students will want to read about and debate—are included in the text, with numerous selections from college newspapers and blogs introducing authentic student voices into the text. Topics range from issues that students will want to read about and debate, to real-world plagiarism, to the merits of lowering the drinking age. Many visual selections appear throughout in conjunction with textual readings. Eighteen sample student essays (more than in any other argument book), including complete MLA and APA research papers, provide realistic models for student writers as well as more student voices. (Many of these student essays include helpful annotations.) An additional thirty selections are organized as debates and casebooks, on questions such as whether newspapers are obsolete and whether everyone should have the right to go to college. A collection of nine classic arguments offers more challenging approaches to enduring issues.

Open and Inviting Full-Color Design

The fresh, contemporary look of *Practical Argument* will engage students. This open, colorful design eliminates the sea of dense type that is typical of many other argument books. Over a hundred photographs and other visuals—such as ads, graphic-novel excerpts, cartoons, realia, templates, charts and graphs, Web pages, and fine art—provide appealing, real-world examples. The use of open space and numerous images not only reinforces the currency of the book's themes but also creates an inviting and visually stimulating format that will appeal to students.

Extensive Support for Students and Instructors

You Get More Digital Choices for Practical Argument

Practical Argument doesn't stop with a book. Online, you'll find both free and affordable premium resources to help students get even more out of the print text and your course. You'll also find convenient instructor resources, such as downloadable sample syllabi, classroom activities, and even access to a nationwide community of teachers. To learn more about or order any of the products below, contact your Bedford/St. Martin's sales representative, email sales support (sales_support@bfwpub.com), or visit the Web site at bedfordstmartins.com/practicalargument.

Student Resources   Send students to free resources, upgrade to an expanding collection of innovative digital content, or package a free stand-alone CD-ROM with *Practical Argument*.

Re:Writing, the best free collection of online resources for the writing class, offers clear advice on citing sources in *Research and Documentation Online* by Diana Hacker, thirty sample papers and designed documents, and over 9,000 writing and grammar exercises with immediate feedback and reporting in *Exercise Central*. Updated and redesigned, *Re:Writing* also features five free videos from *VideoCentral* and three new visual tutorials from our popular *ix: visual exercises* by Cheryl Ball and Kristin Arola. *Re:Writing* is free and open (no codes required) to ensure access to all students. Visit bedfordstmartins.com/rewriting.

VideoCentral: English is a growing collection of videos for the writing class that captures real-world, academic, and student writers talking about how and why they write. Writer and teacher Peter Berkow interviewed hundreds of people—from Michael Moore to Cynthia Selfe—to produce fifty brief videos about topics such as revising and getting feedback. *VideoCentral: English* can be packaged with *Practical Argument* at a significant discount. (An activation code is required.) To learn more, visit bedfordstmartins.com/videocentral. To order *VideoCentral* packaged with the print book, use ISBN-10 0-312-65407-3 or ISBN-13 978-0-312-65407-8.

Re:Writing Plus gathers all of Bedford/St. Martin's premium digital content for composition into one online collection. It includes hundreds of model documents, the first-ever peer-review game, and *VideoCentral*. *Re:Writing Plus* can be purchased separately or packaged with the print book at a significant discount. (An activation code is required.) To learn more, visit bedfordstmartins.com/rewriting. To order *Re:Writing Plus* packaged with the print book, use ISBN-10 0-312-65411-1 or ISBN-13 978-0-312-65411-5.

i·series on CD-ROM presents multimedia tutorials in a flexible format. To learn more, visit bedfordstmartins.com/practicalargument.

- *ix: visual exercises* helps students with key rhetorical and visual concepts. To order *ix: visual exercises* packaged with the print book, use ISBN-10 0-312-65410-3 or ISBN-13 978-0-312-65410-8.

- *i·claim: visualizing argument* offers a new way to see argument—with six tutorials, an illustrated glossary, and over seventy multimedia arguments. To order *i·claim: visualizing argument* packaged with the print book, use ISBN-10 0-312-65409-X or ISBN-13 978-0-312-65409-2.

- *i·cite: visualizing sources* brings research to life through an animated introduction, four tutorials, and hands-on source practice. To order *i·cite: visualizing sources* packaged with the print book, use ISBN-10 0-312-65408-1 or ISBN-13 978-0-312-65408-5.

Instructor Resources   You have a lot to do in your course. Bedford/St. Martin's wants to make it easy for you to find the support you need. To learn about everything that is available with *Practical Argument*, visit bedfordstmartins.com/practicalargument.

Resources for Teaching Practical Argument provides not only sample syllabi for semester and quarter-system courses, chapter overviews, summaries of all the selections, suggested student responses, and teaching tips, but also additional suggestions for classroom activities.

TeachingCentral offers instructors the entire list of Bedford/St. Martin's print and online professional resources in one place. You'll find landmark reference works, sourcebooks on pedagogical issues, award-winning collections, and practical advice for the classroom—all free.

Bits collects creative ideas for teaching a range of composition topics in an easily searchable blog. A community of teachers—leading scholars, authors, and editors—discusses revision, research, grammar and style, technology, peer review, and much more. Take, use, adapt, and pass the ideas around. Then, come back to the site to comment or share your own suggestion. See blogs.bedfordstmartins.com/bits.

Content cartridges for the most common course management systems—Blackboard, WebCT, Angel, and Desire2Learn—allow you to easily download digital materials from Bedford/St. Martin's for your course.

Acknowledgments

The following reviewers examined the manuscript and gave us valuable feedback: Heidi E. Ajrami, Victoria College; Sonja Andrus, Collin College; Joseph E. Argent, Gaston College; Jerry Ball, Arkansas State University; Christine Berni, Austin Community College; Mary Cantrell, Tulsa Community College; Irene Clark, California State University–Northridge; Cathy A. D'Agostino, New Trier Township High School; Sidney Dobrin, University of Florida; MacGregor Frank, Guilford Technical Community College; David Gruber, North Carolina State University; Joseph Haske, South Texas College; Ann Jagoe, North Central Texas College; Loretta McBride, Southwest Tennessee Community College; Susan Miller-Cochran, North Carolina State University; Susan O'Neal, Tulsa Community College; Brian Reed, Langston University; Sylvia Ross, Tidewater Community College; John Schaffer, Blinn College; Ann Spurlock,

Mississippi State University; Mary Stahoviak-Hall, Victoria College; John Williamson, Highlands High School; and our anonymous reviewer from American River College. We are grateful for their help.

We thank Mark Gallaher, Sara Gaunt, Karin Paque, John Sisson, Jessica Carroll, Ester Bloom, Jeff Ousborne, Courtney Novosat, Barbara Fister, and Cara Snider for their assistance.

At Bedford/St. Martin's, Joan Feinberg, Denise Wydra, Karen Henry, Steve Scipione, Leasa Burton, and John Sullivan were involved and supportive from the start of the project. John, in particular, helped us shape this project and was with us every step of the way with encouragement and valuable advice. It's been a genuine pleasure working with him. Alicia Young and Shannon Walsh were an important part of our team, helping with many details. Peter Jacoby, production editor, patiently and efficiently shepherded the book through the production process, along with Shuli Traub. Others who made valuable contributions were Jerilyn Bockorick, Anna Palchik, and Lucy Krikorian, who developed the design; Karita dos Santos and Molly Parke, who were instrumental in marketing the book; Rosemary Winfield and Fran Weinberg, who expertly copyedited the manuscript; Rachel Youdelman, who found art and obtained permission; and Sue Brekka and Sandy Schechter, who handled text permisssions. We are grateful for their help.

Finally, we would like to thank each other for lunches past—and for many, many lunches to come.

Laurie G. Kirszner
Stephen R. Mandell

BRIEF CONTENTS

CONTENTS

PART
4 Using Sources to Support Your Argument   217

8 Evaluating Sources   219

PART

5 Patterns and Purposes   313

12 Argument by Definition   315

13 Causal Argument 353

PART

6 Debates, Casebooks, and Classic Arguments   519

DEBATES

18   Should We Eat Meat?   521

1

Understanding Argument

Understanding Argument

Encountering Arguments

Arguments are everywhere. Whenever you turn on the television, read a newspaper or magazine, talk to friends and family, enter an online discussion, or engage in a debate in one of your classes, you encounter arguments. In fact, it is fair to say that much of the interaction that takes place in society involves argument. Consider, for example, a lawyer who tries to persuade a jury that his or her client is innocent, a doctor who wants to convince a patient to undergo a specific form of treatment, a lawmaker who wants to propose a piece of legislation, an executive who wants to institute a specific policy, an activist who wants to pursue a particular social agenda, a parent who wants to convince a child to study harder, a worker who wants to propose a more efficient way of carrying out a particular task, an employee who thinks that he or she deserves a raise, or a person who is writing a job application letter: all of these people are engaging in argument. Because argument is so widespread, the better your arguing skills, the better able you will be to function not just in school but also in the wider world.

In college, you encounter arguments on a daily basis; in fact, both class discussions and academic writing often take the form of argument. Consider, for example, the following questions that might be debated (and written about) in a first-year writing class:

- Do the benefits of bottled water outweigh the costs?
- Should college campuses go "green"?
- Is *Wikipedia* a legitimate research source?
- Should credit card companies be permitted to target college students?
- How far should colleges go to keep campuses safe?
- Is distance learning as effective as classroom instruction?

What these questions have in common is that they all call for argumentation. To answer these questions, students would be expected to state their opinions and support them.

WHY INSTRUCTORS ASSIGN ARGUMENT

Instructors assign argumentative essays for a number of reasons. Here are just a few:

- To encourage students to develop and defend a position on a topic
- To help students learn to look closely at their own and other people's ideas
- To give students the tools they need to convince others of the validity of their ideas
- To help students learn to mediate or resolve conflicting points of view

World War I propaganda poster (1917)

Defining Argument

Now for the obvious question: exactly what is an argument? Perhaps the best way to begin is by explaining what argument is *not*. An argument (at least an academic argument) is not a **quarrel**. The object of argument is not to attack someone who disagrees with you or to beat an opponent into submission. For this reason, the shouting matches that you routinely see on television or hear on talk radio are not really arguments. Argument is also not **spin**—the positive or biased slant that politicians routinely put on facts—or **propaganda**—information (or misinformation) that is spread to support a particular viewpoint. Finally, argument is not just a contradiction or denial of someone else's position. Even if you establish that an opponent's position is wrong, you still have to establish that your own position has merit by presenting evidence to support it.

There is a basic difference between **formal arguments**—those that you develop in academic discussion and writing—and **informal arguments**—those that occur in daily life, where people often get into arguments about politics, sports, social issues, and personal relationships. These everyday disputes are often just verbal fights in which one person tries to outshout another. Although they sometimes include facts, they tend to rely primarily on emotion and unsupported opinions. Moreover, such everyday arguments do not have the formal structure of academic arguments: they do not establish a logical link between a particular viewpoint and reliable supporting evidence. Moreover, there is no real effort to address opposing arguments. In general, these arguments tend to be disorganized, emotional disputes that have more to do with criticizing an opponent than with advancing and supporting a position on an issue. Although such informal arguments can serve as starting points for helping you think about issues, they do not have the structure or the intellectual rigor of formal arguments.

So exactly what is an argument? An **argument** takes a stand and presents evidence that helps to convince people to accept the writer's position. Keep in mind that arguments make statements with which reasonable people may disagree. For this reason, an argument never actually proves anything. (If it did, there would be no argument.) The best an argument can do is convince other people to accept (or at least acknowledge) the validity of a position.

An academic argument is not a fight.

WHAT KINDS OF STATEMENTS ARE NOT DEBATABLE?

To be suitable for argument, a statement must be **debatable**: in other words, there must be conflicting opinions or conflicting facts that call the validity of the statement into question. For this reason, the following types of statements are generally *not* suitable for argument:

(*continued*)

(*continued*)

- **Statements of fact:** A statement of fact can be verified by research, so it is not debatable. For example, there is no point in arguing that your school makes instructors' lectures available as podcasts. This is a question of fact that can easily be checked. You can, however, argue that making instructors' lectures available as podcasts would (or would not) enhance education at your school. This is a debatable statement that can be supported by facts and examples.

- **Statements of personal preference or taste:** Expressions of personal preference or taste are not suitable for argument. For example, if you say that you don't like the taste of diet soft drinks, no one can legitimately argue that you are wrong. This statement is beyond dispute because it is a matter of personal taste. You could, however, argue that diet soft drinks should not be sold in school cafeterias because they contribute to obesity. To support this claim, you would supply evidence—facts, statistics, and expert opinion—to establish that your position is reasonable.

Note: Unsupported expressions of religious faith or belief, or other statements that express strongly held personal convictions, are often problematic for argument. You may believe such statements are self-evident, but they may not be self-evident to your audience.

Statement of personal conviction: Because my religious beliefs hold that the commandment not to kill should be taken literally, it is clear that the death penalty should be abolished.

Revised: Because it violates the Constitution's guarantee of equal protection under the law, it is clear that the death penalty should be abolished.

It is a mistake to think that all arguments have just two sides—one right side and one wrong side. In fact, most arguments that you encounter in college focus on issues that are quite complex. For example, if you were considering the question of whether the United States should ban torture, you could certainly answer this question with a yes or a no, but this would be an oversimplification. To thoroughly examine the issue, you would have to consider it from a number of angles:

- Should torture be banned in all situations?

- Should torture be used to elicit information that could prevent an imminent attack?

- What actually constitutes torture? For example, is sleep deprivation torture? What about a slap on the face? Loud music? A cold cell? Is more intense interrogation—such as waterboarding—torture?

- Who should have the legal right to approve interrogation techniques?

If you were going to write an argument about this issue, you would have to take a position that adequately represented its complex nature—for example, "It is easy to be against torture, but problems begin when we begin to ask exactly what constitutes torture." To do otherwise would be to commit the **either/or fallacy** (see p. 116)—to offer only two choices when there are actually many others.

Protest against waterboarding

Logos, Pathos, and *Ethos*

To be effective, an argument has to be persuasive. **Persuasion** is a general term that refers to how a speaker or writer influences an audience to adopt a particular belief or to follow a specific course of action.

In the fifth century BCE, the philosopher Aristotle considered the issue of persuasion. Because ancient Greece was primarily an oral culture (as opposed to written or print culture), persuasion—in the form of persuasive

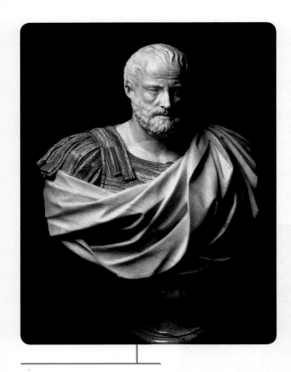

Aristotle

speeches—was extremely important. Public officials had to speak before a citizens' assembly, and people had to make their cases in front of various judicial bodies. The more persuasive the presentation, the better the speaker's chance of success. In *The Art of Rhetoric*, Aristotle examines the different means of persuasion that a speaker can use to persuade listeners (or writers):

- The appeal to logic (*logos*)
- The appeal to emotion (*pathos*)
- The appeal to authority (*ethos*)

The Appeal to Logic

According to Aristotle, argument is the appeal to logic or reason (**logos**). Aristotle assumed that at their core, human beings were logical and that they would therefore respond to a well-constructed argument. Such an argument would resonate with people and convince them that the conclusion that they were hearing or reading was correct. (See Chapter 5 for a discussion of logic.)

The Appeal to Emotion

Aristotle also knew that an appeal to the emotions (**pathos**) could be very persuasive. For example, after December 7, 1941, graphic photographs of the Japanese attack on Pearl Harbor helped to convince Americans that entry into World War II was both justified and desirable. Contemporary American audiences respond in a similar way when they are shown images of planes crashing into the World Trade Center on September 11, 2001.

The Appeal to Authority

Finally, Aristotle knew that the character and authority of a speaker or writer (**ethos**) could contribute to the persuasiveness of an argument. If the person making an argument is known to be honorable, truthful, knowledgeable, and trustworthy, audiences are likely to accept what he or she is saying. If, on the other hand, the person is known to be deceitful, ignorant, dishonest, uninformed, or dishonorable, audiences are likely to dismiss his or her argument—no matter how persuasive it might seem. For this reason, when you analyze an argument, you should try to determine whether the writer is worth listening to—in other words,

Pearl Harbor attack
(December 7, 1941)

whether the writer has **credibility**. You can do this by asking the following questions:

- Does the writer demonstrate knowledge of the subject?
- Does the writer maintain a reasonable tone?
- What steps does the writer take to present himself or herself as a reasonable person?
- Does the writer seem fair?

In the chapters that follow, you will learn to use these appeals to help you construct effective arguments in the classroom and beyond.

CHAPTER

1

The Structure of Argument

AT ISSUE

Do the Benefits of Bottled Water Outweigh the Costs?

Bottled water has become a popular accessory in recent years, making an appearance at the gym, on the hiking trail, and in the hands of numerous actors and supermodels. Bottled water is clean and convenient, but it is also expensive: a gallon of premium bottled water costs more than a gallon of gas. Many people question whether bottled water is really necessary in countries whose water supply is both safe and abundant. Even more important, they ask whether the production of bottled water, as well as the disposal of the bottles and other packaging material, actually threatens our environment.

Later in this chapter, you will be introduced to essays and visuals that highlight the pros and cons of bottled water, and you will be asked to write an argumentative essay in which you take a position on this controversial topic.

In a sense, you already know a lot more than you think you do about how to construct an argumentative essay. After all, an argumentative essay is a variation of the thesis-and-support essays that you have been writing in your college classes: you state a position on a topic, and then you support this position. However, argumentative essays also require some special strategies in terms of structure, style, and purpose. Throughout this book, we introduce you to the unique features of argument. In this chapter, we focus on structure.

The Pillars of Argument

In basic terms, an argumentative essay includes the same three sections—*introduction*, *body*, and *conclusion*—as any other essay. In an argumentative essay, however, the introduction includes an argumentative *thesis statement*, the body includes both the *evidence* (material that supports the thesis) and the *refutation* of opposing arguments, and the conclusion includes a strong, convincing *concluding statement* that reinforces the position stated in the thesis.

The following diagram illustrates one way to organize an argumentative essay:

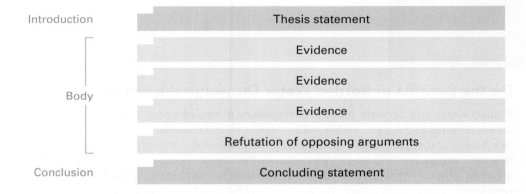

Introduction	Thesis statement
Body	Evidence
	Evidence
	Evidence
	Refutation of opposing arguments
Conclusion	Concluding statement

The elements of an argumentative essay are like the pillars of an ancient Greek temple. Together, the four elements—thesis statement, evidence, refutation of opposing arguments, and concluding statement—help you build a strong argument.

Ancient Greek temple

Thesis Statement

A **thesis statement** in an argumentative essay is a single sentence that states your position on an issue. An argumentative essay must have an argumentative thesis—one that takes a firm stand on a debatable issue. For example, on the issue of whether colleges should require all students to study a language other than English, your thesis statement could be any of the following:

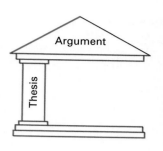

- Colleges should require all students to study a foreign language.

- Colleges should require all liberal arts majors to study a foreign language.

- Colleges should require all students to take Spanish, Chinese, or Farsi.

- Colleges should not require any students to study a foreign language.

Other positions are also possible. (For more on thesis statements, see Chapter 7.)

Evidence

Evidence is the material—facts, observations, expert opinion, examples, or statistics—that supports your thesis statement. For example, you might support your position that foreign-language study should be required for all college students by arguing that this requirement will make them more employable, and you could cite employment statistics to support this point. You might also use the opinion of an expert on the topic— for example, an experienced college language instructor—to support the opposite position, arguing that students without an interest in language study are wasting their time in such courses.

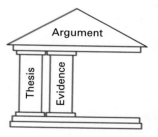

Refutation

Because every argument has more than one side, you should always assume that your readers are skeptical—that they must be convinced. For this reason, you should be prepared to acknowledge and then **refute** (argue against) points that they may make to challenge your argument, showing them to be false or incorrect. For example, if you favor requiring foreign-language study for all students, you should understand that some readers may think college students already have to take too many required courses. After acknowledging this point, you could refute it by suggesting that a required foreign-language course could replace another, less important course. (For more on refutation, see Chapter 7.)

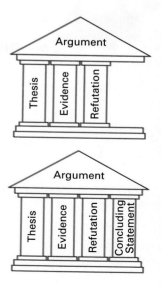

Concluding Statement

After you have provided convincing support for your position and refuted opposing arguments, you should leave your readers with a strong **concluding statement** that reinforces your position. (The position you want them to remember is the one stated in your thesis, not the ones you have refuted.) For example, you might conclude an essay in support of a foreign-language requirement by making a specific recommendation or by predicting the possible negative outcome of *not* implementing this requirement.

CHECKLIST

Does Your Argument Stand Up?

When you write an argumentative essay, check to make sure it includes all four of the elements that you need to build a strong argument:

☐ Do you have an argumentative **thesis**?

☐ Do you include solid, convincing **evidence** to support your thesis?

☐ Do you include a **refutation** of arguments against your position?

☐ Do you include a strong **concluding statement**?

The following student essay includes all four of the elements that are needed to build a convincing argument.

WHY FOREIGN-LANGUAGE STUDY SHOULD BE REQUIRED

NIA TUCKSON

Introduction

"What do you call someone who speaks three languages? Trilingual. 1 What do you call someone who speaks two languages? Bilingual. What do you call someone who speaks only one language? American." As this old joke illustrates, many Americans are unable to communicate in a language other than English. Given our global economy and American companies' need to conduct business with other countries, this problem needs to be

Thesis statement

addressed. A good first step is to require all college students to study a foreign language.

Evidence: First point in support of thesis

After graduation, many students will work in fields in which 2 speaking (or reading) another language will be useful or even necessary.

For example, healthcare professionals will often be called on to communicate with patients who do not speak English; in fact, a patient's life may depend on their ability to do so. Those who work in business and finance may need to speak Mandarin or Japanese; those who have positions in the military or in the foreign service may need to speak Persian or Arabic. A working knowledge of one of these languages can help students succeed in their future careers, and it can also make them more employable.

3   In addition to strengthening a résumé, foreign-language study can also give students an understanding of another culture's history, art, and literature. Although such knowledge may never be "useful" in a student's career, it can certainly enrich the student's life. Too narrow a focus on career can turn college into a place that trains students rather than educates them. In contrast, expanding students' horizons to include subjects beyond those needed for their careers can better equip them to be lifelong learners.

Evidence: Second point in support of thesis

4   When they travel abroad, Americans who can speak a language other than English will find that they are better able to understand people from other countries. As informal ambassadors for the United States, tourists have a responsibility to try to understand other languages and cultures. Too many Americans assume that their own country's language and culture are superior to all others. This shortsighted attitude is not likely to strengthen relationships between the United States and other nations. Understanding a country's language can help students to build bridges between themselves and others.

Evidence: Third point in support of thesis

5   Some students say that learning a language is not easy and that it takes a great deal of time. College students are already overloaded with coursework, jobs, and family responsibilities, and a new academic requirement is certain to create problems. In fact, students may find that adding just six credits of language study will limit their opportunities to take advanced courses in their majors or to enroll in electives that interest them. However, this burden can be eased if other, less important course requirements—such as physical education—are eliminated to make room for the new requirement.

First opposing argument

Refutation

6   Some students may also argue that they, not their school, should be able to decide what courses are most important to them. After all, a student

Second opposing argument

Refutation

who struggled in high school French and plans to major in computer science might understandably resist a foreign-language requirement. However, challenging college language courses might actually be more rewarding than high school courses were, and the student who struggled in high school French might actually enjoy a college-level French course (or take another language). Finally, a student who plans to major in computer science may actually wind up majoring in something completely different— or taking a job in a country in which English is not spoken.

Conclusion

Entering college students sometimes find it hard to envision their   7
personal or professional futures or to imagine where their lives may take them. Still, a well-rounded education, including foreign language, can prepare them for many of the challenges that they will face. Colleges can help students keep their options open by requiring at least a year (and preferably two years) of foreign-language study. Instead of focusing narrowly on what interests them today, American college

Concluding statement

students should take the extra step to become bilingual—or even trilingual—in the future.

◉ EXERCISE 1.1

The following essay, "An Immigrant Writes," by Arnold Schwarzenegger— champion body builder, movie star, and governor of California—includes all the basic elements of argument discussed so far. Read the essay, and then answer the questions that follow it, consulting the diagram on page 12 if necessary.

This editorial appeared in the *Wall Street Journal* on April 10, 2006.

AN IMMIGRANT WRITES
ARNOLD SCHWARZENEGGER

President Reagan memorably described his "shining city on a hill" as a place 1
that "hummed with commerce and creativity, and if there had to be city walls, the walls had doors and the doors were open to anyone with the will and the heart to get here." Perhaps because he'd been a border state governor, Reagan understood the challenges and the opportunities presented by immigration. He believed, as I do, that we can have an immigration policy that both strengthens our borders and welcomes immigrants.

2   Immigration is not just a theory debated on talk shows and on Capitol Hill; in California, it's a reality that we live with every day in our schools, hospitals and workplaces. When Congress returns from its Easter recess, it must immediately address immigration reform again. I urge Congress to remember that immigrants are good people; but our current immigration system is bad policy. We need a new law.

3   Already we hear so much talk about so many false choices. We are told that in a free society it's not possible to have border security. We are advised that in order to secure the borders, we must deport 12 million people. Never mind that we don't know who they are or where they are, and that it could cost up to $230 billion to do it.

4   I reject these false choices, and Congress should too. I salute the members of both parties in Congress who are conducting a civil, serious discussion on this issue. I urge them to agree on legislation based on a simple philosophy: control of the border . . . and compassion for the immigrant. These are the twin pillars around which

> "I reject these false choices."

we must construct a new immigration policy. They are both essential elements in our overall immigration strategy. Without both, our strategy is destined to collapse.

5   To pursue a policy of stronger borders, Congress must get serious about our security. Before 9/11, we gambled that everyone entering our country had good intentions. After 9/11, we cannot afford to take that chance again. A stronger border means more border patrol agents, better equipment and greater resources. We cannot ask state and local officials to bear the cost and responsibility of enforcing federal immigration laws. They are not trained or equipped to do it. The presence of the citizens' groups along our border is a reminder of the federal government's failure to do its job. Government officials, not private citizens, are responsible for our borders. They need to do it right—and to do it right now.

6   A stronger border also requires real solutions, not soundbites or symbolic gestures. Building a wall sounds good and a fence may do some good in certain places. But every wall can be scaled with a ladder. Brick walls and chain link fences will not stop the desires and dreams of a father who is desperate to feed his family. And making it a felony to cross the border crosses the line into pure politics. Instead, we need to bring the 12 million undocumented workers out of the shadows and into the light. I support a temporary worker program to allow American businesses to hire foreign workers when no one else will do the job. How ironic it is to hear some of the same voices who complain about the outsourcing of jobs also complain about the use of immigrant workers here in America.

7   Still, we can do more to address the root of immigration. That's why President Clinton was right to help stabilize Mexico's economy in the '90s, and why President Bush is right today to propose a free trade zone° throughout the Americas. By fostering economic growth in other countries, we foster greater security in our own.

An area of international trade that is designed to keep taxes and other costs low

To pursue a policy of compassion, Congress must attack the problem, 8 not people. A compassionate immigration policy will fight this battle at the borders, not in our schools and not in our hospitals. Teachers, doctors and charity workers should not have to choose between helping those in need and enforcing the law. A compassionate immigration policy will acknowledge that immigrants are just like us: They're moms and dads looking for work, wanting to provide for their kids. Any measure that punishes charities and individuals who comfort and help immigrants is not only unnecessary, but un-American.

Yes, immigration reform is a difficult issue. But it must be guided by a 9 simple goal: compassion for the immigrant, control of the borders. Congress should not rest until it achieves both.

Identifying the Elements of Argument

1. What is this essay's thesis? Restate it in your own words.

2. List the three arguments that the writer presents as evidence to support his thesis.

3. Summarize the opposing arguments that the writer identifies. Then, summarize the writer's refutations of these arguments.

4. Restate the essay's concluding statement in your own words.

Do the Benefits of Bottled Water Outweigh the Costs?

Reread the At Issue box on page 11, which summarizes questions raised on both sides of this issue. As the following sources illustrate, these questions have no easy answers, and reasonable people may disagree on this controversial topic.

As you read the essays and study the visuals, you will be asked to answer some questions and to complete some simple activities. This work will help you understand both the content and the structure of the selections. When you have finished, you will be ready to write an essay in which you take a position on the topic, "Do the Benefits of Bottled Water Outweigh the Costs?"

SOURCES

 New York Times, "In Praise of Tap Water"

 Zak Moore, "Defying the Nalgene"

 Tom Standage, "Bad to the Last Drop"

 PolandSpring.com, "Poland Spring Water"

 PureWater2Go.com, "Pure Water 2Go"

This unsigned editorial was published on August 1, 2007.

IN PRAISE OF TAP WATER

NEW YORK TIMES

On the streets of New York or Denver or San Mateo this summer, it seems the 1
telltale cap of a water bottle is sticking out of every other satchel. Americans
are increasingly thirsty for what is billed as the healthiest, and often most
expensive, water on the grocery shelf. But this country has some of the best
public water supplies in the world. Instead of consuming four billion gallons
of water a year in individual-sized bottles, we need to start thinking about
what all those bottles are doing to the planet's health.

Here are the hard, dry facts: Yes, drinking water is a good thing, far better 2
than buying soft drinks, or liquid candy, as nutritionists like to call it. And almost
all municipal water in America is so good that nobody needs to import a single
bottle from Italy or France or the Fiji Islands. Meanwhile, if you choose to get
your recommended eight glasses a day from bottled water, you could spend up to
$1,400 annually. The same amount of tap water would cost about 49 cents.

Next, there's the environment. Water bottles, like other containers, are 3
made from natural gas and petroleum. The Earth Policy Institute in Washington
has estimated that it takes about 1.5 million barrels of oil to make the water bottles Americans use each year. That could fuel 100,000 cars a year instead. And,
only about 23 percent of those bottles are recycled, in part because water bottles are often not included in local redemption plans that accept beer and soda
cans. Add in the substantial amount of fuel used in transporting water, which is
extremely heavy, and the impact on the environment is anything but refreshing.

Tap water may now be the equal of bottled water, but that could change. The 4
more the wealthy opt out of drinking tap water, the less political support there
will be for investing in maintaining America's public water supply. That would
be a serious loss. Access to cheap, clean water is basic to the nation's health.

Some local governments have begun to fight back. Earlier this summer, San 5
Francisco Mayor Gavin Newsom pro-
hibited his city's departments and agencies from buying bottled water, noting
that San Francisco water is "some of the
most pristine on the planet." Salt Lake
City has issued a similar decree, and
New York City recently began an advertising campaign that touted its water as
"clean," "zero sugar" and even "stain free."

> "Save money, and save the planet, by . . . turning on the tap."

The real change, though, will come when millions of ordinary consumers 6
realize that they can save money, and save the planet, by turning in their water
bottles and turning on the tap.

AT ISSUE: THE STRUCTURE OF ARGUMENT

1. Restate the editorial's thesis in your own words.

2. List the arguments the writer uses in paragraphs 1–3 to support the thesis.

3. Restate the editorial's concluding statement.

4. Do you think the writer considers enough arguments against his position? Can you think of others? Try to refute each of these opposing arguments.

5. Paragraph 5 does not present arguments in support of or against the writer's position. What is the purpose of this paragraph?

This opinion piece appeared online at *TheDartmouth.com*, the student newspaper of Dartmouth College, on August 17, 2007.

DEFYING THE NALGENE

ZAK MOORE

1 The latest environmental craze is taking hold. We have already been told, inconveniently though perhaps of dubious truthiness, that driving, eating meat, non-local produce, flying, turning the lights on, etc. are bad for the environment. Now we are being told that bottled water is bad for the environment.

2 The most common environmental arguments for eschewing bottled water are based on waste of producing and disposing bottles and inefficiencies in transportation of water bottles. It is also argued that consumers should choose tap water or fountain water because of the high cost and insufficient health benefits of bottled water.

3 These arguments are unconvincing.

4 Waste and transportation are not big problems. The waste of plastic should not be a concern either, because cheap plastic is not hard to come by; if plastic were that valuable then it would not be used to hold water and would cost more money. Ditto for the argument that the disposal of water bottles is filling up landfills: if it is not getting more expensive to put things in them, then there is no problem—such price signals are also a fine argument for privatizing public landfills. Similarly, the low price of water bottles indicates that neither is the cost of transportation of bottled water very high. Also, if we are going to compare all the energy that is used to make and transport bottles we should not assume that tap or fountain water is "free." We have to look at the cost of drainage, piping, electricity, treatment, etc. for fountains and sinks too.

5 An intermediate position suggests that maybe drinking bottled water is acceptable if only people would recycle. While I still do it, I do not understand how recycling can be that valuable. If it were cost effective, bottling companies would buy their bottles back from us for a nickel or a dime. Instead, under most circumstances deposit schemes are mandated by the government—if depositing saved companies money we would not need legislation to force the issue.

6 More pragmatic are arguments that we should stop drinking bottled water based on quality and cost. These days there is even more ammunition since it has come out that Aquafina and Dasani use purified tap water rather than spring water. Well, Aquafina tastes the best to me and not only is it bottled in compliance with various specifications by the government, but there is also the more reassuring market quality control of reputation. When Pepsi or Coke or another firm puts a bottle of water on the market they stand behind it with their multibillion-dollar name. If, for example, chemicals or toxins were found in a major brand of water, they would lose millions due to decreased consumption of their product (not to mention negligence law suits). This is an incentive structure I am comfortable drinking water behind. More importantly, bottled water tastes better and cleaner and that is good enough for me.

7   An argument can also be made that bottled water costs too much. Maybe it is more expensive to buy bottled water than to consume sink water, but the 24-pack of Poland Spring I just bought at Wal-Mart for 4 dollars and change did not set me back too far. Indeed water is cheaper than beer, OJ, milk and just about every other beverage—at least at a supermarket if not at Topside or The Hop.

8   While there are no convincing reasons not to buy bottled water there are quite a few arguments in its favor. One is the alternative of walking around with a Nalgene.° I took the Nalgene approach one summer and maybe it works for other people but mine got dirty and moldy after not too long and the top was not big enough to stick my hand in to clean it. And maybe this is okay for a college student walking around campus with a camping backpack to clip it on to, but for most people a water bottle is much more convenient.

A brand of refillable plastic water bottle

> "For most people a water bottle is much more convenient."

9   More importantly, many places in the world do not have running water, much less clean running water. Water bottlers competing like crazy to meet American demand drives prices down and allows people in these parts of the world to afford water. In the market for medicines and technologies, companies in the developed-world innovate new products for wealthy people who test the first models at higher prices, subsidizing these products for the poor who get them cheaper and better. Why should the market for water be any different? If we stopped buying bottled water, people in undeveloped countries would be badly hurt. Buying that new bottle of water in the morning just might be the most humanitarian thing you do all day.

10   Behind the looming hysteria about the perils of bottled water there is not a lot of fact and some quite convincing reasons to keep buying bottled. So grab a bottle, toast to your favorite brand and drink up.

⊘ AT ISSUE: THE STRUCTURE OF ARGUMENT

1. Paragraph 3, which is just one sentence long, states the essay's thesis. Rewrite this thesis statement to make it more specific.

2. In paragraph 2, Moore summarizes the arguments against his position, which he goes on to refute in the body of his essay. What are these arguments? Does he refute them convincingly? What other opposing arguments can you think of?

3. In paragraphs 8 and 9, Moore presents the arguments in support of his thesis. What are these arguments? Can you think of others?

4. In your own words, summarize Moore's concluding statement.

5. Do you think Moore should have defined the word *Nalgene*? Why do you suppose he does not?

This piece appeared in the *New York Times* on August 1, 2005.

BAD TO THE LAST DROP

TOM STANDAGE

It's summertime, and odds are that at some point during your day you'll reach 1
for a nice cold bottle of water. But before you do, you might want to consider
the results of an experiment I conducted with some friends one summer evening last year. On the table were 10 bottles of water, several rows of glasses
and some paper for recording our impressions. We were to evaluate samples
from each bottle for appearance, odor, flavor, mouth, feel and aftertaste—and
our aim was to identify the interloper among the famous names. One of our
bottles had been filled from the tap. Would we spot it?

We worked our way through the samples, writing scores for each one. 2
None of us could detect any odor, even when swilling water around in large
wine glasses, but other differences between the waters were instantly apparent.
Between sips, we cleansed our palates with wine. (It seemed only fair, since
water serves the same function at a wine tasting.)

The variation between waters was wide, yet the water from the tap did 3
not stand out: only one of us correctly identified it. This simple experiment
seemed to confirm that most people cannot tell the difference between tap
water and bottled water. Yet they buy it anyway—and in enormous quantities.

In 2004, Americans, on average, drank 24 gallons of bottled water, making 4
it second only to carbonated soft drinks in popularity. Furthermore, consumption of bottled water is growing more quickly than that of soft drinks and has
more than doubled in the past decade. This year, Americans will spend around
$9.8 billion on bottled water, according to the Beverage Marketing Corporation.

Ounce for ounce, it costs more than gasoline, even at today's high gaso- 5
line prices; depending on the brand, it costs 250 to 10,000 times more than tap
water. Globally, bottled water is now a $46 billion industry. Why has it become
so popular?

It cannot be the taste, since most people cannot tell the difference in a 6
blind tasting. Much bottled water is, in any case, derived from municipal water
supplies, though it is sometimes filtered, or has additional minerals added to it.

Nor is there any health or nutritional benefit to drinking bottled water 7
over tap water. In one study, published in *The Archives of Family Medicine*,
researchers compared bottled water with tap water from Cleveland, and found
that nearly a quarter of the samples of bottled water had significantly higher
levels of bacteria. The scientists concluded that "use of bottled water on the
assumption of purity can be misguided." Another study carried out at the
University of Geneva found that bottled water was no better from a nutritional
point of view than ordinary tap water.

Admittedly, both kinds of water suffer from occasional contamination 8
problems, but tap water is more stringently monitored and tightly regulated

than bottled water. New York City tap water, for example, was tested 430,600 times during 2004 alone.

9   What of the idea that drinking bottled water allows you to avoid the chemicals that are sometimes added to tap water? Alas, some bottled waters contain the same chemicals anyway—and they are, in any case, unavoidable.

10   Researchers at the University of Texas found that showers and dishwashers liberate trace amounts of chemicals from municipal water supplies into the air. Squirting hot water through a nozzle, to produce a fine spray, increases the surface area of water in contact with the air, liberating dissolved substances in a process known as "stripping." So if you want to avoid those chemicals for some reason, drinking bottled water is not enough. You will also have to wear a gas mask in the shower, and when unloading the dishwasher.

11   Bottled water is undeniably more fashionable and portable than tap water. The practice of carrying a small bottle, pioneered by supermodels, has become commonplace. But despite its association with purity and cleanliness, bottled water is bad for the environment. It is shipped at vast expense from one part of the world to another, is then kept refrigerated before sale, and causes huge numbers of plastic bottles to go into landfills.

> "Our choice of water has become a lifestyle option."

12   Of course, tap water is not so abundant in the developing world. And that is ultimately why I find the illogical enthusiasm for bottled water not simply peculiar, but distasteful. For those of us in the developed world, safe water is now so abundant that we can afford to shun the tap water under our noses, and drink bottled water instead: our choice of water has become a lifestyle option. For many people in the developing world, however, access to water remains a matter of life or death.

13   More than 2.6 billion people, or more than 40 percent of the world's population, lack basic sanitation, and more than one billion people lack reliable access to safe drinking water. The World Health Organization estimates that 80 percent of all illness in the world is due to water-borne diseases, and that at any given time, around half of the people in the developing world are suffering from diseases associated with inadequate water or sanitation, which kill around five million people a year.

14   Widespread illness also makes countries less productive, more dependent on outside aid, and less able to lift themselves out of poverty. One of the main reasons girls do not go to school in many parts of the developing world is that they have to spend so much time fetching water from distant wells.

15   Clean water could be provided to everyone on earth for an outlay of $1.7 billion a year beyond current spending on water projects, according to the International Water Management Institute. Improving sanitation, which is just as important, would cost a further $9.3 billion per year. This is less than a quarter of global annual spending on bottled water.

16   I have no objections to people drinking bottled water in the developing world; it is often the only safe supply. But it would surely be better if they had

access to safe tap water instead. The logical response, for those of us in the developed world, is to stop spending money on bottled water and to give the money to water charities.

If you don't believe me about the taste, then set up a tasting, and see if you really can tell the difference. A water tasting is fun, and you may be surprised by the results. There is no danger of a hangover. But you may well conclude, as I have, that bottled water has an unacceptably bitter taste. 17

⊘ AT ISSUE: THE STRUCTURE OF ARGUMENT

1. In paragraphs 1–5, Standage presents a long introduction about an experiment that he conducted. How does this introduction prepare readers for his thesis?

2. In paragraph 6, Standage begins to present and refute arguments against his position. Why does he start by explaining the popularity of bottled water?

3. In your own words, summarize the opposing arguments Standage presents in paragraphs 8–12. How does he refute these arguments? Why doesn't he wait to refute opposing arguments until after he makes his case?

4. In paragraphs 13–15, Standage presents the arguments in support of his thesis. What are these arguments?

5. Standage does not state his thesis until paragraph 16. In your own words, state this thesis. Why does he wait so long to state his thesis? Do you think presenting it late in the essay is a mistake?

6. In your own words, summarize Standage's concluding statement. How does the phrase "bitter taste" (17) strengthen this statement?

POLAND SPRING WATER

POLANDSPRING.COM

Is 100% recyclable

Features a label that's 30% smaller than our previous half-liter bottle

Is made with 30% less plastic than the average half-liter beverage bottle*

Is easy to carry

Is flexible so it's easier to crush for recycling

⊘ AT ISSUE: THE STRUCTURE OF ARGUMENT

The visual above presents an argument in favor of bottled water by refuting arguments against it. What are these opposing arguments?

PURE WATER 2GO

PUREWATER2GO.COM

Pretty amazing! Just imagine what we could do if we used filter bottles every day!

⊙ AT ISSUE: THE STRUCTURE OF ARGUMENT

The visual above, from an ad for water filters, makes an argument against bottled water. In your own words, summarize this argument.

⊘ EXERCISE 1.2

Write a one-paragraph argument taking a position on the bottled-water debate. Follow the template below, filling in the lines to create your argument.

Template for Structuring an Argument

The use of bottled water is a controversial topic. Some people claim that _____

_____

_____.

Others, however, believe that _____

_____

_____.

Although both sides of this issue have merit, I believe that _____

_____

because _____

_____

_____.

⊘ EXERCISE 1.3

Interview two friends on the topic of bottled water. Revise the one-paragraph argument that you drafted above so that it includes your friends' views on the issue.

⊘ EXERCISE 1.4

Write an essay on the topic, "Do the Benefits of Bottled Water Outweigh the Costs?" Cite the readings on pages 20–28, and be sure to document your sources and to include a works-cited page. (See Chapter 10 for information on documenting sources.)

⊘ EXERCISE 1.5

Review the four-point checklist on page 14, and apply each question to your essay. Does your essay include all four elements of an argumentative essay? Add any missing elements. Then, label your essay's thesis statement, evidence, refutation of opposing arguments, and concluding statement.

Reading and Responding to Arguments

2

Thinking and Reading Critically

Do Violent Media Images Trigger Violent Behavior?

In recent years, the popular media seem to have become increasingly violent. This is particularly true of visuals in video games and on some Internet sites, but graphically violent images also appear regularly in films, on TV, in comic books, and even in newspapers. Some research has suggested that these violent images can have a negative effect on those who view them, particularly on adolescents and young children. In fact, some media critics believe that these violent images have helped to create an increasingly violent culture, which in turn has inspired young people to commit violent crimes (including school shootings). Others, however, argue that violent media images are not to blame for such events—and that, in fact, they provide a safe outlet for aggression.

In this chapter and in the chapter that follows, you will be asked to read essays and study images that shed light on the relationship between media violence and violent behavior. In the process, you will learn active reading strategies that will help you learn to examine and interpret texts and images critically.

Now that you understand the structure of an argumentative essay, you can turn your attention to reading arguments more closely. These arguments may be the subject of class discussion, or they may be source material for the essays you write. In any case, you will need to know how to get the most out of reading them.

Reading Critically

When you read an argument, you should approach it with a critical eye. Contrary to popular opinion, **reading critically** does not mean challenging or arguing with every idea you encounter. What it does mean is commenting, questioning, and judging.

As a critical reader, you do not simply accept that what you are reading is true. Instead, you try to assess the accuracy of the facts in your sources, and you consider whether opinions are supported by evidence. You try to judge the appropriateness and reliability of a writer's sources, and you evaluate the scope and depth of the evidence and the relevance of that evidence to the topic. You also consider opposing arguments carefully, measuring them against the arguments in your sources. Finally, you watch out for possible **bias** in your sources—and you work hard to keep your own biases in check.

GUIDELINES FOR READING CRITICALLY

As a critical reader, you need to read carefully, keeping the following guidelines in mind:

- Check the accuracy of a source's facts.
- Be sure opinions are supported convincingly.
- Evaluate the sources.
- Evaluate the evidence.
- Consider opposing arguments.
- Be on the lookout for bias—in your sources and in yourself.

Becoming an Active Reader

Reading critically means being an *active* rather than a *passive* reader. Being an **active reader** means participating in the reading process by taking the time to read the entire source and then to reread it, highlighting and annotating. This process will prepare you to discuss the source with others or to respond in writing to what you have read.

Reading

When you read an argument for the first time, try to get a sense of the writer's position on the issue and the argument's key supporting points. Begin by focusing on the title, the first paragraph (which often contains a thesis statement or overview), and the last paragraph (which often includes a concluding statement or a summary of the writer's key points). You should also look at the topic sentences of the essay's body paragraphs.

As you read, look for words and phrases that help shape the structure of the argument and the writer's ideas. These words and phrases will help you understand the flow of ideas as well as the content and emphasis of the argument.

COMPREHENSION CLUES

- Phrases that signal emphasis (the *primary* reason, the *most important* problem)

- Repeated words and phrases

- Words and phrases that signal addition (*also, in addition, furthermore*)

- Words and phrases that signal time sequence (*first, after that, next, then, finally*)

- Words and phrases that identify causes and effects (*because, as a result, for this reason*)

- Words and phrases that introduce examples (*for example, for instance*)

- Words and phrases that signal comparison (*likewise, similarly, in the same way*)

- Words and phrases that signal contrast (*although, in contrast, on the other hand*)

- Words and phrases that signal contradiction (*however, on the contrary*)

- Words and phrases that signal a move from general to specific (*in fact, specifically, in other words*)

- Words and phrases that introduce summaries or conclusions (*to sum up, in conclusion*)

When you have finished reading the argument, you should have a good general sense of what the writer wants to communicate.

◯ EXERCISE 2.1

"Violent Media Is Good for Kids" is a magazine article by Gerard Jones, a comic book writer and author of several books about popular media. In this article, Jones argues that violent comic books and video games serve a useful function for young people.

In preparation for class discussion and other activities that will be assigned later in this chapter, read the article and answer the questions that follow it.

This article appeared in *Mother Jones* on June 28, 2000.

VIOLENT MEDIA IS GOOD FOR KIDS

GERARD JONES

At 13 I was alone and afraid. Taught by my well-meaning, progressive, English-teacher parents that violence was wrong, that rage was something to be overcome and cooperation was always better than conflict, I suffocated my deepest fears and desires under a nice-boy persona. Placed in a small, experimental school that was wrong for me, afraid to join my peers in their bumptious rush into adolescent boyhood, I withdrew into passivity and loneliness. My parents, not trusting the violent world of the late 1960s, built a wall between me and the crudest elements of American pop culture.

A scene from Gerard Jones and Will Jacobs's comic

Then the Incredible Hulk smashed through it.

One of my mother's students convinced her that Marvel Comics, despite their apparent juvenility and violence, were in fact devoted to lofty messages of pacifism and tolerance. My mother borrowed some, thinking they'd be good for me. And so they were. But not because they preached lofty messages of benevolence. They were good for me because they were juvenile. And violent.

The character who caught me, and freed me, was the Hulk: overgendered and undersocialized, half-naked and half-witted, raging against a frightened world that misunderstood and persecuted him. Suddenly I had a fantasy self to carry my stifled rage and buried desire for power. I had a fantasy self who was a self: unafraid of his desires and the world's disapproval, unhesitating and effective in action. "Puny boy follow Hulk!" roared my fantasy self, and I followed.

I followed him to new friends—other sensitive geeks chasing their own inner brutes—and I followed him to the arrogant, self-exposing, self-assertive, superheroic decision to become a writer. Eventually, I left him behind, followed more sophisticated heroes, and finally my own lead along a twisting path to a career and an identity. In my 30s, I found myself writing action movies and comic books. I wrote some Hulk stories, and met the geek-geniuses who created him. I saw my own creations turned into action figures, cartoons, and computer games. I talked to the kids who read my stories. Across generations, genders, and ethnicities I kept seeing the same story: people pulling themselves out of emotional traps by immersing themselves in violent stories. People integrating the scariest, most fervently denied fragments of their psyches° into fuller senses of selfhood through fantasies of superhuman combat and destruction.

Minds or selves

6   I have watched my son living the same story—transforming himself into a bloodthirsty dinosaur to embolden himself for the plunge into preschool, a Power Ranger to muscle through a social competition in kindergarten. In the first grade, his friends started climbing a tree at school. But he was afraid: of falling, of the centipedes crawling on the trunk, of sharp branches, of his friends' derision. I took my cue from his own fantasies and read him old Tarzan comics, rich in combat and bright with flashing knives. For two weeks he lived in them. Then he put them aside. And he climbed the tree.

7

A scene from Gerard Jones and Gene Ha's comic book *Oktane*

8
9
10

But all the while, especially in the wake of the recent burst of school shootings, I heard pop psychologists insisting that violent stories are harmful to kids, heard teachers begging parents to keep their kids away from "junk culture," heard a guilt-stricken friend with a son who loved Pokémon lament, "I've turned into the bad mom who lets her kid eat sugary cereal and watch cartoons!"

That's when I started the research.

"Fear, greed, power-hunger, rage: these are aspects of our selves that we try not to experience in our lives but often want, even need, to experience vicariously through stories of others," writes Melanie Moore, Ph.D., a psychologist who works with urban teens. "Children need violent entertainment in order to explore the inescapable feelings that they've been taught to deny, and to reintegrate those feelings into a more whole, more complex, more resilient selfhood."

Moore consults to public schools and local governments, and is also raising a daughter. For the past three years she and I have been studying the ways in which children use violent stories to meet their emotional and developmental needs—and the ways in which adults can help them use those stories healthily. With her help I developed *Power Play*, a program for helping young people improve their self-knowledge and sense of potency through heroic, combative storytelling.

11   We've found that every aspect of even the trashiest pop-culture story can have its own developmental function. Pretending to have superhuman powers helps children conquer the feelings of powerlessness that inevitably come with being so young and small. The dual-identity concept at the heart of many

superhero stories helps kids negotiate the conflicts between the inner self and the public self as they work through the early stages of socialization. Identification with a rebellious, even destructive, hero helps children learn to push back against a modern culture that cultivates fear and teaches dependency.

At its most fundamental level, what we call "creative violence"—head-bonking   12 cartoons, bloody videogames, playground karate, toy guns—gives children a tool to master their rage. Children will feel rage. Even the sweetest and most civilized of them, even those whose parents read the better class of literary magazines, will feel rage. The world is uncontrollable and incomprehensible; mastering it is a terrifying, enraging task. Rage can be an energizing emotion, a shot of courage to push us to resist greater threats, take more control, than we ever thought we could. But rage is also the emotion our culture distrusts the most. Most of us are taught early on to fear our own. Through immersion in imaginary combat and identification with a violent protagonist, children engage the rage they've stifled, come to fear it less, and become more capable of utilizing it against life's challenges.

> "Rage can be an energizing emotion."

I knew one little girl who went around exploding with fantasies so violent   13 that other moms would draw her mother aside to whisper, "I think you should know something about Emily. . . ." Her parents were separating, and she was small, an only child, a tomboy at an age when her classmates were dividing sharply along gender lines. On the playground she acted out *Sailor Moon*° fights, and in the classroom she wrote stories about people being stabbed with knives. The more adults tried to control her stories, the more she acted out the roles of her angry heroes: breaking rules, testing limits, roaring threats.

A Japanese cartoon series about magical girls

Then her mother and I started helping her tell her stories. She wrote   14 them, performed them, drew them like comics: sometimes bloody, sometimes tender, always blending the images of pop culture with her own most private fantasies. She came out of it just as fiery and strong, but more self-controlled and socially competent: a leader among her peers, the one student in her class who could truly pull boys and girls together.

I worked with an older girl, a middle-class "nice girl," who held herself   15 together through a chaotic family situation and a tumultuous adolescence with gangsta rap. In the mythologized street violence of Ice T, the rage and strutting of his music and lyrics, she found a theater of the mind in which she could be powerful, ruthless, invulnerable. She avoided the heavy drug use that sank many of her peers, and flowered in college as a writer and political activist.

The title character of *Oktane* gets nasty.

I'm not going to argue that   16 violent entertainment is harmless. I think it has helped inspire some people to real-life violence. I am going to argue that it's helped hundreds of people for every one it's hurt, and that it can help far more if we learn to use it well. I am going to argue that our fear of "youth violence" isn't well-founded on reality, and that the fear can do more harm than the reality. We act as though our highest priority is to prevent our children from growing up into murderous thugs—but modern kids are far more likely to grow up too passive, too distrustful of themselves, too easily manipulated.

17   We send the message to our children in a hundred ways that their craving for imaginary gun battles and symbolic killings is wrong, or at least dangerous. Even when we don't call for censorship or forbid "Mortal Kombat," we moan to other parents within our kids earshot about the "awful violence" in the entertainment they love. We tell our kids that it isn't nice to play-fight, or we steer them from some monstrous action figure to a pro-social doll. Even in the most progressive households, where we make such a point of letting children feel what they feel, we rush to substitute an enlightened discussion for the raw material of rageful fantasy. In the process, we risk confusing them about their natural aggression in the same way the Victorians° confused their children about their sexuality. When we try to protect our children from their own feelings and fantasies, we shelter them not against violence but against power and selfhood.

The people who lived during the reign of Victoria (1819–1901), queen of Great Britain and Ireland, who are often associated with prudish behavior

Identifying the Elements of Argument

1. What is Jones's thesis? Restate it in your own words.

2. What arguments does Jones present as evidence in support of his thesis?

3. What arguments against his position does Jones identify? How does he refute them?

4. Paraphrase Jones's concluding statement.

Highlighting

After you read an argument, read through it again, this time highlighting as you read. When you **highlight**, you use underlining and symbols to identify the essay's most important points. This active reading strategy will help you to understand the writer's ideas and to see connections among those ideas when you reread.

How do you know what to highlight? As a general rule, you look for the same signals that you looked for when you read the essay the first time—for example, the essay's thesis and topic sentences and the words and phrases that identify the writer's intent and emphasis. This time, however, you identify these elements and use various symbols to show your reactions to them.

SUGGESTIONS FOR HIGHLIGHTING

- Underline key ideas—for example, topic sentences.

- Box or circle words or phrases you want to remember.

- Place a check mark or a star next to an important idea.

- Place a double check mark or double star next to an especially significant idea.

- Draw lines or arrows to connect related ideas.

- Put a question mark near an unfamiliar reference or a word you need to look up.

- Number the writer's key supporting points or examples.

Here is how a student, Katherine Choi, highlighted a short magazine article, "When Life Imitates Video" by John Leo. Choi was preparing to write an essay about the effects of media violence on children and adolescents. She began her highlighting by underlining and starring the thesis statement (para. 2). She then circled references to Leo's two key examples, "Colorado massacre" (1) and "Paducah, Ky." (7). In addition, she underlined and starred some particularly important points (2, 8, 9) as well as what she identified as the essay's concluding statement (11).

This piece first appeared in *U.S. News & World Report* on May 3, 1999.

WHEN LIFE IMITATES VIDEO

JOHN LEO

? Marching through a large building using various bombs and guns to pick off   1
victims is a conventional video-game scenario. In the Colorado massacre,
Dylan Klebold and Eric Harris used pistol-grip shotguns, as in some video-
arcade games. The pools of blood, screams of agony, and pleas for mercy must
have been familiar—they are featured in some of the newer and more realistic
kill-for-kicks games. "With each kill," the *Los Angeles Times* reported, "the
teens cackled and shouted as though playing one of the morbid video games
they loved." And they ended their spree by shooting themselves in the head,
the final act in the game *Postal*, and, in fact, the only way to end it.

2   Did the sensibilities created by the modern, video kill games play a role in the Littleton massacre? Apparently so. Note the cool and casual cruelty, the outlandish arsenal of weapons, the cheering and laughing while hunting down victims one by one. All of this seems to reflect the style and feel of the video killing games they played so often.

3   No, there isn't any direct connection between most murderous games and most murders. And yes, the primary responsibility for protecting children from dangerous games lies with their parents, many of whom like to blame the entertainment industry for their own failings.

4   But there is a cultural problem here: We are now a society in which the chief form of play for millions of youngsters is making large numbers of people die. Hurting and maiming others is the central fun activity in video games played so addictively by the young. A widely cited survey of 900 fourth-through eighth-grade students found that almost half of the children said their favorite electronic games involve violence. Can it be that all this constant training in make-believe killing has no social effects?

5   **Dress rehearsal.** The conventional argument is that this is a harmless activity among children who know the difference between fantasy and reality. But the games are often played by unstable youngsters unsure about the difference. Many of these have been maltreated or rejected and left alone most of the time (a precondition for playing the games obsessively). Adolescent feelings of resentment, powerlessness, and revenge pour into the killing games. In these children, the games can become a dress rehearsal for the real thing.

6   Psychologist David Grossman of Arkansas State University, a retired Army officer, thinks "point and shoot" video games have the same effect as military strategies used to break down a soldier's aversion to killing. During World War II only 15 to 20 percent of all American soldiers fired their weapon in battle. Shooting games in which the target is a man-shaped outline, the Army found, made recruits more willing to "make killing a reflex action."

7   Video games are much more powerful versions of the military's primitive discovery about overcoming the reluctance to shoot. Grossman says Michael Carneal, the schoolboy shooter in Paducah, Ky. showed the effects of video-game lessons in killing. Carneal coolly shot nine times, hitting eight people, five of them in the head or neck. Head shots pay a bonus in many video games. Now the Marine Corps is adapting a version of *Doom*, the hyperviolent game played by one of the Littleton killers, for its own training purposes.

8   More realistic touches in video games help blur the boundary between fantasy and reality—guns carefully modeled on real ones, accurate-looking wounds, screams, and other sound effects, even the recoil of a heavy rifle. Some newer games seem intent on erasing children's empathy and concern for others. Once the intended victims of video slaughter were mostly gangsters or aliens. Now some games invite players to blow away ordinary people who have done nothing wrong—pedestrians, marching bands, an elderly woman with a walker. In these games, the shooter is not a hero, just a violent sociopath. One

ad for a Sony game says: "Get in touch with your gun-toting, testosterone-pumping, cold-blooded murdering side."

These killings are supposed to be taken as harmless over-the-top jokes. 9 But the bottom line is that the young are being invited to enjoy the killing of vulnerable people picked at random. This looks like the final lesson in a course to eliminate any lingering resistance to killing.

SWAT teams and cops now turn up as the intended victims of some 10 video-game killings. This has the effect of exploiting resentments toward law enforcement and making real-life shooting of cops more likely. This sensibility turns up in the hit movie *Matrix*: world-saving hero Keanu Reeves, in a mandatory Goth-style, long black coat packed with countless heavy-duty guns, is forced to blow away huge numbers of uniformed law-enforcement people.

"We have to start worrying about what we are putting into the minds of 11 our young," says Grossman. "Pilots train on flight simulators, drivers on driving simulators, and now we have our children on murder simulators." If we want to avoid more Littleton-style massacres, we will begin taking the social effects of the killing games more seriously.

➔ EXERCISE 2.2

Read Katherine Choi's highlighting of John Leo's essay on pages 40–42. How would your own highlighting of this essay be similar to or different from hers?

➔ EXERCISE 2.3

Reread "Violent Media Is Good for Kids" (pp. 36–39). As you reread, highlight the article by underlining and starring important points, boxing or circling key words, or drawing lines and arrows to connect related ideas. If you do not understand a word or a reference, circle it and put a question mark above it.

Annotating

As you highlight, you should also annotate what you are reading. **Annotating** means making notes—of your questions, reactions, and ideas for discussion or writing—in the margins of the essay or between the lines. Keeping this kind of informal record of ideas as they occur to you will prepare you for class discussion and provide a useful source of material when you write.

As you read an argument and think critically about what you are reading, use the questions in the following checklist to help you make useful annotations.

CHECKLIST

Questions for Annotating

☐ What issue is the writer focusing on?

☐ Does the writer take a clear stand on this issue?

☐ What is the writer's thesis?

☐ What is the writer's purpose (his or her reason for writing)?

☐ What kind of audience is the writer addressing?

☐ Does the writer seem to assume readers will agree with the essay's position?

☐ What evidence does the writer use to support the essay's thesis? Does the writer include enough evidence?

☐ Does the writer consider (and refute) opposing arguments?

☐ Do you understand the writer's vocabulary?

☐ Do you understand the writer's references?

☐ Do you agree with the points the writer makes?

☐ Do the views the writer expresses agree or disagree with the views presented in other essays you have read?

🔽 The following passage, which reproduces Katherine Choi's highlighting of John Leo's essay on pages 40–42, also includes her marginal annotations. In these annotations, Choi put Leo's thesis and some of his key points into her own words and recorded a few questions that she intended to explore further. She also identified arguments against Leo's position and his refutation of these arguments.

This piece first appeared in *U.S. News & World Report* on May 3, 1999.

WHEN LIFE IMITATES VIDEO
JOHN LEO

1 Marching through a large building using various bombs and guns to pick off victims is a conventional video-game scenario. In the Colorado massacre, Dylan Klebold and Eric Harris used pistol-grip shotguns, as in some video-arcade games. The pools of blood, screams of agony, and pleas for mercy must have been familiar—they are featured in some of the newer and more realistic kill-for-kicks games. "With each kill," the *Los Angeles Times* reported, "the teens cackled and shouted as though playing one of the morbid video games they loved." And they ended their spree by shooting themselves in the head, the final act in the game *Postal*, and, in fact, the only way to end it.

Columbine h.s., 1999

Thesis ✳

His position: "video kill games" can lead to violent behavior

Opposing arguments

Refutation

True? ———————→
Date of survey?

(He means "training" does have negative effects, right?)

Opposing argument

Refutation

Quotes psychologist (= authority)

1997 ————————

✳

Did the sensibilities created by the modern, video kill games play a role 2
in the Littleton massacre? Apparently so. Note the cool and casual cruelty, the
outlandish arsenal of weapons, the cheering and laughing while hunting down
victims one by one. All of this seems to reflect the style and feel of the video
killing games they played so often.

No, there isn't any direct connection between most murderous games 3
and most murders. And yes, the primary responsibility for protecting children
from dangerous games lies with their parents, many of whom like to blame the
entertainment industry for their own failings.

But there is a cultural problem here: We are now a society in which the 4
chief form of play for millions of youngsters is making large numbers of
people die. Hurting and maiming others is the central fun activity in video
games played so addictively by the young. A widely cited survey of 900 fourth-
through eighth-grade students found that almost half of the children said
their favorite electronic games involve violence. Can it be that all this constant
training in make-believe killing has no social effects?

Dress rehearsal. The conventional argument is that this is a harmless 5
activity among children who know the difference between fantasy and reality.
But the games are often played by unstable youngsters unsure about the difference. Many of these have been maltreated or rejected and left alone most of
the time (a precondition for playing the games obsessively). Adolescent feelings of resentment, powerlessness, and revenge pour into the killing games. In
these children, the games can become a dress rehearsal for the real thing.

Psychologist David Grossman of Arkansas State University, a retired 6
Army officer, thinks "point and shoot" video games have the same effect as
military strategies used to break down a soldier's aversion to killing. During World War II only 15 to 20 percent of all American soldiers fired their
weapon in battle. Shooting games in which the target is a man-shaped outline, the Army found, made recruits more willing to "make killing a reflex
action."

Video games are much more powerful versions of the military's primitive 7
discovery about overcoming the reluctance to shoot. Grossman says Michael
Carneal, the schoolboy shooter in Paducah, Ky., showed the effects of video-
game lessons in killing. Carneal coolly shot nine times, hitting eight people,
five of them in the head or neck. Head shots pay a bonus in many video games.
Now the Marine Corps is adapting a version of *Doom*, the hyperviolent game
played by one of the Littleton killers, for its own training purposes.

More realistic touches in video games help blur the boundary between 8
fantasy and reality—guns carefully modeled on real ones, accurate-looking
wounds, screams, and other sound effects, even the recoil of a heavy rifle.
Some newer games seem intent on erasing children's empathy and concern for
others. Once the intended victims of video slaughter were mostly gangsters or
aliens. Now some games invite players to blow away ordinary people who have
done nothing wrong—pedestrians, marching bands, an elderly woman with a
walker. In these games, the shooter is not a hero, just a violent sociopath. One

ad for a Sony game says: "Get in touch with your gun-toting, testosterone-pumping, cold-blooded murdering side."

9   These killings are supposed to be taken as harmless over-the-top jokes. But the bottom line is that the young are being invited to enjoy the killing of vulnerable people picked at random. This looks like the final lesson in a course to eliminate any lingering resistance to killing.

10   SWAT teams and cops now turn up as the intended victims of some video-game killings. This has the effect of exploiting resentments toward law enforcement and making real-life shooting of cops more likely. This sensibility turns up in the hit movie *Matrix*: world-saving hero Keanu Reeves, in a mandatory Goth-style, long black coat packed with countless heavy-duty guns, is forced to blow away huge numbers of uniformed law-enforcement people.

11   "We have to start worrying about what we are putting into the minds of our young," says Grossman. "Pilots train on flight simulators, drivers on driving simulators, and now we have our children on murder simulators." If we want to avoid more Littleton-style massacres, we will begin taking the social effects of the killing games more seriously.

Recommendation for action

● EXERCISE 2.4

Reread Gerard Jones's "Violent Media Is Good for Kids" (pp. 36–39). As you read, refer to the "Questions for Annotating" checklist (p. 43), and use them as a guide as you write your own reactions and questions in the margins of Jones's article. In your annotations, note where you agree or disagree with Jones, and briefly explain why. Quickly summarize any points that you think are particularly important. Take the time to look up any unfamiliar words or references you have circled and to write down brief definitions or explanations. Think of these annotations as you prepare to discuss the Jones article in class (and, eventually, to write about it).

● EXERCISE 2.5

Exchange annotated essays with another student, and read his or her highlighting and annotating. How are your written responses similar to the other student's? How are they different? Do your classmate's responses help you to see anything new about Jones's article?

● EXERCISE 2.6

The following two brief newspaper opinion pieces from readers of *USA Today* were published on April 17, 2007, following the massacre at Virginia Tech University. Read the readers' comments, and highlight and annotate them. As you read, identify points that support or contradict Gerard Jones's argument. Then, write one or two additional annotations in the margins of Jones's essay to acknowledge these points.

MEDIA VIOLENCE MAY BE REAL CULPRIT BEHIND VIRGINIA TECH TRAGEDY

TIM MILEY, KALAMAZOO, MICHIGAN

Guns are not creating the problem in our society. Rather, it is our mentality ("33 dead after gunfire at dorm, in classrooms," News, Tuesday). 1

Gratuitous violence is accepted as normal. Our television programs and movies are awash in mindless death and destruction, and that sickness spreads into the city streets. Every day, more U.S. soldiers, sailors, Marines and helpless Iraqi and Afghani citizens die in the Middle East. Our culture implicitly believes that violence solves problems. 2

Politicians cannot solve this problem. They created it, with our consent. No law will be able to fix our broken world view. 3

To put an end to the violence, we must rethink our very relationship with the world. Would our society start to get better if every time we saw a violent TV program we changed the channel or, better yet, turned off the television? Would our collective sickness start to fade if every time a violent scene started in a movie, we walked out of the theater? 4

TAKE AIM AT GUNS

PATRICK MACKIN, THE VILLAGES, FLORIDA

A careful observer would have noted that there hardly has been any commentary on the cause of the horrible Virginia Tech shootings: guns. Why? It probably is because many fear bringing on the wrath of the National Rifle Association and gun owners throughout the world. The NRA will toss out its old cry about our Constitution, a well-regulated militia and the right to bear arms. 1

The Bureau of Alcohol, Tobacco, Firearms and Explosives estimates that there are more than 215 million guns in the hands of private citizens. That's a gun for almost every man, woman and child in our country. The USA leads the world in gun ownership. 2

Why should we be surprised about what happened at Virginia Tech? We will continue to have horrible, tragic days like those at Columbine High School 3 and Virginia Tech until we wake up and rid ourselves of guns. One disturbed young man buys two guns and then kills 32 students and himself in his expression of his "right to bear arms." When will we ever learn?

➔ EXERCISE 2.7

The following letter to the editor of a college newspaper takes a position on the issue of how violent media—in this case, video games—influence young people. Read the letter, highlighting and annotating it.

Now, consider how this letter is like and unlike Gerard Jones's essay (pp. 36–39). First, identify the writer's thesis, and restate it in your own words. Then, consider the benefits of violent video games the writer identifies. Are these benefits similar to or different from the benefits Jones identifies?

In paragraph 4, the writer summarizes arguments against her position. Does Jones address any of these same arguments? If so, does he refute them in the same way this writer does? Finally, read the letter's last paragraph. How is this writer's purpose for writing different from Jones's?

> This letter to the editor was published on October 22, 2003, In *Ka Leo o Hawai'i*, the student newspaper of the University of Hawaii at Manoa.

DON'T WITHHOLD VIOLENT GAMES

JESSICA ROBBINS

Entertainment and technology have changed. Video games today are more graphic   1
and violent than they were a few years ago. There is a concern about children being influenced by the content of some of these video games. Some states have already passed laws which ban minors from the viewing or purchasing of these video games without an accompanying adult. I believe this law should not exist.

Today's technology has truly enriched our entertainment experience.   2
Today's computer and game consoles are able to simulate shooting, killing, mutilation and blood through video games. It was such a problem that in 1993 Congress passed a law prohibiting the sale or rental of adult video games to minors. A rating system on games, similar to that placed on movies, was put into place which I support. This helps to identify the level of violence that a game might have. However, I do not believe that this rating should restrict people of any age from purchasing a game.

Currently there is no significant evidence that supports the argument that   3
violent video games are a major contributing factor in criminal and violent behavior. Recognized Universities such as MIT and UCLA described the law as

misguided citing that "most studies and experiments on video games containing violent content have not found adverse effects." In addition there actually are benefits from playing video games. They provide a safe outlet for aggression and frustration, increased attention performance, along with spatial and coordination skills.

> "There actually are benefits from playing video games."

Some argue that there is research that shows real life video game play is related to antisocial behavior and delinquency, and that there is need for a law to prevent children from acting out these violent behaviors. This may be true, but researchers have failed to indicate that this antisocial and aggressive behavior is mostly short-term. We should give children the benefit of the doubt. Today's average child is competent and intelligent enough to recognize the difference between the digital representation of a gun and a real 28 inch military bazooka rocket launcher. They are also aware of the consequences of using such weapons on real civilians.   4

Major software companies who create video games should write congress and protest this law on the basis of a nonexistent correlation between violence and video games. If the law is modified to not restrict these games to a particular age group, then these products will not be unfairly singled out.   5

Writing a Critical Response

Sometimes you will be asked to write a **critical response**—one or more paragraphs in which you examine ideas presented in an argument and express your reactions to them.

Before you can respond in writing to an argument, you need to be sure that you understand what the writer means to get across and that you have a sense of how ideas are arranged—and why. You also need to consider how convincingly the writer conveys his or her position.

If you have highlighted and annotated the argument according to the guidelines outlined in this chapter, you should have a good idea what the writer wants to communicate to readers as well as how successfully the argument makes its point.

Before you begin to write a critical response to an argument, you should consider the questions in the checklist on page 49.

When you write a critical response, begin by identifying your source and its author; then, write a clear, concise summary of the writer's position. Next, analyze the argument's supporting points one by one, considering the strength and breadth of the evidence that is presented. Also consider whether the writer addresses all significant opposing arguments and whether those arguments are refuted convincingly. Quote, summarize, and paraphrase the writer's key points as you go along, being careful to

CHECKLIST

Questions for Critical Reading

☐ What is the writer's general subject?

☐ What purpose does the writer have for presenting this argument?

☐ What is the writer's position?

☐ Does the writer support ideas mainly with facts or with opinion?

☐ What evidence does the writer present to support this position?

☐ Is the evidence convincing? Is there enough evidence?

☐ Does the writer present opposing ideas and refute them effectively?

☐ What kind of audience does the writer seem to be addressing?

☐ Does the writer see the audience as hostile, friendly, or neutral?

☐ Does the writer establish himself or herself as well informed? As a fair and reasonable person?

☐ Does the writer seem to exhibit bias? If so, how does this bias affect the argument?

quote accurately and not to misrepresent the writer's ideas or distort them by quoting out of context. (For information on summarizing, paraphrasing, quoting, and synthesizing sources, see Chapter 9.) As you write, identify arguments you find unconvincing, poorly supported, or irrelevant. At the end of your critical response, sum up your assessment of the argument in a strong concluding statement.

⏺ Katherine Choi, the student who highlighted and annotated the essay "When Life Imitates Video" by John Leo (pp. 43–45), used her highlighting and annotations to help her develop the following critical response to Leo's essay.

RESPONSE TO "WHEN LIFE IMITATES VIDEO"

KATHERINE CHOI

1   In "When Life Imitates Video," John Leo takes the position that "video kill games" can actually lead to violent behavior. In fact, he suggests a cause-and-effect connection between such games and the

Article's source and author identified

Summary of writer's position

notorious 1999 murder spree at Colorado's Columbine High School, which occurred shortly before Leo wrote his essay.

Analysis of supporting evidence

Although Leo acknowledges that there is no "direct connection" between video games and this crime and agrees that parents bear the "primary responsibility" for keeping violent games out of the hands of their children, he insists that our culture is also responsible. He is very critical of our society's dependence on violent video games, which he considers "training in make-believe killing." This argument is convincing, up to a point. The problem is that Leo's primary support for this argument is a reference to an unnamed "widely cited survey," for which he provides no date. In addition, his use of a weak rhetorical question at the end of paragraph 4 instead of a strong statement of his position does little to help to support his argument.

2

Analysis of Leo's discussion of an opposing argument

Leo cites an opposing argument at the beginning of paragraph 5—the "conventional argument" that video games are harmless because children can tell the difference between fantasy and reality. He refutes this argument with unsupported generalizations rather than with specifics, pointing out the possibility that the games will often be played by "unstable youngsters" who channel their "adolescent feelings of resentment, powerlessness, and revenge" into the games.

3

Analysis of supporting evidence

The key piece of supporting evidence for Leo's claim that video games are dangerous is the expert opinion of a psychology professor who is also a retired army officer. The professor, David Grossman, draws an analogy between adolescents' video games and military training games designed to encourage soldiers to shoot their enemies. Although this analogy is interesting, it is not necessarily valid. For one thing, the army training Grossman refers to took place during World War II; for another, the soldiers were aware that the games were preparing them for actual combat.

4

Analysis of supporting evidence

Leo goes on to cite Grossman's comments about the young shooter in a 1997 attack in Paducah, Kansas, and the Marines' use of *Doom* to train soldiers. Again, both discussions are interesting, and both are relevant to the connection between video games and violence. The problem is that neither discussion establishes a cause-and-effect relationship between violent video games and violent acts.

5

6   It may be true, as Leo observes, that video games are becoming more and more violent and that the victims in these games are increasingly likely to be police officers. Still, Leo fails to make his point because he never establishes that real-life violence is also increasing; therefore, he is not able to demonstrate a causal connection. His conclusion—"If we want to avoid more Littleton-style massacres, we will begin taking the social effects of the killing games more seriously"— combines a frightening prediction and a strong recommendation for action. Unfortunately, although Leo's essay will frighten many readers, it does not convincingly establish the need for the action he recommends.   *Conclusion*

    Concluding statement

➲ EXERCISE 2.8

Write a one-paragraph critical response to Gerard Jones's essay on pages 36–39. Use the following template to shape your paragraph.

Template for Writing a Critical Response

According to Gerard Jones, violent media can actually have positive effects on young people because _____. Jones also believes that violent media are a positive influence on children because _____.

Jones makes some good points. For example, he says that _____. However, _____. All in all, _____.

➲ EXERCISE 2.9

Consulting the one-paragraph critical response that you wrote above, write a more fully developed critical response to Gerard Jones's essay on pages 36–39. Refer to the highlighting and annotations that you did for Exercises 2.3 and 2.4.

3

Decoding Visual Arguments

Do Violent Media Images Trigger Violent Behavior?

(continued)

In Chapter 2, you read two essays that discuss the question of whether violence on TV and in other popular media can be blamed (at least in part) for the violence in our society. Now, you will be introduced to a variety of visual texts that offer insights into this issue. At the same time, you will learn how to use the critical reading strategies that you practiced in Chapter 2 to help you **decode**, or interpret, visual texts and to use them as springboards for discussion or writing or as sources in your essays.

A **visual argument** can be an advertisement, a chart or graph or table, a diagram, a Web page, a photograph, or a painting. Like an argumentative essay, a visual argument can take a position. Unlike an argumentative essay, however, a visual argument communicates its position (and offers evidence to support that position) largely through images rather than words.

Thinking Critically about Visual Arguments

When you approach a visual argument—particularly one that will be the subject of class discussion or writing—you should do so with a critical eye. Your primary goal is to understand the point that the creator of the visual is trying to make, but you also need to understand how the message is conveyed. In addition, you need to evaluate whether the methods used to persuade the audience are both logical and fair.

VISUAL TEXTS VERSUS VISUAL ARGUMENTS

Not every visual is an argument; many simply present information. For example, a diagram of a hunting rifle, with its principal parts labeled, tells viewers what the weapon looks like and how it works. However, a photo of two toddlers playing with a hunting rifle could make a powerful argument about the need for gun safety. Conversely, a photo of a family hunting trip featuring a teenager proudly holding up a rifle while his parents look on might make a positive argument for access to guns.

Using Active Reading Strategies with Visual Arguments

As you learned in Chapter 2, being a critical reader involves responding actively to the text of an argument. The active reading strategies that you practiced in Chapter 2—*highlighting* and *annotating*—can also be applied to visual arguments.

When you study a visual argument, you should look for clues to its main idea, or *message*. Some visuals, particularly advertising images, include words (sometimes called *body copy*) as well, and this written text often conveys the main ideas of the argument. Apart from words, however, the images themselves can help you understand the visual's purpose, its intended audience, and the argument that it is making.

COMPREHENSION CLUES

- The individual images that appear
- The relative distance (close together or far apart) between individual images
- The relative size of the images
- The relationship between images and background
- The use of empty space
- The use of color and shading (for example, contrast between light and dark)

- The presence of people
- People's activities, gestures, facial expressions, positions, body language, dress, and the like

APPEALS: *LOGOS, PATHOS,* AND *ETHOS*

As you study visual arguments, you should consider the appeal (or appeals) that the visual uses to convince its audience. For example, an ad produced by Mothers against Drunk Drivers (MADD) that includes statistics about alcohol-related auto fatalities might appeal to logic (*logos*). Another MADD ad could appeal to emotion (*pathos*) by showing photographs of an accident scene. Still another ad could appeal to authority (*ethos*) by featuring a well-known sports figure warning of the dangers of drunk driving. (For more on these appeals, see the introduction to this book.)

When you have studied the visual carefully, you should have a sense of what it was designed to communicate.

Look at the following cartoon.

Rob Rogers/Copyright © The Pittsburgh Post-Gazette/Dist. by United Feature Syndicate, Inc.

The cartoon on the preceding page treats subject matter—video games, TV family dynamics, the Iraq war (and war in general)—that is likely to be familiar to (and of interest to) many readers, making an emotional appeal to those concerned about children's exposure to violence. The cartoon includes no subtle allusions (verbal or visual) or challenging vocabulary; the dialogue is conversational, and the "punch line" is accessible. For these reasons, the cartoon seems to be aimed at a wide general audience (rather than, for example, soldiers, television critics, or child psychologists).

In their dress and actions, the people pictured in the cartoon—a mother and son—are familiar, even stereotypical characters: the mother has arrived home from work or from running errands, and the son is glued to the TV. The television set, placed at the right side of the image, is made to seem important by the large type of the words denoting sounds—"BOOM" and so on—that are coming from it.

All these details work together to support the cartoon's main idea—that for most young children, the real violence of war is a greater threat than the much-criticized make-believe violence of video games. Thus, the cartoon's purpose seems to criticize both war and those who blame violent societal behavior (including war) on violent video games.

Now, turn your attention to the following graph.

Crime Victims per 1,000 Citizens

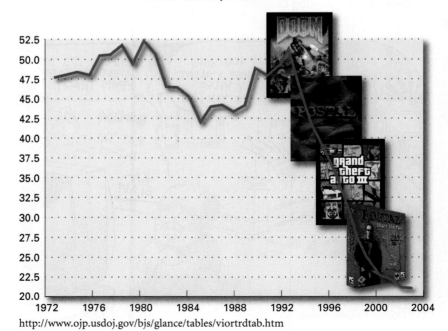

http://www.ojp.usdoj.gov/bjs/glance/tables/viortrdtab.htm

The graph on the preceding page appeals to logic by using statistics as evidence to support its position. In so doing, it makes a powerful visual argument about the relationship between violent video games and crime. The visual uses accessible graphics and has an open, inviting design; its format is designed to make its information clear to most people who will look at it. The main idea that it conveys might be summarized as follows: "While video games have become more and more violent, the number of crime victims has actually declined."

This idea is likely to come as a surprise to most people, who might assume a causal relationship between violent video games and violent crime. But as the graph shows, in 1972—when video games did not exist—the crime rate was considerably higher than it was in 2004. Because the information in the graph is intended to contradict its audience's probable assumptions, it seems to have been created to convince people to change the way they look at video games. In other words, it is an argument (and, in fact, it is a *refutation*).

◉ EXERCISE 3.1

Look at the visuals on the pages that follow, and then answer the questions on page 59.

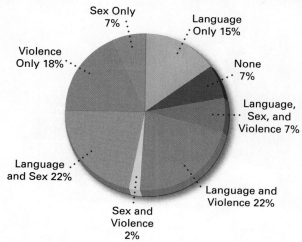

Distribution of Language, Sex, and Violence Codes in PG-Rated Movies

This chart is from "Protecting Children from Harmful Television: TV Ratings and the V-chip," parenthood.library.wisc.edu/Nathanson/Nathanson.html.

Homicides per 100,000 Population

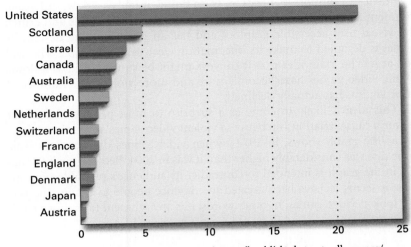

This graph appears in "Violence in the United States," published at netwellness.org/healthtopics/domestictv/violenceUS.cfm.

I saw 7,000 People Killed

This image is from Everylifecounts.info, a Web site dedicated to raising awareness of media violence.

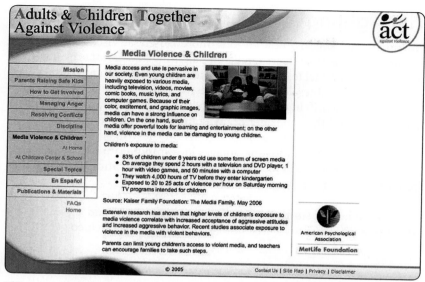

This screen shot is from the Web site Adults and Children Together against Violence, found at http://actagainstviolence.apa.org/mediaviolence/index.html.

Identifying the Elements of Visual Arguments

1. Do you consider all of the visuals on pages 57–59 to be visual arguments, or do you think some were designed solely to present information?

2. What main idea does each visual communicate? State this idea in a single sentence.

3. What elements in each visual support this main idea?

4. What general purpose does the visual seem designed to achieve?

5. To what kind of audience do you think each visual is likely to appeal?

Highlighting and Annotating Visuals

Now it is time to learn how to look more closely at visuals and how to *highlight* and *annotate* them. Unlike highlighting and annotating a written text, marking a visual text involves focusing your attention not only on any words that appear but also on the images.

Begin by identifying key images—perhaps by starring, boxing, or circling them—and then consider drawing lines or arrows to connect related images. Then, go on to make annotations on the visual, commenting on the effectiveness of its individual images in communicating the message of the whole. As in the case of a written text, your annotations can be in the form of comments or questions.

⏺ Here is how a student, Jason Savona, highlighted and annotated an advertisement for *Grand Theft Auto IV*, a popular violent video game.

This desktop wallpaper shows a scene from the popular video game.

Top of gun = taller than tallest building

Huge lone figure looking down on city

"Liberty City" skyline (looks like NY)

Hazy yellow sky

Dark image stands out against lighter background

Name of game centered; large type in contrasting black and white for emphasis

⊃ EXERCISE 3.2

Look at the following visual, and then highlight and annotate it to identify its most important images and their relationship to one another. When you have finished, think about how the images work together to communicate a central message to the audience. What argument does this visual make?

Media Violence

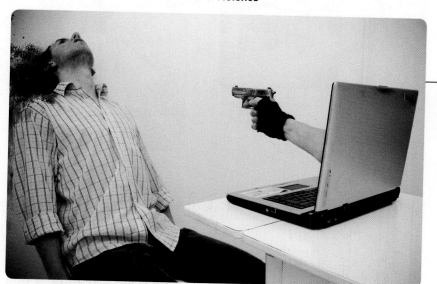

The creator of this image says it is not a statement against video games but is intended to draw attention to their complexity.

⊃ EXERCISE 3.3

Interview a classmate about his or her experiences with video games—or with actual violence. Does your classmate see any links between the kinds of videos that are watched by friends and family members and the violence (or lack of violence) that occurs in his or her community? Write a paragraph summarizing your interview.

⊃ EXERCISE 3.4

Study the three visuals on the following page, all of which appear in Gerard Jones's essay, "Violent Media Is Good for Kids" (pp. 36–39). Look at each visual with a critical eye, and then consider how effectively they support the central argument that Jones makes in his essay.

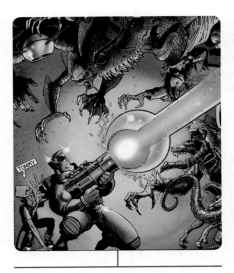

A scene from Gerard Jones and Will Jacobs's comic

A scene from Gerard Jones and Gene Ha's comic book *Oktane*

The title character of *Oktane* gets nasty.

Responding Critically to Visual Arguments

As you learned in Chapter 2, a *critical response* examines the ideas in a text and expresses your reactions to them. When you respond in writing to a visual argument, you should rely on your highlighting and annotations to help you understand the writer's ideas and see how the words and images work together to make a particular point.

As you prepare to write a critical response to a visual argument, you should keep in mind questions like those in the following checklist.

Questions for Responding to Visual Arguments

☐ In what source did the visual appear? What is the target audience for this source?

☐ For what kind of audience do you think that this visual was created? Hostile? Friendly? Neutral?

☐ Who (or what organization) created the visual? What do you know about the goals of this person or group?

☐ What issue is the visual addressing?

☐ What position does the visual take on this issue? How can you tell? Do you agree with this position?

☐ Does the visual include words? If so, are they necessary? What points do they make? Does the visual need more—or different— written text?

☐ Does the visual seem to be a *refutation*—that is, an argument against a particular position?

☐ Is the visual effective? Attractive? Interesting? Clear? Convincing?

When you write a critical response, begin by identifying the source and purpose of the visual. Then, state your reaction to the visual, and examine its elements one at a time, considering how effective each is and how well the various elements work together to create a convincing visual argument. End with a strong concluding statement that summarizes your reaction.

⬇ The critical response that follows was written by the student who highlighted and annotated the advertisement for *Grand Theft Auto IV* on page 60.

RESPONSE TO *GRAND THEFT AUTO IV*

JASON SAVONA

Identification of visual's
source

Reaction to visual

The advertisement for *Grand Theft Auto IV* presents a disturbing   1
preview of the game. Rather than highlighting the game's features and
challenges, this ad promotes the game's violence. As a result, it appeals
more to those who are looking for video games that depict murder and
other crimes than to those who choose a video game on the basis of the
skill it requires.

Analysis of visual's
elements

The "hero" of this game is Niko Bellic, a war veteran from Eastern   2
Europe who has left his country to build a new life in the fictional Liberty
City. Instead of finding peace, he has found a new kind of war. Now,
trapped in the corrupt world of organized crime, Bellic is willing to do
whatever it takes to fight his way out. His idea of justice is vigilante
justice: he makes his own rules. The ad conveys this sense of Bellic
as a loner and an outsider by showing him as a larger-than-life figure
standing tall and alone against a background of the Liberty City skyline.

In the ad, Niko Bellic holds a powerful weapon in his huge hands,   3
and the weapon extends higher than the tallest building behind it,
dominating the picture. Clearly, Bellic means business. As viewers
look at the picture, the dark image of the gun and the man who holds
it comes to the foreground, and everything else—the light brown
buildings, the city lights, the yellow sky—fades into the background. In
the center, the name of the game is set in large black-and-white type
that contrasts with the ad's hazy background, showing the importance of
the product's name.

This image, clearly aimed at young players of violent video games,   4
would certainly be appealing to those who want to have a feeling of
power. What it says is, "A weapon makes a person powerful." This is a
very dangerous message.

Concluding statement

◐ EXERCISE 3.5

Write a one-paragraph critical response to the visual you highlighted and annotated in Exercise 3.2 on page 61. Use the following template to shape your paragraph.

Template for Responding to Visual Arguments

A visual posted on Flickr.com shows _____.

_____. This visual makes a powerful statement about

_____. Its images

show _____

_____. At first glance, the photographer's

goal seems to be to _____

_____

_____. The photo's stark images support this position.

For example, _____

_____, and

_____.

A note that accompanies the photo states that it is not a statement against video games. Still, the impact on its audience is likely to be

_____

_____.

◐ EXERCISE 3.6

Consulting the one-paragraph critical response that you wrote above, write a more fully developed critical response to the visual on page 61. Refer to the highlighting and annotating that you did for Exercise 3.2.

Writing a Rhetorical Analysis

Is It Ethical to Buy Counterfeit Designer Merchandise?

The demand for counterfeit designer merchandise—handbags, shoes, and jewelry—has always been high. Wishing to avoid the high prices of genuine designer goods, consumers spend hundreds of millions of dollars per year buying cheap imitations that are made primarily in factories in China (and in other countries as well). According to United States Customs and Border Protection statistics, the value of counterfeit goods seized in 2008 was $273 million, an increase of more than $72 million over the year before. Naturally, much more counterfeit merchandise gets into the United States than is seized. However hard they try, law enforcement officials cannot seem to stem the tide of counterfeit merchandise that is sold in stores, in flea markets, and by street vendors as well as through the Internet. As long as people want status symbols, there will be a market for these illegal goods.

However, purchasing counterfeit designer goods is not a victimless crime. Buyers are stealing the intellectual property of legitimate businesses that, unlike the manufacturers of fakes, pay their employees fair wages and provide good working conditions. The result is that the sale of counterfeit products eventually drives up prices for legitimate consumers. In addition, because counterfeit goods are of low quality, they do not last as long as the genuine articles. This is not a serious problem when people are buying fake watches and handbags, but it can be life threatening when the counterfeit products include pharmaceuticals, tools, baby food, or automobile parts.

Later in this chapter you will read a rhetorical analysis of an essay that takes a position on this issue, and you will be asked to write a rhetorical analysis of your own about another essay on this topic.

What Is a Rhetorical Analysis?

In everyday use, the term **rhetoric** has distinctly negative connotations. When a speech is described as being nothing but *rhetoric*, the meaning is clear: the speech consists of empty words and phrases that are calculated to confuse and manipulate listeners. When composition instructors use the term *rhetoric*, however, it means something entirely different. Applied to argument, *rhetoric* refers to how various elements work together to form a convincing and persuasive argument.

When you write a **rhetorical analysis** of an argument, you systematically examine the strategies a writer employs to achieve his or her purpose. To carry out this task, you consider the argument's **rhetorical situation**, the writer's **means of persuasion**, and the **rhetorical strategies** that the writer uses to make his or her argument.

OVERVIEW: "LETTER FROM BIRMINGHAM JAIL" BY MARTIN LUTHER KING JR.

Here and throughout the rest of this chapter, we will be analyzing "Letter from Birmingham Jail" by Martin Luther King Jr., which can be found on page 698 of this book.

In 1963, civil rights leader Martin Luther King Jr. organized a series of nonviolent demonstrations to protest the climate of segregation that existed in Birmingham, Alabama. He and his followers met opposition not only from white moderates but also from some African American clergymen who thought that King was a troublemaker. During the demonstrations, King was arrested and jailed for eight days. He wrote his "Letter from Birmingham Jail" on April 16, 1963, from the city jail in response to a public statement by eight white Alabama clergymen entitled "A Call for Unity." This statement asked for an end to the demonstrations, which the clergymen called "untimely," "unwise," and "extreme." (Their letter was addressed to the "white and Negro" population of Birmingham, not to King, whom they considered an "outsider.")

King knew that the world was watching and that his response to the white clergymen would have both national and international significance. As a result, he used a variety of rhetorical strategies to convince readers that his demands were both valid and understandable and that contrary to the opinions of some, his actions were well within the mainstream of American social and political thought. Today, King's "Letter from Birmingham Jail" stands as a model of clear and highly effective argumentation.

Martin Luther King Jr. in Birmingham Jail (April 1963)

Considering the Rhetorical Situation

The **rhetorical situation** consists of the following five elements, all of which you should consider as you write your analysis:

- The writer
- The writer's purpose
- The writer's audience
- The topic
- The context

STRATEGIES FOR ANALYZING THE RHETORICAL SITUATION

You can use the following three strategies to find out information about the rhetorical situation of an argument:

1. **Look at the essay's headnote:** If the essay you are reading has a headnote, it can contain useful information about the writer, the issue being discussed, and the structure of the essay. For this reason, it is a good idea to read headnotes carefully.

2. **Look for clues within the essay:** The writer's use of particular words and phrases can sometimes provide information about his or her preconceptions as well as about the cultural context of the argument. Historical or cultural references can indicate what ideas or information the writer expects readers to have.

3. **Search Google:** Google both the author and the essay's topic. Often, just a few minutes online can give you a lot of useful information—such as the background of a particular debate or the biography of the writer. By looking at titles of the other books or essays the writer has written, you may also be able to get an idea of his or her biases or point of view.

The Writer

Begin by trying to determine whether anything in the writer's background (for example, the writer's education, experience, race, gender, political beliefs, religion, age, and experiences) has influenced the content of the argument. Also consider whether the writer seems to have any preconceptions about the subject.

QUESTIONS FOR ANALYZING THE WRITER

- What is the writer's background?
- How does the writer's background affect the content of the argument?
- What preconceptions about the subject does the writer seem to have?

If you were analyzing "Letter from Birmingham Jail," it would help to know that Martin Luther King Jr. was pastor of the Dexter Avenue Baptist Church in Montgomery, Alabama. In 1956, he organized a bus boycott that led to a United States Supreme Court decision that outlawed segregation on Alabama's buses. In addition, King was a leader of the Southern Christian Leadership Conference and strongly believed in nonviolent protest. His books include *Stride towards Freedom* (1958) and *Why We Can't Wait* (1964). His "I Have a Dream" speech, which he delivered on the steps of the Lincoln Memorial on August 28, 1963, is considered by scholars to be one of the most influential speeches of the twentieth century. In 1964, King won the Nobel Prize for peace.

In his letter, King addresses the injustices that he sees in America—especially in the South—and makes a strong case for civil rights for all races. Throughout his argument, King includes numerous references to the New Testament, to philosophers, and to political and religious thinkers. By doing so, he makes it clear to readers that he is aware of the social,

"I Have a Dream" speech, Washington, D.C. (August 1963)

cultural, religious, and political implications of his actions. Because he is a clergyman, King suggests that by battling injustice, he is doing God's work. This point is made clear in the following passage (para. 3):

> But more basically, I am in Birmingham because injustice is here. Just as the prophets of the eighth century B.C. left their villages and carried their "thus saith the Lord" far beyond the boundaries of their home towns, and just as the Apostle Paul left his village of Tarsus and carried the gospel of Jesus Christ to the far corners of the Greco-Roman world, so am I compelled to carry the gospel of freedom beyond my own home town. Like Paul, I must constantly respond to the Macedonian call for aid.

The Writer's Purpose

Next, consider what the writer hopes to achieve with his or her argument. In other words, ask yourself why the author wrote the argument.

QUESTIONS FOR ANALYZING THE WRITER'S PURPOSE

- Does the writer state his or her purpose directly, or is the purpose implied?
- Is the writer's purpose simply to convince or to encourage action?
- Does the writer rely primarily on logic or on emotion?
- Does the writer have a hidden agenda?

It is clear that Martin Luther King Jr. wrote "Letter from Birmingham Jail" to convince readers that even though he was arrested, his actions were both honorable and just. To get readers to understand that, like Henry David Thoreau, he is protesting laws that he considers wrong, he draws a distinction between just and unjust laws. For him, a law is just if it "squares with the moral law or the law of God" (16). A law is unjust if it "is out of harmony with the moral law" (16). As a clergyman and a civil rights leader, King believed that he had an obligation both to point out the immorality of unjust laws and to protest them—even if it meant going to jail.

The Writer's Audience

Consider whether the writer seems to see readers as friendly, hostile, or neutral. Also try to determine what preconceptions the writer thinks readers have about the subject. Finally, see if the writer shares any common ground with readers.

QUESTIONS FOR ANALYZING THE WRITER'S AUDIENCE

- Who is the writer's intended audience?

- Does the writer see the audience as hostile, friendly, or neutral?

- What values does the writer think the audience holds?

- Does the writer see the audience as informed or uninformed?

In "Letter from Birmingham Jail," King aims his letter at more than one audience. First, he speaks directly to eight clergymen from Birmingham, who are at worst a hostile audience and at best a skeptical one. They consider King to be an outsider whose actions are "unwise and untimely" (1). Before addressing their concerns, King tries to establish common ground, referring to his readers as "fellow clergymen" and "my Christian and Jewish brothers." He then goes on to say that he wishes that the clergymen had supported his actions instead of criticizing them. King ends his letter on a conciliatory note by asking his readers to forgive him if he has overstated his case or been unduly harsh.

In addition to addressing clergymen, King also speaks to white moderates, who he assumes are sympathetic to his cause but concerned about his methods. He knows that he has to influence this segment of his audience if he is to gain wide support for his cause. For this reason, King uses a restrained tone and emphasizes the universality of his message, ending his letter with a plea that is calculated to reassure and inspire those people who need reassurance (50):

> Let us all hope that the dark clouds of racial prejudice will soon pass away and the deep fog of misunderstanding will be lifted from our fear-drenched communities, and in some not too distant tomorrow the radiant stars of love and brotherhood will shine over our great nation with all their scintillating beauty.

The Topic

Try to learn why the writer has decided to write about a particular topic. Also consider how narrow or broad the topic is, and decide if an argument is sufficiently well developed for the topic.

QUESTIONS FOR ANALYZING THE TOPIC

- What is the topic of the argument?

- Why did the writer decide to write about this particular topic?

- Has the writer developed the argument fully enough for the topic?

King addresses complex and emotional issues in "Letter from Birmingham Jail." His topic is apparently racial segregation in Alabama, but he also addresses indifference among white moderates. In addition, he feels he needs to explain his actions (for example, engaging in nonviolent protests) and to answer those who are urging him to call off the demonstrations. Because of the complexity of his topic, his argument is long and somewhat difficult.

The Context

The context is the situation that creates the need for the argument. As you analyze an argument, try to determine the social, political, and cultural events that set the stage for the argument and the part that these events play in the argument itself.

QUESTIONS FOR ANALYZING THE CONTEXT

- What situation (or situations) set the stage for the argument?
- What social, political, and cultural events triggered the argument?
- What historical references situate this argument in a particular place or time?

The immediate context of "Letter to Birmingham Jail" is well known: Martin Luther King Jr. wrote an open letter to eight white clergymen in which he defended his protests against racial segregation. However, the wider social and political context of the letter is less well known.

In 1896, the U.S. Supreme Court ruled in *Plessy v. Ferguson* that "separate but equal" accommodations on railroad cars gave African Americans the equal protection guaranteed by the Fourteenth Amendment of the U.S. Constitution. Well into the twentieth century, this decision was used to justify separate public facilities—including restrooms, water fountains, and even schools and hospitals—for blacks and whites.

In the mid-1950s, state support for segregation of the races and discrimination against African Americans had begun to be challenged. For example, Supreme Court decisions in 1954 and 1955 found that segregation in the public schools and other publically financed locations was unconstitutional. At the same time, whites and blacks alike were calling for an end to racial discrimination. Their actions took the form of marches, boycotts, and sit-ins (organized protests whose participants refused to move from a public area). Many whites, however, particularly in the South, strongly resisted any sudden changes in race relations.

King's demonstrations in Birmingham, Alabama, took place within this larger social and political context. His campaign was a continuation of

Segregated water fountains in North Carolina (1950)

the push for equal rights that had been gaining momentum in the United States for decades. King, along with the Southern Christian Leadership Conference, had dispatched hundreds of people to Birmingham to engage in nonviolent demonstrations against those who were determined to keep African Americans from gaining their full rights as citizens.

Considering the Means of Persuasion: Logos, Pathos, Ethos

In the introduction to this book, you read about how writers of argument use three means of persuasion—*logos*, *pathos*, and *ethos*—to appeal to their readers. Most effective arguments combine two or more of these appeals. In "Letter from Birmingham Jail," Martin Luther King Jr. uses all three of these appeals:

The Appeal to Logic (Logos)

In "Letter from Birmingham Jail," King attempts to demonstrate the logic of his position. In paragraph 15, for example, he says that there are two types of laws—just and unjust. He then points out that he has both a legal and a moral responsibility to "disobey unjust laws." In paragraph 16, King supports his position with references to various philosophers and theologians—for example, St. Thomas Aquinas, Martin Buber, and Paul Tillich. He also develops the argument that even though all Americans should obey the law, they are responsible to a higher moral authority—God.

The Appeal to Emotion (Pathos)

Throughout "Letter from Birmingham Jail," King attempts to create sympathy for his cause. In paragraph 14, for example, he catalogues the injustices of life in the United States for African Americans. He makes a particularly emotional appeal by quoting a hypothetical five-year-old boy who might ask, "Daddy, why do white people treat colored people so mean?" In addition, he includes vivid images of racial injustice to create anger toward those who deny African Americans equal rights. In this way, King creates sympathy (and possibly empathy) in readers.

The Appeal to Authority (Ethos)

To be persuasive, King has to establish that he has the credibility or authority to speak on behalf of the African American community. In paragraph 2, for example, he reminds readers that he is the president of the Southern Christian Leadership Conference, "an organization operating in every southern state." In paragraph 3, he compares himself to the apostle Paul, who carried the gospel "to the far corners of the Greco-Roman world." In addition, King attempts to show readers that what he is doing is well within the mainstream of American political and social thought. By referring to Thomas Jefferson, Henry David Thoreau, and the 1954 U.S. Supreme Court decision that outlawed segregation in public schools, he tries to demonstrate that he is not the wild-eyed radical that some believe him to be. Thus, in his letter, King establishes himself in both secular and religious terms as a leader who has both the stature and the authority to present his case.

Considering the Writer's Rhetorical Strategies

Writers use various **rhetorical strategies** to present their ideas and opinions. Here are a few of the strategies that you should consider when analyzing and evaluating an argument.

Thesis

The **thesis**—the position that the argument supports—is an important rhetorical strategy in every argument. When you analyze an argument, you should always ask, "What is the essay's thesis, and why does the writer state it as he or she does?" You should also consider at what point in the argument the thesis is stated and what the effect of this placement is.

In "Letter from Birmingham Jail," Martin Luther King Jr. begins by telling readers that he is "confined here in the Birmingham city jail" and that he is writing his letter to answer clergymen who have called his demonstrations "unwise and untimely." King clearly (and unapologetically) states his thesis ("But more basically, I am in Birmingham because injustice is here") at the beginning of the third paragraph, right after he explains his purpose, so that readers will have no doubt what his position is as they read the rest of his argument.

Organization

The **organization** of an argument—how a writer arranges ideas—is also important. For example, after stating his thesis, King tells readers why he is in Birmingham and what he hopes to accomplish: he wants unjust laws to be abolished and the 1954 Supreme Court ruling to be enforced. King then **refutes**—argues against—the specific charges that were leveled at him by the white clergymen who want him to stop his protests.

The structure of "Letter from Birmingham Jail" enables King to make his points clearly, logically, and effectively:

- King begins his argument by addressing the charge that his actions are untimely. If anything, says King, his actions are not timely enough—after all, African Americans have waited more than 340 years for their "constitutional and God-given rights" (14).

- He then addresses the issue of his willingness to break laws and makes the distinction between just and unjust laws.

- After chiding white moderates for not supporting his cause, he discusses the fact that some people have accused him of being extreme. According to King, this charge is false: if he had not embraced a philosophy of nonviolent protest, the streets of the South would "be flowing with blood" (29).

- King then makes the point that the contemporary church must recapture the "sacrificial spirit of the early church" (42). He does this by linking his struggle for freedom with the "sacred heritage of the nation and the eternal will of God" (44).

- King ends his argument by asserting both his humility and his unity with the white clergy.

Evidence

To convince an audience, a writer must support the thesis with **evidence**—facts, observations, expert opinion, and so on. King brings in a great deal of evidence to support his arguments. For instance, he uses numerous examples (both historical and personal) as well as many references to philosophers, political thinkers, and theologians (such as Jesus, St. Paul, St. Augustine, Amos, Martin Luther, William Gladstone, and Abraham Lincoln). According to King, these figures, who were once considered "extremists," were not afraid of "making waves" when the need arose. Now, however, they are well within the mainstream of social, political, and religious thought. King also presents reasons, facts, and quotations to support his points.

Stylistic Techniques

Writers also use stylistic techniques to make their arguments more memorable and more convincing. For example, in "Letter from Birmingham Jail," King uses *similes*, *metaphors*, and *allusions* to enhance his argument.

Simile A **simile** is a figure of speech that compares two unlike things using the word *like* or *as*.

> Like a boil that can never be cured so long as it is covered up but must be opened with all its ugliness to the natural medicines of air and light, injustice must be exposed, . . . before it can be cured. (24)

> Isn't this like condemning a robbed man because his possession of money precipitated the evil act of robbery? (25)

Metaphor A **metaphor** is a comparison in which two dissimilar things are compared without the word *like* or *as*. A metaphor suggests that two things that are very different share a quality.

> Frankly, I have yet to engage in a direct-action campaign that was "well-timed" in the view of those who have not suffered unduly from the disease of segregation. (13)

> [W]hen you have seen the vast majority of your twenty million Negro brothers smothering in the airtight cage of poverty . . . (14)

Allusion An **allusion** is a reference within a literary work to another work. An allusion is a kind of shorthand that depends on a reference to a person, literary work, or historical event to enlarge the context of the situation being written about. The writer expects readers to recognize the allusion and to make the connection to the text they are reading.

> I would agree with St. Augustine that "an unjust law is no law at all." (16)

> Of course, there is nothing new about this kind of civil disobedience. It was evidenced sublimely in the refusal of Shadrach, Meshach, and Abednego to obey the laws of Nebuchadnezzar, on the ground that a higher moral law was at stake. (21) [King expects his audience of clergymen to recognize this reference to the Book of Daniel in the Old Testament.]

King also uses *parallelism*, *repetition*, and *rhetorical questions* to further his argument.

Parallelism **Parallelism** is the use of a similar structure in the repetition of pairs or series of words, phrases, or clauses. The use of parallelism emphasizes related ideas and makes a passage easier to follow.

> In any nonviolent campaign there are four basic steps: collection of the facts to determine whether injustices exist; negotiation; self-purification; and direct action. (6)

> Shallow understanding from people of good will is more frustrating than absolute misunderstanding from people of ill will. Lukewarm acceptance is much more bewildering than outright rejection. (23)

> I wish you had commended the Negro sit-inners and demonstrators of Birmingham for their sublime courage, their willingness to suffer, and their amazing discipline in the midst of great provocation. (47)

Repetition Intentional **repetition** involves repeating a word or phrase for emphasis, clarity, or emotional effect.

> "Are you able to accept blows without retaliating?" "Are you able to endure the ordeal of jail?" (8)

> If I have said anything in this letter that overstates the truth and indicates an unreasonable impatience, I beg you to forgive me. If I have said anything that understates the truth and indicates my having patience that allows me to settle for anything less than brotherhood, I beg God to forgive me. (49)

Rhetorical questions A **rhetorical question** is a question that is asked to encourage readers to reflect on an issue, not to call for a reply.

> One may well ask: "How can you advocate breaking some laws and obeying others?" (15)

> Will we be extremists for hate or for love? (31)

Assessing the Argument

No rhetorical analysis of an argument would be complete without an assessment of its effectiveness: whether the rhetorical strategies the writer uses result in a clear and persuasive argument, or whether they fall short. In other words, has the writer achieved his or her purpose? When you write a rhetorical analysis, you can begin with an assessment and go on to support it, or you can begin with a discussion of the various rhetorical strategies that the writer uses and then end with an assessment.

After analyzing "Letter from Birmingham Jail," you could reasonably conclude that King has written an effective argument that is likely to convince his readers that his presence in Birmingham is both justified and necessary. Using *logos*, *pathos*, and *ethos*, he constructs a multifaceted argument that is calculated to appeal to the various segments of his audience—Southern clergymen, white moderates, and African Americans. In addition, King uses similes, metaphors, and allusions to enrich his argument and to make it more memorable, and he uses parallelism, repetition, and rhetorical questions to emphasize ideas and to reinforce his points. Because it is so clear and powerful, King's argument—in particular, the distinction between just and unjust laws—addresses not only the injustices that were present in 1963 when it was written but also the injustices and inequalities that exist today. In this sense, King has written an argument that has broad significance beyond the audiences for which it was originally intended.

CHECKLIST

Preparing to Write a Rhetorical Analysis

As you read, ask yourself the following questions:

☐ Who is the writer? Is there anything in the writer's background that might influence what is (or is not) included in the argument?

☐ What is the writer's purpose? What does the writer hope to achieve?

☐ What topic has the writer decided to write about? How broad is the topic?

☐ What situation created the need for the argument?

☐ At what points in the argument does the writer appeal to logic? To emotion? How does the writer try to establish his or her credibility?

☐ What is the argument's thesis? Where is it stated? Why?

☐ How does the writer organize the argument? How effective is this arrangement of ideas?

☐ What evidence does the writer use to support the argument? Does the writer use enough evidence?

☐ Does the writer use similes, metaphors, and allusions?

☐ Does the writer use parallelism, repetition, and rhetorical questions?

☐ Given your analysis, what is your overall assessment of the argument?

Sample Rhetorical Analysis

Deniz Bilgutay, a student in a composition class, read the following essay, "Terror's Purse Strings" by Dana Thomas, which makes an argument against buying counterfeit designer goods. Deniz then wrote the rhetorical analysis that appears on pages 82–84. Notice how she considers many of the rhetorical elements discussed above. (Deniz Bilgutay's research paper, "The High Cost of Cheap Counterfeit Goods," uses "Terror's Purse Strings" as a source. See Appendix B.)

This piece appeared in the *New York Times* on August 30, 2007.

TERROR'S PURSE STRINGS

DANA THOMAS

1 Luxury fashion designers are busily putting final touches on the handbags they will present during the spring-summer 2008 women's wear shows, which begin next week in New York City's Bryant Park. To understand the importance of the handbag in fashion today consider this: According to consumer surveys conducted by Coach, the average American woman was buying two new handbags a year in 2000; by 2004, it was more than four. And the average luxury bag retails for 10 to 12 times its production cost.

2 "There is a kind of an obsession with bags," the designer Miuccia Prada told me. "It's so easy to make money."

3 Counterfeiters agree. As soon as a handbag hits big, counterfeiters around the globe churn out fake versions by the thousands. And they have no trouble selling them. Shoppers descend on Canal Street in New York, Santee Alley in Los Angeles and flea markets and purse parties around the country to pick up knockoffs for one-tenth the legitimate bag's retail cost, then pass them off as real.

4 "Judges, prosecutors, defense attorneys shop here," a private investigator told me as we toured the counterfeit section of Santee Alley. "Affluent people from Newport Beach." According to a study by the British law firm Davenport Lyons, two-thirds of British consumers are "proud to tell their family and friends" that they bought fake luxury fashion items.

5 At least 11 percent of the world's clothing is fake, according to 2000 figures from the Global Anti-Counterfeiting Group in Paris. Fashion is easy to copy: counterfeiters buy the real items, take them apart, scan the pieces to make patterns and produce almost-perfect fakes.

> "At least 11 percent of the world's clothing is fake."

6 Most people think that buying an imitation handbag or wallet is harmless, a victimless crime. But the counterfeiting rackets are run by crime syndicates that also deal in narcotics, weapons, child prostitution, human trafficking and terrorism. Ronald K. Noble, the secretary general of Interpol,° told the House of Representatives Committee on International Relations that profits from the sale of counterfeit goods have gone to groups associated with Hezbollah, the Shiite terrorist group, paramilitary organizations in Northern Ireland and FARC, the Revolutionary Armed Forces of Colombia.

An international criminal police organization

7 Sales of counterfeit T-shirts may have helped finance the 1993 World Trade Center bombing, according to the International AntiCounterfeiting Coalition. "Profits from counterfeiting are one of the three main sources of income

supporting international terrorism," said Magnus Ranstorp, a terrorism expert at the University of St. Andrews, in Scotland.

Most fakes today are produced in China, a good many of them by chil- 8 dren. Children are sometimes sold or sent off by their families to work in clandestine factories that produce counterfeit luxury goods. Many in the West consider this an urban myth. But I have seen it myself.

On a warm winter afternoon in Guangzhou, I accompanied Chinese police 9 officers on a factory raid in a decrepit tenement. Inside, we found two dozen children, ages 8 to 13, gluing and sewing together fake luxury-brand handbags. The police confiscated everything, arrested the owner and sent the children out. Some punched their timecards, hoping to still get paid. (The average Chinese factory worker earns about $120 a month; the counterfeit factory worker earns half that or less.) As we made our way back to the police vans, the children threw bottles and cans at us. They were now jobless and, because the factory owner housed them, homeless. It was *Oliver Twist* in the 21st century.

What can we do to stop this? Much like the war on drugs, the effort to 10 protect luxury brands must go after the source: the counterfeit manufactur- ers. The company that took me on the Chinese raid is one of the only luxury- goods makers that works directly with Chinese authorities to shut down facto- ries, and it has one of the lowest rates of counterfeiting.

The people who lived during the reign of Victoria (1819–1901), queen of Great Britain and Ireland, who are often associated with prudish behavior

Luxury brands also need to teach consumers that the traffic in fake goods 11 has many victims. But most companies refuse to speak publicly about coun- terfeiting—some won't even authenticate questionable items for concerned customers—believing, like Victorians,° that acknowledging despicable actions tarnishes their sterling reputations.

So it comes down to us. If we stop knowingly buying fakes, the supply 12 chain will dry up and counterfeiters will go out of business. The crime syndi- cates will have far less money to finance their illicit activities and their terrorist plots. And the children? They can go home.

A POWERFUL CALL TO ACTION
DENIZ BILGUTAY

Context

Topic

In her *New York Times* editorial, "Terror's Purse Strings," writer 1 Dana Thomas uses the opening of New York's fashion shows as an opportunity to expose a darker side of fashion—the impact of imitation designer goods. Thomas explains to her readers why buying counterfeit luxury items, like fake handbags, is a serious problem. Her first goal is to raise awareness of the dangerous ties between counterfeiters who sell fake luxury merchandise and international criminal organizations that support terrorism and child labor. Her second goal is to explain how people can be a part of the solution by refusing to buy the counterfeit goods that finance these criminal activities. By gaining her audience's confidence and goodwill, building her case slowly, and appealing to both our logic and our emotions, Thomas succeeds in writing an informative and inspiring piece.

2   For Thomas's argument to work, she has to earn her readers' trust. She does so first by anticipating a sympathetic, well-intentioned, educated audience and then by establishing her own credibility. To avoid sounding accusatory, Thomas assumes that her readers are unaware of the problem posed by counterfeit goods. She demonstrates this by offering basic factual information and by acknowledging what "most people think" or what "many in the West consider": that buying counterfeit goods is harmless. She also acknowledges her readers' high level of education by drawing comparisons with history and literature—specifically, the Victorians and *Oliver Twist*. Second, to earn the audience's trust, she uses her knowledge and position to gain credibility. As the Paris correspondent for *Newsweek* and as the author of a book on luxury goods, Thomas has credibility on her topic. Showing her familiarity with the world of fashion by referring to a conversation with renowned designer Miuccia Prada, she further emphasizes this authority. Later in the article, she shares her experience of witnessing the abuse that accompanies the production of fake designer handbags. This story allows her to say, "I've seen it myself," confirming her knowledge not just of the fashion world but also of the world of counterfeiting. However, despite her authority, she does not distance herself from readers. In fact, she goes out of her way to identify with them, using informal style and first person, noting "it comes down to us" and asking what "we" can do.

3   In Thomas's argument, both the organization and the use of evidence are very effective. She begins her article with statements that are easy to accept, and as she proceeds, she addresses more serious issues. In the first paragraph, she simply asks readers "to understand the importance of the handbag in fashion today." She demonstrates

Analysis of writer's purpose

Thesis statement: Assessment of essay

Analysis of writer's audience

Writer's use of similes, metaphors, allusions

Writer's use of ethos

Analysis of the writer

Analysis of essay's organization

Writer's use of logos

the wide-ranging influence and appeal of counterfeit designer goods, pointing out that "at least 11 percent of the world's clothing is fake." Thomas then makes the point that the act of purchasing these seemingly frivolous goods can actually have serious consequences. For example, crime syndicates and possibly even terrorist organizations

Writer's use of evidence

actually run "the counterfeiting rackets" that produce these popular items. To support this point, she relies on two kinds of evidence— quotations from terrorism experts (specifically, the leader of a respected international police organization as well as a scholar in the field) and her own personal experience at a Chinese factory. Both kinds of

Writer's use of *pathos*

evidence appeal to our emotions. Discussions of terrorism, especially those that recall terrorist attacks on America, spark fear. Thomas deliberately chooses her one specific example—the "sales of counterfeit T-shirts" that "may have helped finance the 1993 World Trade Center bombing"—to evoke that fear. Next, to elicit her readers' compassion, she describes her experience of witnessing child labor in China. After using her readers' emotions to make them empathize with the situation, she asks, "What can we do to stop this?"

Thomas waits until the end of the article to present her thesis, 4 which is stated in the form of a clear-cut solution: to avoid financing terror and abuse, we should not give our money to the terrorists and abusers by buying counterfeit goods. Her appeals to emotion have

Writer's use of *pathos*

made readers ready to act. Her subsequent reference to the "war on drugs" evokes emotionally charged images of evil drug lords and drug-addicted children, reinforcing the readers' sense that change is

Writer's use of *logos*

needed. Ultimately, however, the solution that Thomas presents relies on the simple logic of cause and effect. Those who buy counterfeit goods are supporting criminal practices and, as a result, are responsible for the harm that these organizations do. If we want to change this situation, then we need to change our buying practices.

⊘ EXERCISE 4.1

Read the essay "Sweatshop Oppression," by Rajeev Ravisankar, on pages 86–87. Then, write a one-paragraph rhetorical analysis of the essay. Follow the template below, filling in the blanks to create your analysis.

Template for Writing a Rhetorical Analysis

Ravisankar begins his essay by _____

_____

_____. The problem he identifies is _____

_____

_____. He assumes his readers are _____

_____

_____. His purpose is to _____

_____.

In order to accomplish this purpose, he appeals mainly to _____

_____

_____. He also appeals to _____

_____.

In his essay, Ravisankar addresses the main argument against his thesis, the idea that _____

_____

_____

_____. He refutes this argument by saying _____

_____

_____.

Finally, he concludes by making the point that _____

_____.

Overall, the argument Ravisankar makes is effective [or ineffective] because

_____

_____

_____.

This opinion piece was published in *The Lantern*, the student newspaper of the Ohio State University, on April 19, 2006.

SWEATSHOP OPPRESSION

RAJEEV RAVISANKAR

Being the "poor" college students that we all are, many of us undoubtedly 1
place an emphasis on finding the lowest prices. Some take this to the extreme
and camp out in front of a massive retail store in the wee hours of the morning
on Black Friday,° waiting for the opportunity to buy as much as we can for as
little as possible.

The Friday after Thanksgiving, traditionally the biggest shopping day of the year

What often gets lost in this rampant, low-cost driven consumerism is the 2
high human cost it takes to achieve lower and lower prices. Specifically, this
means the extensive use of sweatshop labor.

Many of us are familiar with the term sweatshop,° but have difficulty 3
really understanding how abhorrent the hours, wages and conditions are.
Many of these workers are forced to work 70–80 hours per week making pennies per hour. Workers are discouraged or intimidated from forming unions.

A work environment with long hours, low wages, and difficult or dangerous conditions

They must fulfill certain quotas for the day and stay extra hours (with no 4
pay) if these are not fulfilled. Some are forced to sit in front of a machine for
hours as they are not permitted to take breaks unless the manager allows them
to do so. Unsanitary bathrooms, poor ventilation and extreme heat, upward of
90 degrees, are also prevalent. Child labor is utilized in some factories as well.

Facing mounting pressure from labor rights activists, trade unions, student 5
protests and human-rights groups, companies claimed that they would make
improvements. Many of the aforementioned conditions, however, persist. In
many cases, even a few pennies more
could make a substantial difference in
the lives of these workers. Of course,
multinational corporations are not interested in giving charity; they are interested
in doing anything to increase profits. Also, many consumers in the West refuse
to pay a little bit more even if it would improve the lives of sweatshop workers.

> "Corporations . . . are interested in doing anything to increase profits."

Free-market economic fundamentalists have argued that claims made by 6
those who oppose sweatshops actually have a negative impact on the plight of
the poor in the developing world. They suggest that by criticizing labor and
human-rights conditions, anti-sweatshop activists have forced companies to
pull out of some locations, resulting in workers losing their jobs. To shift the
blame in this manner is to neglect a simple fact: Companies, not the anti-
sweatshop protestors, make the decision to shift to locations where they can
find cheaper labor and weaker labor restrictions.

Simply put, the onus should always be on companies such as Nike, Reebok, Adidas, Champion, Gap, Wal-Mart etc. They are to blame for perpetuating a system of exploitation which seeks to get as much out of each worker for the least possible price.   7

By continuing to strive for lower wages and lower input costs, they are taking part in a phenomenon which has been described as "the race to the bottom." The continual decline of wages and working conditions will be accompanied by a lower standard of living. This hardly seems like the best way to bring the developing world out of the pits of poverty.   8

So what can we do about it? Currently, the total disregard for human well-being through sweatshop oppression is being addressed by a number of organizations, including University Students against Sweatshops. USAS seeks to make universities source their apparel in factories that respect workers' rights, especially the right to freely form unions.   9

According to an article in *The Nation*, universities purchase nearly "$3 billion in T-shirts, sweatshirts, caps, sneakers and sports uniforms adorned with their institutions' names and logos." Because brands do not want to risk losing this money, it puts pressure on them to provide living wages and reasonable conditions for workers. Campaigns such as this are necessary if we are to stop the long race to the bottom.   10

➲ EXERCISE 4.2

Write an essay-length rhetorical analysis of "Sweatshop Oppression" by Rajeev Ravisankar. Be sure to consider the rhetorical situation, the means of persuasion, and the writer's rhetorical strategies. Include an assessment of the strengths and weaknesses of Ravisankar's argument in your essay.

5

Understanding Logic and Recognizing Fallacies

Do Merit-Based Scholarships Make Sense?

Colleges in the United States have always provided need-based aid to students. As early as the eighteenth century, colleges gave "charitable aid" to help needy students, and after World War II, with the enrollment of veterans on the G.I. Bill, many colleges increased the amount of need-based aid that they provided. At the same time, however, many private colleges (and some state universities) awarded merit-based scholarships to recruit the best students. Recently, however, this situation has begun to change: many elite private colleges have started to phase out merit-based aid in favor of need-based aid.

There has always been a debate between supporters of need-based aid and supporters of merit-based scholarships. Those who favor need-based aid say that without such aid, many students could not afford to attend private colleges. According to them, eligibility for aid should be determined solely by financial need, not by test scores, athletic ability, or academic standing. Those who favor merit-based scholarships say that ability, not need, should be the determining factor for aid. Merit-based scholarships, they argue, reward hard work as well as participation in sports and other extracurricular activities. In addition, merit-based aid enables students from families who cannot afford tuition—but nevertheless do not qualify for need-based aid—to attend expensive private colleges.

Later in this chapter, you will be asked to think more about this issue. You will be given several sources to consider and asked to write a logical argument that takes a position on whether merit-based scholarships make sense.

Elizabeth Hasselbeck versus Rosie O'Donnell on *The View*

The word *logic* comes from the Greek word *logos*, roughly translated as "word," "thought," "principle," or "reason." **Logic** is concerned with the principles of correct reasoning. By studying logic, you learn the principles that determine the validity of arguments. In other words, logic enables you to tell whether a conclusion correctly follows from a set of statements or assumptions.

Why should you study logic? One answer is that a knowledge of logic enables you to make valid points and draw sound conclusions, which in turn helps you to present your ideas clearly and effectively. An understanding of logic also enables you to evaluate the arguments of others. When you understand the basic principles of logic, you know how to tell the difference between a strong argument and a weak argument—between one that is well reasoned and one that is not. This ability can help you cut through the tangle of jumbled thought that characterizes many of the arguments you encounter daily—on television, radio, and the Internet; in the press; and from friends. Finally, knowledge of logic enables you to communicate clearly and forcefully. Understanding the characteristics of good arguments helps you to present your own ideas in a coherent and even compelling way.

Specific rules determine the criteria you use to develop (and to evaluate) arguments logically. For this reason, you should become familiar with the basic principles of *deductive* and *inductive reasoning*—two important ways information is organized in argumentative essays. (Keep in mind that a single argumentative essay might contain both deductive reasoning and inductive reasoning. For the sake of clarity, however, we will be discussing them separately.)

What Is Deductive Reasoning?

Deductive reasoning begins with **premises**—statements or assumptions on which an argument is based or from which conclusions are drawn. Deductive reasoning moves from general statements (or premises) to specific conclusions. The process of deduction has traditionally been illustrated with a **syllogism**, which consists of a *major premise*, a *minor premise*, and a *conclusion*:

Thomas Jefferson

MAJOR PREMISE	All good students should get financial aid.
MINOR PREMISE	Sarah is a good student.
CONCLUSION	Therefore, Sarah should get financial aid.

A syllogism begins with a **major premise**—a general statement that relates two terms. It then moves to a **minor premise**—an example of the statement that was made in the major premise. If these two premises are linked correctly, a **conclusion** that is supported by the two premises should logically follow. (Notice that the conclusion in the syllogism above contains no terms that do not appear in the major and minor premises.) The strength of deductive reasoning is that if the major and minor premises are true, then the conclusion necessarily follows.

Thomas Jefferson used deductive reasoning in the Declaration of Independence (included on p. 679). When, in 1776, the Continental Congress asked him to draft this document, Jefferson knew that he had to write a powerful argument that would convince the world that the American colonies were justified in breaking away from England. He knew how compelling a deductive argument could be, and so he organized the Declaration of Independence to reflect the traditional structure of deductive logic. It contains a major premise, a minor premise (supported by evidence), and a conclusion. Expressed as a syllogism, here is the argument that Jefferson used:

MAJOR PREMISE	When a government oppresses people, the people have a right to abolish that government.
MINOR PREMISE	The government of England is oppressing the American people.
CONCLUSION	Therefore, the American people have the right to abolish that government.

Most of us use deductive reasoning every day—at home, in school, on the job, and in our communities—usually without even realizing it. In practice, deductive arguments are more complicated than the simple three-part syllogism suggests. Still, it is important to understand the basic structure of a syllogism because a syllogism enables you to map out your argument, to test it, and to see if it makes sense.

Constructing Sound Syllogisms

A syllogism is **valid** when its conclusion follows logically from its premises. A syllogism is **true** when the premises are consistent with the facts. To be **sound**, a syllogism must be *both* valid and true.

Consider the following valid syllogism:

MAJOR PREMISE	All state universities give need-based aid.
MINOR PREMISE	UCLA is a state university.
CONCLUSION	Therefore, UCLA gives need-based aid.

In the valid syllogism above, both the major premise and the minor premise are factual statements. If both these premises are true, then the conclusion must also be true. Because the syllogism is both valid and true, it is also sound.

However, a syllogism can be valid without being true. For example, look at the following syllogism:

MAJOR PREMISE	All recipients of merit-based aid are wealthy.
MINOR PREMISE	Dillon is a recipient of merit-based aid.
CONCLUSION	Therefore, Dillon is wealthy.

As illogical as it may seem, this syllogism is valid: its conclusion follows logically from its premises. The major premise states the proposition that *all recipients of merit-based aid*—the entire class of *recipients*—are wealthy. However, this premise is false: some recipients of merit-based aid are wealthy, but many are not. For this reason, even though this syllogism is valid, it is not true.

Keep in mind that validity is a test of an argument's structure, not of its soundness. Even if a syllogism's major and minor premises are true, its conclusion may not necessarily be valid. For example, consider this syllogism:

MAJOR PREMISE	Rain makes streets wet.
MINOR PREMISE	Chestnut Street is wet.
CONCLUSION	Therefore, the rain made Chestnut Street wet.

In the syllogism above, the major premise is true: rain does make streets wet. It is also true that Chestnut Street is wet. The conclusion that it must have rained follows logically from these two premises. However, it is also possible that other factors—not just rain—could have caused the street to be wet. For example, a broken water main, a flood, or a street-cleaning truck could have caused the street to be wet. Therefore, even though the major and minor premises of this syllogism *may* be true, you cannot say for certain that the conclusion is valid.

A flaw in logic can also undercut the validity of a syllogism. Consider the following examples of invalid syllogisms.

Syllogism with an Illogical Middle Term

A syllogism with an illogical middle term cannot be valid. The **middle term** of a syllogism is the term that occurs in both the major and minor premises but not in the conclusion. (It links the major term and the minor term together in the syllogism.) A middle term of a valid syllogism must refer to *all* members of the designated class or group—for example, all dogs, all people, all men, or all women.

Consider the following invalid syllogism:

MAJOR PREMISE	All dogs are mammals.
MINOR PREMISE	Some mammals are porpoises.
CONCLUSION	Therefore, some porpoises are dogs.

Even though the statements in the major and minor premises are true, the syllogism is not valid. *Mammals* is the middle term because it appears in both the major and minor premises. However, because the middle term *mammal* does not refer to *all mammals*, it cannot logically lead to a valid conclusion.

In the syllogism that follows, the middle term *does* refer to all members of the designated group, so the syllogism is valid:

MAJOR PREMISE	All dogs are mammals.
MINOR PREMISE	Ralph is a dog.
CONCLUSION	Therefore, Ralph is a mammal.

Syllogism with a Key Term Whose Meaning Shifts

A syllogism that contains a key term whose meaning shifts cannot be valid. For this reason, the meaning of a key term must remain consistent throughout the syllogism.

Consider the following invalid syllogism:

MAJOR PREMISE	Only man is capable of analytical reasoning.
MINOR PREMISE	Kim is not a man.
CONCLUSION	Therefore, Kim is not capable of analytical reasoning.

In the major premise, *man* refers to mankind—that is, to all human beings. In the minor premise, however, *man* refers to males. Notice how in the following valid syllogism the key terms remain consistent:

MAJOR PREMISE	All educated human beings are capable of analytical reasoning.
MINOR PREMISE	Kim is an educated human being.
CONCLUSION	Therefore, Kim is capable of analytical reasoning.

Syllogisms with Negative Premises

If *either* premise in a syllogism is negative, then the conclusion must also be negative.

The following syllogism is not valid:

MAJOR PREMISE	Only senators can vote on legislation.
MINOR PREMISE	No students are senators.
CONCLUSION	Therefore, students can vote on legislation.

Because one of the premises of the syllogism above is negative ("No students are senators"), the only possible valid conclusion must also be negative ("Therefore, no students can vote on legislation").

If *both* premises are negative, however, the syllogism cannot have a valid conclusion:

MAJOR PREMISE	Needy students may not be denied financial aid.
MINOR PREMISE	Jen is not a needy student.
CONCLUSION	Therefore, Jen may not be denied financial aid.

In the syllogism above, both premises are negative. For this reason, the syllogism cannot have a valid conclusion. (For example, how can Jen get financial aid if she is not a needy student?) To have a valid conclusion, this syllogism must have only one negative premise:

MAJOR PREMISE	Needy students may not be denied financial aid.
MINOR PREMISE	Jen is a needy student.
CONCLUSION	Therefore, Jen may not be denied financial aid.

Recognizing Enthymemes

An **enthymeme** is a syllogism with one or two parts of its argument—usually, the major premise—missing. In everyday life, we often leave out parts of arguments—most of the time because we think they are so obvious (or clearly implied) that they don't need to be stated. We assume that the people hearing or reading the arguments will easily be able to fill in the missing parts.

Many enthymemes are presented as a conclusion plus a reason. Consider the following enthymeme:

Robert has lied, so he cannot be trusted.

In the statement above, the minor premise and the conclusion are stated, but the major premise is only implied. Once the missing term has been supplied, the logical structure of the enthymeme becomes clear:

MAJOR PREMISE	People who lie cannot be trusted.
MINOR PREMISE	Robert has lied.
CONCLUSION	Therefore, Robert cannot be trusted.

It is important to identify enthymemes in arguments you read because some writers, knowing that readers often accept enthymemes uncritically, use them intentionally to unfairly influence readers.

Consider this enthymeme:

Because Liz receives a tuition grant, she should work.

Although some readers might challenge this statement, others will accept it uncritically. When you supply the missing premise, however, the underlying assumptions of the enthymeme become clear—and open to question:

MAJOR PREMISE	All students who receive a tuition grant should work.
MINOR PREMISE	Liz receives a tuition grant.
CONCLUSION	Therefore, Liz should work.

Perhaps some people who receive tuition grants should work, but should everyone? What about those who are ill or who have disabilities? What about those who participate in varsity sports or have unpaid internships? The enthymeme oversimplifies the issue and should not be accepted at face value.

At first glance, the following enthymeme might seem to make sense:

North Korea is ruled by a dictator, so it should be invaded.

However, consider the same enthymeme with the missing term supplied:

MAJOR PREMISE	All countries governed by dictators should be invaded.
MINOR PREMISE	North Korea is a country governed by a dictator.
CONCLUSION	Therefore, North Korea should be invaded.

Once the missing major premise has been supplied, the flaws in the argument become clear. Should *all* nations governed by dictators be invaded? Who should do the invading? Who would make this decision? What would be the consequences of such a policy? As this enthymeme illustrates, if the major premise of a deductive argument is questionable, then the rest of the argument will also be flawed.

BUMPER-STICKER THINKING

Bumper stickers often take the form of enthymemes:

- Self-control beats birth control.
- Peace is patriotic.
- A woman's place is in the White House.
- Ban cruel traps.
- Extinction is forever.
- It's never too late to have a happy childhood.
- No one needs a mink coat except a mink.
- Celebrate diversity.

Most often, bumper stickers state just the conclusion of an argument and omit both the major and minor premises. Careful readers, however, will supply the missing premises and thus determine whether the argument is sound.

Bumper stickers on a car

⬆ EXERCISE 5.1

Read the following paragraph. Then, restate its main argument as a syllogism.

Drunk Driving Should Be Legalized

In ordering states to enforce tougher drunk driving standards by making it a crime to drive with a blood-alcohol concentration of .08 percent or higher, government has been permitted to criminalize the content of drivers' blood instead of their actions. The assumption that a driver who has been drinking automatically presents a danger to society even when no harm has been caused is a blatant violation of civil liberties. Government should not be concerned with the probability and propensity of a drinking driver to cause an accident; rather, laws should deal only with actions that damage person or property. Until they actually commit a crime, drunk drivers should be liberated from the force of the law. (From "Legalize Drunk Driving," by Llewellyn H. Rockwell Jr., WorldNetDaily .com, November 2, 2000)

⬆ EXERCISE 5.2

Read the following excerpt. Then, answer the questions that follow.

Animals Are Equal to Humans

According to the United Nations, a person may not be killed, exploited, cruelly treated, intimidated, or imprisoned for no good reason. Put another way, people should be able to live in peace, according to their own needs and preferences.

Who should have these rights? Do they apply to people of all races? Children? People who are brain damaged or senile? The declaration makes it clear that basic rights apply to everyone. To make a slave of someone who is intellectually handicapped or of a different race is no more justifiable than to make a slave of anyone else.

The reason why these rights apply to everyone is simple: regardless of our differences, we all experience a life with its mosaic of thoughts and feelings. This applies equally to the princess and the hobo, the brain surgeon and the dunce. Our value as individuals arises from this capacity to experience life, not because of any intelligence or usefulness to others. Every person has an inherent value, and deserves to be treated with respect in order to make the most of their unique life experience. (Excerpted from "Human and Animal Rights," by Animal Liberation, www.animalliberation.org.au, 1998)

1. What unstated assumptions about the subject does the writer of this excerpt make? Does the writer expect readers to accept these assumptions? How can you tell?

2. What kind of supporting evidence does the writer of this excerpt provide?

3. What is the major premise of this argument?

4. Express the argument that is presented in these paragraphs as a syllogism.

5. Evaluate the syllogism you constructed. Is it true? Is it valid? Is it sound?

⊖ EXERCISE 5.3

Read the following five arguments, and determine whether each is sound. (To help you evaluate the arguments, you may want to try arranging them as syllogisms.)

1. All humans are mortal. Max is human. Therefore, Max is mortal.

2. Alison should order eggs or oatmeal for breakfast. She won't order eggs, so she should order oatmeal.

3. The cafeteria does not serve steak on Friday. Today is not Friday. Therefore, the cafeteria will not serve steak.

4. All reptiles are cold blooded. Geckos are reptiles. Therefore, geckos are cold blooded.

5. All triangles have three equal sides. The figure on the board is a triangle. Therefore, it must have three equal sides.

⊖ EXERCISE 5.4

Read the following ten enthymemes, which come from bumper stickers. Supply the missing premises, and then evaluate the logic of each argument.

1. If you love your pet, don't eat meat.

2. War is terrorism.

3. Real men don't ask for directions.

4. There are no foreigners.

5. The best things in life aren't things.

6. Don't blame me; I didn't vote for him.

7. Retirement is the best medicine.

8. Love is the only solution.

9. It's a child, not a choice.

10. Live music is better.

Writing Deductive Arguments

Deductive arguments begin with a general principle and reach a specific conclusion. They develop that principle with logical arguments that are supported by evidence—facts, observations, the opinions of experts, and so on. Keep in mind that no single structure is suitable for all deductive (or inductive) arguments. Different issues and different audiences will determine how you arrange your ideas.

In general, deductive essays can be structured in the following way:

INTRODUCTION	Presents an overview of the issue
	States the thesis
BODY	Presents evidence: point 1 in support of the thesis
	Presents evidence: point 2 in support of the thesis
	Presents evidence: point 3 in support of the thesis
	Refutes the arguments against the thesis
CONCLUSION	Concluding statement reinforces the thesis

The following student essay, "Higher Education for All," includes all the elements of a deductive argument. The student who wrote this essay was responding to the question, "Should everyone be encouraged to go to college?" After you read the essay, answer the questions on page 102, consulting the outline above if necessary.

HIGHER EDUCATION FOR ALL

CRYSTAL SANCHEZ

1   Before the middle of the twentieth century, college was a privilege reserved for the rich. The G.I. Bill, which paid for the education of veterans returning from World War II, helped change this situation. By 1956, nearly half of those who had served in World War II, almost 7.8 million people, had taken advantage of this benefit ("U.S. Department of Veterans Affairs"). Even so, college graduates are still a minority of the population. According to the U.S. Census Bureau, in 2004 only 28 percent of Americans had a bachelor's degree. In many ways, this situation is not good for the country. Why should college be just for the privileged few? Because a college education

Introduction

Overview of issue

Thesis statement

provides important benefits, such as increased wages for our citizens and a stronger democracy for our nation, every U.S. citizen should be encouraged to earn a college degree.

Evidence: point 1

One reason everyone should be encouraged to go to college is   2
that a college education gives people an opportunity to discover what they are good at. It is hard for people to know if they are interested in statistics or public policy or marketing unless they have the chance to learn about these subjects. College—and only college—can give them this opportunity. Where else can a person be exposed to a large number of courses taught by experts in a variety of disciplines? Such exposure can open new areas of interest and lead to a much wider set of career options—and to a better life. Without college, most people have limited options and never realize their true potential as human beings. Although life and work experiences can teach a person a lot of things, the best education is the broad kind that a college education offers.

Evidence: point 2

Another reason everyone should be encouraged to go to college is   3
that many current jobs will not exist in this country in ten years; many will be phased out or shipped overseas. Americans should go to college to develop the skills that they will need to get the best jobs that will remain in the United States. According to recent surveys, in the near future, the American workforce will be divided in two. One part will consist of low-wage, low-skill service jobs, such as those in food preparation and retail sales, and the other part will be high-skill, high-wage jobs, such as those in computer engineering and management. (Manufacturing jobs and technical jobs—such as computer programming—that can be done more cheaply overseas will disappear.) To compete for the remaining jobs, Americans have to be educated (New America Foundation). If they do not go to college, then they will not be prepared for the high-growth, high-skill jobs of the future.

Evidence: point 3

Perhaps the best reason everyone should be encouraged to go   4
to college is that education is an essential component of a strong democracy. Those without the ability to understand and analyze news reports are not capable of contributing to the growth and development of society. Democracy requires an informed citizenry who will be able to critically analyze complicated, life-and-death issues in areas such as finance, education, and public health; weigh competing claims of those

running for public office; and assess the job performance of elected officials. By providing students with the opportunity to study subjects such as history, philosophy, English, and political science, colleges and universities help them acquire the critical-thinking skills that they will need to fully participate in American democracy.

5   Of course, many oppose the idea that everyone should attend college. One objection is that educational resources are limited. Some say that if students enter colleges in great number, they will simply overwhelm the higher-education system (Stout). This argument exaggerates the problem. As with any other product in our economy, if demand rises, supply will rise to meet that demand. In addition, new approaches to education—distance learning and computer-assisted learning, for example—will make it possible to educate large numbers of students at a reasonable cost (U.S. Census). Another objection to encouraging everyone to attend college is that underprepared students will require so much help that they will take time and attention away from better students. This argument is actually a red herring.° Most schools already provide resources, such as tutoring and writing centers, for students who need them. With some additional funding, these schools could expand the services they already provide. This course of action might be expensive, but it is a lot less expensive than leaving millions of young people unprepared for jobs of the future.

Refutation of opposing arguments

An irrelevant side issue used as a diversion

6   A college education gave the returning veterans of World War II many opportunities and increased their value to the nation. Today, a college education could do the same for all our citizens. This country has an obligation to offer all students access to an affordable and useful education. Not only will the students benefit personally, but the nation will also. If we do not adequately prepare students for the future, then we will all suffer the consequences.

Conclusion

Concluding statement

Works Cited

New America Foundation. "Should Everyone Go to College?" *New America Foundation.* New America Foundation, 30 Oct. 2006. Web. 21 Oct. 2008.

Stout, Chris. "Top Five Reasons Why You Should Choose to Go to College." *Ezine Articles.* EzineArticles.com, 2008. Web. 21 Oct. 2008.

United States Census Bureau. "College Degree Nearly Doubles Annual
Earnings, Census Bureau Reports." *US Census Bureau Press
Release.* U.S. Census Bureau, 28 Mar. 2005. Web. 21 Oct. 2008.

United States Department of Veterans Affairs. "Born of Controversy:
The GI Bill of Rights." *GI Bill History.* United States Department of
Veterans Affairs, 20 Oct. 2008. Web. 21 Oct. 2008.

Identifying the Elements of Deductive Argument

1. Paraphrase this essay's thesis.

2. What arguments does the writer present as evidence to support her thesis? Which do you think is the strongest argument? Which is the weakest?

3. What opposing arguments does the writer address? What other opposing arguments could she have addressed?

4. What points does the conclusion emphasize? Do you think any other points should be emphasized?

5. Construct a syllogism that expresses the essay's argument. Then, check your syllogism to make sure it is sound.

What Is Inductive Reasoning?

Inductive reasoning begins with specific observations (or evidence) and moves to a general conclusion. You can see how induction works by looking at the following list of observations:

- Nearly 80% of ocean pollution comes from runoff.

- Runoff pollution can make ocean water unsafe for fish and people.

- In some areas, runoff pollution has forced beaches to be closed.

- Drinking water can be contaminated by runoff.

- More than one third of shellfish growing in waters in the United States are contaminated by runoff.

- Each year, millions of dollars are spent to restore polluted areas.

- There is a causal relationship between agricultural runoff and water-borne organisms that damage fish.

Excessive rainfall can cause untreated sewage to pollute ocean water.

After studying these observations, you can use inductive reasoning to reach the conclusion that runoff pollution (rainwater that becomes polluted after it comes in contact with earth-bound pollutants such as fertilizer, pet waste, sewage, and pesticides) is a problem that must be addressed as soon as possible. If it is not addressed, the consequences for people and for wildlife will be severe.

Children learn about the world by using inductive reasoning. For example, very young children see that if they push a light switch up, the lights in a room go on. If they repeat this action over and over, they reach the conclusion that every time they push a switch, the lights will go on. Of course, this conclusion is not always true. For example, the light bulb may be burned out or the switch may be damaged. Even so, their conclusion usually holds true. Children also use induction to generalize about what is safe and what is dangerous. If every time they meet a dog, the encounter is pleasant, then they begin to think that all dogs are friendly. If at some point, however, a dog snaps at them, then they question the strength of their conclusion and modify their behavior accordingly.

Scientists also use induction. In 1620, Sir Francis Bacon first proposed the **scientific method**—a way of using induction to find answers to questions. When using the scientific method, a researcher proposes a hypothesis and then makes a series of observations to test this hypothesis. Based on these observations, the researcher arrives at a conclusion that confirms, modifies, or disproves the hypothesis.

REACHING INDUCTIVE CONCLUSIONS

Here are some of the ways you can use inductive reasoning to reach conclusions:

- **Particular to general:** This form of induction occurs when you reach a generalization based on particular pieces of evidence. For example, suppose you walk into a bathroom and see that the mirrors are fogged. You also notice that the bathtub has drops of water on its sides and that the bathroom floor is wet. In addition, you see a damp towel draped over the sink. Putting all these observations together, you reach the conclusion that someone has recently taken a shower. (Detectives use induction when gathering clues to solve a crime.)

- **General to general:** This form of induction occurs when you draw a general conclusion based on the consistency of your observations. For example, if Apple Corporation has made good products for a long time then it will continue to make good products.

- **General to particular:** This form of induction occurs when you draw a conclusion based on what you generally know to be true. For example, if you have owned several cars made by General Motors and they have been good cars, then a Chevy Volt will probably be a good car as well.

- **Particular to particular:** This form of induction occurs when you assume that because something works in one situation, it will also work in another similar situation. For example, if Krazy Glue fixed the broken handle of one cup, then it will probably fix the broken handle of another cup.

Making Inferences

Unlike deduction, which reaches a conclusion that is based on information provided by the major and minor premises, induction uses what you know to make a statement about something that you don't know. While deductive arguments can be judged in absolute terms (they are either valid or invalid), inductive arguments are judged in relative terms (they are either strong or weak).

You reach an inductive conclusion by making an **inference**—a statement about what is unknown based on what is known. (In other words, you look at the evidence and try to figure out what is going on.) For this reason, there is always a gap between your observations and your conclusion. To bridge this gap, you have to make an **inductive leap**—a stretch of the imagination that enables you to draw an acceptable conclusion. Therefore, inductive conclusions are never certain (as deductive conclusions are) but only probable. The more evidence you provide, the stronger and more probable your conclusions (and your argument) are.

Public opinion polls illustrate how inferences are used to reach inductive conclusions. Politicians and news organizations routinely use public opinion polls to assess support (or lack of support) for a particular policy, proposal, or political candidate. After surveying a sample population—registered voters, for example—pollsters reach conclusions based on their responses. In other words, by asking questions and studying the responses to these questions, pollsters make inferences about issues—for example, which political candidate is ahead and by how much. How solid these inferences are depends on the sample populations they survey. In an election, for example, a poll of randomly chosen individuals will be less accurate than a poll of registered voters or likely voters. In addition, other factors (such as the size of the sample and the way questions are worded) can determine the relative strength of the inductive conclusion.

As with all inferences, a gap exists between a poll's data—the responses to the questions—and the conclusion. The larger and more representative the sample, the smaller the inductive leap necessary to reach a conclusion and the more accurate the poll. If the gap between the data and the conclusion is too big, however, the pollsters will be accused of making a **hasty generalization** (see page 115). Remember, no matter how much support you present, an inductive conclusion is only probable, never certain. The best you can do is present a convincing case and hope that your audience will accept it.

Constructing Strong Inductive Arguments

When you use inductive reasoning, your conclusion is only as strong as the **evidence**—the facts, details, or examples—that you use to support it. For this reason, you should be on the lookout for the following problems that can occur when you try to reach an inductive conclusion:

Generalization Too Broad

The conclusion you state cannot go beyond the scope of your evidence. Your evidence must support your generalization. For instance, you cannot look at just three students in your school and conclude that merit-based scholarships give money to students who don't need it. To reach such a conclusion, you would have to look at a large number of merit-scholarship students from different majors and programs at your school.

Insufficient Evidence

The evidence on which you base an inductive conclusion must be representative, not atypical or biased. For example, you cannot conclude that students are satisfied with the financial aid office at your school by sampling just first-year students. To be valid, your conclusion should be based on responses from a cross-section of students from all years.

Irrelevant Evidence

Your evidence has to support your conclusion. If it does not, it is **irrelevant**. For example, if you assert that students with athletic scholarships strengthen your school, your supporting examples must be students with athletic scholarships, not those with scholarships based on need or on academic merit.

Exceptions to the Rule

There is always a chance that you will overlook an exception that may affect the strength of your conclusion. For example, not everyone who gets a merit-based scholarship is wealthy, and not everyone who gets a need-based scholarship is poor. For this reason, you should avoid using words like *every*, *all*, and *always* and instead use words like *most*, *many*, and *usually*.

⊘ EXERCISE 5.5

Read the following arguments. Then, beside each argument, write a *D* if it is a deductive argument and an *I* if it is an inductive argument.

1. Freedom of speech is a central principle of our form of government. For this reason, students should be allowed to wear T-shirts that call for the legalization of marijuana. _____

2. The Dodge Charger gets eighteen miles a gallon in the city and twenty-six miles a gallon on the highway. The Ford Crown Victoria gets twelve miles a gallon in the city and seventeen miles a gallon on the highway. Therefore, it makes more sense for me to buy the Dodge Charger. _____

3. In Poe's short story "The Cask of Amontillado," Montresor flatters Fortunato. He lures him to his vaults where he stores wine. Montresor then gets Fortunato drunk and chains him to the wall of a crypt. Finally, Montresor uncovers a pile of building material and walls up the entrance to the crypt. Clearly, Montresor has carefully planned to murder Fortunato for a very long time. _____

4. All people should have the right to die with dignity. Garrett is a terminally ill patient, so he should have access to doctor-assisted suicide. _____

5. Last week, we found unacceptably high levels of pollution in the ocean. On Monday, we also found high levels of pollution. Today, we found even higher levels of pollution. We should close the ocean beaches to swimmers until we can find the source of this problem. _____

➲ EXERCISE 5.6

Read the following arguments. Then, decide whether they are deductive or inductive. If they are inductive arguments, evaluate their strength. If they are deductive arguments, evaluate their soundness.

1. *The Farmer's Almanac* says that this winter will be very cold. The national weather service also predicts that this winter will be very cold. So, this should be a cold winter.

2. Many walled towns in Europe do not let people drive cars into their centers. San Gimignano is a walled town in Europe. It is likely that we will not be able to drive our car into its center.

3. The window at the back of the house is broken. There is a baseball on the floor. A few minutes ago, I saw two boys playing catch in a neighbor's yard. They must have thrown the ball through the window.

4. Every time I go to the beach I get sunburned. I guess I should stop going to the beach.

5. All my instructors have advanced degrees. George Martin is one of my instructors. Therefore, George Martin has an advanced degree.

6. My last two boyfriends cheated on me. All men are terrible.

7. I read a study published by a pharmaceutical company that said that Vioxx was safe. Maybe the government was too quick to pull this drug off the market.

8. Chase is not very good looking, and he dresses badly. I don't know how he can be a good architect.

9. No fictional character has ever had a fan club. Harry Potter does, but he is the exception.

10. Two weeks ago, my instructor refused to accept a late paper. She did the same thing last week. Yesterday, she also told someone that because his paper was late, she wouldn't accept it. I'd better get my paper in on time.

⊘ EXERCISE 5.7

Read the inductive paragraph below, written by student Pooja Vaidya, and answer the questions that follow it.

When my friend took me to a game between the Philadelphia Eagles and the Dallas Cowboys in Philadelphia, I learned a little bit about football and a lot about the behavior of football fans. Many of the Philadelphia fans were dressed in green and white football jerseys, each with a player's name and number on the back. One fan had his face painted green and wore a green cape with a large white *E* on it. He ran up and down the aisles in his section and led cheers. When the team was ahead, everyone joined in. When the team fell behind, this fan literally fell on his knees, cried, and begged the people in the stands to support the Eagles. (After the game, several people asked him for his autograph.) A group of six fans sat without shirts. They wore green wigs, and each had one letter of the team's name painted on his bare chest. Even though the temperature was below freezing, none of these fans ever put on his shirt. Before the game, many fans had been drinking at tailgate parties in the parking lot, and as the game progressed, they continued to drink beer in the stadium. By the beginning of the second half, fights were breaking out all over the stadium. Guards grabbed the people who were fighting and escorted them to a holding area under the stadium where a judge held "Eagles Court." At one point, a fan wearing a Dallas jersey tried to sit down in the row behind me. Some of the Eagles fans were so aggressive and threatening that the police had to escort the Dallas fan out of the stadium for his own protection. When the game ended in an Eagles victory, the fans sang the team's fight song as they left the stadium. I concluded that for many Eagles fans, a day at the stadium is an opportunity to engage in behavior that in any other context would be unacceptable and even abnormal.

1. Which of the following statements could you *not* conclude from this paragraph?

   a. All Eagles fans act in outrageous ways at games.

   b. At football games, the fans in the stands can be as violent as the players on the field.

Philadelphia Eagles fans

c. The atmosphere at the stadium causes otherwise normal people to act abnormally.

d. Spectator sports encourage fans to act in abnormal ways.

e. Some people get so caught up in the excitement of a game that they act in uncharacteristic ways.

2. Paraphrase the writer's conclusion. What evidence is provided to support this conclusion?

3. What additional evidence could the writer have provided? Is this additional evidence necessary, or does the conclusion stand without it?

4. The writer makes an inductive leap to reach the paragraph's conclusion. Do you think this leap is too great?

5. Does this paragraph make a strong inductive argument? Why or why not?

Writing Inductive Arguments

Inductive arguments begin with evidence (specific facts, observations, expert opinion, and so on), draw inferences from the evidence, and reach a conclusion by making an inductive leap. Keep in mind that inductive arguments are only as strong as the link between the evidence and the conclusion, so the stronger this link, the stronger the argument.

Inductive essays frequently have the following structure:

INTRODUCTION   Presents the issue
State the thesis

BODY   Presents evidence: facts, observations, expert opinion, and so on
Draws inferences from the evidence
Refutes the arguments against the thesis

CONCLUSION   Concluding statement reinforces the thesis

⬇ The following essay includes all the elements of an inductive argument. After you read the essay, answer the questions on page 112, consulting the outline above if necessary.

This piece appeared in *Slate* on September 2, 2006.

PLEASE DO NOT FEED THE HUMANS

WILLIAM SALETAN

Dug

In 1894, Congress established Labor Day to honor those who "from rude 1 nature have delved° and carved all the grandeur we behold." In the century since, the grandeur of human achievement has multiplied. Over the past four decades, global population has doubled, but food output, driven by increases in productivity, has outpaced it. Poverty, infant mortality, and hunger are receding. For the first time in our planet's history, a species no longer lives at the mercy of scarcity. We have learned to feed ourselves.

We've learned so well, in fact, that we're getting fat. Not just the United 2 States or Europe, but the whole world. Egyptian, Mexican, and South African women are now as fat as Americans. Far more Filipino adults are now overweight than underweight. In China, one in five adults is too heavy, and the rate of overweight children is 28 times higher than it was two decades ago. In Thailand, Kuwait, and Tunisia, obesity, diabetes, and heart disease are soaring.

Hunger is far from conquered. But since 1990, the global rate of mal- 3 nutrition has declined an average of 1.7 percent a year. Based on data from the World Health Organization and the U.N. Food and Agriculture Organization, for every two people who are malnourished, three are now overweight or obese. Among women, even in most African countries, overweight has surpassed underweight. The balance of peril is shifting.

Fat is no longer a rich man's disease. For middle- and high-income 4
Americans, the obesity rate is 29 percent. For low-income Americans, it's
35 percent. Among middle- and high- income kids aged 15 to 17, the rate of
overweight is 14 percent. Among low-income kids in the same age bracket,
it's 23 percent. Globally, weight has tended to rise with income. But a study
in Vancouver, Canada, published three months ago, found that preschool-
ers in "food-insecure" households were twice as likely as other kids to be
overweight or obese. In Brazilian cities, the poor have become fatter than
the rich.

Technologically, this is a triumph. In the early days of our species, even 5
the rich starved. Barry Popkin, a nutritional epidemiologist at the University
of North Carolina, divides history into several epochs. In the hunter-gatherer
era, if we didn't find food, we died. In the agricultural era, if our crops per-
ished, we died. In the industrial era, famine receded, but infectious diseases
killed us. Now we've achieved such control over nature that we're dying not of
starvation or infection, but of abundance. Nature isn't killing us. We're killing
ourselves.

You don't have to go hungry anymore; we can fill you with fats and carbs 6
more cheaply than ever. You don't have to chase your food; we can bring it to
you. You don't have to cook it; we can deliver it ready-to-eat. You don't have
to eat it before it spoils; we can pump it full of preservatives so it lasts forever.
You don't even have to stop when you're full. We've got so much food to sell,
we want you to keep eating.

What happened in America is happening everywhere, only faster. Fewer 7
farmers' markets, more processed food. Fewer whole grains, more refined
ones. More sweeteners, salt, and trans fats. Cheaper meat, more animal fat.
Less cooking, more eating out. Bigger portions, more snacks.

Kentucky Fried Chicken and Pizza Hut are spreading across the planet. 8
Coca-Cola is in more than 200 countries. Half of McDonald's business is
overseas. In China, animal-fat intake has tripled in 20 years. By 2020, meat
consumption in developing countries will grow by 106 million metric tons,
outstripping growth in developed countries by a factor of more than five.
Forty years ago, to afford a high-fat diet, your country needed a gross national
product per capita of nearly $1,500. Now the price is half that. You no longer
have to be rich to die a rich man's death.

Soon, it'll be a poor man's death. The rich have Whole Foods, gyms, and 9
personal trainers. The poor have 7-Eleven, Popeye's, and streets unsafe for
walking. When money's tight, you feed your kids at Wendy's and stock up on
macaroni and cheese. At a lunch buffet, you do what your ancestors did: store
all the fat you can.

That's the punch line: Technology has changed everything but us. We 10
evolved to survive scarcity. We crave fat. We're quick to gain weight and slow
to lose it. Double what you serve us, and we'll double what we eat. Thanks to
technology, the deprivation that made these traits useful is gone. So is the link

between flavors and nutrients. The modern food industry can sell you sweetness without fruit, salt without protein, creaminess without milk. We can fatten you and starve you at the same time.

And that's just the diet side of the equation. Before technology, adult men had to expend about 3,000 calories a day. Now they expend about 2,000. Look at the new Segway scooter. The original model relieved you of the need to walk, pedal, or balance. With the new one, you don't even have to turn the handlebars or start it manually. In theory, Segway is replacing the car. In practice, it's replacing the body.

> "We evolved to survive scarcity." 11

In country after country, service jobs are replacing hard labor. The folks who field your customer service calls in Bangalore are sitting at desks. Nearly everyone in China has a television set. Remember when Chinese rode bikes? In the past six years, the number of cars there has grown from six million to 20 million. More than one in seven Chinese has a motorized vehicle, and households with such vehicles have an obesity rate 80 percent higher than their peers. 12

The answer to these trends is simple. We have to exercise more and change the food we eat, donate, and subsidize. Next year, for example, the U.S. Women, Infants, and Children program, which subsidizes groceries for impoverished youngsters, will begin to pay for fruits and vegetables. For 32 years, the program has fed toddlers eggs and cheese but not one vegetable. And we wonder why poor kids are fat. 13

The hard part is changing our mentality. We have a distorted body image. We're so used to not having enough, as a species, that we can't believe the problem is too much. From China to Africa to Latin America, people are trying to fatten their kids. I just got back from a vacation with my Jewish mother and Jewish mother-in-law. They told me I need to eat more. 14

The other thing blinding us is liberal guilt. We're so caught up in the idea of giving that we can't see the importance of changing behavior rather than filling bellies. We know better than to feed buttered popcorn to zoo animals, yet we send it to a food bank and call ourselves humanitarians. Maybe we should ask what our fellow humans actually need. 15

Identifying the Elements of Inductive Argument

1. What is this essay's thesis? Restate it in your own words.

2. Why do you think Saletan places the thesis where he does?

3. What evidence does Saletan use to support his conclusion?

4. What inductive leap does Saletan make to reach his conclusion? Do you think he should have included more evidence?

5. Overall, do you think Saletan's inductive argument is relatively strong or weak?

Recognizing Logical Fallacies

When you write arguments in college, you are obligated to follow certain rules that ensure fairness. Not everyone who writes arguments is this fair or thorough, however. Sometimes you will encounter arguments in which writers attack the opposition's intelligence or patriotism and base their arguments on questionable (or even false) assumptions. As convincing as these arguments can sometimes seem, they are actually not valid because they contain **fallacies**— inaccurate or intentionally misleading arguments. Familiarizing yourself with the most common logical fallacies can help you to evaluate the arguments of others and to construct better, more effective arguments of your own.

The following pages define and illustrate some logical fallacies that you should learn to recognize and avoid.

Begging the Question

The fallacy of **begging the question** assumes that a statement is self-evident (or true) when it actually requires proof. A conclusion based on such assumptions cannot be valid. For example, someone who is very religious could structure an argument the following way:

MAJOR PREMISE	Everything in the Bible is true.
MINOR PREMISE	The Bible says that Noah built an ark.
CONCLUSION	Therefore, Noah's Ark really existed.

A person can accept the conclusion of this syllogism only if he or she also accepts the major premise, which has not been proven true. Some people might find this line of reasoning convincing, but others would not—even if they were religious.

Begging the question occurs any time someone presents a debatable statement as if it were true. For example, look at the following statement:

> You have unfairly limited my right of free speech by refusing to print my editorial in the college newspaper.

This statement begs the question because it assumes what it should be proving—that refusing to print an editorial violates a person's right to free speech.

Circular Reasoning

A form of begging the question, **circular reasoning** occurs when a person attempts to support a statement by simply repeating the statement in different terms. Consider the following statement:

> Stealing is wrong because it is against the law.

The conclusion of the statement on the previous page is essentially the same as its beginning: stealing (which is illegal) is against the law. In other words, the argument goes in a circle.

Here are some other examples of circular reasoning:

- Lincoln was a great president because he is the best president we ever had.

- I am for equal rights for women because I am a feminist.

- Illegal immigrants commit crimes because they are illegal.

All of the statements above have one thing in common: they illogically use the claims themselves as the evidence to support those claims.

Weak Analogy

An **analogy** is a comparison between two items (or concepts)—one familiar and one unfamiliar. When you make an analogy, you explain the unfamiliar item by comparing it to the familiar item. (For a discussion of argument by analogy, see Chapter 16.)

Although analogies can be effective in arguments, they have limitations. For example, a senator who opposed a government bailout of the financial industry in 2008 made the following argument:

> This bailout is doomed from the start. It's like pouring milk into a leaking bucket. As long as you keep pouring milk, the bucket stays full. But when you stop, the milk runs out the hole in the bottom of the bucket. What we're doing is throwing money into a big bucket and not fixing the hole. We have to find the underlying problems that have caused this part of our economy to get in trouble and pass legislation to solve them.

The problem with using analogies such as this one is that analogies are never perfect. There is always a difference between the two things being compared. The larger this difference, the weaker the analogy—and the weaker the argument that it supports. For example, someone could point out to the senator that the financial industry—and by extension, the whole economy—is much more complex and multifaceted than a leaking bucket. To analyze the economy, the senator would have to expand his discussion beyond this one analogy—which, although striking and accessible, is not strong enough to carry the weight of the entire argument.

Ad Hominem Fallacy (Personal Attack)

The **ad hominem fallacy** occurs when someone attacks the character or the motives of a person instead of focusing on the issues. This line of reasoning is illogical because it focuses attention on the person making the argument, sidestepping the argument itself.

Consider the following statement:

> Dr. Thomson, I'm not sure why we should believe anything you have to say about this community health center. Last year, you left your husband for another man.

The attack on Dr. Thomson's character is irrelevant; it has nothing to do with her ideas about the community health center. Sometimes, however, a person's character may have a direct relation to the issue. For example, if Dr. Thomson had invested in a company that supplied medical equipment to the health center, this fact would have been relevant to the issue at hand.

The ad hominem fallacy also occurs when you attempt to undermine an argument by associating it with individuals who are easily attacked. For example, consider this statement.

Ad hominem attack against Charles Darwin, originator of the theory of evolution

> I think your plan to provide universal heath care is interesting. I'm sure Marx and Lenin would agree with you.

Instead of focusing on the specific provisions of the healthcare plan, the opposition unfairly associates it with the ideas of Karl Marx and Vladimir Lenin, two well-known communists.

Hasty or Sweeping Generalization (Jumping to a Conclusion)

A **hasty or sweeping generalization** (also called **jumping to a conclusion**) occurs when someone reaches a conclusion that is based on too little evidence. Many people commit this fallacy without realizing it. For example, when Richard Nixon was elected president in 1972, film critic Pauline Kael is supposed to have remarked, "How can that be? No one I know voted for Nixon!" The general idea behind this statement is that if Kael's acquaintances didn't vote for Nixon, then neither did other people. This assumption is flawed because it is based on a small sample.

Sometimes people make hasty generalizations because they strongly favor one point of view over another. At other times, a hasty generalization

Politicians frequently engage in the either/or fallacy.

is simply the result of sloppy thinking. For example, it is easier to simply say that an instructor is an unusually hard grader than to survey the instructor's classes to see if this conclusion is warranted (or to consider other reasons for your poor performance in a course).

Either/Or Fallacy (False Dilemma)

The **either/or fallacy** (also called a **false dilemma**) occurs when a person says that there are just two choices when there are actually more. In many cases, the person committing this fallacy tries to force a conclusion by presenting just two choices, one of which is clearly more desirable than the other. (Parents do this with young children all the time: "Eat your carrots, or go to bed.")

Politicians frequently engage in this fallacy. For example, according to some politicians, you are either pro-life or pro-choice, pro–gun control or anti–gun control, pro-stem-cell research or anti-stem-cell research. Many people, however, are somewhere in the middle, taking a much more nuanced approach to complicated issues.

Consider the following statement:

I can't believe you voted against the bill to build a wall along the southern border of the United States. Either you're for protecting our border, or you're against it.

This statement is an example of the either/or fallacy. The person who voted against the bill might be against the wall but not against all immigration restrictions. The person might favor loose restrictions for some people (for example, migrant workers) and strong restrictions for others (for example, drug smugglers). By limiting the options to just two, the speaker oversimplifies the situation and attempts to force the listener to accept a fallacious argument.

Equivocation

The fallacy of **equivocation** occurs when a key term has one meaning in one part of an argument and another meaning in another part. (When a term is used **unequivocally**, it has the same meaning throughout the argument.) Consider the following old joke:

> The sign said, "Fine for parking here," so because it was fine, I parked there.

Obviously, the word *fine* has two different meanings in this sentence. The first time it is used, it means "money paid as a penalty." The second time, it means "good" or "satisfactory."

Most words have more than one meaning, so it is important not to confuse the various meanings. For an argument to work, a key term has to have the same meaning every time it appears in the argument. If the meaning shifts during the course of the argument, then the argument cannot be sound.

Consider the following syllogism:

MAJOR PREMISE	All men are rational.
MINOR PREMISE	No women are men.
CONCLUSION	Therefore, no women are rational.

Although this syllogism is valid, it doesn't make sense. In the major premise the word *men* refers to *people*. In the minor premise, it means *males*. This shift in the meaning of *men* makes the argument unsound.

The same fallacy is apparent in the following statement:

> This is supposed to be a free country, but nothing worth having is ever free.

Just as in the syllogism above, the meaning of a key term shifts. The first time the word *free* is used, it means "not under the control of another." The second time, it means "without charge."

Red Herring

This fallacy gets its name from the practice of dragging a smoked fish across the trail of a fox to mask its scent during a fox hunt. As a result, the hounds lose the scent and are thrown off the track. The **red herring** fallacy occurs when a person raises an irrelevant side issue to divert attention from the real issue. Used skillfully, this fallacy can distract people and change the focus of an argument.

Political campaigns are good sources of examples of the red herring fallacy. Consider this example from the 2008 presidential race:

> I know Senator McCain says he is for the middle class, but he and his wife own seven houses. How can we believe his tax proposals will help the middle class?

The focus of this argument should have been on Senator McCain's tax proposals—not on the fact that he and his wife own seven houses.

Here is another red herring fallacy from the same political campaign:

> Barack Obama wants us to vote for him, but his father was a Muslim. How can we possibly trust him with national security?

Again, the focus of these remarks should have been Obama's qualifications, not the fact that his father was a Muslim.

Slippery Slope

The **slippery-slope** fallacy occurs when a person argues that one thing will inevitably result from another. Other names for the slippery-slope fallacy are the foot-in-the-door fallacy and the floodgates fallacy. Both these

A very slippery slope

names suggest that once you permit certain acts, you inevitably permit additional acts that eventually lead to disastrous consequences. Typically, the slippery-slope fallacy presents a series of increasingly unacceptable events that lead to an inevitable, unpleasant conclusion. (Usually, there is no evidence that such a sequence will actually occur.)

We encounter examples of the slippery-slope fallacy almost daily. During a debate on same-sex marriage, for example, an opponent advanced this line of reasoning:

> If we allow gay marriage, then there is nothing to stop polygamy. And once we allow this, where will it stop? Will we have to legalize incest— or even bestiality?

Whether or not you support same-sex marriage, you should recognize the fallacy of this slippery-slope reasoning. By the last sentence of the passage above, the assertions have become so outrageous that they approach parody. People can certainly debate this issue, but not in such a dishonest and highly emotional way.

You Also (Tu Quoque)

The **you also** fallacy asserts that a statement is false because it is inconsistent with what the speaker has said or done. In other words, a person is attacked for doing what he or she is arguing against. Parents often encounter this fallacy when they argue with their teenage children. By introducing an irrelevant point—"You did it too"—the children attempt to distract parents and put them on the defensive:

- How can you tell me not to smoke when you used to smoke?
- Don't yell at me for drinking. I bet you had a few beers before you were twenty-one.
- Why do I have be home by midnight? Didn't you stay out late when you were my age?

Arguments such as these are irrelevant. People may not follow their own advice, but that doesn't mean that their points have no merit.

Appeal to Doubtful Authority

Writers of research papers frequently use the ideas of recognized authorities to strengthen their arguments. However, the sources offered as evidence need to be respected and credible. The **appeal to doubtful authority** occurs when people use the ideas of nonexperts to support their arguments.

Not everyone who speaks as an expert is actually an authority on a particular issue. For example, when movie stars give their opinions about

Singer-songwriter
Sheryl Crow speaking
about global warming

climate change or foreign affairs—things they may know little about—they are not speaking as experts; therefore, they have no authority. (They *are* experts when they discuss the film industry.) A similar situation occurs with the pundits who appear on television news shows. Some of these individuals have solid credentials in the fields they discuss, but others offer opinions even though they know little about the subjects. Unfortunately, many viewers accept the pronouncements of these "experts" uncritically and think it is acceptable to cite them to support their own arguments.

How do you determine whether a person you read about or hear is really an authority? First, make sure that the person actually has expertise in the field he or she is discussing. You can do this by checking his or her credentials on the Internet. Second, make sure that the person is not biased. No one is entirely free from bias, but the bias should not be so extreme that it undermines the person's authority. Finally, make sure that you can substantiate what the so-called expert says or writes. Check one or two pieces of information in other sources, such as a basic reference text or online encyclopedia. Determine if others—especially recognized experts in the field—confirm this information. If there are major points of discrepancy, dig further to make sure you are dealing with a legitimate authority.

Misuse of Statistics

The **misuse of statistics** occurs when data are misrepresented. Statistics can be used persuasively in an argument, but sometimes they are distorted—intentionally or unintentionally—to make a point. For example, a classic ad for toothpaste says that four out of five dentists recommend Crest toothpaste. What the ad neglects to mention is the number of dentists who were questioned. If the company surveyed several thousand dentists, then this statistic would be meaningful. If the company surveyed only ten, however, it would not be.

Misleading statistics can be much subtler (and much more complicated) than the example above. For example, in 2000, there were 16,653 alcohol-related deaths in the United States. According to the National Highway Traffic Safety Administration (NHTSA), 12,892 of these 16,653 alcohol-related deaths involved at least one driver or passenger who was legally drunk. Of the 12,892 deaths, 7,326 were the drivers themselves, and

1,594 were legally drunk pedestrians. The remaining 3,972 fatalities were nonintoxicated drivers, passengers, or nonoccupants. These 3,972 fatalities present a problem because the NHTSA does not indicate which drivers were at fault. In other words, if a sober driver ran a red light and killed a legally drunk driver, the NHTSA classified this death as alcohol-related. For this reason, the original number of alcohol-related deaths—16,653—is somewhat misleading. (The statistic becomes even more questionable when you consider that a person is automatically classified as intoxicated if he or she refuses to take a sobriety test.)

Post Hoc, Ergo Propter Hoc (After This, Therefore Because of This)

The *post hoc* fallacy asserts that because two events occur closely in time, one event must cause the other. Professional athletes commit the post hoc fallacy all the time. For example, one major league pitcher wears the same shirt every time he has an important game. Because he has won several big games while wearing this article of clothing, he believes it brings him luck.

Many events seem to follow a sequential pattern even though they actually do not. For example, some people refuse to get a flu vaccine because they say that the last time they got one, they came down with the flu. Even though there is no scientific basis for this link, many people insist that it is true. (The more probable explanation for this situation is that the flu vaccination takes at least two weeks to take effect, so it is possible for someone to be infected by the flu virus before the vaccine starts working.)

Another health-related issue also illustrates the post hoc fallacy. Recently, the U.S. Food and Drug Administration (FDA) studied several products that claim to cure the common cold. Because the study showed that these medications were not effective, the FDA ordered the manufacturers to stop making false claims about their products. Despite this fact, however, many people still buy these products. When questioned, they say the medications actually work. Again, the explanation for this phenomenon is simple. Most colds last just a few days. As the FDA pointed out in its report, people who took the medications would have begun feeling better with or without them.

Non Sequitur (It Does Not Follow)

The **non sequitur** fallacy occurs when a conclusion does not follow from the premises. Frequently, the conclusion is supported by weak or irrelevant evidence—or by no evidence at all. Consider the following statement:

Megyn drives an expensive car, so she must be earning a lot of money.

Megyn might drive an expensive car, but this is not evidence that she has a high salary. She could, for example, be leasing the car or paying it off over a five-year period, or it could have been a gift.

Non sequiturs are common in political arguments. Consider this statement:

> Gangs, drugs, and extreme violence plague today's prisons. The only way to address this issue is to release all nonviolent offenders as soon as possible.

This assessment of the prison system may be accurate, but it doesn't follow that because of this situation, all nonviolent offenders should be released immediately.

Scientific arguments also contain non sequiturs. Consider the following statement that was made during a debate on global warming:

> Recently, the polar ice caps have thickened, and the temperature of the oceans has stabilized. Obviously, the earth is healing itself. We don't need to do more to control global warming.

Even if you accept the facts of this argument, you need to see more evidence before you can conclude that no action against global warming is necessary. For example, the cooling trend could be temporary, or other areas of the earth could still be growing warmer.

Bandwagon Appeal (Ad Populum)

The fallacy of the **bandwagon appeal** occurs when you try to convince people that something is true because it is widely held to be true. It is easy to see the problem with this line of reasoning. Hundreds of years ago, most people believed that the sun revolved around the earth and that the earth was flat. As we know, the fact that many people held these beliefs did not make them true.

The underlying assumption of the bandwagon appeal is that the more people who believe something, the more likely it is to be true. Without supporting evidence, however, this form of argument cannot be valid. For example, consider the following statement made by a driver who was stopped by the police for speeding:

> Officer, I didn't do anything wrong. Everyone around me was going the same speed.

As the police officer was quick to point out, the driver's argument missed the point: he was doing fifty-five miles an hour in a thirty-five-mile-an-hour zone, and the fact that other drivers were also speeding was irrelevant. If the driver had been able to demonstrate that the police officer was mistaken—that he was driving more slowly or that the speed limit was

The bandwagon appeal

Mike Baldwin/www.CartoonStock.com

actually sixty miles an hour—then his argument would have had merit. In this case, the fact that other drivers were going the same speed would be relevant because it would support his contention.

Since most people want to go along with the crowd, the bandwagon appeal can be very effective. For this reason, advertisers use it all the time. For example, a book publisher will say that a book has been on the *New York Times* bestseller list for ten weeks, and a pharmaceutical company will say that its brand of aspirin outsells other brands four to one. These appeals are irrelevant, however, because they don't address the central questions: Is the book actually worth reading? Is one brand of aspirin really better than other brands?

❯ EXERCISE 5.8

Determine which of the following statements are logical arguments and which are fallacies. If the statement is not logical, identify the fallacy that best applies.

1. Almost all the students I talked to said that they didn't like the senator. I'm sure he'll lose the election on Tuesday.

2. This car has a noisy engine; therefore, it must create a lot of pollution.

3. I don't know how Professor Resnick can be such a hard grader. He's always late for class.

4. A vote for the bill to limit gun sales in the city is a vote against the Second Amendment.

5. It's only fair to pay your fair share of taxes.

6. I had an internship at a government agency last summer, and no one there worked very hard. Government workers are lazy.

7. It's a clear principle of law that people are not allowed to yell "Fire!" in a crowded theater. By permitting protestors to hold a rally downtown, Judge Cohen is allowing them to do just this.

8. Of course this person is guilty. He wouldn't be in jail if he weren't a criminal.

9. Schools are like families; therefore, teachers (like parents) should be allowed to discipline their kids.

10. Everybody knows that staying out in the rain can make you sick.

11. When we had a draft in the 1960s, the crime rate was low. We should bring back the draft.

12. I'm not a doctor, but I play one on TV. I recommend Vicks Formula 44 cough syrup.

13. Some people are complaining about public schools, so there must be a problem.

14. If you aren't part of the solution, you're part of the problem.

15. All people are mortal. James is a person. Therefore, James is mortal.

16. I don't know why you gave me an F for handing in someone else's essay. Didn't you ever copy something from someone else?

17. First the government stops us from buying assault rifles. Then, it limits the number of handguns we can buy. What will come next? Soon, they'll try to take away all our guns.

18. Shakespeare was the world's greatest playwright; therefore, *Macbeth* must be a great play.

19. Last month I bought a new computer. Yesterday, I installed some new software. This morning my computer wouldn't start up. The new software must be causing the problem.

20. Madonna is against testing pharmaceutical and cosmetics products on animals, and that's good enough for me.

⊃ EXERCISE 5.9

Read the following essay, and identify as many fallacies in it as you can. Make sure you identify each fallacy by name and are able to explain the flaws in the writer's arguments.

This article is from Buchanan.org. It appeared on October 31, 1994.

IMMIGRATION TIME-OUT
PATRICK J. BUCHANAN

Proposition 187 "is an outrage. It is unconstitutional. It is nativist. It is   1
racist."—Al Hunt, *Capital Gang*, CNN

That outburst by my columnist colleague, about California's Prop. 187—   2
which would cut off social welfare benefits to illegal aliens—suggests that this savage quarrel is about more than just money. Indeed, the roots of this dispute over Prop. 187 are grounded in the warring ideas that we Americans hold about the deepest, most divisive issues of our time: ethnicity, nation, culture.

What do we want the America of the years 2000, 2020 and 2050 to be like? Do   3
we have the right to shape the character of the country our grandchildren will live in? Or is that to be decided by whoever, outside America, decides to come here?

By 2050, we are instructed by the chancellor of the University of Califor-   4
nia at Berkeley, Chang Lin-Tin, "the majority of Americans will trace their roots to Latin America, Africa, Asia, the Middle East and Pacific Islands."

Now, any man or woman, of any nation or ancestry can come here—   5
and become a good American.

We know that from our history. But by my arithmetic, the chancellor is   6
saying Hispanics, Asians and Africans will increase their present number of 65 million by at least 100 million in 60 years, a population growth larger than all of Mexico today.

What will that mean for America? Well, South Texas and Southern Cali-   7
fornia will be almost exclusively Hispanic. Each will have tens of millions of people whose linguistic, historic and cultural roots are in Mexico. Like Eastern Ukraine, where 10 million Russian-speaking "Ukrainians" now look impatiently to Moscow, not Kiev, as their cultural capital, America could see, in a decade, demands for Quebeclike status for Southern California. Already there is a rumbling among militants for outright secession. A sea of Mexican flags was prominent in that L.A. rally against Prop. 187, and Mexican officials are openly urging their kinsmen in California to vote it down.

If no cutoff is imposed on social benefits for those who breach our bor-   8
ders, and break our laws, the message will go out to a desperate world: America is wide open. All you need to is get there, and get in.

Consequences will ensue. Crowding together immigrant and minority 9 populations in our major cities must bring greater conflict. We saw that in the 1992 L.A. riot. Blacks and Hispanics have lately collided in D.C.'s Adams-Morgan neighborhood, supposedly the most tolerant and progressive section of Washington. The issue: bilingual education. Unlike 20 years ago, ethnic conflict is today on almost every front page.

Before Mr. Chang's vision is realized, the United States will have at least 10 two official languages. Today's steady outmigration of "Anglos" or "Euro-Americans," as whites are now called, from Southern Florida and Southern California, will continue. The 50 states will need constant redrawing of political lines to ensure proportional representation. Already we have created the first "apartheid districts" in America's South.

Ethnic militancy and solidarity are on the rise in the United States; the old 11 institutions of assimilation are not doing their work as they once did; the Melting Pot is in need of repair. On campuses we hear demands for separate dorms, eating rooms, clubs, etc. by black, white, Hispanic and Asian students. If this is where the campus is headed, where are our cities going?

> "Ethnic militancy and solidarity are on the rise."

If America is to survive as "one nation, one people," we need to call a 12 "time-out" on immigration, to assimilate the tens of millions who have lately arrived. We need to get to know one another, to live together, to learn together America's language, history, culture and traditions of tolerance, to become a new national family, before we add a hundred million more. And we need soon to bring down the curtain on this idea of hyphenated-Americanism.

If we lack the courage to make the decisions—as to what our country will 13 look like in 2050—others will make those decisions for us, not all of whom share our love of the America that seems to be fading away.

❯ EXERCISE 5.10

Choose three of the fallacies that you identified in "Immigration Time-Out" for Exercise 5.9. Rewrite each statement in the form of a logical argument.

Do Merit-Based Scholarships Make Sense?

Go back to page 89, and reread the At Issue box that gives background on whether merit-based scholarships make sense. As the following sources illustrate, this question has a number of possible answers.

As you read this source material, you will be asked to answer questions and to complete some simple activities. This work will help you understand both the content and the structure of the sources. When you are finished, you will be ready to write an argument—either inductive or deductive—that takes a position on whether merit-based scholarships for college students make sense.

SOURCES

 Peter Schmidt, "At the Elite Colleges—Dim White Kids"

 Zoe Mendelson, "Paying for College"

 Brent Staples, "A Broader Definition of Merit: The Trouble with College Entry Exams"

 Associated Press, "Hamilton College to End Merit Scholarships in Favor of Need-Based Aid"

 Lewis & Clark College, "Merit-Based Scholarships for Incoming Students"

This piece appeared in the *Boston Globe* on September 28, 2007.

AT THE ELITE COLLEGES—DIM WHITE KIDS

PETER SCHMIDT

1 Autumn and a new academic year are upon us, which means that selective colleges are engaged in the annual ritual of singing the praises of their new freshman classes.

2 Surf the websites of such institutions and you will find press releases boasting that they have increased their black and Hispanic enrollments, admitted bumper crops of National Merit scholars or became the destination of choice for hordes of high school valedictorians. Many are bragging about the large share of applicants they rejected, as a way of conveying to the world just how popular and selective they are.

3 What they almost never say is that many of the applicants who were rejected were far more qualified than those accepted. Moreover, contrary to popular belief, it was not the black and Hispanic beneficiaries of affirmative action, but the rich white kids with cash and connections who elbowed most of the worthier applicants aside.

4 Researchers with access to closely guarded college admissions data have found that, on the whole, about 15 percent of freshmen enrolled at America's highly selective colleges are white teens who failed to meet their institutions' minimum admissions standards.

5 Five years ago, two researchers working for the Educational Testing Service, Anthony Carnevale and Stephen Rose, took the academic profiles of students admitted into 146 colleges in the top two tiers of Barron's college guide and matched them up against the institutions' advertised requirements in terms of high school grade point average, SAT or ACT scores, letters of recommendation, and records of involvement in extracurricular activities. White students who failed to make the grade on all counts were nearly twice as prevalent on such campuses as black and Hispanic students who received an admissions break based on their ethnicity or race.

6 Who are these mediocre white students getting into institutions such as Harvard, Wellesley, Notre Dame, Duke, and the University of Virginia? A sizable number are recruited athletes who, research has shown, will perform worse on average than other students with similar academic profiles, mainly as a result of the demands their coaches will place on them.

7 A larger share, however, are students who gained admission through their ties to people the institution wanted to keep happy, with alumni, donors, faculty members, administrators, and politicians topping the list.

8 Applicants who stood no chance of gaining admission without connections are only the most blatant beneficiaries of such admissions preferences. Except

perhaps at the very summit of the applicant pile—that lofty place occupied by
young people too brilliant for anyone in
their right mind to turn down—colleges
routinely favor those who have connections over those who don't. While some
applicants gain admission by legiti-

> "Many others get into exclusive colleges the same way people get into trendy night clubs."

mately beating out their peers, many others get into exclusive colleges the same
way people get into trendy night clubs, by knowing the management or flashing
cash at the person manning the velvet rope.

Leaders at many selective colleges say they have no choice but to instruct 9
their admissions offices to reward those who financially support their institutions, because keeping donors happy is the only way they can keep the place
afloat. They also say that the money they take in through such admissions
preferences helps them provide financial aid to students in need.

But many of the colleges granting such preferences are already well- 10
financed, with huge endowments. And, in many cases, little of the money they
take in goes toward serving the less-advantaged.

A few years ago, *The Chronicle of Higher Education* looked at colleges with 11
more than $500 million in their endowments and found that most served
disproportionately few students from families with incomes low enough to
qualify for federal Pell Grants. A separate study of flagship state universities
conducted by the Education Trust found that those universities' enrollments
or Pell Grant recipients had been shrinking, even as the number of students
qualifying for such grants had gone up.

Just 40 percent of the financial aid money being distributed by public col- 12
leges is going to students with documented financial need. Most such money is
being used to offer merit-based scholarships or tuition discounts to potential
recruits who can enhance a college's reputation, or appear likely to cover the
rest of their tuition tab and to donate down the road.

Given such trends, is it any wonder that young people from the wealthiest 13
fourth of society are about 25 times as likely as those from the bottom fourth
to enroll in a selective college, or that, over the past two decades, the middle
class has been steadily getting squeezed out of such institutions by those with
more money?

A degree from a selective college can open many doors for a talented 14
young person from a humble background. But rather than promoting social
mobility, our nation's selective colleges appear to be thwarting it, by turning away applicants who have excelled given their circumstances and offering
second chances to wealthy and connected young people who have squandered
many of the advantages life has offered them.

When social mobility goes away, at least two dangerous things can happen. 15
The privileged class that produces most of our nation's leaders can become complacent enough to foster mediocrity, and less-fortunate segments of our society
can become resigned to the notion that hard work will not get them anywhere.

Given the challenges our nation faces, shouldn't its citizens be at least 16 a little worried that the most selective public universities—state flagships—dominate the annual Princeton Review rankings of the nation's best party schools, as measured largely by drug and alcohol consumption and time spent skipping class and ditching the books?

Should Harvard, which annually turns away about 2,000 valedictorians 17 and has an endowment of nearly $35 billion, be in the business of wasting its academic offerings on some students admitted on the basis of pedigree?

⊘AT ISSUE: SOURCES FOR DEVELOPING A LOGICAL ARGUMENT

1. What is Schmidt's thesis? Why do you think he states it where he does?

2. What opposing argument does Schmidt address? How effectively does he refute this argument?

3. The aid that Schmidt disapproves of is neither merit-based nor need-based. What name would you give it?

4. What are the major objections Schmidt has to the aid that colleges give to "connected" students?

5. Schmidt is a deputy editor of the *Chronicle of Higher Education*, a publication that is read by college and university faculty members and administrators. Should he have mentioned this fact in his essay? What might he have gained (or lost) by doing so?

This opinion piece appeared in the *Los Angeles Times* on August 24, 2008.

PAYING FOR COLLEGE

ZOE MENDELSON

1   I start college this week—Barnard, on a full scholarship. I never thought I'd feel lucky that my parents have virtually no income. I live with my mom, who is a full-time student; my dad teaches part time. Although I'd like to think my scholarship is merit-based, were my parents more comfortably middle class, I would not have been so fortunate. And without a scholarship, there's no way I could afford a school such as Barnard.

2   The situation is more complicated for my friend E.G., who will be a freshman at his first-choice school this fall, Johns Hopkins University. He was at my house when his dad text-messaged me, asking that I pass along that his ACT score had come—34 out of a perfect 36. Last year, he competed in the Intel International Science and Engineering Fair with a project in which he figured out how to extract a chemical from sassafras root that treats parasites in beehives and could prevent colony collapse disorder.

3   His parents met in South Korea, where his father was based during his U.S. military service. E.G.'s mom is an overnight supervisor for Kmart, and his dad is a civil engineer working with flood relief/recovery operations in the Air National Guard. This is information that he has volunteered to me proudly.

4   E.G. got some scholarship money, but he is having trouble coming up with his share of the costs for one year—$30,875—because, as his dad put it, his family is "in the nether region." Their household income is too much to qualify for substantial financial aid but not enough to pay that amount. In other words, being middle class makes it nearly impossible to afford the college of your choice, even if you get in.

5   Sure, E.G. could accept one of his more lucrative scholarship offers at another school. But E.G. wants the best, and suggesting that all brilliant middle-class kids should just go to the schools they can afford undermines the meritocracy° that we claim as a nation. Those worthy of the best are not the richest or the poorest but the brightest.

> "Those worthy of the best are not the richest or the poorest but the brightest."

A system under which advancement is based on individual ability

6   The latest U.S. census figures put the median household income in 2006 at $48,200. According to the College Board, the average tuition at a public four-year college is $6,185; for a private one, $23,712. Most top-tier universities are edging up on $40,000. The total cost—room and board, books, transportation—at E.G.'s college for the 2008–09 year is $52,578.

7   Here's another example. My friend Maggie is far more disciplined and hardworking than me and, like me, she graduated in the top 10 of our high

school class. She emigrated from Russia when she was 5. Her dad is a limo driver and earns just enough to support their family of four. Maggie has been accepted at Bard College, which gave her a significant aid package, but she is still responsible for $8,000 a year. Bard assumed that she'd be able to get a loan for that. She applied for a dozen and was rejected for all of them.

The school suggested to Maggie that she defer for a year to give her time to come up with the cash. But the reality is an 18-year-old would be lucky to get a job paying $10 an hour. And the college expects her to save $8,000 in 12 months? Her family finally raised the money, paying Bard in installments from assets back in Russia. But what about next year? 8

This year, according to the Bureau of Economic Analysis, the average American's savings may be near .0% of their disposable income. What this means is that in a startling number of households, college is even more out of reach, even without an unexpected expense such as a mother with cancer, a grandparent who requires live-in help or even dental work or repairs on the car that a parent needs to get to work. Combine that with the difficult economic times we're in and it makes little sense to me that financial-aid policies consider an income large enough to *pay* the bulk of tuition large enough to *afford* it. Colleges need to recognize the difference between the two. 9

The schools that accepted my friends have endowments—Johns Hopkins' is nearly $3 billion, and its website says that it is "a community committed to sharing values of diversity and inclusion." Something is not adding up. The university has billions of dollars and seeks a diverse student body. But it must mean "diverse" with an asterisk: It only applies to those who can afford $52,578 a year, or the very few who are both impoverished and qualified. 10

An annual college bill that exceeds the median household income, and an income level set too low for families like E.G.'s to qualify for aid, seem designed to exclude the middle class. 11

With the $30,875 that E.G. is responsible for each year, he says that by the time he's a junior, he will have dried up all the money his father has saved over 25-plus years. I asked him how his 15-year-old sister was going to pay for college. He said he would "make it back" and help her. 12

Although the thought is sweet, the reality is that when E.G. graduates, even if he gets a high-paying job, he will have massive loans to deal with. (The American college undergrad leaves with an average of nearly $20,000 in student debt, and many have loans that are much higher.) We are all prepared to take out loans for our education but, say, $40,000? That may as well be Monopoly money. 13

Academically, colleges know there are indicators that help give a more complete picture of whether a student will thrive at their schools. These factors can be far from—even contradict—a standardized test score or GPA. That's why the admissions process includes essays and interviews. Economically, colleges have to apply the same reasoning and recognize that a family's financial profile on paper often says very little about what that family can afford. Although the application for federal aid does take into account 14 college-age siblings and parents' marital status, schools don't give this information enough weight.

A few universities have moved in the right direction. Harvard, for instance, announced its "sweeping middle-income initiative" last year. According to the *Harvard University Gazette Online*, "factors such as family size, healthcare costs, sibling educational expenses and other non-discretionary expense that place a drain on family finances are considered carefully . . . and there is no income cut-off for need-based scholarship eligibility." 15

This is common sense and the only way to get the best kids going to the best schools. Maggie and E.G. are eager to start learning at their schools, but I am eager for their schools to start learning from them. The concept of "need-based" financial aid is due for an overhaul in an economy that has redefined college for most families as a "want" and not a "need." 16

⊙ AT ISSUE: SOURCES FOR DEVELOPING A LOGICAL ARGUMENT

1. According to Mendelson, what is wrong with suggesting that "brilliant middle-class kids should just go to the schools they can afford" (para. 5)? Do you agree with her?

2. In your own words, summarize Mendelson's thesis. Does she actually state this thesis in her essay?

3. Do Mendelson's examples in paragraphs 2–8 constitute convincing evidence? What other kinds of evidence does she use to support her thesis? What other evidence could she have used?

4. Mendelson does not address arguments against her position. Do you think she should have? What specific arguments might she have addressed? How could she have refuted them?

5. Is this primarily an inductive or a deductive argument? How can you tell?

This editorial is from the October 1, 2008, issue of the *New York Times*.

A BROADER DEFINITION OF MERIT: THE TROUBLE WITH COLLEGE ENTRY EXAMS

BRENT STAPLES

Imagine yourself an admissions director of a status-seeking college that wants 1 desperately to move up in the rankings. With next year's freshman class nearly filled, you are choosing between two applicants. The first has very high SAT scores, but little else to recommend him. The second is an aspiring doctor who tests poorly but graduated near the top of his high school class while volunteering as an emergency medical technician in his rural county.

This applicant has the kind of background that higher education has always 2 claimed to covet. But the pressures that are driving colleges—and the country as a whole—to give college entry exams more weight than they were ever intended to have would clearly work against him. Those same pressures are distorting the admissions process, corrupting education generally and slanting the field toward students whose families can afford test preparation classes.

Consider the admissions director at our hypothetical college. He knows 3 that college ranking systems take SAT's and ACT's into account. He knows that bond-rating companies look at the same scores when judging a college's credit worthiness. And in lean times like these, he would be especially eager for a share of the so-called merit scholarship money that state legislators give students who test well.

These and related problems are the subject of an eye-opening report from 4 a commission convened by the National Association for College Admission Counseling. The commission, led by William R. Fitzsimmons, the dean of admissions and financial aid at Harvard, offers a timely reminder that tests like the SAT and ACT were never meant to be viewed in isolation but considered as one in a range of factors that include grades, essays and so on.

But the report goes further, urging schools to move away from traditional 5 admissions tests in favor of exams that would be more closely related to high school achievement and that are at least currently exempt from the hype and hysteria that surround the SAT. Mr. Fitzsimmons said that Harvard would always use tests. But he raised eyebrows when he said the school might one day join the growing number of colleges that have made the SAT and the ACT optional.

The commission deals bluntly with the parties it blamed for inflating the 6 importance of college entry exam scores. It calls on college guides and bond-rating agencies to stop using test scores as proxies for academic quality or financial health. And it wants an end to the increasingly common practice of using minimum admissions test scores to determine eligibility for merit aid. The commission insists that the tests have not been validated for that purpose and often rule out applicants based on a single missed item.

The National Merit Scholarship Program, which uses a test to screen 7 thousands of applicants every year, comes in for a drubbing. The commission believes that the program has played a destructive role by helping to narrow the public's view of merit, giving it an exclusively test-related meaning. This commission draws on the work of Patrick Hayashi, a former associate president at The University of California, who has been fiercely critical of the National Merit program—and has even described it as "bogus."

He first questioned the scholarship program during the 1990s out of disappointment with highly sought-after national merit scholarship students who had enrolled at Berkeley. He later wrote that those students had been outshone by students from the university's more broadly defined merit program and had done "nothing to distinguish themselves academically or otherwise."

The commission has also called on the states to stop the practice of using 9 college entry exams in the public school accountability system. By inserting exams that weren't designed for this purpose, the states have unintentionally encouraged students to believe that course work matters less than gaming the test that gets them into college.

Critics will inevitably view the report as an attempt to undermine objec- 10 tive admissions and awards systems. But the commission is arguing for a richer and more expansive view of merit that could include test scores but does not end with them. And the commission's central contention—that the obsession with admissions tests is damaging education— is indisputably true.

> "The obsession with admissions tests is damaging education."

⊙ AT ISSUE: SOURCES FOR DEVELOPING A LOGICAL ARGUMENT

1. Why do you think Staples begins his essay with a hypothetical situation? Would another strategy have been more successful?

2. What is the thesis of this essay? At what point in the essay is this thesis stated?

3. According to Staples, how do most colleges determine merit?

4. What definition of merit does the National Association for College Admission Counseling suggest? How is their definition of merit different from the traditional view? Which of the two definitions do you think is more accurate? Why?

5. Formulate a syllogism that presents the main points of Staples's argument. Do you think his conclusion at the end of paragraph 10 is "indisputably true," as Staples says it is?

6. Can you find any fallacies in Staples's argument?

This article is an Associated Press report from March 16, 2007.

HAMILTON COLLEGE TO END MERIT SCHOLARSHIPS IN FAVOR OF NEED-BASED AID

ASSOCIATED PRESS

Hamilton College said Thursday it will stop offering merit scholarships to incoming students in 2008 and use the money instead to provide more need-based assistance to low- and middle-income families. 1

The move won praise from educators who said they hope it will inspire other colleges to follow suit. 2

The decision by the small liberal arts college would affect only a few dozen students. But it comes at a time when colleges have been criticized for using their resources to lure high-achieving students—many of whom don't need the money to attend college—thereby improving a school's academic standing at the expense of its economic diversity. 3

"This is a true act of leadership . . . and hopefully it will begin to restore the system to a more sensible one," said Barmak Nassirian, associate executive director of the American Association of College Registrars and Admissions Officers. 4

> ""This is a true act of leadership.""

Hamilton, a 195-year-old liberal arts college in upstate New York with about 1,800 students, has awarded a limited number of merit scholarships since 1997. On average, 15 to 20 students out of a first-year class of 470 have received merit scholarships of up to half tuition. 5

Approximately 5 percent of Hamilton's $21 million financial aid budget is spent on merit aid, according to Monica Inzer, dean of admission and financial aid. The new policy will reallocate about $1 million each year for additional need-based aid, she said. 6

Those who study groups in terms of race, age, sex, income, and other factors

Inzer said demographers° predict a college student population with greater financial need in the coming decade, and colleges and universities must prepare for that reality. 7

Currently, more than half of all Hamilton students receive need-based financial aid. The average financial aid package (grant, work-study, loan) for those students exceeds $26,000, Inzer said. It costs $43,890 a year to attend Hamilton. 8

"Everyone is saying it would be great to slow this merit aid trend down, but no schools have been willing to do it," said Sandy Baum, senior policy analyst for The College Board and professor of economics at Skidmore College. 9

While a few schools across the country—among them George Washington and Dickinson College—have reduced the amount of merit aid they give out 10 or the number of students who receive it, Hamilton is believed to be the first school to entirely abandon its merit scholarship program, she said.

Some highly selective schools, which have plenty of applicants to choose 11 from, award aid only on the basis of need. But many schools spend millions on merit aid to lure more accomplished students.

⊘ AT ISSUE: SOURCES FOR DEVELOPING A LOGICAL ARGUMENT

1. The Associated Press, an agency that distributes news articles throughout the country, published this story based on a Hamilton College press release. Does it present information objectively, or does it take a stand on the issue? Explain.

2. Do you think other colleges and universities will be able to follow Hamilton College's lead? What factors might limit their ability to do so?

3. At what point does the article explain the context for Hamilton's actions? Should it have supplied more background information? If so, what kind?

This posting is from the Student Financial Services Web site at Lewis & Clark College, Portland, Oregon.

MERIT-BASED SCHOLARSHIPS FOR INCOMING STUDENTS

LEWIS & CLARK COLLEGE

Neely and Trustee Scholarships

The Barbara Hirschi Neely Scholarships, Lewis & Clark's highest merit awards, recognize men and women of exceptional academic achievement and distinctive personal accomplishment. Up to 10 scholarships are awarded to entering first-year students and are renewable annually, based on continued academic excellence as evidenced by maintaining a cumulative GPA of 3.3 or higher. The scholarships provide full tuition and fees, valued at more than $134,900 over four years. 1

> "The scholarships provide full tuition and fees, valued at more than $134,000 over four years."

The Neely Scholarships are made possible by Barbara Hirschi Neely, who established numerous trust funds to benefit Lewis & Clark College. When she died in January 1990, these trust funds totaled $6.2 million—all designated as endowment° funds for student aid. 2

Money that is donated to an institution, often for a specific purpose, and that the institution invests and uses for various annual expenses

Up to 15 merit-based Trustee Scholarships will also be awarded. These scholarships are valued at one half of tuition and fees per year and are renewable annually for the next three years based on continued academic excellence as evidenced by maintaining a cumulative GPA of 3.3 or higher—a cumulative value of more than $67,450. Both scholarships are renewable annually. Lewis & Clark's Neely and Trustee scholarship winners have earned many additional honors, including: the Rhodes Scholarship, the Truman Scholarship, the Goldwater Scholarship, the James Madison Fellowship, and the Fulbright Fellowship; membership in Phi Beta Kappa and Dr. Robert B. Pamplin Jr. honor societies; and awards from the Mellon Foundation and the National Science Foundation. 3

Basis of Eligibility

Neely and Trustee Scholarships are available to first-year applicants for admission. Transfer students are not eligible. The faculty selection committee considers candidates on the basis of academic record, preferred areas, and character and personality. 4

Academic Record: Past recipients have followed an exceptionally challenging curriculum and attained superior records. Standardized test scores place them well above national norms. (Standardized tests are optional for students applying through the Portfolio Path to Admission.) 5

Preferred Areas: Special preference is given to: 6

1. *Math/sciences*: students whose interests, curiosities, and commitments lie in the sciences, with the intent of advancing the understanding of natural systems and promoting responsible use of resources, or

2. *International education/issues*: students who possess an unusually keen interest in the history, arts, and political and social realities of other nations or cultures and who are prepared to become citizens of the world.

Character and Personality: Previous winners had superior recommenda- 7 tions. Candidates should utilize both the personal essay and admission interview to enhance their credentials. In all they did, past finalists sought challenges and made the most of opportunities presented to them. They were leaders both in and out of the classroom.

Selection Process

The Office of Admissions and a faculty selection committee review top can- 8 didates for Neely and Trustee Scholarships. Emphasis is given to candidates' intellectual interests and academic performance. Strong candidates demonstrate interest in one of the preferred areas described above through course selection, grades, and activities beyond the classroom (e.g., summer activities). Candidates are not required to achieve a minimum GPA or test score; however, standards are high. The following is an academic profile of the 2008 Trustee and Neely Scholars:

GPA: 95% had a GPA of 3.9 or higher
Rank: 100% were in the top tenth of their class.
SAT: Middle 50% range 1500–1580 (CR+M)
ACT: Middle 50% range 33–35

Student Applications

To be eligible for consideration, the student must submit all credentials 9 required for completed application to the College no later than February 1. No nomination is required.

Notification of Winners

Winners are announced by March 15. 10

Dean's Scholarships

More than 100 of these merit-based scholarships are available to entering first- 11 year and transfer students based on their academic program and performance. The awards average $7,000. Scholarships are renewable for three additional years based on continued academic excellence by achieving a cumulative GPA of 3.0 or higher. All students admitted to the excellence by achieving a cumulative GPA of 3.0 or higher. All students admitted to the College are considered for these scholarships; no separate form other than the application for admission is required. The following is an academic profile of the 2008 Dean's Scholars:

GPA: Middle 50% range 3.84–4.0
Rank: Nearly 83% were in the top tenth of their class.
SAT: Middle 50% range 1310–1410 (CR+M)
ACT: Middle 50% range 29–31

Leadership and Service Awards

These awards recognize students who have demonstrated outstanding aca- 12
demics combined with exemplary leadership and/or service in their school
or community. Scholarships are worth $5,000 per year and are renewable for
three additional years based on continued leadership and/or service combined
with academic success. All admitted students are considered for these scholarships; no separate form other than the application for admission is required.
The following is an academic profile of the 2008 recipients:

GPA: Middle 50% range 3.64–4.0
Rank: 96% were in the top quarter of their class.
SAT: Middle 50% range 1230–1340
ACT: Middle 50% range 26–29

Herbert Templeton National Merit Scholarships

Lewis & Clark offers awards of $1,000 to entering first-year students who have 13
been selected as National Merit finalists and who have named Lewis & Clark as
their first-choice college with the National Merit Corporation by May 1.

Music and Forensics Scholarships

Students who demonstrate exceptional talent and commitment in music or 14
forensics may be considered for awards. For details, contact:

Music scholarship information:
Dave Becker
Department of Music
Lewis & Clark College
0615 S.W Palatine Hill Road
Portland, Oregon 97219-7899
503-768-7460
music@lclark.edu

Forensics scholarship information:
Steve Hunt
Director of Forensics
Lewis & Clark College
0615 S.W. Palatine Hill Road
Portland, Oregon 97219-7899
503-768-7617
hunt@lclark.edu

Private Scholarships

Private scholarships, many of which are based on merit or special crite- 15
ria, are an increasingly important source of funding for students. Last year,
Lewis & Clark students garnered over $1 million in external scholarship
money awarded by businesses, community groups, and religious and fraternal
organizations. Your high school counselor should be able to refer you to local
scholarship sources. If you are on campus, you are also welcome to use the
reference information located in the Office of Student Financial Services and
in Watzek Library to research sources of private scholarships.

Information about All Other Merit-Based Scholarships

Office of Admissions
Lewis & Clark College
0615 S.W. Palatine Hill Road
Portland, Oregon 97219-7899
503-768-7040
800-444-4111 toll free
503-768-7055 fax
admissions@lclark.edu

⊙ AT ISSUE: SOURCES FOR DEVELOPING A LOGICAL ARGUMENT

1. What criteria do the merit-based scholarships listed on the Lewis & Clark College Student Financial Services Web site have in common? What criteria differentiate them from one another?

2. Where does the money for these merit-based scholarships come from?

3. On the basis of their descriptions on the Web site, do the merit-based scholarships take aid away from needy students?

➲ **EXERCISE 5.11**

Write a one-paragraph **deductive** argument in which you argue *in favor of* merit-based scholarships. Follow the template below, filling in the blanks to create your argument.

Template for Writing a Deductive Argument

Merit-based scholarships make sense for society as well as for students. As a rule, society should encourage good students to _____

_____

_____. Everyone benefits when _____

_____.

For example, _____

_____

_____. By identifying good students and providing them with merit-based scholarships, _____

_____

_____

_____. Therefore,_____

_____.

Not everyone agrees with this position, however. Some people argue that

_____

_____

_____. This argument misses the point. When colleges give merit-based scholarships, _____

_____

_____.

For this reason, colleges should provide merit-based scholarships

_____

_____.

➲ **EXERCISE 5.12**

Write a one-paragraph **inductive** argument in which you argue *against* merit-based scholarships. Follow the template below, filling in the blanks to create your argument.

Template for Writing an Inductive Argument

Today, many students cannot afford to go to college. Tuition _____

_____.

In addition, books and _____

_____

_____. To meet these costs, some students _____

_____.

Other students _____

_____.

In addition, many colleges have less money for financial aid. This means that, when they give merit-based scholarships, they _____

_____

_____.

Those who favor merit-based scholarships, however, argue that _____

_____

_____. Although this may be true, in today's

financial environment, _____

_____

_____. As result, it is clear that _____

_____.

➲ EXERCISE 5.13

Interview several of your classmates as well as one or two of your instructors about what they think of merit-based scholarships. Then, edit the deductive and inductive arguments you wrote in Exercises 5.11 and 5.12 so that they include some of these comments.

➲ EXERCISE 5.14

Write an essay in which you argue for or against merit-based scholarships for college students. Make sure that your essay is organized primarily as either a deductive argument or an inductive argument. Use the readings on pages 128–141 as source material, and be sure to document all information that you get from these sources. (See Chapter 10 for information on documenting sources.)

➲ EXERCISE 5.15

Review the logical fallacies discussed on pages 113–123. Then, reread the essay you wrote for Exercise 5.14, and check to see if it contains any fallacies. Underline any fallacies you find, and identify them by name. Then, rewrite each statement so it expresses a logical argument. Finally, revise your draft to eliminate any fallacies you found.

➲ EXERCISE 5.16

Review the four pillars of argument discussed in Chapter 1. Does your essay include all four elements of an effective argument? Add anything that is missing. Then, label the key elements of your essay.

6 Rogerian Argument, Toulmin Logic, and Oral Arguments

Is Distance Learning as Good as Classroom Learning?

Distance learning (sometimes called **e-learning**) is a type of instruction designed to take place over a computer network. It has its roots in the correspondence courses that became popular in the nineteenth century and also in classroom television instruction, which was seen as an alternative to face-to-face teaching in the 1950s. Beginning in the 1990s, increasing college costs and advances in technology made distance learning a practical and cost-effective option for educators.

The advantages of distance learning are clear. For colleges and universities, distance-learning programs are very profitable, allowing schools to reach new student populations both nationally and internationally. In addition, schools can provide instruction without the expense of providing classrooms, offices, libraries, and bookstores. For students, distance learning offers the freedom of flexible scheduling, creating extra time for work or family. Finally, students like saving the cost of commuting to and from school.

Despite the advantages of distance learning, however, questions remain about its effectiveness. Some educators wonder whether online courses can ever duplicate the dynamic educational atmosphere that face-to-face instruction can provide. Others question whether students learn as well from education delivered by technology as they do from classroom instruction. Finally, many instructors observe that because distance-learning classes require more self-discipline than on-campus classes, students find it easy to procrastinate and fall behind in their work.

Later in this chapter, you will be asked to think more about this issue. You will be given several sources to consider and asked to write an argument—using one of the three approaches discussed in this chapter—that takes a position on whether distance learning is as good as classroom instruction.

The traditional model of argument is confrontational: one side wins, and the other loses.

Understanding Rogerian Argument

The traditional model of argument is **confrontational**—characterized by conflict and opposition. This has been the tradition since Aristotle wrote about argument in ancient Greece. The end result of this model of argument is that someone is guilty and someone is innocent, someone is a winner and someone is a loser, or someone is right and someone is wrong.

Arguments do not always have to be confrontational, however. In fact, the twentieth-century psychologist Carl Rogers contended that this method of arguing can actually be counterproductive, making it impossible for two people to reach agreement. According to Rogers, attacking opponents and telling them that they are wrong or misguided puts them on the defensive. The result of this tactic is frequently ill will, anger, hostility—and conflict. If you are trying to negotiate an agreement or convince someone to do something, these are exactly the responses that you do not want. To solve this problem, Rogers developed a new approach to argument—one that emphasizes cooperation over confrontation.

Rogerian argument begins with the assumption that people of good will can find solutions to problems that they have in common. Rogers recommends that you consider those with whom you disagree as colleagues, not opponents. Instead of entering into the adversarial relationship that is assumed in classical argument, Rogerian argument encourages you to enter into a cooperative relationship in which both you and your readers search for **common ground**—points of agreement about a problem. By taking this approach, you are more likely to find a solution that will satisfy everyone.

Structuring Rogerian Arguments

Consider the following situation. Assume that you bought a camera that broke one week after the warranty expired. Also assume that the manager of the store where you purchased the camera has refused to exchange it for another camera. His point is that because the warranty has expired, the store has no obligation to take the camera back. As a last resort, you write a letter to the camera's manufacturer. If you were writing a traditional argument, you would state your thesis—"It is clear that I should receive a new camera"—and then present arguments to support your position. You would also refute opposing arguments, and you would end your letter with a strong concluding statement.

Because Rogerian arguments begin with different assumptions, however, they are structured differently from classical arguments. In a Rogerian argument, you would begin by establishing common ground—by pointing out the concerns you and the camera's manufacturer share. For example, you could say that as a consumer, you want to buy merchandise

Rogerian argument focuses on helping each side meet its goals.

A malfunctioning camera might provide an opportunity to use Rogerian argument.

that will work as advertised. If the company satisfies your needs, you will continue to buy its products. This goal is shared by the manufacturer. Therefore, instead of beginning with a statement that demands a yes or no response, you would point out that both you and the manufacturer have an interest in solving your problem.

Next, you would describe *in neutral terms* the manufacturer's view of the problem, defining the manufacturer's concerns and attempting to move toward a compromise position. For example, you would explain that you understand that the company wants to make a high-quality camera that will satisfy customers. You would also say that you understand that despite the company's best efforts, mistakes sometimes happen.

In the next section of your letter, you would present your own view of the problem fairly and objectively. This section plays a major role in convincing the manufacturer that your position has merit. Here, you should also try to concede the strengths of the manufacturer's viewpoint. For example, you can say that although you understand that warranties have time limits, your case has some unique circumstances that justify your claim.

Next, you would explain how the manufacturer would benefit from granting your request. Perhaps you could point out that you have been satisfied with other products made by this manufacturer and expect to purchase more in the future. You could also say that instead of requesting a new camera, you would be glad to send the camera back to the factory to be repaired. This suggestion shows that you are fair and willing to compromise.

Finally, your Rogerian argument would reinforce your thesis and end with a concluding statement that emphasizes the idea that you are certain that the manufacturer wants to settle this matter fairly.

◑ EXERCISE 6.1

Read through the At Issue topics listed in this book's table of contents. Choose one topic, and then do the following:

1. Identify some common ground that you and someone who holds the opposite position might have.

2. Summarize your own position on the issue.

3. In a few sentences, summarize the main concerns of someone who holds the opposite position.

4. Write a sentence that explains how your position on the issue might benefit individuals (such as those who hold opposing views) or society in general.

Writing Rogerian Arguments

Rogerian arguments are typically used to address highly controversial, emotionally charged issues. This strategy attempts to downplay disagreement and to instead reinforce agreement and compromise. Thus, Rogerian argument makes an effort to acknowledge the reader's perspective and to address his or her concerns.

> **Note:** Although the Rogerian approach to argument can be used to develop a whole essay, it can also be part of a more traditional argument. In this case, it frequently appears in the refutation section, where opposing arguments are addressed.

In general, a Rogerian argument can be structured in the following way:

INTRODUCTION	Introduces the problem, pointing out how both the writer and reader are affected (establishes common ground)
BODY	Presents the reader's view of the problem
	Presents the writer's view of the problem (includes evidence to support the writer's viewpoint)
	Shows how the reader would benefit from moving toward the writer's position (includes evidence to support the writer's viewpoint)
	Lays out possible compromises that would benefit both reader and writer (includes evidence to support the writer's viewpoint)
CONCLUSION	Includes a strong concluding statement that reinforces the thesis

⬇ The following student essay includes all the elements of a Rogerian argument. After you read the essay, answer the questions on page 153, consulting the outline above if necessary.

DO THE OLYMPIC GAMES NEED PERMANENT HOST SITES?

CHRISTOPHER CHU

Introduction

The decision to hold the 2008 Summer Olympics in Beijing, China, was controversial. Many people protested, and some wanted to boycott the games because of China's history of human-rights violations. Months after the Olympics ended, people still wondered if a country's political and human-rights actions should affect its eligibility to host the Olympics. For many people, the Olympics is a symbol of world unity, and for this reason, they reject the idea of boycotting the event. They believe this act would be a rejection of the Olympic values of peace, understanding, and international cooperation. However, these ideals are undercut when the games are held in a country known to violate human rights. If we truly support the spirit of the Olympics, we should not hold the games in

Thesis statement

countries that do not share the games' core values. To avoid this problem, we should consider creating permanent Olympic sites in countries that embody the basic values that are symbolized by the games.

Reader's view of the situation

Understandably, boycotting the Olympic Games because of a country's politics seems problematic to many. Some say that a boycott unfairly denies athletes' rights, fosters a "politically correct" value system, and undermines the spirit of the games. Supporters of the Olympics argue that when the games are boycotted (as they were in Moscow in 1980 and in Los Angeles 1984) it is the athletes, not the host countries who suffer. Anita DeFrantz, a former U.S. Olympian who was kept from participating in the 1980 games because the United States boycotted the Olympics that year, thinks that political boycotts of the games deny the rights of both citizens and athletes. Remembering her own experience, she says that in the event of a boycott, "the rights of the U.S. Olympians will be sacrificed at the whim of our political leaders." When a country boycotts the Olympics, it undercuts the games' support for peaceful communication and understanding. And as DeFrantz points out, the boycott did not change Russia's decision to invade Afghanistan. "Even though the games went on without us," she says, "the boycott had zero effect on the issues that caused it." In the end, the boycott did nothing but punish the United States's own athletes.

3   China, the host country for the 2008 Olympics, presented an even more difficult problem than the Soviet Union did. Not only did China invade Tibet in the 1950s, but it has continued to use harsh measures to repress political dissent ("Speak Out"). During the torch relays before the games, protesters in several major cities such as London, Paris, and San Francisco (shown in Fig. 1) turned out in force to highlight China's human-rights violations (Wendel). In addition to its actions concerning Tibet, China also sold weapons to Sudan that were used to carry out the genocide in Darfur (Nabaum 1). In addition, China is Sudan's major oil importer, buying about 66% of its exported petroleum (Ruibal). In the *New Republic,* Alex Nabaum asks, "Can we really send our athletes to compete in a country that tortures its own citizens merely for expressing political thoughts?" (1). Although a boycott would punish our athletes, we have to consider the suffering that we ignore if we hold the games in

Writer's view of the situation

Fig.1. Morris, David Paul. *Pro-Tibetan Activists March Across Golden Gate Bridge.* 2008. Gettyimages.com. JPEG file.

a country with a long history of human-rights violations. We may not think it is our place to judge the political practices of another nation, but when that nation engages in torture, helps to support genocide, and slaughters protesters, we cannot silently stand by as if these actions do not matter.

Benefits of writer's position

Although boycotting the Olympic Games may not be the best solution for athletes or nations, neither is holding the games in a country whose political practices undermine their values. We should support the athletes of every participating country, but it is also important to support the mission of the games. As DeFrantz says, "The Olympic Games are, and should be, about the athletes, competition and the promise of peace." But the promise of peace is threatened when the games are held in a country that either rejects or threatens peace, as China does in Tibet, Sudan, and Burma. So, we should consider how we can protect the rights of the athletes without supporting countries whose political actions are at odds with the games' mission. A possible solution to this problem is to choose several permanent sites for the games, one on each major continent. Tim Wendel points out that alternating among a few "non-superpower locales" would end the "insane bidding wars to host the games" and allow nations to improve security because sites would be permanent. Establishing permanent Olympic sites would ensure that every athlete could compete without fear and also keep the integrity of the games intact.

Possible compromise

4

Conclusion

Boycotts are not a good way to maintain the spirit of the Olympics, but we cannot in good conscience endorse games that are held in countries that challenge the values of the Olympic Games. We can, however, establish permanent Olympic sites in countries that have a history of supporting the values that the games promote. In spite of our positions on the Moscow or Beijing games, we should concede the fact that politics and the actions of the country holding the games affect everyone's perception of the games. For this reason, it would be in everyone's best interest to build several permanent host sites that share one common goal: the idea of an Olympics whose host sites support the games' basic values.

Concluding statement

5

Works Cited

DeFrantz, Anita L. "Athletes, Not Politics, Define Olympics." *USA Today* 16 May 2008: 19. Print.

Nabaum, Alex. "Gold Meddle." *New Republic* 22 Oct. 2007: 1+. Print.

Ruibal, Sal. "Activists: Beijing Boycott No Solution." *USA Today* 8 June
2007: 9. Print.

"Speak Out on Tibet." Editorial. *New York Times*. New York Times,
24 Mar. 2008. Web. 10 Nov. 2008.

Wendel, Tim. "Embattled Games Should Consider Permanent Sites."
USA Today 17 July 2008: 9. Print.

Identifying the Elements of Rogerian Argument

1. Where in the essay does the writer attempt to establish common ground? Do you think he is successful?

2. What evidence does the writer supply to support his viewpoint?

3. Where does the writer address opposing points of view? Summarize these opposing views. Do you think the writer does enough to acknowledge them?

4. What points does the conclusion emphasize? Other than reinforcing the thesis, what else is the conclusion trying to accomplish?

5. How would this essay be different if it were written as a traditional (as opposed to a Rogerian) argument?

Understanding Toulmin Logic

Another way of describing the structure of argument was introduced by the philosopher Stephen Toulmin in his book *The Uses of Argument* (1958). Toulmin observed that although formal logic is effective for analyzing highly specialized arguments, it is inadequate for describing the arguments that occur in everyday life. Although Toulmin was primarily concerned with the structures of arguments at the level of sentences or paragraphs, his model is useful when dealing with longer arguments.

In its simplest terms, a **Toulmin argument** has three parts—the *claim*, the *grounds*, and the *warrant*. The **claim** is the main point of the essay—usually stated as the thesis. The **grounds** are the evidence that a writer uses to support the claim. The **warrant** is the inference—either stated or implied—that connects the claim to the grounds.

A basic argument using Toulmin logic would have the following structure.

CLAIM	Distance learning should be a part of all students' education.
GROUNDS	Students who take advantage of distance learning get better grades and are under less stress than students who do not.
WARRANT	Anything that improves students' grades and lowers stress is a valuable educational option.

Notice that the three-part structure above resembles the **syllogism** that is the backbone of classical argument. When you use Toulmin logic to construct an argument, you still use deductive and inductive reasoning. You arrive at your claim inductively from facts, observations, and examples, and you connect the grounds and the warrant to your claim deductively.

Constructing Toulmin Arguments

Real arguments—those you encounter in print or online every day—are not as simple as the three-part model above implies. To be convincing, they often contain additional elements. To account for the demands of everyday debates, Toulmin expanded his model.

CLAIM	The **claim** is the main point of your essay. It is a debatable statement that the rest of the essay will support. *Distance learning should be a part of all students' education.*
REASON	The **reason** is a statement that supports the claim. Often the reason appears in the same sentence, with the claim connected to it by the word *because*. (In an argumentative essay, this sentence is the thesis statement.) *Distance learning should be a part of all students' education **because** it enables them to have a more successful and enjoyable college experience.*
WARRANT	The **warrant** is the inference that connects the claim and the grounds. The warrant is often an unstated assumption. Ideally, the warrant should be an idea with which your readers will agree. (If they do not agree with it, you will need to supply **backing**.) *Distance learning is a valuable educational option.*
BACKING	The **backing** is the evidence that supports the warrant. *My own experience with distance learning was positive. Not only did it enable me to schedule classes around my job, but it also enabled me to work at my own pace in my courses.*

GROUNDS   The **grounds** are the concrete evidence that a writer uses to support the claim. These are the facts and observations that support the thesis. They can also be the opinions of experts that you locate when you do research.

Studies show that students who take advantage of distance learning often get better grades than students who do not.

Research indicates that students who take advantage of distance learning are under less stress than those who are not.

QUALIFIERS   The **qualifiers** are statements that limit the claim. For example, they can be the real-world conditions under which the claim is true. These qualifiers can include words such as *most, few, some, sometimes, occasionally, often,* and *usually.*

Distance learning should be a required part of most students' education.

REBUTTALS   The **rebuttals** are refutations of opposing arguments.

Some people argue that distance learning deprives students of an interactive classroom experience, but a class chat room can give students a similar opportunity to interact with their classmates.

◑ EXERCISE 6.2

Look through this book's table of contents, and select an At Issue topic that interests you (ideally, one that you know something about). Write a sentence that states your position on this issue. (In terms of Toulmin argument, this statement is the *claim*.)

Then, list as many of the expanded Toulmin model elements as you can, consulting the description of these elements on pages 154–155.

Reason: _____

_____

Grounds: _____

_____

Warrant: _____

_____

_____

Backing: _____

_____

_____

Qualifiers: _____

_____

_____

Rebuttals: _____

_____

Writing Toulmin Arguments

One of the strengths of the Toulmin model of argument is that it emphasizes that presenting effective arguments involves more than stating ideas as
absolute facts. Unlike the classical model of argument, the Toulmin model
encourages writers to make realistic and convincing points by including
claims and qualifiers and by addressing opposing arguments in down-to-
earth and constructive ways. In a sense, this method of constructing an
argument reminds writers that arguments do not exist in a vacuum. They
are aimed at real readers who may or may not agree with them.

In general, a Toulmin argument can be organized in the following way:

INTRODUCTION	Introduces the problem
	States the claim (and possibly the qualifier)
BODY	Includes a strong concluding statement that rein-forces the claim
	Possibly states the warrant
	Presents the backing that supports the warrant
	Presents the grounds that support the claim
	Presents the conditions of rebuttal
CONCLUSION	Includes a strong concluding statement that rein-forces the claim

⬇ The following student essay includes all the elements of a Toulmin
argument. (Note that labels identifying these elements appear in the
margins.) The student who wrote this essay was responding to the question, "Should Congress pass a constitutional amendment banning the
burning of the American flag?" After you read the essay, answer the questions on page 160, consulting the outline above if necessary.

OUR RIGHT TO BURN OR BURNING OUR RIGHTS?

FRANCO GHILARDI

1   Recently, several members of Congress have tried to amend the   Introduction
Constitution to prohibit the desecration of the United States flag. Some
supporters of the proposed amendment say that burning the flag (as
shown in Fig. 1) is not only offensive but also an attack against our
country. They say that by showing disrespect for the symbol of our
country, protesters are actually giving aid and comfort to our enemies. As
disagreeable as flag desecration—especially flag burning—is, however,
legislators should think twice before amending the Constitution to
prohibit it. Flag burning is considered political speech and is protected by
the Constitution. Because prohibiting flag burning would undermine one of   Claim and reason
our most basic constitutional rights—the right to protest—it should remain
protected.

Fig. 1. Bowmer, Riok. *A Protester Throws an American Flag over Burning
Debris Outside the Democratic National Convention at the Staples Center
in Los Angeles.* 2000. APimages.com. JPEG file.

Warrant

Backing

Grounds

Although some argue that it is un-American to desecrate the flag, 2 it is more un-American to deny citizens their constitutional right to free expression. Freedom of speech is the first right in our Bill of Rights, and most Americans would agree that the founding fathers placed it first for a reason. They believed that freedom to criticize the government was the most basic defense a free people could have against tyranny—in their case, the tyranny of the English monarchy. Reinforcing this freedom, the United States Supreme Court ruled in 1989 that the First Amendment protects flag burning. To counter this ruling, members of Congress have repeatedly introduced bills to amend the Constitution to prohibit the desecration of the flag. One of the most recent bills, proposed in 2006, even equated flag burning with cross burning ("Senator Clinton"). This comparison, however, is misguided. First, the Court has always recognized the distinction between a violation of civil rights and the protection of free expression, and for this reason, it permits cross burning only when it rises to the level of political speech. In addition, cross burning has always been associated with the persecution of African Americans, while flag burning has usually been associated with protest against the government. Thus, flag burning (unlike cross burning) gives citizens a way of exercising their constitutional right to criticize their government.

Backing

Passing a constitutional amendment to ban the desecration of the flag 3 could inevitably lead to other restrictions of liberty. For example, owning, using, or laundering a bathing suit, T-shirt, or other item of clothing with the image of an American flag on it could be considered desecration. And what would happen if someone sat on a towel that had an image of an American flag on it? This too could be considered desecration. The absurdity of these

Grounds

examples raises the question of how to define *desecration*. *Desecration* could mean almost anything—from accidentally dirtying a flag blanket at a picnic to burning a flag to protest a war. The restrictions imposed by a flag-desecration amendment could also interfere with the private-property rights of both individuals and businesses. For example, if the flag became a symbol controlled by the government, could the government then tell people how to display it? Would the government be able to impose restrictions on businesses that produce flags or flag merchandise? Those who support a constitutional amendment to prohibit flag desecration should carefully consider these possible consequences.

4   Despite the Supreme Court's ruling that the First Amendment protects flag burning, some argue that it is unacceptable for citizens to protest by burning an important national symbol. In 2003, during the Iraq war, General Wesley K. Clark announced that he was in favor of the American flag amendment (Wyatt). However, Clark qualified his support by saying, "No administration should ever say that if you disagree with [the administration], you're not being patriotic." Robert Scales, a Vietnam War veteran, takes a different position on the question of flag burning. Scales, who remembers feeling shocked that protesters would burn the American flag during the Vietnam War, also remembers questioning how other nations would see those protesters. He writes, "Undoubtedly [the Vietnamese government] would have punished those protesters if they burned the North Vietnamese flag in Hanoi" (Scales). Even so, Scales never questions people's right to protest by burning the flag. He even goes on to say that a soldier's duty is "to defend the right to free speech with [her or his] life even if that 'speech' is expressed in despicable ways." As these examples show, even though flag burning may be highly objectionable, in many cases it is a legitimate expression of free speech and American civil liberties.

Conditions for rebuttal

Grounds

Qualifier

5   Passing an amendment banning flag desecration interferes with citizens' First Amendment rights of free speech. Like all of the liberties listed in the Bill of Rights, freedom of speech is basic to our way of life and should not be restricted by a constitutional amendment that could eventually affect other liberties, such as the right to private property and the freedom to engage in political dissent. Although some people may argue that it is un-American to desecrate the flag, it is more un-American to deny us our freedom of expression in a country founded on principles of personal liberty.

Conclusion

Concluding statement

Works Cited

Scales, Robert. "Forget Flag Burning." *Time* 3 July 2006: 100. Print.

"Senator Clinton, in Pander Mode." Editorial. *New York Times.* New York Times, 7 Dec. 2005. Web. 10 Dec. 2008.

Wyatt, Edward. "Clark Tells Veterans He Backs Amendment on Flag Desecration." *New York Times.* New York Times, 12 Nov. 2003. Web. 10 Dec. 2008.

Identifying the Elements of Toulmin Argument

1. Summarize the position this essay takes as a three-part argument—including the claim, the grounds, and the warrant.

2. Do you think the writer includes enough backing for his claim? What other supporting evidence could he have included?

3. Find the qualifier in the essay. How does it limit the argument? How else could the writer have qualified the argument?

4. Do you think the writer addresses enough objections to his claim? What other arguments could he have rebutted?

5. Based on your reading of this essay, what advantages do you think Toulmin logic offers to writers? What disadvantages does it present?

Understanding Oral Arguments

Many everyday arguments—in school, on the job, or in your community—are presented orally. In many ways, an oral argument is similar to a written one: it has an introduction, a body, and a conclusion, and it addresses and refutes opposing points of view. In other more subtle ways, however, an oral argument is different from a written one. Before you plan and deliver an oral argument, you should be aware of these differences.

The major difference between an oral argument and a written one is that an audience cannot reread an oral argument to clarify information. Listeners have to understand an oral argument the first time they hear it. To help your listeners, you need to design your presentation with this limitation in mind, considering the following guidelines:

- **An oral argument should contain verbal signals that help guide listeners.** Transitional phrases such as "My first point," "My second point," and "Let me sum up" are useful in oral arguments, where listeners do not have a written text in front of them. They foreshadow information to come and alert listeners to shifts from one point to another.

- **An oral argument should use simple, direct language and avoid long sentences.** Complicated sentences that contain elevated language and numerous technical terms are difficult for listeners to follow. For this reason, your sentences should be straightforward and easy to understand.

- **An oral argument should repeat key information.** A traditional rule of thumb for oral arguments is, "Tell listeners what you're going to tell them; then tell it to them; and finally tell them what you've told them." In other words, in the introduction of an oral argument, tell your listeners what they are going to hear; in the body, discuss your points, one at a time; and finally, in your conclusion, restate your points. This intentional repetition ensures that your listeners follow (and remember) your points.

■ **An oral argument should include visuals.** Visual aids can make your argument easier to follow. You can use visuals to identify your points as you discuss them. You can also use visuals—for example, charts, graphs, or tables—to clarify or reinforce key points as well as to add interest. Carefully selected visuals help increase the chances that what you are saying will be remembered.

Planning an Oral Argument

The work you do to plan your presentation is as important as the presentation itself. Here is some advice to consider as you plan your oral argument:

1. **Choose your topic wisely.** Try to select a topic that is somewhat controversial so listeners will want to hear your views. You can create interest in a topic, but it is easier to appeal to listeners if they already have some interest in what you have to say. In addition, try to choose a

Visual aids can help listeners follow an oral presentation.

topic that you know something about. Even though you will probably have to do some research, the process will be much easier if you are already familiar with the basic issues.

2. **Know your audience.** Try to determine what your audience already knows about your topic. Also, assess their attitudes toward your topic. Are they friendly? Neutral? Hostile? The answers to these questions will help you decide what information to include and which arguments will most likely be effective (and which will not).

3. **Know your time limit.** Most oral presentations have a time limit. If you run over your allotted time, you risk boring or annoying your listeners. If you finish too soon, it will seem as if you don't know much about your subject. As you prepare your argument, include all the information that you can cover within your time limit. Keep in mind that you will not be able to go into as much detail in a short speech as you will in a long speech, so plan accordingly.

4. **Identify your thesis statement.** Like a written argument, an oral argument should have a debatable thesis statement. Keep this statement simple, and make sure that it clearly conveys your position on your topic. Remember that in an oral argument, your listeners have to understand your thesis the first time they hear it. (See Chapter 7 for more on developing a thesis statement.)

5. **Gather support for your thesis.** You need to support your thesis convincingly if you expect listeners to accept it. Supporting evidence can be in the form of facts, observations, expert opinion, or statistics. Some of your support can come from your own experiences, but most will come from your research.

6. **Acknowledge your sources.** Remember that all of the information you get from your research needs to be documented. As you deliver your presentation, let listeners know where the information you are using comes from—for example, "According to a 2009 editorial in the *New York Times* . . ." or "As Kenneth Davis says in his book *America's Hidden History*. . . ." This strategy enhances your credibility by showing that you are well informed about your topic. (Including source information also helps you protect yourself from inadvertent **plagiarism**. See Chapter 11.)

7. **Prepare your speaking notes.** Effective speakers do not read their speeches. Instead, they prepare **speaking notes**—usually on index cards—that list the points they want to make. (Some speakers write out the full text of their speech or make a detailed outline of their speech and then prepare the notes from this material.) These notes guide you as you speak, so you should make sure that there are not too

many of them and that they contain just key information. (It is a good idea to number your note cards so you can be sure that they stay in the correct order.)

8. **Prepare visual aids.** Visual aids help you to communicate your thesis and your supporting points more effectively. Visuals increase interest in your presentation, and they also strengthen your argument by reinforcing your points and making them easier for listeners to understand. In addition, visuals can help establish your credibility and thus improve the persuasiveness of your presentation.

    You can use the following types of visual aids in your presentations:

    - Diagrams
    - Photographs
    - Slides
    - Flip charts
    - Overhead transparencies
    - Document cameras
    - Handouts
    - Objects

    In addition to these kinds of visual aids, you can also use **presentation software**, such as Microsoft's PowerPoint or Adobe's Persuasion. With presentation software, you can easily create visually appealing and persuasive slides. You can insert scanned photographs or drawings into slides, or you can cut and paste charts, graphs, and tables into them. You can even include video and sound clips. Keep in mind, however, that the images, film clips, or sound files that you use must support your thesis; if they are irrelevant, they will distract or confuse your listeners. (See the oral argument on p. 168 for examples of PowerPoint slides.)

9. **Practice your presentation.** As a general rule of thumb, you should spend as much time rehearsing your speech as you do preparing it. In other words, practice, practice, practice. Be sure you know the order in which you will present your points and when you will move from one visual to another. Rehearse your speech aloud with just your speaking notes and your visuals until you are confident that you can get through your presentation effectively. Try to anticipate any problems that may arise with your visuals, and solve them at this stage of the process. If possible, practice your speech in the room in which you will actually deliver it. Bring along a friend, and ask for feedback. Finally, cut or add material as needed until you are certain that you can stay within your time limit.

CHECKLIST

Designing and Displaying Visuals

☐ Use images that are large enough for your audience to see and that will reproduce clearly.

☐ Make lettering large enough for your audience to see. Use 40- to 50-point type for titles, 25- to 30-point type for major points, and 20- to 25-point type for less important points.

☐ Use bulleted lists, not full sentences or paragraphs.

☐ Put no more than three or four points on a single visual.

☐ Make sure there is a clear contrast between your lettering and the background.

☐ Don't show your listeners the visual before you begin to speak about it. Display the visual only when you discuss it.

☐ Face your listeners when you discuss a visual. Even if you point to the screen, always look at your listeners. Never turn your back on your audience.

☐ Introduce and discuss each visual. Don't simply show or read the visual to your audience. Always tell listeners more than they can read or see for themselves.

☐ Don't use elaborate special effects or visuals that will distract your audience.

⬤ **EXERCISE 6.3**

Look through the table of contents of this book, and select three At Issue topics that interest you. Imagine that you are planning to deliver an oral argument to a group of college students on each of these topics. For each topic, list three visual aids you could use to enhance your presentation.

Delivering Oral Arguments

Delivery is the most important part of a speech. The way you speak, your interactions with the audience, your posture, and your eye contact all affect your overall presentation. In short, a confident, controlled speaker will have a positive effect on an audience, while a speaker who fumbles with note cards, speaks in a shaky voice, or seems disorganized will have a negative effect. To make sure that your listeners see you as a credible, reliable source of information, follow these guidelines:

1. **Accept nervousness.** For most people, nervousness is part of the speech process. The trick is to convert this nervousness into energy that you can channel into your speech. The first step in dealing with nervousness is to make sure that you have rehearsed enough. If you have prepared adequately, you will probably be able to handle any problem you may encounter. If you make a mistake, you can correct it. If you forget something, you can fit it in later. In short, try to relax.

2. **Look at your audience.** When you speak, look directly at the members of your audience. At the beginning of the speech, make eye contact with a few audience members who seem to be responding positively. As your speech progresses, look directly at as many audience members as you can. Try to sweep the entire room. Don't focus excessively on a single person or on a single section of your audience.

3. **Speak naturally.** Your presentation should sound like conversational speech, not like a performance. This is not to suggest that your presentation should include slang, ungrammatical constructions, or colloquialisms; it should conform to the rules of standard English. The trick is to maintain the appearance of a conversation while following the conventions of public speaking. Achieving this balance takes practice, but it is a goal worth pursuing.

Michelle Obama projects confidence and control as she speaks.

4. **Speak slowly.** When you give an oral presentation, you should speak more slowly than you do in normal conversation. This strategy gives listeners time to process what they hear—and gives you time to think about what you are saying.

5. **Speak clearly and correctly.** As you deliver your presentation, speak clearly. Do not drop endings, and be careful to pronounce words correctly. Look up the pronunciation of unfamiliar words in a dictionary, or ask your instructor for help. If you go though an entire speech pronouncing a key term or name incorrectly, your listeners will question your credibility.

6. **Move purposefully.** As you deliver your speech, don't pace, move your hands erratically, or play with your note cards. Try to stand in one spot, with both feet flat on the floor. Move only when necessary—for example, to point to a visual or to display an object. If you intend to distribute printed material to your listeners, do so only when you are going to discuss it. (Try to arrange in advance for someone else to give out your handouts.) If you are not going to refer to the material in your presentation, wait until you have finished your speech before you distribute it. Depending on the level of formality of your presentation and the size of your audience, you may want to stand directly in front of your audience or behind a podium.

7. **Be prepared for the unexpected.** Don't get flustered if things don't go exactly as you planned. If you forget material, work it in later. If you make a mistake, correct it without apologizing. Most of the time, listeners will not realize that something has gone wrong unless you call attention to it. If someone in the audience looks bored, don't worry. You might consider changing your pace or your volume, but keep in mind that the person's reaction might have nothing to do with your presentation. He or she might be tired, preoccupied, or just a poor listener.

8. **Leave time for questions.** End your presentation by asking if your listeners have any questions. As you answer questions, keep in mind the following advice:

   - *Be prepared.* Make sure you have anticipated the obvious counterarguments to your position, and be prepared to address them. In addition, prepare a list of Web sites that you can refer your audience to for more information.

   - *Repeat a question before you answer it.* This technique enables everyone in the audience to hear the question, and it also gives you time to think of an answer.

   - *Keep control of interchanges.* If a questioner repeatedly challenges your answer or monopolizes the conversation, say that you will be glad to discuss the matter with him or her after your presentation is finished.

- *Be honest.* Answer questions honestly and forthrightly. If you don't know the answer to a question, say so. Tell the person you will locate the information that he or she wants and send it by email. Above all, do not volunteer information that you are not sure is correct.

- *Use the last question to summarize.* When you get to the last question, end your answer by restating the main point of your argument.

Writing an Oral Argument

The written text of an oral argument is organized just as any other argument is: it has an introduction that gives the background of the issue and states the thesis, it has a body that presents evidence that supports the thesis, it addresses arguments against the thesis, and it ends with a concluding statement. (In addition, the person making the speech often concludes by asking if the members of the audience have any questions.)

In general, an oral argument can be structured in the following way:

INTRODUCTION	Presents the background of the issue
	States the thesis
BODY	Presents evidence: Point 1 in support of the thesis
	Presents evidence: Point 2 in support of the thesis
	Presents evidence: Point 3 in support of the thesis
	Refutes opposing arguments
CONCLUSION	Concluding statement restates thesis
	Speaker asks for questions

⊙ The following oral argument was presented by a student in a speech course. After you read this argument, answer the questions on page 173, consulting the outline above if necessary.

AN ARGUMENT IN SUPPORT OF THE "GAP YEAR"

CHANTEE STEELE

Introduction

College: even the word sounded wonderful when I was in high   1
school. Everyone I knew told me it would be the best time of my life.
They told me that I would take courses in exciting new subjects and that
I'd make life-long friends. **[Show slide 1]** What they didn't tell me was
that I would be anxious, confused, and uncertain about my major and
about my future. Although this is only my second year in college, I've
already changed my major once, and, to be honest, I'm still not sure I've
made the right decision. But during the process of changing majors,
my adviser gave me some reading material that included information
about a "gap year." A gap year is a year off between high school and
college when students focus on work or community service and learn
about themselves. Although it's gaining popularity in the United States,
the gap year still suggests images of spoiled rich kids who want to play
for a year before going to college. According to educator Christina Wood,
however, in the United Kingdom a gap year is common; it is seen as a time
for personal growth that helps students mature (36). **[Show slide 2]** In fact,
230,000 British students take a gap year before going to college. As the rest
of my speech will demonstrate, a well-planned gap year gives students
time to mature, to explore potential careers, and to volunteer or travel.

Thesis statement

Evidence: Point 1   **[Show slide 3]** Apparently I'm not alone in my uncertainty about   2
in support of thesis   my major or about my future. As Holly Bull reports in the *Chronicle of
Higher Education,* "The National Research Center for College and
University Admissions estimates that over 50% of students switch
majors at least once." As they go from high school to college, most
students have little time to think about what to do with their lives. A
gap year before college would give them time to learn more about
themselves. According to Wood, "Gap years provide valuable life
experiences and maturity so students are more ready to focus on their
studies when they return" (37). A year off would give some students

the perspective they need to mature and to feel more confident about their decisions. Bull agrees, noting that many students "choose a gap year because they are drawn to the extraordinary range of options, or because they prefer to head to college with a clearer idea of a major."

3   The gap year gives students many options to explore before going to college. [Show slide 4] This slide shows just some of the resources students can use as they prepare for their gap year. As you can see, they can explore opportunities for employment, education, and volunteer work. There are even resources for students who are undecided. As David Lesesne, the dean of admissions at Sewanee, says, "Some students do very interesting and enriching things: hike the Appalachian Trail, herd sheep in Crete, play in a signed rock band, [or even] attend school in Guatemala" (qtd. in Wood 37). As long as the year is well planned and approached seriously, students are certain to gain perspective from their time away from school.

Evidence: Point 2 in support of thesis

4   A gap year can also help students get into better colleges. According to Joel Bauman, the vice president of enrollment services at Westminster College, the gap year can give students material to write about in admissions essays that could give them competitive edges against other applicants (Wood 37). And, depending on the scope of their service or work, a gap year could enable students to earn scholarships that they were not eligible for before. In fact, some colleges actually encourage time off for students. In "The Creditability in Your Gap Year," Ben Harder reports that for some applicants, taking a year off is not optional. For example, Harvard makes some applicants' admission dependent on a gap year (99). Given this support for the gap year, and given the resources that are now available to help students plan it, the negative attitudes about it in the United States are beginning to change.

Evidence: Point 3 in support of thesis

5   In spite of the benefits I've outlined, parental concerns about "slackerdom" and money are common. Supporters of the gap year acknowledge that students have to be motivated to make the most of their experiences. Clearly, the gap year is not for everyone. For example, students who are not self-motivated may not benefit from a gap year. In addition, parents worry about how much money the gap year will cost them. This is a real concern when you add the

Refutation of opposing arguments

year off to the expense of four years of college (Wood 37). However, if finances are a serious concern, students can choose to spend their gap year in their own communities or take advantage of a paid experience like AmeriCorps—which, as the AmeriCorps Web site shows, covers students' room and board *and* offers an educational award after students complete the program. **[Show slide 5]**

Conclusion

After considering the benefits of a gap year, I think that we should 6 encourage more students to postpone college for a year. Many students (like me) are uncertain about their goals. We welcome new opportunities and are eager to learn from new experiences and may find a year of service both emotionally and intellectually rewarding. Given another year to mature, many of us would return to school with a greater sense of purpose, focus, and clarity. In some cases, the gap year could actually help us get into better schools and possibly get more financial aid. If we intend to take the college experience seriously,

Concluding statement

spending a gap year learning about our interests and abilities would help us to become better, more confident, and ultimately more focused students. **[Show slide 6]**

Are there any questions? 7

Works Cited

Bull, Holly. "The Possibilities of the Gap Year." *Chronicle of Higher Education* 52.44 (2006): 77. Print.

Harder, Ben. "The Creditability in Your Gap Year." *U.S. News & World Report* 141.7 (2006): 98–99. Print.

Wood, Christina. "Should You Take a 'Gap Year'?" *Careers and Colleges* Fall 2007: 36–37. Print.

Slide 1

Slide 2

230,000 students between 18 and 25 take a Gap
Year in the U.K.

—Tom Griffiths, founder and director
of www.gapyear.com

(qtd. in Christina Wood, "Should You Take a 'Gap Year'?,"
Careers and Colleges Fall 2007)

Slide 3

50% of students change their major at least once.

—National Research Center for College
and University Admissions

Slide 4

A Few Links for the Potential "Gapster"

(links from Holly Bull, "The Possibilities of the Gap Year," *Chronicle of Higher Education* 52.44 [2006])

Employment

Cool Works: coolworks.com (domestic jobs)

Working Abroad: workingabroad.org (jobs overseas)

Education

Global Routes: globalroutes.org (semester-long courses)

Sea-mester: seamester.com (sea voyage programs)

Volunteer Work

AmeriCorps: americorps.org

City Year: cityyear.org

Thoughtful Texts for Fence Sitters

Karl Haigler and Rae Nelson, *The Gap-Year Advantage* (Macmillan, 2005)

Colin Hall, *Taking Time Off* (Princeton Review, 2003)

Charlotte Hindle and Joe Bindloss, *The Gap Year Book* (Lonely Planet, 2005)

Slide 5

Slide 6

Identifying the Elements of an Oral Argument

1. Where does this oral argument include verbal signals to help guide readers?

2. Does this oral argument use simple, direct language? What sections of the speech, if any, could be made simpler?

3. Where does this oral argument repeat key information for emphasis? Is there any other information that you think should have been repeated?

4. What opposing arguments does the speaker identify? Does she refute them convincingly?

5. How effective are the visuals that accompany the text of this oral argument? Are there enough visuals? What other information do you think could have been displayed in a visual?

6. What questions would you ask this speaker at the end of her speech?

Is Distance Learning as Good as Classroom Learning?

Go back to page 145, and reread the At Issue box, which gives background about whether distance learning is as good as classroom instruction. As the following sources illustrate, this question has a number of possible answers.

After you review the sources listed below, you will be asked to answer some questions and to complete some simple activities. This work will help you to understand both the content and the structure of the sources. When you are finished, you will be ready to develop an argument—using one of the three alternative approaches to argument discussed in this chapter—that takes a position on whether distance learning is as effective as classroom learning.

SOURCES

 Sandra C. Ceraulo, "Online Education Rivals 'Chalk and Talk' Variety"

 Suzanne M. Kelly, "The Sensuous Classroom: Focusing on the Embodiment of Learning"

 Marilyn Karras, "Calling a University 'Virtual' Creates an Actual Oxymoron"

 eLearners.com, "Frequently Asked Questions about eLearning"

 Naugatuck Valley Community College, "Distance Learning"

 "Two Views of Distance Learning"

This piece appeared in the *Buffalo News* on May 29, 2002.

ONLINE EDUCATION RIVALS "CHALK AND TALK" VARIETY

SANDRA C. CERAULO

Like many people whose formal education was based entirely on "chalk and 1 talk" lectures, I was skeptical about the value of online education. But in 1999, I was in a bind. I wanted to take information technology courses, but was unable to commute to nighttime lectures. So I decided to give an online course a try.

Though it was only a noncredit adult education course, I was immediately 2 impressed with the caliber of my online classmates. The students really wanted to learn, and their introductory remarks revealed that most of them were taking the course by choice.

Intelligent and insightful dialogue, posted by students at times convenient 3 for them in our online discussion board, flowed naturally. Like most of my classmates, I mastered the material, saved all of the commuting time and never had to miss a class. I was surprised to find myself thinking that the quality of this education was as good as that in my undergraduate courses at Cornell or my graduate courses at the University of Chicago.

There was one major difference this time. I attended lectures when and 4 where I chose. I, the student, was in the driver's seat. I reasoned that if I liked the convenience and independence of online learning, so would many other people. As a professor myself, I saw that my experiment with online learning had given me an unexpected preview of where education was going. I continued taking information technology courses and also enrolled in a certification program in online teaching, a program that was offered entirely online.

Today, I have taught the material I learned online in online and tradi- 5 tional college courses. I am certified in online teaching and am an expert in e-learning and information technology. I am impressed by the fact that my online students become as skilled as their peers in the traditional classroom. The lesson seems clear: Online courses can provide as good an education as traditional classes.

But online courses aren't for everyone. Students who like a "live demon- 6 stration" and hands-on help are better off in traditional classrooms. Likewise, those who prefer to personally check in with their instructor and classmates will find that traditional courses better meet their needs. Still, online education is ideal in many other cases.

For example, a computer science major who wants to learn one more 7 programming language could easily learn it online. Online education also can help avoid scheduling difficulties. Students must assess their own personal and educational needs and weigh all of their options to create the course of study that is best for them.

As is true of traditional courses, the fact that an online course exists does not guarantee it is a good one. Institutions with state-of-the-art technology and financial resources to hire and train the best technical staffs are likely to have the best programs. Research has shown that the most important factor in determining the quality of an online program is the technical expertise of those who work in it. 8

> "The fact that an online course exists does not guarantee it is a good one."

I think all students can benefit from trying online education. Since many companies and software manufacturers are rapidly converting their training programs to e-learning format, college students who are experienced in online learning may find themselves at an advantage in the workplace. The current generation of students must train for the 21st century workplaces, not those of the past. 9

Quite unexpectedly, I took to e-learning like a fish to water, and I encourage others to give it a try, too. 10

⊙ AT ISSUE: SOURCES FOR USING ALTERNATIVE APPROACHES TO ARGUMENT

1. Where does Ceraulo state her thesis? Summarize this thesis statement. Why do you think she waits so long to state it?

2. What is a "chalk and talk" lecture? How is it different from an online lecture?

3. Does Ceraulo use any techniques of Rogerian argument in her essay? Where?

4. According to the author, why are online courses not for everyone?

5. What does Ceraulo consider to be the most important factor in determining the quality of an online program?

6. What, according to Ceraulo, are the advantages of online education? Can you think of any other advantages that she neglects to mention?

This article is from the July 25, 2008, issue of the *Chronicle Review*, a magazine of the *Chronicle of Higher Education*.

THE SENSUOUS CLASSROOM: FOCUSING ON THE EMBODIMENT OF LEARNING

SUZANNE M. KELLY

1 Not long ago, a soon-to-be-minted Ph.D. sat in on one of my women's-studies classes, placing herself in the midst of the undergraduates. Afterward the two of us stayed behind to discuss her impressions of the class. "I'd forgotten what it's like to sit with them," she said.

2 I nodded in agreement, and she smiled slightly. I could see she wanted to say something else, so I probed. "What else did you think?"

3 "Well," she said, "I'd also forgotten how they smell!"

4 I'm still not entirely sure what she meant, but her delivery was so earnest—and so free from judgment—that I couldn't write her comment off. In fact, it tapped into some very deep part of me that understands the potency of sensual bodies, both the students' and the professor's, in the classroom.

5 Even in my undergraduate days, I had a sense that my education was never independent of the bodies seated beside me. I was the kind of student who sometimes felt pressed to stand on top of my desk to confront my philosophical enemies. I can still see the contours of one foe's head and hear his slow, monotonous speech, even though it's been nearly 20 years since we met. Memories of my body in that room still fill me with the old readiness to pounce. How I must have appeared to people then—in my long hippie skirt and combat boots, hair wild as the night, a foot shorter than my foe. Climbing up on my desk was obviously about making myself appear larger, but it was also about literally getting above the impeding banter° so I could be heard.

Chatter that blocks communication

6 I suspect that some of our peers didn't care for our contentious displays, and I can appreciate that now. But I believe that without that classroom, without being framed by the presence of one another, we could not have come to know all that we did. Words and ideas were the intangible, abstract stuff of our learning. But they were always moving through the matter of our bodies in time and space, looping, feeding in and around our fleshly selves.

7 Of course, none of what I've described could have been experienced online. I have colleagues who are passionate about the virtues of online courses. They tell me students "speak" more online, that conversations are more open, fruitful, and inclusive.

8 But in women's studies, my field, many courses grapple with the body as they cover eating disorders, ideas about beauty, violence against women, and other issues. In one of my courses, for instance, we talk about modernity's policing of the body and what that has meant for women in body practices like dieting, ornamentation, and hair removal. In a physical classroom, we

177

are witnesses to at least some of each other's practices: me to my students' makeup and dyed hair; them to my shaved legs and high wedge sandals. What does it do to our discussions when bodies are hidden behind computers and software—when the sensuous classroom is lost?

Every spring, when the weather begins to warm up, the outdoors calls students and professors alike to move class outside. That always sounds like a good idea until we are actually out there, and we can't hear ourselves talk over the combined sounds of cars, leaf blowers, and other conversations. 9

I like being outside anyway. As we step beyond the walls of the building, a new classroom is formed by the circle of our bodies on the grass. A leaf falls on my papers; a spider crawls on my bag. A student plucks a dandelion and puts it behind her ear. The wind brushes the hairs on my arm, and I smell the fresh-cut hay from the field beyond the quad. Memories and emotions from my outdoor past are fused with the ideas of the day's class. 10

> "A student plucks a dandelion and puts it behind her ear."

Despite not being able to hear one another as well as inside the building, we manage to communicate without the walls of the traditional classroom. It seems ironic that online learning is often referred to as "a classroom without walls," given that the phrase once referred to a kind of experiential learning, one rooted in taking students out into the world, not cordoning them away into the far corner of their home offices. Either way, education isn't simply a question of walls or no walls. It's the bodies that matter. 11

It should come as no surprise that educators consider the body expendable, given the long Western tradition of playing down the body's knowledge in favor of the mind's. Some weeks before we had an outdoor class last semester, my students and I had been discussing Donna Haraway's "A Cyborg Manifesto," on the potential of the cyborg.° With cellphones and computers, pacemakers and hearing aids, we are already, Haraway tells us, part human and part machine. 12

A combination of human and machine

My students often initially find Haraway's arguments compelling, seeing the good in what we now are, and the potential to apply it in positive ways. "There's no turning back," they argue. What lies ahead is the promise of the cyborg, the benefits of which would include breaking down oppressive gender roles through the anonymity made possible online. 13

But eventually the old notions of nature and origin come rushing back, and my students begin to mourn the possibility of losing their sensuous selves even in relationship to their peers. Timid or brave, most students delight in having an attentive audience. Body language matters—a glance, a smile, a nod, and even the way a student holds a thought for a bit, visibly considers it, and then speaks it out loud. 14

Obviously distance learning has merits. People who might not otherwise have access to education can take online courses. That is particularly true for women, who must often balance mothering with paid work and find it impossible to be a student in the parameters of traditional education. But online courses are just a substitute for traditional education because a classroom full of bodies is quite literally full of real, living matter. In other words, it's the real thing. 15

At the most basic level, to be a student has always meant actually dragging 16
one's exhausted body into class with readings in hand, being (more or less)
awake, alert, listening, and ready to open one's mouth. And to be a teacher, for
me, means seeing the faces of the students and how their bodies reflect their
thoughts and emotions, hearing the timbre of their voices or the lilts in their
dialects, experiencing them before me in the rich mix of ideas.

After one class not long ago, a student caught me to discuss some ideas for 17
her final paper. It wasn't until we had been talking for half an hour that I happened to look down and notice that I had buttoned up my coat wrong. The left
side was hanging way below the right.

"Look at me," I said, laughing, humiliated. "I'm turning into one of those 18
oblivious professors!" I had stood there going on about this theorist and that idea,
all the while looking as if my not-yet-2-year-old nephew had helped me dress. The
student was kind enough to laugh with me and to try to cheer me up by telling me
about a friend of hers who was bored by the constraining lectures of law school.

"Sounds awful," I said. 19

"Yes. I told my friend how different it was for me at college," she said. 20
"How one of my professors sits on top of her desk, flailing her hands here and
there, sometimes even eating oranges!"

My heart sank as I quickly realized that she was talking about me. I do some- 21
times eat oranges in class. I do occasionally wave my hands around. And I do sometimes sit on my desk—in that way, I guess not much has changed since my college
days. The student's description was a useful reminder, helping me to better see myself
as a professor with a body, and to think about the meanings—both known and not
yet understood—that are embedded in our physical proximity to one another.

⊘ AT ISSUE: SOURCES FOR USING ALTERNATIVE APPROACHES TO ARGUMENT

1. Kelly begins her article with a brief anecdote about women's-studies class. What are the advantages of opening with this story? Do you see any disadvantages?

2. According to Kelly, what does classroom learning provide that distance learning does not offer?

3. Why does the author think that women's-studies courses are not suitable for distance learning? Do you think her point has merit? Explain.

4. Do you think Kelly's points about women's-studies courses apply to other kinds of courses as well? Why or why not?

5. The author ends her article with another anecdote. What is the point of this story? Can you think of a more effective way to end her essay?

This piece is from the December 18, 1997, *Deseret News*, Salt Lake City.

CALLING A UNIVERSITY "VIRTUAL" CREATES AN ACTUAL OXYMORON

MARILYN KARRAS

The concept of a "virtual" university concerns me. Though Gov. Mike Leavitt 1 and others who are promoting the Western Governors University and a Utah Electronic Community College have begun shying away from using the term *virtual* still is an apt word to define a high-tech transfer of information.

According to the dictionary definition of the word, a virtual university 2 would be a university in effect but not in actual fact. And while we're consulting Mr. Webster, it's interesting to note that he defines a *university* as "an educational institution of the highest level."

Putting the two words together creates an actual oxymoron of the highest 3 level.

I have nothing against distance learning when it's necessary. People who 4 cannot attend classes on campus should not be denied a certificate for completing their studies. But to confer on them a degree signifying they have a university education would be dishonest.

A university education involves, among other things, debate, discussion 5 and an exchange of ideas among classmates and professors, both inside and outside the classroom. Stimulating independent thinking is one of its primary objectives. It is doubtful that students in remote areas, listening to a television set or a computer, can get that kind of interactive stimulation.

It's a question deserving academic and practical debate: How much should 6 we give up or adjust in order to take advantage of technology? Just because we CAN teach people facts without requiring them to attend traditional classes doesn't mean we necessarily should. Except in cases where it would be impossible for them to be educated on campus.

If a high school student doesn't meet the requirements to receive a diploma 7 with his class, he cannot later earn that diploma. He can study and take a test later and receive an equivalency certificate but not a high school diploma.

That kind of distinction should be made among those who earn a 8 certificate from a "virtual" educational institution. Those graduates should not be recognized as having achieved the same education as those who attended the traditional university.

It's not a matter of elitism. It's a distinction between types of learning. 9 A graduate of a distance-learning institution has not been educated as thoroughly as a university graduate, though the same facts have been transferred. That person has not had the same experience.

> "It's not a matter of elitism."

Utah has already made some mistakes in its higher education system that 10
tend to diminish the university degrees offered here. Weber State University is
not a university, and the name never should have been changed. Weber State
College was a fine college, and I am proud to have received a degree from that
school.

But it is not a university. Universities have graduate programs offering 11
master's degrees and doctorates. They operate on a different level, with different requirements of their faculties and curricula. To call WSC a university is
simply an attempt to change the image of the school by changing its name. It's
simple pretense and should never have been allowed.

The logical way to run an educational system in this state would be to 12
have one system, as California does, with various campuses specializing in certain areas. Universities should offer and participate in greater research experiences and community colleges would offer students a more basic education.
But that's a subject for another column.

Let's call things what they are. Let's be honest as well as practical in pro- 13
viding educational opportunities at various levels for our residents. To put a
particular name to an institution does not change its nature. Virtual is still
virtual and should not be confused with a "real" university degree.

⊘ AT ISSUE: SOURCES FOR USING ALTERNATIVE APPROACHES TO ARGUMENT

1. Why does Karras think that *virtual* is "an apt word to define the high-tech transfer of information" (1)?

2. According to the author, why does putting together the words *virtual* and *education* create an **oxymoron**—a figure of speech in which two contradictory terms are combined?

3. What does Karras see as the difference between a university educa-tion and a virtual education?

4. In paragraph 9, Karras says that the distinction she is making is "not a matter of elitism." Do you agree? Do you think she is making a distinction between two types of learning or between two types of students?

5. Do you think a virtual degree should have the same status as a tradi-tional university degree? Why or why not?

6. Identify as many elements of Toulmin argument in Karras's essay as you can. Does analyzing her essay in this way help you to better understand her argument? If so, how?

This set of frequently asked questions is from eLearners.com.

FREQUENTLY ASKED QUESTIONS ABOUT eLEARNING

eLEARNERS.COM

What are the positive and negative aspects of online learning? 1

You might find that distance learning requires more discipline and self- 2
motivation than traditional courses that meet face-to-face.

One method to determine how well online 3
learning might work for you is to consider its
benefits and disadvantages.

> "Consider its benefits and disadvantages."

To get the most from this list, consider your 4
learning needs, professional priorities, and personal circumstances to help you
decide what is best for you.

Pros	Cons
No time spent commuting/traveling to a campus	Allow for time required to boot up computer, software programs, and connect to the Internet.
No additional travel costs to add to the family budget	Budget for additional high-speed Internet costs (if applicable).
Continue working at your current job while you take classes, thus allowing you to earn a living *and* gain work experience, applying your course work.	Need the discipline not to log into your class while at work (unless your employer permits you to complete your course work at the office)
Your learning options are not constrained by your geographic location (e.g., you live in California and attend the University of Massachusetts).	Plan and adjust your studying schedule around assignment due dates (e.g., you live in California and your final project is due to your instructor at 5 p.m. Eastern time).
You can learn at your own pace and study at your convenience (e.g., after the kids are asleep or before work).	At times, you may experience feelings of isolation or a sense of detachment from your school.
If you prefer to express yourself in writing rather than verbally, you may find distance learning more effective.	Lack of face-to-face interaction—especially in self-paced courses—or difficulty in developing relationships with classmates
Classes typically centered and focused on student responses	Students may need to wait for feedback and responses from peers

and virtual discussion rather than instructor-led lectures

and instructors (especially if you study between the hours of 11 p.m. to 6 a.m.).

Instruction and course work can be highly customized to your field and subject—especially computer based training (CBT).

Equipment needs of students and learning providers (e.g., generally a personal computer, office software, and an Internet connection are required)

Additional benefits of learning new technologies and practicing the use of the Internet, office software, etc.

May require you to learn new or enhance computer and troubleshooting skills

You will meet and work with classmates from all over the United States and throughout the world.

Possibility of limited local networking opportunities

All students are 100 percent equal: your work will stand on merits alone, and you will not be treated differently based upon race, sex, creed, sexual orientation, religion, disability, etc.

You will be required to be able to work unsupervised (i.e., you will have to problem solve solutions independently).

Requires 100 percent participation from each and every classmate (e.g., the most outgoing students will not monopolize the discussions)

You must be self-motivated and disciplined to progress through your program in a timely manner.

⊙ AT ISSUE: SOURCES FOR USING ALTERNATIVE APPROACHES TO ARGUMENT

1. This Web page is from eLearners.com, a site that promotes distance learning. Do you think the site's treatment of the pros and cons of distance learning is balanced? Why or why not?

2. Can you think of any positive or negative aspects of distance learning that this page neglects to mention?

3. Assume you are writing an argument in favor of distance learning. From the eLearners.com Web page, identify the three strongest arguments *against* distance learning. How would you refute each of these opposing arguments?

4. Assume you are writing an argument against distance learning. From the Web pages, identify the three strongest arguments *in favor of* distance learning. How would you refute each of these arguments?

This Web page, accessed January 19, 2010, explains the NVCC distance-learning program.

DISTANCE LEARNING

NAUGATUCK VALLEY COMMUNITY COLLEGE

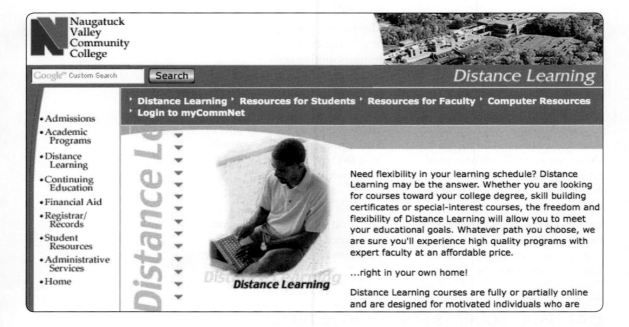

⊘ AT ISSUE: SOURCES FOR USING ALTERNATIVE APPROACHES TO ARGUMENT

1. What is the purpose of this Web page?

2. What kind of audience does this Web page seem to be addressing? How can you tell?

3. Is the Web page's treatment of distance learning balanced? Explain.

4. What additional information—if any—do you think should have been provided?

5. How do you think Marilyn Karras (p. 180) would respond to this Web page?

The photo at left is by Andy Nelson. The photo at right is by Tanya Constantine.

TWO VIEWS OF DISTANCE LEARNING

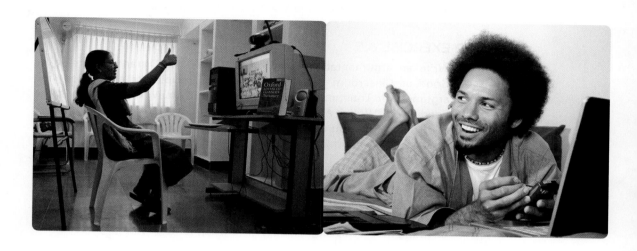

↪ AT ISSUE: SOURCES FOR USING ALTERNATIVE APPROACHES TO ARGUMENT

1. The picture at left above shows an instructor teaching in a distance-learning program. What is your reaction to this picture? Does it present distance learning in a favorable or unfavorable light? Explain.

2. The other picture—a student taking a distance-learning class—is from a university's Web site that promotes its distance-learning program. What advantages of distance learning does this picture try to show?

3. Do you think you would do well in an e-learning environment? Why or why not?

⊘ EXERCISE 6.4

Discuss your feelings about distance learning with one or two of your classmates. Consider both the strengths and the limitations of this method of teaching. What types of classes do you think it is best suited for? Which classes do you think it would not work for? Then, write a paragraph that presents the key ideas of your discussion.

⊘ EXERCISE 6.5

Write an argumentative essay on the topic, "Is Distance Learning as Good as Classroom Learning?" Use the principles of either Rogerian argument or Toulmin logic to structure your essay. Cite sources in the Reading and Writing about the Issue section on pages 174–185, and be sure to document the sources you use and to include a works-cited page. (See Chapter 10 for information on documenting sources.)

⊘ EXERCISE 6.6

Review the four pillars of argument that are discussed in Chapter 1. Does your essay include all four elements of an effective argument? Add anything that is missing. Then, label the elements of your argument.

⊘ EXERCISE 6.7

Assume that you have been asked to present the information in the essay you wrote for Exercise 6.5 as an oral argument. What information would you include? What information would you eliminate? Select two or three visuals that you would use when you deliver your speech. Then, make an outline of your speech and indicate at what points you would display these visuals.

3

Writing an Argumentative Essay

CHAPTER

7

Planning, Drafting, and Revising an Argumentative Essay

AT ISSUE

Should College Campuses Go "Green"?

In recent years, more and more American colleges and universities have been moving toward becoming "green" campuses, emphasizing **sustainability**—the use of systems and materials that will not deplete the earth's natural resources. Various schools have taken steps such as the following to become green:

- Placing an emphasis on recycling and reducing nonbiodegradable waste
- Creating green buildings and using eco-friendly materials in construction projects
- Instituting new curricula in environmental science
- Monitoring their greenhouse gas emissions and evaluating their carbon footprint
- Growing crops on campus to feed students
- Hiring full-time "sustainability directors"
- Encouraging students to use bikes instead of cars
- Purchasing wind-generated electricity to supply the campus's energy

- Eliminating trays in college cafeterias

Although many schools have launched ambitious programs and projects to reduce their energy dependence, some have been more cautious, citing the high cost of such programs and the need to allocate resources elsewhere. Moreover, some critics of the green movement object to the notion that colleges should help make students "sustainability literate." Such critics consider the green movement to be an expression of political correctness that at best gives lip service to the problem and at worst threatens academic freedom by furthering a political agenda.

The question remains whether the green movement that is spreading rapidly across college campuses is here to stay or just a fad—or something between these two extremes. This chapter takes you through the process of writing an argumentative essay on the topic, "Should College Campuses Go 'Green'?" (Exercises guide you through the process of writing your own argumentative essay.)

189

Before you can write a convincing argumentative essay, you need to understand the **writing process**. You are probably already familiar with the basic outline of this process, which includes *planning, drafting,* and *revising.* This chapter reviews this familiar process and explains how it applies to the specific demands of writing an argument.

Choosing a Topic

The first step in planning an argumentative essay is to choose a topic you can write about. Your goal is to select a topic that you have some emotional stake in—not simply one that interests you. If you are going to spend hours planning, writing, and revising an essay, then you should care about your topic. At the same time, you should have an open mind about your topic and be willing to consider various viewpoints. Your topic also should be narrow enough to fit the boundaries of your assignment—the time you have to work on the paper and its length and scope.

Typically, your instructor will give you a general assignment, such as the following.

Assignment: Write a three- to five-page argumentative essay on a topic related to college services, programs, facilities, or curricula.

The first thing you need to do is narrow this general assignment to a topic, focusing on one particular campus service, program, facility, or curriculum. You could choose to write about any number of topics—financial aid, the writing center, athletics, the general education curriculum—taking a position, for example, on who should receive financial aid, whether to expand the writing center, whether college athletes should receive a salary, or why general education requirements are important for business majors.

If you are interested in the environment, however, you might decide to write about the "green" movement that is spreading across college campuses, perhaps using your observations of your own campus's programs and policies to support your position.

Topic: The "green" movement on college campuses

TOPICS TO AVOID

Certain kinds of topics are not appropriate for argumentative essays. For one thing, some topics are just not arguable. For example, you could not write an argumentative essay on a statement of fact, such as the fact that many colleges saw their endowments decline during the financial crisis of 2008. (A fact is not debatable, so there can be no argument.)

Some familiar topics—particularly those that involve questions of personal taste or matters of faith—also present problems. For example, you might have a hard time convincing some readers that the death penalty is immoral or that abortion is a woman's right. These topics are overused, and in many people's minds, they are "settled." When you write on topics such as these, your readers' strong religious or cultural beliefs are likely to prevent them from considering your arguments, however original or well supported they might be.

Finally, topics that are very narrow or depend on subjective value judgments—or that take a stand on issues readers simply will not care much about, such as whether one particular video game or TV reality show is more entertaining than another—are unlikely to engage your audience (even if these topics are compelling to you or your friends).

⊛ EXERCISE 7.1

In response to the boxed assignment on the previous page, list ten topics that you could write about. Then, cross out any that do not meet the following criteria:

- The topic interests you.

- You know something about the topic.

- You care about the topic.

- You have an open mind about the topic.

Thinking about Your Topic

Before you can start to do research, develop a thesis statement, or plan the structure of your argument, you need to think a bit about the topic you have chosen. You can use *invention strategies*, such as **freewriting** (writing without stopping for a predetermined time) or **brainstorming** (making quick notes on your topic) to help you discover ideas you might write about. You can also explore ideas in a writing journal or in conversations with friends, classmates, family members, or instructors.

Brainstorming Notes

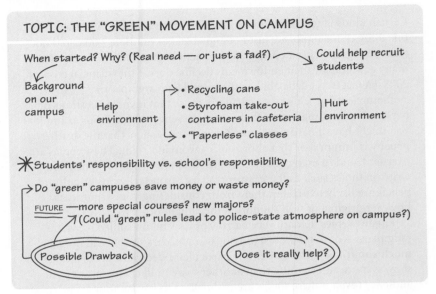

TOPIC: THE "GREEN" MOVEMENT ON CAMPUS

When started? Why? (Real need — or just a fad?) → Could help recruit students

Background on our campus   Help environment   • Recycling cans   • Styrofoam take-out containers in cafeteria   • "Paperless" classes   ] Hurt environment

✳ Students' responsibility vs. school's responsibility

→ Do "green" campuses save money or waste money?

FUTURE — more special courses? new majors?
(Could "green" rules lead to police-state atmosphere on campus?)

(Possible Drawback)   (Does it really help?)

➲ EXERCISE 7.2

Choose one of the three remaining topics from the list you prepared in Exercise 7.1, and brainstorm to think of ideas you might write about.

When you finish your informal exploration of ideas, you should be able to construct a quick **informal outline** that lists the ideas you plan to discuss.

Informal Outline

Topic: The "Green" Movement on College Campuses
    History/background
        National
        Our campus
    Positive aspects
        Helps environment
        Attracts new students
    Negative aspects
        Cost
        Enforcement
    Future

By grouping your ideas and arranging them in a logical order, an informal outline like the one above can help lead you to a thesis statement that expresses the position you will take on the issue.

⊙ EXERCISE 7.3

Construct an informal outline for an essay on the topic you brainstormed about in Exercise 7.2.

Taking a Stand

After you have decided on a topic and thought about how you want to approach it, your next step is to **take a stand** on the issue you are going to discuss. You do this by expressing your position as a thesis statement.

An argumentative thesis must be **debatable**—that is, it must have at least two sides, presenting a position with which some people might disagree. To confirm that your thesis is debatable, you should see if you can formulate an **antithesis**, or opposing statement. For example, the statement "Our school is going 'green'" has no antithesis because it is simply a statement of fact; you could not take the opposite position because the facts would not support it. However, the following thesis statement takes a position that *is* debatable (and, therefore, suitable for an argumentative essay):

> **THESIS**   College campuses should go "green."
>
> **ANTITHESIS**   College campuses should not go "green."

At this point, any thesis that you come up with is only **tentative**. As you think about your topic and as you read about it, you will very likely modify your thesis statement, perhaps expanding or narrowing its scope, rewording it to make it more precise, or even changing your position. Still, the tentative thesis statement that you decide on at this point can help you focus your exploration of your topic.

> **Tentative Thesis:** *College campuses should go "green."*

⊙ EXERCISE 7.4

List five possible thesis statements for the topic you brainstormed about in Exercise 7.2. Can you formulate an antithesis for each thesis? Which thesis statement seems most promising for an essay? Why?

Understanding Your Audience

When you write an argument, your goal is to convince your audience to accept your position as sensible (or even compelling). Sometimes you will even be able to change your readers' minds and get them to accept your position—or even take some action in support of it. To make the best possible case to your audience, you need to understand who your audience is—what knowledge, values, beliefs, and opinions your readers might have. You will also need to have some idea whether your audience is likely to be receptive, hostile, or neutral to the ideas you propose.

In most cases, it makes sense to assume that your readers are **skeptical**—that they have open minds but still need to be convinced. However, if you are writing about a topic that is controversial (stem-cell research, the death penalty, abortion rights, and so on), you will need to assume that at least some of your readers will not support your position and may, in fact, be hostile to it. If this is the case, they will be scrutinizing your arguments very carefully, looking for opportunities to argue against them. Your goal in this case is not necessarily to win them over but to make them more receptive to your position—or at least to get them to admit that you have made a good case even though they may disagree with you. At the same time, however, you also have to work to convince those who probably agree with you or are neutral (perhaps because the issue you are discussing is something they haven't thought much about).

An audience of first-year college students who are used to the idea of recycling might find the idea of a "green" campus appealing—and, in fact, natural and obvious. An audience of faculty or older students might be more skeptical, realizing that the benefits of green practices might be offset by the time and expense they might involve. College administrators might find the long-term goal of a green campus attractive (and see it as a strong recruitment tool), but they might also be somewhat hostile to your position, anticipating the considerable expense that would be involved. If you wrote an argument on the topic of green campuses, you would need to consider many of these positions—and, if possible, address them.

⊖ EXERCISE 7.5

Consider how different audiences might respond to the thesis statement you found the most promising in Exercise 7.4. Identify five possible groups of readers on your college campus—for example, athletes, history majors, or part-time faculty. Would you expect each group to be neutral, positive, or hostile to your thesis? Why?

Gathering Evidence

After you have a sense of who your audience will be and how they might react to your thesis, you can begin to collect **evidence** to support your thesis. As you look for evidence, you need to understand the difference between fact and opinion, and you need to look for bias in your sources.

Kinds of Evidence

You will use both facts and opinions to support your points, and to build a convincing argument you will need to know which is which.

A **fact** is a statement that can be verified (proven to be true). An **opinion** is always open to debate because it is a personal judgment. In general, the more knowledgeable the writer is, the more credible his or her opinion. The opinion of a respected expert on environmental issues will carry more weight than the opinion of a student with no particular expertise on the issue. However, if the student's opinion is supported by facts or statistics, it will be much more convincing than an unsupported opinion would be.

FACTS

- Drexel University has solar-powered recycling and litter receptacles.
- Philadelphia University has introduced a bachelor's degree in environmental sustainability.
- A Swarthmore College dorm has a "green" roof.

UNSUPPORTED OPINIONS

- Sustainability should be a top priority on university campuses.
- "Sustainability literacy" is really a political agenda rather than an educational goal.

SUPPORTED OPINION

- The university encourages students to live a "green" lifestyle, but it is not doing enough to help them. For example, it has no separate trash receptacles for paper, plastic, bottles, and cans.

⊘ EXERCISE 7.6

What evidence might you use to support the thesis statement you decided on in Exercise 7.4?

Criteria for Evaluating Evidence in Your Sources

As you read each potential source, consider the quality of the supporting evidence that the writer marshals to support his or her position. The more compelling the evidence, the more willing you should be to accept the writer's ideas—and, perhaps, to integrate these ideas into your own essay. (Don't forget that if you use any of your sources' ideas, you must document them. See Chapter 10 for information on MLA documentation format and Appendix B for information on APA documentation format.)

To be convincing, the evidence that is presented in the sources you review should be *accurate, relevant, representative,* and *sufficient:*

- **Accurate** evidence comes from reliable sources that you have quoted carefully—and not misrepresented by quoting out of context.

- **Relevant** evidence applies specifically (and not just tangentially) to the topic under discussion.

- **Representative** evidence is drawn from a fair range of sources, not just those that support your position.

- **Sufficient** evidence is enough facts, statistics, expert opinion, and so on to support the essay's thesis.

(For more detailed information on evaluating sources, see Chapter 8.)

Note: Remember, the evidence you use to support your own arguments should also satisfy these four criteria.

Detecting Bias in Your Sources

As you select sources, you should be alert for **bias**—a writer's use of preconceived ideas (rather than factual evidence) as support for his or her arguments. A writer who demonstrates bias may not be trustworthy, and you should approach such a writer's arguments with skepticism. To determine whether a writer is biased, follow these guidelines:

- Consider what a writer explicitly tells you about his or her beliefs or opinions. For example, if a writer mentions that he or she is a lifelong member of the Sierra Club, a vegan, and the owner of a house heated by solar energy, then you should consider the possibility that he or she might downplay (or even disregard) valid arguments against a green campus rather than presenting a balanced view.

- Look for slanted language. For example, a writer who mocks supporters of environmental issues as *politically correct* or uses pejorative terms such as *hippies* for environmentalists should not earn your trust.

- Consider the supporting evidence the writer chooses. Does the writer present only examples that support his or her position and ignore valid opposing arguments? Does the writer quote only those experts who agree with his or her position—for example, only pro- (or only anti-) environmental writers? A writer who does this is presenting an unbalanced (and therefore biased) case.

- Consider the writer's tone. A writer whose tone is angry, bitter, or sarcastic should be suspect.

- Finally, consider any overtly offensive statements or characterizations that a writer makes. A writer who makes negative assumptions about college students (for example, characterizing them as selfish and self-involved and therefore dismissing their commitment to campus environmental projects) should be viewed with skepticism.

> **Note:** Keep in mind that it is important to be aware of any biases you hold that might affect the strength or logic of your own arguments. See "Being Fair," page 204.

⊘ EXERCISE 7.7

In writing an essay that supports the thesis statement you have been working with in this chapter, you might not be objective. What biases do you have that you might have to watch for as you research and write about your topic?

⊘ EXERCISE 7.8

Gather evidence to support your thesis statement, evaluating each source carefully (consulting Chapter 8 as necessary). Be on the lookout for bias in your sources.

Refuting Opposing Arguments

As you plan your essay and read sources that will supply your supporting evidence, you will encounter evidence that contradicts your position. You may be tempted to ignore this evidence, but if you do, your argument will be less convincing. Instead, as you do your research, identify the most convincing arguments against your position and prepare yourself to **refute** (argue against) them, showing them to be false or incorrect. Indicating to readers that you are willing to address these arguments—and that you can respond effectively to them—will help convince them to accept your position.

Of course, simply saying that your opponent's position is "wrong" or "stupid" is not very convincing. You need to summarize opposing arguments accurately and explain why these arguments are weak, untrue, unimportant, or irrelevant. In the case of a strong opposing argument, acknowledge its strengths before you refute it; if you do not, readers may see you as uninformed or unfair. Also be careful not to create a **straw man**—distorting an opposing argument by oversimplifying it so it can be easily refuted (for example, claiming that environmentalists believe that sustainability should always be the first priority for schools in their decisions about allocating resources). This unfair tactic will discourage readers from trusting you and thus will undermine your credibility.

⊘ EXERCISE 7.9

"Putting a Plague in Perspective" by Daniel Halperin is a refutation argument. Read it carefully, and then answer the questions that follow it.

This article appeared in the *New York Times* on January 1, 2008.

PUTTING A PLAGUE IN PERSPECTIVE

DANIEL HALPERIN

Although the United Nations recently lowered its global H.I.V. estimates, 1 as many as 33 million people worldwide are still living with the AIDS virus. This pandemic requires continued attention; preventing further deaths and orphans remains imperative. But the well-meaning promises of some presidential candidates to outdo even President Bush's proposal to nearly double American foreign assistance to fight AIDS strike me, an H.I.V.-AIDS specialist for 15 years, as missing the mark.

Some have criticized Mr. Bush for requesting "only" $30 billion for the 2 next five years for AIDS and related problems, with the leading Democratic candidates having pledged to commit at least $50 billion if they are elected. Yet even the current $15 billion in spending represents an unprecedented amount of money aimed mainly at a single disease.

Meanwhile, many other public health needs in developing countries are being ignored. The fact is, spending $50 billion or more on foreign health assistance does make sense, but only if it is not limited to H.I.V.-AIDS programs.

> "Many other public health needs in developing countries are being ignored."

3

Last year, for instance, as the United 4 States spent almost $3 billion on AIDS programs in Africa, it invested only about $30 million in traditional safe-water projects. This nearly 100-to-1 imbalance is disastrously inequitable—especially considering that in Africa H.I.V. tends to be most prevalent in the relatively wealthiest and most developed countries. Most African nations have stable adult H.I.V. rates of 3 percent or less.

Many millions of African children and adults die of malnutrition, pneu- 5 monia, motor vehicle accidents and other largely preventable, if not headline-grabbing, conditions. One-fifth of all global deaths from diarrhea occur in just three African countries—Congo, Ethiopia and Nigeria—that have relatively low H.I.V. prevalence. Yet this condition, which is not particularly difficult to cure or prevent, gets scant attention from the donors that invest nearly $1 billion annually on AIDS programs in those countries.

I was struck by this discrepancy between Western donor's priorities and 6
the real needs of Africans last month, during my most recent trip to Africa.
In Senegal, H.I.V. rates remain under 1 percent in adults, partly due to that
country's early adoption of enlightened policies toward prostitution and other
risky practices, in addition to universal male circumcision which limits the
heterosexual spread of H.I.V. Rates of tuberculosis, now another favored disease of international donors, are also relatively low in Senegal, and I learned
that even malaria, the donors' third major concern, is not quite as rampant as
was assumed, with new testing finding that many fevers aren't actually caused
by the disease.

Meanwhile, the stench of sewage permeates the crowded outskirts of 7
Dakar, Senegal's capital. There, as in many other parts of West Africa and the
developing world, inadequate access to safe water results in devastating diar-
rheal diseases. Shortages of food and basic health services like vaccinations,
prenatal care and family planning contribute to large family size and high
child and maternal mortality. Major donors like the President's Emergency
Plan for AIDS Relief, known as Pepfar, and the Global Fund to Fight AIDS,
Tuberculosis and Malaria have not directly addressed such basic health issues.
The Global Fund's director, Michel Kazatchkine, has acknowledged, "We are
not a global fund that funds local health."

Botswana, which has the world's most lucrative diamond industry and 8
is the second-wealthiest country per capita in sub-Saharan Africa, is nowhere
near as burdened as Senegal with basic public health problems. But as one
of a dozen Pepfar "focus" countries in Africa, this year it will receive about
$300 million to fight AIDS—in addition to the hundreds of millions already
granted by drug companies, private foundations and other donors. While in
that sparsely populated country last month, I learned that much of its AIDS
money remains unspent, as even its state-of-the-art H.I.V. clinics cannot
absorb such a large influx of cash.

As the United States Agency for International Development's H.I.V. pre- 9
vention adviser in southern Africa in 2005 and 2006, I visited villages in poor
countries like Lesotho, where clinics could not afford to stock basic medicines
but often maintained an inventory of expensive AIDS drugs and sophisticated
monitoring equipment for their H.I.V. patients. H.I.V.-infected children are
offered exemplary treatment, while children suffering from much simpler-to-
treat diseases are left untreated, sometimes to die.

In Africa, there's another crisis exacerbated by the rigid focus on AIDS: 10
the best health practitioners have abandoned lower-paying positions in family planning, immunization and other basic health areas in order to work for
donor-financed H.I.V. programs.

The AIDS experience has demonstrated that poor countries can make 11
complex treatments accessible to many people. Regimens that are much simpler to administer than anti-retroviral drugs—like antibiotics for respiratory
illnesses, oral rehydration for diarrhea, immunizations and contraception—
could also be made widely available. But as there isn't a "global fund" for safe

water, child survival and family planning, countries like Senegal—and even poorer ones—cannot directly tackle their real problems without pegging them to the big three diseases.

To their credit, some AIDS advocates are calling for a broader approach 12 to international health programs. Among the presidential candidates, Senator Barack Obama, for example, proposes to go beyond spending for AIDS, tuberculosis and malaria, highlighting the need to also strengthen basic health systems. And recently, Mr. Bush's plan, along with the Global Fund, has become somewhat more flexible in supporting other health issues linked to H.I.V.—though this will be of little use to people, especially outside the "focus" countries, who are dying of common illnesses like diarrhea.

Based on a study of the cause and spread of disease

But it is also important, especially for the United States, the world's largest 13 donor, to re-examine the epidemiological° and moral foundations of its global health priorities. With 10 million children and a half million mothers in developing countries dying annually of largely preventable conditions, should we multiply AIDS spending while giving only a pittance for initiatives like safe-water projects?

If one were to ask the people of virtually any African village (outside 14 some 10 countries devastated by AIDS) what their greatest concerns are, the answer would undoubtedly be the less sensational but more ubiquitous ravages of hunger, dirty water and environmental devastation. The real-world needs of Africans struggling to survive should not continue to be subsumed by the favorite causes du jour of well-meaning yet often uninformed Western donors.

Identifying the Elements of a Refutation Argument

1. What is Halperin's thesis? Does he offer enough evidence to support it?

2. What position is Halperin refuting? Where does he summarize this argument? Restate it in your own words.

3. On what basis does Halperin refute the opposing argument?

4. How does he establish his credibility?

Revising Your Thesis Statement

Before you can begin drafting your argumentative essay, and even before you can decide how to arrange your ideas, you need to revise your tentative thesis statement so it says exactly what you want it to say.

After you have gathered and evaluated evidence to support your position and considered the merits of opposing ideas, you are ready to refocus your thesis and state it in more definite terms. Although a tentative thesis statement such as "College campuses should go 'green'" is a good start, the thesis that guides your essay's structure should be more specific. In fact, it will be most useful as a guide if it actually acknowledges opposing arguments in its phrasing.

> **Revised thesis statement:** Despite the expense, colleges should make every effort to create "green" campuses because by doing so they will improve their own educational environment, ensure their own institution's survival, and help solve the global climate crisis.

⊘ EXERCISE 7.10

Consulting the sources you gathered in Exercise 7.8, list all the arguments against the position that you took in your thesis statement. Then, list possible refutations of these arguments. When you have finished, revise your thesis statement so that it is more specific, acknowledging and refuting the most important argument against your position.

Once you have revised your thesis statement, you will have a concise blueprint for the essay you are going to write. Now, you are ready to plan your essay's structure and write a first draft.

Understanding Essay Structure

As you learned in Chapter 1, an argumentative essay, like other essays, includes an introduction, a body, and a conclusion. In the introduction, you state your thesis; in the body paragraphs, you present evidence to support your thesis, and you **refute** opposing arguments; and in your conclusion, you bring your argument to a close and reinforce your thesis with a strong

SUPPLYING BACKGROUND INFORMATION

Depending on what you think your readers know—and what you think they need to know—you might decide to include some background on the issue you are discussing. For example, in an essay about green campuses, you might briefly sum up the history of the U.S. environmental movement and trace its rise on college campuses. If you decide to include a background paragraph, it should be placed right after your introduction, where it can prepare readers for the discussion to follow.

concluding statement. These four elements—thesis, evidence, refutation, and concluding statement—are like the four pillars of the ancient Greek temple, supporting your argument so that it will stand up to scrutiny.

Understanding basic essay structure can help you shape your essay. Two other strategies—*using induction and deduction* and *constructing a formal outline*—can also be helpful.

Using Induction and Deduction

Many argumentative essays are structured either **inductively** or **deductively.** (See Chapter 5 for explanations of induction and deduction.) For example, the body of an essay with the thesis statement that is shown on page 201 could have either of the following general structures:

INDUCTIVE STRUCTURE

- Colleges are taking a number of steps to follow "green" practices.
- Through these efforts, campuses have become more environmentally responsible, and their programs and practices have made a positive difference.
- Because these efforts are helping to save the planet, they should be expanded.

DEDUCTIVE STRUCTURE

- Saving the planet is vital.
- "Green" campuses can help to save the planet.
- Therefore, colleges should create green campuses.

These patterns offer two options for structuring your essay. Many argumentative essays, however, combine induction and deduction or use other strategies to shape their ideas.

Constructing a Formal Outline

If you like, you can construct a **formal outline** before you begin your draft. (You can also construct an outline of your finished paper to check the logic of its structure.) A formal outline, which is more detailed and more logically organized than the informal outline shown on page 192, presents your main points and supporting details in the order in which you will discuss them.

A formal outline of the first body paragraph of the student essay on page 212 would look like this:

I. Background of the term *green*
   A. 1960s environmental movement
      1. Political agenda
      2. Environmental agenda

   B. Today's movements
      1. Eco-friendly practices
      2. Green values

Following a formal outline makes the drafting process flow smoothly, but many writers find it hard to predict exactly what details they will use for support or how they will develop their arguments. In fact, your first draft is likely to move away from your outline as you develop your ideas. Still, if you are the kind of writer who prefers to know where you are going before you start on your way, you will probably consider the time you devote to outlining to be time well spent.

⊙ EXERCISE 7.11

Look back at the thesis you decided on earlier in this chapter, and review the evidence you collected to support it. Then, construct a formal outline for your paper.

Preparing to Write

Before you begin writing your draft, you need to think about how to approach your topic and your audience. The essay you write will use a combination of *logical, emotional,* and *ethical* appeals, and you will have to be careful to use these appeals reasonably. (See the introduction to this book for information on these appeals.) As you write, you will concentrate on establishing yourself as informed, reasonable, and fair.

Establishing Your Credibility

If you expect your readers to accept your ideas, you will need to establish yourself as someone they should believe and trust. This involves showing your audience that you know what you are talking about as well as making sure that your tone is reasonable.

- **Demonstrating your command of the material:** If you want readers to listen to what you are saying, you need to earn their respect by showing them that you have done your research, that you have collected evidence that supports your argument, and that you understand the most compelling arguments against your position. For example, discussing your own experiences as a member of a campus or community environmental group, your observations at a Greenpeace convention, and essays and editorials that you have read on both sides of the issue will encourage your audience to accept your ideas on the subject of "green" campuses.

MAINTAINING YOUR CREDIBILITY

An argument is no place for modesty. Be careful to avoid phrases that undercut your credibility ("Although this is not a subject I know much about") and to avoid apologies ("This is just my opinion"). Be as clear, direct, and forceful as you can, showing readers you are confident as well as knowledgeable. And, of course, be sure to proofread carefully: grammatical and mechanical errors and typos will weaken your credibility.

- **Demonstrating that you are a reasonable person:** Even if your evidence is strong, your argument will not be convincing if it does not seem reasonable. One way to present yourself as a reasonable person is to **establish common ground** with your readers, stressing possible points of agreement instead of attacking those who might disagree with your position. For example, saying, "We all want our planet to survive" is a more effective strategy than saying, "Those who do not support the concept of a green campus are going to destroy our planet." (For more on establishing common ground, see the discussion of Rogerian argument in Chapter 6.)

  Another way to present yourself as a reasonable person is to **maintain a reasonable tone**. Try to avoid absolutes (words like *always* and *never*); instead, use more conciliatory language (*in many cases, much of the time,* and so on). Try not to use words and phrases like *obviously* or *as anyone can see* to introduce points whose strength may be obvious only to you. Do not brand opponents of your position as misguided, uninformed, or deluded; remember, some of your readers may hold opposing positions and will not appreciate your unfavorable portrayal of them.

  Finally, be very careful to treat your readers with respect, addressing them as your intellectual equals. Avoid statements that might insult them or their beliefs ("Although some ignorant or misguided people may still think . . ."). And never assume that your readers know less about your topic than you do; they may actually know a good deal more.

Being Fair

If you want readers to respect your point of view, you need to demonstrate respect for them by being fair. It is not enough to support your ideas convincingly and maintain a reasonable tone. You also need to avoid unfair tactics in your argument and take care to avoid **bias**. (See Chapter 8 for information on avoiding **confirmation bias** in your writing.)

In particular, you should be careful not to *distort evidence, quote out of context, slant evidence,* or *make unfair appeals.* These unfair tactics may influence some readers in the short term, but in the long run such tactics will alienate your audience.

- **Do not distort evidence. Distorting** (or misrepresenting) **evidence** is an unfair tactic. It is not ethical or fair, for example, to present your opponent's views inaccurately or to exaggerate his or her position and then argue against it. If you want to argue that green programs on college campuses are a good idea, then it is not fair to attack someone who expresses reservations about their cost by writing, "Mr. McNamara's concerns about cost reveal that he has basic doubts about saving the planet." (His concerns reveal no such thing.) It is, however, fair to acknowledge your opponent's reasonable concerns about cost and then go on to argue that the long-term benefits of such programs justify their expense.

- **Do not quote out of context.** It is perfectly fair to challenge someone's stated position. It is not fair, however, to misrepresent that position by **quoting out of context**—that is, by taking the words out of the original setting in which they appeared. For example, if a college dean says, "For schools with limited resources, it may be more important to allocate resources to academic programs than to environmental projects," you are quoting the dean's remarks out of context if you say, "According to Dean Levering, it is 'more important to allocate resources to academic programs than to environmental projects.'"

- **Do not slant evidence.** An argument based on slanted evidence is not fair. **Slanting** involves choosing only evidence that supports your position and ignoring evidence that challenges it. This tactic makes your position seem stronger than it actually is. Another kind of slanting involves using biased language to unfairly characterize your opponents or their positions—for example, using a dismissive term such as *tree-hugger* to describe a concerned environmentalist.

- **Do not make unfair appeals.** If you want your readers to accept your ideas, you need to avoid **unfair appeals** to the emotions, such as appeals to your audience's fears or prejudices. For example, if you try to convince readers of the importance of using green building materials by saying, "Construction projects that do not use green materials doom future generations to a planet that cannot sustain itself," you are likely to push neutral (or even receptive) readers to skepticism or outright hostility.

- **Do not use logical fallacies.** Using **logical fallacies** (flawed arguments) in your writing will alienate your readers. (See Chapter 5 for information about logical fallacies.)

Writing a Draft

Once you understand how to approach your topic and your audience, you will be ready to draft your essay. At this point, you will have selected the sources you will use to support your position as well as identified the strongest arguments against your position (and decided how to refute them). You may also have prepared a formal outline, or perhaps just a list of points to follow.

Now, you need to focus on some guidelines for drafting your essay. As you write, keep the following points in mind:

- **Follow the structure of an argumentative essay.** State your thesis in your first paragraph, and discuss each major point in a separate paragraph, moving from least to most important point to emphasize your strongest argument. Introduce each body paragraph with a clearly worded topic sentence. Discuss each opposing argument in a separate paragraph, and be sure your refutation appears directly after each opposing argument. Finally, don't forget to include a strong concluding statement in your essay's last paragraph.

- **Use coordination and subordination to make your meaning clear.** Readers shouldn't have to guess how two points are connected; you should use coordination and subordination to show them the relationship between ideas.

  Choose **coordinating conjunctions**—*and, but, or, nor, for, so,* and *yet*—carefully, making sure you are using the right word for your purpose. (Use *and* to show addition; *but, for,* or *yet* to show contradiction; *or* to present alternatives; and *so* to indicate a causal relationship.)

  Choose **subordinating conjunctions**—*although, because,* and so on—carefully, and place them accurately in your sentences. For example, the ideas in the following two sentences are not connected:

  > Achieving a green campus is vitally important. Creating a green campus is expensive.

To communicate your point clearly, you need to subordinate one idea to the other.

  If you want to stress the idea that green measures are called for, you would write the following:

  > Although creating a green campus is expensive, achieving a green campus is vitally important.

If, on the other hand, you want to place emphasis on the high cost, you would write the following:

> Although achieving a green campus is vitally important, creating a green campus is expensive.

■ **Include transitional words and phrases.** Be sure you have enough transitions to guide your readers through your discussion. You need to supply signals that move readers from sentence to sentence and paragraph to paragraph, and the signals you choose need to make sense in the context of your discussion.

SOME TRANSITIONS FOR ARGUMENT

- ■ To show causal relationships: *because, as a result, for this reason*

- ■ To indicate sequence: *first, second, third; then; next; finally*

- ■ To introduce additional points: *also, another, in addition, furthermore, moreover*

- ■ To move from general to specific: *for example, for instance, in short, in other words*

- ■ To identify an opposing argument: *however, although, even though, despite*

- ■ To grant the validity of an opposing argument: *certainly, admittedly, granted, of course*

- ■ To introduce a refutation: *however, nevertheless, nonetheless, still*

■ **Define your terms.** If the key terms of your argument have multiple meanings—as *green* does—be sure to indicate what the term means in the context of your argument. Terms like *environmentally friendly, environmentally responsible, sustainable,* and *sustainability literacy* may mean very different things to different readers.

■ **Use clear language.** An argument is no place for vague language or wordy phrasing. If you want readers to understand your points, your writing should be clear and direct. Avoid vague words like *good, bad, right,* and *wrong,* which are really just unsupported judgments that do nothing to help you make your case. Also avoid wordy phrases such as *revolves around* and *is concerned with,* particularly in thesis statements and topic sentences.

- **Finally, show your confidence and your mastery of your material.** Avoid qualifying your statements with phrases like *I think, I believe, it seems to me,* and *in my opinion.* These qualifiers weaken your argument by suggesting that you are unsure of your material or that the statements to follow may not be true.

⊙ EXERCISE 7.12

Keeping the above guidelines in mind, write a draft of an essay that develops the thesis statement you have been working with.

Revising Your Argumentative Essay

After you have drafted your essay, read it over carefully to see if it says what you want it to say. As you prepare to revise, consider both how you support your ideas and how you present them.

Asking Questions

Asking some basic questions, such as those in the two checklists that follow, can help you start the revision process.

The answers to the above questions may lead you to revise your essay's content, structure, and style. For example, you may want to look for additional sources that can provide the kind of supporting evidence you need. Or, you may notice you need to revise the structure of your essay, perhaps rearranging your points so that the most important point is placed last, for emphasis. You may also want to revise your essay's introduction and conclusion, sharpening your thesis statement or adding a stronger concluding

CHECKLIST

Questions about Your Essay's Supporting Evidence

☐ Do you support your opinions with *evidence*—facts, observations, examples, statistics, expert opinion, and so on?

☐ Do you have enough evidence to support your thesis?

☐ Do the sources you rely on present information accurately and without bias?

☐ Are your sources' discussions directly relevant to your topic?

☐ Have you consulted sources that represent a wide range of viewpoints, including sources that disagree with your position?

> **CHECKLIST**
>
> ## Questions about Your Essay's Structure and Style
>
> ☐ Do you have a clearly stated thesis?
>
> ☐ Are your topic sentences clear and concise?
>
> ☐ Do you provide all necessary background and definitions?
>
> ☐ Do you refute opposing arguments effectively?
>
> ☐ Do you include enough transitional words and phrases to guide readers smoothly through your discussion?
>
> ☐ Have you avoided vague language and wordy phrasing?
>
> ☐ Do you have a strong concluding statement?

statement. Finally, you may decide to add more background material to help your readers understand the issue you are writing about.

Getting Feedback

After you have done as much as you can on your own, it is time to get feedback from your instructor and (with your instructor's permission) from your school's writing center or from other students in your class.

Instructor Feedback You can get feedback from your instructor in a variety of different ways. For example, your instructor may ask you to email a draft of your paper to him or her with some specific questions ("Do I need paragraph 3, or do I have enough evidence without it?" "Does my thesis statement need to be more specific?"). The instructor will then email the draft back to you with corrections and recommendations. If your instructor prefers the traditional face-to-face conference, you may still want to email your draft ahead of time so that he or she will have had time to read it.

Writing Center Feedback You can get feedback from a writing center tutor, who can be either a student or a professional. The tutor can give you another point of view about your paper's content and organization and also help you focus on specific questions of style, grammar, punctuation, and mechanics. (Keep in mind, however, that a tutor will not edit or proofread your paper for you; that is your job.)

Peer Review You can get feedback from your classmates. **Peer review** can be an informal process in which you ask a classmate for advice, or it can be a more structured process, involving small groups working with copies of students' work. Peer review can also be conducted electronically. For example, students can exchange drafts by email or respond to one another's drafts that are posted on the class's Web site. They can also use Word's comment tool, as illustrated in the following example.

DRAFT

Comment: Your first two sentences are a little abrupt. Maybe you could ease into your argument more slowly?

Comment: I like these two questions. They really got me thinking.

Comment: Could you be more specific? I'm not sure what you mean.

Comment: You definitely talk about this in your paper, but you also talk about other reasons to go green. You might consider revising this thesis statement so it matches your argument.

Colleges and universities have no excuse for ignoring the threat of global warming. Campus leaders need to push beyond efforts to recycle or compost and instead become models of sustainability. Already, many universities are hard at work demonstrating that reducing their institution's environmental impact is not only possible but worthwhile. They are overhauling their entire infrastructure, their buildings, systems, and even curriculum. While many students, faculty, staff and administrators are excited by these new challenges, some still question this need to go green. Is it worth the money? Is it promoting "a moral and behavioral agenda rather than an educational one"? (Butcher). In fact, "greening" will ultimately save institutions money while providing their students with a good education. Colleges should make every effort to create green campuses because by doing so they will help solve the global climate crisis.

FINAL VERSION

Over the last few years, the pressure to go "green" has led colleges and universities to make big changes. The threats posed by global warming are inspiring campus leaders to push beyond efforts to recycle to become models of sustainability. Today, in the interest of reducing their environmental impact, many campuses are seeking to overhaul their entire infrastructure—their buildings, their systems, and even their curriculum. While many students, faculty, staff, and administrators are excited by these new challenges, some question this need to go green. Is it worth the money? Is it promoting "a moral and behavioral agenda rather than an educational one"? (Butcher). In fact, greening will ultimately save institutions money while providing their students with the educational opportunities necessary to help them solve the crisis of their generation. Despite the expense, colleges should make every effort to create green campuses because by doing so they will improve their own educational environment, ensure their own institution's survival, and help solve the global climate crisis.

⊘ EXERCISE 7.13

Following the guidelines for revision discussed earlier, get some feedback from others, and then write another draft of your essay.

Adding Visuals

After you have gotten feedback about the ideas in your paper, you might want to consider adding a **visual**—a chart, graph, table, photo, or diagram—to help you make a point more forcefully. For example, in a paper on the green campus movement, you could include anything from photos of students recycling to a chart comparing energy use at different schools. You can create a visual yourself, or you can download one from the Internet, beginning your search with Google Images. If you download a visual and paste it into your paper, be sure to include a reference to the visual in your discussion to show readers how it supports your argument. You should also take care to label your visual with a figure number, to use proper documentation, and to include a caption explaining what the visual shows, as the student paper that begins on the following page does. (For information on how to document visuals, see Chapter 10.)

Editing and Proofreading

The final step in the revision process is **editing and proofreading** your essay. At this point, you need to make sure that your paper is well organized, convincing, and clearly written, with no distracting grammatical or mechanical errors, typos, or spelling errors. This is also the time to make sure that your paper conforms to your instructor's requirements for documentation and manuscript format. (The student paper that begins on the following page follows MLA style and manuscript format; for additional sample papers illustrating both MLA and APA documentation style and manuscript format, see Chapter 10 and Appendix B, respectively.)

CHOOSING A TITLE

Your title should give readers clear information about the subject of your essay, and it should also be appropriate for your topic. A serious topic should have a serious title, and a thoughtfully presented argument deserves a thoughtfully selected title. It is not necessary to think of a title that will attract attention or shock readers. A simple statement of your topic ("Going 'Green'") or of your position on the issue ("College Campuses Should Go 'Green'") is usually all that is needed. If you like, you can use a quotation from one of your sources as a title ("Green Is Good").

⬇ The following student paper, "Going 'Green,'" argues that colleges should make every effort to create green campuses.

GOING "GREEN"

SHAWN HOLTON

Introduction

Over the last few years, the pressure to go "green" has led colleges 1 and universities to make big changes. The threats posed by global warming are inspiring campus leaders to push beyond early efforts, such as recycling, to become models of sustainability. Today, in the interest of reducing their environmental impact, many campuses are seeking to overhaul their entire infrastructure—their buildings, their systems, and even their curriculum. While many students, faculty, staff, and administrators are excited by these new challenges, some question this need to go green. Is it worth the money? Is it promoting "a moral and behavioral agenda rather than an educational one"? (Butcher). In fact, greening will ultimately save institutions money while providing their students with the educational opportunities necessary to help

Thesis statement

them solve the crisis of their generation. Despite the expense, colleges should make every effort to create green campuses because by doing so they will improve their own educational environment, ensure their own institution's survival, and help solve the global climate crisis.

Background of green movement

Although the green movement has been around for many years, 2 *green* has only recently become a buzzword. Green political parties and groups began forming in the 1960s to promote environmentalist goals ("Environmentalism"). These groups fought for "grassroots democracy, social justice, and nonviolence" in addition to environmental protections and were "self-consciously activist and unconventional" in their strategies ("Environmentalism"). Today, however, *green* denotes much more than a political movement; it has become a catch-all word for anything eco-friendly. People use *green* to describe everything from fuel-efficient cars to fume-free house paint. Green values have become more mainstream in response to evidence that human activities, particularly those that result in greenhouse-gas emissions, may be causing global warming at a dramatic rate ("Call for Climate Leadership" 4). To fight this climate change, many individuals, businesses, and organizations are choosing to go green, making sustainability and preservation of the environment a priority.

3   Greening a college campus means moving toward a sustainable campus, one that works to conserve the earth's natural resources. More specifically, it means reducing the university's carbon footprint by focusing on energy efficiency in every aspect of campus life. This is no small task. Although replacing incandescent light bulbs with compact fluorescent ones and offering more locally grown food in dining halls are valuable steps, meaningful sustainability requires more comprehensive changes. For example, universities also need to invest in alternative energy sources, construct new buildings and remodel old ones with energy efficiency as a priority, and work to reduce campus demand for nonrenewable products. These changes will eventually save universities money, but, in most cases, the institutions will need to spend money now to reduce costs in the long term. To achieve this transformation, many colleges are—individually or in cooperation with other schools—establishing formal "climate commitments," setting specific goals, and developing tools to track their investments and evaluate their progress.

Definition of green *as it applies to colleges*

4   Despite the challenges of making a university campus sustainable, there are many compelling reasons to act now. Saving money on operating costs, thus making the school more competitive in the long-term, is an appealing incentive. In fact, many schools have made solid, and sometimes immediate, gains by greening some aspect of their campus. For example, by installing windows, mirrors, and solar panels, "the University of South Carolina has reduced heating costs in its new residence hall by 20 percent and electricity costs by 40 percent, compared with a similarly sized dorm" (Egan). By changing their parking and transit systems to encourage more carpooling, biking, and walking, Cornell University has saved 417,000 gallons of fuel and cut costs by $36 million over the last twelve years ("Call for Climate Leadership" 10). And Oberlin College not only saves money by generating its own solar energy (as shown in Fig. 1) but also makes money by selling its excess

First argument in support of thesis

electricity back to the local power company (Petersen). Many other schools have taken similar steps, with similarly positive results.

5

Attracting the attention of the media, donors, and—most significantly—prospective students is another practical reason for schools to go green. As one *New York Times* journalist put it, "Green is good for the planet, but also for a college's public image" (Zernike). The *Princeton Review* now includes a "green rating," and schools are finding that going green is an effective

Fig. 1. Solar panels on the roof of the Adam Joseph Lewis Center for Environmental Studies, Oberlin College. 2008. Oberlin.edu.

way to recruit students. According to one recent survey, "63 percent [of respondents] said that a college's commitment to the environment could affect their decision to go there" (Zernike). A school's commitment to the environment can also bring in large private donations. For example, Carnegie Mellon University has attracted $1.7 million from the National Science Foundation for its new Center for Sustainable Engineering (Egan). The University of California, Davis, will be receiving up to $25 million from the Chevron Corporation to research biofuel technology ("Call for Climate Leadership" 10). While greening certainly costs money, a green commitment can also help a school remain financially viable.

Second argument in support of thesis

Third argument in support of thesis

In addition to these practical reasons for going green, universities also have another, perhaps more important, reason to promote and model sustainability: doing so may help solve the climate crisis. Although

6

an individual school's reduction of emissions will not have a noticeable impact on global warming, its graduates will be in a position to make a huge impact. College is a critical time in most students' personal and professional development. Students are making choices about what kind of adults they will be, and they are also receiving the training, education, and experience that they will need to succeed in the working world. If universities can offer time, space, and incentives—both in and out of the classroom—to help students develop creative ways to live sustainably, these schools have the potential to change the thinking and habits of a whole generation.

7   Many critics of greening claim that becoming environmentally friendly is too expensive and will result in higher tuition and fees. However, often a very small increase in fees, as little as a few dollars a semester, can be enough to help a school institute significant change. For example, at the University of Colorado–Boulder, a student-initiated one-dollar increase in fees allowed the school to purchase enough wind power to reduce its carbon emissions by 12 million pounds ("Call for Climate Leadership" 9). Significantly, the students were the ones who voted to increase their own fees to achieve a greener campus. Although university faculty and administrators' commitment to sustainability is critical for any program's success, few green initiatives will succeed without the enthusiastic support of the student body. Ultimately, students have the power. If they think their school is spending too much on green projects, then they can make a change or choose to go elsewhere.

First opposing argument (and refutation)

8   Other critics of the trend toward greener campuses believe that schools with commitments to sustainability are dictating how students should live rather than encouraging free thought. As one critic says, "Once [sustainability literacy] is enshrined in a university's public pronouncements or private articles, then the institution has diminished its commitment to academic inquiry" (Butcher). This kind of criticism overlooks the fact that figuring out how to achieve sustainability requires and will continue to require rigorous critical thinking and creativity. Why not apply the academic skills of inquiry, analysis, and problem solving to the biggest problem of our day? Not doing so would be irresponsible and would only confirm the perception that universities are ivory towers of irrelevant knowledge. In fact,

Second opposing argument (and refutation)

the presence of sustainability as both a goal and a subject of study has the potential to reaffirm academia's place at the center of civil society.

Conclusion

Creating a green campus is a difficult task, but universities must rise to [9] the challenge or face the consequences. If they do not commit to changing their ways, they will become less and less able to compete for students and for funding. If they refuse to make a comprehensive commitment to sustainability, they also risk irrelevance at best and institutional collapse at worst. Finally, by not rising to the challenge, they will be giving up the opportunity to establish themselves as leaders in addressing the climate crisis. As the coalition of American College and University Presidents states in its Climate Commitment, "No other institution has the influence, the critical mass and the diversity of skills needed to successfully reverse global warming" ("Call for Climate Leadership" 13). Now is the time for

Concluding statement

schools to make the choice and pledge to go green.

Works Cited

Butcher, Jim. "Keep the Green Moral Agenda off Campus." *Times Higher Education.* TSL Education, 19 Oct. 2007. Web. 16 Sept. 2008.

"A Call for Climate Leadership." *American College and University Presidents Climate Commitment.* Presidents Climate Commitment, Mar. 2007. Web. 15 Sept. 2008.

Egan, Timothy. "The Greening of America's Campuses." *New York Times.* New York Times, 8 Jan. 2006. Web. 10 Sept. 2008.

"Environmentalism." *Encyclopaedia Britannica Online.* Encyclopaedia Britannica, Inc., 2008. Web. 14 Sept. 2008.

Petersen, John. "A Green Curriculum Involves Everyone on Campus." *Chronicle of Higher Education* 54.41 (2008): A25. *Academic Search Premier.* Web. 12 Sept. 2008.

Zernike, Kate. "Green, Greener, Greenest." *New York Times.* New York Times, 27 July 2008. Web. 12 Sept. 2008.

⊘ EXERCISE 7.14

Find a visual that will strengthen your argument, and add it to your essay. Be sure to document it appropriately and to include a descriptive caption. Then, edit and proofread your paper, paying special attention to parenthetical documentation and your works-cited page. When you have finished, add a title, and print out a final copy of your essay.

Using Sources to Support Your Argument

Evaluating Sources

Should Data Posted on Social-Networking Sites Be "Fair Game" for Employers?

Many—if not most—college students use social-networking sites such as Facebook and MySpace. The popularity of these sites has grown rapidly, and it is expected to increase even more in the near future. For example, MySpace has more than 110 million monthly active users and has an average of 300,000 new registrations every day. An advantage of these sites is that they enable friends, family, coworkers, and people with common interests to communicate. However, they also allow almost anyone to view and forward information—sometimes very personal information—without asking permission.

In recent years, a debate has been growing about the practice of using social-networking sites to find information about job applicants. Currently, about 20% of employers regularly check a job candidate's personal information on social-networking sites, and they use this information when they make their hiring decisions.

In one high-profile case, a graduating senior had his job offer rescinded after a prospective employer saw material that he deemed inappropriate on the student's MySpace page. The student's defense was that much of what was on his page was not meant to be taken seriously and that it was not fair for the employer to take it out of context. In addition, the student argued that the information on the site was posted for his friends, not for potential employers.

Many employers disagree with this student's position, however. They say that when someone posts information on a social-networking site, it is there for others to see. They point out that there are ways to limit access to a site, and if a person doesn't use them, then his or her site is available to everyone. Thus, if the information is public, there is no reason that a prospective employer shouldn't look at it. Employers add that because an employee represents the company outside of the workplace, it makes sense to

(*continued*)

(continued)

evaluate a candidate based on information on his or her social-networking site.

In this chapter's exercises, you will be asked to evaluate a number of research sources to determine if they are acceptable for an argumentative essay that takes a stand on whether it is acceptable for employers to use data posted on social-networking sites. Later, in Chapter 9, you will learn how to integrate sources into an essay on this topic. In Chapter 10, you will see an MLA paper on the topic, "Should Data Posted on Social-Networking Sites Be 'Fair Game' for Employers?"

Whenever you locate a source—print or electronic—you should always take the time to evaluate it. When you **evaluate** a source, you assess the objectivity of the author, the credibility of the source, and its relevance to your argument. Although a librarian or an instructor has screened the sources in your college library for general accuracy and trustworthiness, you cannot assume that all these sources are suitable for your particular writing project.

Material that you access on the Internet presents even more problems. As you probably know, anyone can publish on the Internet. For this reason, the information you find there has to be evaluated very carefully for accuracy. Although some material on the Internet (for example, journal articles that are published in both print and digital format) is reliable, other material (for example, personal Web sites and blogs) may be totally unsuitable as a research source.

To be reasonably certain that the information you are accessing is appropriate, you have to approach it critically. This chapter will give you some of the tools you will need to evaluate your sources.

Evaluating Print Sources

As you locate print sources, you need to evaluate them to make sure that they are suitable for your research. After all, if you use an untrustworthy source, you undercut your credibility.

To evaluate print sources, you use the same process that you use when you evaluate anything else. For example, if you are thinking about buying a computer, you will decide on several criteria to help you make your decision—for example, price, speed, memory, reliability, and availability of technical support. The same is true for evaluating research sources. You can use the following criteria to decide whether a print source is (or is not) appropriate for your research:

- Accuracy
- Credibility

Print sources must be evaluated carefully.

- Objectivity
- Currency
- Comprehensiveness

The illustrations on page 222 show where to find information that can help you evaluate a print source.

Accuracy

A print source is **accurate** if is factual and free of errors. One way to judge the accuracy of a source is to compare the information it contains to that same information in several other sources. If a source has factual errors, then it probably includes other types of errors as well. Needless to say, errors in spelling and grammar should also cause you to question a source's general accuracy.

You can also judge the accuracy of a print source by checking to see if the author cites sources for the information he or she discusses. Documentation can help readers determine both the quality of information in a source and the range of sources used. It can also show readers what sources a writer has failed to consult. (Failure to cite an important book or article should cause you to question the writer's familiarity with a subject.) If possible, verify the legitimacy of some of the books and articles that a writer cites. You can do this by choosing several titles and seeing what you can

TOMMIE SHELBY ——————— Author

We Who Are Dark

The Philosophical Foundations
of Black Solidarity

Publisher

The Belknap Press of
Harvard University Press
Cambridge, Massachusetts
London, England 2005

Date of publication

Library of Congress Cataloging-in-Publication Data

Shelby, Tommie, 1967–
We who are dark: the philosophical foundations of
Black solidarity/Tommie Shelby.
p.   cm.

Includes bibliographical references and index.
Contents: Two conceptions of Black nationalism—Class, poverty, and
shame—Black power nationalism—Black solidarity after Black power—Race,
culture, and politics—Social identity and group solidarity.

ISBN 0-674-01936-9 (alk. paper)

1. African Americans—Politics and government. 2. African Americans—
Race identity. 3. African Americans—Social conditions—1975–
4. Black nationalism—United States. 5. Black power—United States.
6. Ethnicity—Political aspects—United States. 7. Racism—Political
aspects—United States. 8. United States—Race relations—Political aspects.
I. Title.

E185.615.S475   2005
305.896'073—dc22   2005045329

Sources cited

find out about them on the Web. If a print source has caused a great deal of debate or if it is disreputable, you will probably be able to find information about it by searching it on Google.

Credibility

A print source is **credible** when it is believable. You can begin checking a source's credibility by determining if a writer has the expertise to write about a subject. Is the writer an authority or simply a person who has decided to write about a particular topic? Has your instructor ever mentioned the writer's name? Is the writer mentioned in your textbook? What other books (or articles) has the author written? Are these publications on the same subject or on a variety of other subjects? (You can usually find this information on the Amazon.com site.)

You can also look at where a book or article was published. Was a book published by a university press or by a popular press? If a university press published the book, you can be reasonably certain that it was **peer reviewed**—read by experts in the field to confirm the accuracy of the information. If a commercial press published the book, you will have to consider other criteria—author and date of publication, for example—to determine quality. If your source is an article, see if it appears in a **scholarly journal**—a periodical aimed at experts in a particular field—or in a **popular magazine**—a periodical aimed at general readers. Journal articles are almost always acceptable research sources because they are usually documented, peer reviewed, and written by experts. (They can, however, be difficult for general readers to understand.) Articles in high-level popular magazines, such as the *Atlantic* and the *Economist*, may also be suitable—provided experts write them. However, articles in lower-level popular magazines—such as *Sports Illustrated* and *Newsweek*—may be easy to understand, but they are seldom acceptable sources for research.

You can determine how well respected a source is by looking at reviews written by critics. You can find reviews of books by consulting *Book Review Digest*—either in print or online—which lists books that have been reviewed in at least three magazines or newspapers and includes excerpts of reviews. In addition, you can consult the *New York Times Book Review* Web site—<www.nytimes.com/pages/books/index.html>—to access reviews printed by the newspaper since 1981. (Both professional and reader reviews are also available at Amazon.com.)

Finally, you can determine how well respected a source is by seeing how often other scholars in the field refer to it. **Citation indexes** list books and articles by how often they are mentioned by other sources in a given year. This information can give you an idea of how important a work is in a particular field. Citation indexes for the humanities, the social sciences, and the sciences are available online and in your college library.

Objectivity

A print source is **objective** when it is not unduly influenced by personal opinions or feelings. Ideally, you want to find sources that are completely objective, but to one degree or another, all sources are *biased*—prejudiced in favor of or against something. In short, all sources—especially those that take a stand on an issue—reflect the opinions of their authors, regardless of how hard they may try to be impartial. (Of course, an opinion is perfectly acceptable—as long as it is supported by evidence.)

As a researcher, you should recognize that bias exists and ask yourself whether a writer's assumptions are justified by the facts or are the result of emotion or preconceived ideas. You can make this determination by looking at a writer's choice of words and seeing if the language is slanted or by reviewing the writer's points and seeing if his or her argument is one-sided. Get in the habit or asking yourself whether you are being offered a legitimate point of view or simply being fed propaganda.

The covers of the liberal and conservative magazines shown here suggest different biases about the results of the 2006 midterm elections (which gave the Democrats control of Congress).

 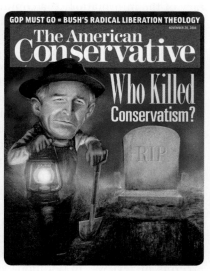

Currency

A print source is **current** when it is up-to-date. (For a book, you can find the date of publication on the same page that lists the publisher. For an article, you can find the date on the front cover of the magazine or journal.) If you are dealing with a scientific subject, the date of publication can be very important. Older sources might contain outdated information, so you want to use the most up-to-date source that you can find. For other subjects—literary criticism, for example—the currency of the information may not be as important as it is in the sciences. Even so, you want to be sure that the source you are consulting is the most current one and that it has not been updated with a newer edition.

Comprehensiveness

A print source is **comprehensive** when it covers a subject in sufficient depth. Does the source deal specifically with your subject? (If it treats your subject only briefly, you will have to consult other sources.) Does it treat your subject in enough detail? Does the source include the background information that you need to understand the discussion? Does the source mention other important sources that discuss your subject? Are the facts and interpretations that are discussed supported by the other sources you have read, or are there major points of disagreement? Finally, does the author include documentation?

How comprehensive a source needs to be depends on your purpose and audience as well as on your writing assignment. For a short essay, an op-ed piece from the *New York Times* and a chapter in a book might give you enough information to support your argument. If you are writing a research paper, however, you might need to consult journal articles (and possibly books) about your subject.

◉ EXERCISE 8.1

Each of the following three print sources was found in a university library:

- Michael Gregoris, "Stay Informed on Facebook's Third-Party Privacy Policies"

- Maria Aspan, "How Sticky Is Membership on Facebook? Just Try Breaking Free"

- Lew McCreary, "What Was Privacy?"

Read the articles (pp. 226–231), and decide if each is acceptable for a three- to five-page argumentative essay on the topic of whether information posted on social-networking sites should be "fair game" for employers. Be sure to evaluate each source on the basis of its accuracy, credibility, objectivity, currency, and comprehensiveness.

This article appeared on June 14, 2007, in the *Gazette,* the newspaper of the University of Western Ontario, Canada.

STAY INFORMED ON FACEBOOK'S THIRD-PARTY PRIVACY POLICIES

MICHAEL GREGORIS

At face value—no pun intended—Facebook appears to be a safe, reliable connection to one's various social networks. 1

Its agency is like no other, brimming with utility and functionality that mimics the addictive properties of Paris Hilton's favorite party favour. But there's another side to Facebook hidden under the photo tags and wall posts. For starters, Facebook's privacy agreement indicates personal information is collected and sold to third parties. 2

Most would be suspicious if the clause weren't disguised in a flurry of legal jargon. But some people ignore that stage, scrolling down and hitting the accept button without reading what they are signing. 3

Some might say 'Who cares?' Others feel comfortable forking over their private information, which inevitably reaches the faceless corporate entities that own and operate the world in which we live. 4

The website http://www.albumoftheday.com/facebook/ claims the CIA used its corporate fronts to fund Facebook's development and, along with assistance from the Department of Defense, that Facebook data-mines our personal information on a daily basis to create a compendium of political views, known affiliations, et cetera for perusal at the government's leisure. 5

These allegations have yet to be proven, but at the very least it's thought-provoking. What, exactly, are we getting ourselves into? 6

Calls for amendments to Facebook's privacy policy have been made to ensure user information is protected and remains within Facebook. In response to mounting criticism, Facebook's owners have acknowledged they intend on releasing an updated version of the policy that will comply with requests for privacy. 7

Unfortunately, Facebook's owners haven't revealed a launch date for the enactment of this revised policy. Is the already incurred damage irreversible? 8

As of Feb. 2007, Facebook had more than 27 million members, and it shows no signs of slowing down. If these allegations have the slightest truth, governmental and corporate entities have already won. 9

> "Is the already incurred damage irreversible?"

Herein lies the conflict: utility vs. privacy. To its credit, Facebook has revolutionized how we interact and relate with one another. Where else can you find out about a party you weren't invited to? 10

The ability to reunite with a friend from long ago enables us to reclaim the 11 past, therefore Facebook has become a staple of everyday life. Perhaps that's what happens when a promising idea is swallowed-up by a market-driven western world, where ethics are replaced with dollar figures.

In this day and age, we're over stimulated to a point where we no longer 12 realize the extent of our actions.

It's important for us to make an effort to stay informed, and reject the 13 enticing pull of ignorance.

This article appeared in the February 11, 2008, *New York Times*.

HOW STICKY IS MEMBERSHIP ON FACEBOOK? JUST TRY BREAKING FREE

MARIA ASPAN

Are you a member of Facebook.com? You may have a lifetime contract. 1

Some users have discovered that it is nearly impossible to remove them- 2 selves entirely from Facebook, setting off a fresh round of concern over the popular social network's use of personal data.

While the Web site offers users the option to deactivate their accounts, 3 Facebook servers keep copies of the information in those accounts indefinitely. Indeed, many users who have contacted Facebook to request that their accounts be deleted have not succeeded in erasing their records from the network.

"It's like the Hotel California," said Nipon Das, 34, a director at a biotech- 4 nology consulting firm in Manhattan, who tried unsuccessfully to delete his account this fall. "You can check out any time you like, but you can never leave."

It took Mr. Das about two months and several e-mail exchanges with 5 Facebook's customer service representatives to erase most of his information from the site, which finally occurred after he sent an e-mail threatening legal action. But even after that, a reporter was able to find Mr. Das's empty profile on Facebook and successfully sent him an e-mail message through the network.

In response to difficulties faced by ex-Facebook members, a cottage 6 industry of unofficial help pages devoted to escaping Facebook has sprung up online—both outside and inside the network.

"I thought it was kind of strange that they save your information without 7 telling you in a really clear way," said Magnus Wallin, a 26-year-old patent examiner in Stockholm who founded a Facebook group, "How to perma- nently delete your facebook account." The group has almost 4,300 members and is steadily growing.

The technological hurdles set by Facebook have a business rationale: 8 they allow ex-Facebookers who choose to return the ability to resurrect their accounts effortlessly. According to an e-mail message from Amy Sezak, a spokeswoman for Facebook, "Deactivated accounts mean that a user can reactivate at any time and their information will be available again just as they left it."

But it also means that disenchanted users cannot disappear from the site 9 without leaving footprints. Facebook's terms of use state that "you may remove your user content from the site at any time," but also that "you acknowledge that the company may retain archived copies of your user content."

Its privacy policy says that after someone 10 deactivates an account, "removed information may persist in backup copies for a reasonable period of time."

> "Removed information may persist in backup copies for a reasonable period of time."

Facebook's Web site does not inform 11 departing users that they must delete information from their account in order to close it fully—meaning that they may unwittingly leave anything from e-mail addresses to credit card numbers sitting on Facebook servers.

Only people who contact Facebook's customer service department are 12 informed that they must painstakingly delete, line by line, all of the profile information, "wall" messages and group memberships they may have created within Facebook.

"Users can also have their account completely removed by deleting all of 13 the data associated with their account and then deactivating it," Ms. Sezak said in her message. "Users can then write to Facebook to request their account be deleted and their e-mail will be completely erased from the database."

But even users who try to delete every piece of information they have ever 14 written, sent or received via the network have found their efforts to permanently leave stymied. Other social networking sites like MySpace and Friendster, as well as online dating sites like eHarmony.com, may require departing users to confirm their wishes several times—but in the end they offer a delete option.

"Most sites, even online dating sites, will give you an option to wipe your 15 slate clean," Mr. Das said.

Mr. Das, who joined Facebook on a whim after receiving invitations from 16 friends, tried to leave after realizing that most of his co-workers were also on the site. "I work in a small office," he said. "The last thing I want is people going on there and checking out my private life."

"I did not want to be on it after junior associates at work whom I have to 17 manage saw my stuff," he added.

Facebook's quiet archiving of information from deactivated accounts has 18 increased concerns about the network's potential abuse of private data, especially in the wake of its fumbled Beacon advertising feature.

That application, which tracks and publishes the items bought by 19 Facebook members on outside Web sites, was introduced in November without a transparent, one-step opt-out feature. After a public backlash, including more than 50,000 Facebook users' signatures on a MoveOn.org protest petition, Facebook executives apologized and allowed such an opt-out option on the program.

Tensions remain between making a profit and alienating Facebook's 20 users, who the company says total about 64 million worldwide (MySpace has an estimated 110 million monthly active users).

The network is still trying to find a way to monetize its popularity, mostly 21 by allowing marketers access to its wealth of demographic and behavioral information. The retention of old accounts on Facebook's servers seems like another effort to hold onto—and provide its ad partners with—as much demographic information as possible.

"The thing they offer advertisers is that they can connect to groups of peo- 22 ple. I can see why they wouldn't want to throw away anyone's information, but there's a conflict with privacy," said Alan Burlison, 46, a British software engineer who succeeded in deleting his account only after he complained in the British press, to the country's Information Commissioner's Office and to the TRUSTe organization, an online privacy network that has certified Facebook.

Mr. Burlison's complaint spurred the Information Commissioner's 23 Office, a privacy watchdog organization, to investigate Facebook's data-protection practices, the BBC reported last month. In response, Facebook issued a statement saying that its policy was in "full compliance with U.K. data protection law."

A spokeswoman for TRUSTe, which is based in San Francisco, said its 24 account deletion process was "inconvenient," but that Facebook was "being responsive to us and they currently meet our requirements."

"I kept getting the same answer and really felt that I was being given the 25 runaround," Mr. Burlison said of Facebook's customer service representatives. "It was quite obvious that no amount of prodding from me on a personal level was going to make a difference."

Only after he sent a link to the video of his interview with Britain's 26 Channel 4 News to the customer service representatives—and Facebook executives—was his account finally deleted.

Steven Mansour, 28, a Canadian online community developer, spent two 27 weeks in July trying to fully delete his account from Facebook. He later wrote a blog entry—including e-mail messages, diagrams and many exclamations of frustration—in a post entitled "2504 Steps to closing your Facebook account" (www.stevenmansour.com).

Mr. Mansour, who said he is "really skeptical of social networking sites," 28 decided to leave after a few months on Facebook. "I was getting tired of always getting alerts and e-mails," he said. "I found it very invasive."

"It's part of a much bigger picture of social networking sites on the Inter- 29 net harvesting private data, whether for marketing or for more sinister purposes," he said. His post, which wound up on the link-aggregator Digg.com, has been viewed more than 87,000 times, Mr. Mansour said, adding that the traffic was so high it crashed his server.

And his post became the touchstone for Mr. Wallin, who was inspired to 30 create his group, "How to permanently delete your Facebook account," after joining, leaving and then rejoining Facebook, only to find that all of his information from his first account was still available.

"I wanted the information to be available inside Facebook for all the users 31 who wanted to leave, and quite a few people have found it just by using internal search," said Mr. Wallin. Facebook has never contacted Mr. Wallin about the group.

Mr. Wallin said he has heard through members that some people have suc- 32 cessfully used his steps to leave Facebook. But he is not yet ready to leave himself.

"I don't want to leave yet; I actually find it really convenient," he said. 33 "But someday when I want to leave, I want it to be simple."

Harvard Business Review published this article in October 2008.

WHAT WAS PRIVACY?

LEW McCREARY

As best he can, Logan Roots safeguards his privacy by living off the informa- 1 tion grid. In a short article in *CSO* magazine (which serves an audience of top security executives), Roots defined privacy as "the freedom to selectively reveal one's self." He described going to great lengths to preserve that freedom by actively frustrating the mechanisms that collect those spores of fact most of us routinely release about ourselves.

"I pay in cash and use false names for as many goods and services as pos- 2 sible," Roots told *CSO* in 2003. "I'm even in a local pool of people who swap [grocery store] club cards. . . . For the past few months I've been using the card of a person who died two years ago. I'm almost sad it's time to switch cards again. I love the dead thing so much."

Most answers to the question "What is privacy?" begin with the individual 3 (usually a living one). Privacy is partly a form of self-possession—custody of the facts of one's life, from strings of digits to tastes and preferences. Matters of personal health and finance, everyone agrees, are in most instances nobody's business but our own—unless we decide otherwise. This version of privacy considers everything we know about ourselves and wish to control but that the continuous capture of our digital existence—the Google searches, the e-mail traffic, the commercial transactions, the cookie-tracked footprints° of treks through cyberspace—makes increasingly uncontrollable. All of this behavioral cast-off is the raw material for a granular understanding of what we want or need (whether we know it or not), what we will or won't put up with, and what we might buy or undertake to do—now and in the future.

Cookies are data files created by Web browsers, indicating (among other information) which sites have been visited.

Today's highly efficient data-gathering and -disseminating mechanisms 4 provoke another, rueful question: "What *was* privacy?" The answer may be that people could once feel confident that what others might find out about them would be treated with reasonable care and consideration, and thus would probably do them no harm. They can no longer. Moreover, the frictionless ease with which government records can now be found online means that reckless-driving citations and SEC violations are accessible to just about anyone.

The face-off between information privacy and information exploitation is 5 a storm ever in the making. Judicial remedies are unlikely to produce a satisfying or sensible balance between companies' economic prerogatives and customers' privacy interest. New technologies—too heedlessly adopted or opportunistically applied—will continue to threaten personal privacy. Business will have to find ways to address this uneasiness. If companies remain complacent, under-estimating the degree to which privacy matters to customers, harsh regulation may be waiting in the wings. The best way out is for businesses and customers to negotiate directly over where to draw the lines.

> "New technologies . . . will continue to threaten personal privacy."

⊘ EXERCISE 8.2

Write a one- or two-paragraph evaluation of each of the three sources you read in Exercise 8.1. Be sure to support your points with specific references to the sources.

Evaluating Web Sites

The Internet is like a freewheeling frontier town in the old West. Occasionally, a federal marshal may pass through, but for the most part, there is no law and order, so you are on your own. On the Internet, literally anything goes—exaggerations, misinformation, errors, and even complete fabrications. Many Web sites contain reliable content, but many do not. The main reason for this situation is that there is no authority—as there is in a college library—who evaluates sites for accuracy and trustworthiness. That job falls to you, the user. (Even if someone wanted to take on such a task, the amount of new information that appears daily on the Internet would make it impossible.)

Another problem is that Internet sources often lack some of the publication information that you find in print sources. For example, an article on a Web site may lack a date, a place of publication, or even a named author. For this reason, it is not always easy to evaluate the material you find online.

Most sources found in a college library have been evaluated by a reference librarian for their suitability as research sources, but this is not true of material you find on the Internet.

When you evaluate an Internet source, you need to begin by viewing it skeptically—unless you know for certain that it is reliable. In other words, assume that its information is questionable until you establish that it is not. Then apply the same criteria you use to evaluate print sources—*accuracy, credibility, objectivity, currency,* and *comprehensiveness.*

The Web page pictured on page 233 shows where to find information that can help you evaluate Web sites.

Accuracy

A Web site is **accurate** when it contains information that is factual and free of errors. Information in the form of facts, opinions, stories, statistics, and interpretations is everywhere on the Internet, and in the case of Wiki sites, this information is continuously being rewritten and revised. Given the volume and variety of this material, it is a major challenge to determine its accuracy. You can assess the accuracy of information on a Web site by asking the following questions:

- **Does the site contain errors of fact?** Factual errors—inaccuracies that relate directly to the central point of the source—should immediately disqualify a site as a possible source.

- **Does the site contain a list of references or any other type of documentation?** Reliable sources indicate where their information comes from. The authors know that people want to be sure that the information they are using is accurate and reliable.

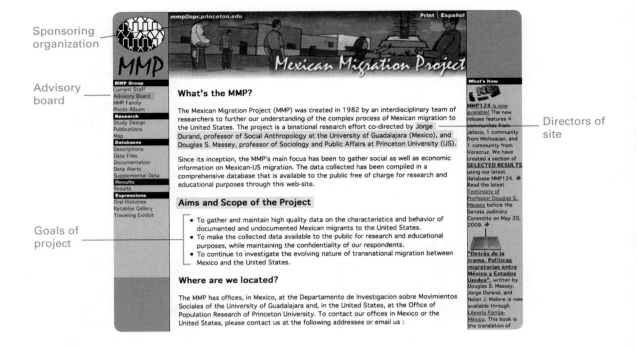

Sponsoring organization

Advisory board

Directors of site

Goals of project

- **Does the site provide links to other sites?** Does the site have links to reliable Web sites that are authored by well-respected authorities or sponsored by trustworthy institutions? If it does, then you can conclude that your source is at least trying to maintain a certain standard of quality.

- **Can you verify information?** A good test for accuracy is to try to verify key information from a site. You can do this by checking it in a reliable print source or on a good reference Web site such as *Encyclopedia.com*.

Credibility

Information on a Web site is **credible** when it is believable. Just as you would not naively believe a stranger who approached you on the street, you should not automatically believe a site that you randomly encounter on the Web. You can assess the credibility of a Web site by asking the following questions:

- **Does the site list authors, directors, or editors?** Anonymity—whether on a Web site or on a blog—should be a red flag for a researcher who is considering a source. When a site lists an author, does it include his or her credentials? If it does not, use a search engine such as Google to find out if the author is a recognized authority on the topic discussed.

- **Is the site refereed?** Does a panel of experts or an advisory board decide what material appears on the Web site? If not, what standards are used to determine suitability?

- **Does the site contain errors in grammar, spelling, or mechanics?** If it does, you should be on the alert for other types of errors. If the person maintaining the site does not care enough to make sure that the site is free of small errors, you have to wonder if he or she will take the time to verify the accuracy of the information presented.

- **Does an organization sponsor the site?** If so, have you heard of the sponsoring organization? Use a search engine such as Google to determine the purpose and point of view of the organization.

Objectivity

Information on a Web site is **objective** when it limits the amount of bias that it displays. Some sites—such as those that support a particular political position or social cause—make no secret of their biases. They present them clearly in their policy statements on their home pages. Others, however, try to hide their biases—for example, by referring only to articles that praise a particular point of view and not mentioning those that do not. Keep in mind that bias does not automatically disqualify a source. It should, however, alert you to the fact that you are seeing only one side of an issue and that you will have to look further to get a complete picture. You can assess the objectivity of a Web site by asking the following questions:

- **Does advertising appear on the site?** If the site contains advertising, check to make sure that the commercial aspect of the site does not affect its objectivity. The site should keep advertising separate from content.

- **Does a commercial entity sponsor the site?** A for-profit company may sponsor a Web site, but it should not allow commercial interests to determine content. If it does, there is a clear conflict of interest. For example, if a site is sponsored by a company that sells organic products, it may include information that emphasizes the virtues of organic products and ignores information that is skeptical of their benefits.

- **Does a political organization or special-interest group sponsor the site?** Just as you would for a commercial site, you should make sure that the sponsoring organization is presenting accurate information. It is a good idea to check the information you get from a commercial site against information you get from an educational or a reference site—*Ask.com* or *Encyclopedia.com,* for example. Organizations have specific agendas, and you should make sure that they are not bending the truth to satisfy their own needs.

USING A SITE'S URL TO ASSESS OBJECTIVITY

A Web site's **URL** (uniform resource locator) can give you information that can help you assess the site's objectivity.

Look at the domain name to identify sponsorship. The last part of a site's URL can tell you whether a site is a commercial site (.com and .net), an educational site (.edu), a nonprofit site (.org), or a governmental site (.gov, .mil, and so on).

Identify the site's purpose. Knowing who sponsors a site can help you determine whether a site is trying to sell you something (.com and .net) or just trying to provide information (.edu, .org, or .gov).

See if the URL has a tilde (~) in it. A tilde in a site's URL indicates that information was published by an individual and is unaffiliated with the sponsoring organization. Individuals can have their own agendas, which may be different from the agenda of the site where their information appears or to which it is linked.

- **Does the site link to biased sites?** Even if a site seems trustworthy, it is a good idea to check some of its links. Just as you can judge people by the company they keep, you can also judge Web sites by the sites they link to. Links to biased sites should cause you to reevaluate the information on the original site.

AVOIDING CONFIRMATION BIAS

Confirmation bias is the tendency that people have to accept information that supports their own beliefs and to ignore information that does not. People might see false or inaccurate information on Web sites, for example, and because it reinforces their deeply held beliefs—especially political and social beliefs—they forward it to others. This misinformation then becomes so widely distributed that people simply assume that it must be true. Consider the following false charges that appeared in chain emails during the 2008 presidential race:

- Michelle Obama called a New York hotel's room service and ordered $400 worth of lobster and caviar for her lunch.

- Sarah Palin, the Republican candidate for vice president, tried to have a list of books banned at the Wasilla, Alaska, public library.

(continued)

(continued)

- Barack Obama is not a native-born American.

- John McCain is senile.

Although these and other rumors were false, people continued to believe and circulate them. Even if a piece of information supports your own beliefs, you should not automatically accept it. Before using this information in an argumentative essay, check to make sure that it is actually true.

Currency

Information on a Web site is **current** when it is up-to-date. Some works—such as novels and poetry—are timeless and are useful whatever their age. Other works, however—such as those in the hard sciences—must be current because advances in some disciplines can quickly make information outdated. For this reason, you should be aware of the shelf life of information in the discipline you are researching and choose information accordingly. You can assess the currency of a Web site by asking the following questions:

- **Does the Web site include the date when it was last updated?** As you look at Web pages, check the date on which they were created or updated. Some Web sites automatically display the current date, and you should not confuse the date on which you are viewing the page with the date the page was last updated.

- **Are all links on the site live?** If a Web site is properly maintained, all the links it contains will be **live**—that is, they will take you to other Web sites. If a site contains a number of links that are not live, you should question its currency.

- **Is the information on the Web site up-to-date?** A site might have been updated, but this does not necessarily mean that it contains the most up-to-date information. In addition to checking when a Web site was last updated, look at the dates of the individual articles it lists to make sure they are not outdated.

Comprehensiveness

Information on a Web site is **comprehensive** when it covers a subject in depth. A site that presents itself as an authoritative source should include (or link to) the major sources of information that you need to understand a subject. (A site that leaves out an important source of information or that ignores opposing points of view cannot be called comprehensive.) In addition, certain sites may not be appropriate for college-level research because they do not discuss a subject in detail. You can assess the comprehensiveness of a Web site by asking the following questions:

- **Does the site provide in-depth coverage?** Articles in professional journals—which are available both in print and online—generally treat subjects in enough depth for college-level research. Other types of articles—especially those in popular magazines and in general encyclopedias, such as *Wikipedia*—may be too superficial (or uneven) for college-level research.

- **Does the site provide information that is not available elsewhere?** The Web site should provide information that is not available from other sources. In other words, it should make a contribution to your knowledge and do more than simply repackage information from other sources.

- **Who is the intended audience for this site?** Knowing the audience for a Web source can help you to judge its comprehensiveness. Is it aimed at general readers or at experts? Is it aimed at high school students or at college students? It stands to reason that a site that is aimed at experts or college students will be more comprehensive than one that is aimed at general readers or high school students.

- **Does the site suit your needs?** You are the ultimate judge of whether a site is comprehensive enough for your purposes. You have to determine whether the information on a Web site is relevant and appropriate as a source for your argumentative essay. If it is not, even if it contains a large amount of information, the site will not have enough material for your particular project.

⊙ EXERCISE 8.3

Each of the following three sources was found on the Internet:

- Jonathan Kleiman, "The Importance of User Education in Privacy"

- Facebook.com, "Facebook Principles"

- Kim Hart, "A Flashy Facebook Page, at a Cost to Privacy"

Assume you are preparing to write an essay on the topic of whether information posted on social-networking sites should be "fair game" for employers. Read the sources (pp. 238–244), and decide if each is acceptable for your essay. Evaluate each source on the basis of its accuracy, credibility, objectivity, currency, and comprehensiveness.

This posting from All Facebook: The Unofficial Facebook Resource is from February 7, 2008.

THE IMPORTANCE OF USER EDUCATION IN PRIVACY

JONATHAN KLEIMAN

I've been having a back-and-forth with an acquaintance of mine over Facebook 1 for a while now. Whenever I see him post pictures of his young grandchildren I send him a message warning him that his Facebook friends can see them, and that perhaps his privacy settings should be stronger.

Every time he asks me "can you see them now?" and every time I say 2 "yep" a few times until he finally fixes it.

I also have a friend who bragged to me that she has very few con- 3 tacts, and that nobody can see any of her pictures unless she adds them as friends. Well, she was right. At least, she was right about all of the pictures that hadn't at one point been used as her profile picture (which happened to be virtually none of them). All a person would have to do to access them is message her and any response would open up her not-so-limited profile.

She certainly didn't know that this was the case. Does she realize that 4 applications encourage me to add her pictures to a public database, like the celebrity face matcher that I mentioned earlier today?

I'm not making any complaints about Facebook's privacy settings. In fact, 5 aside from the Beacon° fiasco and the fact that applications can access my pictures through my friends' profiles, I'm generally very impressed.

Facebook's targeted advertising system, shut down after a class-action lawsuit raised privacy concerns

I'm merely suggesting that the average 6 users may be overconfident in their sense of privacy. Is it Facebook's responsibility to make sure we take the time to learn how to use the sites we're using properly? Also, is there really any legitimate expectation of privacy?

> "Average users may be overconfident in their sense of privacy."

. . . and if not, and we've entered the public sphere by joining Facebook, 7 will this have legal implications? People who enter the public sphere give up a ton of privacy rights.

Let me know what you think. 8

Facebook's privacy policy was updated on November 26, 2008.

FACEBOOK PRINCIPLES

FACEBOOK.COM

Facebook Principles

We built Facebook to make it easy to share information with your friends [1] and people around you. We understand you may not want everyone in the world to have the information you share on Facebook; that is why we give you control of your information. Our default privacy settings limit the information displayed in your profile to your networks and other reasonable community limitations that we tell you about.

> "You may not want everyone in the world to have the information you share."

Facebook follows two core principles: [2]

1. **You should have control over your personal information.** Facebook helps you share information with your friends and people around you. You choose what information you put in your profile, including contact and personal information, pictures, interests and groups you join. And you control the users with whom you share that information through the privacy settings on the Privacy page.

2. **You should have access to the information others want to share.** There is an increasing amount of information available out there, and you may want to know what relates to you, your friends, and people around you. We want to help you easily get that information.

Sharing information should be easy. And we want to provide you with [3] the privacy tools necessary to control how and with whom you share that information. If you have questions or ideas, please send them to privacy@ facebook.com.

Safe Use of Facebook

For information for users and parents about staying safe on Facebook, click here. [4]

Facebook's Privacy Policy

Facebook's Privacy Policy is designed to help you understand how we collect [5] and use the personal information you decide to share, and help you make informed decisions when using Facebook, located at www.facebook.com and its directly associated domains (collectively, "Facebook" or "Website").

By using or accessing Facebook, you are accepting the practices described 6 in this Privacy Policy.

Facebook is a licensee of the TRUSTe Privacy Program. TRUSTe is an 7 independent, non-profit organization whose mission is to build user's trust and confidence in the Internet by promoting the use of fair information practices. This privacy statement covers the site www.facebook.com and its directly associated domains. Because this Web site wants to demonstrate its commitment to your privacy, it has agreed to disclose its information practices and have its privacy practices reviewed for compliance by TRUSTe.

If you have questions or concerns regarding this statement, you should 8 first contact our privacy staff at privacy@facebook.com. If you do not receive acknowledgment of your inquiry or your inquiry has not been satisfactorily addressed, you should contact TRUSTe Watchdog at http://www.truste.org/consumers/watchdog_complaint.php. TRUSTe will then serve as a liaison with us to resolve your concerns.

EU Safe Harbor Participation

We participate in the EU Safe Harbor Privacy Framework as set forth by the 9 United States Department of Commerce. As part of our participation in the safe harbor, we have agreed to TRUSTe dispute resolution for disputes relating to our compliance with the Safe Harbor Privacy Framework. If you have any complaints regarding our compliance with the Safe Harbor you should first contact us at privacy@facebook.com. If contacting us does not resolve your complaint, you may raise your complaint with TRUSTe at http://www.truste.org/users/users_watchdog_intro.html.

The Information We Collect

When you visit Facebook you provide us with two types of information: 10 personal information you knowingly choose to disclose that is collected by us and Web Site use information collected by us as you interact with our Web Site.

When you register with Facebook, you provide us with certain personal 11 information, such as your name, your email address, your telephone number, your address, your gender, schools attended and any other personal or preference information that you provide to us.

When you enter Facebook, we collect your browser type and IP address. 12 This information is gathered for all Facebook visitors. In addition, we store certain information from your browser using "cookies." A cookie is a piece of data stored on the user's computer tied to information about the user. We use session ID cookies to confirm that users are logged in. These cookies terminate once the user closes the browser. By default, we use a persistent cookie that stores your login ID (but not your password) to make it easier for you to login when you come back to Facebook. You can remove or block this cookie using the settings in your browser if you want to disable this convenience feature.

When you use Facebook, you may set up your personal profile, form relationships, send messages, perform searches and queries, form groups, set up events and applications, and transmit information through various channels. We collect this information so that we can provide you the service and offer personalized features. In most cases, we retain it so that, for instance, you can return to view prior messages you have sent or easily see your friend list. When you update information, we usually keep a backup copy of the prior version for a reasonable period of time to enable reversion to the prior version of that information.   13

You post User Content (as defined in the Facebook Terms of Use) on the Site at your own risk. Although we allow you to set privacy options that limit access to your pages, please be aware that no security measures are perfect or impenetrable. We cannot control the actions of other Users with whom you may choose to share your pages and information. Therefore, we cannot and do not guarantee that User Content you post on the Site will not be viewed by unauthorized persons. We are not responsible for circumvention of any privacy settings or security measures contained on the Site. You understand and acknowledge that, even after removal, copies of User Content may remain viewable in cached and archived pages or if other Users have copied or stored your User Content.   14

Any improper collection or misuse of information provided on Facebook is a violation of the Facebook Terms of Service and should be reported to privacy@facebook.com.   15

If you choose to use our invitation service to tell a friend about our site, we will ask you for information needed to send the invitation, such as your friend's email address. We will send your friend an email or instant message in your name inviting him or her to visit the site, and may send up to two reminders to them. Facebook stores this information to send invitations and reminders, to register a friend connection if your invitation is accepted, to allow you to see invitations you have sent, and to track the success of our referral program. Your friend may contact us at privacy@facebook.com to request that we remove this information from our database.   16

Facebook may also collect information about you from other sources, such as newspapers, blogs, instant messaging services, and other users of the Facebook service through the operation of the service (e.g., photo tags) in order to provide you with more useful information and a more personalized experience.   17

By using Facebook, you are consenting to have your personal data transferred to and processed in the United States.   18

The following piece was published in the *Washington Post* on June 12, 2008.

A FLASHY FACEBOOK PAGE, AT A COST TO PRIVACY

KIM HART

Facebook fanatics who have covered their profiles on the popular social net- 1 working site with silly games and quirky trivia quizzes may be unknowingly giving a host of strangers an intimate peek at their lives.

Those mini-programs, called widgets or applications, allow users to person- 2 alize their pages and connect with friends and acquaintances. But they could pose privacy risks. Some security researchers warn that developers of the software have assembled too much information—home town, schools attended, employment history—and can use the data in ways that could harm or annoy users.

"Everything requires you to give access to personal information or it 3 forces you to ask your friends to do the same—it becomes a real nuisance," said David Dixon, 40, an information technology consultant in Columbia who recently deleted most of the applications he had downloaded to his Facebook profile after reading on a blog that developers may have access to his information. "Why does a Sudoku puzzle have to know I have two kids? Why does a postcard need to know where I went to college?"

Even private profiles, in which personal details are available only to 4 specific friends, reveal personal information, said Chris Soghoian, a cyber-security researcher at Indiana University. And they're allowing access to their friends' information—even if their friends are not using the application. That's because MySpace and Facebook, the largest online social networks, let outside developers see a member's information when they add a program.

"You want to be social with your friends, but now you're giving 20 guys you've never met vast amounts of information from your profile," he said. "That should be troubling to people." 5

> "Now you're giving 20 guys you've never met vast amounts of information."

A year ago, Facebook started allow- 6 ing outside developers to create small software programs for members to download. Since then, the company said, about 24,000 applications have been built by 400,000 developers. They've become enormously popular, with users playing poker, getting daily horoscopes and sending one another virtual cocktails, to name a few. More than 95 percent of Facebook users have installed at least one application, the company said.

Applications have grown so much that venture-capital firms have formed 7 exclusively to fund their development, and there is a Stanford University course devoted to creating them.

In February, MySpace also opened up to developers. It has more than 1,000   8
applications. The company, along with other social networks such as Hi5 and
AOL's Bebo, allows applications under OpenSocial, a Google-led initiative that lets
developers distribute games and other programs across multiple social networks.

Each site has come up with its own policies on the data that develop-   9
ers are allowed to see. MySpace, the largest social network, with 110 million
members, said developers can see users' public details—name, profile picture
and friend lists—when they download a program. When a user installs one on
Facebook, which has 70 million members, the developer can see everything in
a profile except contact information, as well as friends' profiles. Members can
limit what is seen by changing privacy controls, and both companies say developers are allowed to keep those data for only 24 hours.

Developers can collect other data from members once they've down-   10
loaded the applications.

Ben Ling, director of Facebook's platform, said that developers are not   11
allowed to share data with advertisers but that they can use it to tailor features to users. Facebook now removes applications that abuse user data by, for
example, forcing members to invite all of their friends before they can use it.

"When we find out people have violated that policy, there is swift enforce-   12
ment," he said.

But it is often difficult to tell when developers are breaking the rules by,   13
for example, storing members' data for more than 24 hours, said Adrienne
Felt, who recently studied Facebook security at the University of Virginia.

She examined 150 of the most popular Facebook applications to find out   14
how much data could be gathered. Her research, which was presented at a
privacy conference last month, found that about 90 percent of the applications
have unnecessary access to private data.

"Once the information is on a third-party server, Facebook can't do any-   15
thing about it," she said. Developers can use it to provide targeted ads based
on a member's gender, age or relationship status.

Consumer advocates have voiced concerns over how software developers are   16
using such data. The Center for Digital Democracy is urging the Federal Trade
Commission to look into the privacy policies surrounding third-party applications.

Some developers acknowledge the value of the data at their fingertips but   17
say they're careful not to abuse it.

"We don't care who their favorite musicians are, and we're not looking   18
at their pictures," said Dan Goodman, co-founder of Loladex, an application
that lets users find friend-recommended businesses, such as plumbers and piz-
zerias. Loladex does keep track of user-provided data, such as Zip codes.

Goodman said he hasn't ruled out using the data for targeted advertising,   19
but "we're not trying to push the privacy envelope."

Hungry Machine, based in Georgetown, has created 25 Facebook applica-   20
tions, including programs that let users recommend movies, books and music.

"Leveraging that data would make a lot of sense," said Tim O'Shaughnessy,   21
a co-founder of the company. But he said no plans are in the works.

Slide, which designed three of the most popular Facebook applications— 22 SuperPoke, FunWall and Top Friends—said it uses personal details only to make applications more relevant to users. For example, Slide collects friends' birthdays so it can remind you to "poke" them on the right day.

Many Facebook users don't mind using the tools to express themselves. 23 Gabby Jordan of Baltimore uses the Flirtable and Pimp Wars programs to connect with friends.

"If there are too many, you could easily delete them off your profile and 24 not have to worry about it," she wrote in an e-mail.

But revealing information on quizzes or maps of places visited, for 25 instance, may also make it easier for strangers to piece together tidbits to create larger security threats, said Alessandro Acquisti, assistant professor of public policy and information systems at Carnegie Mellon University.

Some online activities ask users to list pets' names or to display their high 26 school's mascot, answers to common security questions asked by financial companies.

"Nowadays, some people have downloaded so many [applications], it's 27 a constant flow of information about what they've done, what they're doing, which can be mined by your friends and also by someone you don't know anything about," he said.

⊘ EXERCISE 8.4

Read the blog post and comments below, and then answer the questions that follow.

> This blog post, followed by a number of comments, first appeared on the Legal Blog Watch Web site on March 11, 2008.

DO EMPLOYERS USING FACEBOOK FOR BACKGROUND CHECKS FACE LEGAL RISKS?

CAROLYN ELEFANT

As employers increasingly turn to social networking sites like Facebook to 1 conduct background checks on job applicants and employees, a potential face-off is brewing regarding the legality of this practice, according to reports from *Financial Week* and the *New York Daily News*. Long ago, most employers stopped requiring applicants to submit photographs or inquiring about marital status or age to avoid accusations that they rejected a candidate for discriminatory reasons. Now, social networking profiles make this once off-limits information readily available, thus reopening the potential for liability. And demographic data isn't the only concern for employers. Facebook profiles may also include information about employees' political activities, a factor that employers are prohibited from considering under most states' laws.

A recent study suggests that in fact, many employers are taking advantage of the treasure trove of information that social networking sites provide. A survey of 350 employers by the Vault found that 44% of employers use social networking sites to examine the profiles of job candidates, and 39% have looked up the profile of a current employee.

> "Many employers are taking advantage of the treasure trove of information that social networking sites provide."

2

Despite increased employer use of social networking sites, most experts advise employers against the practice in light of the potential risks. Says Neal D. Mollen, an attorney with Paul Hastings, Janofsky & Walker, "I think it's unlikely employers are going to learn a good deal of job-related information from a Facebook page they won't learn in the context of a well-run interview, so the potential benefit of doing this sort of search is outweighed by the potential risk." And for those employers who can't resist peeking at social networking sites, Jennifer M. Bombard, an attorney with Morgan Brown & Joy, recommends that they document a "legitimate business rationale for rejecting applicants" and make sure that hiring decisions are not motivated by information found on an applicant's social networking site. Yet even with these prophylactic° measures, a discrimination case will be "more problematic to defend" where an employer admits to having looked at a social networking site, says Gerald L. Maatman Jr., an attorney with Seyfarth Shaw.

3

Protective

If employers want to review social networking profiles to get a sense of what a potential employee is like, I say let them (so long as they don't use the information to unlawfully discriminate against protected groups). But first, require them to disclose the practice to job applicants and employees. Just as the information that we post on Facebook says something about us, employers' use of Facebook to ferret out personal information about prospective or current employees conveys a lot about them.

4

Posted by Carolyn Elefant on March 11, 2008 at 12:45 PM | Comments (8)

Comments

I've never understood how employers are able to look at peoples' Facebook profiles anyway, unless I'm Facebook-impaired. Can't you change your privacy settings so that only friends you've added can see your profile? I'm pretty sure that's the way mine's set. . . . not even people in my network can see my profile unless they're a friend.

5

Posted by: birdy | Mar 11, 2008 6:28:50 PM

It's true that you can set your Facebook privacy settings to only show your 6 profile to your friends, or even just your name and no location—but then nobody can find you on there, and you're typically on there to be findable. An employer can tell a lot from a picture—your race, whether you are attractive, whether you are overweight, if you are wearing a yarmulke or a veil. These are all bases for discrimination beyond what's on your resume. So, safer with no picture—but that also defeats the purpose of social contacts finding you.

> Posted by: Carol Shepherd | Mar 12, 2008 9:19:03 AM

good post. I just put a copy on our employment screening blog: blog. 7 employeescreen.com.

> Posted by: Jason Morris | Mar 14, 2008 10:02:09 AM

Tactics like utilizing searches on major social networking sites are very ques- 8 tionable. First, employee screening in general has a very subversive stigma associated with it b/c of what it does. Following stated regulated approaches as it relates to the FCRA and by being open about the type of information being requested will ensure a compliant employee background search. Using certi- fied professionals and doing your home[work] by checking with Employee Screening resources should guide you properly.

> Posted by: Bob Maxwell | Jun 27, 2008 10:32:50 PM

Hey! I am doing a legal research paper on this same topic for an independent 9 graduate study course and was wondering what your sources were. Also, can you send me direction on how to find the Vault survey you referenced in the blog? Thanks so much!

> Posted by Monica Dunham | July 3, 2008 12:10:19 PM

depends of the type of employment. . . . many jobs require applicants to con- 10 sent to a background check process.

> Posted by: | Sep. 15, 2008 8:56:56 PM

1. What steps would you take to determine whether Elefant's informa- tion is accurate?

2. How could you determine whether Elefant is respected in her field?

3. Is Elefant's blog written for an audience that is knowledgeable about her subjects? How can you tell?

4. Do you think this blog post is a suitable research source? Why or why not?

5. What insights about this blog post do the comments that accompany it give you?

⊘ EXERCISE 8.5

Read this page from an online journal. Then, locate and label the information that enables you to determine its suitability as a source.

MISSION STATEMENT

ELECTRONIC JOURNAL OF HUMAN SEXUALITY

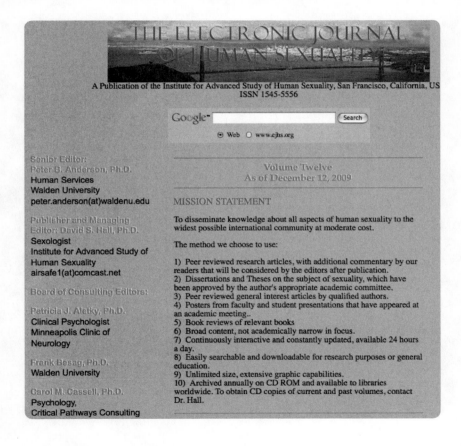

THE ELECTRONIC JOURNAL OF HUMAN SEXUALITY

A Publication of the Institute for Advanced Study of Human Sexuality, San Francisco, California, US
ISSN 1545-5556

Google [   ] [Search]
⦿ Web ○ www.ejhs.org

Senior Editor:
Peter B. Anderson, Ph.D.
Human Services
Walden University
peter.anderson(at)waldenu.edu

Publisher and Managing Editor: David S. Hall, Ph.D.
Sexologist
Institute for Advanced Study of
Human Sexuality
airsafe1(at)comcast.net

Board of Consulting Editors:

Patricia J. Aletky, Ph.D.
Clinical Psychologist
Minneapolis Clinic of
Neurology

Frank Besag, Ph.D.
Walden University

Carol M. Cassell, Ph.D.
Psychology,
Critical Pathways Consulting

Volume Twelve
As of December 12, 2009

MISSION STATEMENT

To disseminate knowledge about all aspects of human sexuality to the widest possible international community at moderate cost.

The method we choose to use:

1) Peer reviewed research articles, with additional commentary by our readers that will be considered by the editors after publication.
2) Dissertations and Theses on the subject of sexuality, which have been approved by the author's appropriate academic committee.
3) Peer reviewed general interest articles by qualified authors.
4) Posters from faculty and student presentations that have appeared at an academic meeting..
5) Book reviews of relevant books
6) Broad content, not academically narrow in focus.
7) Continuously interactive and constantly updated, available 24 hours a day.
8) Easily searchable and downloadable for research purposes or general education.
9) Unlimited size, extensive graphic capabilities.
10) Archived annually on CD ROM and available to libraries worldwide. To obtain CD copies of current and past volumes, contact Dr. Hall.

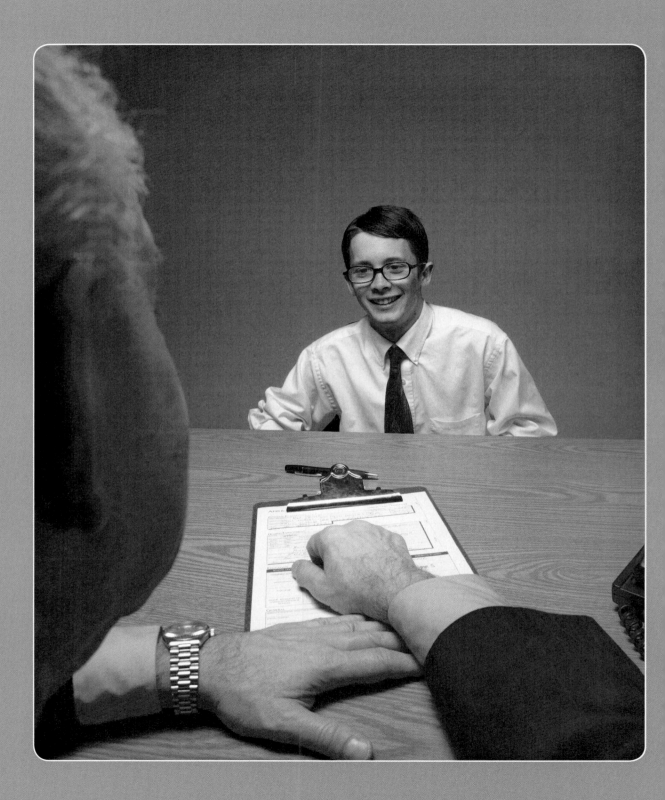

9

Summarizing, Paraphrasing, Quoting, and Synthesizing Sources

(AT ISSUE)

Should Data Posted on Social-Networking Sites Be "Fair Game" for Employers? (continued)

In the readings in the At Issue topic that was introduced in Chapter 8, you learned about the dangers students may face when they post personal information on social-networking sites—particularly how potential employers might view this information. (This is the issue explored in the MLA paper in Chapter 10.) In this chapter, you will learn how to take notes from various sources that address this issue.

As you saw in Chapter 8, before you can decide which material to use to support your arguments, you need to evaluate a variety of potential sources. After you know what sources you will use, you can begin thinking about where you might use each source and how to integrate the sources you have chosen into your essay in the form of *summary, paraphrase,* and *quotation.* When you actually write your argument, you will *synthesize* the sources into your paper, blending them with your own ideas and interpretations, as the student writer did when she wrote the MLA research paper in Chapter 10.

Summarizing Sources

A **summary** restates the main idea of a passage (or even an entire book or article) in concise terms. Because a summary leaves out the examples, explanations, and stylistic devices of the source, it is always much shorter than the original. Sometimes it is just a sentence or two.

WHEN TO SUMMARIZE

Summarize when you want to give readers a general sense of a source's position on an issue.

When you summarize information, you use your own words and phrasing, not those of your source. If you want to use an author's particularly distinctive word or phrase, you may do so—but you must always place such words in quotation marks and **document** them. If you do not, you will be committing **plagiarism**. (See Chapter 10 for information on documenting sources; see Chapter 11 for information on avoiding plagiarism.)

The following paragraph is from a newspaper op-ed piece.

ORIGINAL SOURCE

When everyone has a blog, a MySpace page or Facebook entry, everyone is a publisher. When everyone has a cellphone with a camera in it, everyone is a paparazzo. When everyone can upload video on YouTube, everyone is a filmmaker. When everyone is a publisher, paparazzo or filmmaker, everyone else is a public figure. We're all public figures now. The blogosphere has made the global discussion so much richer—and each of us so much more transparent. ("The Whole World Is Watching," Thomas L. Friedman, *New York Times*, June 27, 2007, 23).

The following summary conveys a general but accurate sense of the original paragraph without including the source's phrasing or the writer's own opinions. (One distinctive phrase is placed in quotation marks.) Parenthetical documentation indicates the source of the material.

SUMMARY

The popularity of blogs, social-networking sites, cell phone cameras, and YouTube has enhanced the "global discussion" but made it very hard for people to remain anonymous (Friedman 23).

Notice that this summary is much shorter than the original passage and that it does not include all the original's examples. Still, it accurately communicates a general sense of the source's main idea.

SUMMARIZING SOURCES

When you summarize a source, *do*

- Convey the main idea of the original.
- Be concise.
- Use your own original words and phrasing.
- Place any words from your source in quotation marks.
- Include documentation.

Do not

- Include your own analysis or opinions.
- Include digressions.
- Argue with your source.
- Use your source's syntax and phrasing.

⊙ EXERCISE 9.1

Write a two-sentence summary of the following paragraph. Then, edit your summary so that it is only one sentence long. Be sure your summary conveys the main idea of the original paragraph and includes proper documentation.

> The time has come for a line to be drawn in the war for Internet privacy. Web sites such as MySpace and Facebook are quasi-private mediums that deserve to be treated as such. Sure, opponents of the stance will say that employers and universities are completely within legal boundaries when looking at someone's Facebook or MySpace account. Hey, that's true. There's no law against it. The Internet is a public domain. The fact that it's not illegal, however, doesn't necessarily make it ethical. (David Hall, "Legal Online Behavior No Basis for Work Discrimination," *Daily Skiff*, Texas Christian University, August 29, 2007)

Paraphrasing Sources

A **paraphrase** is different from a summary. While a summary gives a general overview of the original, a paraphrase presents the source's ideas in detail, including its main idea, its key supporting points, and possibly its examples. For this reason, a paraphrase is longer than a summary. In fact, it may be as long as the original.

WHEN TO PARAPHRASE

Paraphrase when you want readers to understand a source's position in specific terms.

Like a summary, a paraphrase uses your own words and phrasing, not the language and syntax of the original. Any words or phrases that you quote must be placed in quotation marks. When you paraphrase, you may not always follow the order of the original source, but you should try to convey the writer's emphasis.

The following paragraph is from an editorial that appeared in a student newspaper.

ORIGINAL SOURCE

Additionally, as graduates retain their Facebook accounts, employers are increasingly able to use Facebook as an evaluation tool when making hiring decisions. Just as companies sometimes incorporate social functions into their interview process to see if potential hires can handle themselves responsibly, they may also check out a student's Facebook account to see how the student chooses to present him or herself. This may seem shady and underhanded, but one must understand that social networks are not anonymous; whatever one chooses to post will be available to all. Even if someone goes to great pains to keep an employer-friendly profile, his or her friends may still tag pictures of him or her which will be available to whoever wants to see them. Not only can unexpected Facebook members get information by viewing one's profile, but a user's personal information can also leak out by merely registering for the service. Both the user agreement and the privacy policy indicate that Facebook can give information to third parties and can supplement its data with information from newspapers, blogs and instant messages. ("Beware What You Post on Facebook," *The Tiger*, Clemson University, August 4, 2006)

The following paraphrase reflects the original paragraph's emphasis and communicates its key points.

PARAPHRASE

Because students keep their accounts at social-networking sites after they graduate, potential employers can use the information they find there to help them evaluate candidates' qualifications. This process is comparable to the way a company might evaluate an applicant in person in a social situation. Some people may see the practice of employers checking applicants' Facebook pages as "shady and underhanded," but these sites are not intended to be anonymous or private. For example, a person may try to maintain a profile that will be appropriate for employers, but friends may post inappropriate pictures. Also, people can reveal personal information not only in profiles but also simply by registering with Facebook. Finally, as Facebook states in its membership information, it can supply information to others as well as provide data from other sources. ("Beware")

Notice that this paraphrase includes many of the details presented in the original passage, and quotes a key phrase, but its style and sentence structure are different from those of the original.

PARAPHRASING SOURCES

When you paraphrase a source, *do*

- Convey the source's ideas fully and accurately.
- Use your own words and phrasing.
- Convey the emphasis of the original.
- Put any words from the source in quotation marks.
- Include documentation.

Do not

- Use the exact words or phrasing of your source (unless you are quoting).
- Include your own analysis or opinions.
- Digress or contradict your source.

➲ EXERCISE 9.2

Write a paraphrase of the paragraph from David Hall's article, which you summarized in Exercise 9.1. How is your paraphrase different from your summary?

➲ EXERCISE 9.3

The following paragraph is also from the Clemson University student newspaper article excerpted on page 252. Read the paragraph, and then write a paraphrase that communicates its key ideas. Before you begin, circle any distinctive word and phrases that might be difficult to paraphrase, and consider whether you should quote them. Be sure to include documentation.

All these factors make clear the importance of two principles: Responsibility and caveat emptor. First, people should be responsible about how they portray themselves and their friends, and employers, authorities and the owners must approach this information responsibly and fairly. Second, "let the buyer beware" applies to all parties involved. Facebook users need to understand the potential consequences of the information they share, and outside viewers need to understand that the material on Facebook is often only a humorous, lighthearted presentation of one aspect of a person. Facebook is an incredibly valuable communications tool that will link the college generation more tightly than any before it, but users have to understand that, like anything good in life, they have to be aware of the downsides.

Quoting Sources

When you **quote** words from a source, be sure that you are quoting accurately—that is, that every word and every punctuation mark in your quotation matches the source *exactly*. You also need to be sure that your quotation conveys the meaning its author intended and that you are not distorting the meaning by quoting out of context or by omitting a key part of the quotation.

WHEN TO QUOTE

Quote a source's words only in the following situations:

- Quote when your source's words are distinctive or memorable.

- Quote when your source's words are so direct and concise that a paraphrase would be awkward or convoluted.

- Quote when your source's words add authority or credibility to your argument (for example, when your source is a well-known expert on your topic).

- Quote an opposing point when you will go on to refute it.

Remember, quoting from a source adds interest to your paper—but only when the writer's words are compelling. Too many quotations—especially long quotations—distract readers and make it difficult for them to follow your discussion. Quote only when you must. If you include too many quotations, your paper will be a patchwork of other people's words, not an original, unified whole.

QUOTING SOURCES

When you quote a source, *do*

- Enclose borrowed words in quotation marks.
- Quote accurately.
- Include documentation.

Do not

- Quote out of context.
- Distort the source's meaning.
- Include too many quotations.

⊙ EXERCISE 9.4

Read the following paragraphs from an article that appeared in *New Scientist*. (The full text of this article begins on p. 256.) If you were going to use these paragraphs as source material for an argumentative essay, which particular words or phrases do you think you might want to quote? Why?

Cols likes a smoke and has tried many different drugs. He has three piercings and is in the process of tattooing his arm. He earns between $75,000 and $100,000 a year and doesn't see his dad.

I know all about Cols even though I have never met him and probably never shall. Five years ago only a close friend of his would have known such personal details about him. Yet thanks to his profile on the social networking website MySpace, I even know the first thing he thinks about in the morning.

There's nothing unusual about this. Millions of people share some of their most personal details with total strangers on the Internet via sites such as MySpace, Friendster and Facebook. The dangers this can pose to children are well publicized, but it also has powerful if less well known implications for us all. The sheer volume of personal information that people are publishing online—and the fact that some of it could remain visible permanently—is changing the nature of personal privacy. Is this a good thing, or will the "MySpace generation" live to regret it? (Alison George, "Things You Wouldn't Tell Your Mother," *New Scientist,* September 16, 2006)

⊘ EXERCISE 9.5

Read the essay that follows, and highlight it to identify its most important ideas. (For information on highlighting, see Chapter 2.) Then, write a summary of one paragraph and a paraphrase of another paragraph. Assume that this article is a source for a paper you are writing on the topic, "Should Data Posted on Social-Networking Sites Be 'Fair Game' for Employers?" Be sure to include documentation.

> This selection is from *New Scientist*, where it appeared on September 16, 2006.

THINGS YOU WOULDN'T TELL YOUR MOTHER

ALISON GEORGE

Cols likes a smoke and has tried many different drugs. He has three piercings   1
and is in the process of tattooing his arm. He earns between $75,000 and
$100,000 a year and doesn't see his dad.

I know all about Cols even though I have never met him and probably   2
never shall. Five years ago only a close friend
of his would have known such personal
details about him. Yet thanks to his profile
on the social networking website MySpace, I
even know the first thing he thinks about in
the morning.

> "I know all about Cols even though I have never met him."

There's nothing unusual about this. Millions of people share some of   3
their most personal details with total strangers on the Internet via sites such
as MySpace, Friendster and Facebook. The dangers this can pose to children
are well publicized, but it also has powerful if less well known implications
for us all. The sheer volume of personal information that people are publishing online—and the fact that some of it could remain visible permanently—
is changing the nature of personal privacy. Is this a good thing, or will the
"MySpace generation" live to regret it?

The change has been made possible by the way social networking sites   4
are structured. They allow users to create a profile of themselves for others to
peruse, and to build networks with hundreds or thousands of people who share
their interests or just like the look of their page. It's an opportunity to present
yourself in a way you want others to see you. Many people reveal everything
from their musical tastes and political and sexual orientation to their drinking
and drug habits and their inner thoughts and feelings. And it's a very recent
phenomenon. "There is no real-world parallel. You don't go walking round
the mall telling people whether you are straight or gay," says Fred Stutzman,

a researcher at the University of North Carolina at Chapel Hill who studies identity and social networks.

What's more, people can end up having multiple identities online. The picture you present of yourself on the dating site Match.com, for instance, will likely be different to the one you give on Facebook, restricted mainly to universities and high schools. This can be confusing if someone is trying to find out more about you by searching on Google—if they're thinking of employing you, for example, or dating you. In recognition of this online identity crisis, Stutzman and his colleague Terrell Russell have set up a service called ClaimID (claimid.com) that allows you to track, verify, annotate and prioritise the information that appears about you online, so that when someone searches you they get representative information.

Such a service could prove increasingly useful for people entering the workforce with a few years of social networking behind them. Tasteless in-jokes are fine within the network, says Stutzman. "But when you're going for that job interview, they can really come back and bite people." A survey by the U.S. National Association of Colleges and Employers published in July found that 27 percent of employers have Googled their job candidates or checked their profiles on social networking sites. It is not just employers who are interested in your online revelations. U.S. college athletes who posted pictures of themselves behaving badly on their social networking profiles unwittingly found themselves on Bob Reno's badjocks.com site, which publishes stories about scandals in sport.

How does this happen? Offline, it is easy to compartmentalise the different aspects of your life—professional, personal, family—but online, where social networks are so much larger and looser, the distinctions become blurred. These issues have not gone unnoticed by social network providers. They are reluctant to offer too much privacy because this makes it harder for users to communicate with people they don't know. Yet too little privacy means that users lose control over the information they post. "There is a fine balance between protecting and revealing—for users as well as providers," says Alessandro Acquisti of Carnegie Mellon University in Pittsburgh, Pennsylvania, who researches privacy and information security and is looking at the difference between online and offline behaviour.

In everyday life, says Acquisti, we are better equipped to manage our privacy—we are unlikely to give strangers our phone number and date of birth. So why do some people give out this information freely online? According to Acquisti, it's because people expect that the more information they give, the more they gain from the network. His research also shows that some users are not well informed about the reach of the network, and how their profile could potentially be viewed by millions of people. Internet researcher Steve Jones of the University of Illinois at Chicago agrees. "A social network where you create a circle of friends feels private," he says. "It's more of a feeling of a website shared with a small, closed group of people."

For those wishing to keep out prying eyes, most social networks do offer additional privacy tools. Users of MySpace and Facebook can choose to reveal their profiles only to friends, for example. But recent research shows that many users don't make use of these tools, even if they are worried about privacy. A survey of Facebook users published in June by Acquisti and his colleague Ralph Gross found that even among users who were concerned about a stranger knowing their address or class schedule, 22 percent still gave their address on their Facebook profile, and 40 percent published their class schedule.

What can be done to prevent what Acquisti and Gross call "an eternal   10 memory of our indiscretions"? Some recommend drastic measures. "Anything you put on the Internet has the potential to be made public and you should treat it as such," says Jones. "If you put something on MySpace or Facebook ask yourself whether you would be comfortable shouting it out at a family reunion. If the answer is no, then don't put it up." As newspapers report more stories about students being kicked off their courses and bloggers being sacked because of their online revelations, users might well feel compelled to tighten up their online privacy. This semester, students moving into campus accommodation at the University of California, Berkeley, will even be required to attend a class in social networking to make them aware of the risks.

It could go another way, though. As people become more tolerant of   11 online openness, we could see a shift in attitudes and a rethinking of what we consider private. "People tend to adapt to new environments of revelations," says Acquisti. "The new generation may be used to people talking online about their drug use and sex lives."

Their attitudes may depend on what profession they end up in. Lindsey,   12 a law student in Philadelphia who we contacted, has noticed some interesting trends among her friends. "Friends who work as DJs, record-store owners or graphic designers express themselves far more freely than friends who work in more traditional professions," she says. She has also noticed that most of her friends who are teachers don't have online profiles. "They've realized that there's nothing worse than walking in to teach your calculus class only to have them holding copies of the photograph of you on the beach."

Working Source Material into Your Argument

When you use source material in an argumentative essay, your goal is to integrate the material smoothly into your discussion, blending summary, paraphrase, and quotation with your own ideas.

To help readers follow your discussion, you need to indicate the source of your information clearly and distinguish your own ideas from those of your sources. Never simply drop source material into your discussion. Whenever possible, introduce quotations, paraphrases, and summaries with a phrase that identifies their source, and always follow them with documentation. This strategy helps readers identify the boundaries between your own ideas and those of your sources.

It is also important that you include signals to help readers understand why you are using a particular source and what the exact relationship is between your source material and your own ideas (for example, that a source supports a point you are making or that you disagree with a source).

Using Identifying Tags

Using an **identifying tag**—a phrase that introduces the quotation, paraphrase, or quotation—will help you accomplish these goals (as well as avoid accidental plagiarism).

SUMMARY WITH IDENTIFYING TAG

<u>According to Thomas L. Friedman</u>, the popularity of blogs, social-networking sites, cell phone cameras, and YouTube has enhanced the "global discussion" but made it hard for people to remain anonymous (23).

VERBS IN IDENTIFYING TAGS

To avoid repeating phrases like *he says* in identifying tags, try using some of the following verbs to introduce your source material:

notes	observes	points out
acknowledges	explains	predicts
proposes	comments	implies
suggests	warns	concludes
believes	reports	

(You can also use "According to . . . ," as in the example above.)

Note that you do not always have to place the identifying tag at the beginning of the summarized, paraphrased, or quoted material. You can also place it in the middle or at the end:

IDENTIFYING TAG AT THE BEGINNING

<u>Thomas L. Friedman notes</u> that the popularity of blogs, social-networking sites, cell phone cameras, and YouTube has enhanced the "global discussion" but made it hard for people to remain anonymous (23).

IDENTIFYING TAG IN THE MIDDLE
The popularity of blogs, social-networking sites, cell phone cameras, and YouTube, <u>Thomas L. Friedman observes,</u> has enhanced the "global discussion" but made it hard for people to remain anonymous (23).

IDENTIFYING TAG AT THE END
The popularity of blogs, social-networking sites, cell phone cameras, and YouTube has enhanced the "global discussion" but made it hard for people to remain anonymous, <u>Thomas L. Friedman points out</u> (23).

Working Quotations into Your Sentences

When you use quotations in your essays, you may need to edit them so they fit smoothly into your sentences. If you do so, be careful not to distort your sources' meaning.

Adding or Changing Words When you add or change words in a quotation, use **brackets** to indicate your edits:

ORIGINAL QUOTATION
"Web sites such as MySpace and Facebook are quasi-private mediums that deserve to be treated as such" (Hall).

WORDS ADDED FOR CLARIFICATION
"[Social networking] Web sites such as MySpace and Facebook are quasi-private mediums that deserve to be treated as such" (Hall).

ORIGINAL QUOTATION
"The blogosphere has made the global discussion so much richer—and each of us so much more transparent" (Friedman 23).

WORDS CHANGED TO MAKE VERB TENSE LOGICAL
As Thomas Friedman explains, increased access to cell phone cameras, YouTube, and the like continues to "[make] the global discussion so much richer—and each of us so much more transparent" (23).

Deleting Words When you delete words from a quotation, use **ellipses**—three spaced periods—to indicate your edits. However, do not use ellipses to indicate a deletion at the beginning of a quotation:

ORIGINAL QUOTATION
"Just as companies sometimes incorporate social functions into their interview process to see if potential hires can handle themselves

responsibly, they may also check out a student's Facebook account to see how the student chooses to present him or herself" ("Beware").

UNNECESSARY WORDS DELETED
"Just as companies sometimes incorporate social functions into their interview process, . . . they may also check out a student's Facebook account . . . " ("Beware").

DISTORTING QUOTATIONS

Be careful not to distort a source's meaning when you add, change, or delete words from a quotation. In the following example, the writer unfairly deletes material from the original quotation that would weaken his argument.

Original quotation
"This incident is by no means an isolated one. Connecticut authorities are investigating reports that seven girls were sexually assaulted by older men they met on MySpace" ("Beware").

Distorted
"This incident is by no means an isolated one. [In fact,] seven girls were sexually assaulted by older men they met on MySpace" ("Beware").

◉ EXERCISE 9.6

Reread the summary you wrote for Exercise 9.1 and the paraphrase you wrote for Exercise 9.3. Add three different identifying tags to each, varying the verbs you use and the position of the tags. Then, check to make sure you have used correct parenthetical documentation. (If the author's name is included in the identifying tag, then it does not appear in the parenthetical citation.)

Synthesizing Sources

In a **synthesis**, you combine summary, paraphrase, and quotation from several sources with your own ideas to support an original conclusion. A synthesis identifies similarities and differences among ideas, indicating where sources agree and disagree and how they support or challenge one another's ideas. Transitional words and phrases identify points of similarity (*also, like, similarly,* and so on) or difference (*however, in contrast,* and so on). When you write a synthesis, you include parenthetical documentation to identify each piece of information you get from a source and to distinguish your sources' ideas from one another and from your own ideas.

The following synthesis is excerpted from the student paper with MLA documentation in Chapter 10. Note how the synthesis blends information from three sources with the student's own ideas to support her point about how the Internet has affected people's concepts of "public" and "private."

Student's original point	Part of the problem is that the Internet has fundamentally altered our notions of "private" and "public" in ways that we are still only beginning to understand. As Alison George writes in *New Scientist*
Quotation	magazine, "the sheer volume of personal information that people are publishing online—and the fact that some of it could remain visible permanently—is changing the nature of personal privacy" (50).
Student's own ideas	On a site such as MySpace, people can reveal the most intimate details of their lives to millions of total strangers. This development is unprecedented and, at least for the foreseeable future, irreversible.
Quotation	As *New York Times* columnist Thomas Friedman observes, "When everyone has a blog, a MySpace page or Facebook entry, everyone is a publisher. . . . When everyone is a publisher, paparazzo or film-
Student's evaluation of source	maker, everyone else is a public figure" (23). Given the changes in our understanding of privacy and the essentially public nature of the Internet, the analogy that Hall makes between a MySpace post and a private conversation seems of limited use. In the Internet age, more and more of "what you say or do or write will end up as a digital fin-
Quotation	gerprint that never gets erased" (Friedman 23).

CHAPTER 10

Documenting Sources: MLA

When you are building an argument, you use sources for support. To acknowledge the material you borrow and to help readers evaluate your sources, you need to supply documentation. In other words, tell them where you found your sources. If you use documentation responsibly, you will also avoid **plagiarism**, an ethical offense with serious consequences. (See Chapter 11 for more on plagiarism.)

MLA documentation consists of two parts: **parenthetical references** in the text of your paper and a **works-cited list** at the end of the paper. (The references are keyed to the works-cited list.)

Using Parenthetical References

The basic parenthetical citation consists of the author's last name and a page number before the final period of a sentence:

(Fielding 213)

If the author is referred to in the sentence, include only the page number.

According to environmental activist Brian Fielding, the number of species affected is much higher (213).

Here are some other situations you may encounter:

- When referring to a work by two authors, include both authors' names.

(Stange and Hogarth 53)

- When citing a work with no listed author, include a short version of the title.

("Small Things" 21)

- When citing a source that is quoted in another source, indicate this by including the abbreviation *qtd. in.*

According to Kevin Kelly, this narrow approach is typical of the "hive mind" (qtd. in Doctorow 168).

- When citing two or more works by the same author, include a short title after the author's name.

(Anderson, *Long Tail* 47)

- If a source does not include page numbers, or if you are referring to the entire source rather than to a specific page, cite the author's name in the text of your paper rather than in a parenthetical reference.

Parenthetical citations must be included for *all* sources that are not **common knowledge**, whether you are summarizing, paraphrasing, or quoting directly from a source. (See p. 284 for an explanation of common knowledge.) With direct quotations, include the parenthetical reference and period *after* the closing quotation marks.

According to Doctorow, this is "authorship without editorship. Or authorship fused with editorship" (166).

When quoting a prose passage of more than four lines, introduce it with a complete sentence, followed by a colon. Indent the entire passage one inch from the margin, and do not use quotation marks. Place the parenthetical reference *after* the final punctuation mark.

Doctorow points out that *Wikipedia*'s history pages can be extremely informative:

This is a neat solution to the problem of authority—if you want to know what the fully rounded view of opinions on any controversial subject look like, you need only consult its entry's history page for a blistering eyeful of thorough debate on the subject. (170)

Preparing the Works-Cited List

Start your works-cited list on a new page following the last page of your paper. Center the heading Works Cited at the top of the page. Double-space your list, and list entries alphabetically by the author's last name—or by the first word (other than an article such as *a* or *the*) of the title if an author is not given. Each entry should begin at the left-hand margin, with the other lines in the same entry indented one-half inch from the margin. (This format can be automatically generated if you use the "hanging indent" option in your word processing program.)

Here are some additional guidelines:

- Italicize all book and periodical titles.

- Use a short version of a publisher's name (Penguin rather than Penguin Books), and abbreviate University Press (as in Princeton UP or U of Chicago P).

- If you are listing more than one work by an author, include the author's name in the first entry, and substitute three unspaced hyphens followed by a period for the second and subsequent entries.

- Put quotation marks around the title of an article in a periodical or around a section of an edited book or anthology, and provide the inclusive page numbers: 44–99. For page numbers larger than 99, give the last two digits of the second number if the first is the same: 147–69, 286–301.

- Include the medium of publication—print, Web, CD, and so on—for all entries.

When you have completed your list, double-check your parenthetical references to make sure they match the items in your works-cited list.

The following models illustrate the most common kinds of references.

Periodicals

For periodical articles found online or through a full-text database, see page 273.

Journals

Journals are periodicals published for experts in a field. Cite both volume number and issue number when available. In cases where only an issue number is available, cite the issue.

> Minkler, Lanse. "Economic Rights and Political Decision-Making."
> *Human Rights Quarterly* 31.2 (2009): 369–93. Print.
> Picciotto, Joanna. "The Public Person and the Play of Fact."
> *Representations* 105 (2009): 85–132. Print.

Magazines

Magazines are periodicals published for a general audience. Do not include a magazine's volume and issue number, but do include the date (day, month, and year for weekly publications; month and year for those published less frequently). If pages are not consecutive, give the first page followed by a plus sign.

> Gladwell, Malcolm. "Open Secrets." *New Yorker* 8 Jan. 2007:
> 44–53. Print.
> Rice, Andrew. "Mission from Africa." *New York Times Magazine*
> 12 Apr. 2009: 30+. Print.

Newspapers

Include both section letter and page number. If an article continues on to another page, provide the first page followed by a plus sign.

> Darlin, Damon. "Software That Monitors Your Work, Wherever You
> Are." *New York Times* 12 Apr. 2009: B2+. Print.

Editorial, Letter to the Editor, or Review

Include authors and titles where available as well as a descriptive label—for example Editorial, Letter, or Review. In the case of reviews, include the title and author of the work that is reviewed.

> Bernath, Dan. Letter. *Washington Post* 12 Apr. 2009: A16. Print.
> Franklin, Nancy. "Whedon's World." Rev. of *Dollhouse,* dir. Joss
> Whedon. *New Yorker* 2 Mar. 2009: 45. Print.
> "World Bank Responsibility." Editorial. *Wall Street Journal* 28 Mar.
> 2009: A10. Print.

Political Cartoon or Comic Strip

> Adams, Scott. "Dilbert." Comic strip. *Chicago Tribune* 10 March
> 2009: C9. Print.
> Pett, Joel. Cartoon. *Lexington Herald-Leader* 30 Apr. 2009: A12. Print.

Advertisement

Cite the name of the product or company that is advertised, followed by the descriptive label and the publication information.

> RosettaStone. Advertisement. *Atlantic* May 2009: 98. Print.

Books

Books by One Author

List the author, last name first, followed by the title (italicized). Include the city of publication and a short form of the publisher's name. End with the date of publication.

> Davidson, James West. *They Say: Ida B. Wells and the
>   Reconstruction of Race.* New York: Oxford UP, 2009. Print.

Books by Two or Three Authors

List authors in the order in which they are listed on the book's title page. List the first author with last name first, but list the second and third authors with first names first.

> Singer, Peter, and Jim Mason. *The Way We Eat: Why Our Food
>   Choices Matter.* Emmaus: Rodale, 2006. Print.

Books by More than Three Authors

List only the first author, last name first, followed by the abbreviation et al. ("and others").

> Gould, Harvey, et al. *Advanced Computer Simulation Methods.* San
>   Francisco: Pearson, 2009. Print.

Two or More Books by the Same Author

List the entries alphabetically by title. In each entry after the first, substitute three unspaced hyphens, followed by a period, for the author's last name.

> Friedman, Thomas L. *Hot, Flat, and Crowded: Why We Need a
>   Green Revolution—and How It Can Renew America.* New York:
>   Farrar, 2008. Print.
> ---. *The World Is Flat: A Brief History of the Twenty-First Century.*
>   New York: Farrar, 2005. Print.

Edited Book

If the book is by one author, the editor's name goes after the title, preceded by the abbreviation Ed. (for "edited by"). If the book is an edited collection of essays by different authors, treat it as an anthology.

> Whitman, Walt. *The Portable Walt Whitman.* Ed. Michael Warner.
>   New York: Penguin, 2004. Print.

Translation

Hernández Chávez, Alicia. *Mexico: A Brief History*. Trans. Andy Klatt. Berkeley: U of California P, 2006. Print.

Revised Edition

Smith, Steven S., Jason M. Roberts, and Ryan J. Vander Weilen. *The American Congress*. 4th ed. Cambridge: Cambridge UP, 2006. Print.

Anthology

Include the name of the editor (or editors) of the anthology, followed by the abbreviation ed. (for "editor") or eds. (for "editors").

Bob, Clifford, ed. *The International Struggle for New Human Rights*. Philadelphia: U of Pennsylvania P, 2009. Print.

Work in an Anthology

Malone, Dan. "Immigration, Terrorism, and Secret Prisons." *Keeping Out the Other: Immigration Enforcement Today*. Ed. David C. Brotherton and Philip Kretsedemas. New York: Columbia UP, 2008. 44–62. Print.

More than One Work in the Same Anthology

To avoid repeating the entire anthology entry, you may provide a cross-reference from individual essays to the entire anthology.

Adelson, Glenn et al., eds. *Environment: An Interdisciplinary Anthology*. New Haven: Yale UP, 2008. Print.

Lesher, Molly. "Seeds of Change." Adelson 131–37.

Marshall, Robert. "The Problem of the Wilderness." Adelson 288–92.

Section or Chapter of a Book

Leavitt, Steven D., and Stephen J. Dubner. "Why Do Drug Dealers Still Live with Their Moms?" *Freakonomics: A Rogue Economist Explores the Hidden Side of Everything*. New York: Morrow, 2006. 49–78. Print.

Introduction, Preface, Foreword, or Afterword

Christiano, Thomas, and John Christman. Introduction. *Contemporary Debates in Political Philosophy*. Ed. Thomas Christiano and John Christman. Malden: Wiley, 2009. 1–20. Print.

Multivolume Work

> McNeil, Peter, ed. *Fashion: Critical and Primary Sources.* 4 vols.
> Oxford: Berg, 2009. Print.

Article in a Reference Work

If the entries in a reference work are arranged alphabetically, do not include page numbers or volumes. When citing a familiar encyclopedia that publishes new editions regularly, include only the edition (if given) and year. If the article's author is given, include that as well.

> "Human Rights." *Encyclopedia Americana.* 2003 ed. Print.
> Sisk, David W. "Dystopia." *New Dictionary of the History of Ideas.*
> New York: Scribner's, 2005. Print.

Internet Sources

Web sources can create problems because they sometimes lack basic information—for example, dates of publication or authors' names. When citing Internet sources, however, you should supply all the information you can reasonably find.

For sites that exist only on the Web, include (when available) the author, title, overall Web site title (if part of a larger project), version, sponsor of the site, date, medium (Web), and date of access. For sites that are online editions of printed works, include as much of the original print information as is available as well as the medium and date accessed. Works that are accessed through a library database should also include the name of the database.

It is not necessary to include a URL for a Web source unless your instructor requires it. In such cases, the URL should be placed in angle brackets (< >) followed by a period and set as the final element in the citation: <http://www.eff.org>.

Entire Web Site

Include (if available) the author, title of the Web site, version, publisher or sponsor, date, medium (Web), and date that the site was accessed. If the site has no title, use the designation Home page.

> *Human Rights Watch.* Home page. Human Rights Watch. Web. 11
> May 2009.

Document within a Web Site

> "Uniform Impunity: Mexico's Misuse of Military Justice to Prosecute
> Abuses in Counternarcotics and Public Security Operations."
> *Human Rights Watch.* Human Rights Watch, Apr. 2009. Web. 6
> May 2009.

Online Video

Baggs, Amanda. "In My Language." *YouTube.* YouTube, 14 Jan. 2007. Web. 21 May 2009.

Blog Posts and Blog Comments

Friedman, Kerim. "Information Foraging." *Savage Minds* 12 Apr. 2009. Web. 14 May 2009.

McCreary, John. Weblog comment. *Savage Minds.* Your Name Here, 12 Apr. 2009. Web. 14 May 2009.

Podcast

Glass, Ira. "Scenes from a Recession." *This American Life.* Chicago Public Radio, 27 Mar. 2009. Web. 10 May 2009.

Ogg, Erica. "Google Tries to Rehab Its Antitrust Image." *CNET News Daily Podcast.* CBS Interactive, 8 May 2009. Web. 12 May 2009.

Message from an Email Discussion Group

Kagan, Richard. "Mother's Day and Abortion." Message to H-Human-Rights Discussion. Michigan State U, 3 May 2009. Email. 12 May 2009.

Online Book

Doctorow, Cory. *Content: Selected Essays on Technology, Creativity, Copyright, and the Future of the Future.* San Francisco: Tachyon, 2008. *Craphound.com.* Cory Doctorow. Web. 10 Apr. 2009.

Part of an Online Book

Zittrain, Jonathan L. "The Lessons of Wikipedia." *The Future of the Internet and How to Stop It.* New Haven: Yale UP, 2008. *futureoftheinternet.org.* Jonathan L. Zittrain. Web. 10 May 2009.

Article in an Online Scholarly Journal

Johnston, Rebecca. "Salvation or Destruction: Metaphors of the Internet." *First Monday* 14.4 (2009): n. pag. Web. 15 Apr. 2009.

Article in an Online Magazine

Gourevich, Philip, and Errol Morris. "Exposure: The Woman behind the Camera at Abu Ghraib." *The New Yorker.* Condé Nàst, 24 Mar. 2008. Web. 20 Apr. 2009.

Article in an Online Newspaper

Possley, Maurice, and Ken Armstrong. "The Verdict: Dishonor." *Chicago Tribune.* Tribune, 11 Jan. 1999. Web. 12 May 2009.

Article from a Library Database

Hartley, Richard D. "Sentencing Reform and the War on Drugs: An Analysis of Sentence Outcomes for Narcotics Offenders Adjudicated in the US District Courts on the Southwest Border." *Criminal Justice Policy Review* 19.4 (2008): 414–37. *Sage Premier.* Web. 12 May 2009.

Legal Case

When citing a court opinion, provide the plaintiffs' names, the legal citation (volume, abbreviation of the source, page numbers), the name of the court, the year of the decision, and any relevant information about where you found it. In many cases, online versions of the opinions will include only the first page; in those cases, supply that page number followed by a plus sign.

Miranda v. Arizona, 384 US 436+. Supreme Ct. of the US. 1966. *FindLaw.* Thompson Reuters, 2009. Web. 15 May 2009.

Government Document

Include the government agency or body issuing the document, followed by publication information.

United States. Dept. of Homeland Security. *Estimates of the Unauthorized Immigrant Population Residing in the United States: January 2008.* Washington: Office of Immigration Policy, Feb. 2009. Web. 12 May 2009.

⟳ The following student research paper, "Should Data Posted on Social-Networking Sites Be 'Fair Game' for Employers?" by Erin Blaine, follows MLA format and documentation style as outlined in the preceding pages.

Blaine 1

Erin Blaine

Professor Adams

Humanities 101

4 March 2010

Should Data Posted on Social-Networking Sites Be

"Fair Game" for Employers?

The popularity of social-networking sites such as MySpace   1

and Facebook has exploded over the last several years, especially

among college students and young professionals. These sites

provide valuable opportunities for networking and for connecting

socially. At the same time, potential employers, human resources

professionals, and even college admissions officers have begun

to use these sites to help them evaluate applicants. Because of

the ease with which social-networking sites can be accessed,

and because of the valuable information they can provide, this

use seems certain to become more widespread in the years to

come. Some people are concerned about this trend, arguing that

social-networking sites should be off-limits to potential employers

because they do not have the context they need to evaluate

information. As long as this information is freely posted in a

public forum, however, it should be considered "fair game."

At present, both employers and universities use   2

social-networking sites to evaluate candidates. A recent survey

found that 10% of college admissions officers acknowledged

visiting such sites as they review applicants' dossiers, and 38%

said that what they saw there "negatively affected" their "views

of the applicant" (Hechinger). This practice can also be seen in the

business world, where recruiters look at sites such as Facebook

and LinkedIn to help them evaluate potential employees, a practice

that is sometimes referred to as "informal reference checking"

(Athavaley). In a recent study, the U.S. National Association of

A parenthetical
reference
identifies the
source, which
is included in
the works-cited
list.

Blaine 2

Colleges and Employees found that "27 per cent of employers have Googled their job candidates or checked their profiles on social networking sites" (George 51).

Not everyone is happy with this practice, and college students in particular seem to have strong objections. Interviewed in the school newspaper, one Tufts University student points out that people use social-networking services to "share uncensored aspects" of their lives, but "now that this system is being used as a way to spy on on [their] lives for the professional sphere, [they] are all in danger" (qtd. in Dince). Writing in the Texas Christian University *Daily Skiff*, David Hall argues that the "time has come for a line to be drawn in the war for Internet privacy." Although Hall acknowledges that there is no law barring employers or universities from looking at Facebook and MySpace accounts, he points out that the fact that the practice is legal "doesn't necessarily make it ethical." Posts on such sites, writes Hall, are like a "conversation between friends" and should therefore be "granted the same level of respect" as "private business." For this reason, these exchanges should not affect a person's "standing with an employer or university." To support his view, Hall also cites the example of a university student who was denied a teaching certificate because of a seemingly innocent photograph posted on her MySpace page.

Despite these objections, admissions committees and job recruiters who visit sites like Facebook and MySpace for "informal reference checking" are acting reasonably given the realities of the digital age. As a practical matter, it would be impossible to prevent employers from reviewing online sites as part of informal background and reference checks. More important, those who believe that it is unethical for recruiters to look at the online profiles of prospective job candidates seem to expect

Parenthetical documentation indicates source quoted in another source.

Source of information from Hall identified by author's name in text; Internet source includes no page number.

Blaine 3

the benefits of social-networking sites without acknowledging
that these new technologies bring new responsibilities and
liabilities as well as opportunities. Moreover, the potential
problems associated with employers' use of social-networking
sites would not be an issue if users of social-networking sites
such as Facebook and MySpace took advantage of available
measures to protect themselves.

Part of the problem is that the Internet has fundamentally   5
altered our notions of "private" and "public" in ways that we
are still only beginning to understand. As Alison George writes
in *New Scientist* magazine, "The sheer volume of personal
information that people are publishing online—and the fact that
some of it could remain visible permanently—is changing the
nature of personal privacy" (50). On a site such as MySpace,
people can reveal intimate details of their lives to millions of
strangers. This situation is unprecedented and, at least for the
foreseeable future, irreversible. As *New York Times* columnist
Thomas L. Friedman observes, "When everyone has a blog, a
MySpace page or Facebook entry, everyone is a publisher. . . .
When everyone is a publisher, paparazzo or filmmaker, everyone
else is a public figure." Given the changes in our understanding
of privacy, and given the essentially public nature of the Internet,
the analogy that Hall makes between a MySpace post and a
private conversation does not hold up. In the Internet age, more
and more of "what you say or do or write will end up as a digital
fingerprint that never gets erased" (Friedman).

Rather than relying on outdated notions of privacy,   6
students and jobseekers should accept these new conditions and
take steps to protect themselves. They must realize that a sensible
approach to the Internet demands both "a caution and an
empowerment," in the words of Jobster CEO Jason Goldberg (qtd.
in Athavaley). The editors of Clemson University's *Tiger* agree,

Because the source is identified in the text of the paper, only a page number is needed in the parenthetical documentation.

Ellipses indicate that words have been left out of a quotation.

Blaine 4

noting that services such as Facebook "make clear the importance of two principles: Responsibility and caveat emptor" ("Beware"). Social-networking sites have features that restrict who can see a profile or access a person's network and private information, but "recent research shows that many users don't make use of these tools, even if they're worried about privacy" (George 51). Simply using such easily available restrictions might drastically reduce the chances of having an indiscreet or unflattering post or photograph remain on a site. In addition, a service called ClaimID allows Internet users to "track, verify, annotate, and prioritize the information that appears about [them] online" (George 50).

The most important way for people to protect themselves   7
against possible misuse of personal information is for them to take responsibility for the information they post online. As one college guidance counselor advises, when they are writing in Facebook or MySpace, users should ask, "Is this something [I] want [my] grandmother to see?" (Hechinger). A potential employer coming across an applicant's humorous membership in a Facebook group such as "I Sold My Grandma for Crack-Cocaine!" or a picture of a student posing with an empty liquor bottle may not understand the tone, the context, or the joke. Students should also be careful about the "friends" who have access to their online social networks. Specifically, they should consider whether these people really know them and would have good things to say about them if a prospective employer contacted them for a reference. As Steven Rothberg, president and founder of CollegeRecruiter.com, says, "If you're going to have friends who are at best questionable in dealing with a potential employer on your behalf, you are probably better off not having those friends visible in your network" (qtd. in Athavaley).

Brackets indicate quotations have been edited for clarity.

Blaine 5

The ease of accessing social-networking sites, which is   8
potentially a downside, also has an advantage: these sites
provide an excellent opportunity for jobseekers to connect with
potential employers and to get their names and resumes in
circulation. Just as Facebook and similar sites are fair game for
potential employers, they are also fair game for prospective
employees. For example, a job seeker can scan the LinkedIn
networks of a company's executives or human resources staff,
searching for mutual connections. In the past, a recruiter or
company might not only check a job candidate's references but
also place candidates in social situations to learn more about
them. In today's job market, people should think of their
networks as an extension of themselves. Writing in the *Wall Street
Journal*, Anjali Athavaley cites the example of Chandan Mahajan,
whose LinkedIn profile displayed his previous work experience
and included several recommendations from former colleagues.
Mahajan credits the site and his extended online network for
helping him land a job at a large information-technology
company. His experience is a good example of the advantages
that the Internet can offer jobseekers.

As Thomas L. Friedman argues, access and open   9
information creates opportunities as well as problems. Friedman
suggests that the most important opportunity may be the one
to "out behave your competition." In other words, just as the
Internet now allows negative information to travel more quickly
than ever, it also allows positive information to spread. So
rather than fearing the dangers of snooping recruiters, students
and job seekers should remember to be careful but should not
miss the opportunity to take advantage of the possibilities that
social-networking sites provide.

Blaine 6

Works Cited

Athavaley, Anjali. "Job References You Can't Control." *Wall Street Journal*. Dow Jones, 27 Sept. 2007. Web. 14 Feb. 2010.

"Beware What You Post on Facebook." Editorial. *Tiger*. Clemson U, 4 Aug. 2006. Web. 15 Feb. 2010.

Dince, Rebecca. "Future Employees Using Facebook to Obtain Info on Applicants." *Tufts Daily*. Tufts U, 8 Feb. 2006. Web. 19 Feb. 2010.

Friedman, Thomas L. "The World Is Watching." *New York Times* 27 June 2007: A23. Print.

George, Alison. "Things You Wouldn't Tell Your Mother." *New Scientist* 16 Sep. 2006: 50–51. Print.

Hall, David. "Legal Online Behavior No Basis for Work Discrimination." *Daily Skiff*. Texas Christian U, 29 Aug. 2007. Web. 19 Feb. 2010.

Hechinger, John. "College Applicants Should Beware of Facebook." *Wall Street Journal*. Dow Jones, 18 Sept. 2008. Web. 14 Feb. 2010.

The works-cited list includes full information for all the sources cited in the paper.

Avoiding Plagiarism

Where Do We Draw the Line with Plagiarism?

In recent years, a number of high-profile plagiarism cases have put a spotlight on how much "borrowing" from other sources is acceptable. Some critics—and many colleges and universities—draw little distinction between intentional and unintentional plagiarism, arguing that any unattributed borrowing is theft. Others are more forgiving, accepting the fact that busy historians or scientists (or students) might not realize that a particular sentence in their notes was not their original idea or might accidentally incorporate a source's exact words (or its unique syntax or phrasing) into their own work without attribution.

In the age of the Internet, with its "cut-and-paste" culture, plagiarism has become easier to commit—but, with the development of plagiarism-detection software, it is also now much easier to detect. Some colleges and universities, however, are uncomfortable with the idea of using such software, arguing that it establishes an atmosphere of distrust.

On college campuses, as in the professional world, questions like the following have arisen: What exactly constitutes plagiarism? How serious a matter is it? Is there a difference between intentional and unintentional plagiarism? Is plagiarizing a few sentences as bad as plagiarizing an entire paper? Why do people commit plagiarism? What should be done to prevent it? How should it be punished? What are its short- and long-term consequences?

These are some (although by no means all) of the questions that you might consider as you read the sources at the end of this chapter. After reading these sources, you will be asked to write an argumentative essay that takes a position on the topic, "Where Do We Draw the Line with Plagiarism?"

Understanding Plagiarism

Plagiarism is using the words or ideas of another person without attributing them to their rightful author—that is, presenting those borrowed words and ideas as if they are your own.

TWO DEFINITIONS OF PLAGIARISM

From *MLA Handbook for Writers of Research Papers,* Seventh Edition (2009)

Derived from the Latin word *plagiarius* ("kidnapper"), *to plagiarize* means "to commit literary theft" and to "present as new and original an idea or product derived from an existing source" (*Merriam-Webster's Collegiate Dictionary* [11th ed.; 2003; print]). Plagiarism involves two kinds of wrongs. Using another person's ideas, information, or expressions without acknowledging that person's work constitutes intellectual theft. Passing off another person's ideas, information, or expressions as your own to get a better grade or gain some other advantage constitutes fraud. Plagiarism is sometimes a moral and ethical offense rather than a legal one since some instances of plagiarism fall outside the scope of copyright infringement, a legal offense.

From *Publication Manual of the American Psychological Association,* Sixth Edition (2009)

Researchers do not claim the words and ideas of another as their own; they give credit where credit is due (APA Ethics Code Standard 8.11, Plagiarism). Quotation marks should be used to indicate the exact words of another. *Each time* you paraphrase another author (i.e., summarize a passage or rearrange the order of a sentence and change some of the words), you need to credit the source in the text.

The key element of this principle is that authors do not present the work of another as if it were their own work. This can extend to ideas as well as written words. If authors model a study after one done by someone else, the originating author should be given credit. If the rationale for a study was suggested in the Discussion section of someone else's article, that person should be given credit. Given the free exchange of ideas, which is very important to the health of intellectual discourse, authors may not know where an idea for a study originated. If authors do know, however, they should acknowledge the source; this includes personal communications.

For many people, defining *plagiarism* is simple—it is not "borrowing" but stealing—and it should be dealt with severely. For others, it is a more slippery term, seen as considerably more serious if it is intentional than if it is accidental (for example, if it is the result of careless research methods). Most colleges and universities have guidelines that define plagiarism strictly and have penalties in place for these who commit it. To avoid plagiarism, you need to use sources responsibly and to understand what kind of information requires documentation and what kind does not.

Using Sources Responsibly

To avoid unintentional plagiarism, you need to take (and maintain) control over your sources, keeping track of all the material you use so that you remember where you found each piece of information.

As you take notes, be careful to distinguish your sources' ideas from your own. If you are integrating a source's words into your notes, put them in quotation marks. (If you are taking notes by hand, circle the quotation marks; if you are typing your notes, put the quotation marks in boldface.) If you photocopy material, write the full source information on the first page. When you download sources from the Web, be sure the URL appears on every page. Finally, never cut and paste material from sources directly into your paper.

INTERNET SOURCES AND PLAGIARISM

The Internet presents a particular challenge for students as they try to avoid plagiarism. Committing plagiarism (intentional or unintentional) with electronic sources is easy because it is so simple to cut and paste material from online sources into a paper. However, inserting even a sentence or two from an Internet source into a paper without quotation marks and attribution constitutes plagiarism.

It is also not acceptable to borrow material from a source when no author is identified. Even when no author's name appears, if the words or ideas you borrow are not your own, you must identify their source.

As you draft your paper, be sure to quote your sources' words accurately (even punctuation must be reproduced exactly as it appears in the source). Be careful not to quote out of context, and be sure that you are presenting your sources' ideas accurately when you summarize or paraphrase. (For information on quoting, paraphrasing, and summarizing source material, see Chapter 9.)

INTENTIONAL PLAGIARISM

Handing in other students' papers as your own or buying a paper from an Internet site is never acceptable. Such acts constitute serious violations of academic integrity. Creating your own original work is an important part of the educational experience, and misrepresenting someone else's work as your own undermines the goals of education.

Knowing What to Document

Documentation of sources means stating where you found the information and exactly what that information is. Different disciplines require different formats for documentation—for example, English uses MLA, and psychology uses APA. For this reason, you should be sure to check with your instructor to find out what documentation style he or she prefers. (For information on MLA and APA documentation formats, see Chapter 10 and Appendix B, respectively.)

Regardless of the discipline, always document the following kinds of information:

- Quotations from a source

- Summaries or paraphrases of a source's original ideas

- Opinions, judgments, and conclusions that are not your original ideas

- Statistics from a source

- Data from charts or graphs in a source

You do not, however, need to document the following kinds of information:

- **Common knowledge**—that is, factual information that can be found in several different sources (for example, a writer's date of birth, a scientific fact, or the location of a famous battle)

- Familiar quotations—anything from proverbs to lines from Shakespeare's plays—that you expect readers will recognize

- Your own original opinions, judgments, and conclusions

⊖ EXERCISE 11.1

Which of the following requires documentation, and why?

1. Doris Kearns Goodwin is a prize-winning historian.

2. Doris Kearns Goodwin's *The Fitzgeralds and the Kennedys* is a 900-page book with about 3,500 footnotes.

3. In 1994, Lynne McTaggart accused Goodwin of borrowing material from a book that McTaggart wrote.

4. My own review of the background suggests that Goodwin's plagiarism was unintentional.

5. Still, these accusations left Goodwin to face the "slings and arrows" of media criticism.

6. As Goodwin explains, "The more intensive and far-reaching a historian's research, the greater the difficulty of citation."

7. In her defense, Goodwin argued that the more research a historian does, the harder it is to keep track of sources.

8. Some people still remain convinced that Goodwin committed plagiarism.

9. Goodwin believes that her careful research methods, which she has described in exhaustive detail, should have presented accidental plagiarism.

10. Goodwin's critics have concluded that her reputation as a historian was hurt by the plagiarism charges.

◉ EXERCISE 11.2

Read the following editorial. If you were using this article as a source, what information would you need to document, and what information would you *not* have to document? Identify two pieces of information you would need to document (for example, statistics). Then, identify two pieces of information you would *not* need to document (for example, common knowledge).

This unsigned editorial appeared on August 11, 2006.

CHEATERS NEVER WIN

AUSTIN AMERICAN-STATESMAN

We live in the era of cut and paste, thanks to the Internet, which provides students with countless materials to plagiarize.   1

If you think that's an exaggeration, do an Internet search of "free term papers." You'll find cheathouse.com, Cheater.com, Schoolsucks.com, echeat .com and Free Essay Network (freeessay.com) among the 603 million results that turn up.   2

One site, 24hourtermpapers.com even boasts of providing "custom ³ term papers" within 24 hours (at $23.95 per page), targeting college students who put off writing papers until the 11th hour. A disclaimer warns that "these term papers are to be used for research purposes only. Use of these papers for any other purpose is not the responsibility of 24 Hour Term Papers." Funny that they say that, because the site provides the student with a nice package to hand directly to the professor: All term papers are "sent within the due date," with a bibliography page thrown in for no extra charge.

A student who pays such a steep price for a term paper is not likely to use ⁴ it only as a resource. One of the perks of being a student today is unlimited access to a slew of research tools, from the library to an online research database the institution pays for the student to use.

Student Judicial Services at the University of Texas defines plagiarism as ⁵ "representing as your own work any material that was obtained from another source, regardless of how or where you acquired it." This includes borrowing ideas or even structure. And "by merely changing a few words or rearranging several words or sentences, you are not paraphrasing. Making minor revisions to borrowed text amounts to plagiarism," the Web site warns.

But those warnings go unheeded by many. The Center for Academic ⁶ Integrity found last year that more than 70 percent of college students admitted to having cheated at least once, more than 60 percent admitted to plagiarizing and nearly 40 percent said they have plagiarized from the Internet.

Strict disciplinary action should follow students who are caught trying ⁷ to claim someone else's work as their own. The more it goes unnoticed, the easier it is for students to keep stealing. Educators should devote time and attention to properly educating students on what plagiarism is and why it's stupid to do it.

In the end, the plagiarizer has the most to lose, whether he or she gets ⁸ caught or not. Many of the online papers are not worthy of copying, especially if a student wants to excel in college. By stealing someone else's work and labeling it as their own, students forgo the opportunity to learn how to research, develop ideas and translate them into quality writing. Not to mention tarnishing a reputation, if the student gets caught.

> "In the end, the plagiarizer has the most to lose."

Cheathouse.com and other sites like it might get students a passing grade ⁹ in a course, but it only puts them a step behind everyone else who is developing the skills needed to thrive in the workplace. Employers won't be as forgiving as teachers or disciplinary committees. The day will come when the "I'm a student. I'm still learning" excuse will fall on deaf ears.

Revising to Eliminate Plagiarism

As you revise your papers, scrutinize your work carefully to be sure you have not inadvertently committed plagiarism.

The following paragraph (from page 28 of Thomas L. Friedman's 2008 book *Hot, Flat and Crowded*) and the guidelines that follow it will help you to understand the situations in which accidental plagiarism is most likely to occur.

> So if you think the world feels crowded now, just wait a few decades. In 1800, London was the world's largest city with one million people. By 1960, there were 111 cities with more than one million people. By 1995 there were 280, and today there are over 300, according to UN Population Fund statistics. The number of megacities (with ten million or more inhabitants) in the world has climbed from 5 in 1975 to 14 in 1995 and is expected to reach 26 cities by 2015, according to the UN. Needless to say, these exploding populations are rapidly overwhelming infrastructure in these megacities—nineteen million people in Mumbai alone—as well as driving loss of arable land, deforestation, overfishing, water shortages, and air and water pollution.

1. **Be sure you have identified your source and provided appropriate documentation.**

   PLAGIARISM
   The world is becoming more and more crowded, and some twenty-six cities are expected to have populations of over 10 million by 2015.

   This writer does not quote directly from Friedman's discussion, but her summary of his comments does not represent her original ideas and therefore needs to be documented. The following responsible use of source material includes both an introductory phrase that identifies Friedman as the source of the ideas and a page number that directs readers to the exact location of the material the student is summarizing.

   CORRECT
   According to Thomas L. Friedman, the world is becoming more and more crowded, and some twenty-six cities are expected to have populations of over 10 million by 2015 (28).

2. **Be sure you have placed quotation marks around borrowed words.**

   PLAGIARISM
   According to Thomas L. Friedman, the exploding populations of megacities around the world are overwhelming their infrastructure (28).

Although the passage above provides parenthetical documentation and includes an introductory phrase that identifies Friedman as the source of its ideas, it uses Friedman's exact words without placing them in quotation marks. The writer needs to either place quotation marks around Friedman's words or paraphrase his comments.

CORRECT (BORROWED WORDS IN QUOTATION MARKS)
According to Thomas L. Friedman, the "exploding" populations of large cities around the world are "rapidly overwhelming infrastructure in these megacities" (28).

CORRECT (BORROWED WORDS PARAPHRASED)
According to Thomas L. Friedman, the rapid rise in population of large cities around the world poses a serious threat to their ability to function (28).

3. Be sure you have indicated the boundaries of the borrowed material.

PLAGIARISM
The world is becoming more and more crowded, and this will lead to serious problems in the future. Soon, as many as twenty-six of the world's cities will have populations over 10 million. It is clear that "these exploding populations are rapidly overwhelming infrastructure in these megacities" (Friedman 28).

In the passage above, the student correctly places Friedman's words in quotation marks and includes appropriate parenthetical documentation. However, she does not indicate that other ideas in the passage, although not quoted directly, are also Friedman's. The student needs to use **identifying tags** (introductory phrases) to indicate the boundaries of the borrowed material, which goes beyond the quoted words:

CORRECT
According to Thomas L. Friedman, the world is becoming more and more crowded, and this will lead to serious problems in the future. Soon, Friedman predicts, as many as twenty-six of the world's cities will have populations of over 10 million, and this rise in population will put a serious strain on the cities' resources, "rapidly overwhelming infrastructure in these megacities" (28).

4. Be sure you have used your own phrasing and syntax.

PLAGIARISM
If you feel crowded now, Thomas L. Friedman says, just wait twenty or thirty years. In 1800, London, with a million inhabitants, was the

largest city in the world; over 111 cities had more than a million people by 1960. Thirty-five years later, there were 280; today, according
to statistics provided by the UN Population Fund, there are more than
300. There were only five megacities (10 million people or more) in
1975 and fourteen in 1995. However, by 2015, the United Nations predicts, there might be twenty-six. These rapidly growing populations
threaten to overwhelm the infrastructure of the megacities (Mumbai
alone has 19 million people), destroying arable land, the forests, and
fishing and causing water shortages and water and air pollution (28).

The student who wrote the passage above does provide an identifying
tag and parenthetical documentation to identify the source of the passage's
ideas. Still, even though she does not use Friedman's exact language, this
passage is plagiarized because its phrasing and syntax are almost identical
to Friedman's. In the following passage, the writer responsibly paraphrases
and summarizes Friedman's ideas, quoting a few distinctive passages. (See
Chapter 9 for information on paraphrase and summary.)

CORRECT

As Thomas L. Friedman warns, the world has been growing more
and more crowded and is likely to grow still more crowded in the
years to come. Relying on UN population data, Friedman estimates
that there will be some twenty more "megacities" (those with more
than 10 million people) in 2015 than there were in 1975. (In 1800, in
contrast, only one city in the world—London—had a million inhabitants.) Obviously, this is an alarming trend. Friedman believes that
these rapidly growing populations are "overwhelming infrastructure
in these megacities" and are bound to strain resources, leading to
"loss of arable land, deforestation, [and] overfishing" and creating
not only air and water pollution but water shortages as well (28).

Note: Do not forget to document statistics that you take from a source.
For example, Thomas L. Friedman's statistics about the threat of rising
population are the result of his original research, so you need to document
them. In addition, always provide documentation for data from graphs and
tables in a source and for visuals downloaded from the Internet.

◉ EXERCISE 11.3

The following student paragraph synthesizes information from two different
sources (which follow the student paragraph), but the student writer has not
used sources responsibly. (For information on synthesis, see Chapter 9.)
Read the sources and the paragraph, and then make the following changes:

■ Insert quotation marks where the student has quoted a source
directly.

- Edit paraphrased and summarized material if necessary so that its syntax and phrasing are not too close to that of a source.

- Add parenthetical documentation where necessary to acknowledge a source's words or original ideas.

- Add introductory phrases where necessary to clarify the scope of the borrowed material or to differentiate material from the two sources.

- Check every quoted passage once more to see if the quotation adds something vital to the paragraph. If it does not, summarize or paraphrase the source's words instead.

STUDENT PARAGRAPH

In recent years, psychologists have focused on the idea that girls (unlike boys) face a crisis of self-esteem as they approach adolescence. Both Carol Gilligan and Mary Pipher did research to support this idea, showing how girls lose their self-confidence in adolescence because of sexist cultural expectations. Women's groups have expressed concern that the school system favors boys and is biased against girls. In fact, boys are often regarded not just as classroom favorites but also as bullies who represent obstacles on the path to gender justice for girls. Recently, however, this impression that boys are somehow privileged while girls are shortchanged is being challenged.

Source 1

That boys are in disrepute is not accidental. For many years women's groups have complained that boys benefit from a school system that favors them and is biased against girls. "Schools shortchange girls," declares the American Association of University Women. . . . A stream of books and pamphlets cite research showing not only that boys are classroom favorites but also that they are given to schoolyard violence and sexual harassment.

In the view that has prevailed in American education over the past decade, boys are resented, both as unfairly privileged sex and as obstacles on the path to gender justice for girls. This perspective is promoted in schools of education, and many a teacher now feels that girls need and deserve special indemnifying consideration. "It is really clear that boys are Number One in this society and in most of the world," says Patricia O'Reilly, a professor of education and the director of the Gender Equity Center, at the University of Cincinnati.

The idea that schools and society grind girls down has given rise to an array of laws and policies intended to curtail the advantage boys have and to redress the harm done to girls. That girls are treated as the second sex in school and consequently suffer, that boys are accorded privileges and consequently benefit—these are things everyone is presumed to know. But they are not true.

—Christina Hoff Sommers, "The War against Boys"

Source 2

Girls face an inevitable crisis of self-esteem as they approach adolescence. They are in danger of losing their voices, drowning, and facing a devastating dip in self-regard that boys don't experience. This is the picture that Carol Gilligan presented on the basis of her research at the Emma Willard School, a private girls' school in Troy, N.Y. While Gilligan did not refer to genes in her analysis of girls' vulnerability, she did cite both the "wall of Western culture" and deep early childhood socialization as reasons.

Her theme was echoed in 1994 by the clinical psychologist Mary Pipher's surprise best seller, *Reviving Ophelia* (Putnam, 1994), which spent three years on the *New York Times* best-seller list. Drawing on case studies rather than systematic research, Pipher observed how naturally outgoing, confident girls get worn down by sexist cultural expectations. Gilligan's and Pipher's ideas have also been supported by a widely cited study in 1990 by the American Association of University Women. That report, published in 1991, claimed that teenage girls experience a "free-fall in self-esteem from which some will never recover."

The idea that girls have low self-esteem has by now become part of the academic canon as well as fodder for the popular media. But is it true? No.

—Rosalind C. Barnett and Caryl Rivers, "Men Are from Earth, and So Are Women. It's Faulty Research That Sets Them Apart"

Where Do We Draw the Line with Plagiarism?

Reread the At Issue box on page 281. Then, read the sources on the following pages. As you read these sources, you will be asked to answer questions and to complete some activities. This work will help you to understand the content and structure of the material you read. When you have read the sources, you will be ready to write an argumentative essay in which you take a position on the topic, "Where Do We Draw the Line with Plagiarism?"

SOURCES

 Jack Shafer, "Sidebar: Comparing the Copy"

 Lawrence M. Hinman, "How to Fight College Cheating"

 Deborah R. Gerhardt, "The Rules of Attribution"

 Richard A. Posner, "The Truth about Plagiarism"

 Doris Kearns Goodwin, "How I Caused That Story"

 Carolyn Foster Segal, "Copy This"

In this *Slate* article, Shafer accuses a *New York Times* reporter of plagiarism. As evidence, he presents the opening paragraphs from the source (a Bloomberg News story), the accused reporter's *New York Times* article, and—for contrast—two other newspaper articles that report the same story without relying heavily on the original source.

This piece appeared in *Slate* on March 5, 2008.

SIDEBAR:° COMPARING THE COPY

JACK SHAFER

A short news story printed alongside a longer related article

1 How different can four news stories generated by the same assignment be? Compare the opening paragraphs of these pieces about the 2005 mad cow disease conference call: the Bloomberg News version; the *New York Times* version, which lifts passages from Bloomberg without attribution; and the starkly different pieces run by the *globeandmail.com* and the *Omaha World-Herald*.

> "How different can four news stories generated by the same assignment be?"

Opening paragraphs from the July 15, 2005, Bloomberg News story by Daniel Goldstein:

2 The U.S. plans to resume imports of Canadian cattle, after an appellate court cleared the way to end a ban imposed two years ago because of mad-cow disease.° Cattle prices fell and shares of beef producer Tyson Foods Inc. surged.

3 The first shipments from Canada may arrive at U.S. slaughterhouses in days, U.S. Agriculture Secretary Mike Johanns said today in a conference call. "If things go well, it could very well be next week." USDA and Canadian officials are coordinating how to certify animals for shipment, he said.

4 A U.S. appellate court° yesterday ruled in favor of the government, which argued Canadian cattle under 30 months of age don't pose a risk of mad-cow disease. Tyson's beef business had a loss of $19 million in the quarter ended April 2, as the lack of available cattle boosted costs and led to plant closings. Canada before the ban supplied about 5 percent of U.S. beef.

A brain disease that can be transmitted to humans through consumption of contaminated beef

A higher court that hears appeals of rulings that were made by a lower court

Opening paragraphs from the July 16, 2005, *New York Times* story by Alexei Barrionuevo:

The United States Agriculture Department said on Friday that it planned   5
to resume imports of Canadian cattle within days, after an appellate court
lifted a two-year-old injunction imposed because of mad cow disease.

The first shipments from Canada could arrive at American slaughter-   6
houses as early as next week, Agriculture Secretary Mike Johanns said in a
conference call with reporters. Officials in Canada and the United States
are coordinating how to certify the animals for shipment, he said.

"We want to make sure everything is in place," he said. "If things go   7
well, it could very well be next week."

The news sent shares of the beef producer Tyson Foods and   8
McDonald's restaurants surging. Cattle prices fell. Shares of Tyson rose
7.5 percent in early trading, and closed at $19.47 a share, a 5 percent
increase, while McDonald's closed at $30.99 a share, up 4.7 percent.

Tyson's beef business recorded a loss of $19 million in the quarter   9
ended April 2. The company was hurt by the ban on cattle from Canada,
which increased costs and led to temporary plant closings. Before the ban,
Canada supplied about 5 percent of the nation's beef.

A United States appeals court ruled on Thursday in favor of the gov-   10
ernment, which had argued that Canadian cows under 30 months of age
did not pose a risk of bovine spongiform encephalopathy, or mad cow
disease.

Opening paragraphs from the July 15 *globeandmail.com* story by Terry Weber, time stamped 12:28 p.m.:

The United States is taking immediate steps to reopen the border to   11
Canadian cattle imports Agriculture Secretary Mike Johanns said Friday.

During a webcast, Mr. Johanns said that Washington has been in   12
touch with Ottawa and that the two sides are now going through the
logistical steps necessary to resume trade of live cattle for the first time
since May, 2003.

"Our hope is we're talking about days and not weeks," he said. "If   13
things go well, it could very well be next week, but we have not set a specific date."

Late Thursday, a three-member U.S. appeal court panel in Seattle   14
overturned a temporary injunction issued by Montana Judge Richard
Cebull halting the U.S. Department of Agriculture's March plan to reopen
the border.

Judge Cebull had sided with U.S. ranchers group R-Calf in its argu-   15
ment that reopening the border exposed U.S. ranchers and consumers to
unnecessary risks from mad-cow disease. The USDA had been planning

to ease restrictions by allowing cattle younger than 30 months to be imported.

Mr. Johanns noted that Canadian officials had already anticipated 16 the ruling and taken steps to meet U.S. requirements, should Thursday's favour reopening the border.

"It [the reopening] could be as early as next week, but we want to 17 make sure everything is in place," he said.

Those requirements, he said, including ensuring that animals being 18 imported into the U.S. meet minimal-risk rule criteria, getting documents to U.S. customs to confirm the shipments are appropriate for entry.

Opening paragraphs from the July 15 *Omaha World-Herald* story by Chris Clayton:

Canadian cattle could start arriving at U.S. feedlots and meatpacking 19 plants as early as next week, U.S. Agriculture Secretary Mike Johanns said Friday.

Thursday's unanimous decision by the 9th U.S. Circuit Court of 20 Appeals lifting a lower court's injunction gives U.S. and Canadian officials a nearly two-week window to begin shipping live cattle from Canada before another court hearing, scheduled late this month in Montana.

No date has been set, but Johanns said he will move as "expedi- 21 tiously as possible" to begin importing Canadian cattle once officials work out the ground rules. Canadian and USDA officials anticipated the requirements would be in place at whatever time the legal issues were resolved.

"Our hope is we are talking about days, not weeks," Johanns said. "It 22 could be as early as next week, but we want to make sure everything is in place. . . . If things go well, it could very well be next week, but we haven't set a specific date" [*ellipsis in the original*].

Johanns has lamented the closed border since becoming agriculture 23 secretary in late January, saying that it hurts U.S. cattle feeders and meatpackers because the United States continued to import boxed beef from Canada.

Higher cattle prices because of tight supplies caused meatpackers to 24 scale back production at U.S. facilities. Industry officials claim to have lost as many as 8,000 meatpacking jobs because of the closed border.

"I'm just worried that many of those jobs were impacted in a very 25 permanent way," Johanns said. "My hope is that restructuring now will be abated and this industry can start getting back to a normal flow of commerce here."

About 1 million cattle were imported from Canada in the year before 26 the border closed in May 2003 when Canada reported its first case of mad-cow disease, or bovine spongiform encephalopathy.

❯ AT ISSUE: SOURCES FOR AVOIDING PLAGIARISM

1. Identify the passages in the *New York Times* story that you think are too close to the original Bloomberg News story.

2. Identify passages in the other two excerpts that convey the same information as the *Times* story (paraphrased or summarized).

3. In his introduction, Shafer says that the passages from the Toronto *Globe and Mail* and the *Omaha World-Herald* are "starkly different" from the Bloomberg News story. Do you agree?

4. Can you identify any passages in the *Globe and Mail* or *Omaha World-Herald* excerpts that you believe are too close to the original source?

5. On the basis of what you see here, do you agree with Shafer that the *New York Times* reporter is guilty of plagiarism? Explain your conclusion.

This article appeared in the *Washington Post* on September 3, 2004.

HOW TO FIGHT COLLEGE CHEATING

LAWRENCE M. HINMAN

Recent studies have shown that a steadily growing number of students cheat or plagiarize in college—and the data from high schools suggest that this number will continue to rise. A study by Don McCabe of Rutgers University showed that 74 percent of high school students admitted to one or more instances of serious cheating on tests. Even more disturbing is the way that many students define cheating and plagiarism. For example, they believe that cutting and pasting a few sentences from various Web sources without attribution is not plagiarism. 1

Before the Web, students certainly plagiarized—but they had to plan ahead to do so. Fraternities and sororities often had files of term papers, and some high-tech term-paper firms could fax papers to students. Overall, however, plagiarism required forethought. 2

Online term-paper sites changed all that. Overnight, students could order a term paper, print it out and have it ready for class in the morning—and still get a good night's sleep. All they needed was a charge card and an Internet connection. 3

One response to the increase in cheating has been to fight technology with more technology. Plagiarism-checking sites provide a service to screen student papers. They offer a color-coded report on papers and the original sources from which the students might have copied. Colleges qualify for volume discounts, which encourages professors to submit whole classes' worth of papers—the academic equivalent of mandatory urine testing for athletes. 4

> "The cost of both plagiarism and its detection will also undoubtedly continue to spiral."

The technological battle between term-paper mills and anti-plagiarism services will undoubtedly continue to escalate, with each side constructing more elaborate countermeasures to outwit the other. The cost of both plagiarism and its detection will also undoubtedly continue to spiral. 5

But there is another way. Our first and most important line of defense against academic dishonesty is simply good teaching. Cheating and plagiarism often arise in a vacuum created by routine, lack of interest and overwork. Professors who give the same assignment every semester, fail to guide students in the development of their projects and have little interest in what the students have to say contribute to the academic environment in which much cheating and plagiarism occurs. 6

Consider, by way of contrast, professors who know their students and who give assignments that require regular, continuing interaction with them about their projects—and who require students to produce work that is a meaningful development of their own interests. These professors create an environment in which cheating and plagiarism are far less likely to occur. 7

In this context, any plagiarism would usually be immediately evident to the professor, who would see it as inconsistent with the rest of the student's work. A strong, meaningful curriculum taught by committed professors is the first and most important defense against academic dishonesty.

The second remedy is to encourage the development of integrity in our students. A sense of responsibility about one's intellectual development would preclude cheating and plagiarizing as inconsistent with one's identity. It is precisely this sense of individual integrity that schools with honor codes seek to promote. 8

Third, we must encourage our students to perceive the dishonesty of their classmates as something that causes harm to the many students who play by the rules. The argument that cheaters hurt only themselves is false. Cheaters do hurt other people, and they do so to help themselves. Students cheat because it works. They get better grades and more advantages with less effort. Honest students lose grades, scholarships, recommendations and admission to advanced programs. Honest students must create enough peer pressure to dissuade potential cheaters. Ultimately, students must be willing to step forward and confront those who engage in academic dishonesty. 9

Addressing these issues is not a luxury that can be postponed until a more convenient time. It is a short step from dishonesty in schools and colleges to dishonesty in business. It is doubtful that students who fail to develop habits of integrity and honesty while still in an academic setting are likely to do so once they are out in the "real" world. Nor is it likely that adults will stand up against the dishonesty of others, particularly fellow workers and superiors, if they do not develop the habit of doing so while still in school. 10

⊙ AT ISSUE: SOURCES FOR AVOIDING PLAGIARISM

1. In the first five paragraphs of this article, Hinman provides background on how plagiarism by students has been changed by the Internet. Summarize the situations before and after the development of the Internet.

2. The author's thesis appears in paragraph 6. Restate this thesis in your own words.

3. Does Hinman view plagiarism-detection sites as a solution to the problem of college cheating? What are the limitations of such sites?

4. According to Hinman, what steps can professors take to eliminate academic dishonesty?

5. In paragraphs 8 and 9, the author suggests two additional solutions to the problem of plagiarism. What are these remedies? Given what you know about college students, do you think Hinman's suggestions are realistic? Explain.

6. Hinman does not address arguments that challenge his recommendations. What opposing arguments might he have presented? How would you refute these opposing arguments?

This article appeared in the *Chronicle Review* on May 26, 2006.

THE RULES OF ATTRIBUTION

DEBORAH R. GERHARDT

Why do smart students commit plagiarism? Why would a top high-school 1
writer—so accomplished that she would eventually attend Harvard—commit
professional suicide by publishing text copied from another author's popular
novel? In reading the gotcha press coverage on Kaavya Viswanathan's novel
How Opal Mehta Got Kissed, Got Wild, and Got a Life, I can't help wondering how much Ms. Viswanathan knew about copyright infringement and
plagiarism while she was writing. We don't send our high-school basketball
stars onto the court without teaching them the rules of the game, but I fear
that too often we send our high-school writing stars to college and graduate
school without teaching them the academic and legal rules that govern their
creative work.

Ms. Viswanathan's book was inspired by two novels that resonated with 2
her own experience: Megan McCafferty's *Sloppy Firsts* and *Second Helpings*.
She readily admits to having read the novels three or four times. Many passages
are so similar that last month the young novelist was accused of plagiarism and
copyright infringement, and her public comments about those charges reflect
genuine contrition and confusion. She told the *New York Times:* "All I really
want to do is apologize to Ms. McCafferty. I don't want her to think I intended
to cause her distress, because I admire her so much." This month she was
accused of using content from another author's work as well.

In college basketball, the rules are not taught once during a brief orien- 3
tation and then forgotten. They are repeatedly discussed as the season progresses. As we push young writers into the creative arena, the rules of the writing game should get the same attention. Plagiarism rules are not there just to
deter literary thieves. They are codes of honor designed to nurture academic
integrity by teaching students to honor the voices of others on the way to finding their own.

Copyright law cannot be understood without thoughtful reflection, 4
because it contains many contradictions. Copyright protection is not supposed
to extend to facts, ideas, or general plot lines, yet the copyright laws tell us that
the right to create derivative works—for example, a movie from a novel—
belongs exclusively to the author. Copyright laws provide broad protection
for authors and publishers by assuring that their work will not be copied without compensation, yet they still permit fair use, such as copying excerpts for
criticism, comment, or parody. Trying to define the scope of fair use can be a
maddening endeavor, but we would serve our students well by at least alerting
them to the known ends of the spectrum, to give them some compass to guide
them in determining when and how they may use another's content.

We should not expect our students to absorb these complex rules on 5 their own. If we stop to look at our cultural environment through the eyes of Ms. Viswanathan and her peers, we will see that the concepts of plagiarism and copyright are counterintuitive. Copying is essential to learning. When a toddler repeats a word, it is great cause for celebration. That same child will learn to write by copying letters seen in print. In high school and college, students memorize their lecture notes and redeliver this content back to professors on exams, often without the expectation of attribution. The ability to repeat back what they learned (generally without attribution) is richly rewarded.

We encourage our students to recycle objects and ideas they get from others. Discarding paper and plastic in appropriate receptacles has become a routine responsibility in our schools. Students create collages and sculptures from discarded items such as milk jugs and magazines. We assign them to groups to share ideas. We teach them that great writers recycled ideas they found in other great works. A high-school student will learn that Shakespeare brilliantly recast the plot of *Tristan and Isolde* to create *Romeo and Juliet*. She may also learn that Thomas Jefferson could not have drafted the Declaration of Independence without recasting the thoughts of other great philosophers such as John Locke. We would serve our students better if we enriched these lessons with discussions about plagiarism and copyright laws so our students would understand the principles that govern their work in different contexts. They need to learn that they can still work within those principles to create new works inspired by their creative heroes.

When the school day ends, students are inundated with an infinite quantity of recycled content in popular culture. They listen to music that uses famous riffs from other songs. They read books that are turned into movies, and then the characters from those movies appear on an endless array of products, such as breakfast cereals, clothing, toys, and video games. Most students do not know that it takes hours of negotiation and boxes of trademark and copyright licenses to make all this borrowing appear so seamless. The recording industry's lawsuits against students who pirate digital music may

> "Sometimes copyright laws also prohibit copying smaller portions of a work."

have taught our students that copying an entire work can get them in trouble. We must alert our students to the reality that sometimes copyright laws also prohibit copying smaller portions of a work.

It is quite possible—and I believe likely—that Ms Viswanathan's editors 8 and advisers pushed her to write and publish without first taking the time to explain to her the basic principles of plagiarism and copyright. Much of the alleged copying in her work is not verbatim lifting but the creative recycling of ideas. The rules of what can be borrowed and when attribution must be given are complex and require vigilant attention. She confessed to the *New York Times:* "I feel as confused as anyone about it, because it happened so many times." It is so unfortunate to see a promising young writer taken out of the game because she did not understand the rules. My hope is that this incident will motivate parents and educators to remember that creative work has its rules, and if they want to stay in the game, our students should know them.

⊝ AT ISSUE: SOURCES FOR AVOIDING PLAGIARISM

1. Gerhardt opens her essay with a question. How (and where) does she answer this question? Can you supply additional answers?

2. On whom (or what) does Gerhardt place the blame for plagiarism? Do you agree with her, or would you argue that the blame lies elsewhere?

3. Explain the analogy that the author makes between student writers and student basketball stars. Is this a valid analogy? Do you think it strengthens her argument?

4. What is the purpose of Gerhardt's discussion of recycling in paragraphs 6 and 7? Is this discussion an effective addition to her argument? Why or why not?

5. Gerhardt's discussion begins by focusing on a college student who committed plagiarism and copyright infringement in a novel she wrote. How does Gerhardt tie this young woman's story to the problems with plagiarism faced by college students in general? Should she have done more to establish this connection?

This article appeared in *Newsday* on May 18, 2003.

THE TRUTH ABOUT PLAGIARISM

RICHARD A. POSNER

Plagiarism is considered by most writers, teachers, journalists, scholars and even members of the general public to be the capital intellectual crime. Being caught out in plagiarism can blast a politician's career, earn a college student expulsion and destroy a writer's, scholar's or journalist's reputation. In recent days, for example, the *New York Times* has referred to "widespread fabrication and plagiarism" by reporter Jayson Blair as "a low point in the 152-year history of the newspaper." 1

In James Hynes' splendid satiric novella of plagiarism, *Casting the Runes*, the plagiarist, having by black magic murdered one of the historians whom he plagiarized and tried to murder a second, is himself killed by the very same black magic, deployed by the widow of his murder victim. 2

There is a danger of overkill. Plagiarism can be a form of fraud, but it is no accident that, unlike real theft, it is not a crime. If a thief steals your car, you are out the market value of the car, but if a writer copies material from a book you wrote, you don't have to replace the book. At worst, the undetected plagiarist obtains a reputation that he does not deserve (that is the element of fraud in plagiarism). The real victim of his fraud is not the person whose work he copies, but those of his competitors who scruple to enhance their own reputations by such means. 3

> "There is a danger of overkill."

The most serious plagiarisms are by students and professors, whose undetected plagiarisms disrupt the system of student and scholarly evaluation. The least serious are those that earned the late Stephen Ambrose and Dorothy Kearns Goodwin such obloquy last year. Popular historians, they jazzed up their books with vivid passages copied from previous historians without quotation marks, though with footnote attributions that made their "crime" easy to detect. 4

(One reason that plagiarism, like littering, is punished heavily, even though an individual act of plagiarism usually does little or no harm, is that it is normally very difficult to detect—but not in the case of Ambrose and Goodwin.) Competing popular historians might have been injured, but I'm not aware of anyone actually claiming this. 5

Confusion of plagiarism with theft is one reason plagiarism engenders indignation; another is a confusion of it with copyright infringement. Wholesale copying of copyrighted material is an infringement of a property right, and legal remedies are available to the copyright holder. But the copying of brief passages, even from copyrighted materials, is permissible under the doctrine of "fair use," while wholesale copying from material that is in the public domain—material that never was copyrighted, or on which the copyright has expired—presents no copyright issue at all. 6

Plagiarism of work in the public domain is more common than otherwise. 7
Consider a few examples: *West Side Story* is a thinly veiled copy (with music
added) of *Romeo and Juliet*, which in turn plagiarized Arthur Brooke's *The
Tragicall Historye of Romeo and Juliet*, published in 1562, which in turn copied
from several earlier Romeo and Juliets, all of which were copies of Ovid's story
of Pyramus and Thisbe.

Paradise Lost plagiarizes the book of Genesis in the Old Testament. Classi- 8
cal musicians plagiarize folk melodies (think only of Dvorak, Bartok, and Cop-
land) and often "quote" (as musicians say) from earlier classical works. Edouard
Manet's most famous painting. *Dejeuner sur l'herbe*, copies earlier paintings by
Raphael, Titian, and Courbet, and *My Fair Lady* plagiarized Shaw's play *Pyg-
malion*, while Woody Allen's movie *Play It Again, Sam* "quotes" a famous scene
from *Casablanca*. Countless movies are based on books, such as *The Thirty-
Nine Steps* on John Buchan's novel of that name or *For Whom the Bell Tolls* on
Hemingway's novel.

Many of these "plagiarisms" were authorized, and perhaps none was 9
deceptive; they are what Christopher Ricks in his excellent book *Allusions to
the Poets* helpfully terms *allusion* rather than *plagiarism*. But what they show is
that copying with variations is an important form of creativity, and this should
make us prudent and measured in our condemnations of plagiarism.

Especially when the term is extended from literal copying to the copying 10
of ideas. Another phrase for copying an idea, as distinct from the form in
which it is expressed, is dissemination of ideas. If one needs a license to
repeat another person's idea, or if one risks ostracism by one's professional
community for failing to credit an idea to its originator, who may be forgotten
or unknown, the dissemination of ideas is impeded.

I have heard authors of history textbooks criticized for failing to document 11
their borrowing of ideas from previous historians. This is an absurd criticism.
The author of a textbook makes no claim to originality; rather the contrary—
the most reliable, if not necessarily the most exciting, textbook is one that
confines itself to ideas already well accepted, not at all novel.

It would be better if the term *plagiarism* were confined to literal copying, 12
and moreover literal copying that is not merely unacknowledged but deceptive. Failing to give credit where credit is due should be regarded as a lesser,
indeed usually merely venial, offense.

The concept of plagiarism has expanded, and the sanctions for it, though 13
they remain informal rather than legal, have become more severe, in tandem
with the rise of individualism. Journal articles are no longer published anony-
mously, and ghostwriters demand that their contributions be acknowledged.

Individualism and a cult of originality go hand in hand. Each of us sup- 14
poses that our contribution to society is unique rather than fungible and so
deserves public recognition, which plagiarism clouds.

This is a modern view. We should be aware that the high value placed on 15
originality is a specific cultural, and even field-specific, phenomenon, rather
than an aspect of the universal moral law.

Judges, who try to conceal rather than to flaunt their originality, far from 16
crediting their predecessors with original thinking like to pretend that there
is no original thinking in law, that judges are just a transmission belt for rules
and principles laid down by the framers of statutes or the Constitution.

Resorting to plagiarism to obtain a good grade or a promotion is fraud and 17
should be punished, though it should not be confused with "theft." But I think the
zeal to punish plagiarism reflects less a concern with the real injuries that it occasionally inflicts than with a desire on the part of leaders of professional communities, such as journalists and historians, to enhance their profession's reputation.

Journalists (like politicians) have a bad reputation for truthfulness, and 18
historians, in this "postmodernist"° era, are suspected of having embraced
an extreme form of relativism and of having lost their regard for facts. Both
groups hope by taking a very hard line against plagiarism and fabrication to
reassure the public that they are serious diggers after truth whose efforts, a
form of "sweat equity," deserve protection against copycats.

Their anxieties are understandable; but the rest of us will do well to keep 19
the matter in perspective, realizing that the term *plagiarism* is used loosely and
often too broadly; that much plagiarism is harmless and (when the term is
defined broadly) that some has social value.

*Postmodernism is a school of
criticism that denies concepts
such as scientific certainty and
absolute truth.*

⊘ AT ISSUE: SOURCES FOR AVOIDING PLAGIARISM

1. According to Posner, how do most people define *plagiarism*? How is
   his definition different from theirs?

2. Why does Posner believe that the plagiarisms committed by students
   and professors are the most serious? Can you present an argument
   against this position?

3. How do the examples Posner cites in paragraphs 7 and 8 strengthen
   the main argument of his essay?

4. Explain the connection the author makes in paragraph 16 between
   judges and plagiarism. (Note that Posner himself is a federal judge.)

5. Why, according to Posner, do journalists and historians think plagiarism should be punished severely?

6. According to Posner, "the truth about plagiarism" is "that much plagiarism is harmless and (when the term is defined broadly) that some
   has social value" (19). Does the evidence he presents in this essay
   support this conclusion? What connection do you see between this
   position and his comments about the rise of individualism and "the
   cult of originality" in paragraphs 13–15?

Time magazine originally published this article on January 27, 2002.

HOW I CAUSED THAT STORY

DORIS KEARNS GOODWIN

1 I am a historian. With the exception of being a wife and mother, it is who I am. And there is nothing I take more seriously.

2 In recent days, questions have been raised about how historians go about crediting their sources, and I have been caught up in the swirl. Ironically, the more intensive and far-reaching a historian's research, the greater the difficulty of citation. As the mountain of material grows, so does the possibility of error.

3 Fourteen years ago, not long after the publication of my book *The Fitzgeralds and the Kennedys*, I received a communication from author Lynne McTaggart pointing out that material from her book on Kathleen Kennedy had not been properly attributed. I realized that she was right. Though my footnotes repeatedly cited Ms. McTaggart's work, I failed to provide quotation marks for phrases that I had taken verbatim, having assumed that these phrases, drawn from my notes, were my words, not hers. I made the corrections she requested, and the matter was completely laid to rest—until last week, when the *Weekly Standard* published an article reviving the issue. The larger question for those of us who write history is to understand how citation mistakes can happen.

4 The research and writing for this 900-page book, with its 3,500 footnotes, took place over 10 years. At that time, I wrote my books and took my notes in longhand, believing I could not think well on a keyboard. Most of my sources were drawn from a multitude of primary materials: manuscript collections, private letters, diaries, oral histories, newspapers, periodicals, personal interviews. After three years of research, I discovered more than 150 cartons of materials that had been previously stored in the attic of Joe Kennedy's Hyannis Port house. These materials were a treasure trove for a historian—old report cards, thousands of family letters, movie stubs and diaries, which allowed me to cross the boundaries of time and space. It took me two additional years to read, categorize and take notes on these documents.

5 During this same period, I took handwritten notes on perhaps 300 books. Passages I wanted to quote directly were noted along with general notes on the ideas and story lines of each book. Notes on all these sources were then arranged chronologically and kept in dozens of folders in 25 banker's boxes. Immersed in a flood of papers, I began to write the book. After each section and each chapter was completed, I returned the notes to the boxes along with notations for future footnoting. When the manuscript was finished, I went back to all these sources to check the accuracy of attributions. As a final protection, I revisited the 300 books themselves. Somehow

> "Somehow . . . a few of the books were not fully rechecked."

in this process, a few of the books were not fully rechecked. I relied instead on my notes, which combined direct quotes and paraphrased sentences. If I had had the books in front of me, rather than my notes, I would have caught mistakes in the first place and placed any borrowed phrases in direct quotes.

What made this incident particularly hard for me was the fact that I take 6 great pride in the depth of my research and the extensiveness of my citations. The writing of history is a rich process of building on the work of the past with the hope that others will build on what you have done. Through footnotes you point the way to future historians.

The only protection as a historian is to institute a process of research and 7 writing that minimizes the possibility of error. And that I have tried to do, aided by modern technology, which enables me, having long since moved beyond longhand, to use a computer for both organizing and taking notes. I now rely on a scanner, which reproduces the passages I want to cite, and then I keep my own comments on those books in a separate file so that I will never confuse the two again. But the real miracle occurred when my college-age son taught me how to use the mysterious footnote key on the computer, which makes it possible to insert the citations directly into the text while the sources are still in front of me, instead of shuffling through hundreds of folders four or five years down the line, trying desperately to remember from where I derived a particular statistic or quote. Still, there is no guarantee against error. Should one occur, all I can do, as I did 14 years ago, is to correct it as soon as I possibly can, for my own sake and the sake of history. In the end, I am still the same fallible person I was before I made the transition to the computer, and the process of building a lengthy work of history remains a complicated but honorable task.

⊃ AT ISSUE: SOURCES FOR AVOIDING PLAGIARISM

1. The purpose of Goodwin's essay is to explain (and perhaps to justify) her plagiarism. What evidence does she offer to support her explanation?

2. Why might Goodwin's audience be hostile to her explanations?

3. What efforts does the author make to establish common ground with her readers? To show that she is a reasonable person? To establish her credibility?

4. Goodwin writes in personal terms, devoting much of her essay to an explanation of her research methods. What does she gain or lose with this approach?

5. Do you find Goodwin's argument convincing? Would her essay have been more convincing if she had included additional support? What other kinds of support could she have included?

This piece first appeared on September 15, 2006 in the *Chronicle Review.*

COPY THIS

CAROLYN FOSTER SEGAL

1 Not all plagiarists achieve fame and in-depth coverage by the *New York Times*, the *Wall Street Journal*, and the *Chronicle*; most are students toiling in relative obscurity, cutting and pasting or lifting in its entirety the work of others. Intellectual-property rights° in the 21st century may indeed be pre-empted by a return to the centuries-earlier, precopyright practice of "If I find a poem nailed to the church door, I can simply change the names and make it mine." In place of the church door, we have the global window of the computer. Technology has raised the crafty business of plagiarism and its detection to a whole new level.

Legal claims on creative products, such as computer codes or literary works

2 My college has both an honor code and an ethics program. It also has an official but vague policy on plagiarism, which leaves the final determination of punitive measures up to the individual instructor; the college does ask instructors to file a report with the provost's office. In the first week of the semester, I hand out a syllabus with a description of and warning about plagiarism. I also spend time in that first week and throughout the semester describing ways to present secondary sources (direct quotation, paraphrase, summary); the categories of plagiarism (poor or lazy formatting of sources, unintentional, intentional); and the consequences of plagiarism (a grade of F for the paper, and, at my discretion, a grade of F for the course).

3 As I outline the categories of venal and mortal transgressions, I'm often reminded of Sister Mary Helen, my second-grade teacher, who drew an illustration of the soul on the backboard: a chalk circle, which she then filled with a snowstorm of dots representing our sins. A colleague of mine has created a marvelous high-tech version of his lecture on the sin of plagiarism, a Web site with allusions to Dante and the eighth circle of hell.° Neither threat of failure nor fear of everlasting damnation, however, seems to deter some students.

Dante Alighieri (1265–1321) was an Italian writer best known for his work The Divine Comedy, *which describes a journey through the afterlife, including a visit to hell.*

4 Even an emphasis on the process of writing—an earthly procedure more concrete than threats of divine retribution, involving drafts and peer-review sessions—does not stop some students, who will brazen their way through a barrage of probing questions in workshops. Their final papers usually feature blocks of silky-smooth contraband prose, interspersed with ungrammatical and unclear changes designed to cover up their theft.

5 For it is theft, plain and simple—or, more accurately, complex—as I tell my students. It is theft of another writer's ideas, work, and time; it is theft of their fellow students' time; it is theft of their own time, honor, and education; and it is theft of my time—minutes, hours, and days—that I'd rather spend

reading, writing, or watching a softball game. And not only is it unethical, it's foolish. One of my husband's degrees is in library science—he once worked as a reference librarian—and I supported myself through most of graduate school by working in libraries. I teach research methods, for God's sake. I also have a tech wizard living in my basement—my 17-year-old daughter. "So just don't do it," I tell my students.

And most of them don't—not because of all my lectures, but because they 6 are honest, love writing, and want to learn how to do it better. Over time, their hard work has made the plagiarism by the few all the more appalling to me.

The most recent incident involved a student's submitting a retitled appro- 7 priation of the poem "When We Two Parted," complete with "thee" and "thy," for her final project in "Creative Writing: Poetry." Charmed by a blogger's use of the lines, the student had apparently traced them to another blog created by someone who is a big fan of a writer he calls "George Gordon" (the poet formerly known as Lord George Gordon Byron). In another inci- dent, in a nonfiction class, a student pre-

> "In terms of detection, this was a personal best: It took me 30 seconds."

sented as her own work the text of a 2004 online human-resources guide. In terms of detection, this was a personal best: It took me 30 seconds to find the site after typing in one of the subheadings.

On another occasion, I didn't have to search at all: After a creative-writing 8 student ended her dramatic reading of her newest attempt, the student sitting next to her said, "Why am I thinking of *The Last Unicorn*?" As a quick click verified, she was thinking of Jimmy Webb's theme song for the animated film because the student had appropriated the lyrics.

The most outstanding act of plagiarism by a student I have encountered— 9 an act of theft surrounded by a virtual web of lies—occurred two years ago in a nonfiction class, "Writing for Publication," and involved a woman who should have known better. G. was in her 40s and in her senior year; her major was information technology. At the beginning of the semester, I gave my usual lecture on the need for both students and professional writers to cite or handle sources responsibly. For the first workshop, G. brought a piece called "Ten Ways for Working Students to Cope with Stress." It was of nearly publishable quality, but there was something strange about it. Polished and professional, it lacked only one thing—or, more precisely, one part of speech. It contained no articles—the omission apparently a clever attempt to disguise the act of plagiarism.

I found "10 Ways the Working Student Can Cope with Stress" online in 10 10 minutes. The eighth listing of a search, the piece was a publication of the Counseling Center at the University of Pittsburgh. (I simply typed in the key words "ten ways cope stress," conscious of the fact that now I too had been reduced to eliminating all articles.) I e-mailed the student, asking her to meet with me before the next day's class; then I returned to the site, hoping to find some additional tips on stress.

The student had agreed to come in at 11 a.m. In preparation, I printed 11
out the online article and typed up a report. I made duplicate copies—of
the article, the student's paper, my report, my assignment sheet, my rubric,
the course's syllabus with the sections on plagiarism highlighted—for the
chairman of my department, the acting provost, the student's adviser, and
the director of the advising center. The student arrived at 12:30 p.m., an
hour and a half late and just half an hour before our class was scheduled
to meet. I asked G. to tell me about her process, and she began: She had to
find a topic, make notes, and "get just the right words." I was tempted to
jump up like Perry Mason, wave the printout of the original article, and say
sternly, "And you got them right here, didn't you?" but I waited. "My only
concern," she said, and then paused. I wanted her to tell me that she didn't
"get" the assignment—really, both of our lives would have been simpler and
happier, and I wouldn't have to send off all those packets of duplicates. "My
only concern," she continued, "is that I didn't do the heading correctly, and
so I won't get an A."

I explained that the format, while incorrect, was not my greatest worry, 12
and that, in fact, I had a far more serious concern—plagiarism. And so began
the stages of plagiarism grief:

Disbelief: How could I accuse her?
Denial: This was her own original work.
Astonishment: How could she and someone else have produced identical
    texts?
Confusion, Part 1: She forgot to acknowledge her source.
Confusion, Part 2: My assignment was not clear; she didn't realize that she
    actually had to produce her own original work.
Plea No. 1: No one could ever produce original work on her topic (which
    had been her choice).
Plea No. 2: Allow her to add a citation now.
Plea No. 3: Allow her to redo the assignment and remain in the course.
Plea No. 4: She didn't just cut and paste; she typed the entire essay herself.
Plea No. 5: Change the grade for the paper to C, on the grounds of the
    above.
Plea No. 6: All right, give the paper an F; just don't award a final grade
    of F.
Defense: I never mentioned plagiarism in class.
Accusation: I am mean and unfair.

My plagiarist tried—unsuccessfully—to withdraw from the course to 13
avoid her F and, when that didn't work, appealed my charges. Despite the student's protests and appeals, both my chairman and acting provost supported
my decision to award the student a final grade of F for the course (possibly the
earliest-recorded final grade in the history of academe). The following semester, G. repeated the course with another instructor in order to, as her adviser
said, "*reclaim* [emphasis mine] her good name."

I've had work of my own used without my permission. One of my essays 14 appeared online both as part of a fundamentalist church's newsletter (the theme of the issue was honesty) and as required reading for a journalism course. In reply to my letter of complaint, the pastor of the church pointed out—uncharitably—that he knew of two other Web sites where my pirated work appeared and that "at least we included your name." The professor of the journalism course never answered my letter. According to her home-page bio, she had a degree in journalism ethics.

It's the brave/sad new world of the Internet, where every blogbaby can 15 have his or her Warholian 15 minutes of fame; it's a global market with everything ripe for the picking; it's the new frontier with no law and no order. On one of the days that the grievance process with G. was tediously unwinding, my in-house information specialist, my technology-savvy daughter, sent me an e-mail message at work. She wanted me to check out a hit she had found on Google: A term-paper company was selling essays about an article of mine on student excuses.

⊃ AT ISSUE: SOURCES FOR AVOIDING PLAGIARISM

1. How does Segal define *plagiarism*? How have her personal and professional experiences shaped her view of plagiarism?

2. How is Segal's definition of *plagiarism* different from Richard Posner's (p. 302)? In what sense are the views she expresses in paragraph 4 a refutation of the comments Lawrence M. Hinman (p. 297) makes about professors' responsibility to eliminate plagiarism?

3. Most of Segal's essay (paragraphs 7–13) consists of anecdotes about students who have committed plagiarism, Segal's discovery of their dishonesty, and her confrontations with them. How do these anecdotes support the sentiments she expresses in paragraph 6?

4. As a student, do you find Segal's essay mean-spirited? Do you think she should have balanced her negative examples with anecdotes about her other students—those who "are honest" and "love writing" (6)? Why or why not?

⊘ EXERCISE 11.4

Write a one-paragraph argument in which you take a position on where to draw the line with plagiarism. Follow the template below, filling in the blanks to create your argument.

Template for Writing an Argument about Plagiarism

To many people, plagiarism is theft; to others, however, it is not a simple issue. For example, some define plagiarism as _____; others see it as _____. Another thing to consider is _____. In addition, _____. Despite these differences of opinion, plagiarism is often dealt with harshly and can ruin careers and reputations. All things considered,_____.

⊘ EXERCISE 11.5

Discuss your feelings about plagiarism with two or three of your class-mates. Consider how you define *plagiarism*, what causes it, whether there are degrees of dishonesty, and so on, but focus on the *effects* of plagiarism—on those who commit it and on those who are its victims. Then, write a paragraph that summarizes the key points of your discussion.

⊘ EXERCISE 11.6

Write an argumentative essay on the topic, "Where Do We Draw the Line with Plagiarism?" Begin by defining what you mean by *plagiarism*, and then narrow your discussion down to a particular group—for example, high school or college students, historians, scientists, or journalists. Cite the sources on pages 293–310, and be sure to document the sources you use and to include a works-cited page. (See Chapter 10 for information on documenting sources.)

⊘ EXERCISE 11.7 🏛

Review the four pillars of argument discussed in Chapter 1. Does your essay include all four elements of an effective argument? Add anything that is missing. Then, label the elements of your argument.

⊗ WRITING ASSIGNMENTS: AVOIDING PLAGIARISM

1. Write an argument in which you take a position on who (or what) is to blame for plagiarism among college students. Is plagiarism always the student's fault, or are other people (or other factors) at least partly to blame?

2. Write an essay in which you argue that an honor code will (or will not) eliminate (or at least reduce) plagiarism and other kinds of academic cheating at your school.

3. Reread the essays by Posner and Goodwin in this chapter. Then, write an argument in which you argue that only intentional plagiarism should be punished.

4. Do you consider student plagiarism a victimless crime that is best left unpunished? If so, why? If not, how does it affect its victims—for example, the student who plagiarizes, the instructor, the class, and the school?

Patterns and Purposes

WIKIPEDIA
The Free Encyclopedia

Argument by Definition

Is *Wikipedia* a Legitimate Research Source?

Wikipedia—the open-source online encyclopedia—is probably the most frequently used reference source on the planet. Recently, however, the reliability of *Wikipedia* has been called into question. Because almost anyone can write and edit entries, articles can—and do—contain errors. Over time, many errors get corrected, but some do not, perhaps because no one person or group is responsible for quality control. As a result, many college instructors question the reliability of *Wikipedia* as a research source. In fact, academic departments at some schools—for example, the history department at Middlebury College—have banned students from citing *Wikipedia* as a source. According to Don Wyatt, chair of the department, "Even though *Wikipedia* may have some value, particularly in leading students to citable sources, it is not itself an appropriate source for citation." Others disagree, pointing out that *Wikipedia* contains no more (and in some cases fewer) factual errors than respected print encyclopedias.

Later in this chapter, you will be asked to think more about this issue. You will be given several research sources to consider and asked to write an **argument by definition** that takes a position on whether *Wikipedia* is a legitimate research source.

What Is Argument by Definition?

When you write an argumentative essay that depends on your definition of a key term, it makes sense to structure your argument as an **argument by definition**. In this type of essay, you will argue that something fits (or does not fit) the definition of a particular class of items. For example, to argue that graffiti is art, you have to define *art* and then show that graffiti fits this definition.

Many arguments focus on definition. In fact, you encounter them so often that you probably do not recognize them for what they are. For example, look at the following questions:

- Do minorities receive quality health care?
- Is product placement in movies unethical?
- Should the rich pay more taxes than others?
- Are SUVs bad for the environment?
- Is cheerleading really a sport?
- Is *Wikipedia* a legitimate research source?

You cannot answer these questions without providing definitions. In fact, if you were writing an argumentative essay in response to one of these questions, much of your essay would be devoted to defining and discussing a key term.

QUESTION	KEY TERM TO BE DEFINED
Do minorities receive quality health care?	*quality*
Is product placement in movies unethical?	*unethical*
Should the rich pay more taxes than others?	*rich*
Are SUVs bad for the environment?	*bad*
Is cheerleading really a sport?	*sport*
Is *Wikipedia* a legitimate research source?	*legitimate research source*

Many contemporary social and legal disputes involve argument by definition. For example, did a coworker's actions constitute *sexual harassment*? Is an individual trying to enter the United States a *political refugee* or an *illegal alien*? Is a combatant a *terrorist* or a *freedom fighter*? Is a person guilty of *murder* or of *manslaughter*? Did soldiers engage in *torture* or in *aggressive questioning*? Was the magazine cover *satirical* or *racist*? Is the punishment *just,* or is it *cruel and unusual*? These and other arguments hinge on definitions of key terms.

Keep in mind, however, that definitions can change as our thinking about certain issues changes. For example, a joke that would have been acceptable thirty years ago might now be considered racist or sexist. Our definition of what constitutes cruel and unusual punishment has also changed. Public hanging, a common method of execution for hundreds of years, is now considered barbaric.

The last public hanging in the United States (Owensboro, Kentucky, August 14, 1936)

Developing Definitions

The success of an argument by definition depends on your ability to define a term so that readers (even those who do not agree with your position) will see its validity. For this reason, the rhetorical strategies you use to develop your definitions are very important. Arguments by definition will typically include one or more of the following approaches.

Dictionary Definitions (Formal Definitions)

When most people think of definitions, they think of the formal definitions they find in a dictionary. Typically, a formal **dictionary definition** consists of the term to be defined, the general class to which the term belongs, and the qualities that differentiate the term from other items in the same class.

TERM	CLASS	DIFFERENTIATION
dog	a domesticated mammal	that has a long snout, a keen sense of smell, and a barking voice
naturalism	a literary movement	whose followers believed that writers should treat their characters' lives with scientific objectivity

Extended Definitions

Although an argument by definition may include a short dictionary definition, a short definition is usually not enough to define a complex or abstract term. For example, if you were arguing that *Wikipedia* was a *legitimate research source,* you would have to include an **extended definition**, explaining to readers in some detail what you mean by this term and perhaps giving examples of research sources that fit your definition.

Writing the Declaration of Independence, 1776 by Jean Leon Gerome Ferris (Virginia Historical Society)

Examples are often used to develop an extended definition in an argumentative essay. For instance, you could give examples to make the case that a particular baseball player, despite his struggles with substance abuse, is a great athlete. You could define *great athlete* solely in terms of athletic prowess, presenting several examples of other talented athletes and then showing that the baseball player you are discussing possesses the same qualities.

For your examples to be effective, they have to be relevant to your argument. Your examples also have to represent (or at least suggest) the full range of opinion concerning your subject. Finally, you have to make sure that your readers will accept your examples as typical, not unusual. For example in the Declaration of Independence (p. 679), Thomas Jefferson presented twenty-five paragraphs of examples to support his extended definition of the king's tyranny. With these examples, he hoped to convince the world that the colonists were justified in breaking away from England. To accomplish his goal, Jefferson made sure that his examples supported his position, that they represented the full range of abuses, and that they were not unusual or atypical.

Operational Definitions

Whereas a dictionary definition tells what a term is, an **operational definition** defines something by telling how it acts or works. An operational definition transforms an abstract concept into something concrete, observable, and possibly measurable. Children instinctively understand the concept of operational definitions. When a parent tells them to *behave,* they know what the components of this operational definition are: clean up your room, obey your parents, come home on time, and do your homework. Researchers in the natural sciences and social sciences constantly have to come up with operational definitions to support their arguments. For example, if they are arguing that childhood obesity is a serious problem, they have to construct an operational definition of *obese.* At what point does a child become obese? Does he or she have to be 10% above the norm? More? Researchers must agree on this operational definition before they can carry out their study.

Structuring an Argument by Definition

In general terms, an argument by definition can be structured as follows:

- **Introduction:** Establishes a context for the argument by explaining the need for defining the term; presents the essay's thesis

- **Evidence (first point in support of thesis):** Provides a short definition of the term as well as an extended definition (if necessary)

- **Evidence (second point in support of thesis):** Shows how the term does or does not fit the definition

- **Refutation of opposing arguments:** Addresses questions about or objections to the definition; considers other possible meanings (if any)

- **Conclusion:** Reinforces the main point of the argument; includes a strong concluding statement

The following student essay includes all the elements of an argument by definition. The student who wrote this essay is trying to convince his university that he is a nontraditional student and is therefore entitled to the benefits such students receive.

WHY I AM A NONTRADITIONAL STUDENT
ADAM KENNEDY

1   Ever since I started college, I have had difficulty getting the extra help I need to succeed. My final disappointment came last week when my adviser told me that I could not take advantage of the programs the school offers to nontraditional students. She told me that because I am not old enough, I simply do not qualify. This is confusing to me because I am anything but a "traditional" student. In fact, I am one of the most nontraditional students I know. In spite of my age—I am twenty-two—I have had experiences that separate me from most other students my age. The problem is that the school's definition of the term *nontraditional* is so narrow that it excludes people like me who should be able to qualify.

2   According to the National Center for Educational Statistics Web site, the term *nontraditional student* is difficult to define. For this reason, the center uses an operational definition to define the term. In other words, the definition is based on whether a student has any of the following characteristics ("Special Analysis"):

- Did not enter college right after high school
- Is a part-time student

Introduction

Thesis statement

Evidence: Operational definition of a *nontraditional student*

- Has a full-time job
- Has children or a spouse
- Has a GED instead of a high school diploma

Many colleges use similar criteria to define *nontraditional student*. 3
For example, Northern Illinois University provides special services
for commuters as well as for older students. In fact, it has a special
department—Commuter and Non-Traditional Student Services—to meet
these students' needs. The university Web site says that a nontraditional
student is someone who lives off campus, commutes from home, has
children, is a veteran, or is over the age of twenty-five ("Commuter").

According to the criteria listed above, I would have no problem 4
qualifying as a nontraditional student at Northern Illinois University. Our
school, however, has a much narrower definition of the term. When I
went to Non-Traditional Student Services, I was told that my case did
not fit into any of the categories that the school had established. Here, a
nontraditional student is someone who is twenty-five or older, period. The
person I spoke to said that the school's intention is to give special help to
older students who are matriculating into the university. I was then told
that I could appeal and try to convince the dean of Non-Traditional Student
Services that I do not fit the definition of a traditional student.

By any measure, I am not a "traditional student." After getting 5
married at seventeen, I dropped out of high school and got a full-time
job. Soon, my wife and I began to resent our situation. She was still a
high school student and missed being able to go out with her friends
whenever she wanted to. I hated my job and missed being a student.
Before long, we decided it was best to get divorced. Instead of going
back to high school, however, I enlisted in the Army National Guard—
just to get my head together. After two years, I had completed a tour in
Iraq as well as my GED. As soon as I was released from active duty, I
enrolled in college—all this before I turned twenty-one.

I can see how someone could say that I am too young to be a 6
nontraditional student. However, I believe that my life experiences
should qualify me for this program. My marriage and divorce, time
in the army, and reentry issues make me very different from the
average first-year student. The special resources available to students
who qualify for this program—tutors, financial aid, special advising,

Evidence: School's definition of a nontraditional student

Evidence: How writer fits the definition of nontraditional student

Refutation

support groups, and subsidized housing—would make my adjustment to college a lot easier. I am only four years older than the average first-year student, but that doesn't mean that I am anything like them. The focus on age to define *nontraditional* ignores the fact that students younger than twenty-five may also have followed very untraditional paths to college. Life experience, not age, should be the main factor in determining whether a student is nontraditional.

7   The university should expand the definition of *nontraditional* to include younger students who have followed unconventional career paths and have postponed college. Even though these students may be younger than twenty-five, they face challenges similar to those faced by older students. Students like me are returning to school in increasing numbers. Our situation may be different from that of others our age, but that is exactly why we need all the help we can get.

Conclusion

Concluding statement

Works Cited

"Commuter and Non-Traditional Student Services." *Division of Student Affairs and Enrollment Management.* Northern Illinois U, 2009. Web. 12 Oct. 2009.

"Special Analysis 2002: Nontraditional Undergraduates." *The Condition of Education.* Natl. Center for Educ. Statistics, 2002. Web. 12 Oct. 2009.

GRAMMAR IN CONTEXT: AVOIDING *IS WHERE* AND *IS WHEN*

When you write an **argument by definition**, you often include a **formal definition**, which is made up of the term that you are defining, the class to which the term belongs, and the characteristics that distinguish your term from other items in the same class.

In a formal definition, you may sometimes find yourself using the phrase *is where* or *is when*. If so, your definition is incomplete because it omits the term's class. The use of *is where* or *is when* signals that you are giving an example of the term, not a definition. You can avoid this problem by making sure that the verb *be* in your definition is always followed by a noun.

(continued)

(*continued*)

INCORRECT	The university Web site says that a nontraditional student **is when** you live off campus, commute from home, have children, are a veteran, and are over the age of twenty-five.
CORRECT	The university Web site says that a nontraditional student is **someone** who lives off campus, commutes from home, has children, is a veteran, and is over the age of twenty-five.

➲ EXERCISE 12.1

The following essay, "The Wife-Beater" by Gayle Rosenwald Smith, includes the basic elements of an argument by definition. Read the essay, and then answer the questions that follow it, consulting the outline on pages 318–319 if necessary.

This essay appeared in the *Philadelphia Inquirer* on July 2, 2001.

THE WIFE-BEATER

GAYLE ROSENWALD SMITH

Everybody wears them. The Gap sells them. Fashion designers Dolce and 1
Gabbana have lavished them with jewels. Their previous greatest resurgence occurred in the 1950s, when Marlon Brando's Stanley Kowalski wore one in Tennessee Williams' *A Streetcar Named Desire*. They are all the rage.

What are they called? 2

The name is the issue. For they are known as "wife-beaters." 3

A Web search shows that kids nation- 4
wide are wearing the skinny-ribbed white T-shirts that can be worn alone or under another shirt. Women have adopted
them with the same gusto as men. A search of boutiques shows that these wearers include professionals who wear them, adorned with designer accessories, under their pricey suits. They are available in all colors, sizes and price ranges.

"The name is the issue."

Wearers under 25 do not seem to be disturbed by the name. But I sure am. 5

It's an odd name for an undershirt. And even though the ugly ste- 6
reotypes behind the name are both obvious and toxic, it appears to be
cool to say the name without fear of (or without caring about) hurting
anyone.

That the name is fueled by stereotype is now an academically established 7
fact, although various sources disagree on exactly when shirt and name came
together. The *Oxford Dictionary* defines the term *wife-beater* as:

1. A man who physically abuses his wife and

2. Tank-style underwear shirts. Origin: based on the stereotype that physically abusive husbands wear that particular type of shirt.

The *World Book Dictionary* locates the origin of the term *wife-beater* in 8
the 1970s, from the stereotype of the Midwestern male wearing an undershirt while beating his wife. The shirts are said to have been popular in the
1980s at all types of sporting events, especially ones at which one sits in the
sun and develops "wife-beater marks." The undershirts also attained popularity at wet T-shirt contests, in which the wet, ribbed tees accentuated con-
testants' breasts.

In an article in the style section of the *New York Times*, Jesse 9
Scheidlower, principal editor of the *Oxford English Dictionary*'s American
office, says the association of the undershirt and the term *wife-beater* arose
in 1997 from varied sources, including gay and gang subcultures and rap
music.

In the article, some sources argued that the reference in the term was not 10
to spousal abuse per se but to popular-culture figures such as Ralph Cramden
and Tony Soprano. And what about Archie Bunker?

It's not just the name that worries me. Fashion headlines reveal that 11
we want to overthrow '90s grunge and return to shoulder pads and hard-
ware-studded suits. Am I reading too much into a fashion statement that
the return is also to male dominance where physical abuse is acceptable as a
means of control?

There has to be a better term. After all, it's a pretty rare piece of clothing 12
that can make both men and women look sexier. You'd expect a term connot-
ing flattery—not violence.

Wearers under 25 may not want to hear this, but here it is. More than 13
4 million women are victims of severe assaults by boyfriends and husbands
each year. By conservative estimate, family violence occurs in 2 million families each year in the United States. Average age of the batterer: 31.

Possibly the last statistic is telling. Maybe youth today would rather ignore 14
the overtones of the term *wife-beater*. It is also true, however, that the children
of abusers often learn the behavior from their elders.

Therein lies perhaps the worst difficulty: that this name for this shirt 15
teaches the wrong thing about men. Some articles quote women who felt the

shirts looked great, especially on guys with great bodies. One woman stated that it even made guys look "manly."

So *manly* equals *violent*? Not by me, and I hope not by anyone on any side 16 of age 25.

Identifying the Elements of an Argument by Definition

1. In your own words, summarize this essay's thesis.

2. According to Smith, what three problems are associated with defining the term *wife-beater*?

3. Why does Smith include dictionary definitions of *wife-beater*? How is her definition different from these dictionary definitions?

4. Where does Smith introduce possible objections to her definition of *wife-beater*? Does she refute them convincingly?

5. Do you think this essay would be strengthened by the addition of a picture such as the one below? Explain.

Marlon Brando as Stanley Kowalski in Tennessee Williams's play *A Streetcar Named Desire*

⊃ EXERCISE 12.2

Write a one-sentence formal definition of each of the following words.
Then, look up each word in a dictionary, and compare your definitions to
the ones you found there.

- Terrorism
- Comic book
- Cell phone

- Marriage
- Blog
- Union

⊃ EXERCISE 12.3

Choose one of the terms you defined in Exercise 12.2, and write a paragraph-
length argument by definition that takes a position related to the term you
define. Make sure you include two or three examples in your definition.

⊃ EXERCISE 12.4

Read the following poem. What characteristics of a "good poem" does
Nikki Grimes include in her definition? What additional characteristics
should she have included? Write a paragraph that argues in favor of your
own definition of *good poem*.

WHAT IS A GOOD POEM?

NIKKI GRIMES

What is a good poem?
A good poem is a slip-of-a-thing
that celebrates language, that takes
you on a short journey and touches your heart,
turns on your imagination,
or tickles your funny-
bone somewhere along the way.

⊃ EXERCISE 12.5

Each of the two pictures on the following page tries to define *courage*. Study
the pictures, and then write a paragraph in which you define this term. Make
sure that your paragraph takes a stand on what constitutes courage. (If you
like, try to find another picture to support your position.)

COURAGE

Courage comes from a reserve of mind more powerful than outside circumstances.

"Courage is not the absence of fear, but rather the judgment that something else is more important than fear."
—Ambrose Hollingworth Redmoon

Is *Wikipedia* a Legitimate Research Source?

WIKIPEDIA
The Free Encyclopedia

Go back to page 315, and reread the At Issue box, which gives some background on the question of whether *Wikipedia* is a legitimate research source. As the following sources illustrate, this question suggests a variety of possible responses.

As you read the sources that follow, you will be asked to answer some questions and to complete some simple activities. This work will help you understand both the content and the structure of the sources. When you are finished, you will be ready to write an **argument by definition** on the topic, "Is *Wikipedia* a Legitimate Research Source?"

SOURCES

 John Seigenthaler, "A False *Wikipedia* Biography"

 Randall Stross, "Anonymous Source Is Not the Same as Open Source"

 Encyclopedia of Earth, "About the *EoE*"

 Neil Waters, "Wikiphobia: The Latest in Open Source"

 Stanford Daily, "*Wikipedia* with Caution"

 Wikipedia, "Revision History of 'Global Warming'"

 Wikipedia, "Global Warming" (differences between two revisions)

USA Today first published this piece on November 29, 2005.

A FALSE *WIKIPEDIA* BIOGRAPHY

JOHN SEIGENTHALER

John Seigenthaler Sr. was the assistant to Attorney General Robert Kennedy in the early 1960's. For a brief time, he was thought to have been directly involved in the Kennedy assassinations of both John and his brother Bobby. Nothing was ever proven.

—WIKIPEDIA

1   This is a highly personal story about Internet character assassination. It could be your story.

2   I have no idea whose sick mind conceived the false, malicious "biography" that appeared under my name for 132 days on *Wikipedia,* the popular, online, free encyclopedia whose authors are unknown and virtually untraceable. There was more:

> "Nothing was ever proven."

3   "John Seigenthaler moved to the Soviet Union in 1971, and returned to the United States in 1984," *Wikipedia* said. "He started one of the country's largest public relations firms shortly thereafter."

4   At age 78, I thought I was beyond surprise or hurt at anything negative said about me. I was wrong. One sentence in the biography was true. I was Robert Kennedy's administrative assistant in the early 1960s. I also was his pallbearer. It was mind-boggling when my son, John Seigenthaler, journalist with *NBC News,* phoned later to say he found the same scurrilous text on *Reference.com* and *Answers.com.*

5   I had heard for weeks from teachers, journalists and historians about "the wonderful world of *Wikipedia,*" where millions of people worldwide visit daily for quick reference "facts," composed and posted by people with no special expertise or knowledge—and sometimes by people with malice.

6   At my request, executives of the three websites now have removed the false content about me. But they don't know, and can't find out, who wrote the toxic sentences.

Anonymous Author

7   I phoned Jimmy Wales, *Wikipedia*'s founder and asked, "Do you . . . have any way to know who wrote that?"

8   "No, we don't," he said. Representatives of the other two websites said their computers are programmed to copy data verbatim from *Wikipedia,* never checking whether it is false or factual.

9   Naturally, I want to unmask my "biographer." And, I am interested in letting many people know that *Wikipedia* is a flawed and irresponsible research tool.

But searching cyberspace for the identity of people who post spuri- 10
ous information can be frustrating. I found on *Wikipedia* the registered IP
(Internet Protocol) number of my "biographer"—65-81-97-208. I traced it
to a customer of BellSouth Internet. That company advertises a phone number to report "Abuse Issues." An electronic voice said all complaints must be
e-mailed. My two-e-mails were answered by identical form letters, advising
me that the company would conduct an investigation but might not tell me
the results. It was signed "Abuse Team."

Wales, *Wikipedia*'s founder, told me that BellSouth would not be helpful. 11
"We have trouble with people posting abusive things over and over and over,"
he said. "We block their IP numbers, and they sneak in another way. So we
contact the service providers, and they are not very responsive."

After three weeks, hearing nothing further about the Abuse Team inves- 12
tigation, I phoned BellSouth's Atlanta corporate headquarters, which led to
conversations between my lawyer and BellSouth's counsel. My only remote
chance of getting the name, I learned, was to file a "John or Jane Doe" lawsuit against my "biographer." Major communications Internet companies are
bound by federal privacy laws that protect the identity of their customers, even
those who defame online. Only if a lawsuit resulted in a court subpoena would
BellSouth give up the name.

Little Legal Recourse

Federal law also protects online corporations—BellSouth, AOL, MCI 13
Wikipedia, etc.—from libel lawsuits. Section 230 of the Communications
Decency Act, passed in 1996, specifically states that "no provider or user of an
interactive computer service shall be treated as the publisher or speaker." That
legalese means that, unlike print and broadcast companies, online service providers cannot be sued for disseminating defamatory attacks on citizens posted
by others.

Recent low-profile court decisions document that Congress effectively 14
has barred defamation in cyberspace. *Wikipedia*'s website acknowledges that
it is not responsible for inaccurate information, but Wales, in a recent C-Span
interview with Brian Lamb, insisted that his website is accountable and that
his community of thousands of volunteer editors (he said he has only one paid
employee) corrects mistakes within minutes.

My experience refutes that. My "biography" was posted May 26. On 15
May 29, one of Wales' volunteers "edited" it only by correcting the misspelling
of the word "early." For four months, *Wikipedia* depicted me as a suspected
assassin before Wales erased it from his website's history Oct. 5. The false-
hoods remained on *Answers.com* and *Reference.com* for three more weeks.

In the C-Span interview, Wales said *Wikipedia* has "millions" of daily 16
global visitors and is one of the world's busiest websites. His volunteer
community runs the *Wikipedia* operation, he said. He funds his website
through a non-profit foundation and estimated a 2006 budget of "about a million dollars."

And so we live in a universe of new media with phenomenal opportunities 17 for worldwide communications and research—but populated by volunteer vandals with poison-pen intellects. Congress has enabled them and protects them.

When I was a child, my mother lectured me on the evils of "gossip." She 18 held a feather pillow and said, "If I tear this open, the feathers will fly to the four winds, and I could never get them back in the pillow. That's how it is when you spread mean things about people."

For me, that pillow is a metaphor for *Wikipedia*. 19

⊙AT ISSUE: SOURCES FOR DEVELOPING AN ARGUMENT BY DEFINITION

1. What specific points in the biographical sketch does Seigenthaler find objectionable?

2. What steps did Seigenthaler take to "unmask" his biographer?

3. Even though much of this essay tells a story, it also makes a point. What point about *Wikipedia* do you think Seigenthaler wants to make?

4. What opposing arguments does Seigenthaler address? Are there other opposing arguments that he should have included?

5. Do you consider this essay an argument? Why or why not?

6. At the end of the essay, Seigenthaler tells a story about his mother. Why? What does he mean by, "that pillow is a metaphor for *Wikipedia*"?

The *New York Times* published this article on March 12, 2006.

ANONYMOUS SOURCE IS NOT THE SAME AS OPEN SOURCE

RANDALL STROSS

1   *Wikipedia,* the free online encyclopedia, currently serves up the following: Five billion pages a month. More than 120 languages. In excess of one million English-language articles. And a single nagging epistemological° question: Can an article be judged as credible without knowing its author?

Concerning the nature of knowledge

2   *Wikipedia* says yes, but I am unconvinced.

3   Dispensing with experts, the Wikipedians invite anyone to pitch in, writing an article or editing someone else's. No expertise is required, nor even a name. Sound inviting? You can start immediately. The system rests upon the belief that a collectivity of unknown but enthusiastic individuals, by dint of sheer mass rather than possession of conventional credentials,° can serve in the supervisory role of editor. Anyone with an interest in a topic can root out inaccuracies and add new material.

Qualifications such as a degree in a field

4   At first glance, this sounds straightforward. But disagreements arise all the time about what is a problematic passage or an encyclopedia-worthy topic, or even whether a putative correction improves or detracts from the original version.

5   The egalitarian nature of a system that accords equal votes to everyone in the "community"—middle-school student and Nobel laureate alike—has difficulty resolving intellectual disagreements.

6   *Wikipedia*'s reputation and internal editorial process would benefit by having a single authority vouch for the quality of a given article. In the jargon of library and information science, lay readers rely upon "secondary epistemic criteria," clues to the credibility of information when they do not have the expertise to judge the content.

7   Once upon a time, *Encyclopaedia Britannica* recruited Einstein, Freud, Curie, Mencken and even Houdini as contributors. The names helped the encyclopedia bolster its credibility. *Wikipedia,* by contrast, provides almost no clues for the typical article by which reliability can be appraised. A list of edits provides only screen names or, in the case of the anonymous editors, numerical Internet Protocol addresses. Wasn't yesterday's practice of attaching "Albert Einstein" to an article on "Space-Time" a bit more helpful than today's "71.240.205.101"?

> "What does *Wikipedia*'s system offer in place of an expert authority?"

8   What does *Wikipedia*'s system offer in place of an expert authority willing to place his or her professional reputation on the line with a signature attached to an article?

When I asked Jimmy Wales, the founder of *Wikipedia,* last week, 9
he discounted the importance of individual contributors to *Britannica.*
"When people trust an article in *Britannica,*" he said, "it's not who wrote
it, it's the process." There, a few editors review a piece and then editing
ceases. By contrast, *Wikipedia* is built with unending scrutiny and ceaseless
editing.

He predicts that in the future, it will be *Britannica*'s process that will seem 10
strange: "People will say, 'This was written by one person? Then looked at by
only two or three other people? How can I trust that process?'"

The Wikipedian hive is capable of impressive feats. The English-language 11
collection recently added its millionth article, for example. It was about the
Jordanhill railway station, in Glasgow. The original version, a few paragraphs,
appeared to say all that a lay reader would ever wish to know about it. But the
hive descended and in a week, more than 640 edits were logged.

If every topic could be addressed like this, without recourse to specialized 12
learning—and without the heated disputes called flame wars—the anonymous
hive could be trusted to produce work of high quality. But the Jordanhill station is an exception.

Biographical entries, for example, are often accompanied by controversy. 13
Several recent events have shown how anyone can tamper with someone else's
entry. Congressional staff members have been unmasked burnishing articles
about their employers and vandalizing those of political rivals. (Sample addition: "He likes to beat his wife and children.")

Mr. Wales himself ignored the encyclopedia's guidelines about "Dealing 14
with Articles about Yourself" and altered his own *Wikipedia* biography; when
other editors undid them, he reapplied his changes. The incidents, even if few
in number, do not help *Wikipedia* establish the legitimacy of a process that is
reluctant to say no to anyone.

It should be noted that Mr. Wales is a full-time volunteer, and that nei- 15
ther he nor the thousands of fellow volunteer editors has a pecuniary interest
in this nonprofit project. He also deserves accolades for keeping *Wikipedia*
operating without the intrusion of advertising, at least so far.

Most winningly, he has overseen a system that is gleefully candid in its 16
public self-examination. If you're seeking a well-organized list of criticisms
of *Wikipedia,* you won't find a better place than *Wikipedia*'s coverage of itself.
Wikipedia also provides a taxonomy of no fewer than 23 different forms of
vandalism that strike it.

It is easy to forget how quickly *Wikipedia* has grown; it began only in 17
2001. With the passage of a little more time, Mr. Wales and his associates may
come around to the idea that identifying one person as a given article's super-
vising editor would enhance the encyclopedia's reputation.

Mr. Wales has already responded to recent negative articles about vandal- 18
ism at the site with announcements of modest reforms. Anonymous visitors
are no longer permitted to create pages, though they still may edit existing
ones.

To curb what Mr. Wales calls "drive-by pranks" that are concentrated 19 on particular articles, he has instituted a policy of "semi-protection." In these cases, a user must have registered at least four days before being permitted to make changes to the protected article. "If someone really wants to write 'George Bush is a poopy head,' you've got to wait four days," he said.

When asked what problems on the site he viewed as most pressing, Mr. 20 Wales said he was concerned with passing along the Wikipedian culture to newcomers. He sounded wistful when he spoke of the days not so long ago when he could visit an article that was the subject of a flame war and would know at least some participants—and whether they could resolve the dispute tactfully.

As the project has grown, he has found that he no longer necessar- 21 ily knows anyone in a group. When a dispute flared recently over an article related to a new dog breed, he looked at the discussion and asked himself in frustration, "Who are these people?"

Isn't this precisely the question all users are bound to ask about contributors? 22

By wide agreement, the print encyclopedia in the English world reached 23 its apogee in 1911, with the completion of *Encyclopaedia Britannica*'s 11th edition. (For the fullest tribute, turn to *Wikipedia*.) But the *Wikipedia* experiment need not be pushed back in time toward that model. It need only be pushed forward, so it can catch up to others with more experience in online collaboration: the open-source software movement.

Wikipedia and open-source projects like Linux are similarly noncommer- 24 cial, intellectual enterprises, mobilizing volunteers who will probably never meet one another in person. But even though Wikipedians like to position their project under the open-source umbrella, the differences are wide.

Jeff Bates, a vice president of the Open Source Technology Group who 25 oversees SourceForge.net, the host of more than 80,000 active open-source projects, said, "It makes me grind my teeth to hear *Wikipedia* compared to open source." In every open-source project, he said, there is "a benevolent dictator" who ultimately takes responsibility, even though the code is contributed by many. Good stuff results only if "someone puts their name on it."

Wikipedia has good stuff, too. These have been designated "featured arti- 26 cles." But it will be a long while before all one-million-and-counting entries have been carefully double-checked and buffed to a high shine. Only 923 have been granted "featured" status, and the consensus-building process is presently capable of adding only about one a day.

Mr. Wales is not happy with this pace and seems open to looking again at 27 the open-source software model for ideas. Software development that relies on scattered volunteers is a two-step process: first, a liberal policy encourages the contributions of many, then a restrictive policy follows to stabilize the code in preparation for release. *Wikipedia,* he said, has "half the model."

There's no question that *Wikipedia* volunteers can address many more 28 topics than the lumbering, for-profit incumbents like *Britannica* and *World Book,* and can update entries swiftly. Still, anonymity blocks credibility. One thing that Wikipedians have exactly right is that the current form of the encyclopedia is a beta test. The quality level that would permit speaking of Version 1.0 is still in the future.

⊖ AT ISSUE: SOURCES FOR DEVELOPING AN ARGUMENT BY DEFINITION

1. In paragraph 3, Stross presents the *Wikipedia* philosophy. In your own words, summarize this philosophy.

2. At what points in his essay does Stross refute the *Wikipedia* philosophy? What aspects of this philosophy does he seem to disagree with most?

3. Do you think Stross should have provided formal definitions of the terms *anonymous source* and *open source*? Why or why not?

4. Where in the essay does Stross acknowledge *Wikipedia*'s strengths? Do you think that the encyclopedia's strengths outweigh its weaknesses? Explain.

5. Do you agree with Jimmy Wales, founder of *Wikipedia*, that in the future, *Britannica*'s process "will seem strange" (para. 10)?

6. What does Stross mean when he says, "Version 1.0 is still in the future" (28)?

This selection is from the *Encyclopedia of Earth* site, at EoEarth.org.

ABOUT THE *EoE*
ENCYCLOPEDIA OF EARTH

Welcome

Welcome to the *Encyclopedia of Earth,* a new electronic reference about the   1
Earth, its natural environments, and their interaction with society. The *Encyclopedia* is a free, fully searchable collection of articles written by scholars, professionals, educators, and experts who collaborate and review each other's work. The articles are written in non-technical language and will be useful to students, educators, scholars, professionals, as well as to the general public.

The Need for a New Reference on the Environment

The motivation behind the *Encyclopedia of Earth* is simple. Go to Google   2
and type in *climate change, pesticides, nuclear power, sustainable development,* or any other important environmental issue. Doing so returns millions of results, some fraction of which are authoritative. The remainder is of poor or unknown quality.

This illustrates a stark reality of the Web: digital information on the envi-   3
ronment is characterized by an abundance of "great piles of content" and a dearth of "piles of great content." In other words, there are many resources for environmental content, but there is no central repository of authoritative information that meets the needs of diverse user communities. Our goal is to make the *Encyclopedia of Earth* the largest reliable information resource on the environment in history.

The People and Institutions Behind the *Encyclopedia*

The Environmental Information Coalition (EIC) is comprised of a diverse   4
group of respected scientists and educators, and the organizations, agencies, and institutions for which they work. The EIC defines the roles and responsibilities for individuals and institutions involved in the Coalition, as well as the editorial guidelines for the *Encyclopedia.*

The Stewardship Committee of the Environmental Information Coalition   5
develops and enforces policies and guidelines for the *Encyclopedia*, with input from Topic Editors and Authors.

The EIC is governed by its own set of bylaws and an International Advi-   6
sory Board with renowned scholars from diverse fields.

The Secretariat for the EIC is the National Council for Science and the   7
Environment (NCSE), Washington D.C., USA. NCSE is a 501(c)(3) non-profit

organization with a reputation for objectivity, responsibility, and achievement in its promotion of a scientific basis for environmental decision-making.

The Department of Geography and Environment and the Center for Energy 8 and Environmental Studies at Boston University also provide editorial support.

Content Sources for the *Encyclopedia of Earth*

The *Encyclopedia* has content from three different sources: 9

- **Original Articles Written by *EoE* Authors.** These are individuals who are experts in their fields as judged by their peers and by their track record of distinguished research, teaching, writing, training, and public outreach in their field. You can view our current list of authors here.

- **Content Partners.** These are organizations who have reached a formal agreement with the *EoE* to have their existing material published in the *Encyclopedia*. In most cases, such material is published verbatim from the Partner organization, with some editing for style and length to make the entry consistent with *EoE* guidelines. Remaining consistent with the *EoE* governance guidelines, once the entry is up on the *EoE*, authors may then add to or edit that material. Every entry from a Content Partner is assigned to, and must be approved by, at least one Topic Editor. You can view our current list of Content Partners here.

- **Free and Open Content Sources.** The typical example here is a government agency whose work rests fully in the public domain, such as many federal government publications. Other examples include non-profit and educational organizations whose copyright allows free use for educational and non-commercial purposes. In most cases, such material is published verbatim from the organization, with some editing for style and length to make the entry consistent with *EoE* guidelines. Remaining consistent with the *EoE* governance guidelines, once the entry is up on the *EoE*, authors may then add to or edit that material. Every entry from a Content Source is assigned to, and must be approved by, at least one Topic Editor. You can view our current list of Content Sources here.

The Scope of the *Encyclopedia of Earth*

The scope of the *Encyclopedia of Earth* is the environment of the Earth broadly 10 defined, with particular emphasis on the interaction between society and the natural spheres of the Earth. The scope of the *Encyclopedia* thus includes:

- The hydrosphere, lithosphere, atmosphere, magnetosphere, cryosphere, and biosphere, and their interactions, especially in regards to how these systems support life and underpin human existence.

- The living organisms on Earth that constitute its biological diversity.

- The interactions and feedbacks among society, biological diversity, and the physical systems of the Earth. This includes the social, economic, political, behavioral, technical, cultural, legal, and ethical driving forces behind environmental change.

- Those parts of traditional disciplines that investigate the environment or its interaction with society. This includes the natural, physical, and social sciences, the arts and humanities, and the professional disciplines (education, journalism, business, law, public health, engineering, medicine, public policy).

- The interdisciplinary fields of environmental science—natural and social—that integrate concepts, methods, and analytical tools from multiple fields in the investigation of the environment or its interaction with society. Examples include:

  - Environmental physical sciences such as atmospheric sciences, Earth systems science, remote sensing, biogeochemistry, oceanography, and other non-biological terrestrial sciences.

  - Environmental life sciences such as environmental biology, ecology, forestry, fisheries, marine biology, agriculture, aquaculture, and related fields.

  - Environmental engineering and other sciences related to the impacts of natural and anthropogenic activities on the environment, including assessment, prevention, control, regulation, remediation, and restoration.

  - Environmental social sciences such as ecological and environmental economics, environmental sociology and history, and other fields that study human social and cultural activities which affect, and are affected by, environmental conditions.

  - Environmental data and information sciences that deal with the collection, storage, standardization, integration, analysis, and management of data related to the analysis of the environment or environmental change.

The Editorial and Publication Process

Authors and Topic Editors are experts in their fields as judged by their peers and 11 by their track record of distinguished research, teaching, writing, training, and public outreach in their field. This community of scholars includes scientists and educators at major research universities as well as teaching-oriented colleges and community colleges; some high school educators; scientists/analysts at think tanks, NGOs, government agencies, etc.; professionals from business, trade groups, professional organizations, etc. who are appropriately qualified.

Content for the *Encyclopedia* is created, maintained, and governed by this 12 community of experts via a specially adapted "wiki"—an online tool that allows experts to collectively add and edit Web content. Unlike other, well-known wikis, such as *Wikipedia,* access is restricted to approved experts and all content is reviewed and approved by Topic Editors prior to being published from the wiki to this public site. Revisions to existing articles are also done on the authors' wiki, and when approved they become the current version at the public site. This process produces a constantly evolving, continuously updated reference.

> "Access is restricted to approved experts and all content is reviewed and approved."

The Commitment to Objectivity

In the interests of encouraging the broadest participation, of assisting people 13 in making up their own minds about controversial issues, and of increasing the likelihood of articulating the whole truth about all subjects, the *Encyclopedia of Earth* adopts the following policies regarding neutrality and fairness.

1. **Neutrality.** *Encyclopedia of Earth* articles shall, when touching upon any issue of controversy, be fair and insofar as possible *neutral*. Following are some examples of what is meant by neutrality in the *Encyclopedia of Earth*:

   - **Controversy.** The *Encyclopedia of Earth* recognizes two classes of controversy: *scientific controversy* and *values controversy. Scientific controversy* describes differences in opinion of scholars on the interpretation of scientific data. For example, the regional changes in weather caused by increases in greenhouse gases in the Earth's atmosphere is a subject of scientific controversy. *Values controversy* describes differences in opinion on values-based decision-making about the environment. For example, whether taking an action to preserve or protect an endangered species is worth the economic or societal costs of such actions is a values controversy.

   When touching upon any issue of controversy, the distinction between scientific and values controversy should be recognized, and every different view on a subject that attracts a significant portion of adherents shall be represented, with each such view and its arguments or evidence being expressed as fairly and sympathetically as possible. This entails, among other things, that:

   - **No Advocacy.** The *Encyclopedia of Earth* itself shall not advocate positions on environmental issues; it shall also be both non-partisan and non-sectarian.

   - **Language.** The *Encyclopedia of Earth* shall not use phraseology or tone that elevates or deprecates particular perspectives or people holding a particular perspective.

   - **Dialectic.** The *Encyclopedia of Earth* shall attempt, iteratively if necessary, to represent fairly and sympathetically the arguments of different disputants against each others' positions.

   - **Balance.** Where there is a need to apportion limited space, space on areas of disagreement shall be apportioned roughly in proportion to their representation (1) among experts, when a dispute exists mainly among scholars; and (2) among the interested population, when a dispute exists mainly among the general population. When a dispute is equally a scholarly and a popular dispute, separate articles will be written to describe each dispute neutrally.

2. **Uncertainties and Assumptions.** The *Encyclopedia of Earth* shall recognize uncertainties in data, interpretation, and understanding, as well as other reasons for different perspectives on a subject, such as assumptions made.

3. **Inclusion.** As access to the broadest array of knowledge has many salutary effects, the *Encyclopedia of Earth* shall be strongly disposed to include rather than exclude content.

4. **Exclusion.**

   - **Harm.** When some content both has no discernible and unique benefit to the advancement of knowledge, and has significant potential to harm the health or moral character of individuals, of human society at large, or of the environment, it may be excluded.

   - **Broad consensus.** To be grounds for exclusion, the harmful nature of some content must be affirmed, or likely to be affirmed, by the majority of the world's population, regardless of political or religious views.

   - **Examples.** Paradigm examples of excluded content are bomb-making instructions, pornography, and Holocaust denial.

Policy on the Use of Content from *Wikipedia*

Authors, Topic Editors, the Stewardship Committee of the Environmental 14 Information Coalition, and the International Advisory Board of the *EoE* have determined that *Wikipedia* contains some content that may be suitable for the *EoE* in terms of subject area, level of writing, and accuracy. The copyright associated with *Wikipedia* allows considerable freedom to re-use its content. There may be, therefore, instances where *Wikipedia* content—appropriately applied and reviewed—can be used in the *EoE*.

We allow Authors and Topic Editors to use content from *Wikipedia* when 15 they write or edit an article, subject to the following conditions.

1. Authors must limit their use of *Wikipedia* content to articles in their core areas of expertise.

2. Authors and Topic Editors are expected to review and judge content from *Wikipedia* with a high level of scrutiny that is consistent with the overall editorial and quality control guidelines for the *EoE* that were described in the previous two sections. This includes vetting content carefully for accuracy, clarity, objectivity, completeness, and balance. Authors are expected to remove any inaccurate or misleading information, and to add additional content that would, in their opinion improve the quality of the article.

3. Articles with *Wikipedia* content undergo the same review prior to publication as other *EoE* content.

4. When *Wikipedia* content is used in an *EoE* article, that article is identified and attributed in accordance with *EoE* policy. *EoE* Authors and Topic Editors who make contributions to an article that contains *Wikipedia* content are also identified in accordance with *EoE* policy.

The decision to allow use of *Wikipedia* was made after careful deliberation by the *EoE*'s Editorial Board, the International Advisory Board, the Stewardship Committee of the Environmental Information Coalition, and, most importantly after an open forum with Authors and Topic Editors. 16

The Connection to the Earth Portal

The *Encyclopedia* is a crosscutting component of the Earth Portal, a comprehensive resource for timely, objective, science-based information about the environment. It is a means for the global scientific community to come together to produce the first free, expert-driven, massively scalable information resource on the environment, and to engage civil society in a public dialogue on the role of environmental issues in human affairs. It contains no commercial advertising and reaches a large global audience. 17

The Earth Portal has three components: 18

1. The *Encyclopedia of Earth.*

2. The Earth Forum, with commentary from scholars and discussions with the general public.

3. The Earth News, with news stories on environmental issues drawn from many sources.

◯ AT ISSUE: SOURCES FOR DEVELOPING AN ARGUMENT BY DEFINITION

1. How is the *Encyclopedia of Earth* different from *Wikipedia*?

2. Some of the sources included in the *Encyclopedia of Earth* are open-content sources. Who is able to add to or edit these sources? Who is *not* able to make changes?

3. How do the editors of the *Encyclopedia of Earth* try to maintain the objectivity of their online publication? Do you think they can be successful?

4. The policy statement of the *Encyclopedia of Earth* (paras. 14–16) refers specifically to *Wikipedia*. What limitations does it place on the use of content from this source?

5. In your opinion, is the *Encyclopedia of Earth* a better, more reliable source than *Wikipedia*? Why or why not?

This article was published in the *Middlebury Campus,* the student weekly newspaper of Middlebury College, on April 11, 2007.

WIKIPHOBIA: THE LATEST IN OPEN SOURCE

NEIL WATERS

It seemed like a no-brainer. Several students in one of my classes included the same erroneous information in final examination essays. Google whisked me immediately to *Wikipedia,* where I found the source of the erroneous information in under a minute. To prevent recurrences of the problem, I wrote a policy for consideration by the history department, in less than two minutes:

> 1) Students are responsible for the accuracy of information they provide, and they cannot point to *Wikipedia* or any similar source that may appear in the future to escape the consequences of errors. 2) *Wikipedia* is not an acceptable citation, even though it may lead one to a citable source.

I brought up this modest policy proposal, suitably framed in whereases and be it resolved, at the next meeting of the department, and it was passed within about three minutes, and we moved on to more pressing business. And that, I thought, was that—a good six minutes worth of work, culminating in clear guidelines for the future. Some colleagues felt I was belaboring the obvious, and they were right. The history department always has held students responsible for accuracy, and does not consider general encyclopedias of the bound variety to be acceptable for citation either. But *Wikipedia* seemed worth mentioning by name because it is omnipresent and because its "open-source" method of compilation makes it a different animal from, say, the *Encyclopedia Britannica*.

The *Campus* published an article on the departmental policy, and the rest, as they say, is history. Alerted by the online version of the *Campus* Tim Johnson of the *Burlington Free Press* interviewed me and a spokesman for *Wikipedia* who agreed with the history department's position, and published an article. Several college newspapers followed suit, and then Noam Cohen of the *New York Times* interviewed Don Wyatt, chair of the History Department, and me, and published the story. Within a day it received more online "hits" than any other *New York Times* feature. Another interview followed with the *Asahi Shimbun* in Tokyo, and additional articles appeared in *El Pais* in Spain, the *Guardian* in England, and then in literally hundreds of newspapers in the U.S. and abroad. Along with other members of the History Department, I found myself giving interviews almost daily—to radio stations, newspaper reporters, inquisitive high school students, WCAX television news in Burlington, and even to the *NBC Nightly*

> "I found myself giving interviews almost daily."

341

News, which sent correspondent Lisa Daniels to Middlebury to interview me and students in my History of Modern Japan class. A stream of phone calls and e-mails from a wide range of people, from *Wikipedia* disciples to besieged librarians who felt free at last to express their *Wikipedia* misgivings, continues to the present. Somehow the modest policy adoption by the History Department at Middlebury College hit a nerve.

Why this overwhelming spate of interest? I can think of three reasons immediately: 1) Timing. *Wikipedia* has existed since 2001, but it has expanded exponentially, and reached a critical mass in the last couple of years. With over 1.6 million entries in its English language edition, *Wikipedia* has something to say about almost everything. Its popularity has soared with its comprehensiveness and ease of use, and its ease of use in turn has been enhanced by popularity-driven algorithms; Google lists a *Wikipedia* article in first or second place more often than not. 2) Passion. There is something exciting about the growth and development of an entity to which anyone can contribute.

At its best, *Wikipedia* works wonders. Anonymous editors actually improve entries over time, including new material, editing away mistakes, polishing the writing. Accordingly, some of *Wikipedia*'s defenders approach their task with near-religious zeal. But *Wikipedia* at its worst excites similarly intense passions, because anonymous, non-accountable editors can include, through ignorance or malice, misinformation that may or may not get "fixed." Further, thousands of high school teachers as well as college professors who try mightily to induce a measure of critical thinking in their students' approach to sources for research grow quietly furious because the very ubiquity of *Wikipedia* tempts people to use it in lieu of other, more reliable sources of information. 3) Scandals. The *Wikipedia* entry for John Seigenthaler, Sr. in 2004 contained spurious accusations that he was a suspect in the assassinations of both John F. Kennedy and Robert Kennedy. The entry was unaltered for four months (thereafter authors of new entries, but not editors of existing entries, had to register their names with *Wikipedia*). A *Wikipedia* "policeman" turned out to have bogus credentials. Sinbad was declared dead (he has since risen again). All this keeps the pot boiling.

In the final analysis, *Wikipedia*'s greatest strength is also its greatest weakness. Anonymous, unaccountable, unpaid, often non-expert yet passionate editors built *Wikipedia,* but their anonymity and lack of accountability assures that *Wikipedia* cannot be considered an authoritative source. And yet it is frequently used as if it were, *Wikipedia*'s own disclaimers notwithstanding. College professors and high school teachers alike need to remember that the impressive computer acumen of their students does not automatically translate into impressive levels of critical thought, particularly when it comes to evaluating the reliability of the new tools at their disposal, and of the information those tools provide. The Internet has opened up new highways of information, but we need to know how to spot the potholes.

❯ AT ISSUE: SOURCES FOR DEVELOPING AN ARGUMENT BY DEFINITION

1. In paragraph 1, Waters, who teaches at Middlebury, lists the two policies he proposed to the history department. Do you think these policies make sense? Do you think they are fair? Explain.

2. Why do you think Waters's "modest policy proposal" (para. 2) attracted so much interest not only on campus but also around the world?

3. Do you think Waters oversimplifies the issue of using *Wikipedia* as a source? What additional points could he have discussed?

4. Where does Waters acknowledge the arguments in favor of using *Wikipedia* as a research source? How does he refute these arguments?

5. Summarize Waters's reasons for concluding that *Wikipedia* is not an acceptable research source.

This editorial appeared in the *Stanford Daily* on March 8, 2007.

WIKIPEDIA WITH CAUTION

STANFORD DAILY

It is difficult not to love *Wikipedia,* the free online encyclopedia to which any- 1
one can contribute (www.wikipedia.org). With 1,674,086 articles in English
alone, it provides anyone with Internet access the ability to get fast, free information on anything from the New Orleans Mint (operational until 1909), to
the biography of Weird Al Yankovic (he started accordion lessons at age seven).

In February, the Department of History at Middlebury College forbade 2
students from citing *Wikipedia* as a source in history papers and tests, also
giving notice that students would not be given any breaks for mistaken knowledge they derived from the site.

The department's decision received national attention, including a Feb- 3
ruary 21 article in the *New York Times,* and much of the response has been
negative. One op-ed printed in the *Middlebury Campus,* the school newspaper,
likened the move to "censorship" and condemned the professors who advocated the ban.

We have a hard time understanding what all of the fuss is about. Mid- 4
dlebury's new rule is hardly censorship. Students are not prohibited from
viewing, discussing or disseminating anything from *Wikipedia.* Rather, history students have simply been officially told what should already be obvious:
Wikipedia, however useful, is not something that should be cited in a serious
academic context, and if it is used, it could reflect poorly on students' work.

Most university-level students should be able to discern between *Wikipedia* 5
and more reliable online sources like government databases and online periodicals. To be fair, some of *Wikipedia*'s entries are specific enough to be extremely
valuable in studying or researching, but
others are shallow, short, and occasionally
completely inaccurate. There are many Web
sites that can provide credible resources, but
Wikipedia is not one of them, nor does it
purport to be. Jimmy Wales, one of the founders of *Wikipedia,* told the *Times*
that he does not even consider Middlebury's action "a negative thing."

> "The articles are not always perfect."

Naturally, because it is a user-generated Web site, the articles are not 6
always perfect, and should not be relied on as much as actual class materials. *Wikipedia* has even introduced a citation function where contributors can
direct readers to other more well-established sources.

Yet even as we point out that college students ought to know better than 7
to rely completely on *Wikipedia,* Middlebury's ban seems a bit overzealous.
Students are also supposed to use proper grammar and spelling in assignments, but rather than having an official policy against poor writing, most
schools simply tell students what the standards are ahead of time.

It is the role of teachers to advise students what is acceptable; for some 8
assignments it is conceivable that referencing *Wikipedia* as an example, rather
than an authoritative source, might be useful. Instead of totally banning *Wikipedia* as an information source departmentally, history professors at Middlebury should have stressed or continued to stress that using it could hurt an
individual's performance in the class. Much like spelling and grammar, if students already know what is expected in terms of citations, any deviation from
expectations will make grading easier for professors.

There was a point in time where all Internet sources were suspect for most 9
academic uses. Thankfully, that is no longer the case. Research has certainly
become easier and more accessible with online help, but some sites, like some
books, are better than others. We still love *Wikipedia* and admit that it can
be great for a quick definition or fact, but we won't be citing it in any papers
anytime soon.

⊘ AT ISSUE: SOURCES FOR DEVELOPING AN ARGUMENT BY DEFINITION

1. In paragraph 4, the editorial says that *Wikipedia* "is not something
   that should be cited in a serious academic context." Later, in paragraph 7, the editorial says, "Middlebury's ban seems a bit overzealous." Do these two statements contradict each other? Explain.

2. Based on your reading of this editorial, write a one-paragraph definition of *acceptable source*.

3. In paragraph 8, the editorial makes a distinction between "referencing
   Wikipedia as an example" and citing it as "an authoritative source."
   What is this distinction? Do you think it is valid?

4. This editorial was written by students at a prestigious university. Do
   you think their position on the issue makes sense for all college students? For high school students? For scholars?

345

REVISION HISTORY OF "GLOBAL WARMING"*

WIKIPEDIA

From *Wikipedia,* the free encyclopedia
View logs for this page
(Latest | Earliest) View (newer 50) (older 50) (20 | 50 | 100 | 250 | 500)
For any version listed below, click on its date to view it.
For more help, see Help:Page history and Help:Edit summary.
(cur) = difference from current version, (last) = difference from preceding version,
m = minor edit, → = section edit, ← = automatic edit summary

(compare selected versions)

- (cur) (last) ⊙ 07:35, 21 July 2008 William M. Connolley (Talk | contribs) 1
  (101,906 bytes) (rv: 1 preferred "a few")

- (cur) (last) ⊙ 00:02, 21 July 2008 Axlq 2
  (Talk | contribs) m (101,914 bytes) (→
  Solar variation: attempt to remove weasel word)

  "Attempt to remove weasel word."

- (cur) (last) ○ 20:21, 20 July 2008 Smptq (Talk | contribs) m (101,906 3
  bytes) (Undid revision 226859199 by Shawine (talk))

- (cur) (last) ○ 19:52, 20 July 2008 Shawine (Talk | contribs) m (101,909 4
  bytes) (→ Solar variation)

- (cur) (last) ○ 06:38, 18 July 2008 SmackBot (Talk | contribs) m (101,906 5
  bytes) (Date the maintenance tags or general fixes)

- (cur) (last) ○ 05:33, 18 July 2008 Orangemarlin (Talk | contribs) m 6
  (101,890 bytes) (Reverted to revision 226389686 by Enuja; Approximately? Not sure it makes grammatical sense..using TW)

- (cur) (last) ○ 05:18, 18 July 2008 Josephprymak (Talk | contribs) 7
  (101,904 bytes)

- (cur) (last) ○ 04:50, 18 July 2008 Enuja (Talk | contribs) 101,890 8
  bytes) Undid revision 226388778 by JPINFV (talk) see www.aps.org;

---

*By clicking on "(*cur*)" or "(*last*)" next to each entry, you can see the current version of a text
or the previous version of the text before it was edited. By clicking on the "Compare selected
versions" button near the top of the page, you can view the changes in the context of the article. Readers can access the revision history by clicking on the "History" box at the beginning
of an article. This history gives readers a sense of how extensively revised the article is.

statement not been rescinded, discussion in newsletter not endorsed by APS)

- (cur) (last) ○ 04:43, 18 July 2008 JPINFV (Talk | contribs) (102,660 bytes) 9

- (cur) (last) ○ 03:49, 18 July 2008 Orangemarlin (Talk | contribs) m 10 (101,890 bytes) (Reverted to revision 226378704 by Enuja; I'm not sure this is appropriate. Highly POV..using TW)

- (cur) (last) ○ 03:47, 18 July 2008 Isis07 (Talk | contribs) (102,010 bytes) 11 (→ See also)

- (cur) (last) ○ 03:47, 18 July 2008 Isis07 (Talk | contribs) (102,010 bytes) 12 (→ See also)

- (cur) (last) ○ 03:43, 18 July 2008 Isis07 (Talk | contribs) (101,971 bytes) 13 (→ See also)

- (cur) (last) ○ 03:22, 18 July 2008 Enuja (Talk | contribs) (101,890 bytes) 14 (Undid revision 226377518 by Isis07 (talk) please put integrate new information into the article; also suggest large changes on talk)

- (cur) (last) ○ 03:14, 18 July 2008 Isis07 (Talk | contribs) (102,993 bytes) 15 (→ See also)

- (cur) (last) ○ 13:41, 17 July 2008 Brusegadi (Talk | contribs) (101,890 16 bytes) (Reverted 3 edits by Sm8900; Not an appropriate source for this article. using TW)

- (cur) (last) ○ 13:33, 17 July 2008 Sm8900 (Talk | contribs) (102,757 17 bytes) (→ Attributed and expected effects)

- (cur) (last) ○ 13:31, 17 July 2008 Sm8900 (Talk | contribs) (102,761 18 bytes) (→ Attributed and expected effects)

- (cur) (last) ○ 13:29, 17 July 2008 Sm8900 (Talk | contribs) (102,763 bytes) 19

- (cur) (last) ○ 21:04, 16 July 2008 Stephan Schulz (Talk | contribs) 20 (101,890 bytes) (Undid revision)

⊙ AT ISSUE: SOURCES FOR DEVELOPING AN ARGUMENT BY DEFINITION

1. Above is an excerpt from a long list of revisions to a *Wikipedia* article on global warming. What information about the revision process do you learn from this excerpt?

2. How does the information on the revision-history pages affect your opinion of *Wikipedia*?

3. Why do you think the editors of *Wikipedia* make this kind of information available to readers?

This page was accessed from *Wikipedia* on July 21, 2008.

GLOBAL WARMING (DIFFERENCES BETWEEN TWO REVISIONS)

WIKIPEDIA

Revision as of 00:02, 21 July 2008 (view source)
Axlq (Talk | contribs)
m (→ Solar variation: attempt to remove weasel word)
← Older edit

Current revision (07:35, 21 July 2008) (view source)
William M. Connolley (Talk | contribs)
(rv: I preferred "a few")

Line 110:

[Image:Solar-cycle-data.png|thumb|280px|right|Solar variation over the last thirty years.]]
{{main|Solar variation}}

At least two studies suggest that the Sun's contribution may have been underestimated. Two researchers at [[Duke University]], Bruce West and Nicola Scafetta, have estimated that the Sun may have contributed about 45–50% of the increase in the average global surface temperature over the period 1900–2000, and about 25–35% between 1980 and 2000.<ref>

{{cite journal | first=Nicola | last=Scafetta | coauthors=West, Bruce J. | title=Phenomenological solar contribution to the 1900–2000 global surface warming | url = http://www.fel.duke.edu/~scafetta/pdf/2005GL025539.pdf | format = [[Portable Document Format|PDF]] | date=[[2006-03-09]] | journal=[[Geophysical Research Letters]] | volume=33 | issue=5 | id=L05708 | doi=10.1029/2005GL025539 | accessdate=2007-05-08 | pages=L05708}}

</ref> A paper by Peter Stott and other researchers suggests that climate models overestimate the relative effect of greenhouse gases compared to solar forcing; they also suggest that the cooling effects of volcanic dust and sulfate aerosols have been underestimated.<ref>{{Cite journal | first=Peter A.| last=Stott | coauthors="et al." | title=Do Models Underestimate the Solar Contribution to Recent Climate Change? | date=[[2003-12-03]] | journal=[[Journal of Climate]] | volume=16 | issue=24 | pages=4079-4093 | doi=10.1175/1520-0442(2003)016<4079:DMUTSC>2.0.CO;2 | accessdate=2007-04-16 | url=http://climate.envsci.rutgers.edu/pdf/StottEtA1.pdf | year=2003}}</ref>

Line 110:

[[Image:Solar-cycle-data.png|thumb|280px|right|Solar variation over the last thirty years.]]
{{main|Solar variation}}

A few papers suggest that the Sun's contribution may have been underestimated. Two researchers at [[Duke University]], Bruce West and Nicola Scafetta, have estimated that the Sun may have contributed about 45–50% of the increase in the average global surface temperature over the period 1900–2000, and about 25–35% between 1980 and 2000.<ref>

{{cite journal | first=Nicola | last=Scafetta | coauthors=West, Bruce J. | title=Phenomenological solar contribution to the 1900–2000 global surface warming | url = http://www.fel.duke.edu/~scafetta/pdf/2005GL025539.pdf | format = [[Portable Document Format|PDF]] | date=[[2006-03-09]] | journal=[[Geophysical Research Letters]] | volume=33 | issue=5 | id=L05708 | doi=10.1029/2005GL025539 | accessdate=2007-05-08 | pages=L05708}}

</ref> A paper by Peter Stott and other researchers suggests that climate models overestimate the relative effect of greenhouse gases compared to solar forcing; they also suggest that the cooling effects of volcanic dust and sulfate aerosols have been underestimated.<ref>{{Cite journal | first=Peter A. | last=Stott | coauthors= "et al." | title=Do Models Underestimate the Solar Contribution to Recent Climate Change? | date=[[2003-12-03]] | journal=[[Journal of Climate]] | volume=16 | issue=24 | pages=4079-4093 | doi=10.1175/1520-0442(2003)016<4079:DMUTSC>2.0.CO;2 | accessdate=2007-04-16 | url=http://climate.envsci.rutgers.edu/pdf/StottEtA1.pdf | year=2003}}</ref>

⊘ AT ISSUE: SOURCES FOR DEVELOPING AN ARGUMENT BY DEFINITION

1. Page 348 compares two versions of a passage (boxed) from the *Wikipedia* article on global warming. What is the nature of the revision it illustrates? Do you think the revision is an improvement over the original?

2. Does the fact that the editor is anonymous affect your assessment of the changes?

3. Look up the term *global warming* on *Wikipedia*. Then, access its revision history. Look at specific revisions, and compare selected versions. How would you characterize these revisions? Are they minor, or do you think they actually improve the entry?

4. Based on the nature of the revisions you see in the global warming entry, do you think *Wikipedia* is a legitimate research source?

⊖ **EXERCISE 12.6**

Write a one-paragraph argument by definition in which you take a position on whether *Wikipedia* is a legitimate research source. Follow the template below, filling in the blanks to create your argument.

Template for Writing an Argument by Definition

Many people are questioning the use of *Wikipedia* as a legitimate research source. A *legitimate source* can be defined as a source that _____

_____

_____.

According to this definition, *Wikipedia* _____

_____

_____. Not every one agrees, however. Some

people say that *Wikipedia* _____

_____

_____

_____. Others say that _____

_____

_____.

Although these points make sense, it is clear that _____

_____

_____. In conclusion, *Wikipedia* _____

_____

_____

_____.

⊖ **EXERCISE 12.7**

Ask two or three of your instructors whether they consider *Wikipedia* a legitimate research source. Then, revise the draft of the paragraph you wrote for Exercise 12.6 so that it includes your instructors' opinions.

⊖ **EXERCISE 12.8**

Write an argument by definition on the topic, "Is *Wikipedia* a Legitimate Research Source?" Make sure that you define the term *legitimate research source* and that you give examples to develop your definition. (If you like, you may incorporate the material you developed in Exercises 12.6 and 12.7

into your essay.) Cite the readings on pages 328–348, and be sure to document the sources you use and to include a works-cited page. (See Chapter 10 for information on documenting sources.)

⊘ EXERCISE 12.9 🏛

Review the four pillars of argument discussed in Chapter 1. Does your essay include all four elements of an effective argument? Add anything that is missing. Then, label the key elements of your essay.

⊘ WRITING ASSIGNMENTS: ARGUMENT BY DEFINITION

1. On most campuses, instructors have the right to pursue, teach, and discuss subjects without restriction. This principle is called *academic freedom*. Do you think that instructors should have academic freedom, or do you believe that this principle should be restricted? For example, are there any subject or ideas an instructor should *not* be allowed to discuss? Write an argument by definition in which you define *academic freedom* and take a position on this issue.

2. Many colleges require students to perform community service before they graduate. Do you think that college students should have to do community service? Before you begin your argument, find a definition of the term *community service*. Be sure your argument focuses on the definition of this term.

3. Take detailed notes about the food and service in your campus cafeteria. Then, write an argumentative essay in which you rate the cafeteria as *excellent*, *good*, *bad*, or *poor*. Keep in mind that you are presenting *operational definitions* of these terms (see p. 318) and that you will have to explain the factors you examined to form your assessment.

National Report

17,000 killed in senseless act

Authorities search for answers on a day of sadness

A nation is in mourning as thousands were suddenly killed yesterday all across the country by people who had been drinking and driving. Traffic was backed up in all 50 states making it difficult for emergency vehicles to reach the victims. Hospitals in every city remain overwhelmed with thousands of critically injured patients. ___ the help of N ional Gua ___ as w s s

simply are not enough resources to meet the demands of this catastrophe. The president spoke early this morning at an emergency press conference expressing his condolences to the friends and families of those who were lost. One official in DeBeau County called this "the most devastating moment in American history." In some places, entire families were killed, leaving many to wonder how something like this could happen in our country today. In a show of support, long lines of volunteers have formed at the ___ of blood and ti ___ enters to ___ to ___ in

If this were today's headline, would you notice?

Last year, drinking and driving actually did kill about 17,000 people. It injured half a million more. But because it happened over a year rather than in a single day, it's not always front-page news. It's a growing problem, with a simple answer. If you drink, find a safe way home. And do your part to keep drunk driving out of the headlines.

MADD.

Activism | Victim Services | Education

www.madd.org

CHAPTER

13

Causal Argument

AT ISSUE

Will Lowering the Drinking Age Solve the Problem of Binge Drinking among College Students?

In 1984, the National Minimum Drinking Age Act encouraged states to raise the drinking age to twenty-one by reducing the federal highway appropriation for any state that did not do so. This act effectively raised the federal minimum drinking age to twenty-one. The intent was to reduce reckless driving among young adults, thereby preventing injuries and deaths caused by drunk driving. (The problem of teenage drinking was exacerbated by young people driving to other states with lower drinking ages.)

In 2008, more than one hundred college presidents, joining together in a group called the Amethyst Initiative, released a statement calling for a "public debate" on the issue of lowering the federal drinking age from twenty-one to eighteen. The statement argues that the current drinking age encourages binge drinking among college students as well as disrespect for the law. Critics of this position, led by Mothers Against Drunk Driving, have called the proposal irresponsible, accusing college presidents of trying to sidestep the difficult task of cracking down on underage drinking. Others have pointed out that the higher drinking age has had beneficial effects—for example, reducing drunken driving deaths among eighteen- to twenty-year-olds—that lowering the drinking age would most likely eliminate.

The question of lowering the drinking age is more complicated than it may seem. For example, did raising the drinking age to twenty-one actually *cause* the rise in binge drinking? If so, is it the most important cause? And even if the higher drinking age is the main cause of the problem, will lowering the age once again to eighteen lessen the problem? And will it create other problems? These are some of the questions that you will be asked to think about as you read the research sources that appear later in this chapter. After reading these selections, you will be asked to write a **causal argument** that takes a position on whether lowering the drinking age will decrease binge drinking among college students.

What Is Causal Argument?

Causal arguments attempt to find causes (Why don't more Americans vote?) or identify possible consequences (Does movie violence cause societal violence?). A causal argument identifies the causes of an event or situation and takes a stand on what actually caused it. Alternatively, a causal argument can focus on results, taking a position on what a likely outcome is, has been, or will be.

Many of the arguments that you read and discuss examine causes and effects. In an essay on one of the following topics, you would search for the causes of an event or a situation, examining a number of different possible causes before concluding that a particular cause was the most likely one. You also could consider the possible outcomes or results of a given event or situation and conclude that one possible result would most likely occur:

- Why don't more Americans vote?
- Does movie violence cause societal violence?
- Is autism caused by childhood vaccines?
- Is fast food making Americans fat?
- Is human activity responsible for climate change?
- Does the death penalty discourage crime?
- Do single-sex schools improve students' academic performance?
- Does profiling decrease the likelihood of a terrorist attack?

⊘ EXERCISE 13.1

Causal arguments are all around us—for example, on cigarette packages, in public-service advertisements, and on bumper stickers. Look at the visuals on the pages that follow, and consider the causes and effects you might discuss if you were writing a causal argument developing one of the statements listed below. List as many possible causes and effects as you can.

- Guns don't kill people; people kill people.
- Caution: Cigarette smoking may be hazardous to your health.
- Friends don't let friends drive drunk.

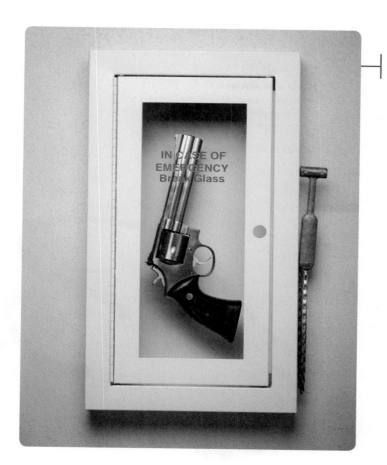

Guns don't kill people; people kill people.

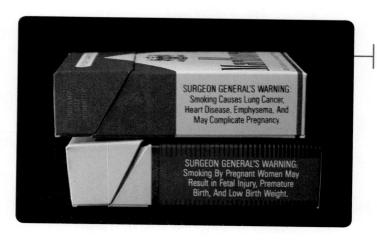

Surgeon general's warning

Friends don't let
friends drive drunk.

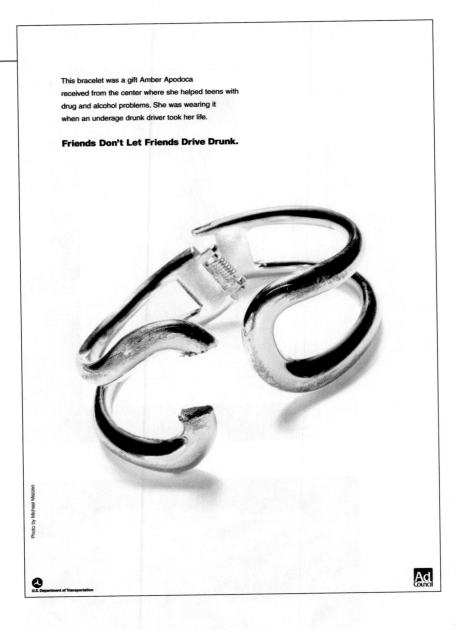

This bracelet was a gift Amber Apodoca
received from the center where she helped teens with
drug and alcohol problems. She was wearing it
when an underage drunk driver took her life.

Friends Don't Let Friends Drive Drunk.

Photo by Michael Mazzeo

U.S. Department of Transportation

Ad Council

Bumper stickers

Understanding Cause-and-Effect Relationships

Before you can write a causal argument, you need to understand the nature of cause-and-effect relationships, some of which can be very complex. For one thing, a single event or situation can have many possible results, and not all of these will be equally significant. In the same way, identifying causes can be particularly challenging because an event or situation can have multiple causes. For example, many factors might explain why more Americans do not vote. (The diagram on page 358 illustrates some possible causes.)

Main and Contributory Causes

In a causal argument, your focus is on identifying what you believe is the most important cause and presenting arguments that convince readers *why* it is the most important (and why other causes are not as important).

The most important cause is the **main cause**; the less important causes are **contributory causes**. Typically, you will present the main cause as your key argument in support of your thesis, and you will identify the contributory causes elsewhere in your argument. (You may also identify factors that are *not* causes and explain why they are not.)

Identifying the main cause is not always easy; the most important cause may not always be the most obvious one. However, you need to decide which cause is most important so you can structure and support your essay with this emphasis in mind.

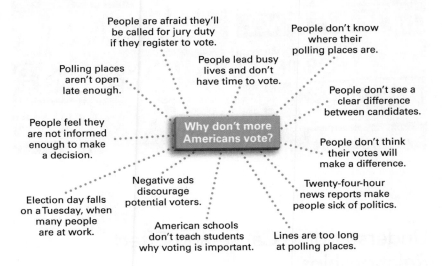

EXERCISE 13.2

Look at the diagram above. Which causes do you see as the most and least important? Why? Do you think that any of the factors presented in the diagram are not really causes? Can you suggest any additional causes? If you were writing a causal argument on the topic of why many Americans do not vote, which cause would you focus on? What kind of evidence would you use to support your argument?

Immediate and Remote Causes

As mentioned earlier, one reason that identifying the main cause of a particular effect can be difficult is that the most important cause is not necessarily the most obvious one. Usually, the most obvious cause is the **immediate cause**—the one that occurs right before an event. For example, a political scandal that erupts the day before an election might cause many disillusioned voters to stay home from the polls. However, this immediate cause, although it is the most obvious, may be less important than one or more **remote causes**—factors that occurred further in the past but may have had a greater impact.

⊘ EXERCISE 13.3

Look once more at the diagram on page 358. Which causes do you consider remote causes, and which do you consider immediate causes? Now, look back at your response to Exercise 13.2. Are there any remote causes that you consider nevertheless to be main causes (of primary importance)? Are there any immediate causes that you consider to be only contributory (less important) causes?

Causal Chains

A **causal chain** is a sequence of events in which one event causes the next, which in turn causes the next, and so on. For example, the problem of Americans who do not vote can be described as a causal chain:

High schools do not stress the importance of elections ⟶ Students are not encouraged to follow election coverage in the media ⟶ Students have little knowledge of the issues ⟶ Students do not understand why their votes are important ⟶ Young adults do not develop a habit of voting ⟶ Americans are less likely to vote.

When you write a causal argument, you can organize your essay as a causal chain, as the following outline illustrates:

Thesis statement: U.S. secondary education is at fault for Americans' failure to see voting as a civic duty.

- High schools do not stress the importance of elections.
- As a result, students do not follow election coverage in the media.
- Because they do not follow election coverage, students have little knowledge of the issues.
- With little knowledge of the issues, students do not understand that it is important to vote.
- Because they do not see voting as important, young adults do not develop a habit of regular voting.
- As a result, American adults are less likely to vote.

Concluding statement: Because the habit of voting is established early, high schools need to take responsibility for encouraging students to vote.

KEY WORDS FOR CAUSAL ARGUMENT

When you write causal arguments, use verbs such as the following to indicate causal connections:

bring about	create	lead to	encourage
influence	contribute to	originate in	cause

Be sure to use transitional words and phrases such as *due to, consequently,* and *as a result* to help readers follow your argument. You should also try to repeat words like *cause, effect, outcome,* and *result* to help identify individual causes and effects.

⊙ EXERCISE 13.4

Fill in the blanks to create a causal chain for each of these sequences:

1. Restaurants should be required to list fat and calorie content on their menus. If they do so, _____. As a result, _____. Eventually, _____.

2. Abstinence programs should be instituted in high schools. One immediate result would be _____. This could bring about _____. This in turn might lead to _____. Ideally, the result would be _____.

3. Taxes on cigarettes should be raised. If this step is taken, the first result would be _____. Another possible effect might be _____. In a few years' time, the outcome might be _____.

Post Hoc *Reasoning*

Post hoc **reasoning** is the incorrect assumption that an event that precedes another event has caused that event. For example, you may notice that few of your friends voted in a recent election, and you may also observe that many of your friends are science majors. This does not mean, of course, that their decision to choose careers in science has made them nonvoters. In fact, a scientist can be very interested in electoral politics, and someone who spends four years as a political science major might actually be a nonvoter. As you develop your causal argument, be very careful not to assume that every event that precedes another event has somehow caused it. (For information on avoiding post hoc fallacies, see Chapter 5.)

⊘ EXERCISE 13.5

The following excerpt from a humorous essay by Nora Ephron takes a lighthearted look at the concept of post hoc reasoning. For each paragraph, identify the cause and the result that Ephron discusses. Then, list several more plausible causes for each effect.

> This piece appeared in the *New York Times* on January 13, 2008.

THE CHICKEN SOUP CHRONICLES

NORA EPHRON

The other day I felt a cold coming on. So I decided to have chicken soup to 1
ward off the cold. Nonetheless I got the cold. This happens all the time: you think you're getting a cold; you have chicken soup; you get the cold anyway. So: is it possible that chicken soup gives you a cold?

> "So: is it possible that chicken soup gives you a cold?"

I will confess a bias: I've never 2
understood the religious fervor that surrounds breast-feeding. There are fanatics out there who believe you should breast-feed your child until he or she is old enough to unbutton your blouse. Their success in conning a huge number of women into believing this is one of the truly grim things about modern life. Anyway, one of the main reasons given for breast-feeding is that breast-fed children are less prone to allergies. But children today are far more allergic than they were when I was growing up, when far fewer women breast-fed their children. I mean, what is it with all these children dropping dead from sniffing a peanut? This is new, friends, it's brand-new new, and don't believe anyone who says otherwise. So: is it possible that breast-feeding causes allergies?

It's much easier to write a screenplay on a computer than on a type- 3
writer. Years ago, when you wrote a screenplay on a typewriter, you had to retype the entire page just to make the smallest change; now, on the computer, you can make large and small changes effortlessly, you can fiddle with dialogue, you can change names and places with a keystroke. And yet movies are nowhere near as good as they used to be. In 1939, when screenwriters were practically still using quill pens, the following movies were among those nominated for best picture: *Gone with the Wind, The Wizard of Oz, Mr. Smith Goes to Washington, Wuthering Heights* and *Stagecoach,* and that's not even the whole list. So: is it possible that computers are responsible for the decline of movies?

There is way too much hand-washing going on. Someone told me the 4 other day that the act of washing your hands is supposed to last as long as it takes to sing the song "Happy Birthday." I'm not big on hand-washing to begin with; I don't even like to wash fruit, if you must know. But my own prejudices aside, all this washing-of-hands and use of Purell before picking up infants cannot be good. (By the way, I'm not talking about hand-washing in hospitals, I'm talking about everyday, run-of-the-mill hand-washing.) It can't possibly make sense to keep babies so removed from germs that they never develop an immunity to them. Of course, this isn't my original theory—I read it somewhere a few weeks ago, although I can't remember where. The *New York Times*? The *Wall Street Journal*? Who knows? Not me, that's for sure. So: is it possible that reading about hand-washing leads to memory loss?

Structuring a Causal Argument

Generally speaking, a causal argument can be structured in the following way:

- **Introduction:** Establishes a context for the argument by explaining the need to examine causes or consider effects; states the essay's thesis

- **Refutation of opposing arguments:** Considers and rejects possible causes or effects

- **Evidence (first point in support of thesis):** Discusses less important causes or effects

- **Evidence (second point in support of thesis):** Discusses major causes or effects

- **Conclusion:** Reinforces the argument's main point; includes a strong concluding statement

Other organizational patterns are also possible. For example, you might decide to refute opposing arguments *after* you have discussed arguments in support of your thesis. You might also include a background paragraph (as the student writer whose essay begins on the following page does). Finally, you might decide to organize your essay as a *causal chain* (see p. 359).

 The following student essay illustrates one possible structure for a causal argument. The student writer argues that, contrary to popular opinion, texting is not causing damage to the English language but is a creative force with the power to enrich and expand the language.

TEXTING: A BOON, NOT A THREAT, TO LANGUAGE

KRISTINA MIALKI

1   Certain technological developments of the last two decades have a   Introduction
lot of people worrying about the state of the English language. Emailing,
blogging, instant-messaging, and texting are bringing with them
new ways of writing and communicating. The fear is that these new
technologies will encourage a sloppy, casual form of written English that
will eventually replace proper English altogether. Texting, in particular,
has people concerned because it encourages the use of a specialized,
nonstandard form of English. However, the effects of this new "textese"
are misunderstood. Texting will not destroy the English language; in fact,   Thesis statement
it is keeping the language alive.

2   A text message is a brief written note sent via a cell phone or a similar   Background
device. Texting has become extremely popular because sending text
messages is instant, mobile, and silent. To make texting more efficient,
texters have developed a shorthand—an abbreviated form of English that
uses numbers and symbols in addition to letters. In textese, common
phrases such as "see you later" or "talk to you later" become "cul8r" and
"T2YL." Feelings and phrases are also expressed with emoticons, such as
"*:-o" (meaning "alarmed") or ">:-<" (meaning "angry"). Today, texting is
the preferred method of communication for many young people, who are
the most enthusiastic users of this technology. Not surprisingly, unwarranted
fears that texting will destroy the language often focus on this group.

3   Some people say texting will destroy the English language because   Opposing argument
it encourages use of an overly simplified form of written English that
does not follow standard rules of spelling, grammar, and punctuation.
The implication is that people who text, particularly children and teens,
will not learn proper written English. However, there is no evidence   Refutation
that texting is having or will have this effect. In fact, *Newsweek* recently
reported on a British study that found just the opposite to be true. The
more children texted, the better they did on reading, writing, spelling,

and vocabulary tests (Huang). If, in fact, young people's language skills are weakening, then researchers should seek out the real cause for this decline rather than incorrectly blaming texting.

Evidence: First point in support of thesis

Texting is a valuable way of communicating that actually encourages more writing and reading. Texters often spend hours each day engaged with language. This is time that would otherwise probably be spent on the phone, not reading or writing. Textese may not be standard written English, but it is a rich and creative form of communication, a modification of English for a particular purpose. For this reason, standard English is not in danger of being destroyed or replaced by textese. Just as most young people know not to talk to their teachers the way they talk to their friends, they know not to write papers the way they write text messages. Texting simply broadens young people's exposure to the written word.

Evidence: Second point in support of thesis

Another reason texting is so valuable is that it encourages creative use of language. The small screen size and limited number of keys require texters to be inventive, so the need for new and clever abbreviations is constant. Texters are continually playing with words and coming up with new ways of expressing themselves. Texting does not, as some fear, encourage sloppy, thoughtless, or careless writing. On the contrary, it rewards ingenuity and precision. One recent study of text messages sent between Toronto teenagers confirmed this. The researchers found imagination and skill in the teens' messages and praised what they saw as "an expansive new linguistic renaissance" ("OMG!"). In other words, these researchers recognized that texting was not killing the English language but actually enriching it and keeping it alive.

Conclusion

According to *Newsweek*, people around the world will send approximately 2.3 trillion text messages this year (Huang). The exceptional popularity of texting and its fast growth over the last ten years explain why it is attracting so much attention. It is not, however, the threat that some believe it to be. It is neither destroying the language

Concluding statement

not deadening people's thoughts and feelings. It is a lively and creative way for people to play with words and stay connected.

Works Cited

Huang, Lily. "The Death of English (LOL)." *Newsweek*. Newsweek, 2 Aug. 2008. Web. 23 Aug 2008.

"OMG! Text Teens Are GR8 at Language After All." Yorkshire
   Post [Leeds, England] 15 May 2008: n. pag. InfoTrac Custom
   Newspapers. Web. 25 Aug. 2008.

GRAMMAR IN CONTEXT: AVOIDING "THE REASON IS BECAUSE"

When you write a **causal argument**, you connect causes to effects. In
the process, you might be tempted to use the ungrammatical phrase
the reason is because. However, the word *because* means "for the reason
that"; therefore, it is redundant to say "the reason is because" (which
actually means "the reason is for the reason that"). Instead, use the
grammatical phrase "the reason is *that*."

INCORRECT	Another <u>reason</u> texting is so valuable <u>is because</u> it encourages creative use of language.
CORRECT	Another <u>reason</u> texting is so valuable <u>is that</u> it encourages creative use of language.

⊜ EXERCISE 13.6

The following essay, "U.S. Needs an Educated Citizenry" by Marjorie
O. Rendell, is a causal argument. Read the essay carefully, and then
answer the questions that follow it, consulting the outline on page 362 if
necessary.

The *Philadelphia Inquirer* published this piece on September 15, 2008.

U.S. NEEDS AN EDUCATED CITIZENRY

MARJORIE O. RENDELL

At the close of the Constitutional Convention in Philadelphia, 221 years ago 1
this week, a crowd approached Benjamin Franklin. They asked whether the
founders had created a monarchy or a republic.

"A Republic, if you can keep it," he replied. 2

Franklin's brief response captures the dual qualities upon which the survival 3 of American democracy depends: an enduring Constitution, and an engaged and informed citizenry. Each depends on the other—citizens need the Constitution to guide them, and the Constitution needs citizens to infuse it with new meaning in each generation.

> "More than two centuries later, many believe that the democratic process Franklin helped create is incapable of meeting America's national challenges." 4

More than two centuries later, many believe that the democratic process Franklin helped create is incapable of meeting America's national challenges. A recent Pew survey reported that only a third of Americans trust the federal government as an institution.

This distrust of government leads to a vicious cycle. Declining participa- 5 tion causes a decline in the quality of governance, leading citizens to further disengage from the political life of their communities and the nation. How can we redress this democracy deficit?

The central feature of the democracy deficit is a knowledge deficit. There 6 is a huge gap between what people need to know to be productive citizens and engage effectively in the democratic process.

On the last national civics assessment, administered in 2006, two-thirds 7 of students scored below proficient and less than a fifth of high school seniors could explain how citizen participation benefits democracy.

Closing this knowledge gap requires us to recognize the role that pub- 8 lic schools, as the single institution affecting more Americans than any other, must play in training young people for active citizenship. Franklin's vision of democracy—"if we can keep it"—requires sustained citizen engagement in local, state and national politics.

This sort of engagement is impossible without the proper education. 9 While until the 1960s many high schools required graduating students to have taken three civics courses, today most schools offer only a single, often optional civics course that overlooks the role of citizens in democracy.

We must once again make civic education the cornerstone of public 10 education. This goal requires a joint commitment on the part of individual schools, as well as policymakers at every level.

My passion for improving civic knowledge and engagement led me to 11 help establish the Pennsylvania Coalition for Representative Democracy (PennCORD) in 2004. PennCORD unites educational, advocacy and governmental organizations committed to improving civic learning for students in grades K–12. The key partners include the Pennsylvania Bar Association, the National Constitution Center, the state Department of Education, and the Governor's Office of the First Lady.

Our goal is to prepare students to understand and participate in their 12
communities, government and society. And, building a solid foundation in
civic learning is the first critical step toward achieving this goal.

As fellow Pennsylvanian and Justice Robert H. Jackson once said, "It is 13
not the function of our government to keep the citizens from falling into error;
it is the function of the citizen to keep the government from falling into error."

Schools should promote civic learning, both in the classroom and through 14
service-based learning, through inclusion in their school mission statements
and integration into curricula at every grade level.

States and the federal government should include civics on mandated 15
assessments to prevent it from being eclipsed by other subjects.

Franklin's message to the crowd outside Independence Hall so many years 16
ago remains the defining challenge for Americans in the coming century.

All of our national challenges—from energy dependence to the rising def- 17
icit to the wars overseas—can be met by citizens who rise to the challenge of
serving their communities and the nation.

Yet we can only keep the Republic if every school in America renews that 18
spirit and preserves the citizenry that can guide us forward.

Identifying the Elements of a Causal Argument

1. What problem does Rendell identify in paragraph 4 of this essay?
   Summarize this problem in your own words.

2. Paragraph 5 presents a causal chain. List the elements of this causal chain.

3. In paragraph 6, Rendell identifies the cause of the problem she discusses. Summarize this cause in your own words.

4. List the recommendations Rendell makes for how to solve the problem she discusses.

5. In paragraph 17, Rendell explains the results of implementing her
   recommendations. What outcome does she expect?

6. Reread the essay's concluding statement. Is it effective? Is it appropriate for the essay?

Will Lowering the Drinking Age Solve the Problem of Binge Drinking among College Students?

Reread the At Issue box on page 353. Then, read the sources on the pages that follow.

As you read each of these sources, you will be asked to respond to a series of questions and complete some simple activities. This work will help you to understand the content and structure of the material you read. When you are finished, you will be prepared to write a **causal argument** in which you take a position on the topic, "Will Lowering the Drinking Age Solve the Problem of Binge Drinking among College Students?"

SOURCES

 Amethyst Initiative, "Statement"

 Radley Balko, "Amethyst Initiative's Debate on Drinking a Welcome Alternative to Fanaticism"

 Joanne Glasser, "Alcohol and Those under Twenty-One Don't Mix"

 Andrew Herman, "Raise the Drinking Age to Twenty-Five"

 Bradley R. Gitz, "Save Us from Youth"

 Robert Voas, "There's No Benefit to Lowering the Drinking Age"

STATEMENT

AMETHYST INITIATIVE

It's Time to Rethink the Drinking Age

In 1984 Congress passed the National Minimum Drinking Age Act, which 1 imposed a penalty of 10% of a state's federal highway appropriation on any state setting its drinking age lower than 21.

Twenty-four years later, our experience as college and university presidents convinces us that . . .

> **"Twenty-one is not working."** 2

Twenty-One Is Not Working

A culture of dangerous, clandestine "binge-drinking"—often conducted off- 3 campus—has developed.

Alcohol education that mandates abstinence as the only legal option has 4 not resulted in significant constructive behavioral change among our students.

Adults under 21 are deemed capable of voting, signing contracts, serving on juries 5 and enlisting in the military, but are told they are not mature enough to have a beer.

By choosing to use fake IDs, students make ethical compromises that erode 6 respect for the law.

How Many Times Must We Relearn the Lessons of Prohibition?

We call upon our elected officials: 7

> To support an informed and dispassionate public debate over the effects of the 21-year-old drinking age.

> To consider whether the 10% highway fund "incentive" encourages or inhibits that debate.

> To invite new ideas about the best ways to prepare young adults to make responsible decisions about alcohol.

We pledge ourselves and our institutions to playing a vigorous, construc- 8 tive role as these critical discussions unfold.

To Sign:

1. Review and print statement 9
2. Sign, indicating your name and institution

369

3. Return by mail to:

The Amethyst Initiative
PO Box 507
Middlebury, VT 05753

Or by fax to: 802-398-2029

Currently, membership in the Amethyst Initiative is limited to college and uni- 10
versity presidents and chancellors. If you are not a president or chancellor, but would
like to become part of this larger effort, please sign-up at chooseresponsibility.org.

Amethyst Initiative
PO Box 507 Middlebury, VT 05753 802.398.2024
info@amethystinitiative.org

⊙ AT ISSUE: SOURCES FOR DEVELOPING A CAUSAL ARGUMENT

1. Two of the headings in this position paper—"It's Time to Rethink the Drinking Age" and "Twenty-One Is Not Working"—together express the college presidents' position. Combine these two headings to create a one-sentence thesis statement that expresses this opinion.

2. Read the argument in paragraph 5 carefully. Then, write a brief refutation of this argument.

3. Does the college presidents' statement actually call for lowering the drinking age, or does it take a different position? Explain.

4. What does the statement ask of elected officials? What does it pledge that college presidents will do?

5. How do the writers of this statement establish their credibility? Do you think they need to do more?

This article is from *FoxNews.com,* where it appeared on August 25, 2008.

AMETHYST INITIATIVE'S DEBATE ON DRINKING A WELCOME ALTERNATIVE TO FANATICISM

RADLEY BALKO

1   It's been nearly 25 years since Congress blackmailed the states to raise the minimum drinking age to 21 or lose federal highway funding. Supporters of the law have hailed it as an unqualified success, and until recently, they've met little resistance.

2   For obvious reasons, no one wants to stand up for teen drinking. The alcohol industry won't touch the federal minimum drinking age, having been sufficiently scolded by groups like Mothers Against Drunk Driving and federal regulators. So the law's miraculous effects have generally gone unchallenged.

3   But that may be changing. Led by John McCardell, the soft-spoken former president of Middlebury in Vermont, a new group called the Amethyst Initiative is calling for a new national debate on the drinking age. And McCardell and his colleagues ought to know. The Amethyst Group consists of current and former college and university presidents, and they say the federal minimum drinking age has contributed to an epidemic of binge drinking, as well as other excessive, unhealthy drinking habits on their campuses.

4   This makes perfect sense. Prohibitions have always provoked overindulgence. Those of us who have attended college over the last 25 years can certainly attest to the fact that the law has done nothing to diminish freshman and sophomore access to alcohol. It has only pushed underage consumption underground. It causes other problems, too. Underage students, for example, may be reluctant to obtain medical aid for peers who have had too much to drink, out of fear of implicating themselves for drinking illegally, or for contributing to underage drinking.

> "It has only pushed underage consumption underground."

5   More than 120 college presidents and chancellors have now signed on to the Amethyst Initiative's statement, including those from Duke, Tufts, Dartmouth, Johns Hopkins, Syracuse, Maryland, and Ohio. Over the last few years several states, including Wisconsin, Montana, Minnesota, Kentucky, South Carolina, and Vermont have also considering lowering their drinking ages back to 18.

6   All of this has the usual suspects predictably agitated. Mothers Against Drunk Driving, not accustomed to striking a defensive posture, calls the Amethyst Initiative's request for an "informed debate" on the issue "deeply

disappointing," and has even raised the possibility that parents shouldn't send their kids to colleges who have signed on to the measure.

Acting National Transportation Safety Board Chairman Mark Rosenker 7 says it would be a "national tragedy" to, for example, allow 19- and 20-year-old men and women returning from Iraq and Afghanistan to have a beer in celebration of completing their tours of duty.

Supporters of the 21 minimum drinking age have long credited the law 8 with the dramatic reduction in traffic fatalities they say took place after it was passed. But a study released last July may pull the rug out from their strongest argument.

The working paper by economic researchers Jeffrey Miron and Elina 9 Tetelbaum finds that the bulk of studies on highway fatalities since the federal minimum drinking age went into effect erroneously include data from 12 states that had already set their drinking ages at 21, without federal coercion. That, Miron and Tetelbaum conclude, may have skewed the data, and indicated a national trend that may not actually exist.

While it's true that highway fatalities have dropped since 1984, it isn't nec- 10 essarily because we rose the drinking age. In fact, the downward trend actually began in 1969, just as many states began *lowering* their drinking ages in recognition of the absurdity of prohibiting servicemen returning from Vietnam from enjoying a beer (the 1984 law was a backlash against those states). As Miron and Tetelbaum explain, 1969 was the year when "several landmark improvements were made in the accident avoidance and crash protection features of passenger cars," a more likely explanation for the drop than a law passed 15 years later.

Miron and Tetelbaum also credit advances in medical technology and 11 trauma treatment for the decline in fatalities, which makes sense, given that we've seen improvements in just about every other area of human development over the same period, including life expectancy, and both incidence and survival rates of major medical conditions like heart disease, cancer, and stroke—none of which have much to do with teen drinking.

The U.S. has the highest minimum drinking age in the world (save for 12 countries where it's forbidden entirely). In countries with a low or no national minimum drinking age, teens are introduced to alcohol gradually, moderately, and under the supervision of their parents.

U.S. teens, on the other hand, tend to first try alcohol in unsupervised 13 environments—in cars, motels, or outdoor settings in high school, or in dorm rooms, fraternity parties, or house parties when they leave home to go to college. During alcohol prohibition, we saw how adults who imbibed under such conditions reacted—they drank way too much, way too fast. It shouldn't be surprising that teens react in much the same way.

Anti-alcohol organizations like MADD and the American Medical Associa- 14 tion oppose even allowing parents to give minors alcohol in supervised settings, such as a glass of wine with dinner, or a beer on the couch while watching the football game. They've pushed for prison time for parents who throw supervised parties where minors are given access to alcohol, even though those parties probably made the roads safer than they otherwise would have been (let's face it—if the kids hadn't been drinking at the supervised party, they'd have been drinking at an unsupervised one). They advocate a "not one drop until 21" policy that's not only unrealistic, it mystifies and glorifies alcohol by making the drug a forbidden fruit—a surefire way to make teens want to taste it.

McCardell and the academics who have signed on to the Amethyst Initiative are asking only for a debate—an honest discussion based on data and common sense, not one tainted by Carry Nation–style fanaticism. In today's hyper-cautious, ban-happy public health environment, that's refreshing. The group comprises serious academics who have collectively spent thousands of years around the very young people these laws are affecting. The nation's policy makers would be foolish to dismiss their concerns out of hand. 15

⊜ AT ISSUE: SOURCES FOR DEVELOPING A CAUSAL ARGUMENT

1. Write a thesis statement for Balko's essay. Where would you locate this thesis statement? Why?

2. In paragraph 4, Balko summarizes two problems that he says have been caused by the higher drinking age. In your own words, summarize these two problems. If you can, list one or two additional problems.

3. What, according to Balko, is the Amethyst Initiative's position on the drinking age? Where does he summarize this position? Is his interpretation of the group's position accurate? (Refer to the Amethyst Initiative's statement on p. 369.)

4. How do Miron and Tetelbaum's findings (summarized in paras. 9–11) challenge the arguments of those who support the current minimum drinking age? Does Balko cite any other experts to support his position? What additional kinds of supporting evidence do you think would be helpful?

5. Consider each of the following words and expressions: *fanaticism* (title), *blackmailed* (1), *scolded* (2), *the usual suspects* (6). Do you think any of this language is inflammatory? Can you find other uses of slanted language? Do you think that more neutral language would be more appropriate (and just as effective) here, or do you see this kind of language as necessary?

This piece is from *ChicagoTribune.com*, where it appeared on August 29, 2008.

ALCOHOL AND THOSE UNDER TWENTY-ONE DON'T MIX

JOANNE GLASSER

About this time last year a 19-year-old Bradley University soccer player died 1 when four of his friends lit Roman candles, accidentally setting his bedroom on fire as he slept. All had been drinking, including the victim. Three of the four students—who would end up in jail—also played soccer for Bradley.

Eight days after that tragedy I arrived in Peoria to start my first year as 2 Bradley president, knowing well what one of my priorities would be. Bradley would rewrite its book on how to deal with alcohol use and abuse. I did not believe then—nor did the committee members who drafted the new policies conclude—that lives would be saved by dumbing those policies down.

I make this point because more than 120 university presidents have signed 3 on to a movement urging lawmakers to consider lowering the drinking age from 21 to 18. The Amethyst Initiative argues that the higher age limit not only isn't working; it's developed "a culture of dangerous, clandestine binge-drinking" among underage students.

I do not believe for a moment that Bradley's tragedy would have been avoided 4 had alcohol been easier to get. And I vehemently disagree that lowering the drinking age would make college campuses safer.

"The facts are with me."

The facts are with me. 5

The National Highway Traffic Safety 6 Administration says that in 1982, two years before Congress effectively raised the minimum national drinking age, 43 percent of underage drivers involved in fatal crashes had been drinking. By 1998, just 21 percent had been. A NHTSA study found that the new law not only reduced drinking and driving but reduced "youth drinking directly."

A 2005 Harvard University study found that binge drinking on college 7 campuses is one-third lower in states where tough laws target high-volume sales. The researchers said states concerned about underage drinking should toughen laws and their enforcement, not ease up.

Reviewing 40 years worth of literature published on the subject, two Uni- 8 versity of Minnesota researchers concluded, "The preponderance of the evidence suggests that higher legal drinking ages reduce alcohol consumption."

One of the leading experts on the misuse of alcohol by college students, 9 Henry Wechsler of the Harvard School of Public Health, says reducing the drinking age would not reduce the misuse of alcohol on college campuses.

The American Medical Association seconds that conclusion: "There is no 10 evidence that there were fewer campus alcohol problems when lower drinking ages were in effect." Conversely, universities have found that the minimum legal drinking age "provides a strong legal rationale to develop effective prevention policies that can reduce high-risk as well as underage drinking," according to the AMA.

That is exactly what we have done at Bradley University. 11

Some highlights: 12

- Weekend, on-campus events dubbed "Late Night BU" provide our students with alcohol-free ways to have fun.
- Our alcohol education program has been expanded and integrated into first-year classes and residence hall programs.

New penalties underscore just how seriously we take alcohol misuse. Students who violate our policy may be fined and may be prohibited from living in fraternity or sorority houses, or elsewhere off campus. Student leaders who are twice cited will be barred from holding leadership positions for a year. Repeat offenders may be suspended from the university. 13

Ask me to describe Bradley, and I'll tell you it's a superb university for serious students, located in a prototypical American city. In coping with an "alcohol culture" on campus, Bradley is the norm, not the exception. What's unusual at Bradley is our determination to change that—and our motivation. I should say that Bradley University doesn't make anyone's list of the nation's top party schools. 14

Not long after our committee began meeting, alcohol played a major role in the death of another student, a young man who fell into traffic while horsing around along a busy street near campus. His blood-alcohol content was more than twice Illinois' legal threshold. This student was 22, one year past the minimum drinking age. Clearly the fact that he could access alcohol legally did not protect him from misusing it. 15

Because of what Bradley went through this past year, I believe I may recognize more than most the serious consequences of allowing 18- and 19-year-olds to belly up to the bar, no questions asked. Our plan is intended both to make a meaningful difference at Bradley and to make the university a national leader in combating the misuse of alcohol. We will be measuring changes in students' perceptions and behavior to see how we're doing. We'll be happy to keep you posted. 16

AT ISSUE: SOURCES FOR DEVELOPING A CAUSAL ARGUMENT

1. This essay is a refutation of the statement by the university presidents on page 369. Where does Glasser explicitly present this refutation in one sentence? Is this sentence her essay's thesis? Explain.

2. In paragraph 5, Glasser says, "The facts are with me." List the facts she uses to support her challenge to the university presidents. Are these statements all actually "facts," or do you think some are opinions?

3. Glasser begins her essay with an anecdote; in paragraph 15, she includes another one. Why does she use each anecdote? Does she achieve her purpose in both cases?

The piece appeared on August 22, 2007, on *BG Views,* a Web site for Bowling Green State University and the citizens of its community.

RAISE THE DRINKING AGE TO TWENTY-FIVE

ANDREW HERMAN

As a new school year begins, as dorms fill with new and returning students alike, a single thought frequents the minds of every member of our population: newfound freedom from a summer of jobs and familial responsibilities. 1

But our return to school coexists with a possibly lethal counterpart: college drinking. 2

Nearly everyone is exposed to parties during college, and one would be hard pressed to find a college party without alcohol. Most University students indicate in countless surveys they have used alcohol in a social setting before age 21. 3

It is startling just how ineffective current laws have been at curbing underage drinking. 4

> "It is startling just how ineffective current laws have been."

A dramatic change is needed in the way society addresses drinking and the way we enforce existing laws, and it can start with a simple change: making the drinking age 25. 5

Access and availability are the principal reasons underage drinking has become easy to do. Not through direct availability, but through access to legal-aged "friends." 6

In a college setting, it is all but impossible not to know a person who is older than 21 and willing to provide alcohol to younger students. Even if unintentional, there is no verification that each person who drinks is of the appropriate age. 7

However, it should be quite easy to ensure underage individuals don't have access to alcohol. In reality, those who abstain from alcohol are in the minority. Countless people our age consider speeding tickets worse than an arrest for underage consumption. 8

Is it truly possible alcohol abuse has become so commonplace, so acceptable, that people forget the facts? 9

Each year, 1,400 [college students] die from drinking too much. 600,000 are victims of alcohol-related physical assault and 17,000 are a result of drunken driving deaths, many being innocent bystanders. 10

Perhaps the most disturbing number: 70,000 people, overwhelmingly female, are annually sexually assaulted in alcohol-related situations. 11

These numbers are difficult to grasp for the sheer prevalence of alcoholic destruction. Yet, we, as college students, are responsible for an overwhelming portion of their incidence. It is difficult to imagine anyone would wish to assume the role of rapist, murderer or victim. We all assume these things could never happen to us, but I am certain victims in these situations thought the same. The simple truth is that driving under the influence is the leading cause of death for teens. For 12

10- to 24-year-olds, alcohol is the fourth-leading cause of death, made so by factors ranging from alcohol poisoning to alcohol-related assault and murder.

For the sake of our friends, those we love, our futures and ourselves, we must take a stand and we must do it now. 13

Advocates of lowering the drinking age assert only four countries worldwide maintain a "21 standard," and a gradual transition to alcohol is useful in reducing the systemic social problems of substance abuse. 14

If those under the age of 21 are misusing alcohol, it makes little sense to grant free rein to those individuals to use it legally. A parent who observes their children abusing the neighbor's dog would be irresponsible to get one of their own without altering such dangerous behavior. 15

Increasing the drinking age will help in the search for solutions to grievous alcoholic problems, making it far more difficult in college environments to find legal-aged providers. 16

By the time we are 25, with careers and possibly families of our own, there is no safety net to allow us to have a "Thirsty Thursday." But increasing the legal age is not all that needs to be done. Drinking to get drunk needs to exist as a social taboo rather than a doorway to popularity. 17

Peer pressure can become a tool to change this. What once was a factor greatly contributing to underage drinking can now become an instrument of good, seeking to end such a dangerous practice as excessive drinking. Laws on drinking ages, as any other law, need to be enforced with the energy and vigor each of us should expect. 18

Alcohol is not an inherently evil poison. It does have its place, as do all things in the great scheme of life. 19

But with alcohol comes the terrible risk of abuse with consequences many do not consider. All too often, these consequences include robbing someone of his life or loved one. All communities in the country, our own included, have been touched by such a tragedy. 20

Because of this, and the hundreds of thousands of victims each year in alcohol-related situations, I ask that you consider the very real possibility of taking the life of another due to irresponsible drinking. 21

If this is not enough, then take time to think, because that life could very well be your own. 22

⊘ AT ISSUE: SOURCES FOR DEVELOPING A CAUSAL ARGUMENT

1. This essay's author is a college student. Given his position on the issue, does his status as a student increase or decrease his credibility?

2. How does Herman establish common ground with his readers?

3. In paragraph 14, Herman mentions an opposing argument. How does he refute it? Do you think his refutation is strong enough? If not, how would you expand or reword it?

The *Arkansas Democrat-Gazette* published this piece on August 31, 2008.

SAVE US FROM YOUTH

BRADLEY R. GITZ

It was Ralph Waldo Emerson who wrote, "A foolish consistency is the hob- 1
goblin of little minds." Seldom has anything so stupid been said by someone
so smart.

Far from a reflection of deficient thinking, consistency is the most impor- 2
tant and elusive quality in politics, if only because without it we are left with
nothing but sheer randomness. For our laws to make sense they must be based
on discernible political principles free of the kind of internal contradictions
that consistency irons out.

A modest case of inconsistency arose recently with newspaper reports that 3
a growing number of American college presidents are agitating for a reduction
in the drinking age from 21. A petition they have circulated to that effect has
already drawn fire from Mothers Against Drunk Driving and various public
safety experts (whatever that means) who have conjured up the usual horror
stories of the carnage on our roads that would supposedly flow from such a
change.

The complaint of the college presidents is a reasonable if hardly decisive 4
one—that it has become too difficult to police
the thing because their students are going to
drink anyway, with such difficulties contributing to a shift toward surreptitious behavior that
undermines respect for the law.

> "Students are going
> to drink anyway."

The interesting part of the spat, and that which brings the consistency 5
angle into play, is the part that is missing: any discussion of whether it is
morally acceptable to deny a certain group of legal adults, in this case those
between 18 and 21, things that other legal adults are not denied.

Ultimately, the most important issue at stake with respect to the drinking 6
age is not whether 18-year-olds are responsible enough to consume alcohol, or
even the consequences of such consumption in legal vs. illegal circumstances,
but whether those who are old enough to be sued in a court of law, carry
a gun into combat on behalf of their fellow citizens and participate in our
democratic process by stepping into a voting booth should be prevented from
occupying a bar stool.

Clearly, even those skeptical of the maturity of 18- and 19-year-olds must 7
recognize that a significant percentage of the military personnel defending their
freedom to drink liquor and do lots of other things is of such age. Indeed, it
takes a rather extraordinary amount of chutzpah for Party A to tell Party B, who
happens to be risking his life on the battlefield on behalf of Party A, that he is
not mature enough to legally enjoy the things in life that Party A gets to enjoy.

American soldiers who have served their country by braving the suicide bombers and snipers in places like Iraq and Afghanistan would seem to deserve better.

All of this becomes more bizarre still when we encounter enthusiastic 8 campaigns to increase the voting rates of those 18 to 21 on the assumption that they don't vote as often as they should. For some inexplicable reason, we feel that such young people are capable of making the kinds of political distinctions compatible with democratic governance but are thoroughly untrustworthy when it comes to a six-pack of Budweiser.

The point here is not that the drinking age should be 18, as opposed to 21 9 or even 40; rather, it is that consistency should prevail so that it is not different from the age of consensual adult behavior in other realms, including serving in the military and voting. No one should be treated with the respect accorded an adult in some areas but not others.

In short, it matters less what the drinking age is than that it corresponds 10 to and is compatible with the other standards of adulthood. So if the idea of 18-year-olds flooding into the bars alarms us, as well it might, then the better solution might be to raise the age requirement for lots of other things to 21 or wherever, thereby providing the logical heft that only consistency can provide to an argument.

The current disparity in age requirements carries with it not only incon- 11 sistency but the implicit assumption that certain activities, such as military service and voting, require less maturity and matter less than the ability to safely consume a glass of cheap wine.

For some of us, the specter of college students at a fraternity keg party is 12 a great deal less terrifying than the fact that a fair number of 18-year-olds who don't know who the vice president is or whether Mexico is to our north or south will be handed ballots on the first Tuesday in November.

⊃ AT ISSUE: SOURCES FOR DEVELOPING A CAUSAL ARGUMENT

1. Gitz develops his thesis in paragraphs 6, 9, and 10. State this thesis in one sentence.

2. Why does Gitz begin his essay with a quotation from Emerson and a commentary on that quotation? Is this an effective opening strategy? What does it tell you about how Gitz sees his audience?

3. In paragraph 5, Gitz presents his argument for legal consistency in moral terms. Do you see his essay as essentially a moral or ethical argument, or do you think it is more an argument of logic? Explain.

This piece appeared in the January 12, 2006, edition of the *Christian Science Monitor.*

THERE'S NO BENEFIT TO LOWERING THE DRINKING AGE

ROBERT VOAS

After nearly four decades of exacting research on how to save lives and reduce injuries by preventing drinking and driving, there is a revanchist attempt afoot to roll back one of the most successful laws in generations: the minimum legal drinking age of 21.

This is extremely frustrating. While public health researchers must produce painstaking evidence that's subjected to critical scholarly review, lower-drinking-age advocates seem to dash off remarks based on glib conjecture and self-selected facts.

It's startling that anybody—given the enormous bodies of research and data—would consider lowering the drinking age. And yet, legislation is currently pending in New Hampshire and Wisconsin to lower the drinking age for military personnel and for all residents in Vermont. Just as bad are the arguments from think-tank writers, various advocates, and even academics (including at least one former college president) that ignore or manipulate the real evidence and instead rely on slogans.

> "It's startling that anybody—given the enormous bodies of research and data—would consider lowering the drinking age."

I keep hearing the same refrains: "If you're old enough to go to war, you should be old enough to drink," or "the drinking-age law just increases the desire for the forbidden fruit," or "lower crash rates are due to tougher enforcement, not the 21 law," or "Europeans let their kids drink, so they learn how to be more responsible," or finally, "I did it when I was a kid, and I'm OK."

First, I'm not sure what going to war and being allowed to drink have in common. The military takes in youngsters particularly because they are not yet fully developed and can be molded into soldiers. The 21 law is predicated on the fact that drinking is more dangerous for youth because they're still developing mentally and physically, and they lack experience and are more likely to take risks. Ask platoon leaders and unit commanders, and they'll tell you that the last thing they want is young soldiers drinking.

As for the forbidden fruit argument, the opposite is true. Research shows that back when some states still had a minimum drinking age of 18, youths in those states who were under 21 drank more and continued to drink more as adults in their early 20s. In states where the drinking age was 21, teenagers drank less and continue to drink less through their early 20s.

And the minimum 21 law, by itself, has most certainly resulted in fewer 7 accidents, because the decline occurred even when there was little enforcement and tougher penalties had not yet been enacted. According to the National Highway Traffic Safety Administration, the 21 law has saved 23,733 lives since states began raising drinking ages in 1975.

Do European countries really have fewer youth drinking problems? No, 8 that's a myth. Compared to American youth, binge drinking rates among young people are higher in every European country except Turkey. Intoxication rates are higher in most countries; in Britain, Denmark, and Ireland they're more than twice the U.S. level. Intoxication and binge drinking are directly linked to higher levels of alcohol-related problems, such as drinking and driving.

But, you drank when you were a kid, and you're OK. Thank goodness, 9 because many kids aren't OK. An average of 11 American teens die each day from alcohol-related crashes. Underage drinking leads to increased teen pregnancy, violent crime, sexual assault, and huge costs to our communities. Among college students, it leads to 1,700 deaths, 500,000 injuries, 600,000 physical assaults, and 70,000 sexual assaults each year.

Recently, New Zealand lowered its drinking age, which gave researchers 10 a good opportunity to study the impact. The result was predictable: The rate of alcohol-related crashes among young people rose significantly compared to older drivers.

I've been studying drinking and driving for nearly 40 years and have been 11 involved in public health and behavioral health for 53 years. Believe me when I say that lowering the drinking age would be very dangerous; it would benefit no one except those who profit from alcohol sales.

If bars and liquor stores can freely provide alcohol to teenagers, parents 12 will be out of the loop when it comes to their children's decisions about drinking. Age 21 laws are designed to keep such decisions within the family where they belong. Our society, particularly our children and grandchildren, will be immeasurably better off if we not only leave the minimum drinking age law as it is, but enforce it better, too.

⊙ AT ISSUE: SOURCES FOR DEVELOPING A CAUSAL ARGUMENT

1. Voas, a research scientist, addresses the "consistency" argument advanced by Bradley R. Gitz (p. 378). Does he do a satisfactory job of presenting arguments against this position? Why or why not?

2. How does Voas view people who favor lowering the drinking age? How can you tell? Do you agree with his characterizations?

3. In paragraph 11, Voas establishes himself as an expert on the issue. Should he have presented his credentials earlier? If so, where?

⊖ EXERCISE 13.7

Write a one-paragraph causal argument in which you take a position on whether lowering the drinking age to eighteen will solve the problem of binge drinking among college students. Follow the template below, filling in the blanks to create your argument.

Template for Writing a Causal Argument

In 1984, the federal drinking age was raised to twenty-one. Since that time, there have been many positive results, such as _____

_____

_____. However, there have also been some negative effects. As over 100 college presidents who favor reconsidering the federal drinking age point out, _____

_____

_____. MADD and others, however, argue against lowering the drinking age, noting that _____

_____. Granted, _____

_____. Still,

_____

_____

_____

_____. For these reasons, _____

_____

_____.

⊖ EXERCISE 13.8

Working with a group of two or three of your classmates, discuss your experiences with alcohol as a high school student and as a college student. What negative behavior have you observed at parties where alcohol was served? What problems have you observed with teenage drivers and alcohol? Does your group believe that these problems were caused or exacerbated by the current drinking age? Write a paragraph that summarizes your group's impressions.

⊖ EXERCISE 13.9

Write a causal argument on the topic, "Will Lowering the Drinking Age Solve the Problem of Binge Drinking among College Students?" Begin by considering all possible causes of binge drinking and explaining why you think that certain factors are most to blame for the situation. Then, consider whether a change in the drinking age will have a positive effect on the problem. (If you like, you may incorporate the material you developed for Exercises 13.7 and 13.8 into your essay.) Cite the readings on pages 369–381, and be sure to document the sources you use and to include a works-cited page. (See Chapter 10 for information on documenting sources.)

➲ EXERCISE 13.10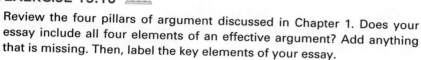

Review the four pillars of argument discussed in Chapter 1. Does your essay include all four elements of an effective argument? Add anything that is missing. Then, label the key elements of your essay.

➲ WRITING ASSIGNMENTS: CAUSAL ARGUMENT

1. What could your school do to encourage students to adopt healthier lifestyles? Write an editorial for your college newspaper in the form of a causal argument. In your editorial, take one of these two positions:

■ If the university takes steps to encourage healthier lifestyles, students will benefit greatly.

■ If the university does not take steps to encourage students to adopt healthier lifestyles, the consequences could be serious.

2. Look at pictures of female celebrities in popular magazines such as *People* or *Us*, and consider the likely effects of these photos on teenage girls. Then, write an essay arguing for or against the charge that photos such as these help to encourage poor self-esteem, risky behavior, or eating disorders. Include some of the pictures in your essay, and analyze the impact of their visual elements as well as the effect of the words in the accompanying articles or captions.

3. In recent years, young children's lives have become more and more structured. Instead of the free play that their parents enjoyed, many of today's elementary-school-age children are busy with scheduled sports, lessons, and play dates. Write an essay structured as a causal chain that traces the probable causes of this change as well as its likely effects on children and on their families. In your thesis statement, indicate whether you consider the effects positive or negative.

CHAPTER 14

Evaluation Arguments

AT ISSUE

Do the Harry Potter Books Deserve Their Popularity?

In 1997, the publication of *Harry Potter and the Philosopher's Stone* introduced a worldwide phenomenon. Both children and adults were fascinated by the adventures of Harry Potter and his friends at the Hogwarts School of Witchcraft and Wizardry as they struggled against the evil Lord Voldemort.

Today, the author of the seven Harry Potter books, J. K. Rowling, is reportedly the highest-earning writer of all time. Around the world, her books have been praised for turning countless children into avid readers. The Harry Potter books have been translated into dozens of languages and have been the subject of films and video games—as well as the subject of some controversy.

Although millions who have followed the exploits of Harry Potter hold the books in high regard, the series has its critics. Some question the books' literary value, arguing that they are repetitious and poorly written. These critics claim that the key elements of the books are little more than clichés of children's literature, perhaps offering entertainment and comfort but not education or enlightenment.

Some conservative Christians object to the books' violent content and question their moral values, arguing that children should not be celebrating witches and wizards, and some feminists believe that the books shortchange their female characters. Other commentators dismiss the series as more of a marketing phenomenon than a groundbreaking literary event. Still others believe that although the books are acceptable entertainment for children, they offer little that is new or original, let alone compelling, for adult readers.

The question of whether the Harry Potter books deserve their popularity is complex. As writer Charles Taylor notes, "Nothing deserves our respect (or scorn) simply because it's popular, no matter how popular" (p. 409).

Later in this chapter, you will return to this topic as you explore readings on both sides of this issue. You will then be asked to write an **evaluation argument** that takes a position on whether the Harry Potter books live up to their reputation.

385

What Is an Evaluation Argument?

You evaluate when you express an opinion about the quality of an item—for example, a product, service, program, performance, work of literature or art, or candidate for public office. When you evaluate, you make a value judgment about something or someone.

When constructing an **evaluation argument**, you have several options: you can make a positive or negative judgment, you can assert that someone else's positive or negative judgment is not accurate or justified, or you can write a comparative evaluation, in which you demonstrate that one thing is (or is not) superior to another.

Evaluation is part of your daily life. Before you make any decision, you need to evaluate your options. For example, you evaluate clothing and electronic equipment before you make a purchase, and you evaluate films, concerts, and TV shows before you decide how to spend your evening. Before you decide to go to a party, you evaluate its positive and negative qualities—who will be there, what music you are likely to hear, and what kind of food and drink will probably be on hand. You also evaluate your teachers, your classes, and even your friends. Without evaluation, you would be unable to function in your daily life.

In your personal life and in your life as a student, you might read (or write) evaluations based on topics like the following:

- Is the college bookstore doing its best to serve students?
- Is the Canadian medical system superior to the U.S. system?
- Is *Moby-Dick* the great American novel?
- Is New Orleans still a worthwhile tourist destination?
- Has the 2002 McCain-Feingold act been successful in reforming campaign finance practices?
- Is the SAT a valid testing instrument?
- Are portable e-book readers such as the Kindle worth buying?
- Are Crocs a marvel of comfort and design or just ugly shoes?
- Are hybrid cars worth the money?
- Are the Beatles the most important band of the twentieth century?

◉ EXERCISE 14.1

List ten additional topics that would be suitable for evaluation arguments.

◉ EXERCISE 14.2

Choose one word in each of the word pairs listed in the box on the next page, and use each word in a sentence that evaluates a service at your school.

MAKING EVALUATIONS

When you write an evaluation, you use terms like the following to express judgments and indicate the relative merits of two items:

- Superior/inferior
- Useful/useless
- Efficient/inefficient
- Effective/ineffective
- Successful/unsuccessful
- Deserving/undeserving

- Important/trivial
- Original/trite
- Innovative/predictable
- Interesting/dull
- Inspiring/depressing

Criteria for Evaluation

When you evaluate something, you cannot just say that it is good or bad, useful or useless, valuable or worthless, or superior or inferior to something else. You need to explain *why* this is so. Before you can begin to develop a thesis and gather supporting evidence for your argument, you need to decide what **criteria for evaluation** you will use: to support a positive judgment, you need to show that something has value because it satisfies certain criteria; to support a negative judgment, you need to show that something lacks value because it does not satisfy those criteria.

In order to make any judgment, then, you need to select the specific criteria you will use to assess your subject. For example, in an evaluation of college bookstores, will you base your evaluation on the user-friendliness of their service? Their prices? The number of books they stock? The efficiency or knowledge of their staff? Your answer to these questions will help you begin to plan your evaluation.

The criteria that you establish will help you decide how to evaluate a given subject. For example, if your criteria for evaluating rock bands focus on their influence on other musicians, you may be able to support the thesis that the Beatles were the most important group of the twentieth century. If, however, your criteria for evaluation is singing ability and complexity of musical arrangements, your case may be less compelling. Similarly, if you are judging healthcare systems on the basis of how many individuals have medical coverage, you may be able to demonstrate that the Canadian system is superior to the U.S. system. If your criteria are referral time and government support for medical research, your evaluation argument will be different. Whatever criteria you decide on, a bookstore (or band or healthcare system) that satisfies them will be seen as superior to one that does not.

Consider another example. Suppose you want to evaluate the government's Head Start program, which was established in 1964 to provide preschool education to children from low-income families. The program also provides medical coverage and social services to the children enrolled, and in recent years it has expanded to cover children of migrant workers and children in homeless families. On what basis would you evaluate this program? Would you evaluate only the children's educational progress or also consider the program's success in providing health care? In considering educational progress, would you focus on test scores or on students' performance in school? Would you measure long-term effects—for example, Head Start students' likelihood of attending college and their annual earnings as adults? Or would you focus on short-term results—for example, students' performance in elementary school? Finally, would you evaluate only the children or also their families? Depending on the criteria you select for your evaluation, the Head Start program could be considered a success or a failure.

⊛ EXERCISE 14.3

Choose one of the topics you listed in Exercise 14.1, and list five possible criteria for an evaluation argument on that topic.

⊛ EXERCISE 14.4

By what criteria do you evaluate the textbooks for your college courses? Design? Content? Clarity? Comprehensiveness? Cost? Work with another student to decide on the most important criteria, and then write a paragraph in which you evaluate this textbook.

Structuring an Evaluation Argument

In general terms, an evaluation argument can be structured like this:

- **Introduction:** Establishes criteria by which you will evaluate your subject; states the essay's thesis

- **Refutation of opposing arguments:** Presents others' evaluations and your arguments against them

- **Evidence (first point in support of thesis):** Supplies facts, opinions, and so on to support your evaluation

- **Evidence (second point in support of thesis):** Supplies facts, opinions, and so on to support your evaluation

- **Evidence (third point in support of thesis):** Supplies facts, opinions, and so on to support your evaluation

■ **Conclusion:** Reinforces the main point of the argument; includes a strong concluding statement

The following student essay includes all the elements of an evaluation argument. The student who wrote the essay is evaluating a character in a 1925 Ernest Hemingway short story, "Hills Like White Elephants." (For more on arguing about literature, see Appendix A, "Writing Literary Arguments," on p. 713.)

NOT JUST A "GIRL"
LOREN MARTINEZ

1   In Ernest Hemingway's famous story "Hills Like White Elephants," a couple, "the American and the girl with him," talk and drink while waiting for a train to Madrid (Hemingway 69). Most readers agree that the subject of their discussion is whether "the girl," called Jig, should have an abortion. Most of the story is told through dialogue, and although the word *abortion* is never mentioned, most readers agree that her pregnancy is the source of the tension between them. However, there are other aspects of the story about which readers do not agree. For example, some critics believe that Hemingway's portrayal of "the girl" is unfair or sexist. More specifically, some see in her the qualities of "the typically submissive Hemingway woman" (Nolan 19). However, a close reading of the story reveals the opposite to be true: "the girl" is not a one-dimensional stereotype but a complex, sympathetically drawn character.

2   Most critics who see Hemingway's portrayal of Jig as sexist base their interpretation on Hemingway's reputation and not on the story itself. For example, feminist critic Katherine M. Rogers points out that because Hemingway himself "openly expressed fear of and hostility to women" (263), it "seems fair" to see his male characters "as representative of Hemingway himself" (248). However, although "the American" in this story may see Jig as just "a pleasant pastime,"

Introduction

Thesis statement

Opposing arguments and refutation

it would be an oversimplification to confuse the character's opinion of her with the writer's as Rogers would encourage us to do (251). For example, one could argue (as many critics have done) that because the name "Jig" has sexual connotations, it reveals the author's sexism (Renner 38). However, as critic Howard Hannum points out, she is referred to by this name only twice in the story, both times by the male character himself, not by the narrator (qtd. in Renner 38). Critic Stanley Renner agrees with Hannum, rejecting the idea that Hemingway's choice to refer to the character as "the girl" is equally "belittling" (38). Renner argues that this use of the word *girl* is necessary to show how the character changes and matures in this story. In fact, he sees "her achievement of mature self-knowledge and assertion [as] the main line of development in the story" (39). All in all, the evidence suggests that "the girl," not "the American," is actually the story's protagonist. Given this central focus on "the girl" and the complexity of her character, the accusations that Hemingway's sexism has led him to create a stereotype do not seem justified.

Evidence (first point in support of thesis)

When students who are not familiar with Hemingway's reputation as a misogynist read "Hills Like White Elephants," they tend to sympathize more often with "the girl" than with "the American" (Bauer 126) and to see the character's thoughtfulness and depth. Although "the American" refers to the abortion as "'really an awfully simple operation'" (Hemingway 72), downplaying its seriousness, "the girl" has a "more mature understanding" of what her decision might mean (Bauer 130). She recognizes that it is not so "simple," and she is not naive enough to think that having the baby will save the relationship. In fact, she responds to his own naive comments with sarcasm. He claims that they will be "'all right and happy'" if she goes through with the operation; he says he's "'known lots of people who have done it.' 'So have I,' said the girl. 'And afterward they were all so happy'" (Hemingway 73). Despite her sarcasm and her resistance to his suggestions, the man continues to insist that this problem will be easy to fix. Finally, the girl becomes irritated with him and, as readers can see by the dashes that end his lines midsentence, cuts him off, finishing his lines for him as he tries to tell her again how "perfectly simple" the operation is (Hemingway 76). Readers understand her pain

3

and frustration when she finally says, "'Would you please please please please please please please stop talking?'" (Hemingway 76).

4   The argument that "the girl" is a flat, stereotypical character portrayed in sexist terms is hard to support. In fact, a stronger argument could be made that it is the man, "the American," who is the stereotype. As critic Charles J. Nolan Jr. points out, "Hemingway highlights Jig's maturity and superiority as he excoriates the selfishness and insensitivity of her companion" (19). Moreover, "the girl" is certainly the central character in this story—the one in conflict, the one who must make the final decision, and the one who grows over the course of the story. At times, she seems willing to listen to the man, even going as far as to say, "'Then I'll do it. Because I don't care about me'" (Hemingway 74). However, soon after, she responds defiantly to his comment, "'You mustn't feel that way'" with "'I don't feel any way'" (Hemingway 75). Thus, as Renner notes, Hemingway's dialogue reveals "the self-centered motives of his male character" while at the same time dramatizing the female character's complex inner struggle (38). By the end of the story, the shallow "American" still expects things to be all right between them. But when the man asks, "'Do you feel better?'" Hemingway shows the girl's quiet power—and her transformation—by giving her the final understated words of the story: "'I feel fine. . . . There's nothing wrong with me. I feel fine'" (Hemingway 77). Though we do not learn what her decision is, we can see that she is now in control: she has decided to shut down the conversation, and what the man has to say no longer matters.

Evidence (second point in support of thesis)

5   In "Hills Like White Elephants," "the girl" proves herself to be neither "'weak *in* character'" nor "'weak *as* character'" as some have described Hemingway's female characters (Bauer 126). Far from being weak *in* character, she constantly questions and pushes against the male character's suggestions. And far from being weak *as* a character, she acts as the protagonist in this story, winning the reader's sympathies. A stereotypically drawn female character would not be able to carry off either of these feats. Although Hemingway may convey sexism in his other stories—and demonstrate it in his own life—readers who evaluate *this* story will discover a complex, conflicted, sympathetic female character.

Conclusion

Concluding statement

Works Cited

Bauer, Margaret D. "Forget the Legend and Read the Work: Teaching Two Stories by Ernest Hemingway." *College Literature* 30.3 (2003): 124–137. *Academic Search Premier.* Web. 22 Oct. 2008.

Hemingway, Ernest. "Hills Like White Elephants." *Men without Women.* New York: Scribner's, 1927. 69–77. Print.

Nolan, Charles J., Jr. "Hemingway's Women's Movement." *Hemingway Review* 4.1 (1984): 14–22. *Academic Search Premier.* Web. 22 Oct. 2008.

Renner, Stanley. "Moving to the Girl's Side of 'Hills Like White Elephants.'" *Hemingway Review* 15.1 (1995): 27–41. *Academic Search Premier.* Web. 22 Oct. 2008.

Rogers, Katharine M. *The Troublesome Helpmate: A History of Misogyny in Literature.* Seattle: U of Washington P, 1996. Print.

GRAMMAR IN CONTEXT: COMPARATIVES AND SUPERLATIVES

When you write an **evaluation argument**, you make judgments, and these judgments often call for comparative analysis—for example, when you argue that one thing is better than another or the best of its kind.

When you compare two items or qualities, you use a **comparative** form: *bigger, better, more interesting, less realistic.* When you compare three or more items or qualities, you use a **superlative** form: *the biggest, the best, the most interesting, the least realistic.* Be careful to use these forms appropriately.

- **Do not use the comparative when you are comparing more than two things.**

    INCORRECT   This couple has many options, but getting married may not be the better one.

    CORRECT   This couple has many options, but getting married may not be the best one.

- **Do not use the superlative when you are comparing only two things.**

    INCORRECT   Of the two characters, "the girl" has the most realistic understanding of what her decision might mean.

    CORRECT   Of the two characters, "the girl" has the more realistic understanding of what her decision might mean.

⊃ EXERCISE 14.5

The following newspaper editorial, "Do We Have the World's Best Medical Care?" includes the basic elements of an evaluation argument. Read the essay, and then answer the questions that follow it, consulting the outline on pages 388–389 if necessary.

The *Kalamazoo Gazette* published this article on August 14, 2007.

DO WE HAVE THE WORLD'S BEST MEDICAL CARE?

KALAMAZOO GAZETTE

Many Americans are under the delusion that we have "the best health care 1 system in the world," as President Bush sees it, or provide the "best medical care in the world," as Rudolph Giuliani declared last week. That may be true at many top medical centers. But the disturbing truth is that this country lags well behind other advanced nations in delivering timely and effective care. . . .

Seven years ago, the World Health Organization made the first major 2 effort to rank the health systems of 191 nations. France and Italy took the top two spots; the United States was a dismal 37th. More recently, the highly regarded Commonwealth Fund has pioneered in comparing the United States with other advanced nations through surveys of patients and doctors and analysis of other data. Its latest report, issued in May, ranked the United States last or next-to-last compared with five other nations—Australia, Canada, Germany, New Zealand and the United Kingdom—on most measures of performance, including quality of care and access to it. Other comparative studies also put the United States in a relatively bad light.

Insurance coverage: All other major industrialized nations provide uni- 3 versal health coverage, and most of them have comprehensive benefit packages with no cost-sharing by patients. The United States, to its shame, has some 45 million people without health insurance and many more millions who have poor coverage. . . .

Access: Citizens abroad often face long waits before they can get to see a 4 specialist or undergo elective surgery. Americans typically get prompter attention, although Germany does better. The real barriers here are the costs facing low-income people without insurance or with skimpy coverage. But even Americans with above-average incomes find it more difficult than their counterparts abroad to get care on nights or weekends without going to an emergency room, and many report having to wait six days or more for an appointment with their own doctors.

Fairness: The United States ranks dead last on almost all measures of 5 equity because we have the greatest disparity in the quality of care given to richer and poorer citizens. Americans with below-average incomes are much less likely than their counterparts in other industrialized nations to see a doctor when sick, to fill prescriptions or to get needed tests and follow-up care.

Healthy lives: We have known for years that America has a high infant 6 mortality rate, so it is no surprise that we rank last among 23 nations by that yardstick. But the problem is much broader. We rank near the bottom in healthy life expectancy at age 60, and 15th among 19 countries in deaths from a wide range of illnesses that would not have been fatal if treated with timely and effective care. The good news is that we have done a better job than other industrialized nations in reducing smoking. The bad news is that our obesity epidemic is the worst in the world.

Quality: In a comparison with five other countries, the Commonwealth 7 Fund ranked the United States first in providing the "right care" for a given condition as defined by standard clinical guidelines and gave it especially high marks for preventive care, like Pap smears and mammograms to detect early stage cancers, and blood tests and cholesterol checks for hypertensive patients. But we scored poorly in coordinating the care of chronically ill patients, in protecting the safety of patients, and in meeting their needs and preferences, which drove our overall quality rating down to last place. American doctors and hospitals kill patients through surgical and medical mistakes more often than their counterparts in other industrialized nations.

Life and death: In a comparison of five countries, the United States 8 had the best survival rate for breast cancer, second best for cervical cancer and childhood leukemia, worst for kidney transplants, and almost-worst for liver transplants and colorectal cancer. In an eight-country comparison, the United States ranked last in years of potential life lost to circulatory diseases, respiratory diseases and diabetes and had the second highest death rate from bronchitis, asthma and emphysema. Although several factors can affect these results, it seems likely that the quality of care delivered was a significant contributor. . . .

Use of information technology: Shockingly, despite our vaunted prowess in 9 computers, software and the Internet, much of our health care system is still operating in the dark ages of paper records and handwritten scrawls. American primary care doctors lag years behind doctors in other advanced nations in adopting electronic medical records or prescribing medications electronically. This makes it harder to coordinate care, spot errors and adhere to standard clinical guidelines. . . .

> "Much of our health care system is still operating in the dark ages."

With health care emerging as a major issue in the presidential campaign 10 and in Congress, it will be important to get beyond empty boasts that this country has "the best health care system in the world" and turn instead to fixing its very real defects. The main goal should be to reduce the huge number of uninsured, who are a major reason for our poor standing globally. But there is also plenty of room to improve our coordination of care, our use of computerized records, communications between doctors and patients, and dozens of other factors that impair the quality of care. The world's most powerful economy should be able to provide a health care system that really is the best.

Identifying the Elements of an Evaluation Argument

1. Identify the editorial's thesis statement. Then, restate it in your own words.

2. The headings list the seven criteria that the editorial establishes for its evaluation. Which two criteria do you consider the most important? Why?

3. The sections labeled "Access," "Quality," and "Life and Death" include arguments against the editorial's thesis. Summarize these opposing arguments and the editorial's refutation of them.

4. Summarize the editorial's concluding statement.

Do the Harry Potter Books Deserve Their Popularity?

Reread the At Issue box on page 385, which provides background on the question of whether the Harry Potter books have earned their reputation. Then, read the sources on the pages that follow.

As you read these sources, you will be asked to respond to some questions and complete some activities. This work is designed to help you understand the content and structure of the selections. When you are finished, you will be ready to decide on the criteria by which you will evaluate the Harry Potter series and to write an **evaluation argument** on the topic, "Do the Harry Potter Books Deserve Their Popularity?"

SOURCES

 Michiko Kakutani, "An Epic Showdown as Harry Potter Is Initiated into Adulthood"

 Carlie Webber, "We're All Still Wild about Harry"

 A. S. Byatt, "Harry Potter and the Childish Adult"

 Charles Taylor, "A. S. Byatt and the Goblet of Bile"

 Christine Schoefer, "Harry Potter's Girl Trouble"

This book review is from the July 19, 2007, issue of the *New York Times*.

AN EPIC SHOWDOWN AS HARRY POTTER IS INITIATED INTO ADULTHOOD

MICHIKO KAKUTANI

So, here it is at last: The final confrontation between Harry Potter, the Boy Who Lived, the Chosen One, the "symbol of hope" for both the Wizard and Muggle worlds, and Lord Voldemort, He Who Must Not Be Named, the nefarious leader of the Death Eaters and would-be ruler of all. Good versus Evil. Love versus Hate. The Seeker versus the Dark Lord.

> "Good versus Evil. Love versus Hate."

J. K. Rowling's monumental, spellbinding epic, 10 years in the making, is deeply rooted in traditional literature and Hollywood sagas—from the Greek myths to Dickens and Tolkien to *Star Wars*. And true to its roots, it ends not with modernist, *Soprano*-esque equivocation, but with good old-fashioned closure: a big-screen, heart-racing, bone-chilling confrontation and an epilogue that clearly lays out people's fates. Getting to the finish line is not seamless—the last part of *Harry Potter and the Deathly Hallows*, the seventh and final book in the series, has some lumpy passages of exposition and a couple of clunky detours—but the overall conclusion and its determination of the main characters' story lines possess a convincing inevitability that make some of the prepublication speculation seem curiously blinkered in retrospect.

With each installment, the Potter series has grown increasingly dark, and this volume—a copy of which was purchased at a New York City store yesterday, though the book is embargoed for release until 12:01 a.m. on Saturday—is no exception. While Ms. Rowling's astonishingly limber voice still moves effortlessly between Ron's adolescent sarcasm and Harry's growing solemnity, from youthful exuberance to more philosophical gravity, *Deathly Hallows* is, for the most part, a somber book that marks Harry's final initiation into the complexities and sadnesses of adulthood.

From his first days at Hogwarts, the young, green-eyed boy bore the burden of his destiny as a leader, coping with the expectations and duties of his role, and in this volume he is clearly more Henry V than Prince Hal, more King Arthur than young Wart: high-spirited war games of Quidditch have given way to real war, and Harry often wishes he were not the de facto leader of the Resistance movement, shouldering terrifying responsibilities, but an ordinary teenage boy—free to romance Ginny Weasley and hang out with his friends.

Harry has already lost his parents, his godfather Sirius and his teacher Professor Dumbledore (all mentors he might have once received instruction from) and in this volume, the losses mount with unnerving speed: at least a half-dozen characters we have come to know die in these pages, and many others are wounded or tortured. Voldemort and his followers have infiltrated Hogwarts and the Ministry of Magic, creating havoc and terror in the Wizard and Muggle worlds alike, and the members of various populations—including elves, goblins and centaurs—are choosing sides.

No wonder then that Harry often seems overwhelmed with disillusion- 6 ment and doubt in the final installment of this seven-volume bildungs-roman. He continues to struggle to control his temper, and as he and Ron and Hermione search for the missing Horcruxes (secret magical objects in which Voldemort has stashed parts of his soul, objects that Harry must destroy if he hopes to kill the evil lord), he literally enters a dark wood, in which he must do battle not only with the Death Eaters, but also with the temptations of hubris and despair.

Harry's weird psychic connection with Voldemort (symbolized by the 7 lightning-bolt forehead scar he bears as a result of the Dark Lord's attack on him as a baby) seems to have grown stronger too, giving him clues to Voldemort's actions and whereabouts, even as it lures him ever closer to the dark side. One of the plot's significant turning points concerns Harry's deci-sion on whether to continue looking for the Horcruxes—the mission assigned to him by the late Dumbledore—or to pursue the Hallows, three magical objects said to make their possessor the master of Death.

Harry's journey will propel him forward to a final showdown with 8 his arch enemy, and also send him backward into the past, to the house in Godric's Hollow where his parents died, to learn about his family history and the equally mysterious history of Dumbledore's family. At the same time, he will be forced to ponder the equation between fraternity and independence, free will and fate, and to come to terms with his own frailties and those of others. Indeed, ambiguities proliferate throughout *The Deathly Hallows*: we are made to see that kindly Dumbledore, sinister Severus Snape and perhaps even the awful Muggle cousin Dudley Dursley may be more complicated than they initially seem, that all of them, like Harry, have hidden aspects to their personalities, and that choice—more than talent or predisposition—matters most of all.

It is Ms. Rowling's achievement in this series that she manages to make 9 Harry both a familiar adolescent—coping with the banal frustrations of school and dating—and an epic hero, kin to everyone from the young King Arthur to Spider-Man and Luke Skywalker. This same magpie talent has enabled her to create a narrative that effortlessly mixes up allusions to Homer, Milton, Shakespeare and Kafka, with silly kid jokes about vomit-flavored candies, a narrative that fuses a plethora of genres (from the boarding-school novel to the detective story to the epic quest) into a story that could be Exhibit A in a Joseph Campbell survey of mythic archetypes.

In doing so, J. K. Rowling has created a world as fully detailed as L. Frank 10 Baum's Oz or J. R. R. Tolkien's Middle Earth, a world so minutely imagined in terms of its history and rituals and rules that it qualifies as an alternate universe, which may be one reason the Potter books have spawned such a passionate following and such fervent exegesis. With this volume, the reader realizes that small incidents and asides in earlier installments (hidden among a huge number of red herrings) create a breadcrumb trail of clues to the plot, that Ms. Rowling has fitted together the jigsaw-puzzle pieces of this long undertaking with Dickensian ingenuity and ardor. Objects and spells from earlier books—like the invisibility cloak, Polyjuice Potion, Dumbledore's Pensieve and Sirius's flying motorcycle—play important roles in this volume, and characters encountered before, like the house-elf Dobby and Mr. Ollivander the wandmaker, resurface, too.

The world of Harry Potter is a place where the mundane and the marvel- 11
ous, the ordinary and the surreal coexist. It's a place where cars can fly and owls can deliver the mail, a place where paintings talk and a mirror reflects people's innermost desires. It's also a place utterly recognizable to readers, a place where death and the catastrophes of daily life are inevitable, and people's lives are defined by love and loss and hope—the same way they are in our own mortal world.

⊃ AT ISSUE: SOURCES FOR DEVELOPING AN EVALUATION ARGUMENT

1. Reread the essay's last paragraph, which sums up Kakutani's evaluation of the book. Then, write a thesis statement that expresses the main idea of this book review.

2. List the positive statements Kakutani makes about the book she is reviewing (and about the Harry Potter books in general).

3. On what criteria does Kakutani base her evaluation? For example, is she evaluating the book in terms of its writing style? Its plot? Its character development? Something else?

4. Go through the review, and identify all the adjectives Kakutani applies to Rowling and to her work. Do all these adjectives have positive connotations? Explain.

5. Where does Kakutani compare the Harry Potter series to other children's books? Is her comparative evaluation of the Harry Potter books positive or negative? In what respects?

This essay first appeared in the *Record*, of Bergen County, New Jersey, on July 15, 2007.

WE'RE ALL STILL WILD ABOUT HARRY

CARLIE WEBBER

With the July 21 release of *Harry Potter and the Deathly Hallows*, J.K. Rowling's 1 series about a boy wizard's coming of age will draw to a close. Readers will finally see who will emerge triumphant in the last battle between Harry Potter and his nemesis, Lord Voldemort.

Raised by his non-magical aunt and uncle, Harry believes for the first 2 11 years of his life that he is an ordinary boy. On his 11th birthday Harry learns of his acceptance to Hogwarts School of Witchcraft and Wizardry, where for the next six years he refines his magical skills in classes such as Potions and Charms.

At Hogwarts Harry makes his first friends, Ron Weasley and Hermione 3 Granger, who are instrumental in his development as both a wizard and a human being. He also discovers the truth of his past: Voldemort killed both of his parents with a curse, but when Voldemort tried to cast the same curse on Harry, it backfired.

Voldemort lost his body and most of his powers, but Harry was left with 4 only a scar on his forehead.

Harry's daily life at Hogwarts includes a lot of everyday humor, from 5 practical jokes to romantic mishaps to a professor telling a student to write repeatedly, "I am a wizard, not a baboon brandishing a stick."

Good, Evil, Love and Death

Despite the funny moments Rowling infuses into the Harry Potter series, 6 these books are not focused on mischief and adventure. Instead, they explore good, evil, love and death. Every year ends in a battle with Voldemort or his followers, the Death Eaters, and as Voldemort gains power, more innocent lives are lost. Rowling has promised at least two more deaths in *Harry Potter and the Deathly Hallows*, leaving readers to wonder if Harry will survive.

With a first-print run of 12 million copies, perhaps the question to ask is 7 not "Will Harry live?" but "Why is this series so compelling?"

One reason may be Rowling's use of the literary tradition of the hero's 8 journey; the *Lord of the Rings* trilogy by J.R.R. Tolkien and *Star Wars* episodes IV–VI employ many of the same plot and character development devices we see in the Harry Potter series, and readers take comfort in these familiarities.

The Harry Potter characters are also delightfully, painfully real in both 9 their endearments and their faults. Deep and often morally ambiguous peripheral characters make for fascinating reading because the reader, like Harry, must struggle to understand a complex world in which good and evil are not easily defined.

> "The Harry Potter characters are delightfully, painfully real."

Regardless of age, readers take joy in watching Harry and his friends grow. 10 Harry, Ron and Hermione, like all teenagers, realize that their world is not perfect. When these realizations happen, the reader is treated to an unfolding of Rowling's multidimensional wizarding society where, as Harry is told by one of Voldemort's servants, "there is no good or evil, there is only power, and those too weak to seek it."

It is Harry's humanity and fallibility rather than his magical talents that 11 make readers want to stay with his story.

Harry and his friends are not immune to subversive actions. They often 12 do the wrong thing for the right reason, such as sneaking off the Hogwarts grounds to fight Voldemort's followers. Harry can sometimes be abrasive, but the reader always comes back to cheer for him because he strives to do what he believes is right, even if it is not the easiest thing to do.

His humanitarian nature is something people of all ages can appreciate 13 and it is this appreciation that makes him resonate with such a wide readership.

In the end we all have to let go of Harry, Ron and Hermione. Saying 14 goodbye to characters who have made us laugh, cry and cheer will be anything but easy. Whether a reader is 11 or 80 he or she is likely to feel some degree of sadness and loss at the end of the last page.

Rather than throw the book across the room or petition J.K. Rowling to 15 bring Harry and his companions back for more adventures, we can sit back and be thankful for the glimpse of Harry's world. We can talk with friends and family about what might or should have been, and let the books spark friendly debate and analysis.

Younger readers may wish to have a trusted adult or older sibling to talk 16 to when they finish the book, because Harry as an adolescent experiences many feelings and social situations they may have yet to encounter, such as dating.

Harry Potter has opened many doors in the world of children's and 17 young adult publishing, too. Thanks to Harry there are thousands more books waiting to be read, and while Harry will always have a special place in our hearts, we should all take the opportunity to explore what he has inspired.

Wands at the ready, everyone, and let's head for the final duel. 18

❯ AT ISSUE: SOURCES FOR DEVELOPING AN EVALUATION ARGUMENT

1. In paragraph 7, Webber poses the question, "Why is this series so compelling?" How does she answer this question? Would you answer it in a different way?

2. Does Webber evaluate the Harry Potter books as literature, or does she have different criteria for evaluation? Explain.

3. How do you suppose A. S. Byatt (p. 403) would respond to the points Webber makes to support her evaluation of the Harry Potter series? Would Byatt dismiss all of Webber's points, or might she agree with some of them?

4. Webber is a librarian, and her article focuses on the value of the Harry Potter books for their young adult audience. Given that she is older and better educated than the typical Harry Potter reader, what do you make of her essay's last sentence? Of her use of *we* and *us*?

The *New York Times* is the source of this selection; it appeared there on July 7, 2003.

HARRY POTTER AND THE CHILDISH ADULT

A. S. BYATT

What is the secret of the explosive and worldwide success of the Harry Potter 1
books? Why do they satisfy children and—a much harder question—why do
so many adults read them? I think part of the answer to the first question is
that they are written from inside a child's-eye view, with a sure instinct for
childish psychology. But then how do we answer the second question? Surely
one precludes the other.

The easy question first. Freud described what he called the "family romance," 2
in which a young child, dissatisfied with its ordinary home and parents, invents
a fairy tale in which it is secretly of noble origin, and may even be marked out as
a hero who is destined to save the world. In J. K. Rowling's books, Harry is the
orphaned child of wizards who were murdered trying to save his life. He lives,
for unconvincingly explained reasons, with his aunt and uncle, the truly dreadful
Dursleys, who represent, I believe, his real "real" family, and are depicted with a
relentless, gleeful, overdone venom. The Dursleys are his true enemy. When he
arrives at wizarding school, he moves into a world where everyone, good and evil,
recognizes his importance, and tries either to protect or destroy him.

The family romance is a latency-period fantasy, belonging to the drowsy 3
years between 7 and adolescence. In *Order of the Phoenix*, Harry, now 15, is
meant to be adolescent. He spends a lot of the book becoming excessively
angry with his protectors and tormentors alike. He discovers that his late (and
"real") father was not a perfect magical role model, but someone who went in
for fits of nasty playground bullying. He also discovers that his mind is linked
to the evil Lord Voldemort, thereby making him responsible in some measure
for acts of violence his nemesis commits.

In psychoanalytic terms, having projected his childish rage onto the cari- 4
cature Dursleys, and retained his innocent goodness, Harry now experiences
that rage as capable of spilling outward, imperiling his friends. But does this
mean Harry is growing up? Not really. The perspective is still child's-eye.
There are no insights that reflect someone on the verge of adulthood. Harry's
first date with a female wizard is unbelievably limp, filled with an 8-year-old's
conversational maneuvers.

Auden and Tolkien wrote about the skills of inventing "secondary worlds." 5
Ms. Rowling's world is a secondary secondary world, made up of intelligently
patchworked derivative motifs from all sorts of children's literature—from
the jolly hockey-sticks school story to Roald Dahl, from *Star Wars* to Diana
Wynne Jones and Susan Cooper. Toni Morrison pointed out that clichés
endure because they represent truths. Derivative narrative clichés work with

children because they are comfortingly recognizable and immediately available to the child's own power of fantasizing.

The important thing about this particular secondary world is that it is symbiotic with the real modern world. Magic, in myth and fairy tales, is about contacts with the inhuman—trees and creatures, unseen forces. Most fairy story writers hate and fear machines. Ms. Rowling's wizards shun them and use magic instead, but their world is a caricature of the real world and has trains, hospitals, newspapers and competitive sport. Much of the real evil in the later books is caused by newspaper gossip columnists who make Harry into a dubious celebrity, which is the modern word for the chosen hero. Most of the rest of the evil (apart from Voldemort) is caused by bureaucratic interference in educational affairs. 6

Supernatural   Ms. Rowling's magic world has no place for the numinous.° It is written for people whose imaginative lives are confined to TV cartoons, and the exaggerated (more exciting, not threatening) mirror-worlds of soaps, reality TV and celebrity gossip. Its values, and everything in it, are as Gatsby said of his own world when the light had gone out of his dream, "only personal." Nobody is trying to save or destroy anything beyond Harry Potter and his friends and family. 7

So, yes, the attraction for children can be explained by the powerful working of the fantasy of escape and empowerment, combined with the fact that the stories are comfortable, funny, just frightening enough. 8

They comfort against childhood fears as Georgette Heyer once comforted us against the truths of the relations between men and women, her detective stories domesticating and blanket-wrapping death. These are good books of their kind. But why would grown-up men and women become obsessed by jokey latency fantasies? 9

Comfort, I think, is part of the reason. Childhood reading remains potent for most of us. In a recent BBC survey of the top 100 "best reads," more than a quarter were children's books. We like to regress. I know that part of the reason I read Tolkien when I'm ill is that there is an almost total absence of sexuality in his world, which is restful. 10

But in the case of the great children's writers of the recent past, there was a compensating seriousness. There was—and is—a real sense of mystery, powerful forces, dangerous creatures in dark forests. Susan Cooper's teenage wizard discovers his magic powers and discovers simultaneously that he is in a cosmic battle between good and evil forces. Every bush and cloud glitters with secret significance. Alan Garner peoples real landscapes with malign, inhuman elvish beings that hunt humans. 11

Reading writers like these, we feel we are being put back in touch with earlier parts of our culture, when supernatural and inhuman creatures—from whom we thought we learned our sense of good and evil—inhabited a world we did not feel we controlled. If we regress, we regress to a lost sense of significance we mourn for. Ursula K. Le Guin's wizards inhabit an anthropologically coherent world where magic really does act as a force. Ms. Rowling's magic wood has nothing in common with these lost worlds. It is small, and on the school grounds, and dangerous only because she says it is. 12

13   In this regard, it is magic for our time. Ms. Rowling, I think, speaks to an adult generation that hasn't known, and doesn't care about, mystery. They are inhabitants of urban jungles, not of the real wild. They don't have the skills to tell ersatz magic from the real thing, for as children they daily invested the ersatz with what imagination they had.

14   Similarly, some of Ms. Rowling's adult readers are simply reverting to the child they were when they read the Billy Bunter books, or invested Enid Blyton's pasteboard kids with their own childish desires and hopes. A surprising number of people—including many students of literature—will tell you they haven't really lived in a book since they were children. Sadly, being taught literature often destroys the life of the books. But in the days before dumbing down and cultural studies° no one reviewed Enid Blyton or Georgette Heyer—as they do not now review the great Terry Pratchett, whose wit is metaphysical, who creates an energetic and lively secondary world, who has a multifarious genius for strong parody as opposed to derivative manipulation of past motifs, who deals with death with startling originality. Who writes amazing sentences.

An academic field that applies a variety of disciplines to the study of subjects such as gender, ethnicity, and social class

15   It is the substitution of celebrity for heroism that has fed this phenomenon. And it is the leveling effect of cultural studies, which are as interested in hype and popularity as they are in literary merit, which they don't really believe exists. It's fine to compare the Brontës with bodice-rippers. It's become respectable to read and discuss what Roland Barthes called "consumable" books. There is nothing wrong with this, but it has little to do with the shiver of awe we feel looking through Keats's "magic casements, opening on the foam / Of perilous seas, in faery lands forlorn."

> "It is the substitution of celebrity for heroism that has fed this phenomenon."

⊃ AT ISSUE: SOURCES FOR DEVELOPING AN EVALUATION ARGUMENT

1. In this essay, Byatt makes numerous allusions to other writers and thinkers as well as to authors of classic children's books. What do these allusions tell you about how Byatt views her audience?

2. Is Byatt criticizing the Harry Potter books themselves? If so, on what basis? Do you think that she might actually be criticizing Harry Potter's readers? The school of literary criticism known as "cultural studies"? The Harry Potter phenomenon itself?

3. How does Byatt explain the appeal of the Harry Potter books to children? How does she explain their appeal to adults?

4. Where does Byatt evaluate the Harry Potter books by showing their inferiority to other works? In what respects does she see the other books as superior?

This piece appeared in *Salon* on July 8, 2003.

A. S. BYATT AND THE GOBLET OF BILE

CHARLES TAYLOR

Byatt once complained that Martin Amis's publisher gave him a large advance payment because Amis needed extensive dental work.

When a book sells 5 million hardcover copies in its first day, it's inevitable that there's going to be someone who slams it and tells us that what we're seeing is merely a pop phenomenon that bears no relation to literature. That esteemed gasbag Harold Bloom, in his guise as self-appointed keeper of the canon, did the honors after the fourth Potter book, *Harry Potter and the Goblet of Fire*, telling us that reading should enrich us (without ever getting around to declaring whether it should entertain us) and shortly thereafter launching his own compendium of children's lit that, in his view, did just that. Right on schedule, just a mere two weeks after the new Harry Potter release, it's A. S. Byatt, apparently having made peace with Martin Amis' dental work,° who steps into the ring against J. K. Rowling's books in a *New York Times* op-ed. 1

Byatt's argument is just what you'd expect from someone shouldering the mantle of high culture. To show that she's not a total killjoy, Byatt allows that Rowling's books are entertaining and reveal "a sure instinct for childish psychology." To answer the bigger question of what explains the series' huge success with adults as well as children (uh, because J. K. Rowling is a master of narrative?), Byatt decides that the books represent "comfort" for their readers, embodying Freud's notion of "family romance" (finding the surrogate family where we are appreciated for ourselves) and the chance to regress to a safe world where good and evil are readily identifiable and we feel that we are given control over the unpredictable. 2

Byatt may have a valid cultural point—a teeny one—about the impulses that drive us to reassuring pop trash and away from the troubling complexities of art. The problem is that her argument has nothing to do with the experience that anyone I know has had reading the Harry Potter books. Perhaps operating from the assumption that anything positive written about J. K. Rowling's work is little more than publicity or evidence of lowered cultural standards, Byatt wastes nary a syllable on the subject that has been widely written about and discussed with both *The Goblet of Fire* and the new *The Order of the Phoenix*: the increasing darkness of the books. Rowling has conceived of the seven-book cycle as tracing Harry's growth from childhood to late adolescence. And as the books have gone on, the dangers he faces have not only increased but, as happens with age, become less easy to shrug off, inflicting physical and psychological wounds that are not so quick to heal. In the climax of *Goblet of Fire*, Harry witnesses the murder of a classmate, an event that is still giving him nightmares in the new book. Having witnessed death, he is now prone to seeing things, not at all reassuring sights, that his classmates who have been 3 spared experiencing death can not. And increasingly, he finds that the power that allowed him to survive the attempt Voldemort made on his life as an infant links his brain with that of the dark lord, making him feel that his goodness is forever imperiled by this access to the dark side.

In *The Order of the Phoenix*, Harry experiences the death of another char- 4 acter, someone very close to him, and increasing alienation from his best friends, Ron and Hermione, who don't bear the burdens he does. Young readers who were the same age as Harry when the series began may be growing with him. But a younger group of readers who are just now beginning the series may find that the later books are too upsetting for them (in the same way that some teenage viewers of *Buffy the Vampire Slayer* abandoned the show when it began dealing with the complications of young adulthood). But even if, at this point, they only read *Harry Potter and the Sorcerer's Stone*, they will find themselves confronted with loss. Remember, this is a character whose parents are murdered when he is an infant, and who himself is under the continual threat of death from his parents' killer. That first book features the devastating scene where Harry encounters a mirror that reveals the heart's truest desire and, looking into it, sees himself happy and smiling with the parents he never knew, a vision that lasts only as long as he looks into the glass, and a metaphor for how fleeting our moments of real happiness are. *This* is Byatt's idea of reassurance?

Of course there's something comforting in the Harry Potter books. I defy 5 Byatt not to find the same qualities in all great children's literature. She has confused comfort with escaping reality. Not only do all great fantasies relate back to the real world, any reassurance they offer always comes at a price. Kids suffer loss in the great works of children's literature and then find that they have the strength to cope. They don't forget their losses, but they learn to live with them. And that's as true of the young heroines in Frances Hodgson Burnett's *The Secret Garden* and *A Little Princess*, or the boys in Walter Farley's *The Black Stallion* and Marjorie Kinnan Rawlings *The Yearling* as it is of Harry Potter.

From the question of comfort and reassurance, Byatt moves on to even 6 shakier ground, complaining that Rowling's form of magic is ersatz. "Ursula K. Le Guin's wizards inhabit an anthropologically coherent world where magic really does act as a force," Byatt writes. "Ms. Rowling's magic wood has nothing in common with these lost worlds. It is small, and on the school grounds, and dangerous only because she says it is." Excuse me? Anything exists in any novel *only because the author says it does.* That does not excuse the author from making it dramatically plausible, and if what Byatt intends to say is that for her Le Guin's worlds are magical and Rowling's are not, then that is an honest admission of taste. But to imply that there's some objective standard dividing books where "magic really does act as a force" from ones where magic is a gimcrack concoction is bunk, and Byatt knows it.

And still Byatt trudges on, claiming that "Rowling speaks to an adult gen- 7 eration that hasn't known, and doesn't care about, mystery. They are inhabitants of urban jungles and not the real wild." Well, if the author biography in my

Modern Library edition of Byatt's *Possession* is correct, the closest she has ever come to the "real wild" is growing up the daughter of a barrister and a school-teacher in darkest Yorkshire. Unless those pages are missing an episode where, Jane-like, Byatt swung from the jungly tendrils, then it's fair to ask how a life spent in boarding school in the British city of York, then Cambridge, Bryn Mawr and Oxford before settling in London, gave her experience of the real wild.

But this is where the crux of Byatt's argument makes itself plain, and she is extraordinarily upfront in its snobbishness. Contemporary adults love Harry Potter, she tells us, because "they don't have the skills to tell ersatz magic from the real thing, for as children they daily invested the ersatz with what imagination they had." In other words, we're too stupid to know the difference between diamonds and cubic zirconia. Byatt names us poor uncultured adult Harry lovers for what we are, "people whose imaginative lives are confined to TV cartoons, and the exaggerated (more exciting, not threatening) mirror-worlds of soaps, reality TV and celebrity gossip." How's that for putting us in our place? 8

It's clear that we're dealing here with an acolyte at the temple of high culture barring the doors as the ignorant masses who love pop culture come a knockin'. Loath as I am to resurrect the old canard accusing writers or critics who dislike a popular work of art of being jealous, in Byatt's case it might be true. Remember, this is the same writer who went into a highly publicized hissy fit some years back when Martin Amis was given a lucrative advance against future books. It's only human for writers or filmmakers or musicians to feel resentful and even contemptuous when what they consider good, serious work is being passed over in favor of some pop artifact. But sooner or later, if you choose the life of a writer, you damn well better be able to make peace with the possibility that in all likelihood you will not enjoy spectacular commercial success. Byatt has it better than most, enjoying a modicum of fame, more than her share of respect, and the distinction of being one of the relative few who has been able to make a living at literary fiction. But success on the scale of J. K. Rowling's clearly gets under her skin. 9

She's not alone. Around the time that *Harry Potter and the Goblet of Fire* was published three years ago, the *New York Times Book Review*, reportedly in response to complaints from publishers and literary agents, created a separate listing of children's bestsellers and relegated the Harry Potter books there. The arguments put forth in favor of that move all claimed to be concerned with fairness. A slot on the *Times*' bestseller list could mean great success for an author, the arguments went, and with Rowling threatening to occupy four slots on the list, it kept some books just bubbling under the top 15 from making it on. Tough. (When the Beatles occupied five slots in the top 10 they weren't relegated to a British list to make room for the Beach Boys.) 10

There's no doubt that publicists and agents use the *Times* list to sell books. But promotion can never be a consideration of people who put together a bestseller list. Either such a list is going to report the bestselling books in the country or it is not. And when a children's novel sells 5 million copies in its first 24 hours on sale, clearly it's not just children who are reading it, and 11 it's a baldfaced lie to pretend that any other book is the No. 1 bestseller. And did Rowling's exile make room for those other lesser-known novelists? Of course it didn't. Occasionally, a left-field success like Alice Sebold's *The Lovely Bones* earns a spot. But the exclusion of Rowling's books means that this week the bestseller list has more room for hacks like Clive Cussler, John Grisham, Nicholas Sparks and the born-again team of Tim LaHaye and Jerry B. Jenkins.

Nothing deserves our respect (or scorn) simply because it's popular, no   12 matter how popular. But literary critics almost never concern themselves with what people actually read. Sometimes there are good reasons not to. Faced with shrinking space for all sorts of reviews, I'd prefer for the novel of some unheralded new writer to get coverage rather than the latest hernia-inducer from Tom

> "Nothing deserves our respect (or scorn) simply because it's popular."

Clancy. But the literary novelists who get themselves worked up over popular fiction never stop to consider what it is that readers are responding to except, like Byatt, to put it down to the stupidity of the masses. It would be disingenuous to claim that literary fiction has altogether abandoned narrative and character. But enough literary fiction seems to have so little connection to the reasons people began reading—and keep reading—that it has to bear at least some of the blame for its own marginalization.

You would think that Byatt, whose most popular book, *Possession*, is a   13 fat, satisfying read that offers the pleasures of narrative and character, would understand that. But maybe the book offers a clue as to why she wouldn't. I don't know anyone who loved *Possession* who didn't skim through all the interpolated Victorian poems. (Reviewing the novel, enthusiastically, for the *New York Review of Books*, Diane Johnson quipped that Byatt's ventriloquism of epic Victorian poetry proved the old adage "nobody likes an epic.") People ate up the parallel stories of the two pairs of lovers, but every few chapters some damn poem about fairies or something got in the way. Byatt admits that she conceived the book as, among other things, a romance in the flavor of her childhood favorite Georgette Heyer, and as a parody of another favorite, Margery Allingham (whose books, she doesn't seem to understand, are already parodies of the English country house mystery). *Possession* is a resounding demonstration that a contemporary novel can be literary and still be a great, engrossing read (not a distinction that would ever have occurred to the great 19th-century novelists). But maybe, for Byatt, those basic pleasures, no matter how nuanced and rich her rendering, were not enough.

In making J. K. Rowling the repository of everything that's cheap and   14 phony in contemporary culture, Byatt seems to be arguing not just against what she sees as the inevitable cheapness of popular culture but also against the basic pleasures that draw people to books. Which is why for Byatt, as an academic as well as a novelist, the advent of cultural studies making their way into the sacred halls of academe is a betrayal. She may admit to loving Georgette Heyer's Regency romances as a child, but now, my God, she has lived to see people actually *reviewing* Heyer. Heaven forfend. What doesn't occur to Byatt is that the excesses of cultural studies (and she's right that some of it betrays an unseemly preoccupation with crap) was a direct response to the academics who deemed any study of popular culture inappropriate at the university level. And it's worth remembering that at one time, that bias would have prevented the study of Shakespeare, Dickens, Mozart or Griffith (or any movies, for that matter).

It's not making distinctions between high culture and pop culture that 15 I object to. It's the either/or scenario proposed by high-culture guardians like Byatt that seems so churlish, so ready to make the appreciation of high culture seem the dreary duty it was when we were schoolchildren. "The only reason people read is pleasure," Leslie Fiedler once said. And I'll end by offering another Fiedler quote that should keep Byatt and the other keepers of the cultural flame up nights. In a *Salon* interview a few weeks before his death, Fiedler related a story about enraging a group of academics by announcing that when he and they were all dead and forgotten, people were still going to be reading Stephen King. The ugly truth that A. S. Byatt and Harold Bloom have yet to face is that when they have been reduced to footnotes, people are still going to be reading and enjoying the Harry Potter books. And somewhere, J. K. Rowling, keeping company with Dumas and Conan Doyle and the other "nonliterary" writers who live on, will be laughing.

⟳ AT ISSUE: SOURCES FOR DEVELOPING AN EVALUATION ARGUMENT

1. In this essay, Charles Taylor offers a refutation of the argument in A. S. Byatt's essay on Harry Potter (p. 403). What points made by Byatt does Taylor address? How does he refute each of these arguments?

2. In paragraph 3, Taylor acknowledges that "Byatt may have a valid cultural point—a teeny one" but then goes on to attack her argument because it "has nothing to do with the experience that anyone I know has had reading the Harry Potter books." What does he mean? What criterion for evaluation do you think is most important to Taylor in assessing the merits of the books? Do you see this criterion as valid?

3. Taylor's essay is much more informal than Byatt's, and his essay includes no literary allusions. Do you see this informality as a strength or a weakness in an essay evaluating works of popular literature? Explain.

4. Do you think paragraph 9 presents a valid criticism of Byatt's essay, or do you see it as an *ad hominem* argument?

This selection is from *Salon.* It appeared on January 12, 2000.

HARRY POTTER'S GIRL TROUBLE

CHRISTINE SCHOEFER

Four factors made me go out and buy the Harry Potter books: Their impres- 1
sive lead on the bestseller lists, parents' raves about Harry Potter's magical
ability to turn kids into passionate readers, my daughters' clamoring and
the mile-long waiting lists at the public library. Once I opened *The Sorcerer's
Stone*, I was hooked and read to the last page of Volume 3. Glittering mystery
and nail-biting suspense, compelling language and colorful imagery, magical
feats juxtaposed with real-life concerns all contributed to making these books
page turners. Of course, Diagon Alley haunted me, the Sorting Hat dazzled
me, Quidditch intrigued me. Believe me, I tried as hard as I could to ignore the
sexism. I really wanted to love Harry Potter. But how could I?

Harry's fictional realm of magic and wizardry perfectly mirrors the 2
conventional assumption that men do and should run the world. From the
beginning of the first Potter book, it is boys and men, wizards and sorcer-
ers, who catch our attention by dominating the scenes and determining the
action. Harry, of course, plays the lead. In his epic struggle with the forces of
darkness—the evil wizard Voldemort and his male supporters—Harry is supported by the dignified wizard Dumbledore and a colorful cast of male characters. Girls, when they are not downright silly or unlikable, are helpers, enablers
and instruments. No girl is brilliantly heroic the way Harry is, no woman is
experienced and wise like Professor Dumbledore. In fact, the range of female
personalities is so limited that neither women nor girls play on the side of evil.

But, you interject, what about Harry's good friend Hermione? Indeed, she is 3
the female lead and the smartest student at Hogwart's School of Witchcraft and
Wizardry. She works hard to be accepted
by Harry and his sidekick Ron, who treat
her like a tag-along until Volume 3. The
trio reminds me of Dennis the Menace,
Joey and Margaret or Calvin, Hobbes
and Suzy. Like her cartoon counterparts, Hermione is a smart goody-goody who
annoys the boys by constantly reminding them of school rules. Early on, she is
described as "a bossy know-it-all," hissing at the boys "like an angry goose." Half-
way through the first book, when Harry rescues her with Ron's assistance, the
hierarchy of power is established. We learn that Hermione's bookish knowledge
only goes so far. At the sight of a horrible troll, she "sinks to the floor in fright . . .
her mouth open with terror." Like every Hollywood damsel in distress, Hermione
depends on the resourcefulness of boys and repays them with her complicity. By
lying to cover up for them, she earns the boys' reluctant appreciation.

> "What about Harry's
> good friend Hermione?"

Though I was impressed by Hermione's brain power, I felt sorry for her. 4
She struggles so hard to get Harry and Ron's approval and respect, in spite of the
boys' constant teasing and rejection. And she has no girlfriends. Indeed, there
don't seem to be any other girls at the school worth her—or our—attention.
Again and again, her emotions interfere with her intelligence, so that she loses
her head when it comes to applying her knowledge. Although she casts successful spells for the boys, Hermione messes up her own and as a result, while they
go adventuring, she hides in the bathroom with cat fur on her face. I find myself
wanting Hermione to shine, but her bookish knowledge and her sincere efforts
can't hold a candle to Harry's flamboyant, rule-defying bravery.

Even though Hermione eventually wins the boys' begrudging respect and 5
friendship, her thirst for knowledge remains a constant source of irritation for
them. And who can blame them? With her nose stuck in books, she's no fun.
Thankfully, she is not hung up on her looks or the shape of her body. But her
relentless studying has all the characteristics of a disorder: It makes her ill-
humored, renders her oblivious to her surroundings and threatens her health,
especially in the third volume.

Ron's younger sister Ginny, another girl student at Hogwart's, can't 6
help blushing and stammering around Harry, and she fares even worse than
Hermione. "Stupid little Ginny" unwittingly becomes the tool of evil when she
takes to writing in a magical diary. For months and months, "the foolish little
brat" confides "all her pitiful worries and woes" ("how she didn't think famous
good great Harry Potter would 'ever' like her") to these pages. We are told how
boring it is to listen to "the silly little troubles of an eleven-year-old girl."

Again and again, we see girls so caught up in their emotions that they lose 7
sight of the bigger picture. We watch them "shriek," "scream," "gasp" and
"giggle" in situations where boys retain their composure. Again and again,
girls stay at the sidelines of adventure while the boys jump in. While Harry's
friends clamor to ride his brand-new Firebolt broomstick, for example, classmate Penelope is content just to hold it.

The only female authority figure is beady-eyed, thin-lipped Minerva 8
McGonagall, professor of transfiguration and deputy headmistress of Hogwart's.
Stern instead of charismatic, she is described as eyeing her students like "a wrath-
ful eagle." McGonagall is Dumbledore's right hand and she defers to him in every
respect. Whereas he has the wisdom to see beyond rules and the power to disregard them, McGonagall is bound by them and enforces them strictly. Although
she makes a great effort to keep her feelings under control, in a situation of crisis
she loses herself in emotions because she lacks Dumbledore's vision of the bigger
picture. When Harry returns from the chamber of secrets, she clutches her chest,
gasps and speaks weakly while the all-knowing Dumbledore beams.

Sybill Trelawney is the other female professor we encounter. She teaches 9
divination, a subject that includes tea-leaf reading, palmistry, crystal gazing—
all the intuitive arts commonly associated with female practitioners. Trelawney
is a misty, dreamy, dewy charlatan, whose "clairvoyant vibrations" are the
subject of constant scorn and ridicule. The only time she makes an accurate

prediction, she doesn't even know it because she goes into a stupor. Because most of her students and all of her colleagues dismiss her, the entire intuitive tradition of fortune-telling, a female domain, is discredited.

A brief description of the guests in the Leaky Cauldron pub succinctly 10 summarizes author J. K. Rowling's estimation of male and female: There are "funny little witches," "venerable looking wizards" who argue philosophy, "wild looking warlocks," "raucous dwarfs" and a "hag" ordering a plate of raw liver. Which would you prefer to be? I rest my case.

But I remain perplexed that a woman (the mother of a daughter, no less) 11 would, at the turn of the 20th century, write a book so full of stereotypes. Is it more difficult to imagine a headmistress sparkling with wit, intelligence and passion than to conjure up a unicorn shedding silver blood? More farfetched to create a brilliant, bold and lovable heroine than a marauder's map?

It is easy to see why boys love Harry's adventures. And I know that 12 girls' uncanny ability to imagine themselves in male roles (an empathic skill that boys seem to lack, honed on virtually all children's literature as well as Hollywood's younger audience films) enables them to dissociate from the limitations of female characters. But I wonder about the parents, many of whom join their kids in reading the Harry Potter stories. Is our longing for a magical world so deep, our hunger to be surprised and amazed so intense, our gratitude for a well-told story so great that we are willing to abdicate our critical judgment? Or are the stereotypes in the story integral to our fascination—do we feel comforted by a world in which conventional roles are firmly in place?

I have learned that Harry Potter is a sacred cow. Bringing up my objections 13 has earned me other parents' resentment—they regard me as a heavy-handed feminist with no sense of fun who is trying to spoil a bit of magic they have discovered. But I enjoyed the fantastical world of wizards, witches, beasts and muggles as much as anyone. Is that a good reason to ignore what's been left out?

⊘ AT ISSUE: SOURCES FOR DEVELOPING AN EVALUATION ARGUMENT

1. What is the central criterion by which Schoefer evaluates the Harry Potter books? Where does she establish this criterion?

2. What positive qualities does Schoefer identify in the Harry Potter books? What other positive features does she ignore? Is she justified in not discussing these positive aspects of the books, or does her failure to do so mean she is unfairly slanting her evidence?

3. How does Schoefer support her argument that the Harry Potter books are sexist? Where does she identify and refute arguments against her position? Can you offer additional refutations?

4. Answer the question Schoefer asks in her last sentence.

⊖ EXERCISE 14.6

Write a one-paragraph evaluation argument in which you take a position on whether the Harry Potter books are worthy of the success they have achieved. Follow the template below, filling in the blanks to create your argument.

Template for Writing an Evaluation Argument

The first Harry Potter book, published in 1997, was a publishing sensation that turned into a worldwide phenomenon. Many people saw the Harry Potter books as valuable, for a variety of reasons. For example,

_____

_____. Also, _____

_____

_____. However, some people have criticized the series. They claim, for example, that _____

_____

_____. Others believe that _____

_____. Depending on the criteria used for evaluation, the Harry Potter books can be seen in positive or negative terms. If we judge them on the basis of _____ , it seems clear that they are _____.

⊖ EXERCISE 14.7

In a group of three or four students, discuss your own reactions (or those of your friends or siblings) to the Harry Potter books. Has reading them been a rewarding experience? What value—literary or otherwise—do you see in these books? Write a paragraph that summarizes your group's conclusions.

⊖ EXERCISE 14.8

Write an evaluation argument on the topic, "Do the Harry Potter books deserve their popularity?" Begin by establishing the criteria by which you will evaluate these books. Then, consider how well the books meet these criteria. (If you like, you may incorporate the material you developed for Exercises 14.6 and 14.7 into your essay.) Cite the sources on pages 397–413, and be sure to document the sources you use and to include a works-cited page. (See Chapter 10 for information on documenting sources.)

⊘ EXERCISE 14.9

Review the four pillars of argument discussed in Chapter 1. Does your essay include all four elements of an effective argument? Add anything that is missing. Then, label the key elements of your essay.

⊘ WRITING ASSIGNMENTS: EVALUATION ARGUMENTS

1. As a college student, you have probably had to fill out course-evaluation forms. Now, you are going to write an evaluation of one of your courses in which you take a strong stand on the quality of the course. Before you begin, decide on the criteria by which you will evaluate it—for example, what practical skills it provided to prepare you for your future courses or employment, whether you enjoyed the course, or what you learned. (If you have access to an evaluation form, you can fill it out as a brainstorming exercise.)

2. Write an evaluation argument challenging a popular position on the quality of a product or service that you know or use. For example, you can defend a campus service that most students criticize or criticize a popular restaurant or film. Be sure you establish your criteria for evaluation before you begin. (You do not have to use the same criteria employed by those who have taken the opposite position.)

3. Write a comparative evaluation—an essay in which you argue that one thing is superior to another. You can compare two teachers, two cell phones, two print advertisements, two part-time jobs, or any other subjects you feel confident you can write about. In your thesis, take the position that one of your two subjects is superior to the other. As you would with any evaluation, begin by deciding on the criteria you will use.

Proposal Arguments

Should All College Instructors Be Required to Make Their Lectures Available as Podcasts?

Despite advances in communication technology, the traditional lecture is still the most widely used method of instruction in U.S. colleges and universities. In the classic lecture method of teaching, an instructor stands in front of a room and presents information to students. (In some cases, lectures are accompanied by audiovisual aids, such as PowerPoint presentations, or by print handouts.) If a student misses a class, he or she is simply out of luck; the only recourse is to get notes from a classmate.

With new digital communication technologies, instructors (and students) have more options for instruction. The most exciting of these technologies—the video podcast— enables students to download lectures onto an iPod or similar device with a visual display. Instructors can record their lectures and upload them onto the course Web site. (Instructors can even use a smart board to store PowerPoint slides that accompany lectures.) Students can then access this material, store it on an iPod or a computer, and retrieve it at their convenience. Supporters of video podcasts say that this technology has many advantages over traditional instruction. For example, it enables students to access material if they miss a class. Opponents say that this technology has its disadvantages. For example, it encourages students to cut class.

Later in this chapter, you will be asked to think more about this issue. You will be given several research sources to consider and asked to write a **proposal** to your instructor arguing that he or she make all course lectures available as podcasts.

Student listening to
podcast

What Is a Proposal Argument?

When you write a **proposal argument**, you suggest a solution to a problem. The purpose of a proposal argument is to convince people that a problem exists and that your solution is both practical and worthwhile.

Proposal arguments are the most common form of argument. You see them every day on billboards and in advertisements, op-ed pieces, editorials, and letters to the editor. The problems proposal arguments address can be local:

- What steps should the city take to protect its historic buildings?
- Should City Council members be limited to two terms?
- How can the city promote the use of public transportation?
- What can the city do to help the homeless?
- What should the city do to encourage recycling?
- How can the city improve community health services?

Or, the problems can be more general:

- Should the United States withdraw its troops from Afghanistan?
- What can be done to lessen our dependence on foreign oil?

- What is the best way to lower the federal deficit?
- How can we solve the health-care crisis in the United States?
- What can countries do to protect themselves against terrorist attacks?
- What should be done to stop nuclear proliferation?

Many proposals try to influence behavior.

Think you can be a meat-eating environmentalist?

Think again!

If you give a damn about the planet, go vegetarian.

Stating the Problem

When you write a proposal argument, you need to begin by demonstrating to readers that a problem exists. In some cases, readers will be familiar with the problem, so you will not have to discuss it in great detail. For example, it would not take much to convince students at your university that tuition is high or that many classrooms are overcrowded. Most people also know about the need to strengthen the levees around New Orleans and to provide health care to the uninsured and are aware of other problems that have received a good deal of media attention.

Other, less familiar, issues need more explanation—sometimes a great deal of explanation. In these cases, you should not assume that readers will accept (or even understand) the significance of the problem you are discussing. For example, why should readers care about the high dropout rate at a local high school? You can answer this question by demonstrating that this problem affects not only the students who drop out but others as well:

- Students who do not have high school diplomas earn substantially less than those who do.

- Studies show that high school dropouts are much more likely to live in poverty than students who complete high school.

- Taxpayers pay for the social services that dropouts often require.

- Federal, state, and local governments lose the taxes that dropouts would pay if they had better jobs.

When you explain the situation in this way, you show that a problem that appears to be limited to just a few individuals actually affects society as a whole.

How much information you need to provide about a problem depends on how much your readers already know about it. In many cases, a direct statement of a problem is not enough: you need to explain the context of the problem and then discuss it with this context in mind. For example, you cannot simply say that the databases in your college library need to be expanded. Why do they need to be expanded? How many new databases should be added? Which ones? What benefits would result from increasing the number of databases? What will happen if they are not expanded? Without answers to these questions, readers will not be able to understand the full extent of the problem. (Statistics, examples, personal anecdotes, and even visuals can also help you demonstrate the seriousness of the problem.) By presenting the problem in detail, you draw readers into your discussion and motivate them to want to solve it.

Advocacy groups frequently publish proposals.

Proposing a Solution

After you have established that a problem exists, you have to propose a solution. Sometimes the solution is so direct and self-evident that you do not need to explain it in much detail. For example, if you want to get a new computer for the college newspaper, you do not have to give a detailed account of how you intend to purchase it. On the other hand, if your problem is more complicated—for example, proposing that your school should sponsor a new student organization—you will have to go into more detail, possibly listing the steps that will be taken to implement your plan as well as the costs associated with it.

Demonstrating That Your Solution Will Work

When you present a solution to a problem, you have to support it with **evidence**—facts, examples, and so on from your own experience and from research. You can also point to proposals like yours that have been successful. For example, if you are proposing that classroom lectures should be made available as podcasts, you could list the reasons why this idea would help students on your campus. You could then show how several other colleges have successfully done what you are proposing. Finally, you could use visuals such as charts or graphs to help you support your position.

You also have to consider the consequences—both intended and unintended—of your proposal. Idealistic or otherwise unrealistic proposals almost always run into trouble when skeptical readers challenge them. If you think, for example, that the federal government should suspend taxes on gasoline until the price of oil drops, you should consider the effects of such a suspension. How much money would drivers actually save? Where would the government get the lost tax revenue? What programs would suffer because the government could no longer afford to fund them? In short, do the benefits of your proposal outweigh its negative effects?

Establishing Feasibility

Your solution not only has to make sense but also has to be **feasible**— that is, it has to be practical. Sometimes a problem can be solved, but the solution may be almost as bad as—or even worse than—the problem. For example, a city could drastically reduce crime by putting police officers on every street corner, installing video cameras at every intersection, and stopping and searching all cars that contain two or more people. These actions might reduce crime, but most people would not want to live in a city that instituted such authoritarian policies.

Even if a solution is desirable, it still may not be feasible. For example, although expanded dining facilities might improve life on campus, the cost of a new student cafeteria would be high. If paying for it means that tuition would have to be increased, many students would find this proposal unacceptable. On the other hand, if you could demonstrate that the profits from the sale of food in the new cafeteria would off-set its cost, then your proposal would be feasible.

Discussing Benefits

By presenting the benefits of your proposal, you can convince undecided readers that your plan has merit. How, for example, would students benefit from an expansion of campus parking facilities? Would student morale improve because students would get fewer parking citations? Would lateness to class decline because students would no longer have to spend time looking for a parking spot? Would the college get more revenue from additional parking fees? Although not all proposals list benefits, many do. This information can help convince readers that your proposal has merit and is worth implementing.

Addressing Possible Objections

You should always assume that any proposal—no matter how strong—will be objectionable to some readers. In addition, even sympathetic readers will have questions that they will want answered before they accept your ideas. That is why you should always anticipate and refute possible objections to your proposal. If there are obvious objections, address and refute them. For example, if all class lectures were available as podcasts, would students stop coming to class? Would some instructors object to making their lectures available as podcasts? If any objections are particularly strong, concede them—respectfully admitting that they have merit but pointing out their shortcomings. For instance, you could concede the point that podcasts might result in some students not coming to class but then point out that instructors could address this issue by making attendance mandatory or by making class participation a course requirement.

Visually illustrating a problem such as an overcrowded campus parking lot can help convince your audience to see the merits of your proposal.

⤵ EXERCISE 15.1

List the evidence you could present to support each of these thesis statements for proposal arguments.

1. Because many Americans are obese, the government should require warning labels on all sugared cereals.

2. The United States should ban all gasoline-burning cars in ten years.

3. Candidates for president should be required to use only public funding for their campaigns.

4. Teachers should carry handguns to protect themselves and their students from violence.

5. To reduce prison overcrowding, the states should release all nonviolent offenders.

○ EXERCISE 15.2

Review the proposals in Exercise 15.1, and list two problems that each one could create if implemented.

○ EXERCISE 15.3

Look at the following ad, which is designed to promote recycling. In what sense is it a proposal argument? For example, what problem does it identify? What solution does it propose? What arguments does it present to support this solution? How does the image in the ad help to support the proposal?

An ad to encourage recycling

⬤ EXERCISE 15.4

Read the following poem, "If I Ran the Zoo" by John Leo. What problem does Leo address? How does he propose to solve this problem? What objections to his proposals does he anticipate? If this were a more fully developed proposal argument, what evidence might Leo have added to support his position?

> This poem was published on the Web site of the National Association of Scholars on June 30, 2008.

IF I RAN THE ZOO

JOHN LEO

If I ran the campus   1
I'd start out anew
I'd make a few changes
That's just what I'd do

Here's a simple suggestion   5
(Avoiding all fads)
I'd have some professors
Who teach undergrads

I hear you all snicker
I hear you all scoff   10
But I've got to believe
That many a prof
Would thrill to be meeting
A freshman or soph

TAs are beloved   15
They're always the rage
Because they all work
For a minimum wage
(But do students want teachers
Who are just their own age?)   20

Remedial classes
I'm sure are a must
For teachers who give
Only A or A-plus

They really must practice   25
At home, if they please,
Traumatically giving
Some Bs and some Cs

There's another idea   30
I can bring to fruition
I know how to cut
The cost of tuition

I really don't care
Whose waters this muddies,   35
This could irritate
The fuddies and duddies
But I'd cancel all courses
Whose names end in "studies."

That's just a start   40
I'll do better than that
My curriculum changes
Will cut out the fat

No courses on Buffy
The Vampire Slayer
Or Batman and Robin   45
Who cares which is gayer?

No bongo or bingo
(Remember I said it)
No study of Yoda
No sex acts for credit   50

No Star Trek theology
No Matrix psychology
No queer musicology
I give no apology

If I ran the campus   55
I'd start out anew
I'd make a few changes
That's just what I'd do

⊘ EXERCISE 15.5

Write a paragraph or two in which you argue for or against the recommendations Leo proposes in "If I Ran the Zoo." Be sure to present a clear statement of the problems he is addressing as well as the strengths or shortcomings of his proposal.

Structuring a Proposal Argument

In general, a proposal argument can be structured in the following way.

- **Introduction:** Establishes the context of the proposal and presents the essay's thesis
- **Explanation of the problem:** Identifies the problem and explains why it needs to be solved
- **Explanation of the solution:** Proposes a solution and explains how it will solve the problem
- **Evidence in support of the solution:** Presents support for the proposed solution (this section can be more than one paragraph)
- **Benefits of the solution:** Explains the positive results of the proposed course of action
- **Refutation of opposing arguments:** Addresses objections to the proposal
- **Conclusion:** Reinforces the main point of the proposal; includes a strong concluding statement

The following student essay contains all the elements of a proposal argument. The student who wrote this essay is trying to convince the college president that the school should adopt an **honor code**—a system of rules that defines acceptable conduct and establishes procedures for handling misconduct.

COLLEGES NEED HONOR CODES
MELISSA BURRELL

1   Today's college students are under a lot of pressure to do well in school, to win tuition grants, to please teachers and family, and to compete in the job market. As a result, the temptation to cheat is greater than ever. At the same time, technology, particularly the Internet, has made cheating easier than ever. Colleges and universities have tried various strategies to combat this problem, from increasing punishments to using plagiarism-detection tools such as Turnitin.com. However, the most comprehensive and effective solution to the problem of academic dishonesty is an honor code, a campuswide contract that spells out and enforces standards of honesty. To fight academic dishonesty, colleges should institute and actively maintain honor codes.

2   Although the exact number of students who cheat is impossible to determine, recent studies estimate that 52% to 90% of students

Introduction

Thesis statement

Explanation of the problem: Cheating

cheat at some point in their college careers (Vandehey, Diekhoff, and LaBeff 468). In my experience, some students cheat by plagiarizing entire papers or stealing answers to tests. Many other students commit so-called lesser offenses, such as collaborating with others when told to work alone, sharing test answers, cutting and pasting material from the Internet, or "fudging" data. All of these acts are dishonest; all amount to cheating. Part of the problem, however, is that students often do not understand what constitutes cheating. According to a *New York Times* article, students' most common excuse for cheating is, "'I didn't mean to.'" If the rules defining cheating are not clear, cheating becomes much easier to justify. In addition, if students see others getting away with cheating, even the most severe punishments do not discourage dishonesty (Zernike).

Explanation of the
solution: Institute an
honor code

An honor code solves these problems by clearly presenting the rules, defining cheating as well as the punishments for various offenses. To enroll for classes, *every* student has to sign a pledge to uphold the honor code. Ideally, students write and manage the honor code themselves, with the help of faculty and administrators. According to Timothy Dodd, however, to be successful, the honor code must be more than a document; it must be a way of thinking. For this reason, all first-year students should receive copies of the school's honor code at orientation. At the beginning of each academic year, students should be required to reread the honor code and renew their pledge to uphold its values and rules. In addition, students and instructors need to discuss the honor code in class. (Some colleges post the honor code in every classroom.) In other words, the honor code must be part of the fabric of the school. It should be present in students' minds, guiding their actions and informing their learning and teaching.

Evidence in support of
the solution

Studies show that serious cheating is 25% to 50% lower at schools with honor codes (Dodd). With an honor code in place, students cannot say that they do not know what constitutes cheating or understand what will happen to them if they cheat. Studies also show that in schools with a strong honor code, instructors are more likely to take action against cheating. One study shows that professors frequently do not confront students who cheat because they are not sure the university will back them up (Vandehey, Diekhoff, and LaBeff 469). When a school has an honor code, instructors can be certain that both the students and the school will support their actions.

5   When a school institutes an honor code, a number of positive results will occur. First, an honor code will create a set of basic rules that students can follow. Students know in advance what is expected of them and what will happen if they commit an infraction. Next, an honor code will promote honesty, placing more responsibility and power in the hands of students and encouraging them to act according to a higher standard. For this reason, schools with honor codes often permit unsupervised exams that require students to monitor one other. Finally, according to Timothy Dodd, an honor code will encourage students to act responsibly. It assumes that students will not take unfair advantage of each other or undercut the academic community. Thus, as Dodd concludes, plagiarism (and cheating in general) becomes a concern for everyone—students as well as instructors.

Benefits of the solution

6   Some people argue that a plagiarism-detection tool such as Turnitin.com would be a simpler and more effective way of preventing cheating than an honor code. However, such tools focus on catching individual acts of cheating, not on preventing a culture of cheating. When schools use these tools, they are telling students that getting caught, not cheating, is their main concern. Thus, these tools do not deal with the real problem—the choice to be dishonest. Rather than trusting students, schools that use plagiarism-detection tools assume that all students are cheating. Unlike plagiarism-detection tools, honor codes fight dishonesty by promoting a culture of integrity, fairness, and accountability. By assuming that most students are trustworthy and punishing only those who are not, schools with honor codes set high standards for students and encourage them to rise to the challenge.

Opposing arguments

Refutation

7   The only long-term, comprehensive solution to the problem of cheating is a campuswide honor code. No solution will be 100% effective in preventing dishonesty, but honor codes go a long way toward addressing the root causes of this problem. The goal of an honor code is to create a campus culture that values and rewards honesty and integrity. By encouraging students to do what is expected of them, honor codes help create a confident, empowered, and trustworthy student body.

Conclusion

Concluding statement

Works Cited

Dodd, Timothy M. "Honor Code 101: An Introduction to the Elements of Traditional Honor Codes, Modified Honor Codes and Academic Integrity Policies." *Center for Academic Integrity*. Clemson Univ., 2007. Web. 1 Sept. 2008.

Vandehey, Michael, George Diekhoff, and Emily LaBeff. "College Cheating: A Twenty-Year Follow-Up and the Addition of an Honor Code." *Journal of College Student Development* 48.4 (2007): 468–80. *Academic OneFile*. Web. 31 Aug. 2008.

Zernike, Kate. "With Cheating on the Rise, More Colleges Are Turning to Honor Codes." *New York Times*. New York Times, 2 Nov. 2002. Web. 1 Sept. 2008.

GRAMMAR IN CONTEXT: *WILL* VERSUS *WOULD*

Many people use the helping verbs *will* and *would* interchangeably. When you write a proposal, however, keep in mind that these words express different shades of meaning.

> **Will** expresses certainty. In a list of benefits, for example, *will* indicates the benefits that will occur if the proposal is accepted.
>
> > First, an honor code will create a set of basic rules that students can follow.
> >
> > Next, an honor code will promote honesty.
>
> **Would** expresses probability. In a refutation of an opposing argument, for example, *would* indicates that another solution might be more effective than the one being proposed.
>
> > Some people argue that a plagiarism-detection tool such as Turnitin.com would be simpler and a more effective way of preventing cheating than an honor code.

⊙ EXERCISE 15.6

The following essay, "My Plan to Escape the Grip of Foreign Oil" by T. Boone Pickens, includes the basic elements of a proposal argument. Read the essay, and answer the questions that follow it, consulting the outline on page 427 if necessary.

This piece appeared in the *Wall Street Journal* on July 9, 2008.

MY PLAN TO ESCAPE THE GRIP OF FOREIGN OIL

T. BOONE PICKENS

One of the benefits of being around a long time is that you get to know a 1
lot about certain things. I'm 80 years old and I've been an oilman for almost
60 years. I've drilled more dry holes and also found more oil than just about
anyone in the industry. With all my experience, I've never been as worried
about our energy security as I am now. Like many of us, I ignored what was
happening. Now our country faces what I believe is the most serious situation
since World War II.

The problem, of course, is our growing dependence on foreign oil—it's 2
extreme, it's dangerous, and it threatens the future of our nation.

Let me share a few facts: Each year we import more and more oil. In 1973, 3
the year of the infamous oil embargo, the United States imported about 24%
of our oil. In 1990, at the start of the first Gulf War, this had climbed to 42%.
Today, we import almost 70% of our oil.

This is a staggering number, particularly for a country that consumes oil 4
the way we do. The U.S. uses nearly a quarter of the world's oil, with just 4% of
the population and 3% of the world's reserves. This year, we will spend almost
$700 billion on imported oil, which is more than four times the annual cost of
our current war in Iraq.

In fact, if we don't do anything about this problem, over the next 10 years 5
we will spend around $10 trillion importing foreign oil. That is $10 trillion
leaving the U.S. and going to foreign nations, making it what I certainly believe
will be the single largest transfer of wealth in human history.

Why do I believe that our dependence on foreign oil is such a danger to 6
our country? Put simply, our economic
engine is now 70% dependent on the
energy resources of other countries, their
good judgment, and most importantly,
their good will toward us. Foreign oil
is at the intersection of America's three
most important issues: the economy, the
environment and our national security. We need an energy plan that maps out
how we're going to work our way out of this mess. I think I have such a plan.

> "Our economic engine is now 70% dependent on the energy resources of other countries."

Consider this: The world produces about 85 million barrels of oil a day, 7
but global demand now tops 86 million barrels a day. And despite three years
of record price increases, world oil production has declined every year since
2005. Meanwhile, the demand for oil will only increase as growing economies
in countries like India and China gear up for enhanced oil consumption.

Add to this the fact that in many countries, including China, the gov- 8
ernment has a great deal of influence over its energy industry, allowing these
countries to set strategic direction easily and pay whatever price is needed to
secure oil. The U.S. has no similar policy, because we thankfully don't have
state-controlled energy companies. But that doesn't mean we can't set goals
and develop an energy policy that will overcome our addiction to foreign oil. I
have a clear goal in mind with my plan. I want to reduce America's foreign oil
imports by more than one-third in the next five to 10 years.

How will we do it? We'll start with wind power. Wind is 100% domestic, 9
it is 100% renewable and it is 100% clean. Did you know that the midsection
of this country, that stretch of land that starts in West Texas and reaches all the
way up to the border with Canada, is called the "Saudi Arabia of the Wind"?
It gets that name because we have the greatest wind reserves in the world. In
2008, the Department of Energy issued a study that stated that the U.S. has the
capacity to generate 20% of its electricity supply from wind by 2030. I think we
can do this or even more, but we must do it quicker.

My plan calls for taking the energy generated by wind and using it to 10
replace a significant percentage of the natural gas that is now being used to fuel
our power plants. Today, natural gas accounts for about 22% of our electricity
generation in the U.S. We can use new wind capacity to free up the natural gas
for use as a transportation fuel. That would displace more than one-third of
our foreign oil imports. Natural gas is the only domestic energy of size that can
be used to replace oil used for transportation, and it is abundant in the U.S.
It is cheap and it is clean. With eight million natural-gas-powered vehicles on
the road world-wide, the technology already exists to rapidly build out fleets
of trucks, buses and even cars using natural gas as a fuel. Of these eight million vehicles, the U.S. has a paltry 150,000 right now. We can and should do so
much more to build our fleet of natural-gas-powered vehicles.

I believe this plan will be the perfect bridge to the future, affording us the 11
time to develop new technologies and a new perspective on our energy use. In
addition to the plan I have proposed, I also want to see us explore all avenues
and every energy alternative, from more R&D into batteries and fuel cells to
development of solar, ethanol and biomass to more conservation. Drilling in
the outer continental shelf should be considered as well, as we need to look at
all options, recognizing that there is no silver bullet.

I believe my plan can be accomplished within 10 years if this country 12
takes decisive and bold steps immediately. This plan dramatically reduces our
dependence on foreign oil and lowers the cost of transportation. It invests
in the heartland, creating thousands of new jobs. It substantially reduces
America's carbon footprint and uses existing, proven technology. It will be
accomplished solely through private investment with no new consumer or
corporate taxes or government regulation. It will build a bridge to the future,
giving us the time to develop new technologies.

The future begins as soon as Congress and the president act. The govern- 13
ment must mandate the formation of wind and solar transmission corridors,

and renew the subsidies for economic and alternative energy development in areas where the wind and sun are abundant. I am also calling for a monthly progress report on the reduction in foreign oil imports, as well as a monthly progress report on the state of development of natural gas vehicles in this country.

We have a golden opportunity in this election year to form bipartisan   14
support for this plan. We have the grit and fortitude to shoulder the responsibility of change when our country's future is at stake, as Americans have proven repeatedly throughout this nation's history.

We need action. Now.   15

Identifying the Elements of a Proposal Argument

1. What is the essay's thesis statement? How effective do you think it is?

2. Where in the essay does Pickens identify the problem he wants to solve?

3. According to Pickens, what are the specific ways dependence on foreign oil threatens the United States?

4. Where does Pickens present his solutions?

5. Where does Pickens discuss the benefits of his proposal? What other benefits could he have addressed?

6. Pickens does not address possible arguments against his proposal. Should he have? What possible arguments might he have addressed? How would you refute each of these arguments?

Should All College Instructors Be Required to Make Their Lectures Available as Podcasts?

 Reread the At Issue box on page 417, which gives background on whether all college lectures should be made available as podcasts. Then, read the sources on the following pages.

As you read this material, you will be asked to answer questions and to complete some simple activities. This work will help you understand both the content and structure of the selections. When you are finished, you will be ready to write a **proposal** that argues for or against requiring all college lectures to be made available as podcasts.

SOURCES

 Murray Jensen, "Lecture Is Dead: Take 3"

 Robert Schneider, "The Attack of the Pod People"

 Jeff Curto, "Globalizing Education One Podcast at a Time"

 Pitt News, "iPod Addiction Goes Academic"

 Fabienne Serriere, "Teaching via iPod"

 Apple.com, "iTunes U"

This reading was published on March 1, 2007, in the *American Biology Teacher*.

LECTURE IS DEAD: TAKE 3

MURRAY JENSEN

I'm not dead.
Ere, he says he's not dead.
Well, he will be soon, he's very ill.

—Monty Python and the Holy Grail, 1975

Large lecture sections are a reality for most of us who teach in public universities. Colleges have been known to put over 1,000 students into an auditorium for a freshman biology course. One thousand people in an auditorium where U2 or The Rolling Stones are performing would be called "intimate," but for the average biology professor explaining the enzymes of glycolysis, well . . . let's just say that the situation is not ideal. 1

Yes—you in row Y, seat 79. You have a question about glucose phosphate isomerase?

Facing a potential PR nightmare (students pay more to see us than they do for most concert tickets), our administrators try to help by equipping us with new technology so as to better educate (or, for some of us, entertain) the masses. I recall three different waves of technology that were intended to improve the educational quality of large lectures, but in each case the technological actually drove students away. 2

At the University of Minnesota in the 1970s, the freshman biology course used a new technology in the lecture auditorium—videotape! It now seems archaic, but at the time the plan was to create a high-quality presentation and record it, and then use the tape for the day's lecture. Students would "engage" in a high quality lecture via videotape, and the professors could go back to their labs and do their research. Since the videotapes were used over and over again each semester, a market emerged for lecture notes. Enterprising students from previous semesters would stand at the back of the lecture hall on the first few days of class and sell copies of the notes for the entire semester. Needless to say, attendance fell off quite a bit after the first week. It was a good attempt, but the videotape experiment ended in about 1980 when the tapes wore thin, or the students tired of paying tuition to watch recorded lectures, and professors again started showing up to give lectures—live and in person. 3

Jump ahead to 2002. I had a single semester leave and was able to attend lectures in many areas of biology. This was the time when PowerPoint was making inroads because book companies were supplying professors with easy-to-use presentations, and many auditoriums were being equipped with high-quality presentation equipment. The slides were typically excellent—very 4 professional images, graphs, etc. And using PowerPoint was easy; you did not need to be a computer geek to press the space bar to advance the slides. Many of the lectures I attended in 2002 involved the lights of an auditorium going off at the start of class, and then being turned on at the end—nothing but PowerPoint slides for the entire time. Depending on the quality of the professor running the slides, most students fell into a cognitive coma (a.k.a. "PowerPoint Paralysis") after a few minutes. But students had no worries about "keeping up" or even staying awake because classroom management systems, like Black-Board or WebCT, enabled them to download the same PowerPoint files that were used in class. Attendance levels fell quickly in lecture courses that were dominated by PowerPoint—why attend if you simply fall asleep and look at the slides later? Like the videotape, PowerPoint was intended to make lectures better, but its misuse, or maybe abuse, drove students away.

Now comes a third technology that is supposed to improve lecture— podcasting. Podcasting is essentially an audio recording that is published on the Internet, either within open or restricted Web sites. Professors at many universities have the option of recording their lectures and then having them podcasted. Students then have a choice of listening to podcasts on their computers, or on their portable MP3 Players, e.g., iPods. (It may sound somewhat complex for professors, but for a college freshman, listening to a podcast is as difficult as accessing e-mail.) And if students elect to listen to the podcasts on their computers, they can combine it with the PowerPoint slides used in the course—it's almost like being there! 5

I started podcasting my lectures for my freshman anatomy and physiol- ogy course this fall as part of a small grant—that, and I'm a sucker for new technology. We post the MP3 files on an open blog site that describes the daily activities of the course (http://blog.lib.umn.edu/msjensen/pstl1135/). I have not run any sort of experiment yet on attendance or student performance, but I did talk to one student who made me think that podcasting might put tradi-tional lecture on life-support. 6

Melissa is a student who works between 20 and 40 hours a week and has about a one-hour commute to campus. On Wednesdays she has only my class on her schedule, and she typically works until midnight on Tuesday nights. 7

I skip class—I just download the podcasts. They're great!

It's important to note that Melissa does attend all labs, where attendance is required, and has successfully competed all the lecture exams—she is pass-ing the class. But it should also be noted that she already has quite a few college credits—not your typical freshman. 8

For good students like Melissa, attendance appears not to be a critical factor for success in the typical class. This is probably true throughout the history of education—the good students can learn from the book, from someone else's notes, by looking at the PowerPoint slides, by listening to the podcasts, etc. If a good student has motivation, he/she will likely succeed no matter how poor the learning environment—he/she will overcome the 9 obstacles. But what about the struggling freshman—the one who has to work hard just to pass. For these students the podcasts represent one more way to learn biology. This is in addition to the book, study groups, labs, PowerPoint files, etc. . . . Podcasts represent one more tool for students to use to understand biology—and if all used together, they might indeed pass. However, the temptation is there—

> "Dude! Just blow-off lecture and listen to the podcast later!"

Dude! Just blow-off lecture and listen to the podcast later!

It is imaginable that someday there will be a biology course meeting in a 10 dark auditorium, the computer projection system quietly humming, and the biology professor talking about the enzymes of glycolysis, and of course, being podcasted—and no students are attending. Will this event mark the death of lecture?

They stab it with their steely knives but they just can't kill the beast.
—HOTEL CALIFORNIA. THE EAGLES

⊘ AT ISSUE: SOURCES FOR DEVELOPING A PROPOSAL ARGUMENT

1. What three new technologies does Jensen discuss?

2. What are Jensen's objections to podcasting his lectures?

3. Where in the essay does Jensen acknowledge the advantages of making lectures available as podcasts?

4. This essay begins with lines from a movie and ends with song lyrics. What point is Jensen making with each of these references?

5. In paragraph 7, Jensen introduces Melissa, a student. What points about podcasting does she help him make?

6. At the end of his essay, Jensen asks, "Will this event mark the death of lecture?" (para. 10). What does he mean? Can you answer his question?

This piece appeared in the *Chronicle of Higher Education* on December 8, 2006.

THE ATTACK OF THE POD PEOPLE

ROBERT SCHNEIDER

1 It was a lovely, crisp autumn day, but a piece in the *Northern Star*, my university's student newspaper, took all the joy out of it. The reporter, Lauren Stott, began on a lyrical note: "It's every student's dream: Wake up for school, stumble over to the computer, and download the day's class lectures . . . then crawl back into bed—iPod in one hand, notebook in the other."

2 The object of the student journalist's enthusiasm was the possibility of having her courses delivered as podcasts, recordings distributed over the Internet and played back on miniature MP3 players like the eponymous Apple iPod. "To most students," she wrote, "podcasting proposes an idea of almost unlimited leisure, letting them learn on their own time and in their preferred location."

3 The article went on to report that my university was planning to set up a central server that would allow instructors to deliver recordings of their lectures to students enrolled in their courses. Asked for her opinion, another student said, "Hopefully professors will give the students a chance to meet in class at least a few times throughout the semester so they can make contacts for study groups and to get help."

4 That dystopian nonsense moved me to pen a dissenting article in support of real-time, nonvirtual class sessions similar to those already offered on our campus. I sent that diatribe to the newspaper's opinion editor. After a week, during which he neither printed it nor acknowledged it, I attached a hard copy to my bulletin board and figured that was the end of that.

5 Shortly afterward, however, I received an e-mail message from a professor at the University of Connecticut, who agreed with me about podcasts but said I should have made allowance for students who couldn't get to campus because of inclement weather. I was flabbergasted—had the professor from UConn been reading my bulletin board?

6 I discovered that an online newsletter, *Podcasting News*, had run a small piece titled "Professor: University Podcasts Are Totally Bogus." The professor was me.

7 The piece included a link to our student newspaper, which led the reader to a mangled version of my opinion piece, reduced to a fifth of its original length and printed as a letter to the editor. The paper had gone at my text with a hedge clipper, then printed it when I was traveling out of state. I never caught my "letter."

8 The shrunken, mangled piece made me sound like a Luddite, a curmudgeon railing against a technology whose self-evident usefulness lay just beyond his intellectual grasp. By the time I found the piece, various readers had added their comments. Most said I was antediluvian, and one cited a survey to prove that. Only the professor from UConn had had the courtesy to look up my e-mail address and contact me directly.

The online piece made no reference to the article that I had originally 9 responded to, which led several of my e-readers to castigate me for neglecting to consider how valuable podcasts would be for handicapped students and students who couldn't come to class because of illness or religious holidays— situations never mentioned in the article that first aroused my ire. Curiously, I had also acquired defenders, one of whom generously forgave my curmudgeonliness on the ground that it was to be expected in a ballet teacher (actually, I teach theater history). Neither my detractors nor my allies had any notion of what I'd written or why. I had been reduced to a silent sound bite in the ether, a floating phenomenon of technophobia.

What the electronic press had done to my arguments was exactly what I 10 suspected podcasting would do to my lectures: shear them of all context and present them at the recipient's convenience, yes, but without style or conviction.

I'm grateful to *The Chronicle* for this opportunity to finally see my whole 11 rant in print.

The subject I teach is largely about events, irrecoverable, ephemeral, you- 12 had-to-be-there events, like the 35 minutes of curtain calls that followed the premiere of Olivier's *Othello*, or the moment—at once stylized and spontaneous—in which a Kabuki actor acknowledges the acclamations of the crowd. Such events can't be recorded, abstracted, time delayed, or transmitted in any form without losing their quality of liveness, one of the essential qualities that qualify them as belonging to my discipline. The specificity of the events, the way they are bound in time and reserved for those present to witness, is one of the most important things I try to convey to my students.

In a more general sense, my class meetings are also events: Participation is 13 reserved for those who manage to get out of bed, put on some clothes, and drag themselves to the appointed classroom at the appointed time. I'm one of those people. It's a nuisance to me to go to class, but my presence is essential: It shows that I care enough about my subject to get out of bed and get dressed in order to transmit its principles to students who've made a similar sacrifice for a similar purpose.

It would be different if I were communicating practical information like 14 a talking clock, or the recording that tells you the campus is closed because of snow. But teaching isn't like that: When you teach, you're also transmitting the values that make information worth having.

So I have to be there. If that means I occasionally have to speak without 15 adequate preparation, misspell words on the blackboard, garble my sentences, and generally work without recourse to a second "take," so be it. At 8 in the morning I may not be beautiful—hell, I may not even be fully awake—but I'm there, and I'm dressed. Any questions?

> "Students have to participate in my classes."

Students have to participate in my 16 classes—and I don't mean "have to" in the sense that if they don't participate, they won't pass. They have to participate because I can't teach if they don't; I have to sense if my **students** are following me or not. Even if their participation takes the form of a blank look or a nodding head—as occasionally happens—I need it.

If forced, I could walk into an empty room to deliver a stream of scholarly 17 syllables into a microphone for an hour and a quarter, but I would never call that teaching.

Students who, in pursuit of "almost unlimited leisure," consent to dilute 18 their classroom experience by forcing it through an iPod are shortchanging themselves. Those of my colleagues who have allowed their teaching to degenerate into mere utterance are shortchanging their students. Lazy students and lazy professors form an insidious alliance whose principal goal is economy of effort, and whose principal product is boredom for all concerned. The new technology supplies an alibi for both groups: It's more convenient, so it must be better, right?

In her "Classroom Is an iPod?" article, Lauren Stott embraces that nox- 19 ious tendency wholeheartedly. I would have preferred a warning: Podcasts of university courses are not "every student's dream"; they're totally bogus, a thin surrogate for real instruction, a fig leaf for disengagement, an excuse for lack of commitment from professors and students alike. People who believe in the transformative value of higher education will resist podcastification with a passion.

Let me add, as a sort of afterthought to my original rant, that there's 20 another, more self-interested reason for professors to be wary: In a world where students can be replaced by iPods, professors can be replaced, too, and quite inexpensively—by tape recorders.

⊘ AT ISSUE: SOURCES FOR DEVELOPING A PROPOSAL ARGUMENT

1. Paragraphs 1 to 11 serve as this introduction to Schneider's essay. What point does he make in this introduction? Why do you think it is so long?

2. What does Schneider mean in paragraph 12 when he says, "The subject I teach is largely about events"? In what sense, according to Schneider, are his class meetings also "events"?

3. What arguments does Schneider present against making his lectures available as podcasts? Do you find these arguments convincing?

4. Identify some words—for example, "nonsense" in paragraph 4—that convey Schneider's attitude toward the issue he is discussing. Does his use of these words strengthen or weaken his case?

5. Schneider never acknowledges any of the advantages of podcasting lectures. Should he have?

This piece is from the October 2006 edition of *TheJournal.com*.

GLOBALIZING EDUCATION ONE PODCAST AT A TIME

JEFF CURTO

In the fall of 2005, I opened the door of my "History of Photography" classroom and found that there were hundreds of students on the other side. These students were Chinese, German, Italian, British, Australian, American, Japanese, and Costa Rican. They ranged in age from 15 to 80. They were professional photographers, amateur photographers, designers, executives, truck drivers, high-schoolers, doctors, and homemakers. There were a lot of them, and they were all interested in the history of photography. While the room only had 25 seats, hundreds of people were sitting in on my class sessions each week.

The room wasn't crowded though, because these students were taking part in a virtual classroom experience by virtue of my recording the class sessions and publishing them as podcasts. These audio files (with images from my Apple Keynote or PowerPoint slides embedded and synchronized with the audio) could be downloaded and heard by anyone with an Internet connection, a bit of time, and an interest in photo history. It wasn't just these "outsiders" who were listening either, as my own classroom-bound students also discovered that listening to and viewing podcasts of class content at a later time aided them in their progress through the course. Most importantly, the students on the inside of my classroom welcomed this diverse group, and were amazed at the level of interest, thought, and overall intellectual discourse that these new students brought to the class.

Fostering Asynchronous Learning

Podcasting is a generic name for a method of distributing audio and other multimedia files over the Internet for playback on mobile devices and personal computers. Although this type of content has long been available on Web pages, a podcast is usually defined by its ability to be automatically downloaded to a user's computer by subscription. That electronic file can then be easily transferred to an iPod or other portable audio player and listened to at any time.

Through podcasting, I have opened the door of my classroom to the rest of the world and started a class discussion that is not constrained by the classroom walls or by the cultural, educational, and personal backgrounds of my physical students. E-mail contact that I get from my virtual students is often read aloud in class, and discussion ensues on topics that my in-classroom students may not have considered. From my classroom students' perspective, the idea that someone is listening to the classes and e-mailing comments from his BlackBerry while riding to work on the Tokyo subway is amazing.

In addition to helping students see that the world is a classroom, I've 5 also been able to help my "live" students learn by providing them with asynchronous delivery of course content. While it might be expected that students would not attend class because they can get the content anytime they want, I've found the opposite to be true, and absences from class are rare. Instead, my students tell me that they often listen to the podcasts each week, a few days after our class session, even though they heard the content presented live. They feel that the repetition helps them identify and recall key concepts and facts. Some listen on their computers, but most listen using their iPods so they can take the class content with them in the car, on the bus, or when they are walking to class.

> "Absences from class are rare."

Streamlining the Podcasting Process

To produce the podcasts, I use ProfCast. The software records my voice 6 through my laptop, takes my Apple Keynote or PowerPoint slides and synchronizes them with the audio as I speak, and advances the slides. As an end product, ProfCast creates an audio file that has embedded images of each of my lecture slides. This file can be listened to and viewed using iTunes or QuickTime Player (on either a Windows or Mac computer), or on a student's iPod.

What's more, ProfCast helps me manage my accumulated audio files, 7 assists me in uploading them to my institution's server, and creates the RSS "feed" file. The RSS file (in the form of an XML document) is what makes the podcast something that can be "subscribed" to so that it is automatically delivered to a student's computer whenever a new class session is ready. It really streamlines the process of producing and distributing the recorded class content.

Aside from my institution-supplied Apple PowerBook and some available 8 Web server space, there isn't much in the way of resources needed to produce this content. An inexpensive microphone is used in lieu of the laptop's built-in mic, and the ProfCast software ($30) is augmented with a couple other freeware or "comes with my computer" software pieces. It takes about 30 minutes a week to finish and upload each new podcast, but that time is more than paid for by the higher quality of learning and the interest and contributions of those "outside of the classroom" students.

Now that I've opened the door to the classroom, I can't imagine ever 9 closing it again, as the benefits for me and my students are genuinely far-reaching.

⊘ AT ISSUE: SOURCES FOR DEVELOPING A PROPOSAL ARGUMENT

1. Curto begins his essay by describing a "virtual classroom experience" (para. 2). How does this strategy create interest in his topic?

2. What is Curto's position on podcasting in the classroom? Where does he state this position?

3. In paragraph 3, Curto defines *podcasting*. Why do you think he includes this definition? Whom does he consider his audience to be? How can you tell?

4. What specific arguments does Curto present to support his thesis?

5. Does Curto seem to be overstating the advantages of podcasting? Should he have acknowledged the possible drawbacks of this teaching technique? If so, where might he have added this new material?

This staff editorial appeared in the March 21, 2006, issue of the *Pitt News,* the student newspaper of the University of Pittsburgh.

iPOD ADDICTION GOES ACADEMIC

PITT NEWS

1   When does a fad become the norm? Probably when colleges issue incoming students shiny new iPods.

2   The integration of iPod technology into academics is an increasing trend for colleges and universities. More than 100 faculty members at Georgia College and State University utilize iPod technology to supplement their curriculum, making iPods a necessity for students. Not only are lectures being offered to download on iPods, but office hours are being replaced by podcasts, providing students with answers to frequently asked questions. The latest generation of technology enables users to screen videos for class on their video-capable iPods.

3   Duke University supplies its freshmen with iPods as welcome gifts and uses the devices to help foreign-language students adapt to coursework, the Associated Press reports. Other colleges, including Pennsylvania's Mansfield University, hope to entice high school students to attend their university through podcasts.

4   Pitt, too, is joining the iRevolution by adding a feature called CourseCasting to its Pick A Prof Web site. Teachers can record their lectures and upload them to pickaprof.com for students to download onto their iPods.

5   You have to congratulate educators for transitioning iPods into an academic tool. Look around—they're everywhere. Students have become so dependent on their mp3 players that the thought of walking from the Cathedral to David Lawrence without popping in their ear buds is unbearable. iPods are a recognized addiction that colleges and universities are manipulating to their advantage.

6   This move by colleges has not only secured Apple a place in the collegiate world for the foreseeable future, but it reinforces the trend of isolationism that is creeping up on Americans everywhere. Now students can avoid falling asleep in class—they can fall asleep in their beds instead, iPod in hand.

7   No longer are the sounds of Oakland stimulating enough. Our lives must move with a soundtrack of our favorite music, news and video. The all-consuming stimulus that we have become accustomed to has made it nearly impossible for us to function without it. Eating lunch alone or studying in Starbucks has turned into a delicate dance between adjusting iPod settings and monitoring cell phone status—all while balancing a latte. Can't we just sit and enjoy ourselves anymore?

> "Can't we just sit and enjoy ourselves anymore?"

The academic iPod invasion has one flaw, though: cost. At around $300 8 for a standard iPod, what happens to students that can't afford one? Will they be at a disadvantage in classes that provide supplementary material via iPod? Sure, they can download a free version of iTunes to their computer, but some students don't even have their own computers, relying instead on campus computer labs. And with technology changing faster and faster, will students be expected to purchase a new iPod every time a feature is added?

The appeal to teachers is understandable. By providing students with pic- 9 tures, movies and other educational supplements prior to lecture, class time can be entirely devoted to discussion. However, making too much available to students is coming dangerously close to making in-class attendance obsolete.

There is no substitution for traditional teaching methods. Often the best 10 teachers are engaging lecturers and it is an undeniable truth that something is lost when lectures move out of the classroom and into the digital world. The use of technology in the classroom is inevitable. Educators must find a way to strike the fragile balance between enriching their teaching and making attendance obsolete. After all, what's the point of going to class when you can listen to your professor anytime, anywhere you want?

⊘ AT ISSUE: SOURCES FOR DEVELOPING A PROPOSAL ARGUMENT

1. This editorial begins with a question. Does it ever answer this question? How would you answer it?

2. According to the editorial, why should educators be congratulated "for transitioning iPods into an academic tool" (para. 5)? Should this comment be taken literally, or is it meant to be sarcastic?

3. According to the editorial, what are the main disadvantages of using the iPod as an educational tool?

4. What is the editorial's position on the issue? Where are opposing arguments acknowledged? How effectively are these opposing arguments refuted?

5. The thesis statement appears in paragraph 10, the editorial's conclusion. Why? Do you think it should have appeared sooner? If so, where might it have been placed?

This post, which is followed by reader comments, appeared on November 23, 2005, on the Unofficial Apple Weblog.

TEACHING VIA iPOD

FABIENNE SERRIERE

Newsweek has an intriguing article about class lectures being made available 1
in mp3 for students. Professors in major universities have been making audio recordings of coursework for quite some time, but recently some of these lecture-casts have replaced actual human-led courses.

Personally I enjoyed having real interaction with my professors during 2
class (which is why I picked courses with low enrollment and hung out in office hours). I can see, however, how this would be useful for distance learning. What do you think? Should some classes be mp3/ videocast only?

> "Personally I enjoyed having real interaction with my professors."

Reader Comments

1. *11-23-2005 @ 7:37PM*

danb said . . .

I am an undergraduate in economics and politics currently in my final 3
year. I think that for the economics portion of the course mp3 cast would be pretty useless. Without the attached diagrams/models/equations the lecture would be particularly difficult to gain from. For my politics lectures however lecture casts are great.

I have been using my iPod mic combo for a while now and distrib- 4
uting my lectures via my blog for other students on my course. With lecturer permission naturally. It's great come revision and much more helpful than a Powerpoint presentation. If only I could somehow index a transcript of the lecture for better searching, now that would be good.

As for economics, I await my lecturer's vodcast with accompanying stills. 5

Reply

2. *11-23-2005 @ 9:56PM*

Andrew said . . .

I am currently taking an online marketing class which uses real audio files. 6
While I'd prefer that they be mp3s, it gets the job done. The class lectures are supplemented with a website that contains notes and pictures, charts, etc. . . .

This method of teaching works but it's no substitute for the real thing.

Reply

3. *11-23-2005 @ 10:53PM*

Noel said . . .

I've taken a virtual course coupled with an active classroom forum. It 7 worked great for some I think, but for me . . . too easy to get distracted and get behind in course work. I think it's great for those 'independent' self-taught, self-motivated type. I on the other hand need the commitment of daily class attendance.

Reply

4. *11-24-2005 @ 10:48PM*

Mike Doan said . . .

Having lectures on MP3 is a great way to *supplement* your notes from 8 the class. In college I had a economics professor who encouraged us to record lectures. The recordings were useful in filling in the blanks in my class notes (too busy drawing those charts and graphs).

Some professor didn't want to be recorded because they claimed that 9 the lectures were their intellectual property. That stance may hinder the number of lecture-casts available.

Reply

5. *11-25-2005 @ 3:44PM*

Pablo said . . .

A very nice initiative, which is not mentioned in the *Newsweek* article, is 10 Open Course Ware from the MIT. They have free audio and video lectures of many undergraduate and graduate courses. You can check them out at: http://ocw.mit.edu/OcwWeb/Global/OCWHelp/avoc. I personally recommend the video lectures on Physics by Walter Lewin. Really cool stuff.

Reply

6. *12-08-2005 @ 6:07PM*

Rahul Malhotra said . . .

Could someone send me some links to all possible electrical engineering 11 courses that are available in the domain of electrical engineering especially information theory/statistical signal processing etc.

Podcasts preferable!

Hare Krishna
Rahul

Reply

⊘ AT ISSUE: SOURCES FOR DEVELOPING A PROPOSAL ARGUMENT

1. Read the various posts on the Unofficial Apple Weblog site. Are the majority of the comments for or against podcasting?

2. What do the readers who comment here like about podcasts? What do they dislike?

3. What, if anything, do the readers think in-person contact adds to a course?

4. Do you think some courses could be taught exclusively via podcast? Explain.

This a screen capture of Apple's iTunes University.

iTUNES U

APPLE.COM

⊘ AT ISSUE: SOURCES FOR DEVELOPING A PROPOSAL ARGUMENT

1. At what audience is this iTunes U ad aimed? Students? Instructors? Administrators? How can you tell?

2. What is iTunes U? What impression is Apple trying to convey with the name of this site?

3. What point does this ad make about podcast lectures?

4. What specific arguments does the ad make to support its position? How effective are these arguments?

5. In what sense, if any, is this ad a proposal argument?

⊙ EXERCISE 15.7

Write a one-paragraph proposal argument in which you try to convince one of your instructors to make lectures available as podcasts. Follow the template below, filling in the blanks to create your proposal.

Template for Writing a Proposal Argument

The traditional lecture method of education has a number of problems. For example, _____ _____. In addition, _____ _____. Making lectures available as podcasts, however, _____ _____.

There are three reasons that this teaching method should be adopted. One reason is that _____ _____.

Another reason is that _____ _____.

Finally, _____ _____.

For these reasons, I believe that _____ _____ _____ _____.

⊙ EXERCISE 15.8

Ask several of your instructors whether they would want to record their lectures as podcasts. Then, add your instructors' comments to the paragraph you wrote for Exercise 15.7.

⊙ EXERCISE 15.9

Write a proposal to one of your instructors arguing that all course lectures should be made available as podcasts. Be sure to present examples from your own experience to support your arguments. (If you like, you may incorporate the material you developed for Exercises 15.7 and 15.8 into your essay.) Cite the readings on pages 435–449, and document your sources. In addition, be sure to include a works-cited page. (See Chapter 10 for information on documenting sources.)

⊙ EXERCISE 15.10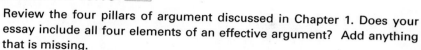

Review the four pillars of argument discussed in Chapter 1. Does your essay include all four elements of an effective argument? Add anything that is missing.

⊙ WRITING ASSIGNMENTS: PROPOSAL ARGUMENTS

1. Each day, students at college cafeterias throw away hundreds of pounds of uneaten food. A number of colleges have found that by simply eliminating the use of trays, they can cut out much of this waste. At one college, for example, students who did not use trays wasted 14.4% less food for lunch and 47.1% less for dinner than those who did use trays. Write a proposal to your college or university in which you suggest banishing trays from dining halls. Use your own experiences as well as information from your research and from interviews with students to support your position. Be sure to address one or two arguments against your position.

2. Look around your campus, and find a service that you think should be improved. It could be the financial aid office, the student health services, or the writing center. Then, write an essay in which you identify the problem (or problems) and suggest a solution. If you wish, interview a few of your friends to get some information that you can use to support your proposal.

3. Assume that your college or university has just received a large donation from an anonymous benefactor. Your school has decided to solicit proposals from both students and faculty on ways to spend the money. Write a proposal to the president of your school in which you identify a good use for this windfall. Make sure you identify a problem, present a solution, and discuss the advantages of your proposal. If possible, address one or two arguments against your proposal—for example, that the money could be put to better use somewhere else.

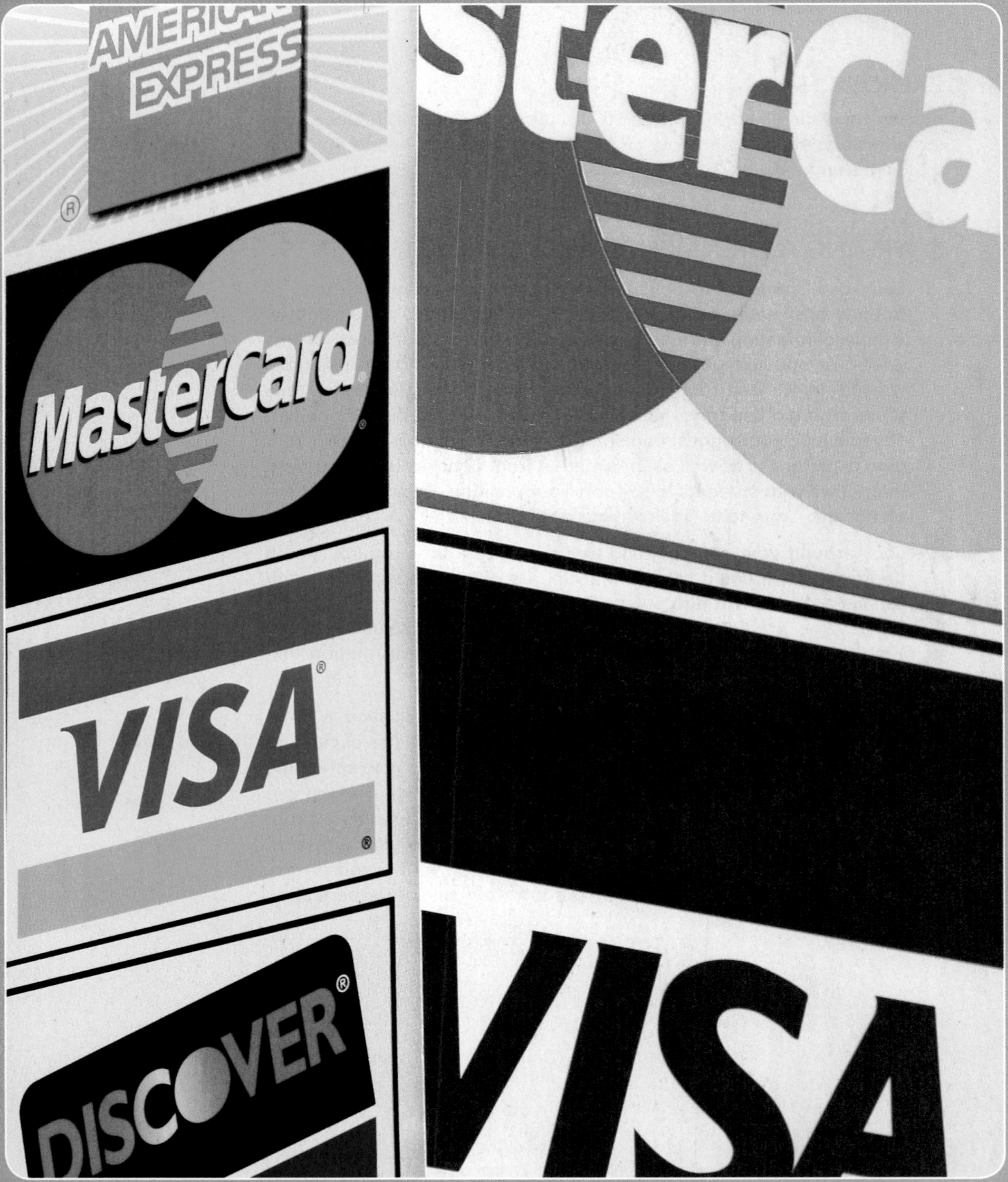

EXPRESS
MasterCard
VISA
DISCOVER
VISA

Argument by Analogy

Should Credit Card Companies Be Permitted to Target College Students?

As the worldwide financial crisis of 2008 revealed, easy credit can be a trap. Still, for those who want to make purchases but do not have the money they need, using credit cards can seem like a perfectly reasonable strategy. College students, who are often cash poor and unwilling (or unable) to postpone purchases, are a tempting target for credit card companies. In fact, these companies have often marketed their products aggressively to students.

College students receive numerous email offers for credit cards, and other offers come through direct mail. Credit card companies also routinely solicit customers at sporting events, concerts, and other venues that attract college students. Until very recently, credit card companies were free to set up tables on campus, offering students free T-shirts and other merchandise in exchange for filling out credit card applications. In some cases, schools even had financial arrangements with credit card compa-

nies, giving them permission to solicit on campus in exchange for a percentage of their profits.

Some of these practices changed with the passage of the Credit Card Act of 2009, which went into effect in early 2010. This law makes it harder for credit card companies to issue cards to students under twenty-one, who now need an adult to cosign their application (unless they can show proof of income). Companies are also prohibited from offering gifts on campus, and colleges now have to disclose any financial agreements they may have with credit card companies.

Still, students remain easy targets for credit card companies. And, despite the convenience of credit cards, their ready availability is a serious problem for students, who may not understand the terms of the agreements they are signing. Some credit cards have hidden fees, outrageous penalties, and very high interest rates; others may reserve the right to

(continued)

(*continued*)

raise customers' interest rates when they miss paying *any* bill (not just their credit card bill). Given these problems, many people believe that schools have a responsibility to protect students from being targeted by credit card companies.

Of course, it could be argued that college students are adults and should therefore have the right to make their own decisions about financial matters, just as they do about other important things in their lives. After all, without credit cards, students might have to give up not just luxuries but also vital purchases, such as textbooks, that contribute to their education. The question is, do the benefits of credit cards outweigh the risks? And if not, should colleges and universities be the ones who act to protect students?

These are some of the issues you should think about as you read the sources at the end of this chapter. After reading this material, you will be asked to write an **argument by analogy** in which you take a position on whether credit card companies should be permitted to target college students.

What Is Analogy?

An **analogy** is an extended comparison between two items, situations, or concepts on the basis of a number of shared characteristics. Unlike a traditional comparison, however, an analogy explains a difficult or unfamiliar concept in terms of something familiar. For example, trying to define an electronic database to readers who are not familiar with electronic communication might be a challenge, but if you begin by telling them that an electronic database is similar to a telephone book, you will be able to get the concept across more easily.

When you set out to develop an analogy, you have a number of options. You can draw an analogy with a historical event—making the case, for example, that a current political campaign, military action, act of legislation, or Supreme Court decision is like an earlier one. You can also compare two current situations that are alike in some respects—two school systems, two fashion trends, two kinds of energy-conservation measures. In each case, you would use a familiar concept to explain a less familiar one.

KEY WORDS FOR ANALOGY

When you develop an analogy, you use words and phrases such as the following to emphasize the parallels between the unfamiliar subject you are explaining and the familiar subject to which it is similar.

like	similarly	in the same way	just as
in comparison	likewise	also	

What Is Argument by Analogy?

When you construct an **argument by analogy**, you make the case that your position about an issue is valid because it is analogous to a comparable position on another issue (a position you expect your readers to accept). For example, most people would agree that laws should protect citizens from danger—speeding cars, epidemics, criminals, and so on. Based on this premise, someone who considers dogs a danger could develop an argument by analogy by saying that it is the government's responsibility to protect its citizens from dogs. Like speeding cars, dogs that are not controlled can injure or even kill someone. For this reason, the government should license dog owners just as it licenses drivers.

Such an argument, however (like all arguments by analogy), has its limitations. For one thing, most dogs are not dangerous, and there is a big difference between a pit bull bred to fight and a toy poodle bred to be a companion. For another, uncontrolled dogs and speeding cars obviously have many significant differences. These weaknesses highlight the major limitation of argument by analogy: an item that is similar to another item in some respects is not necessarily similar in all or even most respects. Because no two items, concepts, or situations are exactly alike, an analogy alone, no matter how convincing, cannot be a substitute for evidence.

Often, brief analogies are included in argumentation essays structured in other ways. For example, in a definition essay, you might draw an analogy to support your definition. In this chapter, however, we focus on analogy as a pattern of development for an entire argumentative essay.

AVOIDING WEAK ANALOGIES

Whether you are using a brief analogy as an example in a support paragraph or an extended analogy to structure an entire essay, be sure it is strong enough to carry the weight of your argument. Be careful not to construct a **weak analogy**—one that is comparable to something else in only a few respects. Remember, the more similar the two items you are comparing, the stronger your analogy will likely be. (See Chapter 4 for more on weak analogies.)

When you write an argument by analogy, you might consider topics such as the following:

- Should the Internet be subject to censorship?
- Is Medicare "socialized medicine"?

- Should the elderly be entitled to discounts in theaters and on public transportation?

- Is plagiarism theft?

- Should SUV owners have to pay an energy surcharge?

- Is it acceptable for parents to spank their children?

- Should prisoners be paid for the work they do while they are in jail?

- Should disabled people be barred from adopting children?

- Should it be legal to share music files on the Internet?

⊙ EXERCISE 16.1

Explain how a position on each of the above topics might be supported by an analogy. Begin by identifying a possible analogy. (For example, in responding to the first topic, you might say that the Internet is analogous to a newspaper.) Then, consider how the situation presented in each topic is like and unlike the analogous situation. Finally, draft a possible thesis statement for an argument by analogy on each topic.

Favorable and Unfavorable Analogies

In an argument by analogy, you can make either favorable or unfavorable comparisons, using either positive or negative examples to help you make your case.

Suppose you were assigned to write an argumentative essay taking a position on the topic, "Should government-issued identity cards be required for all U.S. citizens?" You might decide to structure your essay as an argument by analogy. To make the case that such cards *should* be required, you would use positive examples, drawing favorable analogies with other relatively routine and harmless documents, such as driver's licenses, voter registration cards, and social security cards. To make the case that such cards *should not* be required, you would use negative examples, drawing unfavorable analogies with identity cards issued to citizens of the former Soviet Union or to Jews in Nazi Germany.

Of course, no analogy will actually prove your case. Identity cards are not completely harmless; after all, they are designed in part to identify legal residents (and therefore to identify illegal immigrants). However, they are not inherently evil or dangerous, either. The truth lies somewhere in between.

⊙ EXERCISE 16.2

Write two thesis statements—one using a favorable analogy and one using an unfavorable analogy—for each of the following. Hint: In each case, begin by identifying various ways in which the given item (bicycles, restaurants, or motorcyclists) is like some other item.

- Bicycles should (or should not) have to be licensed because . . .

- Restaurants should (or should not) be required to post calorie counts for all their foods because . . .

- Motorcyclists should (or should not) be required to wear helmets because . . .

Structuring an Argument by Analogy

Generally speaking, an argument by analogy can be structured as follows:

- **Introduction:** Establishes the context for the argument by explaining the central analogy that follows

- **Evidence (first point in support of thesis):** Presents one respect in which the current situation is analogous to another situation

- **Evidence (second point in support of thesis):** Presents another respect in which the current situation is analogous to another situation

- **Opposing arguments:** Explain why the analogy is not valid (or why it has limitations)

- **Refutation:** Explains why the analogy is valid (or why it is valid despite some limitations)

- **Conclusion:** Reinforces the essay's main point; includes a strong concluding statement

The following student essay illustrates one possible way of organizing an argument by analogy. The student writer argues that separate housing for minority students should be permitted just as separate all-female and special-interest dorms are.

DOES SEPARATE HOUSING FOR MINORITY STUDENTS MAKE SENSE?

ANTHONY LUU

1   Students come to college to learn, to expand their horizons, and to become independent adults, but this process is difficult when they do not feel comfortable in their surroundings. Some eighteen-year-olds,   Introduction

especially members of minority groups, may actually do better if they live in like-minded communities that can give them the support and confidence they need to succeed. Although some people see "affinity housing" as controversial, this option can help minority students get the most out of college and help more of them graduate.

Thesis statement

First point in support of thesis: Analogy with other kinds of affinity housing

The idea of allowing students to choose to live with students who share their values and backgrounds is not new. Most schools offer a variety of living options to undergraduates, including single-sex dorms, fraternities and sororities, honors colleges, and dorms based on common interests, such as foreign-language study or environmental activism. Just as women students can choose to live in all-female environments and students who pledge to abstain from alcohol, tobacco, and recreational drugs can opt to live in substance-free areas, minority students should be able to live in a "safe space" where they will not be seen as different or have to constantly explain or defend their values and traditions. Such housing can give them the support they need to survive—and thrive—in school.

Background

Because minority students are underrepresented at most colleges, they can feel isolated from the general campus culture. These days, even public universities are becoming "disproportionally whiter and richer," and their flagship campuses are increasingly "enclaves for the most privileged of their state's young people" (Gerald and Haycock 3). This is partly why, according to a 2008 report by Kevin Carey, "less than half of all black students who start college at a four-year institution graduate in six years or less, 20 percentage points less than the rate for white students" (2). This is a problem that all schools must address, and one way to address it is to create supportive affinity groups for minority students.

Second point in support of thesis (paras. 4–5): Analogy with short-term "living and learning communities"

To help minority students adjust to college, many universities have set up short-term living and learning communities that are in many ways analogous to minority dorms. For example, Florida State University's "summer bridge" program targets at-risk applicants, many of whom are members of ethnic and racial minorities. Here, these students "have the opportunity to meet the university president and senior faculty during a weeklong orientation, followed by six weeks where roughly 300 students live together in a residence hall staffed by hand-picked upperclassman

2

3

4

counselors" (Carey 3). By living in a self-contained community where they can relate to and encourage each other, these students form close bonds. In six years, as Jay Mathews of the *Washington Post* points out, this program has "raised Florida State's six-year graduation rate for black students to 72 percent, higher than its white graduation rate." By raising minority students' comfort level and giving them a community in which to grow and learn together, this program (and many others like it) aids retention and student success among minorities.

5   Using a similar program that includes creating "freshmen learning communities," the University of Alabama has raised its graduation rates eleven percentage points. The school explains its commitment to these learning communities in this way:

> [F]reshmen at big universities can feel lost and anonymous as they struggle alone to contend with disconnected courses taught in depersonalized settings along with hundreds of their peers. Learning communities provide more connected individualized instruction, allowing students to form strong academic relationships with their fellow students, share knowledge, and work together to succeed in school. (Carey 7)

And, according to the *New York Times,* the University of Virginia, which has the highest African American graduation rate of any public university, attributes its success to a peer-mentoring program and other activities that "help knit the black students together as a group" (Olson). Minority dorms are in many ways comparable to these learning communities because they too permit members of minority groups to form separate nurturing communities within their universities.

6   Opponents of minority dorms argue that students need to learn to live together and that racial and ethnic groups should therefore not isolate themselves from the population at large. After all, college is a place for students to meet many different kinds of people—people whose traditions, values, politics, and cultures may be very different from their own. In fact, a *New York Times* opinion piece about housing at Cornell University, "Separate Is Never Equal," calls affinity housing "irrational" and uses the term "Balkanization"—the division of an area into small, hostile units—to describe the way various ethnic groups have chosen their own living spaces on campus (Clark and Meyers). This

Opposing argument

Refutation

dramatic language makes the situation seem much more dire than it is. Unlike the warring Balkan states, minority students and white students *do* interact—in classes, in clubs, on sports teams, and in other public spaces. They do not have to live together for four years to get to know each other or to benefit from their campus's diversity.

Conclusion

7

The idea of allowing students to live in minority dorms is often seen as more controversial than other kinds of affinity housing, but it should not be. As temporary "living and learning communities" on many campuses have recognized, first-year students are especially vulnerable to letting feelings of alienation drive them away from higher education. Among schools that are attempting to raise their minority graduation rates, there is a "broad movement to focus on the first year of college, when students are most likely to drop out" (Carey 8). Even if colleges do not offer minority housing options for all their students, it is crucial to offer these particularly vulnerable entering students the option of living in communities with people whom they consider their allies— those similarly situated students who understand the challenges of being outnumbered on campus. Building on the mutual support of their early years, they will learn to feel like insiders, they will stay enrolled—

Concluding statement

and they will graduate.

Works Cited

Carey, Kevin. "Graduation Rate Watch: Making Minority Student Success a Priority." *Education Sector*. Education Sector, Apr. 2008. Web. 14 Sept. 2009.

Clark, Kenneth B., and Michael Meyers. "Separate Is Never Equal." *New York Times*. New York Times, 1 Apr. 1995. Web. 9 Sept. 2009.

Gerald, Danette, and Katie Haycock. "Engines of Inequality: Diminishing Equity in the Nation's Premier Public Universities." *Education Trust*. Education Trust, 2007. Web. 10 Sept. 2009.

Mathews, Jay. "Raising Minority Graduation Rates in College." *Washington Post*. Washington Post, 16 June 2008. Web. 14 Sept. 2009.

Olson, Elizabeth. "Peer Support Cited in Black Students' Success." *New York Times*. New York Times, 17 May 2006. Web. 9 Sept. 2009.

GRAMMAR IN CONTEXT: USING *LIKE* AND *AS*

When you write an argument by analogy, you may use *like* or *as* to express your comparison. When you do so, be sure to use these two words correctly.

- Use *like* only as a preposition.

CORRECT	Separate college dorms for members of minority groups are in many ways like separate dorms for women.

- Use *as* only to introduce a complete clause.

INCORRECT	Students must learn to live together in college like they do in the rest of their lives.
CORRECT	Students must learn to live together in college as they do in the rest of their lives.

● EXERCISE 16.3

The following essay, "Civil Rights and Anti-Abortion Protests" by Nat Hentoff, is an argument by analogy. Read the essay, and then answer the questions that follow it, consulting the outline on page 457 if necessary.

This editorial first appeared on February 6, 1989, in the *Washington Post.*

CIVIL RIGHTS AND ANTI-ABORTION PROTESTS

NAT HENTOFF

1 Planned Parenthood° recently assembled 13 distinguished civil rights leaders so that they might express their scorn for the notion that there is any moral connection between the Operation Rescue° demonstrations "and the civil rights struggles of the 1960s."

2   The leaders—including Jesse Jackson, Andrew Young, Julian Bond, John Jacob, Mary King and Roger Wilkins—deplored the pro-lifers' "protests to deny Americans their constitutional right to freedom of choice. They want the Constitution rewritten." And in the unkindest cut of all, these leaders—once themselves demonstrators against laws they considered

An organization that advocates for access to birth control and abortion

An organization that advocates for outlawing abortion

profoundly unjust—compared the nonviolent Operation Rescue workers to "the segregationists who fought desperately to block black Americans from access to their rights."

Actually, however, a more accurate analogy would link these pro-lifers 3 to the civil rights workers of the 19th century, the Abolitionists, who would not be deterred from their goal of ensuring equal rights for all human beings in this land. They believed, as these 13 civil rights leaders later did, that social change comes only after social upheaval.

What the Abolitionists were opposing was the rule of law—ultimately 4 underlined by the Supreme Court in its *Dred Scott* decision—that people of African descent, whether free or slaves, had "never been regarded as a part of the people or citizens of the State." They had no rights whatever. They were the property of their owners, no more. The Abolitionists did indeed want the Constitution rewritten.

Now, the pro-lifers, aware that the Supreme Court has declared itself in 5 error before, are protesting the holding in *Roe v. Wade* that "the unborn have never been recognized in the law as persons in the whole sense." Although that decision also spoke of a time when the fetus becomes viable and then may be protected by the state, in fact we have abortion on demand.

As Justice Harry Blackmun said in *Doe v. Bolton*—decided on the same 6 day as *Roe v. Wade*—the mother's health is paramount, and that includes, among other things, "physical, emotional, psychological, familial" factors. Abortions can be obtained for these reasons, and more.

So, like the slave, the fetus is property and its owner can dispose of it. 7 Increasingly, for instance, women are undergoing prenatal testing to find out the gender of the developing human being inside them. If it's the wrong sex, it is aborted.

> "So, like the slave, the fetus is property."

Pro-lifers who maintain the fetus should 8 have equal protection under the law are not limited to those driven by religious convictions. There is the biological fact that after conception, a being has been formed with unique human characteristics. He or she, if allowed to survive, will be unlike anyone born before. From their point of view, therefore, pro-lifers are engaged in a massive civil rights movement. In 16 years, after all, there have been some 20 million abortions.

Some pro-lifers, like some of the abolitionists, feel that nonviolence, how- 9 ever direct, is insufficient. They are of the order of John Brown.° As noted by James McPherson in *Battle Cry of Freedom*, Brown stalked out of a meeting of the New England Antislavery Society, grumbling, "Talk! Talk! Talk! That will never free the slaves. What is needed is action—action!"

A nineteenth-century American antislavery activist who used violence to further his goals

Those relatively few—and invariably isolated—pro-lifers who follow John 10 Brown's flag are surely not in the tradition of Martin Luther King, and the 13 civil rights leaders have reason to keep them at a far distance. But Operation Rescue, and similar demonstrations, are not violent. Entrances are blocked, and so they were in some nonviolent civil rights demonstrations. There is shouting, some of it not very civil, back and forth across the lines, but so there was in the 1960s.

The only actual violence connected with Operation Rescue has been inflicted by the police, most viciously, in Atlanta where one of the Planned Parenthood's 13 civil rights leaders is mayor. A member of the Atlanta City Council, Josea Williams—himself a close associate of Martin Luther King—has said: "We who were the leaders of the movement in the '50s and '60s are now political leaders. And we are doing the same thing to demonstrators that George Wallace and Bull Connor did to us." 11

Twelve years ago, another associate of Dr. King argued against the *Roe v. Wade* thesis that a woman's privacy rights justify abortion. That, he said, "was the premise of slavery. You could not protest the . . . treatment of slaves . . . because that was private." 12

The civil rights leader who said that was Jesse Jackson—before he became a member of the pro-abortion congregation. By then, he was also a political leader. 13

Identifying the Elements of an Argument by Analogy

1. What analogy does Hentoff draw in paragraphs 3 and 4 between Operation Rescue demonstrators and the nineteenth-century abolitionists? List the similarities and differences between these two groups. Considering these similarities and differences, evaluate Hentoff's analogy. Are there any similarities between the two groups that Hentoff does not identify?

2. In addition to the central analogy on which his argument is based, Hentoff also draws analogies between slaves and fetuses and between "some pro-lifers" and the abolitionist John Brown. How do these analogies support his argument?

3. Identify each use of the terms *pro-lifers*, *pro-abortion*, and *abortion on demand*. What connotations do these terms have? What, if anything, does Hentoff's choice of these words tell you about his view of the abortion issue? What other terms could he have used?

4. What is this essay's thesis? If no thesis is explicitly stated, write one.

READING AND WRITING ABOUT THE ISSUE

Should Credit Card Companies Be Permitted to Target College Students?

Reread the At Issue box on pages 453–454, which gives background on the targeting of college students by credit card companies. Then, read the sources on the following pages.

    As you read these sources, you will be asked to respond to questions and to complete various activities. This work will help you understand the content and structure of the material you read. When you are finished, you will be ready to write an **argument by analogy** on whether credit card companies should be permitted to target college students.

SOURCES

 Erica L. Williams and Tim Westrich, "The Young and the Indebted"

 Contra Costa Times, "Non-Issue Needs No Law"

 FindCollegeCards.com, "Start Your Credit Today!"

 Jessica Silver-Greenberg, "Majoring in Credit-Card Debt"

THE YOUNG AND THE INDEBTED

ERICA L. WILLIAMS AND TIM WESTRICH

1   Kali Dun, five years out of the University of Virginia, still owes thousands of dollars to credit card companies from debt she racked up with credit cards in college. On campus, she said, "[credit card companies] were everywhere . . . like vultures. Outside of my dorm, at football games, and in the quad. I took their teddy bears, free pizza, tote bags, and complicated, convoluted sign up forms." But along with the giveaways and incentives, she also took high fees, high interest rates, and complex terms, and by her junior year, Kali had incurred nearly $3,000 in debt on the three cards she signed up for on campus.

2   High fees, high interest rates, and complex terms are among the most common credit card company practices weighing down students. They're also practices that heighten the risk of default. And default Kali did.

3   Kali's story is but one of many that Campus Progress has heard from young people around the country. It illustrates the unique challenges that college students face with regard to credit cards.

4   Credit card companies aggressively market to college students. Their techniques include buying lists from schools and entering into exclusive arrangements to market directly to students through the mail, over the phone, on bulletin boards, and through aggressive on-campus and near-campus soliciting—facilitated by so-called "free gifts."

5   Young people face the high fees, heavy interest rates, and complex terms that all Americans who have credit cards face. Credit cards carry substantially higher costs than other forms of credit due to myriad fees and high interest rates. The result is that many students unwittingly slide deeper and deeper into debt as they fall prey to the lack of transparency in credit cards.

6   This situation is particularly damaging for students because, according to a 2004 study by Nellie Mae,° 76 percent of undergrads have credit cards, and the average undergraduate has $2,200 in credit card debt. And whereas in 1989, 18- to 24-year-olds with credit cards devoted 13 percent of their income to debt payments—both credit card debt and student loan debt— today's 18- to 24-year-olds devote a startling 22 percent of their income to servicing their debt. One in four of the students surveyed in U.S. PIRG's 2008 Campus Credit Card Trap report said that they have paid a late fee, and 15 percent have paid an "over the limit" fee.

A government organization that provides student loans

7   With the price of higher education rapidly increasing, today's young adults have not only been forced to borrow for their education, but also for

their expenses while in college. While some debt is the result of irresponsible spending and late night pizza runs, large percentages of students reported using their cards for tuition, books, and day-to-day expenses, according to research by U.S. PIRG.

Major borrowing from credit card companies is like visiting a Las Vegas casino—it's a gamble, and the odds are against you. For college students, the analogy goes a step further. Imagine that you entered the casino every time you walked out of class, or out of the cafeteria. Or if fliers for the casino were taped on the walls of every bathroom, and blackjack dealers were calling your dorm room with promises of free casino chips. The casino wants college students, and because students need the money, they don't realize that this gamble is one that has implications for the next five, 10, or 20 years.

> "Major borrowing from credit card companies is like visiting a Las Vegas casino."

8

Not only are college students and other young people in perhaps the most vital and vulnerable point of their financial lives, their future economic health often depends on decisions made during this period. College graduates amass, on average, almost $20,000 in student debt. So between credit cards, student loans, and other loans, students can pay up to 22 cents of every dollar they earn after graduation servicing their debt. 9

To add to this, the economy no longer produces the same opportunities for young Americans that it used to. Today's young adults are joining the job market at a time when incomes have been stagnant and costs for health care and retirement benefits are increasingly being shifted from employers to employees. 10

These and other factors paint a bleak picture of life after college. A 2006 poll of 3 million twentysomethings from *USA Today* and credit reporting agency Experian found that nearly half of twentysomethings have stopped paying a debt, forcing lenders to charge off the debt and sell it to collection agencies, repossess cars, or seek bankruptcy protection. The same poll found that 60 percent of young people feel they are facing tougher financial pressures than young people did in previous generations. And "the Boomerang Effect"—young adults returning to live with their parents—is an increasing phenomenon. In 2006, Experience Inc., which provides career services to link college grads with jobs, found that 58 percent of twentysomethings it surveyed had moved back home after college. Of those, 32 percent stayed for more than a year, according to its survey. 11

Campus Progress began engaging students around the country two years ago in a discussion about debt in higher education through our "Debt Hits Hard" campaign. The campaign focused primarily on rising college costs and student loans. 12

As we began that work, we realized that credit card debt and the process through which it is incurred is an equally important part of understanding 13 the financial lives and burdens of young people. At Campus Progress, we give young people the tools to make their voices heard about the issues that affect them the most. And they speak out about predatory credit card practices and the overwhelming weight of that debt loudly and clearly.

Through a series of public forums around the country, from Broward 14 Community College in Fort Lauderdale, Florida to Purdue University in Indiana, we have brought together students and experts to discuss the growing problem of credit card debt on college campuses. And at each event, we have heard the same: Banks and lenders are profiting off of young people's financial inexperience, partnerships and relationships with universities, and strategic targeting.

We now know the scope of the problem. College students are in trou- 15 ble, and credit card companies are partly to blame. But what about the solution?

Students are aggressively campaigning on the state and campus levels 16 to demand that their schools abide by principles of responsible credit card marketing. They are working toward prohibiting the use of gifts on campus, keeping colleges and universities from sharing student lists with credit card marketers, and stopping student group sponsorship by credit card companies. These recommendations, coupled with efforts in state legislatures to promote responsible soliciting—such as bills under consideration in Maryland and Arizona that seek to protect students from predatory practices—are a good start toward keeping young people safe.

Congress also has its role to play in making credit card practices fairer and 17 more transparent at the federal level. One important step would be to mandate a higher level of fairness in credit card terms and conditions by banning several of the most abusive credit card practices.

Young people who want to use credit cards responsibly currently have a 18 difficult time determining the cards' terms and conditions and cost-shopping among different credit cards. Those who do read their voluminous cardholder agreements often find a clause to the effect of: "We reserve the right to change the terms at any time for any reason." Congress should mandate that card issuers give cardholders at least 45 days notice of any interest rate increases and the right to cancel their card and pay off the existing balance before the increase takes place.

Congress could also go a step further by enacting more creative ways of 19 disclosing the most important information. This can be done by requiring credit card companies to disclose the length of time it will take to pay off an account if only the minimum payment is made. In this way, students could better gauge the long-term costs of putting debt on their credit cards.

Legislative action to protect against abuses by credit card companies is 20 a fundamental issue of fairness and protection of America's future—young Americans—when they are arguably in the most vulnerable and important phase of their financial lives.

❯ AT ISSUE: SOURCES FOR DEVELOPING AN ARGUMENT BY ANALOGY

1. According to Williams and Westrich, what problems do college students have that are comparable to those faced by "all Americans who have credit cards" (para. 5)?

2. What financial problems do college students have that other Americans do *not* have? List the problems the authors identify in paragraphs 6–11.

3. The writers begin their essay with an anecdote about one particular student. Is this an effective opening strategy? Should they have included more anecdotes in addition to "Kali's story"?

4. Whom do the writers blame for the problems faced by students who use credit cards? What do they believe should be done to solve the problems?

5. In paragraph 8, Williams and Westrich present an analogy. Summarize this analogy. Do you think it effectively supports the essay's argument? Why or why not?

6. Paraphrase the writers' concluding statement. Do you think this statement is strong enough? Can you suggest an alternative concluding statement?

This unsigned opinion piece appeared in the September 18, 2000, edition of the *Contra Costa Times*.

NON-ISSUE NEEDS NO LAW

CONTRA COSTA TIMES

1   A lot of legislation gets shoveled into the action hopper in Sacramento° during the hectic race to the deadline for introducing bills. Some address the hard and knotty problems faced by the state, its citizens, businesses and institutions. Others look at pet issues, narrow interests or perhaps most irksome of all non-problems that lead to fluffy, feel-good legislation that serves little purpose except to respond to that age-old cure-all: "There oughta be a law!"

The capital of California

2   One proposal that falls into this last category wrings its hands over the tactics of credit card companies in soliciting students on college campuses.

3   No matter that the Legislature has little say over universities' policies. The lawmakers worried that students are too readily falling for free come-ons and racking up debt they can't handle rushed to the rescue in the last days of the legislative session.

4   Both the Senate and the Assembly passed legislation, written by Sen. Joseph Dunn, D–Garden Grove, asking officials at public and private colleges to re-examine their policies on how credit card companies solicit on campus.

5   No fraud or deceitful practices are alleged. The main target of the lawmakers' anxiety seems to be the outpouring of free T-shirts and similar relatively inexpensive goodies to beguile the students in exchange for a little credit history and a signature on the dotted line. For one thing, this shows a shallow and undeserved lack of faith in the good sense of most students.

> "No fraud or deceitful practices are alleged."

6   For another, college is a time and place when schoolboys and schoolgirls begin that dramatic, sometimes traumatic, transition from adolescents into educated young adult men and women.

7   Part of that education out of the classrooms except for possible courses in economics or consumer affairs is learning how to manage one's finances, including credit.

8   The step from parental allowance to personal money via plastic is a heady one. Some won't be able to handle it responsibly. Some will. Others will lag. It's called growing up.

9   College officials can usefully limit the number of credit card vendors and the times they are permitted to operate on campus if their presence is becoming a distraction.

10   Student organizations, some of which profit by sponsoring vendors, can review their policies with a view to balancing values.

There are more appropriate ways than ineffectual, unneeded, feel-good 11 legislation to help young adults learn to discipline themselves as they begin to enter the real world of personal budgeting and responsible use of credit.

Society has enough real problems that, sad to say, may need to be 12 addressed with, "There oughta be a law!"

Cajoling college students with freebies to sign up for credit cards isn't one 13 of them.

⊙ AT ISSUE: SOURCES FOR DEVELOPING AN ARGUMENT BY ANALOGY

1. This editorial has very short paragraphs, even for a newspaper article. (Because newspaper articles are set in columns, paragraphs are typically shorter than those that appear elsewhere.) Should any of these short paragraphs be combined?

2. Some of the paragraphs in this editorial could be developed further. For example, paragraphs 6 and 7 could include additional supporting information. Write two additional sentences for each of these paragraphs.

3. What other paragraphs do you think should be developed further? What kind of information would you add?

4. What position does this argument take? Write a one-sentence thesis statement that communicates this position.

5. In what sense is this editorial a refutation? What argument does it refute?

6. Summarize the argument the editorial makes in paragraph 8.

The following is from the Web site FindCollegeCards.com

START YOUR CREDIT TODAY!

FINDCOLLEGECARDS.COM

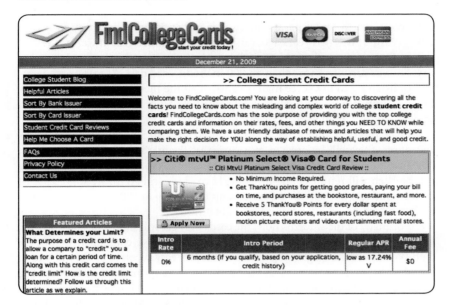

AT ISSUE: SOURCES FOR DEVELOPING AN ARGUMENT BY ANALOGY

1. How does this Web page encourage students to apply for credit cards? How does its language support its message? Do you think this language is sufficiently student friendly?

2. Given that this page is designed to reach students, do you think its design is appealing enough? What visual elements could be added to increase its appeal to its target audience?

3. Does anything on this page attempt to refute familiar arguments against issuing credit cards to college students? Should it?

4. Read the list of bullet points to the right of the image of the credit card. How do these points target a student audience?

5. What information about credit cards does *not* appear on this page?

Business Week first published this piece on September 4, 2007.

MAJORING IN CREDIT-CARD DEBT

JESSICA SILVER-GREENBERG

Seth Woodworth stood paralyzed by fear in his parents' driveway in Moses 1
Lake, Wash. It was two years ago, during his sophomore year at Central Washington University, and on this visit, he was bringing home far more than laundry. He was carrying more than $3,000 in credit-card debt. "I was pretty terrified of listening to my voice mail because of all the messages about the money I owed," says Woodworth. He did get some help from his parents but still had to drop out of school to pay down his debts.

Over the next month, as 17 million college students flood the nation's 2
campuses, they will be greeted by swarms of credit-card marketers. Frisbees, T-shirts, and even iPods will be used as enticements to sign up, and marketing on the Web will reinforce the message. Many kids will go for it. Some 75% of college students have credit cards now, up from 67% in 1998. Just a generation earlier, a credit card on campus was a great rarity.

For many of the students now, the cards they get will simply be an easier way 3
to pay for groceries or books, with no long-term negative consequences. But for Seth Woodworth and a growing number like him, easy access to credit will lead to spending beyond their means and debts that will compromise their futures. The freshman 15, a fleshy souvenir of beer and late-night pizza, is now taking on a new meaning, with some freshman racking up more than $15,000 in credit-card debt before they can legally drink. "It's astonishing to me to see college students coming out of school with staggering amounts of debt and credit scores so abominable that they couldn't rent a car," says Representative Louise Slaughter (D-N.Y.).

Congressional Oversight Weighed

The role of credit-card companies in helping to build these mountains of debt 4
is coming under great scrutiny. Critics say that as the companies compete for this important growth market, they offer credit lines far out of proportion to students' financial means, reaching $10,000 or more for youngsters without jobs. The cards often come with little or no financial education, leaving some unsophisticated students with no idea what their obligations will be. Then when students build up balances on their cards, they find themselves trapped in a maze of jargon and baffling fees, with annual interest rates shooting up to more than 30%. "No industry in America is more deserving of oversight by Congress," says Travis Plunkett, legislative director for Consumer Federation of America, a consumer advocacy group.

The oversight may be coming soon. With Democrats in control of Con- 5
gress and the debt problems for college kids only growing worse, the chances of a crackdown have increased substantially. The Senate is expected to hold

hearings on the credit-card industry's practices this fall. Representative Barney Frank (D-Mass.) has pledged to introduce tough legislation. And Slaughter introduced a bill in August to limit the amount of credit that could be extended to students to 20% of their income or $500 if their parents co-sign for the card.

The major credit-card companies take great issue with the criticisms. 6 Bank of America (BAC), Citibank (C), JPMorgan Chase (JPM), American Express (AXP), and others say they are providing a valuable service to students and they work hard to ensure that their credit cards are used responsibly. Citibank and JPMorgan both offer extensive financial literacy materials for college students. Citibank, for instance, says it distributed more than 5 million credit-education pieces to students, parents, and administrators last year for free. At JPMorgan Chase, bank representative Paul Hartwick says: "Our overall approach toward college students is to help them build good financial habits and a credit history that prepares them for a lifetime of successful credit use."

Questions about the Vetting Process

The banks also make the point that students have to be responsible for their own 7 actions. They are the ones, after all, who sign up for cards and then choose to use them. The banks argue that they have to act like responsible parents, keeping credit cards out of the hands of students who are clamoring for them. A spokesman for Bank of America says that it denies half of the students who apply for cards.

But the experiences of Woodworth and other students raise questions about 8 the rigorousness of the vetting process for getting a credit card. Ryan Rhoades, who graduated from the University of Pittsburgh last year with more than $13,000 of debt, remembers his credit-card company's employees telling him not to worry about being unemployed. Lukasz Kozoil, formerly a student at DePaul University, says that Citibank's representatives told him to fill in his tuition on a card application where it asked for income. (A spokesman for Citibank says, "no representative from Citi is authorized to fill in tuition cost on a credit-card application.") Woodworth got his American Express card without a job, and it had a credit limit of $6,000. "Within three months, they upped it to $10,000," he says.

This is not common practice for the credit-card industry. In most cases, 9 an unemployed person would have a hard time getting a credit card, especially one with a five-figure credit line. Consumer advocates say that banks have modified their practices for college students, because they're vulnerable and their parents will usually bail them out. "When you compare this to the way that credit is extended in the general population, there seems to be something wrong with this system," says Linda Sherry, director of national priorities at Consumer Action, a San Francisco consumer education and advocacy group.

AMEX Restraint Draws Kudos

American Express would not comment specifically on Woodworth's situation. 10 Kim Forde, a spokeswoman, says the company "has a number of sophisticated risk management tools in place to manage credit prudently. The specific criteria are proprietary, but there are a number of factors that we consider in our underwriting process before granting anyone credit. In terms of students in general, students eligible for approval are 18, and can typically show the means for paying the bill. But it's not a one-size-fits-all [approach]."

Unlike many other card companies, American Express does not market to college students on campus, a measure of restraint that has drawn kudos from consumer activists. However, the company does market to college kids online and has a special student card that it bills as "one of the best-looking cards on campus" and "in a class by itself." That is the card that Woodworth obtained. 11

Another unusual characteristic in the relationship between students and credit-card companies is that students are particularly susceptible to the complex fees and charges such companies employ. The practices attract plenty of criticism because few cardholders, in college or not, can understand them easily. For example, in a September, 2006, report, the Government Account- 12

> "Students are particularly susceptible to the complex fees and charges."

ability Office said that bank disclosures "were too complicated for many consumers to understand. The required disclosures were poorly organized, burying important information in text or scattering information about a single topic in numerous places."

Vulnerable to "Universal Default"

Less well-known is that banks often change the rates they charge cardholders as their credit scores change. Students' credit scores can plunge particularly quickly, with one or two missed payments, because their track records are so short. One common practice is called "universal default." Under universal default, a student who has two credit cards and faithfully makes timely payments on one, but misses a payment on the other, can find that the interest rate he's being charged has been raised to 30% on both cards. At Senate hearings in April, several of the leading credit-card issuers pledged to eliminate universal default. But according to a 2007 Consumer Action survey, 8 of the 10 leading credit-card issuers still raise cardholders' interest rates based on information from credit reports. 13

All of this is disclosed in cardholder policies. But students, like many other people, don't read the fine print. "I had no idea that my interest rate would rise the way that it did because I missed one payment," says Woodworth. The average credit-card contract can be 30 pages long, and it's littered with legal jargon in tiny type. "You tell me how any college student can understand the terms of a card, and make rational choices when the agreements themselves are unreadable," says Elizabeth Warren, a law professor at Harvard University. "It's like selling toasters and handing a consumer wiring diagrams." 14

When Woodworth first applied for his American Express card, not having a job meant that money was scarce. His meals out consisted largely of trips to the student dining hall and the occasional late-night pizza. As he made the 71-mile trip 15 between his home in Ellensburg and the school's campus in Moses Lake, he just hoped his bank account wouldn't empty before his gas tank. The Amex card was a blessing, at least at first. "I was really surprised that I could get a card," he says.

Using Plastic to Buy Gas and Food

The credit card helped him connect his wants and his means. Instead of 16 scrounging quarters from the couch cushions, he could charge his meals to the card. "It's not like I was buying a 50-inch television," he says. "It was just basic things, and it was easier not to deal with cash." As Woodworth's balances grew, he kept on telling himself that he would pay it off when he got a better job, or managed to squirrel away some cash.

Like Woodworth, many college students have no fear about credit cards 17 to temper their spending. They tend to be optimistic about the future, anticipating that once they get out of school they'll have a good job and plenty of money. Credit-card ads often echo this optimism with some showing students smiling into the distance as if glimpsing the blissful days ahead.

Students also live in a culture of debt. Many of them are borrowing tens of 18 thousands of dollars to go to school, tapping low-interest loans to pay tuition. "The primary way we help students pay for college is by telling them to take on more and more student loan debt," says Tamara Draut, director of the Economic Opportunity Program at Demos. The message is clear, she says: "Debt is O.K., and you are going to have lots of it." In that context, Woodworth and other students think little of charging another $50 for dinner or groceries.

What Students Don't Know Can Hurt Them

What Woodworth didn't realize is that a $500 card balance at the average inter- 19 est rate of 16% can take nearly 3 years to pay off if only minimum payments are made. Even the minimums grew oppressive for Woodworth. The thought of the looming debt debilitated him: "I would stay up at night thinking about it," he says. "I couldn't get up in the mornings. I wasn't socializing, and sometimes I wouldn't eat, then other days I would eat too much. I felt totally alone."

Instead of tackling the debt immediately or asking for help, Woodworth 20 procrastinated, letting the balance fester until it had spiraled out of control, and he had to return home. When that shiny new card came, he never read the fine print. "I should have read it, and I realize that," says Woodworth.

He didn't know that his interest rate could rise if he made a late payment, 21 and then it did. He didn't know if he made a late payment on one account the rate on another card could be raised, and it was. And he didn't know that there are no regulations governing how hefty late fees can be. Then he got hit each month with a $39 wallop.

Credit-card companies say that they put a heavy emphasis on financial lit- 22 eracy. They distribute materials and make information available online to help students become savvy consumers, while helping them to build a good credit score in the long term. "Each one of our new student account holders receives our *Student Financial Handbook*, an easy-to-use guide for understanding the

475

basics of managing their finances, including how to balance a checkbook, how a credit card works, and so on," said Bruce Hammond, president of card services for Bank of America, in his testimony before the Senate earlier this year.

Long-Term Effects of Mismanaged Debt

But consumer advocates say such efforts aren't nearly enough. They contend that credit-card companies should be banned from marketing on college campuses, in the same way that tobacco and alcohol companies can't market to kids. "Education alone isn't going to solve the problem," says Plunkett, of the Consumer Federation of America. "Credit-card companies are subtly shifting the burden to students when they talk about credit education programs. The companies should not be targeting a population who are not in a position to handle credit wisely." 23

The learning curve with credit cards is steep, and there is little room for trial and error. Mistakes made in college can haunt students long after graduation. Their credit scores can have an impact whether they get their job of choice, whether they qualify for an apartment, and even whether they have to pay more to get their utilities turned on. 24

As for Woodworth, he is finally headed back to school this fall after two years away from campus. He has learned from his experience with credit, but the lessons have a bitter tinge. "If I could do it over again, I never would have gotten a credit card," says Woodworth. 25

⊜ AT ISSUE: SOURCES FOR DEVELOPING AN ARGUMENT BY ANALOGY

1. The story of Seth Woodworth, introduced in paragraph 1 and continued throughout this article, is presented as a cautionary tale for students, and Woodworth is characterized as a victim of credit card companies. What arguments might the companies make to place the blame on Woodworth himself?

2. What position on student credit cards does this essay take? How do you know? Do you think the boldfaced section headings make this position clear, or are they distracting in any way?

3. Where does this article present the credit card companies' position on the issue? Do you think these companies are portrayed fairly? How does the writer refute the companies' arguments in defense of their strategies?

4. Paragraph 24 summarizes some of the problems students encounter with credit cards, and paragraph 25 brings readers back to Seth Woodworth's story. Do you think these paragraphs serve as an effective conclusion, or do you think the essay needs a stronger conclusion—and a stronger concluding statement?

⊜ EXERCISE 16.4

List all the solicitations you receive as a college student—by email, by direct mail, and so on. Then, list all the promotional offers you see on campus—for example, in the dorms, at the bookstore, on tables, or on posters and bulletin boards. Consider how each of these advertised products and services is like and unlike credit cards. Then, write two possible thesis statements for an essay on this chapter's At Issue topic, using each of the following sentence templates.

1. Because credit cards are analogous to useful (and harmless) products such as _____ , credit card companies should be permitted to target college students, just as other businesses do.

2. Because credit cards are analogous to potentially harmful (and even dangerous) products such as _____ _____ , credit card companies should not be permitted to target college students as many other businesses do.

⊜ EXERCISE 16.5

Write a one-paragraph argument by analogy that takes a position on the issue of whether credit card companies should be permitted to target college students. Follow the template below, filling in the blanks to create your argument.

Template for Writing an Argument by Analogy

Credit cards (should/should not) be marketed to college students. Credit cards can be very useful for students, but they can also lead to serious problems. For example, _____ _____ _____. In addition, _____ _____. For these reasons, some people have suggested that colleges have a responsibility to regulate how credit cards are marketed to their students. For example, schools should not _____ _____. Moreover, they should _____ _____ . Some argue that because other items—for example, _____ _____—are marketed on campus, it is acceptable to market credit cards as well. Others point out, however,

that credit cards are potentially dangerous, as are _____
_____, and so
they should not be made available to students. On balance, it seems that
_____
_____.

❂ EXERCISE 16.6

In a group of four students, discuss the advantages and disadvantages of credit cards for college students. What problems do credit cards cause? In what respects do they make your life easier? What habits (positive or negative) do they help you to establish? Write a paragraph that expresses your group's opinions.

❂ EXERCISE 16.7

Write an argument by analogy on the topic, "Should Credit Card Companies Be Permitted to Target College Students?" Begin by establishing a positive or negative analogy between credit cards and other products that might appeal to students. Then, use this analogy to help you support your thesis. (If you like, you may include in your essay one of the thesis statements you wrote for Exercise 16.4 or the paragraphs you wrote for Exercises 16.5 and 16.6.) Cite the sources on pages 465–476, and be sure to document the sources you use and to include a works-cited page. (See Chapter 10 for information on documenting sources.)

❂ EXERCISE 16.8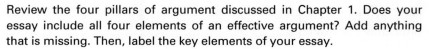

Review the four pillars of argument discussed in Chapter 1. Does your essay include all four elements of an effective argument? Add anything that is missing. Then, label the key elements of your essay.

❯ WRITING ASSIGNMENTS: ARGUMENT BY ANALOGY

1. Many college campuses are now smoke-free, but some people argue that the laws forbidding smoking on campus are too strict. Write an argument by analogy in which you take a position on the issue of whether smoking should be permitted on college campuses.

2. Do you believe that college administrators should be able to censor your school's student newspaper? If so, under what conditions? If not, why not? Establish an analogy between the school newspaper and another campus service (or another media outlet), and use this analogy to help you develop your argument.

3. Should your school mandate community service as a requirement for graduation? Write an argument by analogy in which you take a position on this issue.

CHAPTER

17

Ethical Arguments

AT ISSUE

How Far Should Colleges Go to Keep Campuses Safe?

As the 2007 Virginia Tech massacre tragically illustrated, college campuses are no longer the safe, open environments they once were. In fact, some campuses have become downright dangerous. It is no longer unusual to read reports of shootings, robberies, and muggings (and even murders) on campuses—both urban and rural. As a result, students, parents, and educators have called for action. In response, colleges have increased the number of blue-light phones and security guards, installed card-access systems in dorms and labs, and placed surveillance cameras in parking garages and public areas. Many colleges also use text messages, automated phone calls, and emails to alert students and faculty to emergency situations.

Not everyone is happy about this emphasis on increased security, however. Some faculty members point out that colleges are supposed to be places of free thought. They say that a high level of security undercuts this freedom by limiting access to campus and sanitizing the college experience. Students complain about having to wait in long lines to get into campus buildings as security guards examine and scan IDs. They also complain about having to register guests in advance and having to accompany them to dorm rooms. They point out that colleges tell them they are adults but treat them like children.

Later in this chapter, you will be asked to think more about this issue. You will be given several research sources to consider and asked to write an **ethical argument** considering how far colleges should go to keep students safe.

What Is an Ethical Argument?

Ethics is the field of philosophy that studies the standards by which actions can be judged as right or wrong or good or bad. To make such judgments, either we measure actions against some standard (such as a moral rule like "Thou shall not kill"), or we consider them in terms of their consequences. Usually, making ethical judgments means examining abstract concepts such as *good*, *right*, *duty*, *obligation*, *virtue*, *honor*, and *choice*. **Applied ethics** is the field of philosophy that applies ethics to real-life issues, such as abortion, the death penalty, animal rights, and doctor-assisted suicide.

An **ethical argument** focuses on whether something should be done because it is good or right (or not done because it is bad or wrong). For example, consider the following questions:

- Should teenagers ever be tried as adults?
- Is torture ever justified?
- Should terrorists be tried in civilian courts?
- Should gay and lesbian couples be allowed to marry?
- Is the death penalty ever justified?
- Do animals have rights?

Ethical arguments that try to answer questions like these usually begin with a clear statement that something is right or wrong and then go on to show how a religious, philosophical, or ethical tradition supports this position. Notice how the last three questions on the list above can be examined in ethical arguments.

- **Should gay and lesbian couples be allowed to marry?** You could begin your ethical argument by pointing out that marriage stabilizes society and is therefore good. You could go on to demonstrate how both individuals and society as a whole would be better off if gay and lesbian couples were permitted to marry.

- **Is the death penalty ever justified?** You could begin your ethical argument by pointing out that because killing in any form is immoral, the death penalty is morally wrong. You could go on to demonstrate that despite its utility—it rids society of dangerous criminals—the death penalty hurts all of us. You could conclude by saying that because the death penalty is so immoral, it has no place in a civilized society.

- **Do animals have rights?** You could begin your ethical argument by pointing out that like all thinking beings, animals have certain basic rights. You could go on to discuss the basic rights that all thinking beings have—for example, the right to respect, a safe environment,

One could make an ethical argument in favor of gay marriage.

and a dignified death. You could conclude by saying that the inhumane treatment of animals should not be tolerated, whether those animals are pets, live in the wild, or are raised for food.

Stating an Ethical Principle

The most important part of an ethical argument is the **ethical principle** on which it is based: the set of ideas that guides you to an ethically correct conclusion.

- **You can show that something is good or right** by establishing that it conforms to a particular moral law or that it will result in something good for society. For example, you could argue for a policy restricting access to campus by saying that such a policy will reduce crime on campus or will result in a better educational experience for students.

- **You can show that something is bad or wrong** by demonstrating that it violates a moral law or that it will result in something bad for society. For example, you could argue against the use of torture by saying that respect for individual rights is one of the basic principles of American society and that by ignoring this principle we undermine our Constitution and our way of life.

Whenever possible, you should base your ethical argument on an ethical principle that is **self-evident**—one that needs no proof or explanation. (By doing so, you avoid having to establish the claim that is the basis for your essay.) Thomas Jefferson uses this strategy in the Declaration of Independence (page 679). When he says, "We hold these truths to be self-evident," he is saying that the ethical principle that supports the rest of his argument is so basic (and so widely accepted) that it requires no proof—in other words, that it is self-evident. If readers accept Jefferson's assertion, then the rest of his argument—that the thirteen original colonies owe no allegiance to England—will be much more convincing. (Remember, however, that the king of England, George III, would not have accepted Jefferson's assertion. For him, the ethical argument made in the Declaration of Independence was anything but self-evident.)

Keep in mind that an ethical principle has to be self-evident to most of your readers—not just to those who agree with you or hold a particular set of religious beliefs. For this reason, using a religious doctrine as an ethical principle has its limitations. Doctrines that cut across religions and cultures are more suitable than those that do not. For example, every culture prohibits murder and theft. But other doctrines—such as the Jehovah's Witness prohibition against blood transfusion or the Muslim dietary restrictions—are not universally accepted. In addition, an ethical principle must be stated so that it applies universally. For example, not all readers will find the statement, "As a Christian, I am against killing and therefore against the death penalty" convincing. A more effective statement would be to say, "Because it has not been shown to be an effective deterrent to murder, I am against the death penalty."

Ethics versus Law

Generally speaking, an ethical argument deals with what is right and wrong, not necessarily with what is legal or illegal. In fact, there is a big difference between law and ethics. **Laws** are rules that govern a society and are enforced by its political and legal systems. **Ethics** are standards that determine how human conduct is judged.

Keep in mind that something that is legal is not necessarily ethical. As Socrates, St. Augustine, Henry David Thoreau, and Martin Luther King Jr. have all pointed out, there are just laws, and there are unjust laws. For example, when King wrote his famous "Letter from Birmingham Jail (page 698)", segregation was legal in many Southern states. According to King, unjust laws—such as those that institutionalized segregation—are out of harmony with both moral law and natural law. As King wrote, "We should never forget that everything Adolph Hitler did in Germany was 'legal.'" For King, the ultimate standard for deciding what is just or unjust is morality, not legality.

Women march for the right to vote, New York, 1913.

There are many historical examples of laws that most people would now consider unjust:

- **Laws against woman suffrage:** In the late eighteenth century, various states passed laws prohibiting women from voting.

- **Jim Crow laws:** In the mid-nineteenth century, laws were passed in the American South that legalized discrimination against African Americans.

For decades in America, African Americans were treated unfairly due to unjust laws.

After the Nuremberg laws were passed, many German Jews were sent to concentration camps.

- **Nuremberg laws:** In the 1930s, Nazi Germany passed a series of laws that took away the rights of Jews living in Germany.

- **Apartheid laws:** Beginning in 1948, South Africa enacted laws that defined and enforced racial segregation. These laws stayed in effect until 1994, when Nelson Mandela was elected South Africa's first black president.

Today, virtually everyone would agree that these laws were wrong and should never have been enacted. Still, many people obeyed these laws, with disastrous consequences. These consequences illustrate the importance of doing what is ethically right, not just what is legally right.

The difference between ethics and law can be seen in many everyday situations. Although we have no legal obligation to stop a drunk friend from driving, most people would agree that we should. In addition, although motorists (or even doctors) have no legal obligation to help at the scene of an accident, many people would say that it is the right thing to do.

An example of a person going beyond what is legally required occurred in Lawrence, Massachusetts, in 1995, when fire destroyed Malden Mills, the largest employer in town. Citing his religious principles, Aaron Feuerstein, the owner of the mill and inventor of Polartec fleece, decided to rebuild in Lawrence rather than move his business overseas as many of his competitors had done. In addition, he decided that for sixty days, all employees would receive their full salaries—even though the mill was closed. Feuerstein was not required by law to do what he did, but he decided to do what he believed was ethical and responsible.

Understanding Ethical Dilemmas

Life decisions tend to be somewhat messy, and it is often not easy to decide what is right or wrong or what is good or bad. In many real-life situations, people are faced with **dilemmas**—choices between alternatives that seem equally unfavorable. An **ethical dilemma** occurs when there is a conflict between two or more possible actions—each of which will have a similar consequence or outcome.

The classic ethical dilemma is the so-called lifeboat dilemma. In this hypothetical situation, a boat hits an iceberg, and survivors are crowded into a lifeboat. As a storm approaches, the captain of the boat realizes that he is faced with an ethical dilemma. If he does nothing, the overloaded boat will capsize, and all the people will drown. If he throws some of the passengers overboard, he will save those in the boat, but those he threw overboard will drown.

Another ethical dilemma occurs in William Styron's 1979 novel *Sophie's Choice*. The novel's narrator is fascinated by the story of

Aaron Feuerstein at Malden Mills

A scene from Alfred Hitchcock's *Lifeboat* (1944)

In the 1982 film *Sophie's Choice,* a mother (played by Meryl Streep) is forced to make a terrible decision.

Sophie, a woman who was arrested by the Nazis and sent along with her two children to the Auschwitz concentration camp. When she arrived, she was given a choice by a sadistic guard: one of her children would go to the gas chamber and one would be spared, but she had to choose which one. If she did not choose, both children would be murdered.

Ethical dilemmas are not just the stuff of fiction; people confront them every day. For example, an owner of a business who realizes that costs must be cut faces an ethical dilemma. If the owner takes no action, the business will fail, and all the employees will lose their jobs. If the owner lays off some employees, they will be hurt, but the business will be saved and so will the jobs of the remaining workers. A surgeon who has to separate conjoined twins who share a heart also faces an ethical dilemma. If the surgeon does nothing, both twins will die, but if the surgeon operates, one of the twins will live, but the other will be sacrificed.

Often, the only way to resolve an ethical dilemma is to choose the lesser of two evils. Simple "right or wrong" or "good versus bad" prescriptions will not work in such cases. For example, killing may be morally, legally, and ethically wrong, but what if it is done in self-defense? Stealing is also wrong, but what if a person steals food to feed a hungry child? Although it may be tempting to apply clear ethical principles, you should be careful not to oversimplify the situations you are writing about.

⊖ EXERCISE 17.1

Consider the following topics for ethical arguments. Then, decide what ethical principle you could use for each argument. For example, if you were going to argue that doctors should not participate in doctor-assisted suicide, you could use the principles mentioned in the Hippocratic Oath as the basis for your argument.

- The United States should (or should not) prohibit the use of animals in scientific experiments.

- Students with special needs should (or should not) get preference in college admissions.

- Homeless people should (or should not) be forcibly removed from city streets.

- Gay and lesbian couples should (or should not) be allowed to adopt.

- Everyone should (or should not) be required to sign an organ-donor card.

⊖ EXERCISE 17.2

Make a list of some rules or laws that you think are unjust. Then, next to each item on your list, write down the ethical principle on which you based your conclusion.

⊖ EXERCISE 17.3

Look at the following two images. In what sense do they make ethical arguments? What is the ethical principle underlying each image?

⊝ EXERCISE 17.4

Read the following poem, "Ethics" by Linda Pastan. What ethical dilemma
does the poem present? Does the poem resolve this dilemma?

ETHICS
LINDA PASTAN

In ethics class so many years ago   1
our teacher asked this question every fall:
If there were a fire in a museum
which would you save, a Rembrandt painting
or an old woman who hadn't many   5
years left anyhow? Restless on hard chairs
caring little for pictures or old age
we'd opt one year for life, the next for art
and always half-heartedly. Sometimes
the woman borrowed my grandmother's face   10
leaving her usual kitchen to wander
some drafty, half imagined museum.
One year, feeling clever, I replied
why not let the woman decide herself?
Linda, the teacher would report, eschews   15
the burdens of responsibility.
This fall in a real museum I stand
before a real Rembrandt, old woman,
or nearly so, myself. The colors
within this frame are darker than autumn,   20
darker even than winter—the browns of earth,
though earth's most radiant elements burn
through the canvas. I know now that woman
and painting and season are almost one
and all beyond saving by children.   25

⮕ **EXERCISE 17.5**

How would you resolve the ethical dilemma that Pastan presents in her poem? Write a paragraph or two in which you discuss the dilemma as well as the ethical principle on which you based your conclusion.

Structuring an Ethical Argument

In general, an ethical argument can be structured in the following way.

- **Introduction:** Establishes the ethical principle and states the essay's thesis

- **Background:** Gives an overview of the situation

- **Ethical analysis:** Explains the ethical principle and analyzes the particular situation on the basis of this principle

- **Evidence:** Presents points that support the thesis

- **Refutation of opposing arguments:** Addresses arguments against the thesis

- **Conclusion:** Restates the ethical principle as well as the thesis; includes a strong concluding statement

🕑 The following student essay contains all the elements of an ethical argument. The student is responding to the question, "Should college athletes be paid a salary?"

THE PROMISE TO EDUCATE
CHRIS MUÑOZ

1   College athletics are enormously popular in this country. Fans take their team loyalties very seriously, and college sports are a multi-million-dollar industry. Few people, however, question the logic of the relationship between this sports-entertainment business and the universities that support it. If the goal of a university is to educate, then why are so many resources going to athletics? Now, some people

Introduction

Thesis statement
(includes ethical
principle)

Background: Gives
an overview of the
situation

even argue that we should acknowledge the "professional" nature of high-level college sports by paying salaries to the individual athletes. However, this approach would move schools further from their academic mission. Because the purpose of a university is to educate, universities should not pay their athletes a salary.

Since the middle of the nineteenth century, intercollegiate sports 2
have played an important role in college life. By the beginning of the twentieth century, rivalries between campuses—for example, Harvard and Yale—attracted a great deal of attention in newspapers. According to Murray Sperber, by the 1950s, the presence of professional sports teams in football and basketball and live radio and television broadcasts of collegiate games influenced college sports programs all over the country. Colleges soon realized that sports could generate a great deal of income and could even increase enrollment. As a result, Sperber explains, athletic scholarships became a way of attracting talented high school athletes and increasing the fan base for college sports. By the 1990s, athletes who were participating in big-time football and basketball programs were treated as celebrities and were in fact "unpaid professionals" (73). Concern over this situation prompted a debate that is still going on about the proper place of athletics in American colleges and universities.

Ethical analysis:
Presents the ethical
principle and analyzes
the situation on the
basis of this principle

Most people would agree that universities' primary responsibility is 3
to educate their students. This mission is included in virtually all schools' mission statements to remind everyone that scholarship and learning, not profit and glory, are the goals of these institutions. For example, the University of Michigan, a Big Ten school with high-profile sports teams, clearly states that its mission is "to serve the people of Michigan and the world through preeminence in creating, communicating, preserving and applying knowledge, art, and academic values" ("Mission"). Nowhere in this statement is a commitment to sports—let alone to sports as a business—mentioned. Clearly, paying student athletes would put universities in the sports-entertainment business. By entering bidding wars for the best athletes, universities would be forced to commit large portions of their budgets to nonacademic pursuits. In addition, athletes would choose where to go to school based on how much the school paid them, not on the education they would receive. As a result, the mission of the university would be fundamentally compromised.

4   By paying salaries to student athletes, universities would be failing to keep their commitments to nonathletes—those who enroll to receive, first and foremost, an education. Simply put, the more money spent on acquiring and keeping athletes, the less money allotted to other students and programs. As James L. Shulman and William G. Bowen, two experts on college sports and educational values, point out, "intercollegiate athletics programs involve the expenditure of a great deal of money." Shulman and Bowen go on to say that at most of the schools they studied, the costs of sports far exceeded the revenues they generated. Paying salaries to college athletes would make this imbalance even worse, causing more money to be directed toward athletics and less to research and teaching—the core goals of a university. In fact, if universities want to take their educational missions seriously and keep their promises to their students, they should carefully evaluate the admissions preferences and scholarship money athletes currently receive.

Evidence: First point in support of the thesis

5   Paying students to play sports would send a clear message: athletics come before academics. According to universities' stated missions, however, the message should be the other way around: academics should come before athletics. Even in the current system, in which athletes do not receive salaries, many students who compete in "big-time" college athletics receive what writer Andrew Zimbalist calls a "diluted education" (46). Zimbalist argues that "large numbers of student-athletes . . . are harmed by the system because they neither get an education nor a degree" (52). If universities invested money in player salaries, the pressure to win—and thus to earn back revenue for the school—would be even greater than it is now. A university's primary responsibility is to educate its students. Institutional incentives to play sports undermine this mission.

Evidence: Second point in support of the thesis

6   Finally, universities have an obligation to the community at large. As Shulman and Bowen write, "Colleges and universities are tax-favored, not-for-profit institutions because society agrees that they have a broader role to play in a far more consequential societal game." The fundamental purpose of a university is not to win games and make money; it is to serve the community by educating its citizens. If universities want to develop "leaders and citizens who will challenge the

Evidence: Third point in support of the thesis

present and enrich the future," as the University of Michigan, for one, says that it does, schools need to keep their focus on scholarship and stay out of the sports-entertainment business ("Mission").

Opposing argument

Because "top student-athletes are creating considerably more value   7 for their colleges than they are receiving," some critics argue that they should be paid (Zimbalist 11). The justification is that student athletes are actually employees of the university—employees who are currently being

Refutation

exploited for their labor. However, student athletes, like all students, are accepted into the university as *students* and willingly enroll as *students*. Far from being taken advantage of, most of these top student athletes receive compensation in the form of scholarships that cover tuition, room, board, and books. In addition, most of them leave college with a degree, a valuable asset. The key difference between paying a salary and providing financial support is that the latter puts the emphasis where it belongs—on the student athlete's university education.

Conclusion

Ultimately, universities need to be models of the integrity they   8 seek to instill in their students. By choosing not to hire their students as professional athletes, they can honor their commitment to their students, both nonathletes and athletes, and to their community. They can fulfill their responsibility to educate, and they can acknowledge student athletes as students first and athletes second. Universities must not give in to the pressure to further commercialize college sports. They must do

Concluding statement

as they have promised and use their resources to support and enhance academic goals.

Works Cited

"Mission Statement." *Office of the President.* Univ. of Michigan, 2008. Web. 30 Sept. 2008.

Shulman, James L., and William G. Bowen. "College Athletes Should Not Be Paid Because a College Education Is Valuable." *Should College Athletes Be Paid?* Ed. Geoff Griffin. Detroit: Greenhaven, 2007. N. pag. *Opposing Viewpoints Resource Center.* Web. 20 Sept. 2008.

Sperber, Murray. *Onward to Victory: The Crises That Shaped College Sports.* New York: Holt, 1999. Print.

Zimbalist, Andrew. *Unpaid Professionals: Commercialism and Conflict in Big-Time College Sports.* Princeton: Princeton UP, 1999. Print.

GRAMMAR IN CONTEXT: SUBORDINATION AND COORDINATION

When you write an argumentative essay, you need to show readers the logical and sequential connections between your ideas. You do this by using *coordinating conjunctions* and *subordinating conjunctions*—words that join words, phrases, clauses, or entire sentences. Without these conjunctions, readers will have a difficult time following your discussion and being persuaded by your argument. For this reason, you should choose conjunctions carefully, making sure that they accurately express the relationship between the ideas they join.

Coordinating conjunctions—*and, but, for, nor, or, so,* and *yet*—join ideas of equal importance. In compound sentences, they describe the relationship between the ideas in the two independent clauses and show how these ideas are related.

- College athletics are popular in this country, and their fans take their teams very seriously. (*And* indicates addition.)
- The main job of colleges is to educate students, but some colleges put too much emphasis on sports. (*But* indicates contrast or contradiction.)
- Colleges have to compete for top athletes, so they offer them generous athletic scholarships. (*So* indicates a causal relationship.)
- Universities can decide to emphasize sports, or they can emphasize education. (*Or* indicates alternatives.)

Subordinating conjunctions—*after, although because, if, so that, where,* and so on—join ideas of unequal importance. In complex sentences, they describe the relationship between the ideas in the dependent clause and the independent clause and show how these ideas are related.

- After games were broadcast on radio and television, college sports increased in popularity. (*After* indicates time sequence.)
- Although many colleges award sports scholarships, college athletic programs rarely make a profit. (*Although* indicates contrast.)
- Because colleges and universities are tax-exempt, they have an obligation to their communities. (*Because* indicates a causal relationship.)
- Colleges need to be models of integrity if they hope to instill these values in their students. (*If* indicates condition.)

(*continued*)

(*continued*)

- Colleges should stay out of the sports-entertainment business so that they can fulfill their responsibility to educate. (*So that* indicates a causal relationship.)
- Some student athletes go wherever they get the most scholarship money. (*Wherever* indicates location.)

➲ EXERCISE 17.6

The following essay, "Animals in Scientific Research," includes the basic elements of an ethical argument. Read the essay, and then answer the questions that follow it, consulting the list on page 491 if necessary.

This statement is from the Web site of the National Anti-Vivisection Society.

ANIMALS IN SCIENTIFIC RESEARCH

NATIONAL ANTI-VIVISECTION SOCIETY

As animal advocates, we oppose vivisection, or animal experimentation, on ethical grounds, believing that it is morally wrong to harm one species for the supposed benefit of another. We encourage others to extend the circle of compassion to include all living creatures—human and nonhuman alike.   1

> "We oppose vivisection, or animal experimentation, on ethical grounds."   2

Extending the circle of compassion beyond humankind demands a break with traditional thought, which holds that animals exist for humans to use as they see fit. In a world that is largely anthropocentric (human centered), the idea of compassion, respect and justice for all animals is often disregarded as mere sentimentality. After all, people argue, where would we be if we could not use animals for food, clothing, and transportation—or as research tools? Animals are seen simply as resources—as little more than products to make our lives more convenient and comfortable.

Animal advocates, on the other hand, view animals through a wider ethical prism—and it involves far more than sentimentality. We believe that animals should not be viewed as resources and products, but as fellow living creatures who share our planet . . . and that they deserve moral consideration that recognizes their rightful place in the vast and complex web of life.   3

Both human and nonhuman animals have been blessed with gifts unique to 4 our own species, and we each have our own ecological niche that fits together into the natural world. The right to enter into the circle of compassion cannot be measured by mental, physical or emotional abilities. As the great English philosopher Jeremy Bentham wrote, "The question is not, can they think? But can they suffer?"

Being sentient beings, which means the ability to experience sensation or 5 feelings, animals caught in the web of scientific research suffer enormously both physically and psychologically. Even those few "laboratory" animals that escape outright physical pain and discomfort are almost always subjected to isolation, depression and anxiety. In fact the worst atrocity we inflict upon animals condemned to scientific research may be the act of removing them from the natural habitat, or breeding them in captivity, and then placing them in the artificial environment of a laboratory cage, where they have no hope of having the kind of life nature intended for them.

In the end, we as a society have a choice. Do we treat our fellow creatures 6 with cruelty and callousness? Or with compassion, respect and justice? As humans, we have the freedom to make that choice. With this freedom comes the moral obligation to make responsible decisions.

Animals have no such choice. Because they cannot say no, they are completely vulnerable to whatever the researcher has in store for them, no matter 7 how much pain and suffering is involved. Animals are unable to understand or claim their right to be alive, to be free from pain and suffering, and fulfill their biological potential. Therefore, it is up to humans to recognize and protect those rights for them, just as we are morally obligated to protect infants, the developmentally disabled and the mentally ill.

It has been said that the moral progress of our society can be measured 8 by the way it treats animals. Animal experimentation—an institutionalized form of exploitation—stands in the way of moral progress. Now is the time to extend our sphere of ethical concern to all creatures.

Identifying the Elements of an Ethical Argument

1. What is *vivisection*? On what ethical principle do the writers of this essay base their opposition to vivisection?

2. Do the writers consider their readers friendly, hostile, or neutral? How do you know?

3. At what point does the essay address opposing arguments? How effectively are these arguments refuted?

4. What evidence do the writers present to support their case? Is there enough evidence? What other evidence could they have provided?

5. What ideas are emphasized in the essay's conclusion? Do you think the conclusion is effective?

How Far Should Colleges Go to Keep Campuses Safe?

Go back to page 481, and reread the At Issue box, which gives background on how far colleges should go to keep their students safe. Then, read the sources on the pages that follow.

As you read this source material, you will be asked to answer some questions and to complete some simple activities. This work will help you understand both the content and the structure of the selections. When you are finished, you will be ready to write an **ethical argument** that takes a position on the topic, "How Far Should Colleges Go to Keep Campuses Safe?"

SOURCES

 M. Perry Chapman, "Openness vs. Security on Campus"

 Brett A. Sokolow, "How Not to Respond to Virginia Tech—II"

 Jesus M. Villahermosa Jr., "Guns Don't Belong in the Hands of Administrators, Professors, or Students"

 Timothy Wheeler, "There's a Reason They Choose Schools"

 Isothermal Community College, "Warning Signs: How You Can Help Prevent Campus Violence"

 Amy Dion, "Gone But Not Forgotten"

The *Boston Globe* published this piece on April 28, 2007.

OPENNESS VS. SECURITY ON CAMPUS

M. PERRY CHAPMAN

1   We all react with shock and revulsion at the awful acts of violence that invaded the tranquility of the Virginia Tech campus last week. As a consultant who helped to create the campus plan for Virginia Tech in the 1990s, I was struck at the time by the university's commitment to a permeable, welcoming environment, a vibrant community of learning in the shadow of the Blue Ridge Mountains.

2   The tragedy is especially unsettling to those of us who have endeavored to uphold the central ideas of openness and engagement on American college campuses. It gives rise to a fundamental question of how far higher education institutions will have to go to provide a secure place without undermining the ideals that are so essential to the learning enterprise.

3   To address concerns about personal security over the last 30 years, institutions have employed call boxes, security lighting, key card systems, and, inevitably, surveillance cameras. These can be suitable and appropriate measures. But when do seemingly unobtrusive security measures threaten to turn the open, green campuses we all know and love into inward-looking compounds that are hostile to the presumed "outsider" and alienating to student and visitor alike?

4   College administrators need to be wary of the societal implications of sequestering populations in the name of security. We see the examples all around us—the trend toward privatized, gated residential communities erodes the quality of our civic lives by limiting free and spontaneous encounters among a wide range of humanity. In much the same way, the proliferation of crudely designed "protections" to courthouses and government buildings coarsens civic life and lessens our shared pride in the public realm.

> "College administrators need to be wary of the societal implications of sequestering populations."

5   There is a special poignancy that this horrible event took place at Virginia Tech; its history is emblematic of the best American ideals. The university is one of the 69 land grant institutions that came into being as a result of the Morrill Act° of 1862, signed by none other than Abraham Lincoln. It conferred on each state a grant of federal land as an endowment to be used by "at least one college" in the state to "teach such branches of learning as are related to agriculture and the mechanic arts."

A law that granted land to states for the purpose of establishing public colleges

6   The Morrill Act redefined the role and character of American higher education by offering it to a wide swath of the population, not just an

aristocratic elite. It spurred a new American curriculum that was, at once, more egalitarian and pragmatic than anything that had prevailed from the time of the colonial colleges. Most important, it codified at the state and national levels the quintessential American philosophy that a skilled, educated population was critical to the development of modern civil society.

Land grant universities like Virginia Tech have a special responsibility to 7 remain true to their egalitarian roots and foster learning within an environment of openness and free human interaction. That role extends beyond the traditional gates of the campus to the localities whose social and economic opportunities are linked more than ever to the resources of higher education institutions.

Town and gown are now inseparable in the knowledge-based economy 8 of the 21st century. The boundaries must be more seamless, transparent, and, above all, filled with human activity. The safe campus is the one where this activity is robust and visible, where there are "eyes on the quad," to paraphrase the great urban visionary Jane Jacobs.

In their sorrow, students at Virginia Tech demonstrated the power of 9 the bond they share as collegians. No less a Virginian than Thomas Jefferson understood better than anyone the importance of such symbolism.

In the early 1800s, his most profound gesture for the design of the Uni- 10 versity of Virginia was a great lawn bordered on three sides by buildings, but with the fourth side open to the Blue Ridge mountains. This was an architectural expression of educational enlightenment and a symbolic eschewing of the closed, insular quadrangles that had previously marked English and Continental collegiate design.

American campuses must continue to be microcosms of the open and free 11 societies today's students will some day lead.

⊘ AT ISSUE: SOURCES FOR DEVELOPING AN ETHICAL ARGUMENT

1. What steps are colleges taking to keep campuses safe? What objections does Chapman have to these steps?

2. According to Chapman, why is the tragedy at Virginia Tech especially unsettling?

3. What "special responsibility" does Chapmen think schools like Virginia Tech have (para. 7)? Why? Why does Chapman mention the Morrill Act in his essay?

4. In what sense, if any, is this essay an ethical argument? Explain.

5. What arguments against his position might Chapman have addressed? How could he have refuted them?

Inside Higher Ed published this article on May 1, 2007.

HOW NOT TO RESPOND TO VIRGINIA TECH—II

BRETT A. SOKOLOW

If you believe the pundits and talking heads in the aftermath of the Virginia 1
Tech tragedy, every college and university should rush to set up text-message-based early warning systems, install loudspeakers throughout campus, perform criminal background checks on all incoming students, allow students to install their own locks on their residence hall room doors, and exclude from admission or expel students with serious mental health conditions. We should profile loners, establish lockdown protocols and develop mass-shooting evacuation plans. We should even arm our students to the teeth. In the immediate aftermath, security experts and college and university officials have been quoted in newspapers and on TV with considering all of these remedies, and more, to be able to assure the public that WE ARE DOING SOMETHING.

Since when do we let the media dictate to us our best practices? Do we 2
need to do something? Do we need to be doing all or some of these things? Here's what I think. These are just my opinions, informed by what I have learned so far in the reportage on what happened at Virginia Tech. Because that coverage is inaccurate and incomplete, please consider these my thoughts so far, subject to revision as more facts come to light.

> "Since when do we let the media dictate to us our best practices?"

We should not be rushing to install text-message-based warning 3
systems. At the low cost of $1 per student per year, you might ask what the downside could be? Well, the real cost is the $1 per student that we don't spend on mental health support, where we really need to spend it. And, what do you get for your $1? A system that will send an emergency text to the cell phone number of every student who is registered with the service. If we acknowledge that many campuses still don't have the most current mailing address for some of our students who live off-campus, is it realistic to expect that students are going to universally supply us with their cell phone numbers? You could argue that students are flocking to sign up for this service on the campuses that currently provide it (less than 50 nationally), but that is driven by the panic of current events. Next fall, when the shock has worn off, apathy will inevitably return, and voluntary sign-up rates will drop. How about mandating that students participate? What about the costs of the bureaucracy we will need to collect and who will input this data? Who will track which students have yet to give us their numbers, remind them, and hound them to submit the information? Who will update this database as students switch cell

numbers mid-year, which many do? That's more than a full-time job, with implementation already costing more than the $1 per student. Some students want their privacy. They won't want administrators to have their cell number. Some students don't have cell phones. Many students do not have text services enabled on their phones. More added cost. Many professors instruct students to turn off their phones in classrooms.

Texting is useless. It's useless on the field for athletes, while students are 4 swimming, sleeping, showering, etc. And, perhaps most dangerously, texting an alert may send that alert to a psychopath who is also signed-up for the system, telling him exactly what administrators know, what the emergency plan is, and where to go to effect the most harm. Would a text system create a legal duty that colleges and universities do not have, a duty of universal warning? What happens in a crisis if the system is overloaded, as were cellphone lines in Blacksburg? What happens if the data entry folks mistype a number, and a student who needs warning does not get one? We will be sued for negligence. We need to spend this time, money and effort on the real problem: mental health.

We should consider installing loudspeakers throughout campus. This 5 technology has potentially better coverage than text messages, with much less cost. Virginia Tech used such loudspeakers to good effect during the shootings.

We should not rush to perform criminal background checks (CBCs) on 6 **all incoming students.** A North Carolina task force studied this issue after two 2004 campus shootings, and decided that the advantages were not worth the disadvantages. You might catch a random dangerous applicant, but most students who enter with criminal backgrounds were minors when they committed their crimes, and their records may have been sealed or expunged. If your student population is largely of non-traditional age, CBCs may reveal more, but then you have to weigh the cost and the question of whether you are able to perform due diligence on screening the results of the checks if someone is red-flagged. How will you determine which students who have criminal histories are worthy of admission and which are not? And, there is always the reality that if you perform a check on all incoming students and the college across the street does not, the student with the criminal background will apply there and not to you. If you decide to check incoming students, what will you do about current students? Will you do a state-level check, or a 50-state and federal check? Will your admitted applicants be willing to wait the 30 days that it takes to get the results? Other colleges who admitted them are also waiting for an answer. The comprehensive check can cost $80 per student. We need to spend this time, money and effort on the real problem: mental health.

We should not be considering whether to allow students to install their 7 **own locks on their dormitory room doors.** Credit *Fox News Live* for this deplorably dumb idea. If we let students change their locks, residential life and campus law enforcement will not be able to key into student rooms when they overdose on alcohol or try to commit suicide. This idea would prevent us from saving lives, rather than help to protect members of our community. The Virginia Tech killer could have shot through a lock, no matter whether it was the original or a retrofit. This is our property, and we need to have access to it. We need to focus our attention on the real issue: mental health.

Perhaps the most preposterous suggestion of all is that we need to relax 8 **our campus weapons bans so that armed members of our communities can defend themselves. We should not allow weapons on college campuses.** Imagine you are seated in Norris Hall, facing the whiteboard at the front of the room. The shooter enters from the back and begins shooting. What good is your gun going to do at this point? Many pro-gun advocates have talked about the deterrent and defense values of a well-armed student body, but none of them have mentioned the potential collateral criminal consequences of armed students: increases in armed robbery, muggings, escalation of interpersonal and relationship violence, etc. Virginia, like most states, cannot keep guns out of the hands of those with potentially lethal mental health crises. When we talk about arming students, we'd be arming them too. We need to focus our attention on the real issue: mental health.

We should establish lockdown protocols that are specific to the nature 9 **of the threat.** Lockdowns are an established mass-protection tactic. They can isolate perpetrators, insulate targets from threats and restrict personal movement away from a dangerous line-of-fire. But, if lockdowns are just a random response, they have the potential to lock students in with a still-unidentified perpetrator. If not used correctly, they have the potential to lock students into facilities from which they need immediate egress for safety reasons. And, if not enforced when imposed, lockdowns expose us to the potential liability of not following our own policies. We should also establish protocols for judicious use of evacuations. When police at Virginia Tech herded students out of buildings and across the Drill Field, it was based on their assessment of a low risk that someone was going to open fire on students as they fled out into the open, and a high risk of leaving the occupants of certain buildings in situ, making evacuation from a zone of danger an appropriate escape method.

We should not exclude from admission or expel students with mental 10 **health conditions, unless they pose a substantial threat of harm to themselves or others.** Section 504 of the Rehabilitation Act prohibits colleges and universities from discrimination in admission against those with disabilities. It also prohibits colleges and universities from suspending or expelling disabled students, including those who are suicidal, unless the student is deemed to be a direct threat of substantial harm in an objective process based on the most current medical assessment available. Many colleges do provide health surveys to incoming students, and when those surveys disclose mental health conditions, we need to consider what appropriate follow-up should occur as a result. The Virginia Tech shooter was schizophrenic or mildly autistic, and identifying those disabilities early on and providing support, accommodation—and potentially intervention—is our issue.

We should consider means and mechanisms for early intervention with 11 **students who exhibit behavioral issues, but we should not profile loners.** At the University of South Carolina, the Behavioral Intervention Team makes many early catches of students whose behavior is threatening, disruptive or potentially self-injurious. By working with faculty and staff at opening communication and support, the model is enhancing campus safety in a way that many other campuses are not. In the aftermath of what happened at Virginia Tech, I hope many campuses are considering a model designed to help raise flags for early screening and intervention. Many students are loners, isolated, withdrawn, pierced, tattooed, dyed, Wiccan, skate rats, fantasy gamers or otherwise outside the "mainstream." This variety enlivens the richness of college campuses, and offers layers of culture that quilt the fabric of diverse communities. Their preferences and differences cannot and should not be cause for fearing them or suspecting them. But, when any member of the community starts a downward spiral along the continuum of violence, begins to lose contact with reality, goes off their medication regimen, threatens, disrupts, or otherwise gains our attention with unhealthy or dangerous patterns, we can't be bystanders any longer. Our willingness to intervene can make all the difference.

All of the pundits insist that random violence can't be predicted, but many 12 randomly violent people exhibit a pattern of detectable disintegration of self, often linked to suicide. People around them perceive it. We can all be better attuned to those patterns and our protocols for communicating our concerns to those who have the ability to address them. This will focus our attention on the real issue: mental health.

⊘ AT ISSUE: SOURCES FOR DEVELOPING AN ETHICAL ARGUMENT

1. Why does Sokolow begin his essay by discussing what "pundits and talking heads" think should be done to stop campus violence?

2. In paragraph 2, Sokolow says, "Here's what I think. These are just my opinions." Do these two statements undercut or enhance his credibility? Why do you suppose he includes them?

3. How does Sokolow propose to make campuses safer? Do you agree with his suggestions? Why or why not?

4. Is Sokolow's argument a refutation? If so, what arguments is he refuting?

5. In his concluding statement, Sokolow says that the real issue is "mental health." What does he mean? Do you agree?

This selection is from the April 18, 2008, issue of the *Chronicle of Higher Education.*

GUNS DON'T BELONG IN THE HANDS OF ADMINISTRATORS, PROFESSORS, OR STUDENTS

JESUS M. VILLAHERMOSA JR.

In the wake of the shootings at Virginia Tech and Northern Illinois University, a number of state legislatures are considering bills that would allow people to carry concealed weapons on college campuses. I recently spoke at a conference on higher-education law, sponsored by Stetson University and the National Association of Student Personnel Administrators, at which campus officials discussed the need to exempt colleges from laws that let private citizens carry firearms, and to protect such exemptions where they exist. I agree that allowing guns on campuses will create problems, not solve them. 1

I have been a deputy sheriff for more than 26 years and was the first certified master defensive-tactics instructor for law-enforcement personnel in the state of Washington. In addition, I have been a firearms instructor and for several decades have served on my county sheriff's SWAT team, where I am now point man on the entry team. Given my extensive experience dealing with violence in the workplace and at schools and colleges, I do not think professors and administrators, let alone students, should carry guns. 2

Some faculty and staff members may be capable of learning to be good shots in stressful situations, but most of them probably wouldn't practice their firearms skills enough to become confident during an actual shooting. Unless they practiced those skills constantly, there would be a high risk that when a shooting situation actually occurred, they would miss the assailant. That would leave great potential for a bullet to strike a student or another innocent bystander. Such professors and administrators could be imprisoned for manslaughter for recklessly endangering the lives of others during a crisis. 3

Although some of the legislative bills have been defeated, they may be reintroduced, or other states may introduce similar measures. Thus, colleges should at least contemplate the possibility of having armed faculty and staff members on their campuses, and ask themselves the following questions: 4

- Is our institution prepared to assume the liability that accompanies the lethal threat of carrying or using weapons? Are we financially able and willing to drastically increase our liability-insurance premium to cover all of the legal ramifications involved with allowing faculty and staff members to carry firearms?

- How much time will each faculty and staff member be given each year to spend on a firing range to practice shooting skills? Will we pay them for that time?

- Will their training include exposing them to a great amount of stress in order to simulate a real-life shooting situation, like the training that police officers go through?

- Will the firearm that each one carries be on his or her person during the day? If so, will faculty and staff members be given extensive defensive-tactics training, so that they can retain their firearm if someone tries to disarm them?

- The fact that a college allows people to have firearms could be publicized and, under public-disclosure laws, the institution could be required to notify the general public which faculty or staff members are carrying them. Will those individuals accept the risk of being targeted by a violent student or adult who wants to neutralize the threat and possibly obtain their weapons?

- If the firearms are not carried by faculty and staff members every day, where and how will those weapons be secured, so that they do not fall into the wrong hands?

- If the firearms are locked up, how will faculty and staff members gain access to them in time to be effective if a shooting actually occurs?

- Will faculty and staff members who carry firearms be required to be in excellent physical shape, and stay that way, in case they need to fight someone for their gun?

- Will weapons-carrying faculty and staff members accept that they may be shot by law-enforcement officers who mistake them for the shooter? (All the responding officers see is a person with a gun. If you are even close to matching the suspect's description, the risk is high that they may shoot you.)

- Will faculty and staff members be prepared to kill another person, someone who may be as young as a teenager?

> "Will faculty and staff be prepared to kill another person?"

- Will faculty and staff members be prepared for the possibility that they may miss their target (which has occurred even in police shootings) and wound or kill an innocent bystander?

- Will faculty and staff members be ready to face imprisonment for manslaughter, depending on their states' criminal statutes, if one of their bullets does, in fact, strike an innocent person?

- Even if not criminally charged, would such faculty and staff members be prepared to be the focus of a civil lawsuit, both as a professional working for the institution and as an individual, thereby exposing their personal assets?

If any of us in the law-enforcement field were asked these questions, we 5 could answer them all with absolute confidence. We have made a commitment to train relentlessly and to die, if we have to, in order to protect others. Experienced officers have typically fired tens of thousands of rounds practicing for the time when they might need those skills to save themselves or someone else during a lethal situation. We take that commitment seriously. Before legislators and college leaders make the decision to put a gun in the hands of a professor or administrator, they should be certain they take it seriously, too.

⊘ AT ISSUE: SOURCES FOR DEVELOPING AN ETHICAL ARGUMENT

1. What is Villahermosa's thesis?

2. What is Villahermosa trying to establish in paragraph 2? Do you think this paragraph is necessary?

3. In the bulleted list in paragraph 4, Villahermosa poses a series of questions. What does he want this list to accomplish? Is he successful?

4. What arguments does Villahermosa include to support his thesis? Which of these arguments do you find most convincing? Why?

5. Do you think Villahermosa is making an ethical argument here? If so, on what ethical principle does he base his argument?

6. What points does Villahermosa emphasize in his conclusion? Should he have emphasized any other points? Explain.

This article is from the October 11, 2007, issue of *National Review*.

THERE'S A REASON THEY CHOOSE SCHOOLS

TIMOTHY WHEELER

Wednesday's shooting at yet another school has a better outcome than most in 1
recent memory. No one died at Cleveland's Success Tech Academy except the
perpetrator. The two students and two teachers he shot are in stable condition
at Cleveland hospitals.

What is depressingly similar to the mass murders at Virginia Tech and 2
Nickel Mines, Pennsylvania, and too many others was the killer's choice of
venue—that steadfastly gun-free zone, the school campus. Although murderer
Seung-Hui Cho at Virginia Tech and Asa Coon, the Cleveland shooter were
both students reported to have school-related grudges, other school killers
have proved to be simply taking advantage of the lack of effective security at
schools. The Bailey, Colorado, multiple rapes and murder of September 2006,
the Nickel Mines massacre of October 2006, and Buford Furrow's murderous
August 1999 invasion of a Los Angeles Jewish day-care center were all committed by adults. They had no connection to the schools other than being
drawn to the soft target a school offers such psychopaths.

This latest shooting comes only a few weeks after the American Medical 3
Association released a theme issue of its journal *Disaster Medicine and Public Health Preparedness*. This issue is dedicated to analyzing the April 2007
Virginia Tech shootings, in which 32 people were murdered. The authors
are university officials, trauma surgeons, and legal analysts who pore over
the details of the incident, looking for "warning signs" and "risk factors" for
violence. They rehash all the tired rhetoric of bureaucrats and public-health
wonks, including the public-health mantra of the 1990s that guns are the root
cause of violence.

Sheldon Greenberg, a dean at Johns Hopkins, offers this gem: "Reinforce 4
a 'no weapons' policy and, when violated, enforce it quickly, to include expulsion. Parents should be made aware of the policy. *Officials should dispel the
politically driven notion that armed students could eliminate an active shooter*"
(emphasis added). Greenberg apparently isn't aware that at the Appalachian
School of Law in 2002 another homicidal Virginia student was stopped from
shooting more of his classmates when another student held him at gunpoint.
The Pearl High School murderer Luke Woodham was stopped cold when vice
principal Joel Myrick got his Colt .45 handgun out of his truck and pointed it
at the young killer.

Virginia Tech's 2005 no-guns-on-campus policy was an abject failure at 5
deterring Cho Seung-Hui. Greenberg's audacity in ignoring the obvious is
typical of arrogant school officials. What the AMA journal authors studiously

avoid are on one hand the repeated failures of such feel-good steps as no-gun policies, and on the other hand the demonstrated success of armed first responders. These responders would be the students themselves, such as the trained and licensed law student, or their similarly qualified teachers.

> "Virginia Tech's . . .
> no-guns-on-campus
> policy was an abject
> failure."

6

In Cleveland this week and at Virginia Tech the shooters took time to walk the halls, searching out victims in several rooms, and then shooting them. Virginia Chief Medical Examiner Marcella Fierro describes the locations of the dead in Virginia Tech's Norris Hall. Dead victims were found in groups ranging from 1 to 13, scattered throughout 4 rooms and a stairwell. If any one of the victims had, like the Appalachian School of Law student, used armed force to stop Cho, lives could have been saved.

The people of Virginia actually had a chance to implement such a plan 7 last year. House Bill 1572 was introduced in the legislature to extend the state's concealed-carry provisions to college campuses. But the bill died in committee, opposed by the usual naysayers, including the Virginia Association of Chiefs of Police and the university itself. Virginia Tech spokesman Larry Hincker was quoted in the *Roanoke Times* as saying, "I'm sure the university community is appreciative of the General Assembly's actions because this will help parents, students, faculty, and visitors feel safe on our campus."

It is encouraging that college students themselves have a much better 8 grasp on reality than their politically correct elders. During the week of October 22–26 Students for Concealed Carry on Campus will stage a nationwide "empty holster" demonstration (peaceful, of course) in support of their cause.

School officials typically base violence-prevention policies on irrational 9 fears more than real-world analysis of what works. But which is more horrible, the massacre that timid bureaucrats fear might happen when a few good guys (and gals) carry guns on campus, or the one that actually did happen despite Virginia Tech's progressive violence-prevention policy? Can there really be any more debate?

AMA Journal editor James J. James, M.D., offers up this nostrum: 10

We must meaningfully embrace all of the varied disciplines contributing to preparedness and response and be more willing to be guided and informed by the full spectrum of research methodologies, including not only the rigid application of the traditional scientific method and epidemiological and social science applications but also the incorporation of observational/empirical findings, as necessary, in the absence of more objective data.

Got that?

I prefer the remedy prescribed by self-defense guru Massad Ayoob. When 11 good people find themselves in what he calls "the dark place," confronted by the imminent terror of a gun-wielding homicidal maniac, the picture becomes clear. Policies won't help. Another federal gun law won't help. The only solution is a prepared and brave defender with the proper lifesaving tool—a gun.

◉ AT ISSUE: SOURCES FOR DEVELOPING AN ETHICAL ARGUMENT

1. According to Wheeler, what is "depressingly similar" about the mass murders committed on campuses (para. 2)?

2. What is Wheeler's attitude toward those who say, "guns are the root cause of violence" (3)? How can you tell?

3. Why, according to Wheeler, do college administrators and bureaucrats continue to ignore the answer to the problem of violence on campus? How does he refute their objections?

4. What is Wheeler's position on the issue? Do you find his argument in support of this position convincing? What, if anything, do you think he could have done to strengthen his argument?

5. How does Wheeler's language reveal his attitude toward his subject? (For example, consider his use of "gem" in paragraph 4 and "politically correct" in paragraph 8.) Can you give other examples of language that conveys his point of view?

6. How would you characterize Wheeler's opinion of guns? How is his opinion different from Villahermosa's (p. 505)?

This brochure is available on the Web site for Isothermal Community College, isothermal.edu.

WARNING SIGNS: HOW YOU CAN HELP PREVENT CAMPUS VIOLENCE

ISOTHERMAL COMMUNITY COLLEGE

Things to look out for . . .

- Any direct statement about the intention to harm him/her self or other members of the community

- "Hints" that the individual intends to harm him/her self or other members of the community: For example, "I might not be around after this weekend;" "It would be a good idea for you to stay out of the cafeteria tomorrow;" "People might get hurt, if they're not careful"

- Extreme difficulty adjusting to college life; for example the student is isolated, depressed, and/or very angry with peers

- Significant changes in behavior, appearance, habits, mood or activities

- Statements from individuals about access to fire arms and suggestions that they may be bringing them to the campus or may already have them on campus

- Behaviors that indicate that the individual is settling his/her affairs, which may include telling people goodbye, giving possessions away, and/or making statements about what they would like to have done should something happen to them

- Fascination with violence, including some types of video games and music, and/or focusing on or admiring violent "role models"

- Your own "gut feeling" that someone that you know intends to harm him/her self or others

Campus Security – 289-1393
Isothermal Community College
Improve Life Through Learning
www.isothermal.edu

> "We want all of our students, faculty and staff to be safe and secure on campus."

At Isothermal Community College, we want all of our students, faculty and staff to be safe and secure on campus.

In light of the tragic shootings at Virginia Tech and other recent events on college campuses and in schools around the country, it has become clear that friends, classmates and acquaintances of troubled students may be the most likely individuals to be aware of potentially dangerous and/or self-destructive situations.

However, students often are not certain about what kinds of warning signs they should take seriously and/or whether reporting the signs to faculty or staff members is the right thing to do.

The tips in this brochure are aimed at helping you identify potential problems and behaviors that could lead to incidents of campus violence.

If you ever feel endangered or threatened at any time on campus, we ask that you immediately contact Isothermal security, an instructor or an employee of the college for assistance.

Campus security can be reached at 289-1393. To contact the switchboard operator, dial **0** on any campus phone. You should also report any threatening activity to local law enforcement by dialing **911**. Don't forget to dial **9** for an outside line if using the campus phone system.

A lockdown procedure is in place for Isothermal Community College. Faculty and staff members periodically practice the procedure. **If you are informed of a lockdown situation, please cooperate with the proper authorities.** Leaving the classroom or the building in such a situation may put you at greater risk.

Potential for Violence

Warning Signs in Others

Often people who act violently have trouble controlling their feelings. They may have been hurt by others and may think that making people fear them through violence or threats of violence will solve their problems or earn them respect. This isn't true. People who behave violently lose respect. They find themselves isolated or disliked, and they still feel angry and frustrated.

If you see these immediate warning signs, violence is a serious possibility:

- Loss of temper on a daily basis

- Frequent physical fighting

- Significant vandalism or property damage

- Increase in use of drugs or alcohol

- Increase in risk-taking behavior

- Detailed plans to commit acts of violence

- Announcing threats or plans for hurting others

- Enjoying hurting animals

- Carrying a weapon

If you notice the following signs over a period of time, the potential for violence exists:

- A history of violent or aggressive behavior

- Serious drug or alcohol use

- Gang membership or strong desire to be in a gang

- Access to or fascination with weapons, especially guns

- Threatening others regularly

- Trouble controlling feelings like anger

- Withdrawal from friends and usual activities

- Feeling rejected or alone

- Having been a victim of bullying

- Poor school performance

- History of discipline problems or frequent run-ins with authority

- Feeling constantly disrespected

- Failing to acknowledge the feelings or rights of others

Source: American Psychological Association

AT ISSUE: SOURCES FOR DEVELOPING AN ETHICAL ARGUMENT

1. This brochure is designed to help students recognize people who have the potential to commit campus violence. What warning signs does the brochure emphasize?

2. What additional information do you think should have been included in this brochure? Why?

3. Are there any suggestions in this brochure that could possibly violate a person's right to privacy? Explain.

4. What additional steps do you think students should take to protect themselves from the threat of campus violence?

This poster is from the UCDA Campus Violence Poster Project show at Northern Illinois University

GONE BUT NOT FORGOTTEN

AMY DION

Virginia Tech University
4·17·07 (32 dead)

Louisiana Technical College
2·8·08 (3 dead)

Northern Illinois University
2·14·08 (5 dead)

⊘AT ISSUE: SOURCES FOR DEVELOPING AN ETHICAL ARGUMENT

1. This poster shows a handprint on a background that repeats the phrase "Gone but not forgotten." What central point is the poster making?

2. What other images does the poster include? How do these images reinforce its central point?

3. Do you think posters like this one can actually help to combat campus violence? Can they serve any other purpose? Explain.

⊃ EXERCISE 17.7

Write a one-paragraph ethical argument in which you take a position on how far colleges should go to keep students safe. Follow the template below, filling in the blanks to create your argument.

Template for Writing an Ethical Argument

Recently, a number of colleges have experienced violence on their campuses. For example, _____

_____. Many colleges have gone too far (or not far enough) in trying to prevent violence because _____

_____

_____

_____. One reason _____

_____

Another reason _____

_____

_____.Finally,_____

_____

_____. If colleges really want to remain safe, _____

_____

_____

_____.

⊃ EXERCISE 17.8

Ask your friends and your teachers whether they think any of the steps your school has taken to prevent campus violence are excessive—or whether they think these measures don't go far enough. Then, edit the paragraph you wrote for Exercise 17.7 so that it includes their opinions.

⊃ EXERCISE 17.9

Write an ethical argument in which you consider the topic, "How far should colleges go to keep campuses safe?" Make sure you include a clear analysis of the ethical principle that you are going to apply. (If you like, you may incorporate the material you developed for Exercises 17.7 and 17.8 into your essay.) Cite the readings on pages 499–515, and document the sources you use. In addition, be sure to include a works-cited page. (See Chapter 10 for information on documenting sources.)

⊘ EXERCISE 17.10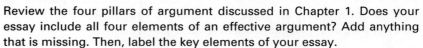

Review the four pillars of argument discussed in Chapter 1. Does your essay include all four elements of an effective argument? Add anything that is missing. Then, label the key elements of your essay.

⊘ WRITING ASSIGNMENTS: ETHICAL ARGUMENTS

1. Write an ethical argument in which you discuss whether hate groups have the right to distribute material on campus. Be sure to explain the ethical principle you are applying and to include several arguments in support of your position. (Don't forget to address arguments against your position.)

2. Should English be made the official language of the United States? Write an ethical argument in which you take a position on this topic.

3. Many people think that celebrities have an ethical obligation to set positive examples for young people. Assume that you are a celebrity, and write an op-ed piece in which you support or dispute this idea. Be sure to identify the ethical principle on which you base your argument.

6

Debates, Casebooks, and Classic Arguments

DEBATE

Should We Eat Meat?

According to the Vegetarian Resource Group, over 4 million vegetarians and vegans live in the United States. Indeed, as health experts increasingly worry about heart disease and obesity, this seems to be an especially good time for Americans to evaluate the merits of meat-eating. But the issue goes well beyond health and nutrition. People become vegetarians for a variety of reasons—nutritional, ethical, environmental, and religious. Thus, these choices are not only personal but also cultural. As Jonathan Safran Foer writes in "Let Them Eat Dog," "Food is not rational. Food is culture, habit, craving, and identity."

Our culture seems obsessed with healthy eating, as shown by the increasing popularity of organic and locally grown food and by the popularity of books and films such as *The Omnivore's Dilemma, Fast Food Nation,* and *Slaughterhouse: The Labor Behind the Profit.* Of course, dietary controversies are not new—and neither is vegetarianism, which has long been associated with certain religious traditions (Jainism and various sects of Hinduism, for example). Western philosophers from Pythagoras to Jean Jacques Rousseau and Rene Descartes also advocated different forms of vegetarianism. In the eighteenth and nineteenth centuries, a vegetarian diet was associated with radical politics. The English Romantic poet Percy Shelley endorsed the practice—and even blamed some of the excesses of the French Revolution on meat-eating. In the United States, vegetarianism has had strong advocates dating back to the founding of the country. Presbyterian minister and dietary reformer Sylvester Graham, for example, helped found the American Vegetarian Society in 1850. He touted the benefits of a high-fiber diet of fruits and vegetables—the staple of which was the "Graham Cracker," made of whole-wheat flour and bran.

For the zealous Graham, who attracted a sizable following, a meatless diet not only improved one's health, but it also improved one's personal morality. Although the language and aims of vegetarians may have changed, many still see the choice to eat—or not to eat—meat as a profoundly moral and ethical decision, not just a matter of personal choice. Both writers in this debate agree that there are social dimensions to being an omnivore. Modeling his essay on Jonathan Swift's famous satire "A Modest Proposal" (p. 672), Jonathan Safran Foer highlights the logical and ethical inconsistency of those who justify consuming animals such as chickens, pigs, and cows for food, even though they would be horrified by killing and eating domesticated dogs and cats. A former vegetarian, Laura Fraser argues that human beings are ultimately omnivores and that people must consider the realities of human society when making dietary choices.

This piece is from the October 31, 2009, *Wall Street Journal.*

LET THEM EAT DOG

JONATHAN SAFRAN FOER

Despite the fact that it's perfectly legal in 44 states, eating "man's best friend" 1
is as taboo as a man eating his best friend. Even the most enthusiastic carnivores won't eat dogs. TV guy and sometimes cooker Gordon Ramsay can
get pretty macho with lambs and piglets when doing publicity for something
he's selling, but you'll never see a puppy peeking out of one of his pots. And
though he once said he'd electrocute his children if they became vegetarian,
one can't help but wonder what his response would be if they poached the
family pooch.

Dogs are wonderful, and in many ways unique. But they are remarkably 2
unremarkable in their intellectual and experiential capacities. Pigs are every bit
as intelligent and feeling, by any sensible definition of the words. They can't
hop into the back of a Volvo, but they can fetch, run and play, be mischievous
and reciprocate affection. So why don't they get to curl up by the fire? Why
can't they at least be spared being tossed on the fire? Our taboo against dog
eating says something about dogs and a great deal about us.

The French, who love their dogs, sometimes eat their horses. 3

The Spanish, who love their horses, sometimes eat their cows. 4

The Indians, who love their cows, sometimes eat their dogs. 5

While written in a much different context, George Orwell's words (from 6
"Animal Farm") apply here: "All animals are equal, but some animals are
more equal than others."

So who's right? What might be the reasons to exclude canine from the 7
menu? The selective carnivore suggests:

Don't eat companion animals. But dogs aren't kept as companions in all 8
of the places they are eaten. And what about our petless neighbors? Would we
have any right to object if they had dog for dinner?

OK, then: Don't eat animals with significant mental capacities. If by "sig- 9
nificant mental capacities" we mean what a dog has, then good for the dog.
But such a definition would also include the
pig, cow and chicken. And it would exclude
severely impaired humans.

Then: It's for good reason that the eternal
taboos—don't fiddle with your crap, kiss your
sister, or eat your companions—are taboo.
Evolutionarily speaking, those things are bad
for us. But dog eating isn't a taboo in many places, and it isn't in any way bad for
us. Properly cooked, dog meat poses no greater health risks than any other meat.

> "Properly cooked,
> dog meat poses no
> greater health risks
> than any other meat."   10

Dog meat has been described as "gamey," "complex," "buttery" and "floral." And there is a proud pedigree of eating it. Fourth-century tombs contain depictions of dogs being slaughtered along with other food animals. It was a fundamental enough habit to have informed language itself: the Sino-Korean character for "fair and proper" (yeon) literally translates into "as cooked dog meat is delicious." Hippocrates praised dog meat as a source of strength. Dakota Indians enjoyed dog liver, and not so long ago Hawaiians ate dog brains and blood. Captain Cook ate dog. Roald Amundsen famously ate his sled dogs. (Granted, he was really hungry.) And dogs are still eaten to overcome bad luck in the Philippines; as medicine in China and Korea; to enhance libido in Nigeria and in numerous places, on every continent, because they taste good. For centuries, the Chinese have raised special breeds of dogs, like the black-tongued chow, for chow, and many European countries still have laws on the books regarding postmortem examination of dogs intended for human consumption. 11

Of course, something having been done just about everywhere is no kind of justification for doing it now. But unlike all farmed meat, which requires the creation and maintenance of animals, dogs are practically begging to be eaten. Three to four million dogs and cats are euthanized annually. The simple disposal of these euthanized dogs is an enormous ecological and economic problem. But eating those strays, those runaways, those not-quite-cute-enough-to-take and not-quite-well-behaved-enough-to-keep dogs would be killing a flock of birds with one stone and eating it, too. 12

In a sense it's what we're doing already. Rendering—the conversion of animal protein unfit for human consumption into food for livestock and pets—allows processing plants to transform useless dead dogs into productive members of the food chain. In America, millions of dogs and cats euthanized in animal shelters every year become the food for our food. So let's just eliminate this inefficient and bizarre middle step. 13

This need not challenge our civility. We won't make them suffer any more than necessary. While it's widely believed that adrenaline makes dog meat taste better—hence the traditional methods of slaughter: hanging, boiling alive, beating to death—we can all agree that if we're going to eat them, we should kill them quickly and painlessly, right? For example, the traditional Hawaiian means of holding the dog's nose shut—in order to conserve blood—must be regarded (socially if not legally) as a no-no. Perhaps we could include dogs under the Humane Methods of Slaughter Act. That doesn't say anything about how they're treated during their lives, and isn't subject to any meaningful oversight or enforcement, but surely we can rely on the industry to "self-regulate," as we do with other eaten animals. 14

Few people sufficiently appreciate the colossal task of feeding a world of billions of omnivores who demand meat with their potatoes. The inefficient use of dogs—conveniently already in areas of high human population (take note, local-food advocates)—should make any good ecologist blush. One could argue that various "humane" groups are the worst hypocrites, spending enormous amounts of money and energy in a futile attempt to reduce the number of unwanted dogs 15 while at the very same time propagating the irresponsible no-dog-for-dinner taboo. If we let dogs be dogs, and breed without interference, we would create a sustainable, local meat supply with low energy inputs that would put even the most efficient grass-based farming to shame. For the ecologically-minded it's time to admit that dog is realistic food for realistic environmentalists.

For those already convinced, here's a classic Filipino recipe I recently came across. I haven't tried it myself, but sometimes you can read a recipe and just know.   16

Stewed Dog, Wedding Style

First, kill a medium-sized dog, then burn off the fur over a hot fire. Carefully remove the skin while still warm and set aside for later (may be used in other recipes). Cut meat into 1" cubes. Marinate meat in mixture of vinegar, peppercorn, salt, and garlic for 2 hours. Fry meat in oil using a large wok over an open fire, then add onions and chopped pineapple and sauté until tender. Pour in tomato sauce and boiling water, add green pepper, bay leaf, and Tabasco. Cover and simmer over warm coals until meat is tender. Blend in purée of dog's liver and cook for additional 5–7 minutes.

There is an overabundance of rational reasons to say no to factory-farmed meat: It is the No. 1 cause of global warming, it systematically forces tens of billions of animals to suffer in ways that would be illegal if they were dogs, it is a decisive factor in the development of swine and avian flus, and so on. And yet even most people who know these things still aren't inspired to order something else on the menu. Why?   17

Food is not rational. Food is culture, habit, craving and identity. Responding to factory farming calls for a capacity to care that dwells beyond information. We know what we see on undercover videos of factory farms and slaughterhouses is wrong. (There are those who will defend a system that allows for occasional animal cruelty, but no one defends the cruelty, itself.) And despite it being entirely reasonable, the case for eating dogs is likely repulsive to just about every reader of this paper. The instinct comes before our reason, and is more important.   18

⊘ READING ARGUMENTS

1. Several times in his essay, Foer uses the term *taboo*, as when he refers to the "eternal taboos" in paragraph 10. What is a taboo? Why do you think he uses this term, rather than a word like "rule"?

2. In what sense is Foer's essay an argument by analogy?

3. In what sense is Foer's essay a proposal argument?

4. What is Foer's thesis? Where is it located? Do you agree with his position on the issue?

This article first appeared on January 7, 2000, on *Salon.com*.

WHY I STOPPED BEING A VEGETARIAN
LAURA FRASER

Until a few of months ago, I had been a vegetarian for 15 years. Like most 1
people who call themselves vegetarians (somewhere between 4 and 10 percent
of us, depending on the definition; only 1 percent of Americans are vegans,
eating no animal products at all), I wasn't strict about it. I ate dairy products
and eggs, as well as fish. That made me a pesco-ovo-lacto-vegetarian, which
isn't a category you can choose for special meals on airlines.

About a year ago, in Italy, it dawned on me that a little pancetta was really 2
good in pasta, too. After failing to convince myself that pancetta was a vegetable, I became a pesco-ovo-lacto-pancetta-vegetarian, with a "Don't Ask, Don't
Tell" policy about chicken broth. It was a slippery slope from there.

Nevertheless, for most of those 15 years, hardly a piece of animal flesh 3
crossed my lips. Over the course of that time, many people asked me why I
became a vegetarian. I came up with vague answers: my health, the environment, the impracticality and heartlessness of killing animals for food when we
can survive perfectly well on soy burgers. It was political, it was emotional and
it made me special, not to mention slightly morally superior to all those bloodthirsty carnivores out there.

The truth is, I became a vegetarian in college for two reasons. One was 4
that meat was more expensive than lentils, and I was broke, or broke enough
to choose to spend my limited budget on other classes of ingestibles. The other
was that I was not a lesbian.

This is not to say that all lesbians are carnivores; in fact, there's probably a higher 5
percentage of vegetarians among lesbians than most other groups. But there was a
fair amount of political pressure to be something in those days. Since, as a privileged
white girl from suburban Denver, I couldn't really identify with any oppressed minority group, I was faced with becoming a lesbian in order to prove my political mettle. I
had to decide between meat and men, and for better or worse, I became a vegetarian.

The identity stuck, even though the political imperative for my label 6
faded. It wasn't an identity that ever really fit: My friends thought it odd that
such an otherwise hedonistic woman should have that one ascetic streak. It
was against my nature, they said. But by then, I'd started to believe the other
arguments about vegetarianism.

First was health. There's a lot of evidence that vegetarians live longer, have 7
lower cholesterol levels and are thinner than meat-eaters. This is somewhat
hard to believe, since for the first few years of not eating meat, I was basically a cheesetarian. Try leafing through some of those vegetarian recipe books
from the early '80s: You added three cups of grated cheddar to everything but
the granola. Then vegetarianism went through that mathematical phase where

you had to figure out which proteins you had to combine with which in order to get a complete protein. Since many nutritionists will tell you people don't need that much protein anyway, I gave up, going for days and days without so much as contemplating beans or tofu.

For whatever haphazard combination of proteins I ate, being a vegetar- 8 ian did seem to have a stunning effect on my cholesterol level. This, of course, could be genetic. But when I had a very involved physical exam once at the Cooper Institute for Aerobic Fitness in Dallas, my total cholesterol level was a super-low 135, and my ratio of HDL (good) cholesterol to LDL (evil) was so impressive that the doctor drawled, "Even if you had heart disease, you would be reversing it." This good news, far from reassuring me that I could well afford a few barbecued ribs now and then, spurred me on in my veg- etarianism, mainly because my cholesterol numbers effectively inoculated me against the doctor's advice that I also needed to lose 15 pounds.

"Why?" I asked. "Don't you lose weight to lower your cholesterol?" 9

He couldn't argue with that. Whether or not most vegetarians are leaner 10 than carnivores, in my case I was happy to more than make up the calories with carbohydrates, which, perhaps not coincidentally, I always craved.

After the health rationale came the animal rights one. Like most vege- 11 tarians, I cracked Peter Singer's philosophical treatise on animal rights, and bought his utilitarian line that if you don't have to kill animals, and it poten- tially causes suffering, you shouldn't do it. (Singer, now at Princeton, has recently come under attack for saying that if a human being's incapacitated life causes more suffering than good, it is OK to kill him.)

It's hard to know where to stop with utilitarianism. Do I need a cashmere 12 sweater more than those little shorn goats need to be warm themselves? Do animals really suffer if they have happy, frolicking lives before a quick and painless end? Won't free-range do?

My animal rights philosophy had a lot of holes from the start. First of all, 13 I excluded fish from the animal kingdom—not only because fish taste deli- cious grilled with a little butter and garlic, but also because they make it a lot easier to be a vegetarian when you go out to restaurants. Now that's utilitarian. Besides, as soon as you start spending your time fretting about the arguments that crowd the inner pens of animal rights philosophy—do fish think?—then you know you're experiencing a real protein deficiency.

I rationalized the fish thing by telling myself I would eat anything I would 14 kill myself. I had been fly-fishing with my dad and figured a few seconds of flopping around was outweighed by the merits of trout almondine. (Notice that I, not the fish, was doing the figuring.) But who was I kidding? If I were hungry enough, I'd kill a cow in a heartbeat. I'd practically kill a cow just for a great pair of shoes.

Which brings me to the leather exception. As long as other people are eat- 15 ing cow, I decided, I might as well recycle the byproducts and diminish the harm by wearing leather jackets and shoes. When everyone stopped eating meat, I'd stop buying leather jackets and shoes. In the meantime, better stock up.

Then there's the environmental rationale. There is no doubt, as Frances 16
Moore Lappe first pointed out in her 1971 book *Food First,* that there is a huge
loss of protein resources going from grain to meat, and that some animals, especially cattle and Americans, use up piggish amounts of water, grain and crop land.

But the problem really isn't meat, 17
but too much meat—over-grazing, over-fishing and over-consumption. If Americans just ate less meat—like driving cars less often—the problem could be alleviated without giving up meat entirely.

> "But the problem really isn't meat, but too much meat."

That approach has worked for centuries, and continues to work in Europe.

All my deep vegetarian questioning was silenced one day when a friend 18
ordered roasted rosemary chicken for two. I thought I'd try "just a bite," and
then I was ripping into it like a starving hyena. Roasted chicken, I realized, is
wonderful. Meat is good.

From a culinary point of view, that's obvious. Consider that most vegetar- 19
ians live in America and England, places tourists do not visit for the food. You
don't find vegetarians in France, and rarely in Italy. Enough said.

As for health, if nutritionists are always telling you to "listen to your body," 20
mine was definitely shouting for more meat. One roasted bird unleashed 15
years' worth of cravings. All of a sudden I felt like I had a bass note playing in
my body to balance out all those soprano carbohydrates. Forget about winning
the low-cholesterol Olympics. For the first time in a long time, I felt satisfied.

As a vegetarian, not only had I denied myself something I truly enjoyed, 21
I had been anti-social. How many times had I made a hostess uncomfortable
by refusing the main course at a dinner party, lamely saying I'd "eat around
it"? How often did my vegetarianism cause other people to go to extra trouble
to make something special for me to eat, and why did it never occur to me
that that was selfish? How about the time, in a small town in Italy, when the
chef had presented me with a plate of very special local sausage, since I was
the American guest—and I had refused it, to the mortification of my Italian
friends? Or when a then-boyfriend, standing in the meat section of the grocery
store, forlornly told a friend, "If only I had a girlfriend who ate meat"? If eating is a socially conscious act, you have to be conscious of the society of your
fellow homo sapiens along with the animals. And we humans, as it happens,
are omnivores.

⊖ READING ARGUMENTS

1. What were some of Fraser's motives for becoming a vegetarian? Why
   does she explain these motives in her essay?

2. In paragraphs 7 and 8, Fraser discusses the health benefits of vegetarianism. How does she use examples from her own life experience to make
   her point?

3. Fraser refers to "utilitarianism" and the "utilitarian" arguments in favor of vegetarianism. What is *utilitarianism*?

4. More than once in her essay, Fraser makes some strong statements in favor of eating meat—for example, "Roasted chicken, I realized, is wonderful. Meat is good" (para. 18). How convincing are such statements? Why does Fraser include them? Should she have used more balanced, less opinionated language? Why or why not?

⊘ AT ISSUE: SHOULD WE EAT MEAT?

1. Near the end of his essay, Foer writes that even people who know all the harmful consequences of eating meat "still aren't inspired to order something else on the menu. Why?" (para. 17). How would you answer this question?

2. Fraser discusses the utilitarian animal rights philosophy of Peter Singer, but then concedes, "It's hard to know where to stop with utilitarianism. Do I need a cashmere sweater more than those little shorn goats need to be warm themselves? Do animals really suffer if they have happy, frolicking lives before a quick and painless end?" (12). How do you answer these questions? What problems of utilitarian arguments do these questions highlight?

3. Foer writes, "Food is not rational. Food is culture, habit, craving, and identity" (18). How does Fraser's experience with vegetarianism support Foer's assertion?

⊘ WRITING ARGUMENTS: SHOULD WE EAT MEAT?

1. Both Fraser and Foer consider the ethics of eating. For example, Fraser writes that, as a "pesco-vegetarian," she would eat anything that she would kill herself (para. 14). Foer examines a number of standards that supposedly guide food choices—for instance, "Don't eat animals with significant mental capacities" (9). He also writes that such rules and taboos say a "great deal about us" (2). Do you have cultural or ethical values that determine what you eat—and what you do not eat? Write an argumentative essay in which you present and defend your values.

2. Write an essay that takes a position on the issue of meat-eating. Should humans eat meat? Why or why not?

DEBATE

Do We Still Need Newspapers?

American newspapers have seen their circulations drop, their advertising revenues plummet, and their profits decline. Thousands of reporters have lost their jobs as publishers have cut back staff in newsrooms and closed foreign bureaus. Although these trends are decades old, they have accelerated in the last two years. The *Seattle Post-Intelligencer*, Seattle's oldest paper, stopped publishing print editions in March 2009 and went entirely online. In April 2009, the New York Times Company, which owns the *Boston Globe*, threatened to close the *Globe* unless that paper could find a way to cut annual labor costs by $20 million. Even the *New York Times*, long considered the paper of record in the United States, has seen its circulation fall sharply. Almost all of the top twenty-five newspapers in the country have experienced similar difficulties, and many smaller papers have gone out of business.

These problems highlight the fact that news is a business. Its history goes back to the early days of the American colonies. Benjamin Franklin, for example, made his name in part as owner and publisher of the *Pennsylvania Gazette*, one of the most successful papers in the colonies. By 1810, there were twenty-seven dailies in the country, and as the century progressed, mass-circulation newspapers became a valuable and profitable industry. But the late nineteenth and early twentieth centuries were the golden age of newspapers, when titans like Joseph Pulitzer and William Randolph Hearst owned hugely popular—and hugely influential—chains of publications such as the *New York World* and the *Seattle Post-Intelligencer*. The industry prospered throughout the twentieth century as large conglomerates like McClatchy and Knight-Ridder bought and operated multiple papers. Daily circulation peaked in 1984—although, despite the recent downturns, most major papers remain profitable.

But newspapers are more than a business. As the playwright Arthur Miller once said, "A good newspaper . . . is a nation talking to itself." If daily and weekly publications have been a lucrative industry, they have also been a medium for national conversations, whether about the American

Revolution, slavery, civil rights, or the war in Afghanistan. Although papers have always been caught up in political partisanship and sensationalism, the ideal of a free press—and the free flow of information that is necessary for citizens of a republic—is enshrined in the First Amendment of the U.S. Constitution. Newspapers help us make political decisions and allow us to keep track of powerful people and institutions, whether in government or in business.

Other media forms also allow citizens to do this, of course. Newspapers have faced competition from radio and television in the past, even as technological advancements such as the telegraph and the Internet actually expanded the possibilities for print publications to gather and present information. For defenders of print, however, newspapers remain relevant because they can provide a depth and breadth of reporting that is difficult to imitate in the image- and sound-bite-driven world of television. Moreover, professional editorial judgment may be more valuable than ever as we are faced with the problem of too much news and information, not too little.

Still, the Web poses a unique threat to newspapers because it siphons off their traditional revenue streams from advertising and classified sections. Paradoxically, then, the Internet provides more access to news content but limits the ability to profit from it. Rather than buying a daily paper, people may simply read news from traditional sources such as the Associated Press online, where it is free.

The two writers in this debate agree that traditional newspapers are facing enormous and perhaps even insurmountable challenges, but their responses to this emerging reality are different. Chris Hedges sees the decline in the newspaper industry in the context of civic life. Gary S. Becker compares television and the Internet with print sources and evaluates their respective capacities to present news, information, and entertainment.

This selection is from the *Pittsburgh Post-Gazette* for July 27, 2008.

REQUIEM FOR REAL NEWS

CHRIS HEDGES

The decline of newspapers is not about the replacement of the antiquated 1
technology of news print with the lightning speed of the Internet. It does not
signal an inevitable and salutary change. It is not a form of progress.

The decline of newspapers is about the rise of the corporate state, the loss 2
of civic and public responsibility on the part of much of our entrepreneurial
class and the intellectual poverty of our post-literate world, a world where
information is conveyed primarily through moving images rather than print.

All these forces have combined to strangle newspapers. And the blood on 3
the floor, this year alone, is disheartening. Some 6,000 journalists nationwide
have lost their jobs, news pages are being radically cut back and newspaper
stocks have tumbled. Advertising revenues are falling off dramatically.
McClatchy Co., publisher of the *Miami Herald*, has seen its shares fall by
77 percent this year. Lee Enterprises Inc., which owns the *St. Louis Post-
Dispatch*, is down 84 percent. Gannett Co., which publishes *USA Today*, is
trading at nearly a 17-year low.

The Internet will not save newspapers. Although all major newspapers, 4
and most smaller ones, have Web sites, they make up less than 10 percent of
newspaper ad revenue. The big advertisers have stayed away, either unsure of
how to use the Internet or suspicious that it can't match the viewer attention
of older media.

Newspapers, when well run, are a public trust. They provide, at their best, 5
the means for citizens to examine themselves, to ferret out lies and the abuse
of power by elected officials and corrupt businesses, to give a voice to those
who would, without the press, have no voice, and to follow, in ways a private
citizen cannot, the daily workings of local, state and federal government.

Newspapers hire people to write about city hall, the state capital, political 6
campaigns, sports, music, art and theater. They keep citizens engaged with
their cultural, civic and political life. When I began as a foreign correspondent 25 years ago, most major city papers had bureaus in Latin America, the
Middle East, Europe, Asia and Moscow. Reporters and photographers showed
Americans how the world beyond our borders looked, thought and believed.
Most of this is vanishing or has vanished.

We live under the happy illusion that we can transfer news gathering to 7
the Internet. News gathering will continue to exist, as it does on sites such as
ProPublica and *Slate*, but journalistic traditions now must contend with a new,
widespread and ideologically driven partisanship that dominates the dissemination of views and information, from Fox News to blogger screeds.

The majority of bloggers and Internet addicts, like the endless rows of 8 talking heads on television, do not report. They are largely parasites who cling to traditional news outlets. They can produce stinging and insightful commentary, but they rarely pick up the phone or go out and find a story. Nearly all reporting is done by newspapers and wire services. Take that away and there's a huge black hole.

Those who rely on the Internet gravitate to sites that reinforce their 9 beliefs. The filtering of information through an ideological lens, which is destroying television journalism, defies the purpose of reporting. Journalism is about transmitting information that doesn't care what you think. Reporting challenges, countermands or destabilizes established beliefs. Reporting, which is time-consuming and often expensive, begins from the premise that there are things we need to know and understand, even if they make us uncomfortable.

If we lose this ethic we are left with pandering, packaging and partisan- 10 ship. We are left awash in a sea of competing propaganda. Bloggers, unlike most established reporters, rarely admit errors. They cannot get fired. Facts, for many bloggers, are interchangeable with opinions. Take a look at the *Drudge Report*. This may be the new face of what we call news.

When the traditional news organizations 11 go belly up we will lose a vast well of expertise and information. Our democracy will suffer a body blow.

> "Our democracy will suffer a body blow."

Not that many will notice. The average 12 time a reader of the *New York Times* spends with the printed paper is about 45 minutes. The average time a viewer spends on the *New York Times* Web site is about seven minutes. There is a difference between browsing and reading. And the Web is built for browsing. When there is a long piece on the Internet, most of us print it out to get through it.

The rise of our corporate state has done the most, however, to decimate 13 traditional news-gathering. Time Warner, Disney, Rupert Murdoch's News Corp., General Electric and Viacom control nearly everything we read, watch, hear and ultimately think. And they think news that does not make a profit is not worth pursuing.

This is why the networks have shut down their foreign bureaus. This is 14 why cable newscasts, with their chatty anchors, all look and sound like the *Today* show. This is why the Federal Communications Commission defines shows like Fox's celebrity gossip program *TMZ* and the Christian Broadcast Network's *700 Club* as "bona fide newscasts."

This is why television news personalities have become celebrities earning, 15 in Katie Couric's case, $15 million a year. This is why newspapers like the *Los Angeles Times* and *Chicago Tribune* are being ruthlessly cannibalized by corporate trolls like Sam Zell, turned into empty husks that focus increasingly on boutique journalism.

Corporations are not in the business of news. They hate real news. Real 16 news makes people ask questions. They prefer to close the prying eyes of reporters. They prefer to transform news into another form of mindless entertainment.

A democracy survives when its citizens have access to trustworthy and 17 impartial sources of information, when it can discern lies from truth. Take this away and a democracy dies.

The fusion of news and entertainment, the rise of a class of celebrity jour- 18 nalists on television who define reporting by their access to the famous and the powerful, the retreat by many readers into the ideological ghettos of the Internet and the ruthless drive by corporations to destroy the traditional news business are leaving us deaf, dumb and blind.

We are cleverly entertained during our descent. We have our own version 19 of ancient Rome's bread and circuses with our elaborate spectacles, sporting events, celebrity gossip and television reality shows. Societies in decline, as the Roman philosopher Cicero wrote, see their civic and political discourse contaminated by the excitement and emotional life of the arena. And the citizens in these degraded societies, he warned, always end up ruled by a despot.

⊘ READING ARGUMENTS

1. What is Hedges's thesis? How does his introductory paragraph set up this thesis?

2. Whom does Hedges blame for the declining influence of newspapers? Why? Can you suggest another explanation?

3. Hedges states that newspapers are a "public trust" (para. 5). What does he mean? What role does he believe newspapers should play in democratic societies?

4. Hedges argues that without trustworthy, impartial reporting, we will be "left awash in a sea of competing propaganda" (10). What does he mean by "competing propaganda"?

5. At the end of his essay, Hedges quotes the ancient Roman philosopher and statesman Cicero. How effective is this reference, both as support for his argument and as a conclusion?

This piece is from a June 29, 2008, posting of the Becker-Posner Blog, located at Becker-Posner-Blog.com.

YES, NEWSPAPERS ARE DOOMED

GARY S. BECKER

The number of general-purpose newspapers has been declining in cities 1
ever since the growth of television, and the decline accelerated after the
Internet was developed. The trend
downward will continue, and perhaps
even accelerate. I do not see much of
a future for the general-purpose hard
copy newspaper that combines opinions,
sports, advertisements, comics, and
information.

> "The trend downward will continue, and perhaps even accelerate."

A telling fact is that young people today do not read general newspapers, 2
whereas they did in the past. When I was a boy my father bought at least five
newspapers every day, and I "read" (that is, looked mainly at sports and comics) three or four of them. It is now rare to see anyone under age 30 reading the
New York Times, *Chicago Tribune*, or any other major newspaper. A teacher
used to be bothered when bored students started reading newspapers in class.
That is no longer a problem since they now turn to their computers and play
video games or email friends.

I find it hard to reconcile the rapid decline in the number of newspapers 3
with Posner's data suggesting that newspapers are quite profitable. Declining
industries, such as the American automobile industry, have always been associated not with profits but with substantial losses, as is happening to Ford, General
Motors, and Chrysler. There is no doubt that the many newspapers which went
out of business did so because they were losing money. Of course, the surviving
newspapers tend to be the ones that are more profitable, but they too are experiencing financial problems. They are cutting staffs, long-term owners are selling
their papers to others—as with the *Wall Street Journal* and *Chicago Tribune*—
and they are trying various approaches to deal with the tough competition from
online advertisements and other online services.

The Internet has gravely wounded the newspaper industry because it 4
provides information, opinion, and entertainment more frequently and effectively than newspapers do. The Web offers as much sports news as desired,
and presents the progress of baseball and other sporting in real time. The
weather is updated every hour, or more frequently, and so are stock market
quotes. Online ads give pictures and personal information about individuals
looking for jobs, and prices and other characteristics of products offered for
sale. Major as well as minor news stories, local and general news, and opinions
on numerous issues are continually being presented.

A case still made for good newspapers and magazines is that they separate 5 facts from opinions, and do enough checking to stand behind the materials presented as facts. I do not know of anything comparable on the Internet, although the reputations of better-known bloggers do rise and fall with changing perceptions about their insights and accuracy. Yet it is not apparent that the demand is very strong for this dimension of what newspapers have traditionally provided.

Newspapers are trying to strengthen their survival prospects by expanding 6 online presentations, and combining these with print editions. In the short run this may help them, which explains why all the major newspapers are moving aggressively to expand online materials, and widen their online customer base. However, I do not believe this approach will succeed in the long run. The reason is that the way newspapers bundle different services is not the right approach to online presentations that usually provide information about the weather on websites that are different from those used to discuss sports or present ads for cars. Some online sites specialize in opinions about domestic politics, others discuss religion, some present pornographic pictures and films, while others focus on economic issues. The traditional newspaper does not readily fit into this format, and so they are generally losing money in their online efforts.

This does not imply that online presentations in the future will continue 7 to be organized in the same way as at present. Perhaps the growing tendency for some websites to link to other sites will coalesce into organized multi-site presentations that deal with many different topics. Already some subscriber-based sites collect and present the best blogs on different topics. How that will evolve is not clear to me, but it is unlikely to develop into anything that looks like the conventional newspaper that has bundled news, information, and advertisements for hundreds of years.

The rapid and continuing decline in the number of major newspapers 8 will be regretted mainly by older persons who are accustomed to reading several newspapers daily—my wife and I still subscribe to four and read others online. However, by voting with how they use their time, the great majority of consumers clearly have shown that they prefer to get their information, entertainment, and opinions from television, and especially from the Internet, than from newspapers.

⮑ READING ARGUMENTS

1. Becker argues that newspapers are "doomed." What evidence does he provide to support his position?

2. In paragraph 4, Becker asserts that the Internet "has gravely wounded the newspaper industry" even more than television harmed it in the past. Why is the Internet such a threat to hard-copy newspapers?

3. According to Becker, good newspapers and magazines check facts and also separate fact from opinion. However, he suggests that the demand for such standards of accuracy is weaker on the Internet. Why do you think that might be the case?

4. According to Becker, what steps are newspapers taking to survive? Why doesn't he believe this approach will be successful?

⊘ AT ISSUE: DO WE STILL NEED NEWSPAPERS?

1. Thomas Jefferson once said, "Were it left to me to decide whether we should have a government without newspapers or newspapers without a government, I should not hesitate to prefer the latter." Do you agree with this statement? What point do you think Jefferson was trying to make about the importance of the press?

2. According to Hedges, "journalism is about transmitting information that doesn't care what you think," and good reporting must "begin with the premise that there are things we need to know and understand, even if they make us uncomfortable" (para. 11). Why does Hedges believe that such information is necessary? Where do you look for this kind of information? Can you think of an example of this kind of reporting?

3. What problems—if any—do you see with the news media in the United States? Do you think there are too many news outlets? Too few? Do you think that ideological biases and sensationalism are serious problems?

⊘ WRITING ARGUMENTS: DO WE STILL NEED NEWSPAPERS?

According to Becker, the "rapid and continuing decline" of major print newspapers will be regretted mainly by older people because younger consumers will get their news elsewhere. Do you think he is correct? What is your own view of the decline of newspapers? Do you think newspapers are necessary, or do you think that other media forms can fill the role that newspapers have traditionally played?

What Should Be Done about Our Nation's Homeless?

According to the National Alliance to End Homelessness, an estimated 1.5 million people will become homeless over the next two years due to the country's economic downturn. They will join the 2.5 to 3.5 million individuals, including 600,000 families, who live on the streets or in shelters at some point over the course of a given year. While some see *homeless person* as a euphemism for harsher terms such as *bum* or *derelict,* the label actually has a legal definition, provided in the 1987 Stewart B. McKinney Homeless Assistance Act. The meaning encompasses a range of people and circumstances, from inhabitants of temporary homeless shelters to those who are discharged from mental institutions and have no place to go. Generally, homeless people are categorized as the *economic* homeless (who are temporarily without a residence because of specific hardships, such as the loss of a job or an eviction) and the *chronic* homeless (who often suffer from mental illness, alcoholism, and addiction and who spend long periods of time living on the street).

Over the years, the United States has dealt with homelessness in a variety of ways. Beginning in the Colonial era, locally operated and charity- or tax-supported almshouses (or poorhouses) were common. Usually, such "county homes" were catch-all facilities that made no distinction among people with mental or physical disabilities, abandoned children, criminals, vagrants, and the elderly. Many of these places were poorly managed and unsanitary. As the nineteenth century progressed, states passed laws regulating the poorhouse system. Hospitals and institutions removed mentally ill patients; children were prohibited from living in poorhouses and transferred to orphanages.

The modern social safety net—Social Security, workers' compensation, unemployment insurance—emerged in the twentieth century. These provisions (and others) were a response to a sharp increase in homelessness after the Great Depression of the 1930s. Thousands all over the country lived in so-called Hoovervilles, shantytowns named after President Herbert Hoover, and these camps became an enduring image of Depression-era hardship and homelessness. Other famous images from the first half of the twentieth century include the footloose hobo, Charlie Chaplin's famous "little tramp" character, and the Joad family in John Steinbeck's 1939 novel *The Grapes of Wrath*.

Today, many people disagree about the causes of and solutions for homelessness as well as about who is responsible for solving the problem. Should private charities and public institutions distinguish between the "worthy poor," who cannot help their circumstances, and the "unworthy poor," who (some argue) choose to be homeless? What obligations do state and federal governments have toward the homeless? Do readily available public services and lax vagrancy laws do harm as well as good?

The two writers in this section have different responses to these questions—and different assumptions about the nature of homelessness, as well. In "Throw the Bums Out: But Do So with Compassion—Coolidge-Style Compassion," John Derbyshire focuses on the chronically homeless in San Francisco and that city's attempts to manage them. In "The Meanest Cities," the editors of *America* (a national Catholic weekly magazine published by the Jesuit order) emphasize the "meanness" of some practical approaches to the problem.

This piece is from *National Review*, November 15, 2008.

THROW THE BUMS OUT: BUT DO SO WITH COMPASSION—COOLIDGE-STYLE COMPASSION

JOHN DERBYSHIRE

On a recent business trip to San Francisco I decided to take a look at the new 1
Asian Art Museum, which is in the old municipal library building, on one side
of the downtown Civic Center Plaza. The museum is very impressive; but in
making my way to it on foot across the downtown area, I acquired impressions
of a different kind, which affected other senses beside the visual. I encountered
San Francisco's appalling vagrancy problem.

It is in the downtown area that the problem is most obvious. I have never 2
seen so many street people in one place. Crossing the plaza to the museum I
found myself weaving my way through pla-
toons, companies, battalions of them. Here
a ragged, emaciated woman mumbling to
herself and making complicated hand gestures like a Buddhist priest; there a huge
black-bearded Rasputin of a man in a floor-
length heavy overcoat, pushing a shopping
cart piled high with filthy bundles; across
the way a little knot of florid winos arguing loudly and ferociously about something; sitting on the sidewalk where I passed, a youngish black woman, gaunt
and nearly bald, with some sort of horrid skin disease all over her face and scalp,
croaking something at me I couldn't understand.

> "I found myself weaving
> my way through
> platoons, companies,
> battalions of them."

As I said, the Asian Art Museum is housed in the old municipal library. 3
There is a $10 door fee, so the vagrants do not enter. On the other side of the
plaza, however, is a spiffy new library, built at a cost of $137 million. It has
practically been colonized by the street people. Defying the best efforts of a
state-of-the-art air-conditioning system, the tang of unwashed bodies pervades
the place. One row of computers (like all modern libraries, the new San Francisco municipal is long on computers and short on books—Nicholson Baker
has written very angrily about this) is occupied entirely by vagrants watching
DVD movies. One of them has his feet, clad in filthy sneakers, up on the desk. I
got chatting with a security guard, a fellow in the last weary stages of cynicism.

He took me to the security office and showed me their "gallery"—an entire 4
wall covered with polaroid snapshots of library patrons apprehended for various offenses. The snapshots were arranged by offense category, each category
tagged with a three-digit police code. The guard interpreted the codes for me.
"These are the assaults . . . here you have the substance abusers . . . these here

were defacing the books . . ." I pointed to a block of 40 or 50 photographs he'd missed. What had their offense been? "Oh, those are the masturbators."

A block east of the museum is U.N. Plaza, boasting a modern-style fountain—a sprawling arrangement of granite slabs and water jets, designed by a world-famous architect. This has naturally proved irresistible to the armies of vagrants. For years they urinated, defecated, and discarded drug paraphernalia there—the last to such a degree that the water was dangerous with chemical contaminants, even if you could bring yourself to ignore the waste products. The city's Department of Public Works used to conduct a daily clean-up. Early this year, though, they decided that the cost was more than could be justified. In March, a chain-link fence was erected around the whole thing, in the teeth of, it goes without saying, vehement protests from "advocates for the homeless." (The word *homeless* is the current euphemism for *vagrants*, publicized by activist New York attorney Robert Hayes in the early 1980s.)

It is not too hard to figure out why San Francisco has so many vagrants. Indigent adults receive cash payments of $320 to $395 a month, with only a nominal work requirement for the able-bodied. Supplemented by a little panhandling, this is a tidy sum in the agreeable Northern California climate. When I wrote about the situation on this magazine's website, I got e-mails from people in neighboring towns and counties saying: "Please don't write about this. We're happy with things just as they are. San Francisco takes in all our homeless people, so we're spared the problem . . ."

Naturally this logic is lost on the city's irredeemably liberal Board of Supervisors and their soulmates in the local press. One of the latter, Ilene Lelchuk of the *San Francisco Chronicle*, recently began a sentence thus: "With San Francisco's homeless population growing despite the millions of dollars the city spends annually to help its most desperate residents . . ." Note that word *despite*. We spend more and more on the homeless, and still their numbers increase. How can this be? What a strange and wonderful thing is the liberal mind! (Recall the similarly clueless *New York Times* headline: "Crime Keeps on Falling, but Prisons Keep on Filling.")

By last year the situation had already got so bad that city voters were presented with a November ballot initiative, Proposition N, under whose terms that $395 monthly cash handout would be reduced to $59, the balance being replaced by city-provided food and shelter. This "Care Not Cash" initiative was passed, with 60 percent of voters in favor. That of course outraged the city's left-wing activists, who immediately challenged the vote in court. On May 8 Superior Court judge Ronald Quidachay ruled that only the Board of Supervisors can set city welfare policy, and that the ballot initiative was therefore invalid. The hundred-dollar-a-week handouts to anyone who shows up will continue—in a city that is looking at a $350 million deficit this year.

The United States of America was founded on the notion of self-support, of people taking care of their families, joining with neighbors to solve common problems in a humane and sensible way. Those common problems would include the occasional citizen, like Huckleberry Finn's pap, who could not, or stubbornly would not, look after himself, and for whom some public provision should be made. When a person "came upon the town," the town would give him some minimal aid, while of course private citizens, if they felt inclined, could exercise the virtue of private charity to any degree they wished. The recipient was, however, expected to defer to community standards. If he persistently committed gross violations of those standards—relieving himself in the town fountain would certainly have counted—he was locked up or institutionalized.

This was a sound system, widely admired outside our borders. Listen to 10 the most American of American presidents, Calvin Coolidge: "The principle of service is not to be confused with a weak and impractical sentimentalism." "Self-government means self support." "The normal must care for themselves."

There was nothing callous about this attitude. Everyone understood 11 that the feeble-minded and insane needed special care in state institutions. (The famously parsimonious Coolidge made a speech in 1916, when he was lieutenant governor of Massachusetts, defending the robust state funding of insane asylums.) Our present age, for all its humanitarian cant, is much crueler. Nationwide, 39 percent of vagrants have some diagnosable mental-health problem—victims, for the most part, of the deinstitutionalization that began after the 1963 Community Mental Health Centers Act.

Crueler, and also more careless of the dignity and independence of the 12 individual. That applies not only to the individual vagrant, but to the self-supporting citizen, too. As you cross Civic Center Plaza they leer at you, yell at you, sometimes harass you. If you are a woman, they make lewd remarks at you. All this we are supposed to put up with in the name of "compassion" and "rights." And put up with it we do! Why?

⊙ READING ARGUMENTS

1. According to Derbyshire, the word *"homeless* is the current euphemism for *vagrants"* (para. 5). What is a euphemism? In what sense is *homeless* a euphemism? What other terms might be used to refer to this population? What connotations does each of these terms have?

2. Derbyshire refers to a fictional character from the nineteenth-century novel *The Adventures of Huckleberry Finn* to show how Americans traditionally dealt with homeless people (9). Do you find this reference effective? Why or why not?

3. Restate the thesis of Derbyshire's essay in your own words.

4. Derbyshire argues that despite all of our "humanitarian cant" (11), our current approach to homelessness is "much crueler" than the approaches of the past. What evidence does he provide to support this statement? What do you think he means by "humanitarian cant"?

This editorial is from the March 6, 2006, issue of *America,* a national Catholic weekly magazine.

THE MEANEST CITIES

AMERICA

Cities vary in their responses to the needs of their homeless populations. 1
Some are very mean indeed as the numbers of homeless people continue to
rise. Take Sarasota, Fla. After state courts overturned two successive anti-
lodging laws as applied to public spaces, the city persisted and this past
summer passed a third ordinance that makes it a crime to sleep without
permission on city property. One requirement for arrest under this new
statute is that a homeless person, on being awakened by police, state that he
or she has no other place to live.

Sarasota tops the list of the 20 meanest cities in a new report by two 2
advocacy groups that have carefully documented a dark phenomenon affecting the growing homeless population—namely, making homelessness a
crime. Released by the National Law Center on Homelessness and Poverty
and the National Coalition for the Homeless, the report is called *A Dream
Denied: The Criminalization of Homelessness in U.S. Cities.* It tracks a trend
toward criminalizing such activities as sitting,
eating or sleeping in public spaces by making them violations of local ordinances. And
violations of this kind may in turn lead to a
criminal record, which makes it still more
difficult for homeless people to find employment or housing. Since a large percentage of
the homeless are mentally ill, these criminal-
izing measures take on an extra edge of cruelty. And yet, one nine-city survey
notes that the cost of holding a person in jail can be three times the cost of
supportive housing.

> "Criminalizing such activities as sitting, eating or sleeping in public spaces."

Statutes in some cities even go so far as to restrict charitable organiza- 3
tions from providing food to poor people in public spaces, with threats of fines
up to $2,000. Many groups that perform this ministry are church related and
view their work as a concrete response to the biblical call to feed the hungry.
Fortunately, as the report notes, in a number of localities "courts have found
restrictions on feedings an unconstitutional burden on religious expression."
Thus Atlanta, which ranks fourth on the list of meanest cities, was forced to
rescind its anti-food-serving measure after it was challenged by a local advocacy group.

But others of Atlanta's onerous restrictions remain, especially in the so- 4
called tourist triangle. A bill passed in August, for example, makes begging illegal there—an area, ironically, near the Martin Luther King Center, where King
and his wife, Coretta Scott King, were buried. This ban, a common type, raises

freedom of speech issues that have prompted the American Civil Liberties Union to initiate a lawsuit. Nationwide, there has been a 12-percent increase in ordinances that prohibit begging in public places. More neutral prohibitions, like those against loitering, are selectively enforced.

Also high on the list of mean cities is Lawrence, Kan. Downtown business 5 leaders urged the city council to pass ordinances targeting homeless persons, and the city responded with a number of "civility ordinances," including one that restricts sitting on sidewalks. Bus stations, too, in some localities, draw negative police activity. In Little Rock, Ark., homeless people have reported being ejected from bus stations even after showing officers their valid bus tickets.

Happily, other localities have taken a more positive approach in dealing 6 with their homeless populations, using what the report calls "constructive alternatives to criminalization." Among them is Broward County, Fla. There, the nonprofit Task Force for Ending Homelessness has partnered with the Fort Lauderdale police to form outreach teams composed of police officers and civil partners. The teams' role is to inform chronically homeless individuals of available social services, encouraging them to make use of these services. It is understood that frequent return visits may be needed before sufficient trust between homeless persons and team members can be established. The teams also partner with local shelters to ensure access to available beds. Since the program began five years ago, it is estimated that there have been 2,400 fewer arrests annually. Similarly positive approaches have been taken in San Diego, Calif., and in Washington, D.C., as well as in several cities in Pennsylvania.

Instead of criminalizing homelessness, greater efforts should be made 7 nationwide to help people move out of this condition, or—better yet—to help them avoid falling into it in the first place. Among the ways to do this would be increasing the supply of transitional and low income housing, making substance abuse and mental health treatment programs more available and raising minimum wage levels throughout the country. Efforts in these directions would address the main causes of homelessness. The current budget cuts in programs that help the poor, along with the proliferation of ordinances that criminalize homeless people, are the wrong way to go.

⊙ READING ARGUMENTS

1. What is the thesis of "The Meanest Cities"? How would the editorial's impact be different if this thesis were stated earlier?

2. What is the "dark phenomenon affecting the growing homeless population" (para. 2)? According to the editorial, what are some of the negative consequences of this "dark phenomenon"?

3. Who is the intended audience for this editorial? How can you tell?

⊖ AT ISSUE: WHAT SHOULD BE DONE ABOUT OUR NATION'S HOMELESS?

1. Both Derbyshire and the editors of *America* are writing about the problem of homelessness. Whose approach seems more ethical? Whose seems more practical?

2. The editors of *America* suggest that government intervention in the homeless problem—whether in the form of more low-income housing, more social services, or a raise in the minimum-wage levels throughout the country—would be helpful. Derbyshire, in contrast, quotes President Calvin Coolidge: "Self-government means self support" (para. 10). What obligation, if any, do you think governments (city, state, and federal) have to help the homeless?

3. The *America* editorial notes that the city of Atlanta has passed a law making begging illegal in major tourist areas. Do you think begging should ever be illegal? If so, under what circumstances? If not, why not?

⊖ WRITING ARGUMENTS: WHAT SHOULD BE DONE ABOUT OUR NATION'S HOMELESS?

How do you view the homeless in your community or city? What kinds of solutions do you think would work best to reduce homelessness?

Should the U.S. Government Drop Its Sanctions against Cuba?

Since 1962, the United States has imposed a Cuban embargo. This policy prohibits trade between the United States and Cuba although it allows food and medicine to be shipped to Cuba from the United States. Additionally, Treasury Department regulations limit the rights of American citizens to travel in Cuba. The embargo officially became law with the 1992 Cuba Democracy Act and the 1996 Helms-Burton Act. The policy is now the longest-standing trade embargo in modern history. (Since taking office, the administration of Barack Obama has loosened travel restrictions for Cuban American citizens, but other economic restrictions remain in force.)

The history of the embargo reflects both international cold war realities and domestic politics within the United States. Fidel Castro assumed control of Cuba in 1959 after his revolutionary forces ousted President Fulgencio Batista. When Castro's government confiscated private property and attempted to institute revolutionary communism, hundreds of thousands of Cubans—stripped of their assets and property—left for the United States. Cuba became an ally of the Soviet Union, leading President John F. Kennedy and the U.S. government to increase restrictions (especially after the Cuban missile crisis). Inside the United States, especially in Florida, numerous Cuban Americans—including exiles and members of exile families—have supported the embargo as a way of delegitimizing the Cuban government, punishing Castro, and possibly hastening the end of his rule.

Although Cuba is free to trade with other countries, the Castro regime has viewed the United States embargo as a blockade and has blamed the policy for the country's economic problems. Supporters of the embargo often see it (in the words of Florida Congressman Lincoln Diaz-Balart) as serving the "cause of freedom in Cuba." Opponents—including most of the members of the United Nations General Assembly—see the policy as an outdated relic of the cold war. In fact, some international and domestic observers worry that the embargo has actually helped the Cuban government hold power over the years.

In his argument against a House of Representatives amendment to lift the Cuban embargo, Lincoln Diaz-Balart views the policy in light of the Organization of American States, a coalition of North, Central, and South American countries whose charter recognizes only representative democracies as legal. In "Thanks for the Sanctions," Jacob Weisberg considers the failures and unintended consequences of the Cuban embargo—and of other attempts by the United States to use sanctions to effect international political change.

Florida Congressman Diaz-Balart spoke on the floor of the U.S. House of Representatives on September 22, 2004.

OPPOSITION TO REP. RANGEL'S AMENDMENT TO LIFT EMBARGO ON CUBAN REGIME

LINCOLN DIAZ-BALART

Mr. Chairman, I rise in opposition to the amendment, and I yield myself 1 such time as I may consume.

A year ago, I was in New York, and I read a newspaper there, the daily 2 called *La Prensa*, and there was an interview with the gentleman from New York, the author of this amendment. It related to the summary executions that had just taken place by Castro of three young black men just a few days before, after they had been arrested by the dictatorship for the crime of trying to come to the United States.

I quote from the gentleman from New York (Mr. Rangel) a little over 3 a year ago: "I am shocked. There is nothing that the Cuban government can tell me that would interest me and that would convince me to speak to them again. It is totally incredible that a government would justify this type of action. The execution of these people puts an end to any possible discussion that there could have been with the Cuban government."

Now, I wish, Mr. Chairman, that I could say that there has been some 4 justice for those summary executions, the murders of those three young men. I wish I could say that the dictator at least had apologized to the grieving family members for their murders.

No, there has been no justice, only increased repression. I showed last 5 night a replica of the punishment box for the best known political prisoner, a physician, Dr. Biscet, who is being held today because he believes in freedom and democracy. After this amendment, I certainly will always recall that it is more important when one truly wants to understand someone to guide oneself by what that person does rather than by what he says.

> "No, there has been no justice, only increased repression."

This, as the gentleman has just stated, is the "normalization of rela- 6 tions" amendment, the "normalization of relations with the Cuban dictatorship" amendment.

Now, the charter of the OAS makes clear that in this hemisphere, only 7 representative democracy is legal, legitimate, and the democratic charter of just 3 years ago says that any interruption in the democratic process in this hemisphere needs to be sanctioned. But this amendment says: you can ban elections for 45 years. You can crush labor unions and crush the free press and eliminate and prohibit all political parties and freedom of expression and execute people, including three young black men just a year ago for trying to get to freedom, and imprison them and torture them. And you can kill Americans, and you can harbor terrorists. And you can harbor fugitives from U.S. justice, including cop killers from our States here.

You can do all of that. And you will get an amendment that says let us 8 normalize relations. You can continue to harbor terrorists, and you can continue to harbor U.S. felony fugitives who murder U.S. citizens and spy on the United States and disrupt antiterrorism operations. We will still normalize with you. That is what this amendment is.

So it is very good that this amendment is on the floor today because 9 this is, after all, the debate about economic interests and debate about the coalition of forces that have advocated for the last years for normalization. This is an important debate for our colleagues to express themselves on. After 45 years of illegal oppression in this hemisphere, the hemisphere that is the only one where its international law requires representative democracy, and great strides have been made in recent decades towards compliance with that legal international law requirement.

This amendment says, no, in the Western Hemisphere it is all right to 10 oppress for 45 years and murder and execute and torture and spy on Americans and harbor fugitives and harbor international terrorists and disrupt the U.S. international war on terrorism. It is all right. We will reward you. We will normalize, we will grant you billions of dollars unilaterally without the dictatorship having to release any political prisoners or move towards freedom for its people. We will reward you unilaterally anyway.

I would ask this Congress of the United States that I hold with such 11 reverence to stand with the Cuban people today and to reject this amendment that simply seeks to reward oppression and reward infamy.

⊘ READING ARGUMENTS

1. Diaz-Balart offers a harsh assessment of the Cuban government, referring explicitly to its authoritarianism, repression, and use of torture. In what sense, if any, is his speech an ethical argument?

2. Restate Diaz-Balart's thesis in your own words.

3. In paragraph 3, Diaz-Balart quotes U.S. Representative Charles Rangel, whose amendment he is speaking against. How does he use Rangel's words to support his own argument? Do you consider Diaz-Balart's argument a refutation? Explain.

4. In his closing paragraph, Diaz-Balart states that he wishes to "stand with the Cuban people today." How is this statement related to his argument as a whole?

This article is from the August 2, 2006, issue of the online magazine *Slate*.

THANKS FOR THE SANCTIONS

JACOB WEISBERG

When trying to rein in the misbehavior of roguish regimes, be it nuclear proliferation, support for terrorism, or internal repression, the United States increasingly turns to a policy of economic sanctions. 1

A quick survey: We began our economic embargo against *North Korea* in 1950. We've had one against *Cuba* since 1962. We first applied economic sanctions to *Iran* during the hostage crisis in 1979 and are currently trying for international sanctions aimed at getting the government there to suspend uranium enrichment. We attached trade sanctions to *Burma* beginning in 1990 and froze the assets of *Sudan* beginning in 1997. President Bush ordered sanctions against *Zimbabwe* in 2003 and against *Syria* beginning in 2004. We have also led major international sanctions campaigns against regimes since brought down by force of arms: Milosevic's *Yugoslavia*, Saddam's *Iraq*, and Taliban *Afghanistan*. 2

America's sanctions policy is largely consistent, and in a certain sense, admirable. By applying economic restraints, we label the most oppressive and dangerous governments in the world pariahs. We wash our hands of evil, declining to help despots finance their depredations, even at a cost to ourselves of some economic growth. We wincingly accept the collateral damage that falls on civilian populations in the nations we target. But as the above list of countries suggests, sanctions have one serious drawback. They don't work. Though there are some debatable exceptions, sanctions rarely play a significant role in dislodging or constraining the behavior of despicable regimes. 3

> "Sanctions have one serious drawback. They don't work."

Sanctions tend to fail as a diplomatic tool for the same reason aerial bombing usually fails. As Israel is again discovering in Lebanon, the infliction of indiscriminate suffering tends to turn a populace against the proximate cause of its devastation, not the underlying causes. People who live in hermit states like North Korea, Burma, and Cuba already suffer from global isolation. Fed on a diet of propaganda, they don't know what's happening inside their borders or outside of them. By increasing their seclusion, sanctions make it easier for dictators to blame external enemies for a country's suffering. And because sanctions make a country's material deprivation significantly worse, they paradoxically make it less likely that the oppressed will throw off their chains. 4

Tyrants seem to understand how to capitalize on the law of unintended consequences. In many cases, as in Iraq under the oil-for-food program, 5 sanctions themselves afford opportunities for plunder and corruption that can help clever despots shore up their position. Some dictators also thrive on the political loneliness we inflict and in some cases appear to seek more of it from us. The pariah treatment suits Bashar Assad, Kim Jong-il, Robert Mugabe, and SLORC just fine. Fidel Castro is another dictator who has flourished in isolation. Every time the United States considers lifting its embargo, Castro unleashes a provocation designed to ensure that we don't normalize relations. It was a disappointment, but no surprise, to learn that the Cuban dictator was in "stable" condition after surgery this week. With our help, Castro has been in stable condition for 47 years.

Constructive engagement, which often sounds like lame cover for 6 business interests, tends to lead to better outcomes than sanctions. Trade prompts economic growth and human interaction, which raises a society's expectations, which in turn prompts political dissatisfaction and opposition. Trade, tourism, cultural exchange, and participation in international institutions all serve to erode the legitimacy of repressive regimes. Though each is a separate case, these forces contributed greatly to undermining dictatorships and fostering democracy in the Philippines, South Korea, Argentina, Chile, and Eastern Europe in the 1980s. The same process is arguably under way in China. Contact also makes us less clueless about the countries we want to change. It is hard to imagine we would have misunderstood the religious and ethnic conflicts in Iraq the way we have if our embassy had been open and American companies had been doing business there for the past 15 years.

As another illustration, take Iran, which is currently the focus of a 7 huge how-do-we-get-them-to-change conversation. Despite decades of sanctions, Iran is full of young people who are culturally attuned to the United States. One day, social discontent there will lead to the reform or overthrow of the ruling theocracy. But there is little reason to think that more sanctions will bring that day any closer. The more likely effect of a comprehensive sanctions regime is that it will push dissatisfied and potentially rebellious Iranians back into the arms of the nuke-building mullahs.

The counterexample always cited is South Africa, where economic and 8 cultural sanctions do seem to have contributed not only to the fall of a terrible regime but to a successful democratic transition. In his new book *The J Curve*, Ian Bremmer argues that South Africa was unusually amenable to this kind of pressure because it retained a functioning multiparty democracy and because, unlike many other pariah states, it didn't actually like being a pariah. Even so, sanctions took a very long time to have any impact. It was nearly three decades from the passage of the first U.N. resolution urging sanctions in 1962 to Nelson Mandela's release from prison in 1990.

If they are so rarely effective, why are Western governments pressing for sanctions more and more often? In a world of trouble, it is partly 9 an exercise in frustration. We often have no good options and need to feel that we're doing something. Sanctions are a palatable alternative to military action and often serve to appease domestic constituencies as well. But we need to learn that tyrants respond more to a deep survival instinct than to economic incentives. To understand their behavior, you can't just read Adam Smith. You need Charles Darwin.

⊘ READING ARGUMENTS

1. How does Weisberg use inductive reasoning to make his argument?

2. Weisberg surveys several decades of U.S. sanctions against various regimes. In what respects is this essay an argument by evaluation? In what respects is it a proposal argument?

3. According to Weisberg, repressive rulers "seem to understand how to capitalize on the law of unintended consequences" (para. 5). What does he mean, and how does he support this statement?

4. Where does Weisberg take opposing viewpoints into consideration? How does he address these opposing arguments?

⊘ AT ISSUE: SHOULD THE U.S. GOVERNMENT DROP ITS SANCTIONS AGAINST CUBA?

1. Weisberg's essay highlights the practical ineffectiveness of sanctions, while Diaz-Balart is more concerned with the ethical necessity of keeping sanctions against Cuba in place. Which of these approaches seems the most persuasive?

2. Diaz-Balart claims that "great strides have been made" (para. 9) in this hemisphere toward establishing representative democracies. Similarly, Weisberg refers to the ongoing "how-do-we-get-them-to-change conversation" (7) with regard to tyrannical regimes. Do you think the United States has the right (or even an obligation) to change other governments in the Western hemisphere and outside of it? Why or why not?

3. Weisberg refers to the "collateral damage" (3) to civilian populations that is caused by sanctions. What does "collateral damage" mean in this context? Do you think the United States bears moral responsibility for such damage? Why or why not?

⊘ WRITING ARGUMENTS: SHOULD THE U.S. GOVERNMENT DROP ITS SANCTIONS AGAINST CUBA?

After reading these two arguments, write an essay that proposes a policy for U.S. relations with Cuba.

Should Undocumented Immigrants Be Entitled to Driver's Licenses?

Few subjects arouse as much political passion in the United States as illegal immigration. According to recent estimates, close to 12 million illegal immigrants are now in the country, which amounts to about 4% of the population. (Undocumented workers make up 5.4% of the nation's workforce.)

Although America is a nation of immigrants, the country has historically shown ambivalence toward immigration—even legal immigration. For example, some American nativists opposed the large influx of Irish Catholics in the nineteenth century. The waves of Italians, Eastern European Jews, and others who arrived in America during the early years of the twentieth century also raised concerns about America's social, ethnic, and cultural identity. Yet many Americans have also seen the country's immigrants as a powerful source of strength, renewal, and national pride. After all, the Statue of Liberty is famously engraved with a poem that reads, in part, "Give me your tired, your poor, / Your huddled masses yearning to breathe free."

The most recent controversies focus on the status of illegal immigrants and raise issues of law, economics, cultural and national identity, and national security. For example, many people worry that undocumented and illegal immigrants take jobs and government resources and services that should be reserved for legal residents. At the same time, most Americans understand that arresting and deporting 11.9 million people is unrealistic. Moreover, these undocumented workers play a significant role in the American economy, and as a practical matter, most of them are here to stay. If you accept this reasoning, what rights and privileges should they have?

At the moment, Hawaii, Maryland, New Mexico, Utah, and Washington State allow illegal immigrants to obtain drivers' licenses (although Maryland plans to end the practice in 2015). In other states, including California and Wisconsin, lawmakers have raised the issue in their state legislatures. Understandably, many Americans oppose these policies because they appear to reward lawless behavior and exacerbate the problem of illegal immigration. But the large number of undocumented residents currently driving without licenses—and without auto insurance—causes many problems, as noted in the National Immigration Law Center's fact sheet. In his testimony before the Maryland state legislature, Michael W. Cutler argues against the practice of allowing illegal immigrants to obtain licenses. The National Immigration Law Center, on the other hand, contends that granting licenses is the wisest and most practical solution to the problems this organization identifies.

This document is from the Web site of the National Immigration Law Center, an organization whose mission is to advocate for the rights of low-income immigrants.

FACT SHEET: WHY DENYING DRIVER'S LICENSES TO UNDOCUMENTED IMMIGRANTS HARMS PUBLIC SAFETY AND MAKES OUR COMMUNITIES LESS SECURE

NATIONAL IMMIGRATION LAW CENTER

The question of whether undocumented immigrants should obtain driver's 1 licenses has been hotly debated in almost every state in the country. But the debate has been a distraction from the real issues that states face in promoting public safety and protecting their communities. States need to create practical, workable solutions, and denying undocumented immigrants licenses is simply bad public policy. It increases uninsurance rates and the number of unlicensed drivers, and it undermines effective law enforcement.

Driver's License Restrictions Won't Fix Our Broken Immigration System.

- Approximately 12 million undocumented immigrants currently live in 2 the U.S. For the most part, these immigrants don't live alone, but with family members who either are U.S. citizens or otherwise authorized to be in the U.S. For the most part, they also are employed, supporting their families and paying U.S. taxes.

- Our immigration system is broken and needs to be fixed, but driver's 3 license restrictions are not the answer. Immigrants do not come to this country to get a driver's license, and they will not leave because they are ineligible for one.

- Congress must act to pass a comprehensive legalization bill that brings 4 undocumented immigrants out of the shadows. In the meantime, states must pass responsible policies that protect everyone's public safety.

State Policymakers Need to Deal with Realistic Solutions, Not Sound Bites and Partisan Politics.

- State policymakers can either ignore reality and offer public policy that 5 flies in its face, or can acknowledge reality and implement a policy that works. Until Congress reforms our immigration system, undocumented immigrants will remain here, and those immigrants who need to drive for work or to transport their children will do so.

■ In defending a 2003 law that granted driver's licenses to all qualified New   6
Mexico residents, Governor Bill Richardson stated, "We're dealing with
a problem, rather than being ideologically senseless. This is a reality in
border states."[1]

■ In supporting a bill that granted driver's licenses to undocumented immi-   7
grants, former Florida governor Jeb Bush stated in 2004, "[O]nce [undoc-
umented immigrants are] here, what do you do? Do you basically say that
they're lepers to society? That they don't exist? . . . A policy that ignores
them is a policy of denial."[2]

■ In defending a 1999 law that allowed undocumented immigrants to drive   8
in Utah, Republican state legislator David Ure stated, "When [undocu-
mented immigrants] got in a wreck, they opened the car door and ran.
Now, they drive better cars and have insurance."[3]

Denying Driver's Licenses to the Undocumented Population Jeopardizes Public Safety and Drives Up Insurance Rates.

■ Unlicensed drivers make our roads more dangerous. The AAA Foundation   9
for Traffic Safety describes unlicensed drivers as "among the worst drivers on the road"[4] and found that unlicensed drivers are almost five times
more likely to be in a fatal crash than are validly licensed drivers.[5]

■ When California's hit-and-run accidents increased by 19 percent from   10
2001 to 2003, law enforcement officers and traffic safety experts pointed
to "an abundance of unlicensed drivers" and "drivers driving without
auto insurance" as two of the reasons for the increase.[6]

■ More than 14 percent of all accidents are caused by uninsured driv-   11
ers, who cause over $4.1 billion in insurance losses per year.[7] This
means that licensed drivers must pay higher premiums for accidents
and injuries caused by unlicensed drivers.[8] An Illinois study estimated
that the average additional auto insurance policy cost per person due
to accidents caused by unlicensed and uninsured immigrant drivers is
$116.90 per year.[9]

■ Four of the six states that provide licenses to undocumented immigrants   12
fall below the national average for uninsured motorists.[10]

   ■ Due to a 2003 New Mexico law that allowed undocumented immigrants to obtain driver's licenses, the uninsurance rate in that state
   dropped from 33 percent in 2002 to 10.6 percent in 2007.[11]

   ■ When Utah changed its policy in 1999, Utah's uninsurance rate
   dropped from 10 percent in 1998 to 5.1 percent in 2007.[12]

   ■ When New York was considering allowing undocumented immigrants
   to obtain driver's licenses, the State Department of Insurance estimated that expanded license access would reduce the premium costs

associated with uninsured motorist coverage by 34 percent, which would have saved New York drivers $120 million each year.[13]

National Security Efforts Are Undermined by Driver's License Restrictions.

- Security experts have made clear that it is counterproductive to deny identification documents to undocumented immigrants, because denying them identification makes the already difficult job of identifying terrorists even harder.[14]

> "Denying them identification makes the already difficult job of identifying terrorists even harder."

- Kim Taipale, executive director of the Center for Advanced Studies in Science and director of the Program on Law Enforcement and National Security in the Information Age at the World Policy Institute, stated, "Denying identity legitimacy to 13 million illegal aliens—the vast majority of whom are not terrorists or otherwise threats to national security—just increases the size of the suspect pool for law enforcement to have to sort through. Since law enforcement resources are already unable to effectively cope with the large illegal alien population, why further complicate their task?"[15]

- According to Margaret Stock, associate professor of law at the U.S. Military Academy at West Point, "Refusing to give driver licenses to illegal immigrants means taking [them] out of the largest law enforcement database in the country. Thus, denial of licenses is a policy prescription that hampers law enforcement far more than it enhances it."[16]

- In 2005, the Government Accountability Office reported that U.S. Immigration and Customs Enforcement found public and private databases, such as driver's license databases, to be more current than the DHS database and more reliable for tracking down immigrants.[17] Denying licenses to undocumented immigrants simply increases the pool of state residents who are not in any database used to track outstanding criminal warrants, child-support delinquents, and threats to national security.

State Law Enforcement Efforts Are Undermined by Driver's License Restrictions.

- Driver's license restrictions cause immigrants to avoid contact with state and local law enforcement. This means that immigrants are unwilling to report crimes and assist local law enforcement in community policing activities. This decreases community trust and undermines efforts to fight crime and save lives.

- Los Angeles Police Chief William Bratton stated in 2007, "It is my belief that by [granting undocumented immigrants driver's licenses] you would reduce the number of hit and runs and increase the number of insured motorists on the road. We would also now have undocumented immigrants' identifying information on record such as photographs and addresses which could prove helpful in the fight against crime and terrorism."[18]

- Drivers have a responsibility to be tested for a license and to obtain auto [19] insurance. License restrictions that prevent drivers from carrying out their legal responsibilities undercut effective use of law enforcement resources because law enforcement officers must divert their attention from catching criminals and protecting public safety to enforcing driver's license restrictions.

State Policymakers Should Support Practical Driver's License Reforms that Improve the Integrity of the License.

- States should require proof of state residency to ensure that only state [20] residents can obtain a driver's license.

- States should implement internal antifraud mechanisms, including staff [21] training on identifying false documents, authenticating security features on identification documents, as well as ensuring that duplicate licenses are not issued.

- States should implement photo comparison technology to compare exist- [22] ing images with each other and compare new images to those on file.

- States should reduce the production and sale of false documents by [23] imposing harsh penalties on those who produce, distribute, or purchase them.

Notes

[1] Aurelio Rojas, "N.M. Steers in Different Direction on Licenses," *Sacramento Bee*, May 23, 2004, http://dwb.sacbee.com/content/politics/story/9399308p-10323630c.html, emphasis added.

[2] Brendan Farrangton, "Illegal Immigrants Could Get Licenses under Bill Backed by Florida's Gov. Jeb Bush," Associated Press, Apr. 6, 2004, emphasis added.

[3] Miriam Jordan, "Driver's Licenses for Illegal Immigrants Divide Congress," *Wall Street Journal*, Dec. 6, 2004, www.rmi.gsu.edu/rmi/faculty/klein/RMI_3500/Readings/Other/Immigration_DriversLicenses.htm, emphasis added.

[4] Robert A. Scopatz, Clayton E. Hatch, Barbara Hilger DeLucia and Kelley A. Tays, *Unlicensed to Kill: The Sequel* (AAA Foundation for Traffic Safety, Jan. 2003), www.aaafoundation.org/pdf/UnlicensedToKill2.pdf, at 16, emphasis added.

[5] "High Risk Drivers Fact Sheet" (AAA Foundation for Traffic Safety, undated), www.aaafoundation.org/multimedia/index.cfm?button=udfacts.

[6]Michael Cabanatuan and Erin McCormick, "California's Hit-and-Run Crisis: More Flee Fatal Accidents Here Than Any Other State," *San Francisco Chronicle*, July 27, 2003, www.sfgate.com/cgibin/article.cgi?file=/chronicle/archive/2003/07/27/MN292165.DTL, emphasis added.

[7]"IRC Estimates More Than 14 Percent of Drivers Are Uninsured" (Insurance Research Council news release, June 28, 2006), www.ircweb.org/news/20060628.pdf.

[8]Stephanie K. Jones, "Uninsured Drivers Travel under the Radar," *Insurance Journal*, Aug. 18, 2003, www.insurancejournal.com/magazines/west/2003/08/18/coverstory/31590.htm.

[9]*Safety and Savings: How Driver's Certificates Would Lower Insurance Premiums and Make Our Roads Safer* (Illinois Coalition for Immigrant and Refugee Rights, May 9, 2007), www.icirr.org/nh/learn/insurancereport.pdf, at 10.

[10]Sam Friedman, "Insurers Silent on Spitzer Licensing Scheme," *National Underwriter*, Nov. 14, 2007, www.property-casualty.com/2007/11/insurers_silent_on_spitzer_lic.html.

[11]Ken Ortiz, "New Driver's Licenses Don't Have 'Loophole,'" *Albuquerque Journal*, Dec. 29, 2007.

[12]"Number of Uninsured Registered Vehicles: Insure-Rite Uninsured Motorist Database" (spreadsheet obtained from the Utah Driver License Division, December 2007).

[13]Nina Bernstein, "Spitzer Grants Illegal Immigrants Easier Access to Driver's Licenses," *New York Times*, Sept. 22, 2007, www.nytimes.com/2007/09/22/nyregion/22licenses.html?ei=5088&en=8d0504cf231fa666&ex=1348113600&adxnnl=1&partner=rssnyt&emc=rss&adxnnlx=1200075859-1WCfvlTaAzrL/CigXEoO2g.

[14]See, e.g., Clark Kent Ervin, "Why N.Y. Driver's License Plan Might Make Us Safer," *USA Today*, Nov. 1, 2007, at http://blogs.usatoday.com/oped/2007/11/why-nv-drivers-.html; Margaret Stock, "Giving Immigrants Licenses May Help Security," *Newsday*, Oct. 2, 2007; and Kim Taipale, "Not Issuing Driver's Licenses to Illegal Aliens Is Bad for National Security" (World Policy Institute, New York, Dec. 17, 2004), http://alien-id.info/.

[15]See Taipale, *supra* note 14, emphasis added.

[16]Margaret Stock, "Driver Licenses and National Security," *Drivers.com*, Jan. 12, 2008, http://drivers.com/article/971/.

[17]*Alien Registration: Usefulness of a Nonimmigrant Alien Annual Address Reporting Requirement Is Questionable* (Government Accountability Office, Jan. 2005, GAO-05-204), www.gao.gov/new.items/d05204.pdf, at 1.

[18]"Former Commissioner of New York City Police Department and Current Chief of Los Angeles Police Department, William J. Bratton Supports Registering Immigrants: Measure Enhances Safety and Security" (New York governor's press release, Oct. 22, 2007), www.ny.gov/governor/press/1022071.html, emphasis added.

⊘ READING ARGUMENTS

1. Does this document from the National Immigration Law Center state a thesis? If so, where?

2. According to the writers, "policymakers need to deal with realistic solutions, not sound bites and partisan politics" (para. 5). What distinction are they making? Why do you think the writers quote New Mexico governor Bill Richardson, former Florida governor Jeb Bush, and Utah state legislator David Ure to make their point?

3. What specific evidence—and what *kinds* of evidence—do the writers use to support their arguments? Is this evidence persuasive? Why or why not?

4. According to this fact sheet, how does refusing to grant driver's licenses to undocumented immigrants undermine homeland security efforts?

5. Why does this fact sheet include so many notes? What purpose do they serve?

This testimony was given before the State of Maryland House of Delegates on February 18, 2004.

STATES SHOULD NOT ISSUE DRIVER'S LICENSES TO ILLEGAL IMMIGRANTS

MICHAEL W. CUTLER

I welcome this opportunity to address you today about the critical issue of the   1
issuance of driver's licenses to illegal aliens. I think it would be appropriate
to begin by telling you about my background. I retired from the Immigration and Naturalization Service (INS) as a Senior Special Agent in New York
in February 2002, having served that agency in various capacities during the
course of my career which spanned some 30 years. I began as an Immigration
Inspector assigned to John F. Kennedy International Airport in October 1971.
For one year I was assigned as an examiner to the unit that adjudicates petitions filed by spouses to accord resident alien status to the husband or wife of
resident aliens or United States citizens.

In 1975, I became a criminal investigator, or special agent as that position is   2
now referred to. I rotated through every squad within the investigations branch,
and in 1988 I was assigned to the Unified Intelligence Division of the Drug
Enforcement Administration's New York office. In 1991, I was promoted to
the position of Senior Special Agent and assigned to the Organized Crime Drug
Enforcement Task Force, where I worked with a wide variety of law enforcement officers from various federal, state, local, and foreign law enforcement
organizations, including the FBI, DEA, IRS, U.S. Customs, ATF, New York State
Police, New Jersey State Police, New York City Police and various county police
departments, as well as with representatives of the Royal Canadian Mounted
Police, New Scotland Yard, British Customs, Japanese National Police, and the
Israeli National Police. Finally, I have testified at several congressional hearings
as an expert witness at hearings that dealt with immigration issues.

I am currently a fellow at the Center for Immigration Studies.   3

My professional experiences have provided me with a unique insight that   4
I hope will be helpful to you as you grapple with this issue.

We currently live in a nation in which being politically correct permeates   5
our society. In some ways this is a good thing, as it causes us to be careful to
not offend any groups of people and show respect for everyone. On the other
hand, it may also cloud issues and perceptions. George Orwell, the author of
the book *1984* devised the concept of "Newspeak" in which words were regularly eliminated from the vernacular to alter perceptions and thought processes. An example of this Orwellian approach to immigration is the use of the
politically correct term, "Undocumented worker" which has supplanted the
legally correct term, "Illegal alien." The term *alien* is not a pejorative term but
rather is a legal term. According to Section 1101 of Title 8 of the United States
Code, the body of law that focuses on immigration issues, the term *alien* is

defined as, ". . . any person who is not a citizen or national of the United States." When citizens of the United States travel outside the United States, they become aliens in the countries to which they travel. I respectfully suggest that by failing to properly recognize the fact that when aliens, especially illegal aliens, enter this country, they are not automatically entitled to every right and privilege enjoyed by United States citizens or by Lawfully Admitted Permanent Resident Aliens. We have sovereign borders that we must enforce if our country's continued existence is to be ensured. A country without borders can no more stand than can a house without walls. By blurring the distinction between what is legal and what is illegal, we encourage the rampant entry of illegal aliens into the United States, and we also encourage other criminal activities. While it is true that the responsibility to enforce the Immigration and Nationality Act falls to the federal government, individual states must do their part in creating an environment that is not conducive to illegal immigration.

> "A country without borders can no more stand than can a house without walls."

We are often told that the immigration laws are not enforceable. Those 6 who take this position will point to the 8 to 14 million illegal aliens currently estimated to be living in the United States today and draw the conclusion that these massive numbers illustrate how unenforceable the laws governing the presence of aliens in the United States are. I would respond by telling you that the immigration laws are no more, nor no less enforceable than any other laws. Motor vehicle laws, drug laws, firearms laws, and others are not more inherently enforceable than the immigration laws, yet no one would seriously suggest we give up attempting to enforce those other laws. The only laws which enjoy a 100 percent compliance rate are the laws of nature. The scientists and engineers at NASA might like to find a way of violating the law of gravity but have thus far been unable to do so.

Man's laws, on the other hand, are imperfect, and so the best we can 7 do, in addition to our limited efforts at enforcing our laws, is to offer deterrence to discourage people from violating our laws. We set up sobriety checkpoints and impose severe penalties for drivers who are caught driving while intoxicated. We seize the assets of criminals who amass money and material property through criminal activities both as a way of generating funds for the government as well as a way of punishing and deterring criminals. We understand that the way to increase the rate of compliance in which law violators are concerned is to devise strategies that discourage the violations of law and to impose penalties on those who break the law nevertheless.

We are here today to discuss whether or not the state of Maryland should 8 issue driver's licenses to illegal aliens. I believe that the issuance of driver's licenses to illegal aliens is the wrong thing to do. The issuance of driver's licenses to illegal aliens aids and abets illegal aliens in living and working illegally in the United States. My understanding of Maryland's motor vehicle law is that the state of Maryland accepts foreign driver's licenses for a period of one year if the license is accompanied by a passport and other such documentation.

It is clear that the desire by aliens who are illegally in the United States [9] to obtain a driver's license goes beyond the need to drive a car in the United States. In the post 9/11 world we have come to use a driver's license as an identity document that can facilitate the bearer's boarding an airplane or train. It can also be used to gain entry into various government buildings. Additionally, the driver's license is one of several documents that are enumerated on the form I-9 which an employer must maintain on file for each employee and may therefore facilitate an illegal alien seeking employment in the United States. Additionally, the driver's license can be used as a so-called "breeder document" in which the bearer of the license obtains other identity documents based on the driver's license.

What I find disturbing about the use of driver's licenses is that there are [10] no guarantees that the bearer of the license is who he or she claims to be. This is a flaw in the system that goes beyond the reach of this hearing, but it is worth considering. The only thing worse than no security is false security. The way we currently use driver's licenses as an identity document provides us with a false sense of security, but it is the method by which we currently do business today. In my career as an immigration officer I have encountered many individuals who had several different driver's licenses in different names that they had procured in an effort to conceal their true identity. This is why we often hear that the illegal aliens who live in our country inhabit the "shadows."

According to recently published statistics, some 400,000 illegal aliens who [11] have been ordered deported from the United States are currently being sought, having failed to turn themselves in. In my experience, many of them will have succeeded in creating false identities for themselves as they seek to evade the immigration authorities. Access to driver's licenses in an assumed identity will go a long way in their quest to create new identities for themselves.

Consider this: aliens who are illegally in the United States became illegal [12] aliens in one of two ways; they either entered the United States by crossing the border without being properly inspected—this includes stowaways who hide in boats or airplanes—or they enter the United States through a port of entry. Some of the aliens who enter through ports of entry do so under assumed identities, concealing their true identities and, perhaps, criminal backgrounds or other issues that if known by the inspector at the time of entry would have served as a basis for denial of admission. Other aliens enter with valid visas or under the Visa Waiver Program which permits aliens from some 28 countries to enter the United States without first obtaining a visa and then, in one way or another, violate their respective immigration status in the United States. That means that they overstay the allotted period of time for which they were admitted, they accept employment without proper authorization, or they get arrested and are subsequently convicted of committing a felony.

According to recently published estimates, perhaps half of all illegal aliens [13] did not enter without inspection but rather entered the United States through a port of entry and then violated the law. This was the case with each and every one of the 19 hijackers who attacked our nation on September 11.

In most cases, the goal of illegal aliens is to obtain employment in the 14 United States, but this is not the only motivation for illegal aliens. While it is only a relatively small proportion of illegal aliens who become involved in serious criminal activity, a disproportionately large percentage of our criminal population is comprised of aliens. In 1988 I was assigned to the DEA Unified Intelligence Division in New York. I conducted an analysis of DEA arrest records and determined that some 60 percent of individuals who were arrested by DEA in the New York City area were identified as being "foreign born," while nationwide, some 30 percent were identified as being "foreign born."

As you may know, the two reasons that law enforcement officials finger- 15 print defendants when they are arrested is to properly identify the suspect in custody and to document the fact that the suspect was indeed arrested. This is essential because criminals often have multiple identities. They conceal their true identities in order to evade detection and when caught, they hope to thwart efforts by law enforcement officers from learning their true identities and their criminal backgrounds. In many cases, illegal aliens who were arrested attempted to conceal the fact that they were aliens and falsely claimed to be United States citizens to avoid being deported after they completed their prison sentences. In my experience, numerous drug suspects, in whose arrest I participated, were found to be in possession of multiple identity documents that they used to attempt to conceal their true identities. The most common identity documents that they carried were false Social Security cards and driver's licenses in different names.

Finally, I would like to remind you that a driver's license is a privilege and 16 not a right. The issuance of driver's licenses to illegal aliens will make it easier for aliens who are living and working illegally in the United States to circumvent our laws. It will also aid criminal aliens and terrorists in concealing themselves within our country. The only reasonable course of action is to not issue driver's licenses to aliens who are illegally in the United States.

⊙ READING ARGUMENTS

1. Cutler argues that language is an important part of this debate, particularly with regard to the phrases "undocumented worker" and "illegal alien" (para. 5). Do you agree that language is an important part of the debate? Why or why not?

2. What is Cutler's thesis? Where is this thesis stated, and why do you think he chose to state it there?

3. In paragraph 6, Cutler addresses the opposing argument that "immigration laws are not enforceable." Does he use inductive reasoning or deductive reasoning? Do you find his refutation of this argument persuasive? Why or why not?

4. What elements of an evaluation argument can you find in Cutler's testimony? Where does he provide an argument by analogy?

5. How does Cutler use causal arguments to make his case? Do you find this kind of argument persuasive here? Why or why not?

⊘ AT ISSUE: SHOULD UNDOCUMENTED IMMIGRANTS BE ENTITLED TO DRIVER'S LICENSES?

1. New Mexico governor Bill Richardson defended a law granting driver's licenses to all qualified state residents by saying, "We're dealing with a problem, rather than being ideologically senseless. This is a reality in border states" (para. 6). What does *ideology* mean, and what does it mean to be "ideologically senseless"? How would you apply this distinction—being ideological versus being realistic—to Cutler's argument?

2. Cutler argues that "being politically correct permeates our society" (5). According to Cutler, this tendency affects our language, leading us to blur distinctions between what is legal and what is illegal with regard to immigration. What is *political correctness*? Do you think the National Immigration Law Center's arguments are undermined by political correctness? Why or why not?

3. While Cutler argues that granting licenses helps criminals and terrorists, the National Immigration Law Center argues that license restrictions actually undermine homeland security. Which side's arguments do you find more convincing on this specific issue, and why?

⊘ WRITING ARGUMENTS: SHOULD UNDOCUMENTED IMMIGRANTS BE ENTITLED TO DRIVER'S LICENSES?

After reading these arguments regarding driver's licenses and undocumented workers, what is your view of the issue? Write an essay that supports your position.

CHAPTER

23

Should the United States Permit Drilling for Oil in Environmentally Sensitive Areas?

The subject of energy in general—and oil in particular—has far-reaching implications and consequences for the United States. Ever since crude oil (or petroleum) began displacing earlier fuel sources such as coal and whale oil in the late nineteenth and early twentieth centuries, it has played an essential part in the growth and prosperity of the country. In fact, the energy provided by oil—much of it extracted and refined in the United States—made modern life possible by powering our factories, electrical appliances, and automobiles. We also use oil to make chemical products such as plastics, fertilizers, and pesticides. Petroleum has now been the dominant source of energy worldwide for more than fifty years. Not surprisingly, it also plays a dominant role in international and domestic politics, affecting everything from our national security and relations in the Middle East to our automobile industry and environmental policies.

Oil has given rise to modern industrial economies and societies, but it has also made those societies oil-dependent. That is especially true of the United States. In 2006, President George W. Bush said that the nation was "addicted to oil." Although oil prices remained relatively low in the 1990s, they have increased significantly since 2001, and the 2008 price spike had a negative effect on American consumers and on the U.S. economy as a whole. But instability in the oil market is nothing new. In the early 1970s, the Arab members of the Organization of the Petroleum Exporting Countries (OPEC) imposed an oil embargo on the United States and

Western Europe in retaliation for their support of Israel. Events like the 1973 embargo have long underscored our excessive reliance on foreign oil, especially as the United States now imports over half the petroleum it consumes. This vulnerability will likely become more apparent as developing nations such as India and China increase the demand for oil worldwide.

For decades now, U.S. policymakers have proposed alternative energy sources, such as solar, nuclear, and wind power. Most experts consider the earth's store of fossil fuels such as petroleum to be finite as well as environmentally hazardous, and these alternatives, they argue, could wean us off an increasingly scarce resource, reduce our foreign dependence, and help the environment. But some argue that due to more practical and immediate needs, the United States should also increase its own domestic oil production to lessen the country's reliance on foreign suppliers. Recently, proponents of this position have contended that the United States should allow drilling in previously reserved or protected areas, such as the Arctic National Wildlife Refuge (ANWR), a 19-million acre national refuge in Alaska that has been federally protected since 1950. Geologists estimate that there may be as many as 11 billion barrels of oil in the refuge.

The following four argumentative essays explore different positions on this issue. Drilling advocates, such as Pete Du Pont in "Drill, Baby, Drill" and Lamar Alexander in "To Drill or . . . ," maintain that we can open the refuge to oil extraction while protecting its pristine wilderness. Opponents, such as Ed Markey in ". . . Not to Drill" and the National Resources Defense Council in "Arctic National Wildlife Refuge: Why Trash an American Treasure for a Tiny Percentage of Our Oil Needs?" see such drilling as unwise and shortsighted.

The *Wall Street Journal* published this opinion piece on September 19, 2008.

DRILL, BABY, DRILL

PETE DU PONT

Energy is essential in America, and 40% of what we use comes from oil and   1
23% from natural gas. That comes to about 21 million barrels of oil and
64 billion cubic feet of natural gas each day. Domestic oil production is
declining—down nearly half since 1970—so imports are up, from one-third
of what we needed in 1970 to just under 60% today. So we need to discover
and access more of our own energy resources.

The good news is that huge resources of oil and gas exist offshore: recover-   2
able oil and gas on America's Outer Continental Shelf comes to some 85 billion
barrels of oil and 420 trillion cubic feet of natural gas, and there are another
10 billion barrels of oil in the North Slope of Alaska. If full access to these
resources were permitted, together they could replace America's imported oil
for some 25 years, and no doubt reduce the price of oil, gas and gasoline.

Until recently there was little chance that greater development of these   3
resources would be permitted. In 1982 Congress began restricting access to
them. In 1990 President George H. W. Bush issued an executive order with-
drawing wide-ranging offshore areas from exploration and drilling, and in
1998 President Clinton extended the ban through 2012. He also vetoed the
1995 legislation Congress passed to allow drilling for the 10 billion barrels of
oil in the Alaska Arctic National Wildlife Refuge. If Mr. Clinton had signed the
bill, we would now be producing a million barrels of oil a day in Alaska instead
of importing that million barrels from the Middle East at an annual cost aver-
aging about $100 a barrel, or $36 billion a year.

A look at the government's Mineral Management Service drilling   4
regulation map . . . shows that drilling is banned off the West Coast
(Washington, Oregon and California), the East Coast (Maine to Florida) and
much of Florida's Gulf Coast, leaving only the western and central Gulf of
Mexico as current permitted drilling areas.

The Interior Department estimates that these restricted areas contain   5
19.1 billion barrels of oil and 77 trillion cubic feet of natural gas, the equivalent of perhaps 30 years of oil we will import from Saudi Arabia. Opening
up these resources would have another advantage: We would have a second
source of Outer Continental Shelf drilling as hurricanes blow through the Gulf
of Mexico.

One of the environmental arguments against offshore drilling is the   6
danger that oil will be spilled and pollute the oceans or coasts. Earlier this
year the Mineral Management Service evaluated the oil spills at the OCS
offshore drilling facilities between 1993 and 2007. About 48,000 barrels of

oil were spilled while 7.5 billion barrels were being produced, or one barrel spilled for every 157,000 produced—less then 0.001%. In terms of oil spillage OCS operations are more than five times as safe as oil tankers, and natural ocean floor seepage puts more oil into our ocean than oil production spillage.

But now energy policies are beginning to change. The price of gasoline 7 rose from $2.22 a gallon in 2007 to more than $4 earlier this year, and people began to wonder why their government thought high gas prices were a good idea when all that offshore oil was out there and available.

The current President Bush has for seven years allowed the offshore drilling 8 bans to stay in place, but in July he lifted the presidential moratorium, and the congressional moratorium expires Sept. 30. So offshore oil and gas drilling can significantly expand our energy resources, and America—which until now has been the only nation in the world that has curtailed access to its own energy supplies—may at last adopt a policy of permitting rather than prohibiting access to our offshore energy resources.

> "Offshore oil and gas drilling can significantly expand our energy resources."

With only two weeks remaining in the congressional session, the antidrill- 9 ing Democratic leadership is under considerable pressure to allow increased offshore oil and gas exploration. They don't much like it—Speaker Nancy Pelosi believes that by stopping offshore drilling "I'm trying to save the planet," and Sen. Chuck Schumer of New York wants Saudi Arabia to increase its production by a million barrels a day but opposes U.S. drilling on the OCS or ANWR—but it has become reality.

The bill that passed the House Tuesday would allow drilling 100 miles off- 10 shore anywhere, and 50 miles off any state that approved drilling. But more than 80% of known oil reserves are inside the 50-mile limit, and ANWR drilling is still not permitted, even though it involves only 2,000 of Alaska's 20 million acres of coastal plain. No royalties would be shared with the states under the House bill, and $18 billion in existing government subsidies for oil companies would be repealed.

The upcoming Senate version proposes to allow drilling off only four 11 states—Georgia, North Carolina, South Carolina and Virginia—and to raise taxes on the oil industry by some $30 billion.

There is no question a great deal of oil and gas is on the Outer Continental 12 Shelf, but the Democratic Party has been opposed to offshore drilling for a long while, and the Republicans have sometimes joined Democrats. Now it is time for a change. As Ronald Reagan said in his 1980 acceptance speech at the Republican National Convention: "Large amounts of oil and natural gas lay beneath our land and off our shores, untouched because the present administration seems to believe the American people would rather see more regulation, taxes, and controls than more energy."

He was talking about the Carter administration, but a quarter-century 13
later the Democratic congressional majority would also like more energy regulation, taxes and controls. But the American people realize more and less
expensive energy is the better goal to be pursuing.

⊘ READING ARGUMENTS

1. Trace the deductive argument in Du Pont's two opening paragraphs.

2. What advantages does Du Pont see in allowing more domestic drilling?

3. Where in this essay does Du Pont address opposing arguments? Does he refute them persuasively?

4. In paragraph 7, Du Pont writes that as the price of gasoline rose to more than $4 per gallon in 2008, "people began to wonder why their government thought high gas prices were a good idea when all that offshore oil was out there and available." Does this seem like an accurate generalization? Why or why not?

5. In paragraph 9, Du Pont quotes Speaker of the House of Representatives Nancy Pelosi, who opposes more domestic drilling. Why does he quote her? How does he use her words to support his argument?

This piece (like the one that follows) is from the journal *Business Perspectives*, published by the University of Memphis, on March 22, 2005.

TO DRILL OR . . .

SENATOR LAMAR ALEXANDER

In 1980, our country made a decision to set aside land in Alaska for conserva- 1
tion and for drilling. Congress debated it and President Carter—during his
administration—approved of and made both parts of the decision. One was
to set aside 100 million acres of land in Alaska, an astonishing amount for a
wilderness area, and then to set aside 1.5 million acres for drilling. That was
the decision our country made.

I grew up in the foothills of the Great Smoky Mountains, and I have 2
always supported conservation. My initial reaction to the proposal of drilling
in the Arctic National Wildlife Refuge (ANWR) was to not do it. I gathered
all possible facts I could find and examined them. I saw that 60 percent of our
nation's oil comes from foreign sources. Also, of the 100 million acres set aside
by President Carter in 1980, 19.5 million are known as ANWR and 17.5 million
acres of that land is off limits to development.

We are a nation that depends upon a reliable supply of energy. ANWR 3
has more oil reserves than the state of Texas. By using just 2,000 of the
19.5 million acres in ANWR, we could produce as much oil as Texas already
produces each year.

I support a plan that calls for responsible oil drilling in Alaska and am 4
currently reviewing other production and conservation solutions. We are a
nation where gasoline prices and natural
gas prices are going up in remarkable
numbers. That means for us fewer jobs.
That means for us cold homes in the winter. We cannot afford to have energy
prices, home heating oil, and natural gas
prices going up to a level our citizens cannot afford. So, we have to strike a
reasonable balance.

> "I support a plan that calls for responsible oil drilling in Alaska."

I am pleased the Senate has included in the Budget Resolution my pro- 5
posal to put the first $350 million a year for three years of revenues from
ANWR into the Land and Water Conservation Fund and other conservation
programs. I believe we should use revenue from oil and gas drilling, and other
activities that deplete our natural resources, to fund conservation efforts.
And, I believe smart development always includes strong environmental
stewardship.

In other words, we would be balancing what we are doing. We might be 6
creating some environmental burden, taking some environmental risk, but we
would be balancing that by a huge environmental benefit on the other side

by helping build state parks and greenways and land trusts, closer to where people live, near their homes.

It's important for us to strike a balance when considering overall energy policy and conservation issues. We have a viable source of energy that should not be ignored, and we have a responsibility to preserving our Great American Outdoors for future generations. I believe by using these 2,000 acres for drilling and putting a portion of the revenues back into the Land and Water Conservation Fund we are doing just that.

◉ READING ARGUMENTS

1. Why do you think Alexander discusses his personal history in the second paragraph? How does this information help support his thesis?

2. According to Alexander, what effects do rising gasoline and natural gas prices have on Americans?

3. What elements of Rogerian argument does Alexander use in this essay? How does Rogerian argument influence the structure and tone of his argument?

Like the previous piece, the following counterpoint is from the March 22, 2005, issue of *Business Perspectives*.

. . . NOT TO DRILL

REPRESENTATIVE ED MARKEY

Our nation's ravenous appetite for oil is one of the most severe threats to our   1
security. Currently, we in the United States comprise less than 5 percent of
the world's population, but we consume 25 percent of its oil. By providing
$8 billion more in tax subsidies to the oil and gas industry, the Energy Bill that
recently passed through the House of Representatives with the support of the
Bush Administration and the Congressional Republican leadership would try
to overcome bad geology with bad economics. Despite the lack of interest on
the part of BP and others familiar with the area, Congress is removing the last
remaining protection from a spectacular untouched national wildlife refuge in
the Arctic. The Congress is placing the drilling bulls eye on the Arctic National
Wildlife Refuge and asking the wildlife to step aside.

The Arctic National Wildlife Refuge is a national treasure, a place of   2
ancient wilderness that remains much the same as it was at the end of the last
Ice Age. The Refuge is one of the few places
remaining in America where man has not
scarred the land; it is a place where roads do
not pave the way, and where the animals
truly do roam free. The Refuge is home to
the 130,000-strong Porcupine Caribou Herd

> "The Arctic National Wildlife Refuge is a national treasure."

as well as polar bears, musk oxen, and more than 130 species of migratory
birds. The Arctic Refuge is the crown jewel of our 544 national wildlife refuges.

Will drilling in the Refuge solve our problems? No. The experts estimate   3
that in all likelihood the Refuge will provide about six-month's worth of oil
at today's rate of consumption. In addition, oil from the Refuge would not
reach the market until a decade after production begins. When it does arrive,
it is estimated that the new production would lower gas prices by less than
one cent per gallon. According to the Bush Administration's Department of
Energy, Arctic Refuge oil would reduce our foreign oil dependence in 20 years
from 70 percent to 66 percent. With only 3 percent of the world's oil reserves,
the United States cannot drill its way to independence.

Do we have a better option? Yes. Our strength lies in technological innova-   4
tion; it always has. Our cars and trucks account for 70 percent of oil consumption. This is auto mechanics, not rocket science. If the scientists of the 1960s
could find a way to respond to President Kennedy's Cold War challenge to put
a man on the moon, surely our technological geniuses of the 21st century would
respond to a presidential challenge to free ourselves of the oil cartel by increasing our automobile fuel economy by 50 percent or more within a decade.

But, President Bush refuses to issue such a challenge. Instead, he chooses 5 to take desperate steps to turn some of our most pristine wildlife and wilderness areas into gas stations. Meanwhile, the average fuel economy of our automobiles and light trucks marches backwards, and our consumption of oil swells.

Drilling for oil in the Arctic Refuge demonstrates a lack of vision that will 6 prolong our dependence on dangerous foreign oil, not solve it. Success lies in setting bold, achievable goals for reducing demand and expanding our use of alternative and renewable sources of the future. We have the technology; all we need is the will.

◇ READING ARGUMENTS

1. Markey begins his essay by referring to America's "ravenous appetite for oil." How does he support this characterization? Why is it significant for his argument?

2. According to Markey, what effect will drilling in the Arctic National Wildlife Refuge (ANWR) have on American energy independence and gas prices? Do you agree with him?

3. In paragraph 3, Markey cites figures from the George W. Bush administration's Department of Energy. Why does he use this source for his information? How effectively does it support his argument?

4. Where in this essay does Markey use a historical analogy? How persuasive do you find this analogy?

The National Resources Defense Council published this article on its Web site, NRDC.org, on July 16, 2008.

ARCTIC NATIONAL WILDLIFE REFUGE: WHY TRASH AN AMERICAN TREASURE FOR A TINY PERCENTAGE OF OUR OIL NEEDS?

NATURAL RESOURCES DEFENSE COUNCIL

On the northern edge of our continent, stretching from the peaks of the Brooks 1 Range across a vast expanse of tundra to the Beaufort Sea, lies Alaska's Arctic National Wildlife Refuge. An American Serengeti, the Arctic Refuge continues to pulse with million-year-old ecological rhythms. It is the greatest living reminder that conserving nature in its wild state is a core American value.

In affirmation of that value, Congress and the American people have consis- 2 tently made clear their desire to protect this treasure and rejected claims that drilling for oil in the Arctic Refuge is any sort of answer to the nation's dependence on foreign oil. Twice in 2005, Congress acted explicitly to defend the refuge from the Bush administration and pro-drilling forces, with House leaders removing provisions that would have allowed for drilling from a massive budget bill, and the Senate withstanding an attempt by Republican leaders to open up the Arctic.

Since then, concerned Americans have continued to push Congress to 3 thwart recurring efforts to see the refuge spoiled. But in the face of soaring gas prices, President Bush has once again offered up Arctic drilling as a solution for America's energy crisis, despite evidence from the government itself that drilling wouldn't make a dent in the price we pay at the pump. Instead, the president is again ignoring the science and valuing oil and gas interests over America's precious natural heritage. In this continuing battle, America's premier wildlife sanctuary is at stake.

Americans Have Steadily Opposed Drilling the Arctic National Wildlife Refuge

The controversy over drilling in the Arctic Refuge—the last piece of America's 4 Arctic coastline not already open to oil exploration—isn't new. Big Oil has long sought access to the refuge's coastal plain, a fragile swath of tundra that teems with staggering numbers of birds and animals. During the Bush administration's first term, repeated attempts were made to open the refuge. But time after time, the American public rejected the idea.

Congress has received hundreds of thousands of emails, faxes and phone 5 calls from citizens opposed to drilling in the Arctic Refuge, an outpouring that has helped make the difference. And polls have consistently shown that a majority of Americans oppose drilling, even in the face of high gas prices and misleading claims from oil interests. A June 2008 poll by the research firm

Belden Russonello & Stewart found that 55 percent of the American public supports continued protection for the Arctic Refuge, and only 35 percent of Americans believe that allowing oil companies to drill in the refuge would result in lower gas prices for American consumers.

Despite repeated failure and stiff opposition, drilling proponents press 6 on. Why? They believe that opening the Arctic Refuge will turn the corner in the broader national debate over whether or not energy, timber, mining and other industries should be allowed into pristine wild areas across the country. Along with the Arctic, oil interests are now targeting America's protected coastal waters. Next up: Greater Yellowstone? Our Western canyonlands?

> "The drive to drill in the Arctic Refuge is about oil company profits."

The drive to drill in the Arctic Refuge is about oil company profits and 7 lifting barriers to future exploration in protected lands, pure and simple. It has nothing to do with energy independence. Opening the Arctic Refuge to energy development is about transferring our public estate into corporate hands so that it can be liquidated for a quick buck.

Arctic Refuge Oil Is a Distraction, Not a Solution

What would America gain by allowing heavy industry into the refuge? Very 8 little. Oil from the refuge would hardly make a dent in our dependence on foreign imports—leaving our economy and way of life just as exposed to wild swings in worldwide oil prices and supply as it is today. The truth is, we simply can't drill our way to energy independence.

Although drilling proponents often say there are 16 billion barrels of oil 9 under the refuge's coastal plain, the U.S. Geological Survey's estimate of the amount that could be recovered economically—that is, the amount likely to be profitably extracted and sold—represents less than a year's U.S. supply.

It would take 10 years for any Arctic Refuge oil to reach the market, and 10 even when production peaks—in the distant year of 2027—the refuge would produce a paltry 3 percent of Americans' daily consumption. The U.S. government's own Energy Information Agency recently reported that drilling in the Arctic would save less than 4 cents per gallon in 20 years. Whatever oil the refuge might produce is simply irrelevant to the larger issue of meeting America's future energy needs.

Handing On to Future Generations a Wild, Pristine Arctic? Priceless.

Oil produced from the Arctic Refuge would come at an enormous, and irre- 11 versible, cost. The refuge is among the world's last true wildernesses, and it is one of the largest sanctuaries for Arctic animals. Traversed by a dozen rivers and framed by jagged peaks, this spectacular wilderness is a vital birthing ground for polar bears, grizzlies, Arctic wolves, caribou and the endangered shaggy musk ox, a mammoth-like survivor of the last Ice Age.

For a sense of what Big Oil's heavy machinery would do to the refuge, just 12
look 60 miles west to Prudhoe Bay—a gargantuan oil complex that has turned
1,000 square miles of fragile tundra into a sprawling industrial zone containing 1,500 miles of roads and pipelines, 1,400 producing wells and three jet-
ports. The result is a landscape defaced by mountains of sewage sludge, scrap
metal, garbage and more than 60 contaminated waste sites that contain—and
often leak—acids, lead, pesticides, solvents and diesel fuel.

While proponents of drilling insist that the Arctic Refuge could be devel- 13
oped by disturbing as little as 2,000 acres within the 1.5-million-acre coastal
plain, an NRDC analysis reveals this to be pure myth. Why? Because U.S. Geological Survey studies have found that oil in the refuge isn't concentrated in a
single, large reservoir. Rather, it's spread across the coastal plain in more than
30 small deposits, which would require vast networks of roads and pipelines
that would fragment the habitat, disturbing and displacing wildlife. . . .

A Responsible Path to Energy Security

The solution to America's energy problems will be found in American ingenuity, 14
not more oil. Only by reducing our reliance on oil—foreign and domestic—
and investing in cleaner, renewable forms of power will our country achieve
true energy security.

The good news is that we already have many of the tools we need to 15
accomplish this. For example, Detroit has the technology right now to produce high-performance hybrid cars, trucks and SUVs. If America made the
transition to these more efficient vehicles, far more oil would be saved than the
Arctic Refuge is likely to produce. Doesn't that make far more sense than selling out our natural heritage and exploiting one of our true wilderness gems?

◯ READING ARGUMENTS

1. At several points in the first five paragraphs, the writers assert that
   the American people have consistently rejected claims that drilling in
   ANWR is "any sort of answer to the nation's dependence on foreign
   oil" (para. 2). How does the article substantiate this generalization
   about Americans? Do you find the supporting evidence persuasive?
   Why or why not?

2. What is the thesis of this article? How would you state it in your
   own words?

3. In paragraph 6, the writers worry that timber, oil, and other industries
   might be allowed to operate in other pristine areas of the country—
   including Yellowstone Park. Does this seem like a real possibility, or
   do you think they are making a fallacious slippery-slope argument?
   Explain.

4. Where does this article take opposing viewpoints into consideration? How do the writers address these opposing arguments? Do they refute them convincingly?

⊘ AT ISSUE: SHOULD THE UNITED STATES PERMIT DRILLING FOR OIL IN ENVIRONMENTALLY SENSITIVE AREAS?

1. Ed Markey writes that although people in the United States comprise less than 5% of the world's population, we consume 25% of its oil. How does this statistic shape your view of energy policy in the United States? Do you think it is significant? Do you think it reflects negatively on the United States? Explain.

2. Ed Markey, Lamar Alexander, and the writers from the National Resources Defense Council claim that ANWR is an environmental treasure and (in Markey's words) "the crown jewel of our 544 national wildlife refuges" (para. 2). Do you believe that protecting such refuges—and offshore coastal areas—is important, even if doing so might limit U.S. energy independence? How do you weigh environmental concerns against energy and economic issues?

3. In what ways, if any, do you see U.S. energy policy—and potential energy independence—as a national security issue?

4. In paragraph 12, Pete Du Pont—referring to U.S. energy policy—says, "Now is a time for a change." What does he mean? Do you agree?

⊘ WRITING ARGUMENTS: SHOULD THE UNITED STATES PERMIT DRILLING FOR OIL IN ENVIRONMENTALLY SENSITIVE AREAS?

1. After reading these four essays, what position do you advocate regarding domestic oil drilling? Write an argumentative essay that takes a stand on the issue.

2. Have you been directly or indirectly affected by energy costs or energy dependence? Where would you rank this issue (and the related issues of domestic drilling, dependence on foreign oil, fuel costs, and the need for new technologies and alternatives) in terms of America's many other priorities? Do you think the government should do more to help solve these problems? Why or why not?

CASEBOOK

Should Felons Permanently Forfeit Their Right to Vote?

Currently, the voting rights of people convicted of serious crimes—such as murder, rape, or kidnapping—vary by state. In Maine and Vermont, felons may vote even while serving prison terms. Some states, such as Massachusetts and Oregon, restore voting rights once prisoners are released, but other states make the process more difficult. For example, in Virginia, those convicted of a felony may acquire voting rights by obtaining a "removal of political disabilities" from the governor; felons become eligible for this status five years after completing their sentences. In Alabama, however, they must obtain a pardon, which—depending on the nature of the felony—can be difficult or even impossible.

The practice of denying the vote to certain criminals and former criminals originates in early English common law. At the founding of the United States, such people were commonly prohibited from serving on a jury and from running for public office as well as from voting. Today, the legacy of these prohibitions is seen not only in restrictions on voting rights but also in federal laws that prohibit felons from receiving food stamps, living in publicly subsidized housing, or receiving federal loans and grants for college.

The right to vote is fundamental to citizenship. Still, over 5 million convicted felons cannot vote—a number larger than the populations of states such as Arkansas or New Hampshire. Moreover, these restrictions on voting tend to have a disproportionate effect on minorities. In Washington, until recently, limits on the voting rights of convicted felons effectively prohibited about 17% of African Americans from voting there. Those in favor of allowing these citizens to vote have cited the Voting Rights Act of 1965, which outlawed discriminatory practices that disenfranchised minority voters. So far, however, the U.S. Supreme Court has not interpreted the Voting Rights Act to apply to felons (although some individual states have loosened their prohibitions).

The following four essays examine this controversy in several different contexts. For example, in "Should Felons Vote?" Edward Feser examines not only the contemporary political implications of the issue but also the broader historical question of whether voting rights are inalienable. Although they approach the issue from different perspectives, all four writers touch on the significance of the vote as a right, the relevance of race, and the meaning of citizenship.

This opinion piece by Florida's attorney general was published on April 2, 2007, in the *St. Petersburg Times*.

FELONS DON'T MERIT AUTOMATIC RIGHTS

BILL McCOLLUM

The campaign to automatically restore civil rights to nearly all felons upon release from prison, with no waiting period and no hearing to determine if those felons will go right back to a life of crime, is reckless and irresponsible. States have enacted laws to take away certain rights of those who commit crimes, reasoning that a person who breaks the law should not make the law.

As a matter of justice, respect for crime victims and public safety, Florida takes away the rights of convicted felons to vote, sit on a jury, or engage in a state-licensed occupation. Felons lose these rights unless Cabinet members, sitting as the Clemency Board, agree to restore them. The 11th U.S. Circuit Court of Appeals upheld Florida's law in 2005, finding it does not violate the U.S. Constitution's equal protection clause or the Voting Rights Act. The federal court stated: "It is not racial discrimination that deprives felons, black or white, of their right to vote but their own decision to commit an act for which they assume the risks of detection and punishment" (*Johnson v. Bush*).

Florida's Constitution and rules provide a safety-conscious process to consider restoring a felon's rights. Felons convicted of less serious crimes may have their rights restored without a hearing. Today, the majority of felons receive restoration of civil rights once their sentences are complete.

But to make sure they remain crime-free and arrest-free once their sentences are served, most felons convicted of serious crimes must wait at least five years before their rights may be restored without a hearing under the current clemency rules. Along with Florida, several other states have at least a waiting period to protect against repeat offenders which, although not common, is a responsible process. The proposal soon coming before the Clemency Board would regrettably eliminate this critical waiting period for all but a few.

The high repeat offender rate in Florida is the central issue in this debate. The revolving door effect of restoring felons' rights only then to revoke them due to a new criminal offense would diminish the integrity of our democratic government and the rule of law. According to the Florida Department of Corrections, nearly 40 percent of offenders commit another crime within three years of release and 45 percent do so within five years; for those under 18 the rate skyrockets to 73 percent. Furthermore, a 2003 Department of Justice report found more than 70 percent

> "The high repeat offender rate in Florida is the central issue in this debate."

of arrestees tested positive for drugs, and studies show that drug traffickers live lives of violence.

The proposal to automatically restore civil rights when leaving prison   6 would restore rights without providing a reasonable period of time to determine if felons are truly rehabilitated or still leading a life of crime. It would include felons who committed heinous offenses such as child pornography, kidnapping and luring a child, armed robbery, carjacking and home invasion, aggravated stalking, aggravated assault, and even battery on a police officer. Furthermore, the proposal would include drug traffickers who are some of society's most dangerous felons often entangled in gang violence and, worst of all, would include offenders who continually plague our society—habitual violent career criminals.

This proposal to automatically restore civil rights to felons would give   7 repeat offenders the same vote at the ballot box as law-abiding citizens. Felons convicted of major crimes would be eligible to sit on a jury to carry out our system of justice. Violent criminals would be able to acquire a state-licensed job, whether as a household pest exterminator, residential building contractor or alarm system installer, allowing felons to regularly access people's homes.

Rather than automatically restore rights to violent repeat offenders, we   8 should ensure fairness in the clemency process by ending the processing backlog. As I previously proposed, this can be accomplished by increasing the number of Clemency Board meetings from a quarterly to a monthly basis to hear more cases and by providing the Parole Commission with additional employees out of Cabinet agencies to conduct timely background checks. I support requiring a decision on the restoration of a felon's rights within one year of eligibility. By adopting these changes, Florida can be proud in having a fair process that protects law-abiding citizens.

⊘ READING ARGUMENTS

1. In his introductory paragraph, McCollum notes that some states "have enacted laws to take away certain rights of those who commit crimes, reasoning that a person who breaks the law should not make the law." Is this statement reasonable? Is it self-evident?

2. According to McCollum, what is the central issue in the debate about whether to restore voting rights to convicted felons?

3. In paragraph 8, McCollum offers an alternative to automatically restoring voting rights to felons. What is this alternative? Does it make sense to you?

4. In what sense is this essay an evaluation argument? What elements of a proposal argument does McCollum use?

This piece is from *City Journal,* where it appeared in the Spring 2005 issue.

SHOULD FELONS VOTE?

EDWARD FESER

Forty-eight states currently restrict the right of felons to vote. Most states for- 1
bid current inmates to vote, others extend such bans to parolees, and still others disenfranchise felons for life. A movement to overturn these restrictions
gained swift momentum during the 2004 presidential campaign, and pending
legal and legislative measures promise to keep the issue in the headlines in the
months to come. It hasn't escaped notice that the felon vote would prove a
windfall for the Democrats; when they do get to vote, convicts and ex-cons
tend to pull the lever for the Left. Had ex-felons been able to vote in Florida in
2000—the state permanently strips all felons of voting rights—Al Gore almost
certainly would have won the presidential election.

Murderers, rapists, and thieves might seem to be an odd constituency for 2
a party that prides itself on its touchy-feely concern for women and victims.
But desperate times call for desperate measures. After three national electoral
defeats in a row, the Democrats need to enlarge their base. If that means reaching out to lock in the pedophile and home-invader vote, so be it. Even newly
moderate Democrat Hillary Clinton has recently endorsed voting rights for
ex-cons. This is inclusiveness with a vengeance.

The liberal advocates and Democratic politicians seeking the enfranchise- 3
ment of felons deny any narrow political motivation, of course. Their interest
is moral, they claim: it is just *wrong* to deny felons the vote. Their various
arguments in support of this conclusion, though, fail to persuade.

The most frequently heard charge is that disenfranchising felons is rac- 4
ist because the felon population is disproportionately black. But the mere
fact that blacks make up a lopsided percentage of the nation's prison population doesn't prove that racism is to blame. Is the mostly male population
of the prisons evidence of reverse sexism? Of course not: men commit the
vast majority of serious crimes—a fact no one would dispute—and that's why
there are lots more of them than women behind bars. Regrettably, blacks also
commit a disproportionate number of felonies, as victim surveys show. In any
case, a felon either deserves his punishment or not, whatever his race. If he
does, it may also be that he deserves disenfranchisement. His race, in both
cases, is irrelevant.

But look where the laws preventing felons from voting arose, the advo- 5
cates say: in bigoted post–Civil War legislatures, keen to keep newly emanci-
pated blacks away from the ballot box. These laws are utterly racist in origin,
like poll taxes and literacy tests. But this argument fails on two counts. First, as
legal writer Roger Clegg notes, many of the same studies appealed to by felon
advocates show that the policy of disenfranchising felons is as old as ancient

Greece and Rome; it made its way to these shores not long after the American Revolution. By the time of the Civil War, 70 percent of the states already had such laws.

Second, even if felon disenfranchisement *did* have a disreputable origin, 6 it wouldn't follow that the policy is bad. To think otherwise would be to commit what logicians call the genetic fallacy. Say Abraham Lincoln drafted the Emancipation Proclamation purely for cynical political reasons, or to exact vengeance on rebellious Southern plantation owners, or just to get rid of some unneeded scratch paper. It would be silly to suggest that therefore freeing the slaves wasn't a good thing.

Felon advocates also argue that to prevent felons from voting, especially 7 after their release from prison, unfairly punishes them twice for the same crime. On this view, the ex-con pays his debt to society by doing time and should suffer no further punishment. But this begs the question at issue: should a felon lose his vote as well as spend time behind bars? Few people would say that the drunk driver sentenced by a judge to lose his driver's license and to pay a hefty fine is punished twice. Most would agree that, given the crime, this one punishment with two components is perfectly apt. Similarly, those who support disenfranchising felons do not believe in punishing criminals twice for the same misdeed; they believe in punishing them once, with the penalty including both jail time and the loss of the vote. A punishment of incarceration without disenfranchisement, they plausibly maintain, would be too lenient.

The claim that disenfranchising felons is wrong because the right to vote 8 is basic and inalienable—another common argument of the advocates—is no more convincing. Obviously, the right is not basic and inalienable in any legal sense, since the laws banning murderers, thieves, and other wrongdoers from voting have stood for a long time. Nor is the right basic and inalienable in a moral sense. Even John Locke, the English philosopher generally regarded as having the greatest influence on the American founding, didn't view the franchise in that light. True, Locke believed that all human beings had certain rights by nature (such as rights to life, liberty, and property), that government existed to protect those rights, and that any legitimate government had to rest on the tacit consent of the people. But the government that the people consented to did not need to be democratic, in Locke's view—it might even be monarchical.

As long as it protected the basic rights of citizens and retained their loy- 9 alty, it remained legitimate, whether or not it allowed its citizens to vote.

Further, Locke added, under certain circumstances we can lose even the 10 rights we do have by nature. Someone who violates another's rights to life, liberty, and property forfeits his own rights to these things; society can legitimately punish him by removing these rights. The criminal has broken the social compact and violated the trust of his fellow citizens. He cannot reasonably complain if they mete out to him a measure of the very harm that he has inflicted on them. Their doing so is a means of dissuading others from breaking the social contract.

Seen in this light, disenfranchisement seems a particularly appropriate pun- 11
ishment for felons. The murderer, rapist, or thief has expressed contempt for his
fellow citizens and broken the rules
of society in the most unmistakable
way. It's fitting that society should
deprive him of his role in determining
the content of those rules or electing
the magistrate who enforces them.

> "Disenfranchisement seems a particularly appropriate punishment for felons."

A *New York Times* editorial this 12
past February favored felon voting—no surprise there—but put forward a
different rationale. The disenfranchisement of felons, the paper held, "may
actually contribute to recidivism by keeping ex-offenders and their families
disengaged from the civic mainstream"—a notion "clearly supported by data
showing that former offenders who vote are less likely to return to jail."

The *Times*'s argument is at least more serious than those considered so far. 13
Still, it doesn't fly. Recidivism doubtless is also less common among ex-cons
who return their videos on time. That doesn't mean they should be rewarded
with free rental privileges at Blockbuster. More to the point, it doesn't seem
to have occurred to the *Times* that it might be misinterpreting the (alleged)
causal connection between voting and keeping out of trouble. Surely it's at
least plausible—in fact, quite plausible—that it is precisely the sort of person
disposed to learn from his mistakes and become more conscientious who is
likely to vote in the first place. That is, it isn't that voting makes someone
responsible but that the responsible person will be likelier to vote.

If that's true, then a former inmate who already has what it takes to clean 14
up his act isn't likely to relapse into a life of crime just because he can't cast
a ballot. By the same logic, an ex-con hell-bent on new rapes and muggings
isn't going to turn over a new leaf just because he gets to vote—even if it's
to vote for a Democrat. The notion that he might is pure sentimentality. It
assumes that deep inside the typical burglar or car jacker lurks a Morgan
Freeman–type character, full of world-weary wisdom and latent civic virtue. A neoconservative, some say, is a liberal mugged by reality. A felon-vote
advocate seems to be a liberal who has seen *The Shawshank Redemption* one
too many times.

It would be a tall order for any moral or political theory, let alone the 15
Lockean one central to the American tradition, to make a convincing case that
the disenfranchisement of felons is particularly unjust. How is depriving felons
of the vote worse than stripping them of their freedom by incarcerating them?
Surely the right to liberty is far more basic and fundamental than the franchise.
Yet few would deny that it's legitimate to deprive serious criminals of their
liberty. To do so, after all, would be to deny the possibility of criminal justice.

Perhaps, though, some advocates of felon voting have trouble with the 16
basic concept of criminal justice. Traditional notions of desert, punishment,
and retribution aren't in fashion among those whose hearts bleed more for
perpetrators than for victims. The movement to give felons the vote may be a

sign that the tough-on-crime New Democrat is as passé as the Kerry campaign: for a whiff of the criminal-as-victim mind-set seems to surround the whole enterprise. The *Times* editorial coos over unnamed "democracies abroad" that "valu[e] the franchise so much that they take ballot boxes right to the prisons." It would have been more accurate to say that they "value the idea of individual responsibility so little that they take ballot boxes right to the prisons."

Such countries devalue the franchise by throwing it away on murderers 17 and other criminals, whose fellow citizens' blood is still fresh on their hands. Such hands can only defile a ballot. If the right to vote is as precious as felon advocates claim to believe it is, we should expect people to uphold at least some minimum moral standards in order to keep it—such as refraining from violating their fellow voters' own inalienable rights.

Those pushing for felon voting will thus need to come up with much bet- 18 ter arguments before they can hope to convince their fellow citizens. They ought at least to try. People might otherwise begin to suspect that the hope of gaining political advantage is the only reason they advocate reform.

⊘ READING ARGUMENTS

1. Feser writes that "the felon vote would prove a windfall for the Democrats" (para. 1). To what degree is the likely party identification of felons relevant to the debate about whether to grant them voting rights?

2. According to Feser, some supporters of restoring voting rights to felons engage in arguments that "fail to persuade" (3). What are these arguments? Do you agree with Feser's assessment of them? Why or why not? Can you identify any fallacies in his reasoning?

3. In paragraph 8, Feser appeals to the authority of seventeenth-century English philosopher John Locke. What support does Locke provide for Feser's position?

4. In paragraph 13, Feser develops an argument by analogy. What analogy does he make? How persuasive is this analogy?

5. What attitude does Feser take toward those who support granting or restoring voting rights to felons? How does the tone of his essay reveal this attitude?

This piece is from the November 6, 2003, issue of the *Nation*.

THE LAST DISENFRANCHISED CLASS

REBECCA PERL

It was 1986, and Jan Warren knew she had to do something to change her life. 1 She wanted to get home to California where her father had just died and left her a produce business. But Warren, 35, was stuck on the East Coast with no money, in a dead-end relationship and pregnant. Desperate, she made a mistake: She agreed to sell cocaine for her cousin. It was the only time Warren had ever sold drugs, and it turned out to be a police sting.

Under strict New York drug laws, Warren was given fifteen years to life. 2 And one sunny Memorial Day in the prison yard, Warren suddenly understood that serving time in prison was going to cost her more than her physical freedom. "I knew people who had died in the wars. I thought of them on Memorial Day—that's what you were supposed to do," said Warren, now 52. "But on that holiday, I realized that something was missing. It was the American flag. It was gone. I couldn't see it. And that should have been my first clue. If you saw the flag you might think of yourself as a citizen with certain inalienable rights, and the truth is, that's wrong."

Warren added, "I didn't realize that part of the whole prison system is set 3 up to alienate you from society, because now I can't vote. And without being able to vote, what politician is going to say, 'Well, Ms. Warren, you have a very good point and because you're one of my constituents I'm going to listen to you'?"

Eventually Warren, a registered Republican, wrote to New York Governor 4 George Pataki after serving six years, and she was later granted clemency—but still not the right to vote. New York laws say any felon in prison or on parole loses that right, and Warren may be on parole for life.

Tough drug laws are one of the primary reasons women like Warren end 5 up in prison. Drug laws are also one of the principal reasons that today one in twenty men can expect to spend part of his life in prison. And an exploding prison population means nearly 5 million people are unable to vote because they have been convicted of a felony— defined as any crime that carries a sentence of a year or more in prison. Today felons and former felons are the single largest group currently barred by law from voting in the United States.

"Today felons and former felons are the single largest group currently barred by law from voting."

Voting rights are left up to the states, so the laws vary. Only Maine and 6 Vermont allow prisoners to vote. Most states take the right away from those in prison and also those on parole or probation. While most states also return the right to vote once the terms of a sentence have been completed, thirteen states, five of them in the South, take voting rights away for life—a punishment extremely rare in the rest of the Western world. As a result, there are now more ex-prisoners than prisoners in the United States who can't vote.

Civil rights advocates predict that voting rights for prisoners and ex-prisoners 7 will be the next U.S. suffrage movement, as lawyers, prison advocates, voting rights groups and foundations have recently begun to join forces and take up the cause. "The United States, this great democracy, was founded as this experiment, and it was a great experiment. But it was a very limited one as well," says Marc Mauer of the Sentencing Project, a prison advocacy group in Washington, D.C. "At the time the country was founded, essentially a group of wealthy white men granted themselves the right to vote." Mauer says that today, we look back on that decision with some degree of national embarrassment, and our history since then has been one of trying to open the franchise.

But if history offers any lessons, it won't be an easy fight or a quick one. 8 That's because, according to some sociologists who study disenfranchisement, the removal of barriers for felons could affect the political balance of power in this country. For one thing, felons who get the chance vote overwhelmingly Democratic, and with a Republican administration in power, there is little chance for change on a national scale.

Disenfranchisement laws can be traced back to ancient Greece and Rome. 9 In Renaissance Europe, people who committed certain crimes were condemned to a "civil death," and lost their civil rights. In the United States, many states passed disenfranchisement laws in the years just after Reconstruction, when blacks were first gaining the right to vote. At the time lawmakers justified the laws by invoking what one Alabama politician called the "menace of negro domination." "This was at the exact same historical period when poll taxes and literacy requirements were being adopted by many Southern legislatures," says Mauer. "All with the express purpose of disenfranchising black voters, so that one Southern legislator at the time referred to the felon disenfranchisement laws as almost an insurance policy." Today the laws are justified on race-neutral grounds, but their discriminatory impact remains.

Also, American laws seem to be out of sync with those of other countries 10 in their severity. Prisoners never lose their right to vote in eighteen countries across Europe, including Ireland, Spain, Switzerland and Poland. In South Africa, prisoners helped to elect one of their own—Nelson Mandela. And last year the Supreme Court of Canada ruled that denying prisoners the vote is "anti-democratic" and "denies the basis of democratic legitimacy."

In the United States the laws affect large numbers of people, and black 11 people in particular. Across the country, one in eight African-American men is barred from voting. In Florida and Alabama, it's one in three. Sometimes felon disenfranchisement laws take the vote away from whole communities. In New York State, 90 percent of prisoners serve their time upstate, yet overwhelmingly these prisoners come from just seven poor, minority neighborhoods in New York City.

Jazz Hayden is from one of those neighborhoods: Harlem. He's one of 131,000 prisoners or parolees in New York State who can't vote because of a felony conviction. As Hayden explains it, just about everyone in Harlem has a brother or a nephew or a cousin who's locked up. Though blacks make up only 15 percent of the state population, they make up more than half the prison population—a situation that is repeated across the country. Because whites are more likely to be offered plea bargains and alternative sentences, they are less likely to spend time in prison and lose the right to vote, according to the New York Civil Liberties Union. 12

In the 1970s Hayden prospered in Harlem. He owned a nightclub and a building on the block where he grew up. But in summer 1987, Hayden was arrested for stabbing and killing a sanitation worker during a fight and was sentenced to prison, where he spent the next thirteen years. There, Hayden had a lot of time to think and read. He got a master's degree in theology. He also filed a lawsuit against the state on behalf of prisoners in New York. "The vote in America represents power because come Election Day, when I go to the voting booth and Bill Gates goes to the voting booth all of us have one vote," he says. "George Bush, Bill Gates and myself—and it's probably the only time in America that we're all equal. And to deny me that right is to say that I'm not a citizen. I'm right back in the same situation that my ancestors were in." 13

Today the NAACP Legal Defense Fund has taken the lead on challenging the voting restriction in court. It reviewed the suit Hayden filed in prison and expanded its scope; in January Hayden's suit became *Hayden v. Pataki*, a class action on behalf of black and Latino prisoners and parolees in New York, and the handful of communities they come from. The suit charges that the law is discriminatory and unconstitutional. "This really shouldn't be viewed any differently than any other struggle for suffrage in this country," says Janai Nelson, a lawyer on the case. "We excluded women from voting for a long time. We excluded non-property holders, we excluded other minorities, despite the fact that this is really the bedrock of our democracy." 14

But not everyone buys Nelson's argument. That includes many crime victims and their relatives. "I don't want these people having access to making changes in my life; they have already done that," says Janice Grieshaber, whose daughter Jenna was murdered in Albany in 1997 one week before she was to graduate from nursing school. Grieshaber says it's really pretty simple: People who don't follow the laws shouldn't have a say in making them. 15

Yet even Grieshaber makes a distinction between the rights of violent and nonviolent criminals. As she sees it, someone locked up because of drugs or a white-collar crime is a more sympathetic figure than, say, someone convicted of manslaughter. And some politicians and criminologists agree. Chris Uggen, a sociologist at the University of Minnesota who studies felon disenfranchisement, says those fighting for felons' right to vote would have a better chance of success if they focused on nonviolent criminals. But Nelson remains unswayed. "This is what it means to be an American," she says. "Regardless of whether or not you're a good American, a law-abiding American, a PC American, really 16 the right to vote does not vary based on our different ideas about what we would ideally like you to be as a person in this country."

Others remain more pragmatic. Legislation introduced by Congressman   17
John Conyers, a Michigan Democrat, seeks (so far unsuccessfully) to grant
the vote to ex-prisoners. An election reform commission on which sit former
Presidents Jimmy Carter and Gerald Ford, set up after the Florida debacle in
2000, made a similar suggestion. "A strong case can be made in favor of restoration of voting rights when an individual has completed the full sentence . . .
including any period of probation or parole," reads their 2001 report. Senator
Harry Reid, a Nevada Democrat, tried to make Carter's suggestion a reality
when he offered an amendment to an election reform package passed last year.
The amendment failed.

Nevertheless, most Americans are in favor of such a move; a poll taken   18
last year showed that 80 percent of Americans support restoring the vote to
ex-felons who have completed their sentences.

Chris Uggen found that had felons been allowed to vote in the last   19
presidential election, hanging chads would have never been an issue. Uggen
looked at the closely contested 2000 election and discovered that had felons
had the vote, Al Gore would have likely won the popular vote by more than
a million votes. In Florida alone, Gore would have picked up 60,000–80,000
votes—enough to swamp the narrow victory margin declared for George
Bush. Uggen also found that had felons—even just those who had completed
their sentences—voted over the past couple of decades, races across the country might have looked very different. One critical difference could have been
control of the U.S. Senate. Republicans including John Warner of Virginia
and Mitch McConnell of Kentucky would likely have lost in past elections,
according to Uggen, which may be part of the reason Senator McConnell told
his senatorial colleagues when Reid's amendment was being debated on the
floor: "We are talking about rapists and murderers, robbers and even terrorists or spies."

For their part, Democrats in Congress have not rushed to champion the   20
issue. Appearing soft on crime might cost Democrats more votes than they
would gain, suggests Uggen. Also, felons are a constituency that can't exactly
fill Democratic coffers, say Washington insiders, so they don't get a lot of
attention. Janai Nelson of the legal defense fund says that when it comes to
expanding the franchise, those in power are content with the status quo. "They
are already successful. They've made their way into office and they've relied on
the political system as it exists, and very few people want to rock the boat and
bring in a new constituency that they may not be familiar with," she says.

At an NAACP candidate forum this summer, presidential candidates   21
John Kerry, Bob Graham, Howard Dean, Carol Moseley Braun, John Edwards
and Al Sharpton said they supported restoring the right to vote to ex-felons,
though Edwards and Graham voted against Reid's amendment last year.
(Kerry voted for it.) Joseph Lieberman, who did not attend, did support Reid.
In 2003, Dennis Kucinich, who was not at the forum, co-sponsored a similar

bill by John Conyers in the House calling for ex-felons to be allowed to vote. Dick Gephardt favors leaving the issue to the states.

For her part, Jan Warren wonders: What happened to rehabilitation? 22 And what about the women she met in prison who struck out in self-defense against violent husbands and rapists? Or those who were wrongly convicted? In January, then-Illinois Governor George Ryan pardoned Madison Hobley, who spent thirteen years on death row for murder. At a nationally televised press conference, the governor said Hobley and three other death-row inmates were wrongly prosecuted, and called the system that convicted them "wildly inaccurate, unjust . . . and, at times, a very racist system."

When it was Hobley's chance to speak, it wasn't the fact that his life was 23 spared that he wanted to talk about. "I said I can't wait to vote again, it was the first thing I wanted to do," said Hobley. "Two weeks after I got out I made sure to get my voter's registration card, and all the officials that turned their head on me, now I've got a chance to get back at them and vote them out."

History is a slow process, but time seems to be on the side of expanding 24 the franchise. "It will be a decades-long struggle but it has the potential to be decade-defining for those members of society who are the most stigmatized and the most invisible," says Robin Templeton, who is now directing an effort in New York, Maryland, Texas, Alabama and Florida focused on restoring voting rights to prisoners. In recent years, Connecticut, Delaware, Maryland and New Mexico have passed less restrictive disenfranchisement laws, and there are legal challenges pending in Florida and Washington State as well as New York. *Hayden v. Pataki* is expected to come to trial in 2005.

◑ READING ARGUMENTS

1. Perl begins her essay with an anecdote. How does this anecdote support her position on the issue?

2. According to Perl, how many U.S. states allow prisoners to vote in elections? Why is this information important?

3. In paragraph 10, Perl claims that American laws that deny felons and prisoners the right to vote are "out of sync with those of other countries." She also notes that 80% of Americans "support restoring the vote to ex-felons who have completed their sentences" (para. 18). Is Perl committing the bandwagon fallacy here?

4. Where does Perl consider arguments against her position? How does she address them?

This editorial appeared in the *New York Times* on July 11, 2004.

FELONS AND THE RIGHT TO VOTE

NEW YORK TIMES

About 4.7 million Americans, more than 2 percent of the adult population, 1
are barred from voting because of a felony conviction. Denying the vote to
ex-offenders is antidemocratic, and undermines the nation's commitment
to rehabilitating people who have paid their debt to society. Felon disenfranchisement laws also have a sizable racial impact: 13 percent of black men have
had their votes taken away, seven times the national average. But even if it
were acceptable as policy, denying felons the vote has been a disaster because
of the chaotic and partisan way it has been carried out.

Thirty-five states prohibit at least some people from voting after they have 2
been released from prison. The rules about which felonies are covered and
when the right to vote is restored vary widely from state to state, and often
defy logic. In four states, including New York, felons on parole cannot vote,
but felons on probation can. In some states, felons must formally apply for
restoration of their voting rights, which state officials can grant or deny on the
most arbitrary of grounds.

Florida may have changed the outcome of the 2000 presidential election 3
when Secretary of State Katherine Harris oversaw a purge of suspected felons
that removed an untold number of eligible voters from the rolls. This year,
state officials are conducting a new purge that may be just as flawed. They have
developed a list of 47,000 voters who may be felons, and have asked local officials to consider purging them. But the *Miami Herald* found that more than
2,100 of them may have been listed in error, because their voting rights were
restored by the state's clemency process. Last week, the state acknowledged
that 1,600 of those on the list should be allowed to vote.

Election officials are also far too secretive about felon voting issues, which 4
should be a matter of public record. When Ms. Harris used inaccurate standards for purging voters, the public did not find out until it was too late.
This year, the state tried to keep the 47,000 names on its list of possible felons
secret, but fortunately a state court ruled this month that they should be open
to scrutiny.

There is a stunning lack of information and transparency surrounding 5
felon disenfranchisement across the country. The rules are often highly technical, and little effort is made to explain them to election officials or to the people affected. In New York, the Brennan Center for Justice at New York University Law School found that local elections offices often did not understand
the law, and some demanded that felons produce documents that do not exist.

Too often, felon voting is seen as a partisan issue. In state legislatures, it is 6 usually Democrats who try to restore voting rights, and Republicans who resist. Recently, Republicans and election officials in Missouri and South Dakota have raised questions about voter registration groups' employment of ex-felons, although they have every right to be involved in political activity. In Florida, the decision about whether a felon's right to vote will be restored lies with a panel made up of the governor and members of his cabinet. Some voting rights activists believe that Gov. Jeb Bush has moved slowly, and reinstated voting rights for few of the state's ex-felons, to help President Bush's re-election prospects.

The treatment of former felons in the electoral system cries out for reform. 7 The cleanest and fairest approach would be simply to remove the prohibitions on felon voting. In his State of the Union address in January, President Bush announced a new national commitment to helping prisoners re-enter society. Denying them the right to vote belies this commitment.

> "The treatment of former felons in the electoral system cries out for reform."

Restoring the vote to felons is difficult, 8 because it must be done state by state, and because ex-convicts do not have much of a political lobby. There have been legislative successes in recent years in some places, including Alabama and Nevada. But other states have been moving in the opposite direction. The best hope of reform may lie in the courts. The Atlanta-based United States Court of Appeals for the 11th Circuit and the San Francisco–based Court of Appeals for the Ninth Circuit have ruled recently that disenfranchising felons may violate equal protection or the Voting Rights Act.

Until the whole idea of permanently depriving felons of their right to vote 9 is wiped away, the current rules should be applied more fairly. The quality of voting roll purges must be improved. Florida should discontinue its current felon purge until it can prove that the list it is using is accurate.

Mechanisms for restoring voting rights to felons must be improved. Even 10 in states where felons have the right to vote, they are rarely notified of this when they exit prison. Released prisoners should be given that information during the discharge process, and helped with the paperwork.

The process for felons to regain their voting rights should be streamlined. 11 In Nevada, early reports are that the restoration of felon voting rights has had minimal effect, because the paperwork requirements are too burdensome. Ex-felons who apply to vote should have the same presumption of eligibility as other voters.

Voting rights should not be a political football. There should be bipartisan 12 support for efforts to help ex-felons get their voting rights back, by legislators and by state and local election officials. American democracy is diminished when officeholders and political parties, for their own political gain, try to keep people from voting.

⊖ READING ARGUMENTS

1. The writers cite several statistics in the first paragraph. How do these statistics introduce and support the main argument of the editorial? What other opening strategy might be more effective? Why?

2. According to the editorial, the policy of "denying felons the vote has been a disaster because of the chaotic and partisan way it has been carried out" (para. 1). What evidence do the writers provide to support this statement? How persuasive is this evidence?

3. The writers claim that restoring voting rights is difficult, in part "because ex-convicts do not have much of a political lobby" (8). What do they mean?

4. The editorial criticizes current policies on the issue of felon disenfranchisement. What alternative policies, if any, do the writers propose?

⊖ AT ISSUE: SHOULD FELONS PERMANENTLY FORFEIT THEIR RIGHT TO VOTE?

1. How does Rebecca Perl characterize felons in her essay? How does Edward Feser characterize felons in his essay? Which description seems more accurate to you? How do these different characterizations affect your response to the writers' respective arguments?

2. Some people believe that lawmakers should take into account the history of African American voting rights when they consider restoring voting rights to felons; however, Edward Feser believes that felons' race is not relevant to the debate. What part, if any, do you think race should play in this discussion—and in the shaping of policy?

3. The *New York Times* editorial notes that President George W. Bush, in his 2004 State of the Union address, "announced a new national commitment to helping prisoners reenter society" (para. 7). Do you believe the restoration of voting rights should be a significant part of this reentry process? Why or why not?

⊖ WRITING ARGUMENTS: SHOULD FELONS PERMANENTLY FORFEIT THEIR RIGHT TO VOTE?

1. In Rebecca Perl's essay, the parent of a murder victim argues that those "who don't follow the laws shouldn't have a say in making them" (para. 15). However, an attorney quoted in the same article claims, "whether or not you're a good American, a law-abiding American, . . . the right to vote does not vary based on . . . what we would ideally

like you to be" as a U.S. citizen (16). After reading the sources in this casebook, write an essay that takes a stand on the issue of whether felons should be permitted to vote.

2. Edward Feser focuses on the punishment of criminals (for example, in paragraph 7), while both the *New York Times* editorial and Rebecca Perl's essay focus on the need for rehabilitation. Presuming that many convicted felons will be returning to society after their sentences, which of these two aspects of our criminal justice system do you see as more important? Write an essay that expresses your view.

Should Openly Gay Men and Women Be Permitted to Serve in the Military?

The current Defense Department position regarding gay men and women in the military is popularly known as "don't ask, don't tell." The policy, which is currently under review, prohibits homosexuals in the military from engaging in homosexual acts, openly declaring their homosexuality, or pursuing gay marriages. Essentially, the government no longer asks recruits or active military personnel if they are gay. As long as their sexual preferences are not made public, gay men and women are permitted to serve. Designed in part by the then-chair of the Joint Chiefs of Staff Colin Powell, the policy began in 1993, during the presidency of Bill Clinton. Clinton had campaigned on a pledge to reverse the rule prohibiting homosexuals in the military, and "don't ask, don't tell" represented an uneasy compromise between the president and those who opposed reversing the previous ban. In March 2010, Defense Secretary Robert Gates approved new rules that will make it harder to discharge gays from the military.

Over the years, the military has had various policies regarding homosexuals. Prior to World War I, U.S. military law did not explicitly address the issue. After the war, sodomy became grounds for court martial—although the rule applied to both homosexuals and heterosexuals. During World War II, military officials attempted to screen out homosexuals, but the draft and the need for a large military force made the issue relatively insignificant. In 1949, the Defense Department instituted a stronger policy against gays in the military, which evolved over the years to include rigorous psychological evaluations of recruits.

No one disputes that gay men and women have served over the years and served honorably. Still, objections persist. Originally, opponents of gays in the military presumed that homosexuals would make poor soldiers, basing that presumption on common stereotypes of gay men as effeminate or unmanly. Now, those who oppose lifting the ban on openly homosexual military personnel are more likely to suggest that homosexuals may undermine unit cohesion and morale, especially the complex bonding necessary for an effective fighting force.* They also argue that because the armed forces are vital to national security, they should not be used as a testing ground for experiments in progressive social policy—particularly while the United States is engaged in wars in Iraq and Afghanistan.

However, those who believe openly gay people should be allowed to serve often see the issue as a simple matter of equal rights before the law and the federal government. There are practical reasons to support this position as well: more than 13,000 gay men and women (including many with much-needed fluency in Arabic and Farsi) have been discharged from the military despite their valuable service. Among countries that belong to the North Atlantic Treaty Organization, only the United States, Turkey, and Greece bar openly gay soldiers from serving, while U.S. allies such as Canada, the United Kingdom, and Israel have no such restrictions.

The six writers in this debate bring a number of different arguments to bear on the issue. For example, retired Army General John M. Shalikashvili, who served as chair of the Joint Chiefs of Staff under President Bill Clinton and originally supported "don't ask, don't tell," reflects on how new evidence has caused him to change his mind. He now thinks the armed services should welcome openly gay Americans. In contrast, Major Daniel L. Davis worries in "Homosexuals in the Military: Combat Readiness or Social Engineering?" that lifting the ban on openly gay personnel may cause problems within harmonious and well-trained units.

---

*In 2009, the military journal *Joint Forces Quarterly* published an article by Colonel Om Prakash that recommended the repeal of "don't ask, don't tell," stating, "There is no scientific evidence to support the claim that unit cohesion will be negatively affected if homosexuals serve openly."

This op-ed essay by a former U.S. Army general appeared in the *New York Times* on January 2, 2007.

SECOND THOUGHTS ON GAYS IN THE MILITARY

JOHN M. SHALIKASHVILI

Two weeks ago, President Bush called for a long-term plan to increase the size of the armed forces. As our leaders consider various options for carrying out Mr. Bush's vision, one issue likely to generate fierce debate is "don't ask, don't tell," the policy that bars openly gay service members from the military. Indeed, leaders in the new Congress are planning to re-introduce a bill to repeal the policy next year. 1

As was the case in 1993—the last time the American people thoroughly debated the question of whether openly gay men and lesbians should serve in the military—the issue will give rise to passionate feelings on both sides. The debate must be conducted with sensitivity, but it must also consider the evidence that has emerged over the last 14 years. 2

When I was chairman of the Joint Chiefs of Staff, I supported the current policy because I believed that implementing a change in the rules at that time would have been too burdensome for our troops and commanders. I still believe that to have been true. The concern among many in the military was that given the longstanding view that homosexuality was incompatible with service, letting people who were openly gay serve would lower morale, harm recruitment and undermine unit cohesion. 3

In the early 1990s, large numbers of military personnel were opposed to letting openly gay men and lesbians serve. President Bill Clinton, who promised to lift the ban during his campaign, was overwhelmed by the strength of the opposition, which threatened to overturn any executive action he might take. The compromise that came to be known as "don't ask, don't tell" was thus a useful speed bump that allowed temperatures to cool for a period of time while the culture continued to evolve. 4

The question before us now is whether enough time has gone by to give this policy serious reconsideration. Much evidence suggests that it has. 5

"Gays and lesbians can be accepted by their peers."

Last year I held a number of meetings with gay soldiers and marines, including some with combat experience in Iraq, and an openly gay senior sailor who was serving effectively as a member of a nuclear submarine crew. These conversations showed me just how much the military has changed, and that gays and lesbians can be accepted by their peers. 6

This perception is supported by a new Zogby poll of more than 500 service members returning from Afghanistan and Iraq, three quarters of whom said 7 they were comfortable interacting with gay people. And 24 foreign nations, including Israel, Britain and other allies in the fight against terrorism, let gays serve openly, with none reporting morale or recruitment problems.

I now believe that if gay men and lesbians served openly in the United 8 States military, they would not undermine the efficacy of the armed forces. Our military has been stretched thin by our deployments in the Middle East, and we must welcome the service of any American who is willing and able to do the job.

But if America is ready for a military policy of nondiscrimination based 9 on sexual orientation, the timing of the change should be carefully considered. As the 110th Congress opens for business, some of its most urgent priorities, like developing a more effective strategy in Iraq, share widespread support that spans political affiliations. Addressing such issues could help heal the divisions that cleave our country. Fighting early in this Congress to lift the ban on openly gay service members is not likely to add to that healing, and it risks alienating people whose support is needed to get this country on the right track.

By taking a measured, prudent approach to change, political and mili- 10 tary leaders can focus on solving the nation's most pressing problems while remaining genuinely open to the eventual and inevitable lifting of the ban. When that day comes, gay men and lesbians will no longer have to conceal who they are, and the military will no longer need to sacrifice those whose service it cannot afford to lose.

⊘ READING ARGUMENTS

1. This essay is called "Second Thoughts on Gays in the Military." What was Shalikashvili's original position on the subject back in 1993? What is his position now?

2. Shalikashvili claims that he changed his mind regarding gays in the military after considering "the evidence that has emerged over the last 14 years" (para. 2). What is the nature of this evidence? How persuasive do you find it in terms of your own view of the issue?

3. In retrospect, how does Shalikashvili view the "don't ask, don't tell" policy? What purpose, if any, does he think it has served?

4. What elements of Rogerian argument does Shalikashvili use in this essay? Given his likely audience, do you think this strategy makes sense?

This statement was delivered by a retired U.S. Army major general on June 23, 2008.

STATEMENT TO THE SUBCOMMITTEE ON MILITARY PERSONNEL, HOUSE ARMED SERVICES COMMITTEE, U.S. HOUSE OF REPRESENTATIVES

VANCE COLEMAN

Madam Chairman, Members of the Committee and my fellow witnesses.   1

During my more than 30 years of service to the United States, I have seen   2
and experienced what happens when our armed forces treat some service personnel as second-class citizens and, conversely, what we can achieve when we
reverse those views and embrace all of our troops as first-class patriots with an
important contribution to make.

I enlisted in the Army when I was 17—in the days before we desegregated   3
our fighting units or our park fountains. My father was a laborer, and my
mother was a domestic worker. And there was, quite simply, no way I was
headed to college. So I decided to head to the military instead.

I served in segregated units in both the United States and Europe before   4
being selected to attend an integrated Leadership Academy and then Officers
Candidate School. After Officers Candidate School, I was assigned to a combat
arms unit. When I reported for duty, however, I was promptly reassigned to a
service unit that was all-black.

The message was clear: It did not matter that I was a qualified Field Artil-   5
lery Officer who was qualified to serve in the all-white combat arms unit. It
only mattered that I was black.

Madam Chairman, I know what it is like to be thought of as second-class,   6
and I know what it is like to have your hard work dismissed because of who
you are or what you look like. I also know what a difference it made when we
placed qualification ahead of discrimination and tore down the walls of racial
prejudice in our fighting forces.

As an Army commander, I also know how disruptive it would be to   7
remove a trained, skilled service member from a unit. It is bewildering, and
counter-intuitive, to me that we maintain a federal law that says, no matter
how well a person does his or her job . . . no matter how integral to their unit
they are . . . they must be removed, disrespected and dismissed because of who
they happen to be, or who they happen to love.

That is why I am grateful to have the opportunity today to urge Congress   8
to repeal "Don't Ask, Don't Tell." The military has shown it excels at blending
people together from different backgrounds and beliefs, putting the mission
first. I ask Congress to repeal "Don't Ask, Don't Tell" and allow the military

to benefit from having the best and the brightest serve regardless of sexual orientation.

In Korea, I was assigned to a Field Artillery Unit that was totally integrated. The unit consisted of individuals from all walks of life who were white, black and brown. There was never a problem of unit morale or unit cohesion. The only thing that the soldiers were interested in was your ability to perform, and whether you could be depended upon when the going got tough. 9

One thing that I learned from serving in the Korean conflict is that in a 24 hour combat situation, the troops are not concerned about who you are or what you believe, but whether you can perform. Performance would mean the difference between winning or losing, life or death. I soon learned from the Senior NCO's that the key to success was performance. That is true fifty years later and it will be true one hundred years into the future. 10

> "Troops are not concerned about who you are or what you believe, but whether you can perform."

As Battery Executive Officer in Korea, I supervised a Sergeant First Class, a communication Chief, who happened to be gay. 11

The Sergeant was in charge of the unit's communication system, including maintenance, organization and design. He was, to put it plainly, essential to the unit's performance, and he was damn good at his job, too. Having to remove him from that position, and from the Army entirely, would have harmed our unit's ability to get our job done. 12

There are some who say that removing a few gay troops won't make a difference. But to commanders who need an Arabic linguist on the ground in Iraq, it can make a very big difference, indeed. And to a parent whose son is bleeding on the battlefield, and being saved by a lesbian nurse, it makes quite a difference, too. Our armed services have always believed in, and promoted, the very true idea that one person can make a real difference in our country and our military. 13

This committee should be concerned, first and foremost, about the readiness of armed forces, and the personnel policies that best serve that readiness. And all of us here today know that, when the federal government gives the order, commanders re-iterate it and service members salute and follow it. 14

As a combat leader, I learned to constantly train my troops to adapt to changing combat conditions, to changing weapons systems, to changing terrain. In the 1980's, I was Division Commander of the 84th Reserve Training Division, testing our mobilization planning by establishing new training models. Military leadership, indeed, is about being able to constantly adapt to change. That is why we are the best military in the world and that is why we are better than the outdated arguments that some still use to prop up "Don't Ask, Don't Tell." 15

Because of this law, five dozen Arabic language experts have been dismissed. Nearly 800 people with skills the DoD admits are "mission-critical" 16 have been sent home. And, according to sound research, another 41,000 lesbian and gay Americans who want to serve have been reluctant to sign up. That's the equivalent of 15 to 20 brigades. And it's unacceptable that we have said we do not want them.

"Don't Ask, Don't Tell" hurts our military readiness. It undermines 17 our commitment to being a nation where we are all equal in the eyes of the law. And it ties the hands of commanders who want to welcome and retain America's best and brightest into the military fold.

It's time, for the sake of our military, to end this modern-day prejudice 18 and embrace all of our troops as first-class patriots with an important contribution to make.

⊙ READING ARGUMENTS

1. Coleman relies on argument by analogy in his statement. What is the analogy? How does it help him make his case?

2. According to Coleman, the military "excels at blending people together from different backgrounds and beliefs" (para. 8). How does he support this statement? Why is it relevant to his argument?

3. Where does Coleman address views that differ from his own? How effectively does he refute these opposing viewpoints?

4. According to Coleman, what is the cost of maintaining the "don't ask, don't tell" policy?

5. In both his opening and closing paragraphs, Coleman uses the phrase "first-class patriots." What do you think he means by this phrase?

A former petty officer in the U.S. Navy wrote this piece, which appeared in the *New York Times* on June 8, 2007.

DON'T ASK, DON'T TRANSLATE

STEPHEN BENJAMIN

Imagine for a moment an American soldier deep in the Iraqi desert. His unit 1 is about to head out when he receives a cable detailing an insurgent ambush right in his convoy's path. With this information, he and his soldiers are now prepared for the danger that lies ahead.

Reports like these are regularly sent from military translators' desks, 2 providing critical, often life-saving intelligence to troops fighting in Iraq and Afghanistan. But the military has a desperate shortage of linguists trained to translate such invaluable information and convey it to the war zone.

The lack of qualified translators has been a pressing issue for some time— 3 the Army had filled only half its authorized positions for Arabic translators in 2001. Cables went untranslated on Sept. 10 that might have prevented the terrorist attacks on Sept. 11. Today, the American Embassy in Baghdad has nearly 1,000 personnel, but only a handful of fluent Arabic speakers.

I was an Arabic translator. After joining the Navy in 2003, I attended the 4 Defense Language Institute, graduated in the top 10 percent of my class and then spent two years giving our troops the critical translation services they desperately needed. I was ready to serve in Iraq.

But I never got to. In March, I was ousted from the Navy under the "don't ask, 5 don't tell" policy, which mandates dismissal if a service member is found to be gay.

My story begins almost a year ago when my roommate, who is also gay, was 6 deployed to Falluja. We communicated the only way we could: using the military's instant-messaging system on monitored government computers. These electronic conversations are lifelines, keeping soldiers sane while mortars land meters away.

Then, last October the annual inspection of my base, Fort Gordon, Ga., 7 included a perusal of the government computer chat system; inspectors identified 70 service members whose use violated policy. The range of violations was broad: people were flagged for everything from profanity to outright discussions of explicit sexual activity. Among those charged were my former roommate and me. Our messages had included references to our social lives—comments that were otherwise unremarkable, except that they indicated we were both gay.

I could have written a statement denying that I was homosexual, but lying did not seem like the right thing to do. My roommate made the same decision, though he was allowed to remain in Iraq until the scheduled end of his tour. 8

> "Lying did not seem like the right thing to do."

The result was the termination of our careers, and the loss to the military 9 of two more Arabic translators. The 68 other—heterosexual—service members remained on active duty, despite many having committed violations far more egregious than ours; the Pentagon apparently doesn't consider hate speech, derogatory comments about women or sexual misconduct grounds for dismissal.

My supervisors did not want to lose me. Most of my peers knew I was   10
gay, and that didn't bother them. I was always accepted as a member of the team. And my experience was not anomalous: polls of veterans from Iraq and Afghanistan show an overwhelming majority are comfortable with gays. Many were aware of at least one gay person in their unit and had no problem with it.

"Don't ask, don't tell" does nothing but deprive the military of talent it   11
needs and invade the privacy of gay service members just trying to do their jobs and live their lives. Political and military leaders who support the current law may believe that homosexual soldiers threaten unit cohesion and military readiness, but the real damage is caused by denying enlistment to patriotic Americans and wrenching qualified individuals out of effective military units. This does not serve the military or the nation well.

Consider: more than 58 Arabic linguists have been kicked out since "don't   12
ask, don't tell" was instituted. How much valuable intelligence could those men and women be providing today to troops in harm's way?

In addition to those translators, 11,000 other service members have been   13
ousted since the "don't ask, don't tell" policy was passed by Congress in 1993. Many held critical jobs in intelligence, medicine and counterterrorism. An untold number of closeted gay military members don't re-enlist because of the pressure the law puts on them. This is the real cost of the ban—and, with our military so overcommitted and undermanned, it's too high to pay.

In response to difficult recruiting prospects, the Army has already taken   14
a number of steps, lengthening soldiers' deployments to 15 months from 12, enlisting felons and extending the age limit to 42. Why then won't Congress pass a bill like the Military Readiness Enhancement Act, which would repeal "don't ask, don't tell"? The bipartisan bill, by some analysts' estimates, could add more than 41,000 soldiers—all gay, of course.

As the friends I once served with head off to 15-month deployments,   15
I regret I'm not there to lessen their burden and to serve my country. I'm trained to fight, I speak Arabic and I'm willing to serve. No recruiter needs to make a persuasive argument to sign me up. I'm ready, and I'm waiting.

⊙ READING ARGUMENTS

1. What is Benjamin's strategy in his three opening paragraphs? What does he gain (or lose) by introducing his argument in this way?

2. Benjamin begins paragraph 4 with the sentence, "I was an Arabic translator." What is the purpose of this statement?

3. The military discovered that Benjamin was gay by monitoring the military's instant-messenging system. Does this action seem like an unfair violation of privacy, or does it seem justified? Explain.

4. Is this essay a causal argument? An argument by evaluation?

A U.S. Army major wrote this opinion piece for the *Washington Times,* where it appeared on August 15, 2007.

HOMOSEXUALS IN THE MILITARY: COMBAT READINESS OR SOCIAL ENGINEERING?

DANIEL L. DAVIS

There has been a great deal of interest in the media in recent days about a renewed   1
movement to strike down the "Don't Ask, Don't Tell" policy regarding homosexuals serving in the military. The debate,
however, has not been a dialogue so much
as a monologue. It seems virtually every
story written or soundbite uttered involves
supporting the ability of homosexual men
and women to serve openly in the armed
services, but remarkably few discuss the
alternative point of view. Such an important issue ought not be decided based on
such an out-of-balance ratio.

> "The debate . . . has not been a dialogue so much as a monologue."

Many of those supporting a repeal of the ban cite the results of a recent   2
Zogby poll they say indicates changing trends within the military toward
acceptance of openly serving homosexuals. According to the Zogby press
release issued with the poll results, Rep. Marty Meehan, Massachusetts Democrat said, "These new data prove that thousands of gay and lesbian service
members are already deployed overseas and are integrated, important members of their units. It is long past time to strike down 'Don't Ask, Don't Tell'
and create a new policy that allows gays and lesbians to serve openly."

But does the data "prove" that so many homosexual service members are   3
deployed overseas? And further, do the poll results really indicate that those
within the military would be accepting of homosexuals?

Some of the more widely repeated findings of the poll are, according to the   4
Zogby release, that 73 percent of respondents "say they are personally comfortable in the presence of gays and lesbians," and only 27 percent of service members
who said they knew for sure a homosexual was a member of their unit "said it has
a negative impact on the morale of their unit." From these two pieces of information it appears that a significant majority of service members are comfortable with
homosexuals and that a small percentage says it would be a problem. But when the
details of the report are examined, a more complicated picture emerges.

As many may know, front-line combat units in the Army and Marines are vir-   5
tually all male. Question 13 of the Zogby poll asked, "Do you agree or disagree with
allowing gays and lesbians to serve openly in the military?" Forty percent of the men
disagreed, and 39 percent of all active-duty personnel likewise disagreed. The Army
had the lowest percentage of those agreeing with the question at 23 percent.

Questions 16 and 17 asked respondents if they knew of any openly serv-   6
ing homosexual service member in their unit. Of all the respondents, only

23 percent said yes, and of these, 75 percent said there were either one or two homosexual service members in their unit. The average unit in the military is the company, which consists of approximately 120 personnel. Therefore, in an average Army combat unit of all or mostly men there are approximately 48 soldiers who do not agree with openly serving homosexual service members, there are only 28 soldiers who are expressly comfortable with them, 42 who are neutral, and one or two homosexual members.

It is clear beyond question that the homosexual person who seeks to serve in the military believes that his or her lifestyle is perfectly moral and no one will ever convince them otherwise. What may be less clear, however, is that many of those religious persons who serve in the military are convinced that the homosexual lifestyle is immoral, and that their views on the subject are as valid as anyone's. By lifting the ban against openly serving homosexuals in the military, therefore, we force a situation whereby unit commanders must deal with an underlying tension that must be perpetually managed, and will likely undermine their best efforts to form a harmonious, well-trained fighting unit.

How is this in the national interest? As noted in the Zogby poll, of those service members who say they are certain homosexuals serve in their unit, the vast majority reports the total in their unit to be one or two. Are we to say, in the name of fairness, that for the sake of these two or three homosexual service members—or even if it's five or six—we will ask the 25–30 religious service members who oppose homosexuality to compromise their convictions?

What must never be compromised, however, is the singular imperative that should be used by our political leaders in determining policies within the armed forces: The only consideration must be determining which policies create the most effective combat unit possible. If policy-makers feel that permitting openly serving homosexuals will make our armed forces better than they are today—with full consideration of how their decision will impact the rest of the force—then they should lift the ban. If lifting the ban would cause disunity among the ranks and lower our war-fighting capability, then the ban must remain.

To make the decision based on any other political or social expedient would be counterproductive to the nation and could potentially compromise our national security.

⊘ READING ARGUMENTS

1. The title of Davis's essay includes the phrase "social engineering." What does this term mean? What connotations does it have?

2. What problems does Davis have with the debate regarding gays in the military? How does he view the evidence used by those who support striking down the "don't ask, don't tell" policy?

3. Where does Davis use a causal argument?

4. According to Davis, what is the only consideration that should determine the policy on whether gays should be able to serve openly in the military?

A retired U.S. Army sergeant major delivered this statement on July 23, 2008.

STATEMENT TO THE SUBCOMMITTEE ON MILITARY PERSONNEL, HOUSE ARMED SERVICES COMMITTEE, U.S. HOUSE OF REPRESENTATIVES

BRIAN JONES

I am a retired sergeant major, U.S. Army. I am a Ranger first and always. The 1
most common attribute that I see on military evaluation reports is "selfless
service." I chose a career path that placed me in a Ranger Battalion, Delta
Force, and as a detachment sergeant major at the Ranger Regiment.

Selfless service is what makes a good team great within the U.S. military. 2
You won't find that, in truth, in the corporate world. Selfless service is what
an individual will do for the good of the team; self-service is doing what is in
a personal self interest, at the expense of the team. Recently, a U.S. Navy Seal
received the Congressional Medal of Honor by throwing himself on a grenade
to protect his team. That is selfless service.

While deployed to Somalia in 1993, commonly referred to as "Blackhawk 3
Down," two of our unit members received the Medal of Honor for asking to
be inserted into a crash site to protect a pilot, knowing what their fate would
be. That is selfless service, and combat effectiveness depends on it. It does not
happen by accident—it must be taught with concentrated training—no dis-
tractions. Selfless service is reinforced with discipline, and encouraged by the
example of combat leaders.

The Ranger way of life trained me for what I do now as the CEO of 4
a company I started three years ago, Adventure Training Concepts. The
concept of ATC is to use the U.S. Army training model to teach the value
of teamwork during corporate team building and leadership development
training.

Our clients are diverse—men and women, adventure seekers of all ages 5
and, I suspect, some who are homosexual. All of them enjoy and benefit pro-
fessionally from the lessons in teamwork taught by ATC programs. There is
a notable difference, however, between the ATC environment and military
units such as the infantry, special operations forces, and submarines. On
my facility, people learn about teamwork and leadership for 6 hours over a
couple of days, but they do not share close, intimate living conditions comparable to those in the military. The difference is critically important and
disregarded at great risk.

In the civilian business world, decisions frequently are based on bonuses 6
and job security. In the military environment, team cohesion, morale, and
esprit de corps is a matter of life and death. Bonus and job security come sec-

ond to the reality of writing the hard letter to a loved one, or holding the hand of a teammate who is fighting for his or her life.

In my 21 years of service in the U.S. Army, I sought, and performed in as many leadership positions that I could. As a leader, my first obligation was to the nation. It meant keeping our soldiers ready for any situation for which our country called upon them. It meant taking care of each soldier I had the honor of leading. It meant being fair and impartial to every soldier. It also meant keeping the soldiers under my charge as safe, secure, trained, equipped, and informed as I possibly could.

On their behalf, I would respectfully like to say that in this time of war, I find it surprising that we are here today to talk about this issue of repealing the 1993 law. Our soldiers are over-tasked with deploying, fighting, redeploying, refitting, and deploying again. These brave men and women have achieved what many Americans thought impossible. With all of the important issues that require attention, it is difficult to understand why a minority faction is demanding that their concerns be given priority over more important issues.

> "It is difficult to understand why a minority faction is demanding that their concerns be given priority."

As a U.S. Army Ranger, I performed long-range patrols in severe cold weather conditions, in teams of 10, with only mission essential items on our backs. No comfort items. The only way to keep from freezing at night was to get as close as possible for body heat—which means skin to skin. On several occasions, in the close quarters that a team lives, any attraction to same sex teammates, real or perceived, would be known and would be a problem. The presence of openly gay men in these situations would elevate tensions and disrupt unit cohesion and morale.

I have served along side many foreign militaries. None of them compares to the U.S. military. In every case, they would give anything to be like ours. Lack of discipline, morale, and values top the list of reasons why. Between 1997 and 2001 I worked with armies from Poland, Italy, England, and France. The discipline, training, and core values are quite different. Here are two specific examples:

- Operation Deep Strike, 1999, 1st deployment exercise into Poland. I personally had to take charge of a logistical transfer point inside Poland when I stopped there (as a SGM) and was horrified at what was going on at this Polish infantry base. The captain (U.S.) in charge displayed incompetence and poor judgment when he placed the females in the Polish infantry barracks. The females were absolutely traumatized. They were surrounded by Polish infantry in the shower, heckled and harassed constantly. I had to control my outrage while giving this captain a lecture on "common sense." My point is that the culture of the Polish military force was very different from the high standards in ours.

■ 2004, Tallil, Iraq. Similar to the Polish Army, the Italian Army occupied a compound at Tallil, Iraq. Again, drinking during deployment is the norm for them. The Italians would lay in wait at the PX, and target females, inviting them to their "bunker" on the Italian compound. There were so many incidents of rape, harassment, and sexual misconduct reported, that the Italian compound had to be placed "off limits." This did not stop further incidents; the Italians always seemed to be one step ahead. Again, the culture, discipline, and leadership of the Italian military is different from ours. I am not a diplomat, and I hope you do not mind my saying this. My concern is our military—the men and women who courageously volunteer to serve.

As an American soldier, I can't imagine comparing our military to that of 11 a foreign nation to justify a change in policy. We should be very proud of the fact that they would rather be like us. Let's keep it that way.

Repealing the 1993 law will not help us win this war on terrorism or any 12 conflict that our military is called upon to fight and win in the future. Too much time is being spent on how we can hinder our great men and women in the military, let's do what we can to lift their morale, give them more resolve, and motivate them to continue the absolutely great job that they are doing. I hope that this Congress will not make their jobs more difficult and dangerous than they already are by repealing a solid law that continues to support the morale, discipline, and readiness of our troops.

⊙ READING ARGUMENTS

1. Throughout the early paragraphs of this statement, Jones repeats the phrase "selfless service." Why does he do this? What does this idea have to do with his main argument?

2. What distinctions does Jones make between the military and the civilian business world? Why does he consider these distinctions important?

3. In paragraph 10, Jones compares the U.S. military to militaries in other countries. Why does he do this? How do these examples support his argument? Are they relevant to the debate over gays in the U.S. military?

This piece appeared on May 10, 2009, at *Fredericksburg.com*, the Web site of the *Free Lance-Star*, a newspaper in Fredericksburg, Virginia.

ALLOW GAYS TO SERVE IN NON-COMBAT ROLES

DAVID BENKOF

Despite campaign promises, President Barack Obama has indicated he wants a deliberative process before repealing the military's "Don't Ask, Don't Tell" policy on gay and lesbian service members. Recently, Defense Secretary Robert Gates echoed those sentiments, calling any change "very difficult." He suggested that a change in policy could take years, if it happens at all.

These sentiments are exactly on target. While gays and lesbians are clearly capable of heroic service in uniform, heroism is not enough to merit serving in the military—which is a privilege, not a right. The military has legitimate concerns about unit cohesion, morale, good order, and discipline that it must explore thoroughly before introducing openly gay individuals into our troops.

But there is another way. The military includes thousands and thousands of non-combat positions. I propose that Congress repeal "Don't Ask, Don't Tell" for non-combat jobs immediately, and then consider extending the change to combat positions in five years, after the initial repeal has had a chance to work.

> "There is another way."

Eliminating gays and lesbians from non-combat positions has had a detrimental effect on the military mission. For example, since 1998 more than 25 Arabic and Farsi linguists have been dismissed from the armed forces because of homosexuality. We need men and women in uniform who speak the languages of Iraq and Iran, and if there's no issue of unit cohesion (because they're not in combat), they should be allowed to serve.

Would it hurt the military mission if a uniformed secretary used the Xerox machine even though she's a lesbian? Who would it harm for a gay man to be a drill sergeant at a Marine base in California? By allowing members of the gay community to sign up for non-combat positions within the military, they are able to serve their country and have access to military benefits, even before a decision to completely repeal "Don't Ask, Don't Tell."

There is some precedent for this: African-Americans in World War I served in mostly non-combat positions. Racial segregation in the military didn't end with President Harry Truman's executive order; it became unnecessary and counterproductive during the Korean War, at which time it was dismantled. The ultimate integration of the military was good for blacks, good for the military, and thus good for America—and repealing "Don't Ask" may be a similar success. But if it's not—and especially in wartime—we want to find out as early as possible.

Do opponents of "Don't Ask, Don't Tell" think women should have been   7
equal combatants in the American Revolution, and slave and free blacks integrated into the Union troops during the Civil War? It seems obvious that the country wasn't ready at those times, but I've spoken to gays and lesbians who say gays should have been welcome to serve openly in World War II, even if that meant we lost to Hitler.

Indeed, the push to repeal "Don't Ask, Don't Tell" is just one manifesta-   8
tion of what I like to call "equality mania," the attitude by gays and lesbians that nothing is more important than complete and total equality—not the welfare of children, not religious freedom, not even national security.

But equality isn't everything. There is literally nothing more important   9
than a strong military. While I'm sympathetic to gays and lesbians who want to serve their country, Obama and Gates are right that we have to be very careful before making a change that can hurt the only military mission—to fight and win wars.

❯ READING ARGUMENTS

1. Is Benkof developing a Rogerian argument? Explain.

2. Where in the essay does Benkof argue by using analogies? How effective are they? Do these analogies reveal any assumptions or biases on his part?

3. In paragraph 7, Benkof says that he has "spoken to gays and lesbians who say gays should have been welcome to serve openly in World War II, even if that meant we lost to Hitler." Do you find this statement convincing? Is it a red herring?

4. Benkof asserts that there is "literally nothing more important than a strong military" (para. 9). Do you agree?

5. In your opinion, is Benkof sidestepping the larger issue of whether the policy of "don't ask, don't tell" should be repealed? Explain your answer.

6. Do you find Benkof's suggestion that gay men and women serve only in noncombat roles reasonable? Or, do you see it as insulting or demeaning?

❯ AT ISSUE: SHOULD OPENLY GAY MEN AND WOMEN BE PERMITTED TO SERVE IN THE MILITARY?

1. Daniel L. Davis argues that a "singular imperative" should be used by political leaders to determine policies in the armed forces—to "create the most effective combat unit possible" (para. 9). Do you agree with

this statement, or do you think there should be other considerations or imperatives?

2. John M. Shalikashvili notes that the idea of gays serving in the military has been a contentious issue and that resolving it "could help heal the divisions that cleave our country" (9). What are these divisions? Do you think he is correct, or do you think he is overstating the importance of resolving this issue? Why do you think the debate over gays in the military has been so divisive and controversial?

3. Vance Coleman compares the current debate about gays in the armed forces to the desegregation of the military. Do you think this is a valid comparison? How are the two issues similar? How are they different?

⊘ WRITING ARGUMENTS: SHOULD OPENLY GAY MEN AND WOMEN BE PERMITTED TO SERVE IN THE MILITARY?

1. After reading these arguments regarding the role of gays in the armed forces, what is your view of the issue? Write an essay that presents your position.

2. All of the readings in this casebook were written by people who are currently serving in the military or who have served in the past. Do you think military officials should be left to decide this issue by themselves, or do you think elected officials or the courts should have the power to make such policies? Answer this question in an argumentative essay.

CASEBOOK

Should Every American Go to College?

Since Harvard College was founded in 1636, the history of American higher education has been closely intertwined with the history of the United States as a whole—economically, socially, and culturally. Both have generally been associated with expanding opportunity, as colleges and universities have become less the privilege of an elite few and more of a training ground for Americans of all backgrounds, as well as for many foreign students. The nineteenth century witnessed the development of the state university system, which educated many engineers, teachers, agricultural experts, and other professionals who participated in the country's industrial boom—especially after the Civil War. In the post–World War I era, the City College of New York provided a free quality college education to many working-class people (including immigrants) at a time when they were effectively barred from attending most colleges. But perhaps the most significant expansion in American higher education occurred after World War II, when millions of returning veterans attended college with the support of federal funding from the 1944 GI Bill. Enrollment skyrocketed— and many credit this bill with helping to create postwar economic prosperity and a large middle class in the United States.

In the decades since the first GI Bill was passed, the number of colleges and universities has increased steadily: there are now over 4,000 such institutions in the United States. Public policy has been shaped to make higher education more accessible—for example, by supporting publicly funded community colleges and creating federal student loan programs. But in recent years, the cost of a four-year degree has increased beyond the rate of inflation, even as more and more people see college as a necessity.

Between 28% and 30% of Americans now have college degrees; roughly two-thirds of high school graduates enroll in college after graduation. Labor statistics show that those with bachelor's degrees earn an average of $20,000 more annually than their counterparts with only a high school diploma. This financial reality, along with the need for a highly educated and competitive workforce in an increasingly global marketplace, has led some to argue that the federal government should do more than it already does to make sure that more—and perhaps even all—Americans attend college. Such proposals raise fundamental questions about the nature of higher education. How should colleges maintain academic standards even as they admit more students? How should such institutions control costs? Is higher education really a right in the same way that a high school education is? Should everyone go to college?

The following four essays address these and other questions from starkly different points of view. For example, in "On 'Real Education,'" Robert T. Perry argues that the United States needs more college-educated workers than ever. In contrast, Charles Murray believes that too many people are going to college. All four writers explore the nature and significance of a college degree in important contexts—and all of the writers suggest new ways of viewing postsecondary education as the United States looks to the future.

This piece appeared on *InsideHigherEd.com* on August 21, 2008.

ON "REAL EDUCATION"

ROBERT T. PERRY

Bell Curve author Charles Murray takes direct aim at higher education in his   1
new book *Real Education* by asserting that we are wasting our time trying to
educate too many people. Murray contends that only 10 to 20 percent of those
enrolled in four-year degree programs should actually be there. His pessimistic
view of people's ability to learn ignores not just good evidence to the contrary
but the real pressures the American economy is facing. Removing some 80–90
percent of our students in my state or just about any state would interrupt the
pipeline of skilled workers, making it nearly impossible to meet the needs of a
society that has defined postsecondary credentials as an entry point for most
professions.

Consider the following: 2

- The U.S. Department of Labor reports that the country needs more graduates if we are to keep up with, let alone lead, other nations in the global
  economy.

- By the end of the next president's first term, there will be three million
  more jobs requiring bachelor's degrees and not enough college graduates
  to fill them.

- 90 percent of the fastest growing job categories, including software engineers, physical therapists, and preschool teachers, 60 percent of all new
  jobs, and 40 percent of manufacturing jobs, will all require some form of
  postsecondary education.

We need *more*, not fewer university and community college graduates,   3
even in rural states like mine. South Dakota's aging population will require
30 percent more health care workers
in the coming decades—and those
workers will require degrees. We're
also facing a teacher shortage; educators of all levels need postsecondary
education to successfully command
and manage a classroom, let alone

> "We need *more*, not fewer
> university and community
> college graduates."

impart wisdom on elementary and secondary students. Our state also lacks
accountants, and the industry has informed us that tomorrow's professionals
will require 150 hours of postsecondary education to successfully complete the
Certified Public Accountant's exam.

Those left out of higher education would have fewer employment options 4 than they do today. Low-wage, low-skill careers are disappearing rapidly, as manufacturing jobs head overseas and American companies are looking for new ways to compete. Those workers who hope to maintain their current standard of living must have some sort of postsecondary credential—participation in the knowledge-based economy demands it. Without some type of degree, their ability to pay for basics like housing, food, and gas will diminish greatly.

We cannot survive in an international economy by simply working 5 cheaper, as there will always be companies overseas who are willing and able to use unskilled work at a lower cost. If we are to work smarter, our workforce needs to acquire more knowledge and skills that are adaptable in a constantly changing world. The people who have proven to be the most knowledgeable, skilled and adaptable are those with postsecondary credentials. Murray's suggestions are completely contrary to this. Dummying down our workforce would result in a lower standard of living for most Americans.

The United States has long enjoyed the enviable position as the leader 6 in educational attainment—just a decade ago, we led all other industrialized nations in this area. That's no longer the case. Now, we rank tenth behind other nations in the percentage of young adults with postsecondary credentials. The National Center for Higher Education Management Systems indicates that the U.S. will need to produce 63.1 million degrees to match leading nations Canada, Japan and South Korea in the percentage of adults with a college degree by 2025. At our current pace, we would fall short of that threshold by 16 million degrees.

Educating a larger percentage of the population does not amount to 7 "educational romanticism," as Murray contends. It simply makes sense—both economically and socially. Higher education allows people of all backgrounds to hone their writing, reading, cognitive and critical thinking skills that enable them to actively participate as citizens. Not everyone who completes a four-year degree will be able to write like William Faulkner—and some may argue that's a good thing. But the papers students have to research and write in college are valuable and marketable experiences to future employers who need workers who can craft memos, reports and strategic plans, all valuable skills in the knowledge economy. Moreover, people with postsecondary degrees also tend to be healthier, are more productive throughout their work lives, are more engaged in their communities, more philanthropic and are less likely to be involved in crime.

The State Higher Education Executive Officers are calling on political 8 leaders make college access and success a national priority. To heed this call, SHEEO believes we need to take immediate action by

- Targeting low-income and first-generation students (populations who are historically least likely to succeed in college and complete their degree programs), by allocating greater public resources to community colleges and regional four-year institutions, while also providing adequate need-based financial aid.

- Overhauling the notoriously complex financial aid system. We can start by making most of the required data for the Free Application for Federal Student Aid directly transferable from the federal income tax form. Also, Pell Grants should be pegged to students' basic living costs, rather than tuition, to highlight the responsibility of states and colleges to moderate tuition and fees and to provide grants for tuition to low-income students.

- Developing information systems to better track students' progress and determine whether they are at risk of dropping out.

In South Dakota, we're committed to raising our graduation rates by 20 percent by 2010, so we can be competitive both nationally and internationally. To do so, the state is reaching out to nontraditional adult learners by offering more university classes in urban centers. The state's public institutions are opening our doors to more out-of-state students by cutting our non-resident tuition rates in half. So far, the increase in students has offset any potential revenue shortfall. The state is also providing $5,000 scholarships to students who take more rigorous courses in high school, maintain a B average, receive a 24 on their ACT and pursue their education in South Dakota. We also want to make sure that those students who start college, finish college. To that end, our Board of Regents has tied retention rates to a pool of performance dollars; retention rates are on the rise.

To Murray's point, people do vary in academic ability, and not everyone 10 can handle the rigors of a postsecondary degree program. I'm not suggesting that everyone needs to spend four years at a flagship state institution, or even two years at their local community college. However, everyone should have at least the option to participate successfully in some form of postsecondary experience—be it a Ph.D. program or a short-term certificate program for dental assistants. Educators need to help more average Americans *and* educational elite succeed. It's common sense. And our future depends on it.

⊖ READING ARGUMENTS

1. This essay is a refutation of ideas expressed in *Real Education*, a 2008 book by Charles Murray (also see page 631). What ideas of Murray's is Perry refuting? Is his refutation convincing?

2. In paragraph 4, Perry refers to the demands of a "knowledge-based economy." What is a knowledge-based economy?

3. Perry argues that the United States needs more college-educated workers, not fewer. How does he use causal argument to make this case?

4. According to Perry, why does higher education benefit people of all backgrounds? What benefits does it provide for the average citizen?

This editorial is from the January–February 2008 issue of *Change.*

THE PRIVILEGES OF THE PARENTS

MARGARET A. MILLER

The apple doesn't fall far from the tree.

—FOLK SAYING

Paul Barton and Anthony Carnevale, in their articles in this issue, are in funda-   1
mental disagreement about the economy's need for college-educated workers.
What they don't disagree about, though, are the benefits that accrue to individuals from having a college education. Barton and Carnevale focus on the
economic benefits—the wage differentials between those with a high-school
education or even some college and those with a bachelor's degree or higher
(which is one reason we need to graduate students, not just admit them). But
when it comes to the private benefits of higher education, possibly even more
important is how advanced intellectual abilities help people navigate contemporary life.

We have to do so many things that other people used to do for us, from   2
making our own plane reservations to making choices about our health to planning for our security in old age (someone has called this the "democratization
of risk," although with a $30 trillion shortfall projected for Social Security and
Medicare, it's more like the "privatization of risk"). We have to be able to
hop from job to job without loss of momentum as we acquire new skills and
knowledge. We have to deal with a wider variety of people in this country and
in an increasingly constricted world. We need to fill out FAFSA forms for our
children (there, even a doctorate may not be enough!).

So I was aware of the stakes when my daughter-in-law told me about a   3
friend of hers who hasn't been to college—indeed, hasn't been in this country
for long. This friend, while having no collegiate ambitions for herself, is very
ambitious for her son and is determined that he will go to college. But when
they spend the afternoon together, Beth notices a difference between herself
and the other mother. "She tells him to study," Beth says, "but she can't help
him with the content, and she doesn't know that she needs to really push him
to do his homework for a certain amount of time after school every day."

I thought of that story when I opened a chart recently produced by Tom   4
Mortenson, which shows the correlation between parental education and children's grades. Sure enough, the more highly educated the parents, the higher
the grades of their children: 60.6 percent of children whose parents have
advanced degrees get mostly A's, whereas only 27.8 percent of high-school
dropouts' children do.

That differential comes about in innumerable small, intangible ways. For   5
instance, educated parents use a wider vocabulary in speaking to their infants
than their less-educated counterparts do. According to ETS's recently released

The Family: America's Smallest School, "by age 4, the average child in a professional family hears about 20 million more words than the average child in a working-class family." Children of educated mothers are also almost twice as likely to be read to as those with less-educated mothers. And if my family is any indication, they are also apt to participate in sustained conversations, even debates (in our household, these periodically featured loud-voiced uncles), which help immeasurably when it comes to writing papers in school and college.

With their sense of entitlement, more highly educated parents are more   6
likely to fight for their children in school, and they know what privileges to fight for. They make sure that their children start algebra in the 8th grade, that they take a college-prep curriculum, that they are placed among the "gifted and talented" students who absorb a disproportionate share of school resources, and that they see college as a realistic possibility and worth taking out loans for (indeed, they may be in a position to subsidize those loans). Having been through the system, they are more knowledgeable about its twists and turns and better able to help their children navigate them.

And they continue to hover over their college-going children. However   7
annoying it may be to us, their involvement has, as the most recent National Survey of Student Engagement (NSSE) reveals, a remarkably good effect on their children's engagement and satisfaction with college, and hence on their ultimate success.

In short, a college education has benefits that ripple down through the gen-   8
erations. Children inherit not just the "sins of the fathers" but their privileges. That's why it is so important that we focus all our intelligence and resources on attracting to our colleges and universities not the children of the privileged (they will come anyway) but first-generation students, whose success we then must do our best to ensure.

> "A college education has benefits that ripple down through the generations."

In this country we've prided ourselves on a system of higher educa-   9
tion by which we, as Carnevale puts it, "mediate opportunity [and] expand merit-based success without surrendering individual responsibility." But with college-going rates stagnating, completion rates a disgrace, and income gaps widening (consider: the richest one percent of Americans hold a third of the nation's wealth), we are becoming as caste-bound a society as any in the Old World.

The children of the less educated will be an increasingly large proportion   10
of the college-going pool. Their parents are equally, if not more, determined to see them succeed than those for whom college is a family tradition, but they can't help them adequately. We need to do for those children what our parents did for us—smooth the way for them to get into college, and once they're there, make sure that they have the same kinds of experiences that help more-privileged students succeed. Again, the NSSE data are revelatory:

First-generation students are less likely than the average student to participate in collegiate activities that lead to student success (learning communities, research with faculty members, study abroad, or capstone experiences). We're the ones who can steer them towards those experiences the way the "helicopter parents" guide their children. This gives a whole new meaning to "in loco parentis."

This attention to the success of first-generation students will entail turning many of higher education's lived values on their heads. Instead of pursuing "the best and brightest," we'll need to look out for the most promising first-generation students; instead of running the rankings race, we'll need to tighten our belts to keep ourselves affordable and spend the resources we have on practices like those that Charles Reed described in the previous issue of *Change* to attract and retain these students. But we need to get better at this job, and fast, because as Carnevale points out, "ultimately, of course, there are no 'other people's children'"—or children's children, for that matter. We need to want the son of Beth's friend to succeed as much as his mother does, for his own, his children's, and our sakes.

⊘ READING ARGUMENTS

1. Miller believes that recent shifts in society make the benefits of higher education more valuable than ever before. What societal changes does she mention? How are these changes related to the need for "advanced intellectual abilities" (para. 1)?

2. In paragraph 4, Miller cites the correlation between parental education and children's grades. How does she use these statistics to support her argument?

3. According to Miller, the United States is "becoming as caste-bound a society as any in the Old World" (9). What does she mean? How does she support this statement?

4. What problems is Miller addressing? In what respects is this essay a proposal argument?

The *Wall Street Journal* published this opinion piece on January 17, 2007.

WHAT'S WRONG WITH VOCATIONAL SCHOOL?

CHARLES MURRAY

The topic yesterday was education and children in the lower half of the intelligence distribution. Today I turn to the upper half, people with IQs of 100 or higher. Today's simple truth is that far too many of them are going to four-year colleges. 1

Begin with those barely into the top half, those with average intelligence. To have an IQ of 100 means that a tough high-school course pushes you about as far as your academic talents will take you. If you are average in math ability, you may struggle with algebra and probably fail a calculus course. If you are average in verbal skills, you often misinterpret complex text and make errors in logic. 2

These are not devastating shortcomings. You are smart enough to engage in any of hundreds of occupations. You can acquire more knowledge if it is presented in a format commensurate with your intellectual skills. But a genuine college education in the arts and sciences begins where your skills leave off. 3

In engineering and most of the natural sciences, the demarcation between high-school material and college-level material is brutally obvious. If you cannot handle the math, you cannot pass the courses. In the humanities and social sciences, the demarcation is fuzzier. It is possible for someone with an IQ of 100 to sit in the lectures of Economics 1, read the textbook, and write answers in an examination book. But students who cannot follow complex arguments accurately are not really learning economics. They are taking away a mishmash of half-understood information and outright misunderstandings that probably leave them under the illusion that they know something they do not. (A depressing research literature documents one's inability to recognize one's own incompetence.) Traditionally and properly understood, a four-year college education teaches advanced analytic skills and information at a level that exceeds the intellectual capacity of most people. 4

There is no magic point at which a genuine-college-level education becomes an option, but anything below an IQ of 110 is problematic. If you want to do well, you should have an IQ of 115 or higher. Put another way, it makes sense for only about 15% of the population, 25% if one stretches it, to get a college education. And yet more than 45% of recent high school graduates enroll in four-year colleges. Adjust that percentage to account for high-school dropouts, and more than 40% of all persons in their late teens are trying to go to a four-year college—enough people to absorb everyone down through an IQ of 104. 5

No data that I have been able to find tell us what proportion of those stu- 6 dents really want four years of college-level courses, but it is safe to say that few people who are intellectually unqualified yearn for the experience, any more than someone who is athletically unqualified for a college varsity wants to have his shortcomings exposed at practice every day. They are in college to improve their chances of making a good living. What they really need is vocational training. But nobody will say so, because "vocational training" is second class. "College" is first class.

Large numbers of those who are intellectually qualified for college 7 also do not yearn for four years of college-level courses. They go to college because their parents are paying for it and college is what children of their social class are supposed to do after they finish high school. They may have the ability to understand the material in Economics 1 but they do not want to. They, too, need to learn to make a living—and would do better in voca-tional training.

Combine those who are unqualified with those who are qualified but 8 not interested, and some large proportion of students on today's college campuses—probably a majority of them—are looking for something that the four-year college was not designed to provide. Once there, they create a demand for practical courses, taught at an intellectual level that can be han-dled by someone with a mildly above-average IQ and/or mild motivation. The nation's colleges try to accommodate these new demands. But most of the practical specialties do not really require four years of training, and the best way to teach those specialties is not through a residential institution with the staff and infrastructure of a college. It amounts to a system that tries to turn out televisions on an assembly line that also makes pottery. It can be done, but it's ridiculously inefficient.

Government policy contributes to the problem by making college schol- 9 arships and loans too easy to get, but its role is ancillary. The demand for col-lege is market-driven, because a college degree does, in fact, open up access to jobs that are closed to people without one. The fault lies in the false premium that our culture has put on a college degree.

For a few occupations, a college degree still certifies a qualification. For 10 example, employers appropriately treat a bachelor's degree in engineering as a requirement for hiring engineers. But a bachelor's degree in a field such as soci-ology, psychology, economics, history or literature certifies nothing. It is a screen-ing device for employers. The college you got into says a lot about your ability, and that you stuck it out for four years says something about your perseverance. But the degree itself does not qualify the graduate for anything. There are better, faster and more efficient ways for young people to acquire credentials to provide to employers.

> "A bachelor's degree in a field such as sociology, psychology, economics, history or literature certifies nothing."

The good news is that market-driven systems eventually adapt to real- 11
ity, and signs of change are visible. One glimpse of the future is offered by
the nation's two-year colleges. They are more honest than the four-year institutions about what their students want and provide courses that meet their
needs more explicitly. Their time frame gives them a big advantage—two
years is about right for learning many technical specialties, while four years is
unnecessarily long.

Advances in technology are making the brick-and-mortar facility increas- 12
ingly irrelevant. Research resources on the Internet will soon make the college
library unnecessary. Lecture courses taught by first-rate professors are already
available on CDs and DVDs for many subjects, and online methods to make
courses interactive between professors and students are evolving. Advances
in computer simulation are expanding the technical skills that can be taught
without having to gather students together in a laboratory or shop. These and
other developments are all still near the bottom of steep growth curves. The
cost of effective training will fall for everyone who is willing to give up the
trappings of a campus. As the cost of college continues to rise, the choice to
give up those trappings will become easier.

A reality about the job market must eventually begin to affect the valua- 13
tion of a college education: The spread of wealth at the top of American society has created an explosive increase in the demand for craftsmen. Finding a
good lawyer or physician is easy. Finding a good carpenter, painter, electri-
cian, plumber, glazier, mason—the list goes on and on—is difficult, and it is a
seller's market. Journeymen craftsmen routinely make incomes in the top half
of the income distribution while master craftsmen can make six figures. They
have work even in a soft economy. Their jobs cannot be outsourced to India.
And the craftsman's job provides wonderful intrinsic rewards that come from
mastery of a challenging skill that produces tangible results. How many white-
collar jobs provide nearly as much satisfaction?

Even if forgoing college becomes economically attractive, the social cachet 14
of a college degree remains. That will erode only when large numbers of high-
status, high-income people do not have a college degree and don't care. The
information technology industry is in the process of creating that class, with
Bill Gates and Steve Jobs as exemplars. It will expand for the most natural of
reasons: A college education need be no more important for many high-tech
occupations than it is for NBA basketball players or cabinetmakers. Walk into
Microsoft or Google with evidence that you are a brilliant hacker, and the job
interviewer is not going to fret if you lack a college transcript. The ability to
present an employer with evidence that you are good at something, without
benefit of a college degree, will continue to increase, and so will the number of
skills to which that evidence can be attached. Every time that happens, the false
premium attached to the college degree will diminish.

Most students find college life to be lots of fun (apart from the boring 15
classroom stuff), and that alone will keep the four-year institution over-
stocked for a long time. But, rightly understood, college is appropriate for a

small minority of young adults—perhaps even a minority of the people who have IQs high enough that they could do college-level work if they wished. People who go to college are not better or worse people than anyone else; they are merely different in certain interests and abilities. That is the way college should be seen. There is reason to hope that eventually it will be.

⊘ READING ARGUMENTS

1. Construct a syllogism for the deductive argument Murray uses in his opening paragraphs. Do you find this argument persuasive? Why or why not?

2. Murray makes a distinction between engineering and the natural sciences (on the one hand) and the humanities and social sciences (on the other). What difference does he see? Why is this difference important to his argument?

3. Murray claims that too many people are going to four-year colleges. What causal arguments does he use to support this claim? How do these arguments support his position on the issue?

4. More than once in his essay, Murray notes that the "intellectually unqualified" probably do not want to attend a four-year college, and he implies that if given the chance, they would choose not to. Do you think this is true? Do you believe Murray's emphasis on personal choice strengthens his argument?

5. According to Murray, more people should go to vocational schools. What advantages does he see for those who choose careers in trades and crafts?

This piece is from an AssociatedContent.com blog posting dated April 25, 2007.

IS COLLEGE FOR EVERYONE?

PHARINET

"You won't get anywhere without your education." We hear this refrain from 1
the time we are in elementary school. This may be true, but is college for everyone? More and more individuals are enrolling in two- and four-year postsecondary schools, but why? Often, a desire for learning is not what drives
students to attend college. Factors that determine reasons for attending college
vary from personal to professional. These factors are the key to our discussion.

There is no doubt that education is important. There is also no doubt that every 2
person has the right to an education. How-
ever, not every person should attend college.
There are too many students enrolled in school
who simply don't belong there. Though dropout rates vary, it is estimated that in the U.S.,
approximately 50% of students who begin college never graduate. There exist students who
are not yet ready for the academic and financial
challenges of college. There exist students who do not have the desire for college or
learning. Some students may be better suited for a different type of education, if any.

> "There are too many students enrolled in school who simply don't belong there."

The student who is not yet ready for the academic and financial challenges 3
of college is the most common. While the cost of college can be offset by grants,
scholarships and work-study programs, too many students find themselves in
desperate financial situations by the end of their first semester. The cost of books
can run several hundred dollars per semester. There are living expenses that students may not have planned for, including the cost of food, rent, gasoline, spending money and supplies other than books. Students find themselves working full-
time jobs while attending school full-time, and their minds, bodies and grades
end up suffering. While it may take a while longer to graduate, many students
who find themselves in a position where they must work may do better to drop
themselves to part-time student status, taking fewer classes. This lowers the cost
of education each semester (though requires a longer-term commitment) and
increases the chances of classroom success. There is more time to dedicate to
coursework without overloading and over-scheduling. Perhaps, certain individuals should consider a different life choice, as the long-term responsibility of repay-
ing student loans can be overwhelming. However, the best financial planning in
the world will not prepare a student for the academic challenges that await them.

Believe it or not, there are students who cannot read [but who are] attend- 4
ing college. While this is an extreme case, it is symptomatic of the problems
with the idea that "college is for everyone." If college is for everyone, why do
we rely on SAT scores and high school transcripts? Why doesn't every school

have an open admissions policy? Quite simply, because not everyone should attend college. If individuals are unable to read, they benefit more from a literacy program than a college course. There are also plenty of literate students who are not up for the challenge. They may have graduated from a high school that did not expect much from them, academically. They may not have the maturity necessary to dedicate themselves to the coursework. For many, this is the first time they have had personal freedom and responsibility without their parents. They aren't necessarily prepared to be "grown ups" yet. College prep courses don't often teach students about being responsible. Teaching responsibility and time and stress management may prepare some students for their college experience, but many will still fall victim to their first taste of "freedom."

"C's get degrees." One of my own students said this to me when inquiring 5 about his progress this semester. Unfortunately, this is an all too common mentality among college students. There is no real desire for learning. Students are "going through the motions" to earn their degrees, hoping to settle into a comfortable job that will pay them well because that "C degree" hangs on their wall. Motivating students to learn is the biggest challenge most educators face. While it may be possible to ignite a spark in some, most students who don't wish to learn simply won't learn. What good is there, then, in attending college? None. What happens when this type of student enters the workforce? Do they exhibit the same lack of motivation in their careers? If so, what type of value is actually attached to that degree?

Once upon a time, college was a place you went when you wished to learn. 6 Now, college is the place you go when you want to get a good job, or appease your parents, or because you are "finding yourself." While admissions representatives and administration share some of the blame (college is a business, after all), it is important to examine other reasons why students who don't belong in college end up there anyway. Students and parents need to examine their options. Is it really going to benefit you (or your child) to attend college? What other options exist? Is a trade school the best option? Perhaps allowing yourself to take a year or two to carefully consider who you are and what you want will save you time and money, and better prepare you should you decide to attend college. Society, too, plays a part in pushing students into college classrooms. We need to start distinguishing between the right to an education, and the benefit of an education. College does not benefit everyone. Not everyone should attend college. It is OK to say this! It is OK to believe this! You are not putting anyone down by saying these things. You may be doing them a favor by letting them know that it is OK not to attend college. Higher education is not the key to happiness and success for every person.

Many people have found happiness in careers that do not require a college edu- 7 cation. If we continue to tell everyone to acquire a college degree, we lessen the pool of people who will do the jobs that keep our world running smoothly. There are jobs that do not require a college education. Some work can be learned on the job or from a trade school. We need fork lift drivers, factory workers, sales clerks and cashiers. What would we do without tractor-trailer drivers, mail carriers and construction workers? Refuse to accept the political correctness that says all of our citizens should receive a higher education. Embrace the reality that college is not for everyone.

⊙ READING ARGUMENTS

1. In her second paragraph, the writer claims that there is "no doubt that every person has the right to an education" but also asserts that "not every person should attend college." Why is this distinction important to her argument? Is it in any sense a contradiction?

2. In her conclusion, the writer advises, "Refuse to accept the political correctness that says all of our citizens should receive a higher education." What is political correctness? Do you agree that "college for all" has its roots in political correctness?

3. According to the writer, what is the biggest challenge that educators face?

⊙ AT ISSUE: SHOULD EVERY AMERICAN GO TO COLLEGE?

1. Margaret A. Miller suggests that higher education is a way of increasing opportunity and equality as well as of expanding "merit-based success" (para. 9). Do you agree? How does widening access to a college or university education keep the United States from being "caste-bound" (9)?

2. Charles Murray bases his argument on "intelligence distribution" (1) in the general population. Why? What are the strengths and limitations of his premises?

3. Pharinet writes, "Once upon a time, college was a place you went when you wished to learn," whereas now people go "to get a good job, or appease [their] parents," or find themselves (6). Do you believe this is true today? If so, do you see it as a problem? Explain.

⊙ WRITING ARGUMENTS: SHOULD EVERY AMERICAN GO TO COLLEGE?

1. After reading and thinking about these essays, do you think more people should be encouraged to attend college, or do you think some people should be discouraged from attending? Do you see higher education as a right (and a necessity) for most—or even all—citizens? Write an argumentative essay that answers these questions.

2. Pharinet writes, "Motivating students to learn is the biggest challenge most educators face" (para. 5). Based on your own observations, what is the biggest challenge—or challenges—that most *students* face as they make their way through postsecondary education?

Do We Still Need Unions?

The influence of organized labor has declined significantly over the last several decades. Currently, around 12% of all salaried employees and workers belong to unions—a number far below these organizations' membership in the mid-twentieth century, when almost 40% of all workers were union members. In some ways, organized labor has been the victim of its own successes. Today, we take many of its historical achievements—the eight-hour work day, workplace safety standards, workers' compensation—for granted. However, higher union wages and more generous benefits in the United States have come at an increasing cost as businesses and manufacturers choose to use cheaper, nonunionized labor overseas.

A labor union is essentially an organization of workers who band together to negotiate with their employer. Such organizations have roots in the guild systems of craftspeople that have existed since the Middle Ages. But modern American unions (as well as all unions worldwide) first became a powerful force during the late nineteenth century with the rise of the industrial revolution, when millions of unskilled workers labored in factories, mills, and coal mines. As individuals, these men, women, and children were disposable and had little power to control their wages or working conditions. Even skilled workers in crafts and trades faced similar challenges. However, by organizing and using tactics such as the strike and the boycott, they were able to win concessions from management.

In 1886, Samuel Gompers founded the American Federation of Labor (AFL), one of the first organizations of its kind, and it became the largest collection of unions in the United States during the first half of the twentieth century. Other historical milestones include the 1894 Pullman Strike, in which 125,000 railroad workers all over the country went on strike to protest a 30% wage cut by a railroad company in Illinois. The infamous 1911 Triangle Shirtwaist Factory fire, which resulted in the deaths of 146 female employees, eventually led to improved working conditions. In 1935, the Wagner Act strengthened and legitimized organized labor and regulated the relationship between unions and ownership.

By the 1950s, when the AFL merged with the Congress for Industrial Organization (CIO), unions were at the peak of their power.

Since that time, the influence of unions has waned. In the late twentieth century, the number of American jobs in manufacturing plants and factories declined radically. Some point to the 1981 air traffic controllers' strike—in which 11,500 workers were fired and replaced by nonunion workers—as a tipping point in organized labor's decreasing power. Others note the widely held perception that today's unions represent another entrenched political-interest group rather than their past idealistic aims. Unlike the writers of the song "Union Label" and the labor leader John L. Lewis, the other writers in this chapter interpret the decline of unions as a trend. Their focus is on how and why this decline occurred and what should be done about it.

"Union Label" was written in 1975 for the International Ladies' Garment Worker's Union.

UNION LABEL

PAULA GREEN AND MALCOLM DODDS

Look for the union label   1
when you are buying that coat, dress or blouse.
Remember somewhere our union's sewing,
our wages going to feed the kids, and run the house.
We work hard, but who's complaining?   5
Thanks to the I.L.G. we're paying our way!
So always look for the union label,
It says we're able to make it in the U.S.A.!

◑ READING ARGUMENTS

1. The lyrics of "Union Label" develop an argument. What is that argument?

2. Analyze "Union Label" as a Toulmin argument. Identify the claim, the grounds, and the warrant.

3. To whom does this song (written over thirty-five years ago) seem to be addressed? That is, who is the *you* referred to in these lyrics? Do you think this audience would have been receptive to the argument presented here? Would this argument still be effective today?

This piece was published in *Business Week* on October 28, 2002.

HOW WAL-MART KEEPS UNIONS AT BAY: ORGANIZING THE NATION'S NO. 1 EMPLOYER WOULD GIVE LABOR A LIFT

WENDY ZELLNER

Sam's Club store No. 6382, Spring Mountain Rd., Las Vegas—epicenter of a 1
critical battle between labor and management. On one side, employees were trying to bring in the United Food & Commercial Workers (UFCW) to represent
5,000 Wal-Mart Stores Inc. (Sam's Club is a subsidiary) workers around the city.
Aided by 15 organizers, a Web site, and a weekly radio call-in show just for Wal-
Mart workers, the union won enough support to petition the National Labor
Relations Board (NLRB) for a vote last fall among the 200 workers at Club 6382.
On the other side, the retailing behemoth, which mounted a blistering counter-
offensive. It parachuted in a dozen labor-relations troops from its Bentonville,
Arkansas headquarters, instructing local managers in a fierce anti-union cam-
paign, including surveillance of employees and the firing of several union sym-
pathizers, the union claims. Wal-Mart denies it did anything illegal.

It was a fight that would end in stalemate—for the time being. Even so, it 2
illustrates just how hard it is for unions to organize in today's workplace—and
how hard employers are resisting. In the case of Sam's Club, the union concluded that workers were too intimidated to proceed with a vote. Instead, it filed
dozens of unfair labor practice complaints with the NLRB, effectively postpon-
ing the election indefinitely. Even today, says Mary Lou Wagoner, an employee
organizer at the Spring Mountain store, "people are just afraid." On Wal-Mart's
side, Coleman Peterson, executive vice-president of the company's People Div.,
says there's no corporate support for illegal tactics. But he's clear that Wal-Mart
doesn't want a union. "Where associates feel free to communicate openly with
their management, why would they need a third party to represent them?" he
asks. Wal-Mart has won all but one of seven union votes in the U.S.

Despite the current impasse, the stakes continue to be high for both sides. 3
Wal-Mart faces the first serious unionization threat since its founding in 1962.
For decades, the company's strategy of placing stores in small towns and rural
areas kept it largely free of exposure to unions. But in recent years, Wal-Mart
has been pushing into the heavily unionized supermarket industry, as well as
into big cities where workers are more familiar with organized labor. Even
though the company has prevailed so far in Las Vegas, the UFCW has an even
more ambitious plan to sign up Wal-Mart workers elsewhere, starting with
117,000 in Michigan, Ohio, Indiana, and Kentucky. If the UFCW gets help
from auto workers and other labor groups in those states, it has a shot at eventually unionizing at least parts of mighty Wal-Mart for the first time.

For its part, the UFCW is fighting to protect the $30,000-a-year wages and   4
benefits of its 800,000 retail members, mostly in the grocery business. Already, it's
getting demands for benefit cuts from big unionized chains such as Kroger Co.
(KR) and Safeway Inc. (SWY), which shoulder labor costs at least 20% higher than
Wal-Mart's, analysts estimate. "We have no choice but to [unionize Wal-Mart] if
we want to survive," says William A. Meyer, the UFCW staffer who's heading up
the Las Vegas effort. A win at Wal-Mart, the country's No. 1 employer, with more
than 1 million workers, also could give the entire labor movement a lift.

Yet for all the drama at the Sam's Club in Vegas, the labor battle there   5
could also be a proxy for many unionization attempts around the country.
And the picture isn't pretty for the future of unions. Interest in unionization
has surged in the U.S., in part as a result of corporate scandals and the troubled economy. Fully half of all nonunion U.S. workers say they would vote yes
if a union election were held at their company today, up from about 40%
throughout the 1990s, according to polls by Peter D. Hart Research Associates
Inc. Yet unions lose about half of the elections they call.

One big reason: Over the past two decades, Corporate America has perfected   6
its ability to fend off labor groups. True, unions themselves bear some blame, since
most run poor sign-up campaigns
and don't spend anywhere near 30%
of their budgets on recruitment, as
AFL-CIO President John J. Sweeney
has long exhorted them to do. Still,
companies facing labor drives routinely employ all the tactics Wal-Mart
has used to get workers to change their
minds. Many of these actions are perfectly legal, such as holding anti-union meetings or inundating workers with anti-union literature and videos.

> "Over the past two decades,
> Corporate America has
> perfected its ability to fend
> off labor groups."

Those that are illegal carry insignificant penalties such as small fines or   7
posting workplace notices about labor rights. Firing activists—as companies
do in fully one-quarter of union drives, according to studies of NLRB cases—
is difficult to prove and takes years to work through the courts. That's long
after a drive has lost steam. Workers may want unions, "but the question is
whether [labor] can overcome the fear generated by an employer's campaign
to get them to take the risk," says Kate Bronfenbrenner, a Cornell University
researcher who did the studies.

Indeed, the extraordinary challenge of winning a union election today is   8
told chapter and verse in the Sam's Club story. Take the tactic of intimida-
tion. Sandy Williams, a five-year Wal-Mart veteran, says that even the clearly
legal actions taken by her managers scared workers away from interest in the
union. Last fall, managers held mandatory employee meetings every week
to express their anti-union sentiments. The corporate labor experts who jet-
ted in stressed such messages as "you can speak for yourself," and "the union
only wants your money." An us-vs.-them atmosphere quickly took hold, and
employees sported buttons that boasted: "I can speak for myself." Executive

Vice-President Peterson says Wal-Mart sends in labor experts to "educate associates about how these [union election] processes work."

Store managers also began to harass union supporters, says Williams and 9 other colleagues. Wagoner, 53, a part-timer at the store, believes she has been "blacklisted" from better-paying full-time jobs because of her pro-union stance. A couple of times, her paperwork was conveniently "lost," she says, and she also was passed over for a worker who shouldn't have been eligible because of a disciplinary action. "They've done just about anything they can to get me to quit," she says.

Sandra L. Mena, a cashier at the Club, says she was fired after three years— 10 officially because of mistakes at her register. But she believes it was because she was pro-union. She says her alleged errors, which employees have no way to verify on their own, surged only after she became active in the union. Peterson declined to comment on either woman's allegations.

Some former Wal-Mart managers say the hardball tactics are standard 11 company policy. Jon M. Lehman says he left Wal-Mart on good terms last fall after 17 years as a store manager but now works for the UFCW. He recounts how he called a Bentonville hotline in 1997 after finding a flyer that said: "This store needs a union" in a bathroom at the store he managed in Hillview, Ky.

The response was a mini version of what occurred in Las Vegas four 12 years later. Three labor experts swooped in from Arkansas to show anti-union videos at mandatory employee meetings, says Lehman, and scoured personnel files for dirt to use against union supporters. The labor experts grilled him and other Hillview managers about potential troublemakers, and the store trained surveillance cameras on suspect workers, he says. Now, as a union organizer, he recently noticed that a store in Scottsburg, Ind., sprouted a multitude of cameras after he began talking to workers there in July. Wal-Mart declined comment on Lehman, although a spokesman says that the 15 cameras installed in Scottsburg have "nothing to do with union activity."

So far, Wal-Mart has been able to stave off unionization, and, given its 13 superior firepower, it may be able to do so for years to come. In that, the country's No. 1 company has a lot in common with most other U.S. employers.

⊘ READING ARGUMENTS

1. Throughout most of its history, Wal-Mart has been largely free from union activity. According to Zellner, what recent changes have made unionization an issue for the company and its workers?

2. Zellner claims that "the picture isn't pretty for the future of unions" (para. 5). In this context, what makes the possibility of unionization at Wal-Mart so significant?

3. Does Zellner take a stand on unionization, or is she neutral? How can you tell? After reading the article, are you more sympathetic to those who support unions or to those who oppose them? Why?

John L. Lewis, an influential labor organizer during the first half of the twentieth century, delivered this speech on September 3, 1937, in Washington, D.C.

LABOR AND THE NATION
JOHN L. LEWIS

Out of the agony and travail of economic America the Committee for Industrial 1 Organization was born. To millions of Americans exploited without stint by corporate industry and socially debased beyond the understanding of the fortunate, its coming was as welcomed as the dawn to the night watcher. To a lesser group of Americans, infinitely more fortunately situated, blessed with larger quantities of the world's goods and insolent in their assumption of privilege, its coming was heralded as a harbinger of ill, sinister of purpose, of unclean methods and non-virtuous objectives. But the Committee for Industrial Organizations is here. It is now henceforth a definite instrumentality, destined greatly to influence the lives of our people and the internal and external course of the republic.

This is true only because the purposes and objectives of the Committee 2 for Industrial Organization find economic, social, political and moral justification in the hearts of the millions who are its members and the millions more who support it. The organization and constant onward sweep of this movement exemplifies the resentment of the many toward the selfishness, greed and the neglect of the few.

The workers of the nation were tired of waiting for corporate industry to 3 right their economic wrongs, to alleviate their social agony and to grant them their political rights. Despairing of fair treatment, they resolved to do something for themselves. They, therefore, have organized a new labor movement, conceived within the principles of the national bill of rights and committed to the proposition that the workers are free to assemble in their own forums, voice their own grievances, declare their own hopes and contract on even terms with modern industry for the sale of their only material possession—their labor.

> "The workers of the nation were tired of waiting for corporate industry to right their economic wrongs."

The Committee for Industrial Organization has a numerical enrollment of 4 3,718,000 members. It has 32 affiliated national and international unions. Of this number 11 unions account for 2,765,000 members. This group is organized in the textile, auto, garment, lumber, rubber, electrical manufacturing, power, steel, coal and transport industries. The remaining membership exists in the maritime, oil production and refining, ship building, leather, chemical, retail, meat packing, vegetable canning, metalliferous mining, miscellaneous manufacturing, agricultural labor, and service and miscellaneous industries. Some 200,000 workers are organized into 507 chartered local unions not yet attached to a national industrial union.

This record bespeaks progress. It is a development without precedent in 5 our own country. Some of this work was accomplished with the enlightened cooperation or the tolerant acquiescence of employers who recognized that a new labor movement was being forged and who were not disposed, in any event, to flout the law of the land. On the other hand, much of this progress was made in the face of violent and deadly opposition which reached its climax in the slaughter of workers paralleling the massacres of Ludlow and Homestead.

In the steel industry the corporations generally have accepted collective bar- 6 gaining and negotiated wage agreements with the Committee for Industrial Organization. Eighty-five per cent of the industry is thus under contract and a peaceful relationship exits between the management and the workers. Written wage contracts have been negotiated with 399 steel companies covering 510,000 men. One thousand thirty-one local lodges in 700 communities have been organized.

Five of the corporations in the steel industry elected to resist collective bar- 7 gaining and undertook to destroy the steel workers' union. These companies filled their plants with industrial spies, assembled depots of guns and gas bombs, established barricades, controlled their communities with armed thugs, leased the police power of cities and mobilized the military power of a state to guard them against the intrusion of collective bargaining within their plants.

During this strike 18 steel workers were either shot to death or had their 8 brains clubbed out by police, or armed thugs in the pay of the steel companies. In Chicago, Mayor Kelly's police force was successful in killing ten strikers before they could escape the fury of the police, shooting eight of them in the back. One hundred sixty strikers were maimed and injured by police clubs, riot guns and gas bombs and were hospitalized. Hundreds of strikers were arrested, jailed, treated with brutality while incarcerated and harassed by succeeding litigation. None but strikers were murdered, gassed, injured, jailed or maltreated. No one had to die except the workers who were standing for the right guaranteed them by the Congress and written in the law.

The infamous Governor Davey, of Ohio, successful in the last election because 9 of his reiterated promises of fair treatment to labor, used the military power of the Commonwealth on the side of the Republican Steel Company and the Youngstown Sheet and Tube Company. Nearly half of the staggering military expenditure incident to the crushing of this strike in Ohio was borne by the federal government through the allocation of financial aid to the military establishment of the state.

The steel workers have now buried their dead, while the widows weep and 10 watch their orphaned children become objects of public charity. The murder of these unarmed men has never been publicly rebuked by any authoritative officer of the state or federal government. Some of them, in extenuation, plead lack of jurisdiction, but murder as a crime against the moral code can always be rebuked without regard to the niceties of legalistic jurisdiction by those who profess to be the keepers of the public conscience.

Shortly after Kelly's police force in Chicago had indulged in their bloody 11 orgy, Kelly came to Washington looking for political patronage. That patronage was forthcoming and Kelly must believe that the killing of the strikers is no liability in partisan politics.

Meanwhile, the steel puppet Davey is still Governor of Ohio, but not for 12
long I think—not for long. The people of Ohio may be relied upon to mete
our political justice to one who has betrayed his state, outraged the public conscience and besmirched the public honor.

While the men of the steel industry were going through blood and gas in 13
defense of their rights and their homes and their families, elsewhere on the
far-flung C.I.O. front the hosts of labor were advancing and intelligent and
permanent progress was being made. In scores of industries plant after plant
and company after company were negotiating sensible working agreements.

The men in the steel industry who sacrificed their all were not merely aiding 14
their fellows at home but were adding strength to the cause of their comrades in all
industry. Labor was marching toward the goal of industrial democracy and contributing constructively toward a more rational arrangement of our domestic economy.

Labor does not seek industrial strife. It wants peace, but a peace with justice. 15
In the long struggle for labor's rights it has been patient and forbearing. Sabotage
and destruction syndicalism have had no part in the American labor movement.
Workers have kept faith in American institutions. Most of the conflicts, which
have occurred have been when labor's right to live has been challenged and denied.

If there is to be peace in our industrial life let the employer recognize his 16
obligation to his employees—at least to the degree set forth in existing statutes. Ordinary problems affecting wages, hours, and working conditions, in
most instances, will quickly respond to negotiation in the council room.

The United States Chamber of Commerce, the National Association of 17
Manufacturers, and similar groups representing industry and financial interests, are rendering a disservice to the American people in their attempts to
frustrate the organization of labor and in their refusal to accept collective bargaining as one of our economic institutions.

These groups are encouraging a systematic organization of vigilante groups to 18
fight unionization under the sham pretext of local interests. They equip these vigilantes with tin hats, wooden clubs, gas masks and lethal weapons and train them in
the arts of brutality and oppression. They bring in snoops, finks, hatchet gangs and
Chowderhead Cohens to infest their plants and disturb the communities.

Fascist organizations have been launched and financed under the shabby 19
pretext that the C.I.O. movement is communistic. The real breeders of discontent and alien doctrines of government and philosophies subversive of good
citizenship are such as these who take the law into their own hands.

No tin-hat brigade of goose-stepping vigilantes or bibble-babbling mob 20
of blackguarding and corporation paid scoundrels will prevent the onward
march of labor, or divert its purpose to play its natural and rational part in the
development of the economic, political and social life of our nation.

Unionization, as opposed to communism, presupposes the relation of 21
employment; it is based upon the wage system and it recognizes fully and unre-
servedly the institution of private property and the right to investment profit.
It is upon the fuller development of collective bargaining, the wider expansion
of the labor movement, the increased influence of labor in our national coun-
cils, that the perpetuity of our democratic institutions must largely depend.

The organized workers of America, free in their industrial life, conscious part- 22
ners in production, secure in their homes and enjoying a decent standard of living,
will prove the finest bulwark against the intrusion of alien doctrines of government.

Do those who have hatched this foolish cry of communism in the C.I.O. 23
fear the increased influence of labor in our democracy? Do they fear its influence will be cast on the side of shorter hours, a better system of distributed
employment, better homes for the underprivileged, social security for the
aged, a fairer distribution of the national income?

Certainly the workers that are being organized want a voice in the determina- 24
tion of these objectives of social justice. Certainly labor wants a fairer share in the
national income. Assuredly labor wants a larger participation in increased productive efficiency. Obviously the population is entitled to participate in the fruits of
the genius of our men of achievement in the field of the material sciences.

Labor has suffered just as our farm population has suffered from a viciously 25
unequal distribution of the national income. In the exploitation of both classes
of workers has been the source of panic and depression, and upon the economic
welfare of both rests the best assurance of a sound and permanent prosperity.

In this connection let me call attention to the propaganda which some of our 26
industrialists are carrying on among the farmers. By pamphlets in the milk cans or
attached to machinery and in countless other ways of direct and indirect approach
the farmers of the nation are being told that the increased price of farm machinery
and farm supplies is due to the rising wage level brought about by the Committee
for Industrial Organization. And yet it is the industrial millions of this country
who constitute the substantial market for all agricultural products.

The interest of the two groups are mutually dependent. It is when the pay roll 27
goes down that the farmer's realization is diminished, so that his loans become over-
due at the bank and the arrival of the tax collector is awaited with fear. On the other
hand it is the prosperity of the farmer that quickens the tempo of manufacturing
activities and brings buying power to the millions of urban and industrial workers.

As we view the years that have passed this has always been true and it 28
becomes increasingly imperative that the farm population and the millions of
workers in industry must learn to combine their strength for the attainment of
mutual and desirable objectives and at the same time learn to guard themselves
against the sinister propaganda of those who would divide and exploit them.

Under the banner of the Committee for Industrial Organization American 29
labor is on the march. Its objectives today are those it had in the beginning: to
strive for the unionization of our unorganized millions of workers and for the
acceptance of collective bargaining as a recognized American institution.

It seeks peace with the industrial world. It seeks cooperation and mutual- 30
ity of effort with the agricultural population. It would avoid strikes. It would
have its rights determined under the law by the peaceful negotiations and contract relationships that are supposed to characterize American commercial life.

Until an aroused public opinion demands that employers accept that rule, 31
labor has no recourse but to surrender its rights or struggle for their realization with its own economic power.

The objectives of this movement are not political in a partisan sense. Yet 32
it is true that a political party which seeks the support of labor and makes
pledges of good faith to labor must, in equity and good conscience, keep that
faith and redeem those pledges.

The spectacle of august and dignified members of Congress, servants of 33
the people and agents of the republic, skulking, in hallways and closets, hiding
their faces in a party caucus to prevent a quorum from acting upon a labor
measure, is one that emphasizes the perfidy of politicians and blasts the confidence of labor's millions in politician's promises and statesmen's vows.

Labor next year cannot avoid the necessity of a political assay of the 34
work and deeds of its so-called friends and its political beneficiaries. It must
determine who are its friends in the arena of politics as elsewhere. It feels that
its cause is just and that its friends should not view its struggle with neutral
detachment or intone constant criticism of its activities.

Those who chant their praises of democracy but who lose no chance to 35
drive their knives into labor's defenseless back must feel the weight of labor's
woe even as its open adversaries must ever feel the thrust of labor's power.

Labor, like Israel, has many sorrows. Its women weep for their fallen and 36
they lament for the future of the children of the race. It ill behooves one who
has supped at labor's table and who has been sheltered in labor's house to
curse with equal fervor and fine impartiality both labor and its adversaries
when they become locked in deadly embrace.

I repeat that labor seeks peace and guarantees its own loyalty, but the 37
voice of labor, insistent upon its rights, should not be annoying to the ears of
justice or offensive to the conscience of the American people.

⊙ READING ARGUMENTS

1. In what sense is Lewis's speech an ethical argument—that is, to what
   degree does his argument address matters of right and wrong?

2. In paragraph 3, Lewis evokes the Bill of Rights of the U.S. Constitution. Why do you think he does this? How does this reference support
   his overall argument?

3. Where does Lewis use emotionally charged rhetoric to make his
   case? Do you find such appeals to emotion effective and persuasive?
   Why or why not?

4. Lewis argues that farmers and workers must "guard themselves
   against the sinister propaganda of those who would divide and
   exploit them" (para. 28). Do you think Lewis's speech is itself propaganda in any sense? Explain.

5. Where does Lewis take opposing views into account? Does he refute
   them effectively?

This piece appears on the Web site of the International Brotherhood of Electrical Workers, Local 1613. The author is a member of Local 1439.

WATCH OUT FOR STEREOTYPES OF LABOR UNIONS

FIELDING POE

I work for the Union, 'cause She's so good to me. And I'm bound to come out on top, 'cause that's where She says I should be.

I am a Union man, and I'll bet you are too, though you may not realize it. I am about as conservative as they come, and I don't vote for my own self-interest. So be careful before you draw your stereotype. 1

I have heard people make disparaging comments about labor unions, and some people even lay the blame for every economic ill at the feet of the unions. But I can say that the union naysayers have several things in common: 2

First, those who express disdain for the organized laborer usually sit in the box seats of life. Many of the opportunities and pleasures that they enjoy are not measured out in daily doses of an hourly wage. 3

Second, the education and positions that allow such people to rail against the malfeasance of labor unions are often purchased by the toil of union workers. I even heard one boss bad-mouth the union when it was well-known that his father's union wage sent him to college. 4

Then there are those who ascribe their success to shrewd moves and hard work—they disdain unions for harboring the lazy and dishonest—yet they fail to recognize that sometimes life's blessings fall upon the worthy and the unworthy. And here's a clue: hard work, intelligence and education are no guarantee of success. Not every person is cut out of doctor material or inventor cloth. Does that mean that the working man or woman should not receive reasonable working benefits? I think they should. And sometimes the only way to secure those benefits and rights is to band together. 5

Most of these self-described individualists participate in a corporate act somewhere along the line. Have you ever signed a petition? Joined a professional organization? Donated to a cause or campaign? Joined a church or synagogue? If so, do you, as a group, believe in something? Would you have opposed those men who pledged their lives, their fortunes and their sacred honor? I am sure breathing people everywhere have joined together at some time to accomplish some common purpose. It's our nature to have a certain social dependence on one another. 6

There are economic dynamics of supply and demand, and in that respect even the unorganized worker, manager or entrepreneur has his economic benefit influenced by the union wage. Put quite simply, if your employer or customer could get away with paying you 50 cents per hour (or per widget), they 7 would. Generally speaking, the prevailing union wage has elevated the benefits of the non-union person. Besides, if every laboring person only made minimum wages, how many people could pay the price of that SUV, McDonald hamburger or that widget you're trying to sell to me? Certainly not enough to support our present economy.

As an electric utility worker, I joined a labor union 20 years ago as a requirement of my job. I was not so pro-union. I wasn't a soft-headed social liberal even then. I had a college degree and I had experience in training and development. I worked hard and I was sure I could excel. I would be promoted. Well, sometimes things don't work out that way. Now I am glad that neither I, nor the company, made the big mistake. But through the years, I have seen many sides of employment that do not support the image of the benevolent family company. Sometimes everyone needs a defender and an advocate. And sometimes a person does not deserve the treatment meted out by his employer. 8

> "Sometimes everyone needs a defender and an advocate."

The company I work for was known 20 years ago as a "family company." Friends told me that I had it made for life when I got that job. Now, at least 15 years from retirement, the very real prospect of unemployment looms on the horizon. In our present contract negotiations, we are bargaining tenuously for every benefit which was purchased by predecessors who struggled before me. It is interesting that this same company has banded with the workers by enlisting our help when it was politically and economically crucial for them. 9

The next time you hear about labor strife, don't tune it out. Don't be a naysayer. It means that real people—good people—are hurting. I'm a union man. And in some way, I bet you are too. 10

⊙ READING ARGUMENTS

1. Why does Poe begin his essay by announcing, "I am a union man"? Is this an effective opening strategy? Why or why not?

2. Poe warns his readers against stereotypes of unions and union workers. What are some of these stereotypes? Why does he see them as dangerous?

3. What point does Poe make about "self-described individualists" (para. 6)? What does this point have to do with his overall argument?

4. Where and how does Poe use deductive reasoning in this essay? Where does he argue by analogy?

5. Could Poe's argument be described as Rogerian? Why or why not?

This piece first appeared in the *Fredericksburg Free Lance-Star* on April 1, 2008.

DO AMERICANS TODAY STILL NEED LABOR UNIONS?

JAMES SHERK

Would you want to work for a company that treats all workers exactly the same, no matter how hard they work? What about one that promotes only on the basis of seniority and not merit? 1

Few Americans want a job with an employer who ignores their individual efforts. Yet that's what labor unions offer employees today. Small wonder membership is steadily declining. 2

> "Few Americans want a job with an employer who ignores their individual efforts."

The premise of collective bargaining is that by representing all employees a union can negotiate a better collective contract than each worker could get through individual negotiations. But because the union negotiates collectively, the same contract covers every worker, regardless of his or her productivity or effort. 3

In the manufacturing economy of the 1930s, this worked reasonably well. An employee's unique talents and skills made little difference on the assembly line. 4

Individual Abilities

In today's knowledge economy, however, collective representation makes little sense. Machines perform most of the repetitive manufacturing tasks of yesteryear. Employers now want employees with individual insights and abilities. The fastest-growing occupations over the past quarter-century have been professional, technical, and managerial in nature. The jobs of the future include Web designers, interior decorators, and public-relations specialists, among others. 5

These jobs depend on the creativity and skills of individual employees. Few workers today want a one-size-fits-all contract that ignores what they individually bring to the bargaining table. Union-negotiated, seniority-based promotions and raises feel like chains to workers who want to get ahead. 6

Additionally, economic changes mean that unions can no longer deliver large gains to their members. Unions boast that their members earn higher wages than non-union workers. But they don't create money out of thin air. They use their bargaining power to take it from someone else. Contrary to popular impression, that someone is usually not business owners. It is consumers, who pay higher prices when companies pass on the added cost of the union-wage bill. 7

But companies can pass union costs on only when customers cannot shop elsewhere. 8

Deregulation and free trade have increased competition, and benefit both consumers and the economy. NAFTA alone saves a typical family $2,000 a year. But increased competition also means that unions cannot win above-market wages through collective bargaining. Companies no longer have monopoly profits to afford those inflated wages. [9]

Take General Motors, which used to pay its janitors and security workers the union rate of $75 an hour. When Toyota and Honda started selling better cars for less, they drove GM to the brink of bankruptcy and forced the United Auto Workers to agree to new contracts paying market rates. As this has happened at company after company, the difference between union and non-union wages has steadily shrunk. [10]

Selective Hiring

The average union member still earns more than the average non-union member, but not because unions are skilled negotiators. It's because unionized companies become very selective about whom they hire. [11]

Since unions make it virtually impossible to lay off under-performing workers, unionized companies take pains to hire more productive workers in the first place. The typical union member naturally earns higher wages—with or without general representation. New workers who vote to join a union, however, do not earn more than they would have if they had stayed non-union. [12]

These modern realities are colliding with problems that have long turned off workers—corruption, unaccountable leadership, and members' dues funding union bosses' lavish salaries. Not to mention excessive political activism. Unions have announced plans to spend $300 million to defeat John McCain. That's great news if you're a partisan Democrat—less so if you're a rank-and-file worker whose dues foot the bill. [13]

The Public Sector

The one sector where unions remain relevant is the government. Almost half of all union members now work in the public sector. The typical union member today works for the DMV, not on the assembly line. [14]

Unions fit more comfortably into government workplaces than the private sector. Government employees are used to bureaucracy that does little to reward individual initiative. And the government faces no competition. [15]

The state of Virginia won't go bankrupt, no matter how much public-sector unions ask for in wages. The state can just raise taxes on everyone else. It's no accident that the typical government employee earns substantially more than an equivalently skilled private-sector worker. Whether it is fair that government unions push for higher taxes to pay their inflated salaries is another question. [16]

The upshot is that unions today have little to offer workers outside of government. By a more than 3-to-1 margin, non-union workers tell pollsters they are happy to stay that way, and union membership has fallen steadily over the past generation. Fewer than one in 25 Virginia workers today belong to a union. [17]

Unions naturally want to reverse their decline. But rather than reform to become relevant, unions want to take away a worker's right to vote on joining a union. 18

Currently workers join unions through secret-ballot elections. If a majority of employees votes in privacy for a union, their company is organized, but neither their employer nor the union knows how each employee voted. This allows workers to vote their convictions. 19

Now organized labor has thrown its weight behind the little-known "Employee Free Choice Act." This misnamed bill abolishes secret-ballot organizing elections and allows unions to press workers to publicly sign a union representation contract. 20

Where no-vote unions are allowed, unions do not take "no" for an answer. Unions train organizers to give workers a high-pressure sales pitch and push them to immediately sign on. If a worker refuses, organizers return again and again to press him to change his mind. Some organizers threaten workers who will not join. 21

Not surprisingly, unions can organize most workplaces where workers are denied a vote. But making it difficult for workers to refuse to join will not make unions more attractive. Nor will it change the competitive realities that prevent unions from raising wages by passing on costs to consumers. Unless unions rethink how they represent workers they will remain irrelevant to 21st-century employees. 22

● READING ARGUMENTS

1. How does Sherk introduce his argument? Do you find this strategy effective? What other opening strategy could he have used?

2. Sherk notes that unions "worked reasonably well" in the early part of the twentieth century (para. 4). According to him, what changes have occurred that have made unions less relevant and less useful?

3. What elements of causal argument does Sherk use to make his case?

4. Sherk structures his argument, in part, as an appeal to the value of individualism as opposed to the need for collective action. Do you see this as a logical appeal or an emotional appeal? Explain.

● AT ISSUE: DO WE STILL NEED UNIONS?

1. After looking back at John L. Lewis's 1937 speech as well as more recent arguments, do you think that the role and the goals of labor unions are essentially the same as they always have been? Or, do you think that they have changed? How have changes in our economy, society, and politics affected our need for unions?

2. James Sherk argues that in today's "knowledge economy," personal economic success depends on individual initiative, creativity, and skill (para. 5). In contrast, Fielding Poe suggests that these factors are "no guarantee of success" (5) and that most "self-described individu-alists" (6) participate in some collective enterprise. Which writer is more persuasive on this point? Do you think this distinction is a use-ful way of assessing the need for labor unions? Why or why not?

3. Writing in the 1930s, John L. Lewis claims that the goals of the labor movement "are not political in a partisan sense" (32) even as he welcomes "the increased influence of labor in our democracy" (23). However, contemporary writer James Sherk chides labor unions for their "excessive political activism" (13). What connections do you see between the labor movement and politics? Do you think such con-nections are helpful? Do you think they are inevitable?

⊘ WRITING ARGUMENTS: DO WE STILL NEED UNIONS?

1. After reading these essays, do you think American workers still need labor unions? Why or why not? Write an argumentative essay that presents your position on this issue.

2. Fielding Poe writes that "hard work, intelligence and education are no guarantee of success" (para. 5). How much control do you think the average person has over his or her career, earning power, and opportunities for financial success? To what degree do you think these things are controlled by external forces? Explain your views in an argumentative essay.

THE ALLEGORY OF THE CAVE
PLATO

Plato (428 BCE–347 BCE) was an important Greek philosopher. In The Republic, *from which "The Allegory of the Cave" is drawn, Plato examines the nature of reality, how we know what we know, and how we should act. An* **allegory** *is a dramatic representation of abstract ideas by characters and events in a story or image. "The Allegory of the Cave" is an imagined dialogue between Plato's teacher (Socrates) and brother (Glaucon).*

And now, I said, let me show in a figure how far our nature is enlightened or 1
unenlightened:—Behold! human beings living in an underground den, which has a mouth open towards the light and reaching all along the den; here they have been from their childhood, and have their legs and necks chained so that they cannot move, and can only see before them, being prevented by the chains from turning round their heads. Above and behind them a fire is blazing at a distance, and between the fire and the prisoners there is a raised way; and you will see, if you look, a low wall built along the way, like the screen which marionette players have in front of them, over which they show the puppets.

    I see.
2
    And do you see, I said, men passing along the wall carrying all sorts of ves- 3
sels, and statues and figures of animals made of wood and stone and various materials, which appear over the wall? Some of them are talking, others silent.

    You have shown me a strange image, and they are strange prisoners. 4

    Like ourselves, I replied; and they see only their own shadows, or the shad- 5
ows of one another, which the fire throws on the opposite wall of the cave?

    True, he said; how could they see anything but the shadows if they were 6
never allowed to move their heads?

    And of the objects which are being carried in like manner they would only 7
see the shadows?

    Yes, he said.
8
    And if they were able to converse with one another, would they not sup- 9
pose that they were naming what was actually before them?

    Very true.
10
    And suppose further that the prison had an echo which came from the 11
other side, would they not be sure to fancy when one of the passers-by spoke that the voice which they heard came from the passing shadow?

    No question, he replied.
12

To them, I said, the truth would be literally nothing but the shadows of 13 the images.

That is certain. 14

And now look again, and see what will naturally follow if the prisoners are 15 released and disabused of their error. At first, when any of them is liberated and compelled suddenly to stand up and turn his neck round and walk and look towards the light, he will suffer sharp pains; the glare will distress him, and he will be unable to see the realities of which in his former state he had seen the shadows; and then conceive someone saying to him, that what he saw before was an illusion, but that now, when he is approaching nearer to being and his eye is turned towards more real existence, he has a clearer vision—what will be his reply? And you may further imagine that his instructor is pointing to the objects as they pass and requiring him to name them,—will he not be perplexed? Will he not fancy that the shadows which he formerly saw are truer than the objects which are now shown to him?

Far truer. 16

And if he is compelled to look straight at the light, will he not have a pain 17 in his eyes which will make him turn away to take refuge in the objects of vision which he can see, and which he will conceive to be in reality clearer than the things which are now being shown to him?

True, he said. 18

And suppose once more, that he is reluctantly dragged up a steep and rugged 19 ascent, and held fast until he is forced into the presence of the sun himself, is he not likely to be pained and irritated? When he approaches the light his eyes will be dazzled, and he will not be able to see anything at all of what are now called realities.

Not all in a moment, he said. 20

He will require to grow accustomed to the sight of the upper world. And 21 first he will see the shadows best, next the reflections of men and other objects in the water, and then the objects themselves; then he will gaze upon the light of the moon and the stars and the spangled heaven; and he will see the sky and the stars by night better than the sun or the light of the sun by day?

Certainly. 22

Earth's star, often associated in Plato's work with reason, absolute good, intellectual illumination, and God

Last of all he will be able to see the sun,° and not mere reflections of him 23 in the water, but he will see him in his own proper place, and not in another; and he will contemplate him as he is.

Certainly. 24

He will then proceed to argue that this is he who gives the season and the 25 years, and is the guardian of all that is in the visible world, and in a certain way the cause of all things which he and his fellows have been accustomed to behold?

Clearly, he said, he would first see the sun and then reason about him. 26

And when he remembered his old habitation, and the wisdom of the den 27 and his fellow prisoners, do you not suppose that he would felicitate himself on the change, and pity them?

Certainly, he would. 28

And if they were in the habit of conferring honors among themselves on those 29 who were quickest to observe the passing shadows and to remark which of them went before, and which followed after, and which were together; and who were therefore best able to draw conclusions as to the future, do you think that he would care for such honors and glories, or envy the possessors of them? Would he not say with Homer,°

      Better to be the poor servant of a poor master,

and to endure anything, rather than think as they do and live after their manner?

A blind Greek poet from the eighth century BCE, author of the epics The Iliad *and* The Odyssey

30   Yes, he said, I think that he would rather suffer anything than entertain these false notions and live in this miserable manner.

31   Imagine once more, I said, such an one coming suddenly out of the sun to be replaced in his old situation; would he not be certain to have his eyes full of darkness?

32   To be sure, he said.

33   And if there were a contest, and he had to compete in measuring the shadows with the prisoners who had never moved out of the den, while his sight was still weak, and before his eyes had become steady (and the time which would be needed to acquire this new habit of sight might be very considerable), would he not be ridiculous? Men would say of him that up he went and down he came without his eyes; and that it was better not even to think of ascending; and if any one tried to loose another and lead him up to the light, let them only catch the offender, and they would put him to death.

34   No question, he said.

35   This entire allegory, I said, you may now append, dear Glaucon,° to the previous argument; the prison house is the world of sight, the light of the fire is the sun, and you will not misapprehend me if you interpret the journey upwards to be the ascent of the soul into the intellectual world according to my poor belief, which, at your desire, I have expressed—whether rightly or wrongly God knows. But, whether true or false, my opinion is that in the world of knowledge the idea of good appears last of all, and is seen only with an effort; and, when seen, is also inferred to be the universal author of all things beautiful and right, parent of light and of the lord of light in this visible world, and the immediate source of reason and truth in the intellectual; and that this is the power upon which he who would act rationally either in public or private life must have his eye fixed.

Plato's brother, who responds to Socrates' questions, ideas, and arguments in The Republic

36   I agree, he said, as far as I am able to understand you.

37   Moreover, I said, you must not wonder that those who attain to this beatific vision are unwilling to descend to human affairs; for their souls are ever hastening into the upper world where they desire to dwell; which desire of theirs is very natural, if our allegory may be trusted.

38   Yes, very natural.

39   And is there anything surprising in one who passes from divine contemplations to the evil state of man, misbehaving himself in a ridiculous manner; if, while his eyes are blinking and before he has become accustomed to the surrounding darkness, he is compelled to fight in courts of law, or in other places, about the images or the shadows of images of justice, and is endeavoring to meet the conceptions of those who have never yet seen absolute justice?

40   Anything but surprising, he replied.

41   Anyone who has common sense will remember that the bewilderments of the eyes are of two kinds, and arise from two causes, either from coming out

of the light or from going into the light, which is true of the mind's eye, quite as much as of the bodily eye; and he who remembers this when he sees anyone whose vision is perplexed and weak, will not be too ready to laugh; he will first ask whether that soul of man has come out of the brighter life, and is unable to see because unaccustomed to the dark, or having turned from darkness to the day is dazzled by excess of light. And he will count the one happy in his condition and state of being, and he will pity the other; or, if he have a mind to laugh at the soul which comes from below into the light, there will be more reason in this than in the laugh which greets him who returns from above out of the light into the den.

That, he said, is a very just distinction. 42

But then, if I am right, certain professors of education must be wrong 43 when they say that they can put a knowledge into the soul which was not there before, like sight into blind eyes.

They undoubtedly say this, he replied. 44

Whereas, our argument shows that the power and capacity of learning 45 exists in the soul already; and that just as the eye was unable to turn from darkness to light without the whole body, so too the instrument of knowledge can only by the movement of the whole soul be turned from the world of becoming into that of being, and learn by degrees to endure the sight of being, and of the brightest and best of being, or in other words, of the good.

Very true. 46

And must there not be some art which will effect conversion in the easiest 47 and quickest manner; not implanting the faculty of sight, for that exists already, but has been turned in the wrong direction, and is looking away from the truth?

Yes, he said, such an art may be presumed. 48

And whereas the other so-called virtues of the soul seem to be akin to 49 bodily qualities, for even when they are not originally innate they can be implanted later by habit and exercise, the virtue of wisdom more than anything else contains a divine element which always remains, and by this conversion is rendered useful and profitable; or, on the other hand, hurtful and useless. Did you never observe the narrow intelligence flashing from the keen eye of a clever rogue—how eager he is, how clearly his paltry soul sees the way to his end; he is the reverse of blind, but his keen eyesight is forced into the service of evil, and he is mischievous in proportion to his cleverness?

Very true, he said. 50

But what if there had been a circumcision of such natures in the days of 51 their youth; and they had been severed from those sensual pleasures, such as eating and drinking, which, like leaden weights, were attached to them at their birth, and which drag them down and turn the vision of their souls upon the things that are below—if, I say, they had been released from these impediments and turned in the opposite direction, the very same faculty in them would have seen the truth as keenly as they see what their eyes are turned to now.

Very likely. 52

Yes, I said; and there is another thing which is likely, or rather a neces- 53 sary inference from what has preceded, that neither the uneducated and uninformed of the truth, nor yet those who never make an end of their education, will be able ministers of State; not the former, because they have no single aim of duty which is the rule of all their actions, private as well as public; nor the latter, because they will not act at all except upon compulsion, fancying that they are already dwelling apart in the islands of the blessed.

Very true, he replied. 54

Then, I said, the business of us who are the founders of the State will be to com- 55 pel the best minds to attain that knowledge which we have already shown to be the greatest of all—they must continue to ascend until they arrive at the good; but when they have ascended and seen enough we must not allow them to do as they do now.

What do you mean? 56

I mean that they remain in the upper world: but this must not be allowed; 57 they must be made to descend again among the prisoners in the den, and partake of their labors and honors, whether they are worth having or not.

But is not this unjust? he said; ought we to give them a worse life, when 58 they might have a better?

You have again forgotten, my friend, I said, the intention of the legislator, 59 who did not aim at making any one class in the State happy above the rest; the happiness was to be in the whole State, and he held the citizens together by persuasion and necessity, making them benefactors of the State, and therefore benefactors of one another; to this end he created them, not to please themselves, but to be his instruments in binding up the State.

True, he said, I had forgotten. 60

Observe, Glaucon, that there will be no injustice in compelling our philos- 61 ophers to have a care and providence of others; we shall explain to them that in other States, men of their class are not obliged to share in the toils of politics: and this is reasonable, for they grow up at their own sweet will, and the government would rather not have them. Being self-taught, they cannot be expected to show any gratitude for a culture which they have never received. But we have brought you into the world to be rulers of the hive, kings of yourselves and of the other citizens, and have educated you far better and more perfectly than they have been educated, and you are better able to share in the double duty. Wherefore each of you, when his turn comes, must go down to the general underground abode, and get the habit of seeing in the dark. When you have acquired the habit, you will see ten thousand times better than the inhabitants of the den, and you will know what the several images are, and what they represent, because you have seen the beautiful and just and good in their truth. And thus our State, which is also yours, will be a reality, and not a dream only, and will be administered in a spirit unlike that of other States, in which men fight with one another about shadows only and are distracted in the struggle for power, which in their eyes is a great good. Whereas the truth is that the State in which the rulers are most reluctant to govern is always the best and most quietly governed, and the State in which they are most eager, the worst.

Quite true, he replied. 62

And will our pupils, when they hear this, refuse to take their turn at the 63 toils of State, when they are allowed to spend the greater part of their time with one another in the heavenly light?

Impossible, he answered; for they are just men, and the commands which we 64
impose upon them are just; there can be no doubt that every one of them will take
office as a stern necessity, and not after the fashion of our present rulers of State.

Yes, my friend, I said; and there lies the point. You must contrive for your 65
future rulers another and a better life than that of a ruler, and then you may
have a well-ordered State; for only in the State which offers this, will they rule
who are truly rich, not in silver and gold, but in virtue and wisdom, which are
the true blessings of life. Whereas if they go to the administration of public
affairs, poor and hungering after their own private advantage, thinking that
hence they are to snatch the chief good, order there can never be; for they will
be fighting about office, and the civil and domestic broils which thus arise will
be the ruin of the rulers themselves and of the whole State.

Most true, he replied. 66

And the only life which looks down upon the life of political ambition is 67
that of true philosophy. Do you know of any other?

Indeed, I do not, he said. 68

❯ READING ARGUMENTS

1. Do you find Plato's allegory persuasive? What are its strengths and weaknesses?

2. According to Plato, what are the benefits of becoming educated about the true nature of reality? What are the drawbacks and costs of this process?

3. "Allegory of the Cave" contains elements of a proposal argument. What does Plato propose? In what sense, if any, does his proposal apply to contemporary politics?

4. This argument is presented in the form of a dialogue, in which Glaucon responds to Socrates. How does Glaucon further Plato's argument?

❯ WRITING ARGUMENTS

Both Plato and Niccolò Machiavelli (p. 663) discuss political leadership. How are their views similar? Where do their beliefs about the proper conduct and nature of political leaders differ? Which writer's argument seems more persuasive, and why? Develop your ideas in an argumentative essay.

FROM *THE PRINCE*
NICCOLÒ MACHIAVELLI

Niccolò Machiavelli (1469–1527), born in Florence, Italy, was a political philosopher who lived during the Renaissance, a period when learning and culture flowered. In The Prince, *Machiavelli argues that the best course of action for a ruler is to do whatever is necessary to hold onto power. This philosophy, now described as* Machiavellian, *is used to characterize someone who acts with deceit and cunning to further his or her own interests rather than working for the common good.*

On the Reasons Why Men Are Praised or Blamed—Especially Princes

It remains now to be seen what style and principles a prince ought to adopt in deal- 1
ing with his subjects and friends. I know the subject has been treated frequently before, and I'm afraid people will think me rash for trying to do so again, especially since I intend to differ in this discussion from what others have said. But since I intend to write something useful to an understanding reader, it seemed better to go after the real truth of the matter than to repeat what people have imagined. A great many men have imagined states and princedoms such as nobody ever saw or knew in the real world, for there's such a difference between the way we really live and the way we ought to live that the man who neglects the real to study the ideal will learn how to accomplish his ruin, not his salvation. Any man who tries to be good all the time is bound to come to ruin among the great number who are not good. Hence a prince who wants to keep his post must learn how not to be good, and use that knowledge, or refrain from using it, as necessity requires.

Putting aside, then, all the imaginary things that are said about princes, 2
and getting down to the truth, let me say that whenever men are discussed (and especially princes because they are prominent), there are certain qualities that bring them either praise or blame. Thus some are considered generous, others stingy (I use a Tuscan term, since "greedy" in our speech means a man who wants to take other people's goods. We call a man "stingy" who clings to his own); some are givers, others grabbers; some cruel, others merciful; one man is treacherous, another faithful; one is feeble and effeminate, another fierce and spirited; one humane, another proud; one lustful, another chaste; one straightforward, another sly; one harsh, another gentle; one serious, another playful; one religious, another skeptical, and so on. I know everyone will agree that among these many qualities a prince certainly ought to have all those that are considered good. But since it is impossible to have and exercise them all, because the conditions of human life simply do not allow it, a prince must be shrewd enough to avoid the public disgrace of those vices that would lose him his state. If he possibly can, he should also guard against

vices that will not lose him his state; but if he cannot prevent them, he should not be too worried about indulging them. And furthermore, he should not be too worried about incurring blame for any vice without which he would find it hard to save his state. For if you look at matters carefully, you will see that something resembling virtue, if you follow it, may be your ruin, while something else resembling vice will lead, if you follow it, to your security and well-being.

On Liberality and Stinginess

Let me begin, then, with the first of the qualities mentioned above, by saying 3 that a reputation for liberality is doubtless very fine; but the generosity that earns you that reputation can do you great harm. For if you exercise your generosity in a really virtuous way, as you should, nobody will know of it, and you cannot escape the odium of the opposite vice. Hence if you wish to be widely known as a generous man, you must seize every opportunity to make a big display of your giving. A prince of this character is bound to use up his entire revenue in works of ostentation. Thus, in the end, if he wants to keep a name for generosity, he will have to load his people with exorbitant taxes and squeeze money out of them in every way he can. This is the first step in making him odious to his subjects; for when he is poor, nobody will respect him. Then, when his generosity has angered many and brought rewards to a few, the slightest difficulty will trouble him, and at the first approach of danger, down he goes. If by chance he foresees this, and tries to change his ways, he will immediately be labeled a miser.

Since a prince cannot use this virtue of liberality in such a way as to 4 become known for it unless he harms his own security, he won't mind, if he judges prudently of things, being known as a miser. In due course he will be thought the more liberal man, when people see that his parsimony enables him to live on his income, to defend himself against his enemies, and to undertake major projects without burdening his people with taxes. Thus he will be acting liberally toward all those people from whom he takes nothing (and there are an immense number of them), and in a stingy way toward those people on whom he bestows nothing (and they are very few). In our times, we have seen great things being accomplished only by men who have had the name of misers; all the others have gone under. Pope Julius II,° though he used his reputation as a generous man to gain the papacy, sacrificed it in order to be able to make war; the present king of France has waged many wars without levying a single extra tax on his people, simply because he could take care of the extra expenses out of the savings from his long parsimony. If the present king of Spain° had a reputation for generosity, he would never have been able to undertake so many campaigns, or win so many of them.

Hence a prince who prefers not to rob his subjects, who wants to be 5 able to defend himself, who wants to avoid poverty and contempt, and who doesn't want to become a plunderer, should not mind in the least if people

The leader of the Roman Catholic Church from 1503 to 1513. Julius (1443–1513) was known for his aggressive foreign policy, which earned him the nickname "The Terrible Pope."

King Ferdinand (1452–1516), who recaptured many Spanish territories from the Moors

consider him a miser; this is simply one of the vices that enable him to reign. Someone may object that Caesar° used a reputation for generosity to become emperor, and many other people have also risen in the world, because they were generous or were supposed to be so. Well, I answer, either you are a prince already, or you are in the process of becoming one; in the first case, this reputation for generosity is harmful to you, in the second case it is very necessary. Caesar was one of those who wanted to become ruler in Rome; but after he had reached his goal, if he had lived, and had not cut down on his expenses, he would have ruined the empire itself. Someone may say: there have been plenty of princes, very successful in warfare, who have had a reputation for generosity. But I answer; either the prince is spending his own money and that of his subjects, or he is spending someone else's. In the first case, he ought to be sparing; in the second case, he ought to spend money like water. Any prince at the head of his army, which lives on loot, extortion, and plunder, disposes of other people's property, and is bound to be very generous; otherwise, his soldiers would desert him. You can always be a more generous giver when what you give is not yours or your subjects'; Cyrus, Caesar, and Alexander were generous in this way. Spending what belongs to other people does no harm to your reputation, rather it enhances it; only spending your own substance harms you. And there is nothing that wears out faster than generosity; even as you practice it, you lose the means of practicing it, and you become either poor and contemptible or (in the course of escaping poverty) rapacious and hateful. The thing above all against which a prince must protect himself is being contemptible and hateful; generosity leads to both. Thus, it's much wiser to put up with the reputation of being a miser, which brings you shame without hate than to be forced—just because you want to appear generous—into a reputation for rapacity, which brings shame on you and hate along with it.

Julius Caesar (100 BCE–44 BCE), leader of the Roman Empire from 49 BCE to 44 BCE

On Cruelty and Clemency: Whether It Is Better to Be Loved or Feared

6 Continuing now with our list of qualities, let me say that every prince should prefer to be considered merciful rather than cruel, yet he should be careful not to mismanage this clemency of his. People thought Cesare Borgia° was cruel, but that cruelty of his reorganized the Romagna, united it, and established it in peace and loyalty. Anyone who views the matter realistically will see that this prince was much more merciful than the people of Florence who, to avoid the reputation of cruelty, allowed Pistoia to be destroyed. Thus, no prince should mind being called cruel for what he does to keep his subjects united and loyal; he may make examples of a very few, but he will be more merciful in reality than those who, in their tenderheartedness, allow disorders to occur, with their attendant murders and lootings. Such turbulence brings harm to an entire community, while the executions ordered by a prince affect only one individual at a time. A new prince, above all others, cannot possibly avoid a

An Italian religious figure, general, and statesman. Cesare (1475–1507) was Machiavelli's model for The Prince.

A Roman poet. Virgil (70 BCE–19 BCE) is known for the epic Aeneid *and other works.*

The queen and founder of Carthage according to Greek and Roman sources, particularly Virgil's Aeneid

name for cruelty, since new states are always in danger. And Virgil,° speaking through the mouth of Dido° says:

> My cruel fate
> And doubts attending an unsettled state
> Force me to guard my coast from foreign foes.

Yet a prince should be slow to believe rumors and to commit himself to action on the basis of them. He should not be afraid of his own thoughts; he ought to proceed cautiously, moderating his conduct with prudence and humanity, allowing neither overconfidence to make him careless, nor overtimidity to make him intolerable.

Here the question arises: is it better to be loved than feared, or vice versa? 7 I don't doubt that every prince would like to be both; but since it is hard to accommodate these qualities, if you have to make a choice, to be feared is much safer than to be loved. For it is a good general rule about men, that they are ungrateful, fickle, liars and deceivers, fearful of danger and greedy for gain. While you serve their welfare, they are all yours, offering their blood, their belongings, their lives, and their children's lives, as we noted above—so long as the danger is remote. But when the danger is close at hand, they turn against you. Then, any prince who has relied on their words and has made no other preparations will come to grief; because friendships that are bought at a price, and not with greatness and nobility of soul, may be paid for but they are not acquired, and they cannot be used in time of need. People are less concerned with offending a man who makes himself loved than one who makes himself feared: the reason is that love is a link of obligation which men, because they are rotten, will break any time they think doing so serves their advantage; but fear involves dread of punishment, from which they can never escape.

Still, a prince should make himself feared in such a way that, even if 8 he gets no love, he gets no hate either; because it is perfectly possible to be feared and not hated, and this will be the result if only the prince will keep his hands off the property of his subjects or citizens, and off their women. When he does have to shed blood, he should be sure to have a strong justification and manifest cause; but above all, he should not confiscate people's property, because men are quicker to forget the death of a father than the loss of a patrimony. Besides, pretexts for confiscation are always plentiful, it never fails that a prince who starts living by plunder can find reasons to rob someone else. Excuses for proceeding against someone's life are much rarer and more quickly exhausted.

But a prince at the head of his armies and commanding a multitude of 9 soldiers should not care a bit if he is considered cruel; without such a reputation, he could never hold his army together and ready for action. Among the marvelous deeds of Hannibal, this was prime: that, having an immense army, which included men of many different races and nations, and which he led to battle in distant countries, he never allowed them to fight among themselves or to rise against him, whether his fortune was good or bad. The reason for this could only be his inhuman cruelty, which, along with his countless other talents, made him an object of awe and terror to his soldiers; and without the cruelty, his other qualities would never have sufficed. The historians who pass snap judgments on these matters admire his accomplishments and at the same time condemn the cruelty which was their main cause.

10   When I say, "His other qualities would never have sufficed," we can see that this is true from the example of Scipio,° an outstanding man not only among those of his own time, but in all recorded history; yet his armies revolted in Spain, for no other reason than his excessive leniency in allowing his soldiers more freedom than military discipline permits. Fabius Maximus° rebuked him in the senate for this failing, calling him the corrupter of the Roman armies. When a lieutenant of Scipio's plundered the Locrians, he took no action in behalf of the people, and did nothing to discipline that insolent lieutenant; again, this was the result of his easygoing nature. Indeed, when someone in the senate wanted to excuse him on this occasion, he said there are many men who knew better how to avoid error themselves than how to correct error in others. Such a soft temper would in time have tarnished the fame and glory of Scipio, had he brought it to the office of emperor; but as he lived under the control of the senate, this harmful quality of his not only remained hidden but was considered creditable.

A Roman general and statesman. Scipio (235 BCE–183 BCE) was considered one of the greatest military leaders in history.

A Roman politician and general (280 BCE–203 BCE)

11   Returning to the question of being feared or loved, I conclude that since men love at their own inclination but can be made to fear at the inclination of the prince, a shrewd prince will lay his foundations on what is under his own control, not on what is controlled by others. He should simply take pains not to be hated, as I said.

The Way Princes Should Keep Their Word

12   How praiseworthy it is for a prince to keep his word and live with integrity rather than by craftiness, everyone understands; yet we see from recent experience that those princes have accomplished most who paid little heed to keeping their promises, but who knew how craftily to manipulate the minds of men. In the end, they won out over those who tried to act honestly.

13   You should consider then, that there are two ways of fighting, one with laws and the other with force. The first is properly a human method, the second belongs to beasts. But as the first method does not always suffice, you sometimes have to turn to the second. Thus a prince must know how to make good use of both the beast and the man. Ancient writers made subtle note of this fact when they wrote that Achilles° and many other princes of antiquity were sent to be reared by Chiron the centaur,° who trained them in his discipline. Having a teacher who is half man and half beast can only mean that a prince must know how to use both these two natures, and that one without the other has no lasting effect.

An ancient Greek warrior and hero of the Trojan War in Homer's Iliad

A creature from Greek mythology who is part human and part horse

14   Since a prince must know how to use the character of beasts, he should pick for imitation the fox and the lion. As the lion cannot protect himself from

traps, and the fox cannot defend himself from wolves, you have to be a fox in order to be wary of traps, and a lion to overawe the wolves. Those who try to live by the lion alone are badly mistaken. Thus a prudent prince cannot and should not keep his word when to do so would go against his interest, or when the reasons that made him pledge it no longer apply. Doubtless if all men were good, this rule would be bad; but since they are a sad lot, and keep no faith with you, you in your turn are under no obligation to keep it with them.

Besides, a prince will never lack for legitimate excuses to explain away his   15
breaches of faith. Modern history will furnish innumerable examples of this behavior, showing how many treaties and promises have been made null and void by the faithlessness of princes, and how the man succeeded best who knew best how to play the fox. But it is a necessary part of this nature that you must conceal it carefully; you must be a great liar and hypocrite. Men are so simple of mind and so much dominated by their immediate needs, that a deceitful man will always find plenty who are ready to be deceived. One of many recent examples calls for mention. Alexander VI° never did anything else, never had another thought, except to deceive men, and he always found fresh material to work on. Never was there a man more convincing in his assertions, who sealed his promises with more solemn oaths, and who observed them less. Yet his deceptions were always successful, because he knew exactly how to manage this sort of business.

In actual fact, a prince may not have all the admirable qualities we listed,   16
but it is very necessary that he should seem to have them. Indeed, I will venture to say that when you have them and exercise them all the time, they are harmful to you; when you just seem to have them, they are useful. It is good to appear merciful, truthful, humane, sincere, and religious; it is good to be so in reality. But you must keep your mind so disposed that, in case of need, you can turn to the exact contrary. This has to be understood: a prince, and especially a new prince, cannot possibly exercise all those virtues for which men are called "good." To preserve the state, he often has to do things against his word, against charity, against humanity, against religion. Thus he has to have a mind ready to shift as the winds of fortune and the varying circumstances of life may dictate. And as I said above, he should not depart from the good if he can hold to it, but he should be ready to enter on evil if he has to.

Hence a prince should take great care never to drop a word that does not   17
seem imbued with the five good qualities noted above; to anyone who sees or hears him, he should appear all compassion, all honor, all humanity, all integrity, all religion. Nothing is more necessary than to seem to have this last virtue. Men in general judge more by the sense of sight than by the sense of touch, because everyone can see but only a few can test by feeling. Everyone sees what you seem to be, few know what you really are; and those few do not dare take a stand against the general opinion, supported by the majesty of the government. In the actions of all men, and especially of princes who are not subject to a court of appeal, we must always look to the end. Let a prince, therefore, win victories and uphold his state; his methods will always be considered worthy,

The leader of the Roman Catholic Church from 1492 to 1503. Alexander (1431–1503) was known for his corruption.

and everyone will praise them, because the masses are always impressed by the superficial appearance of things, and by the outcome of an enterprise. And the world consists of nothing but the masses; the few who have no influence when the many feel secure. A certain prince of our own time, whom it's just as well not to name, preaches nothing but peace and mutual trust, yet he is the determined enemy of both; and if on several different occasions he had observed either, he would have lost both his reputation and his throne.

⊘ READING ARGUMENTS

1. In the first paragraph, how does Machiavelli explain the need for his argument in the context of the "ideal" and the "real"?

2. In what ways is this essay a proposal argument? Where does Machiavelli use elements of a causal argument?

3. What evidence does Machiavelli use to support his arguments? Do you find this evidence persuasive? Why or why not?

4. What is Machiavelli's view of human beings? How does this view help to shape his ideas about the morals and conduct of princes?

5. Where in the essay does Machiavelli address opposing arguments? Does he refute them effectively? Why or why not?

⊘ WRITING ARGUMENTS

1. Does Machiavelli's argument seem relevant to contemporary leaders and politicians, either with regard to how they *should* behave or to how they *do* behave? Why or why not? Explain your views in an argumentative essay.

2. How would Machiavelli assess the goals, methods, and assumptions expressed by Martin Luther King Jr. in "Letter from Birmingham Jail" (p. 698)? Do you think Machiavelli would approve of King's conduct as a social and political leader? Why or why not?

3. Machiavelli is writing to show "what style and principles a prince ought to adopt in dealing with his subjects and friends" (para. 1). Write your own brief version of *The Prince* in the form of an argument that presents guidelines for how a contemporary political leader should behave.

TO HIS COY MISTRESS

ANDREW MARVELL

Andrew Marvell (1621–1678) was a member of the English Parliament for twenty years, starting in 1658. His poetry, which he wrote for his own enjoyment, was not published until after his death. "To His Coy Mistress" is his best-known poem.

Had we but world enough, and time,   1
This coyness, lady, were no crime.
We would sit down, and think which way
To walk, and pass our long love's day.
A river in India   Thou by the Indian Ganges° side   5
A river in England that flows   Should'st rubies find: I by the tide
past the city of Hull   Of Humber° would complain.° I would
To write poems or songs of   Love you ten years before the Flood,
unrequited love   And you should, if you please, refuse
The belief that Jews would   Till the conversion of the Jews.°   10
be converted to Christianity   My vegetable love° should grow
during the Last Judgment; the   Vaster than empires, and more slow.
end of time   An hundred years should go to praise
A slow, unconscious growth   Thine eyes, and on thy forehead gaze:
Two hundred to adore each breast: 15
But thirty thousand to the rest.
An age at least to every part,
And the last age should show your heart.
For, lady, you deserve this state,
Nor would I love at lower rate.   20
    But at my back I always hear
Time's winged chariot hurrying near;
And yonder all before us lie
Deserts of vast eternity.
Thy beauty shall no more be found,   25
Nor in thy marble vault shall sound
My echoing song; then worms shall try
That long preserved virginity,
And your quaint honor turn to dust,
And into ashes all my lust.   30
The grave's a fine and private place,
But none, I think, do there embrace.

Now therefore, while the youthful hue
Sits on thy skin like morning dew,
35 And while thy willing soul transpires
At every pore with instant fires,
Now let us sport us while we may;
and now, like am'rous birds of prey,
Rather at once our time devour,
40 Than languish in his slow-chapt° power,   *Slowly chewing jaws*
Let us roll all our strength, and all
Our sweetness, up into one ball;
And tear our pleasures with rough strife
Thorough° the iron gates of life.   *Through*
45 Thus, though we cannot make our sun
Stand still, yet we will make him run.

⊘READING ARGUMENTS

1. "To His Coy Mistress" is divided into three sections. Paraphrase each section's main idea in one sentence.

2. What does the phrase "coy mistress" suggest about the occasion and audience for the poem? How do you think a "coy mistress" would respond to the speaker's arguments?

3. How does the speaker's attitude toward time—and toward his relationship with the lady he addresses—change in line 21? How does this shift support his argument? What does he say will happen to the lady if she is not persuaded by his poem?

4. The concluding stanza of the poem begins with the phrase, "Now therefore." How does the speaker develop a deductive argument in the lines that follow?

⊘WRITING ARGUMENTS

1. Write a letter from the "coy mistress" to the poem's speaker refuting his arguments.

2. "To His Coy Mistress" is generally considered to be a poem on the theme of *carpe diem,* which means "seize the day." The full quotation comes from the Roman poet Horace: "Seize the day, and place no trust in tomorrow." Does this seem like a good philosophy of life? Write an argumentative essay that develops your position on this issue.

A MODEST PROPOSAL

JONATHAN SWIFT

Jonathan Swift (1667–1745) was a Protestant clergyman (dean of St. Patrick's Cathedral in Dublin) and a member of the Irish ruling class. His other works include A Tale of a Tub *(1704) and* Gulliver's Travels *(1726). "A Modest Proposal," written in 1729, addresses the wretched condition of the Irish people under English rule: drought had caused crop failures in Ireland, and English landowners ignored the widespread famine while thousands died of starvation.*

It is a melancholy object to those who walk through this great town or travel 1
in the country, when they see the streets, the roads, and cabin doors, crowded with beggars of the female sex, followed by three, four, or six children, all in rags and importuning every passenger for an alms. These mothers instead of being able to work for their honest livelihood, are forced to employ all their time in strolling to beg sustenance for their helpless infants: who as they grow up either turn thieves for want of work, or leave their dear native country to fight for the pretender in Spain,° or sell themselves to the Barbadoes.°

I think it is agreed by all parties that this prodigious number of children 2
in the arms, or on the backs, or at the heels of their mothers, and frequently of their fathers, is in the present deplorable state of the kingdom a very great additional grievance; and, therefore, whoever could find out a fair, cheap, and easy method of making these children sound, useful members of the commonwealth, would deserve so well of the public as to have his statute set up for a preserver of the nation.

But my intention is very far from being confined to provide only for the 3
children of professed beggars; it is of a much greater extent, and shall take in the whole number of infants at a certain age who are born of parents in effect as little able to support them as those who demand our charity in the streets.

As to my own part, having turned my thoughts for many years upon this 4
important subject, and maturely weighed the several schemes of our projectors, I have always found them grossly mistaken in their computation. It is true, a child just dropped from its dam° may be supported by her milk for a solar year, with little other nourishment; at most not above the value of 2s., which the mother may certainly get, or the value in scraps, by her lawful occupation of begging; and it is exactly at one year old that I propose to provide for them in such a manner as instead of being a charge upon their parents or the parish, or wanting food and raiment for the rest of their lives, they shall on the contrary contribute to the feeding, and partly to the clothing, of many thousands.

There is likewise another great advantage in my scheme, that it will pre- 5
vent those voluntary abortions, and that horrid practice of women murdering

James Francis Edward Stuart (1688–1766), descendant of the Stuart royal line. After the Stuarts were expelled from Protestant England in 1689, they took refuge in Catholic countries.

A New World colony in the Caribbean. The poor sometimes emigrated from Ireland to Barbados to find work.

Just born

their bastard children, alas! too frequent among us! sacrificing the poor innocent babes I doubt more to avoid the expense than the shame, which would move tears and pity in the most savage and inhuman breast.

The number of souls in this kingdom being usually reckoned one million   6 and a half, of these I calculate there may be about 200,000 couple whose wives are breeders; from which number I subtract 30,000 couple who are able to maintain their own children (although I apprehend there cannot be so many, under the present distress of the kingdom); but this being granted, there will remain 170,000 breeders. I again subtract 50,000 for those women who miscarry, or whose children die by accident or disease within the year. There only remain 120,000 children of poor parents annually born. The question therefore is, how this number shall be reared and provided for? which, as I have already said, under the present situation of affairs, is utterly impossible by all the methods hitherto proposed. For we can neither employ them in handicraft nor agriculture; we neither build houses (I mean in the country) nor cultivate land; they can very seldom pick up a livelihood by stealing, till they arrive at six years old, except where they are of towardly parts, although I confess they learn the rudiments much earlier, during which time they can, however, be properly looked upon only as probationers; as I have been informed by a principal gentleman in the county of Cavan, who protested to me that he never knew above one or two instances under the age of six, even in a part of the kingdom so renowned for the quickest proficiency in that art.

I am assured by our merchants, that a boy or a girl before twelve years   7 old is no salable commodity; and even when they come to this age they will not yield above 3£. or 3£. 2s. 6d. at most on the exchange; which cannot turn to account either to the parents or kingdom, the charge of nutriment and rags having been at least four times that value.

I shall now therefore humbly propose my own thoughts, which I hope will   8 not be liable to the least objection.

I have been assured by a very knowing American of my acquaintance in   9 London, that a young healthy child well nursed is at a year old a most delicious, nourishing, and wholesome food, whether stewed, roasted, baked, or broiled; and I make no doubt that it will equally serve in a fricassee or a ragout.

I do therefore humbly offer it to public consideration that of the 120,000   10 children already computed, 20,000 may be reserved for breed, whereof only one-fourth part to be males; which is more than we allow to sheep, black cattle, or swine; and my reason is, that these children are seldom the fruits of marriage, a circumstance not much regarded by our savages; therefore one male will be sufficient to serve four females. That the remaining 100,000 may, at a year old, be offered in sale to the persons of quality and fortune through the kingdom; always advising the mother to let them suck plentifully in the last month, so as to render them plump and fat for a good table. A child will make two dishes at an entertainment for friends; and when the family dines alone, the fore and hind quarter will make a reasonable dish, and seasoned with a little pepper or salt will be very good boiled on the fourth day, especially in winter.

I have reckoned upon a medium that a child just born will weigh 11
12 pounds, and in a solar year, if tolerably nursed, will increase to 28 pounds.

I grant this food will be somewhat dear, and therefore very proper for 12
landlords, who, as they have already devoured most of the parents, seem to
have the best title to the children.

Infants' flesh will be in season throughout the year, but more plentiful in 13
March, and a little before and after: for we are told by a grave author, an emi-
nent French physician, that fish being a prolific diet, there are more children
born in Roman Catholic countries about nine months after Lent than at any
other season; therefore, reckoning a year after Lent, the markets will be more
glutted than usual, because the number of popish infants is at least three to
one in this kingdom: and therefore it will have one other collateral advantage,
by lessening the number of papists° among us.

Catholics. The term papists
*suggests their allegiance to
the Pope rather than to the
Church of England.*

I have already computed the charge of nursing a beggar's child (in which 14
list I reckon all cottagers, laborers, and four-fifths of the farmers) to be about
2s. per annum, rags included; and I believe no gentleman would repine to give
10s. for the carcass of a good fat child, which, as I have said, will make four
dishes of excellent nutritive meat, when he has only some particular friend or
his own family to dine with him. Thus the squire will learn to be a good landlord, and grow popular among the tenants; the mother will have 8s. net profit,
and be fit for work till she produces another child.

Those who are more thrifty (as I must confess the times require) may flay 15
the carcass; the skin of which artificially dressed will make admirable gloves
for ladies, and summer boots for fine gentlemen.

Butcher shops

As to our city of Dublin, shambles° may be appointed for this purpose in 16
the most convenient parts of it, and butchers we may be assured will not be
wanting: although I rather recommend buying the children alive, and dressing
them hot from the knife as we do roasting pigs.

A very worthy person, a true lover of his country, and whose virtues I 17
highly esteem, was lately pleased in discoursing on this matter to offer a refinement upon my scheme. He said that many gentlemen of this kingdom, having
of late destroyed their deer, he conceived that the want of venison might be
well supplied by the bodies of young lads and maidens, not exceeding fourteen years of age nor under twelve; so great a number of both sexes in every
country being now ready to starve for want of work and service; and these to
be disposed of by their parents, if alive, or otherwise by their nearest relations.
But with due deference to so excellent a friend and so deserving a patriot,
I cannot be altogether in his sentiments; for as to the males, my American
acquaintance assured me from frequent experience that their flesh was generally tough and lean, like that of our schoolboys by continual exercise, and their
taste disagreeable; and to fatten them would not answer the charge. Then as to
the females, it would, I think, with humble submission be a loss to the public,
because they soon would become breeders themselves: and besides, it is not
improbable that some scrupulous people might be apt to censure such a practice (although indeed very unjustly), as a little bordering upon cruelty; which,

I confess, has always been with me the strongest objection against any project, how well soever intended.

18   But in order to justify my friend, he confessed that this expedient was put into his head by the famous Psalmanazar,° a native of the island Formosa, who came from thence to London about twenty years ago: and in conversation told my friend, that in his country when any young person happened to be put to death, the executioner sold the carcass to persons of quality as a prime dainty; and that in his time the body of a plump girl of fifteen, who was cruci- fied for an attempt to poison the emperor, was sold to his imperial majesty's prime minister of state, and other great mandarins° of the court, in joints from the gibbet,° at 400 crowns. Neither indeed can I deny, that if the same use were made of several plump young girls in this town, who without one single groat° to their fortunes cannot stir abroad without a chair, and appear at the playhouse and assemblies in foreign fineries which they never will pay for, the kingdom would not be the worse.

George Psalmanazar (1679?–1763), who falsely claimed to be the first person from Formosa (modern-day Taiwan) to visit Europe. He described Formosan native customs that included cannibalism.

Chinese nobles, court officials, or magistrates

A post for hanging; a gallows

A small coin

19   Some persons of a desponding spirit are in great concern about the vast number of poor people, who are aged, diseased, or maimed, and I have been desired to employ my thoughts what course may be taken to ease the nation of so grievous an encumbrance. But I am not in the least pain upon that matter, because it is very well known that they are every day dying and rotting by cold and famine, and filth and vermin, as fast as can be reasonably expected. And as to the young laborers, they are now in as hopeful condition: They cannot get work, and consequently pine away for want of nourishment, to a degree that if at any time they are accidentally hired to common labor, they have not strength to perform it; and thus the country and themselves are happily deliv- ered from the evils to come.

20   I have too long digressed, and therefore shall return to my subject. I think the advantages by the proposal which I have made are obvious and many, as well as of the highest importance.

21   For first, as I have already observed, it would greatly lessen the number of papists, with whom we are yearly overrun, being the principal breeders of the nation as well as our most dangerous enemies; and who stay at home on pur- pose to deliver the kingdom to the Pretender, hoping to take their advantage by the absence of so many good Protestants, who have chosen rather to leave their country than stay at home and pay tithes against their conscience to an Episcopal curate.

22   Secondly, The poor tenants will have something valuable of their own, which by law may be made liable to distress° and help to pay their landlord's rent, their corn and cattle being already seized, and money a thing unknown.

Able to be seized to pay a debt

23   Thirdly, Whereas the maintenance of 100,000 children from two years old and upward, cannot be computed at less that 10s. a-piece per annum, the nation's stock will be thereby increased £50,000 per annum, beside the profit of a new dish introduced to the tables of all gentlemen of fortune in the kingdom who have any refinement in taste. And the money will circulate among our- selves, the goods being entirely of our own growth and manufacture.

Fourthly, The constant breeders beside the gain of 8s. sterling per annum 24 by the sale of their children, will be rid of the charge of maintaining them after the first year.

Fifthly, This food would likewise bring great custom to taverns, where the 25 vintners will certainly be so prudent as to procure the best receipts for dressing it to perfection, and consequently have their houses frequented by all the fine gentlemen, who justly value themselves upon their knowledge in good eating; and a skillful cook who understands how to oblige his guests, will contrive to make it as expensive as they please.

Sixthly, This would be a great inducement to marriage, which all wise 26 nations have either encouraged by rewards or enforced by laws and penalties. It would increase the care and tenderness of mothers toward their children, when they were sure of a settlement for life to the poor babes, provided in some sort by the public, to their annual profit instead of expense. We should see an honest emulation among the married women, which of them would bring the fattest child to the market. Men would become as fond of their wives during the time of their pregnancy as they are now of their mares in foal, their cows in calf, their sows when they are ready to farrow; nor offer to beat or kick them (as is too frequent a practice) for fear of a miscarriage.

Many other advantages might be enumerated. For instance, the addition 27 of some thousand carcasses in our exportation of barreled beef, the propaga-tion of swine's flesh, and improvement in the art of making good bacon, so much wanted among us by the great destruction of pigs, too frequent at our table; which are no way comparable in taste or magnificence to a well-grown, fat, yearling child, which roasted whole will make a considerable figure at a lord mayor's feast or any other public entertainment. But this and many oth-ers I omit, being studious of brevity.

Supposing that 1,000 families in this city would be constant customers for 28 infants' flesh, besides others who might have it at merry-meetings, particularly at weddings and christenings, I compute that Dublin would take off annually about 20,000 carcasses; and the rest of the kingdom (where probably they will be sold somewhat cheaper) the remaining 80,000.

I can think of no one objection that will possibly be raised against this 29 proposal unless it should be urged that the number of people will be thereby much lessened in the kingdom. This I freely own, and it was indeed one prin-cipal design in offering it to the world. I desire the reader will observe, that I calculate my remedy for this one individual kingdom of Ireland and for no other that ever was, is, or I think ever can be upon earth. Therefore let no man talk to me of other expedients: of taxing our absentees at 5s. a pound: of using neither clothes nor household furniture except what is of our own growth and manufacture: of utterly rejecting the materials and instruments that promote foreign luxury: of curing the expensiveness of pride, vanity, idleness, and gam-ing in our women: of introducing a vein of parsimony, prudence, and temper-ance: of learning to love our country, in the want of which we differ even from Laplanders.° and the inhabitants of Topinamboo:° of quitting our animosities

The indigenous Sami people of Northern European countries, including Sweden, Norway, and Finland. The term is now considered pejorative

Brazil

and factions, nor acting any longer like the Jews, who were murdering one another at the very moment their city° was taken: of being a little cautious not to sell our country and conscience for nothing: of teaching landlords to have at least one degree of mercy toward their tenants: lastly, of putting a spirit of honesty, industry, and skill into our shopkeepers; who, if a resolution could now be taken to buy only our native goods, would immediately unite to cheat and exact upon us in the price the measure, and the goodness, nor could ever yet be brought to make one fair proposal of just dealing, though often and earnestly invited to it.

Jerusalem, which was conquered by the Roman commander Titus in 70

30   Therefore I repeat, let no man talk to me of these and the like expedients, till he has at least some glimpse of hope that there will be ever some hearty and sincere attempt to put them in practice.

31   But as to myself, having been wearied out for many years with offering vain, idle, visionary thoughts, and at length utterly despairing of success, I fortunately fell upon this proposal; which, as it is wholly new, so it has something solid and real, of no expense and little trouble, full in our own power, and whereby we can incur no danger in disobliging England. For this kind of commodity will not bear exportation, the flesh being of too tender a consistence to admit a long continuance in salt, although perhaps I could name a country° which would be glad to eat up our whole nation without it.

England

32   After all, I am not so violently bent upon my own opinion as to reject any offer proposed by wise men, which shall be found equally innocent, cheap, easy, and effectual. But before something of that kind shall be advanced in contradiction to my scheme, and offering a better, I desire the author or authors will be pleased maturely to consider two points. First, as things now stand, how they will be able to find food and raiment for 100,000 useless mouths and backs. And secondly, there being a round million of creatures in human figure throughout this kingdom, whose subsistence put into a common stock would leave them in debt 2,000,000£. sterling, adding those who are beggars by profession to the bulk of farmers, cottagers, and laborers, with the wives and children who are beggars in effect; I desire those politicians who dislike my overture, and may perhaps be so bold as to attempt an answer, that they will first ask the parents of these mortals, whether they would not at this day think it a great happiness to have been sold for food at a year old in the manner I prescribe, and thereby have avoided such a perpetual scene of misfortunes as they have since gone through by the oppression of landlords, the impossibility of paying rent without money or trade, the want of common sustenance, with neither house nor clothes to cover them from the inclemencies of the weather, and the most inevitable prospect of entailing the like or greater miseries upon their breed for ever.

33   I profess, in the sincerity of my heart, that I have not the least personal interest in endeavoring to promote this necessary work, having no other motive than the public good of my country, by advancing our trade, providing for infants, relieving the poor, and giving some pleasure to the rich. I have no children by which I can propose to get a single penny; the youngest being nine years old, and my wife past childbearing.

⊃READING ARGUMENTS

1. Swift's "A Modest Proposal" is satire: it takes a position that is so extreme that readers must necessarily disagree with it. By taking such a position, Swift ridicules the English political system that he considers corrupt and insensitive and implies another, more reasonable argument that the reader must infer. What is the real argument that Swift is making in "A Modest Proposal"? What social reforms does he propose?

2. Where does "A Modest Proposal" use inductive reasoning?

3. In what sense is "A Modest Proposal" an ethical argument?

4. Swift's use of irony—saying one thing but meaning another—is a useful technique for making an argument, yet it also has limitations. What are some of these limitations?

5. What elements of a proposal argument appear in this essay? Which elements, if any, are missing?

⊃WRITING ARGUMENTS

1. Write your own modest proposal. Choose a contemporary issue or controversy (political, cultural, or social). Then, write an argumentative essay that uses irony, satire, and hyperbole (intentional exaggeration) to make your point.

2. "A Modest Proposal" includes population data, economic projections, and other kinds of support. What point do you think Swift is making about actual proposals to solve social or political problems? Do you think his point is relevant today? Why or why not?

3. Both "A Modest Proposal" and Margaret Sanger's "The Cause of War" (p. 686) deal, in large part, with the subject of population control and limited resources. How would you compare and contrast their arguments—and their methods of argumentation? Do you think they express the same general view of human beings and civilization? Which argument do you see as more effective? Explain your views in an argumentative essay.

THE DECLARATION OF INDEPENDENCE
THOMAS JEFFERSON

Thomas Jefferson, born in 1743, was one of the founding fathers of the United States. He served in the Virginia House of Burgesses and the Continental Congress, as governor of Virginia, minister to France, Secretary of State in President George Washington's cabinet, vice president, and president of the United States for two terms. He also founded the University of Virginia. In 1776, he was chosen to draft the Declaration of Independence, the founding document of American liberties. Jefferson died on July 4, 1826.

In Congress, July 4, 1776
The Unanimous Declaration of the
Thirteen United States of America

1   When in the Course of human events it becomes necessary for one people to dissolve the political bands which have connected them with another, and to assume among the powers of the earth, the separate and equal station to which the Laws of Nature and of Nature's God entitle them, a decent respect to the opinions of mankind requires that they should declare the causes which impel them to the separation.

2   We hold these truths to be self-evident, that all men are created equal, that they are endowed by their Creator with certain unalienable Rights, that among these are Life, Liberty, and the pursuit of Happiness. That to secure these rights, Governments are instituted among Men, deriving their just powers from the consent of the governed. That whenever any Form of Government becomes destructive of these ends, it is the Right of the People to alter or to abolish it, and to institute new Government, laying its foundation on such principles and organizing its powers in such form, as to them shall seem most likely to effect their Safety and Happiness. Prudence, indeed, will dictate that Governments long established should not be changed for light and transient causes; and accordingly all experience hath shewn that mankind are more disposed to suffer, while evils are sufferable, than right themselves by abolishing the forms to which they are accustomed. But when a long train of abuses and usurpations, pursuing invariably the same Object evinces a design to reduce them under absolute Despotism, it is their right, it is their duty, to throw off such Government, and to provide new Guards for their future security. Such has been the patient sufferance of these Colonies; and such is now the necessity which constrains them to alter their former Systems of Government. The history of the present King of Great Britain is a history of repeated injuries and usurpations, all having in direct object the establishment of an absolute Tyranny over these States. To prove this, let Facts be submitted to a candid° world.

Impartial, without prejudice

He has refused his Assent to Laws, the most wholesome and necessary for 3
the public good.

He has forbidden his Government to pass laws of immediate and press- 4
ing importance, unless suspended in their operation till his Assent should be
obtained; and when so suspended, he has utterly neglected to attend to them.

He has refused to pass other Laws for the accommodation of large districts 5
of people, unless those people would relinquish the right of Representation in
the Legislature, a right inestimable to them and formidable to tyrants only.

He has called together legislative bodies at places unusual, uncomfortable, 6
and distant from the depository of their Public Records, for the sole purpose
of fatiguing them into compliance with his measures.

He has dissolved Representative Houses repeatedly, for opposing with 7
manly firmness his invasions on the rights of the people.

He has refused for a long time, after such dissolutions, to cause others to 8
be elected; whereby the Legislative Powers, incapable of Annihilation, have
returned to the People at large for their exercise; the State remaining in the
mean time exposed to all the dangers of invasion from without, and convul-
sions within.

He has endeavored to prevent the population of these States; for that pur- 9
pose obstructing the Laws for Naturalization of Foreigners; refusing to pass
others to encourage their migration hither, and raising the conditions of new
Appropriations of Lands.

He has obstructed the Administration of Justice, by refusing his Assent to 10
Laws for establishing Judiciary Powers.

He has made Judges dependent on his Will alone, for the tenure of their 11
offices, and the amount and payment of their salaries.

He has erected a multitude of New Offices, and sent hither swarms of 12
Officers to harass our people, and eat out their substance.

He has kept among us, in times of peace, Standing Armies without the 13
Consent of our legislatures.

He has affected to render the Military independent of and superior to the 14
Civil Power.

He has combined with others to subject us to a jurisdiction foreign to 15
our constitution, and unacknowledged by our laws; giving his Assent to
their Acts of pretended Legislation: For quartering large bodies of armed
troops among us: For protecting them, by a mock Trial, from punishment
for any Murders which they should commit on the Inhabitants of these
States: For cutting off our Trade with all parts of the world: For imposing Taxes on us without our Consent: For depriving us in many cases, of
the benefits of Trial by Jury: For transporting us beyond Seas to be tried
for pretended offenses: for abolishing the free System of English Laws in
a neighboring Province,° establishing therein an Arbitrary government,
and enlarging its Boundaries so as to render it at once an example and fit
instrument for introducing the same absolute rule into these Colonies: For
taking away our Charters, abolishing our most valuable Laws and altering

*Québec, whose residents
were deprived of political
representation by the British
government in 1774*

fundamentally the Forms of our Governments: For suspending our own Legislatures, and declaring themselves invested with power to legislate for us in all cases whatsoever.

He has abdicated Government here, by declaring us out of his Protection 16 and waging War against us.

He has plundered our seas, ravaged our Coasts, burnt our towns, and 17 destroyed the lives of our people.

He is at this time transporting large Armies of foreign Mercenaries to 18 complete the works of death, desolation and tyranny, already begun with circumstances of Cruelty & Perfidy scarcely paralleled in the most barbarous ages, and totally unworthy the Head of a civilized nation.

He has constrained our fellow Citizens taken Captive on the high Seas to 19 bear Arms against their Country, to become the executioners of their friends and Brethren, or to fall themselves by their Hands.

He has excited domestic insurrections amongst us, and has endeavored to 20 bring on the inhabitants of our frontiers, the merciless Indian Savages, whose known rule of warfare, is an undistinguished destruction of all ages, sexes, and conditions.

In every stage of these Oppressions We have Petitioned for Redress in 21 the most humble terms: Our repeated Petitions have been answered only by repeated injury. A Prince, whose character is thus marked by every act which may define a Tyrant, is unfit to be the ruler of a free people.

Nor have We been wanting in attention to our British brethren. We have 22 warned them from time to time of attempts by their legislature to extend an unwarrantable jurisdiction over us. We have reminded them of the circumstances of our emigration and settlement here. We have appealed to their native justice and magnanimity, and we have conjured them by the ties of our common kindred to disavow these usurpations, which would inevitably interrupt our connections and correspondence. They too have been deaf to the voice of justice and of consanguinity. We must, therefore, acquiesce in the necessity, which denounces our Separation, and hold them, as we hold the rest of mankind, Enemies in War, in Peace Friends.

We, THEREFORE the Representatives of the UNITED STATES OF 23 AMERICA, in General Congress, Assembled, appealing to the Supreme Judge of the world for the rectitude of our intentions, do, in the Name, and by Authority of the good People of these Colonies, solemnly publish and declare, That these United Colonies are, and of Right ought to be FREE AND INDEPENDENT STATES; that they are Absolved from all Allegiance to the British Crown, and that all political connection between them and the State of Great Britain, is and ought to be totally dissolved; and that as Free and Independent States, they have full Power to levy War, conclude Peace, contract Alliances, establish Commerce, and to do all other Acts and Things which Independent States may of right do. And for the support of this Declaration, with a firm reliance on the protection of Divine Providence, we mutually pledge to each other our Lives, our Fortunes, and our sacred Honor.

⊘ READING ARGUMENTS

1. What are the purposes of the first and second paragraphs of the Declaration of Independence? Is this opening deductive or inductive?

2. In paragraph 2, Jefferson writes, "Governments long established should not be changed for light and transient causes." Why is this qualification important to his argument? What objections does it anticipate?

3. According to the declaration, what is the purpose of government? What makes a government legitimate?

4. In what sense is the Declaration of Independence a causal argument?

5. What specific evidence does Jefferson supply to support his case? How effective is this evidence? What do you consider his most convincing piece of evidence?

⊘ WRITING ARGUMENTS

1. In a one-page response, analyze and evaluate the Declaration of Independence in terms of the Toulmin model. Begin by identifying the claim, the grounds, and the warrant.

2. In the declaration, Jefferson writes that revolutionary action should not be taken for "light and transient causes" (para. 2). After an armed uprising several years before the American Revolution, he also said, "God forbid we be 20 years without such a rebellion. . . . The tree of liberty must be refreshed from time to time with the blood of patriots and tyrants." In your view, what conditions or actions on the part of an established government justify its overthrow? Explain your answer in an argumentative essay.

3. Jefferson and Niccolò Machiavelli take different views of the proper behavior of political leaders. Using the assumptions and arguments in the excerpt from *The Prince* (p. 663), write an analysis and critique of the Declaration of Independence and its premises and principles.

DECLARATION OF SENTIMENTS AND RESOLUTIONS

ELIZABETH CADY STANTON

Elizabeth Cady Stanton (1815–1902) was a prominent leader in the struggle for the rights of women, advocating for the right of women to vote, divorce, and be equal to men under law. In 1848, when Stanton's Declaration of Sentiments and Resolutions was written for a women's rights convention in Seneca Falls, New York, married women were not allowed to own property. Stanton's declaration is modeled on Thomas Jefferson's Declaration of Independence.

When, in the course of human events, it becomes necessary for one portion of 1 the family of man to assume among the people of the earth a position different from that which they have hitherto occupied, but one to which the laws of nature and of nature's God entitle them, a decent respect to the opinions of mankind requires that they should declare the causes that impel them to such a course.

We hold these truths to be self-evident: that all men and women are created 2 equal; that they are endowed by their Creator with certain inalienable rights; that among these are life, liberty, and the pursuit of happiness; that to secure these rights governments are instituted, deriving their just powers from the consent of the governed. Whenever any form of government becomes destructive of these ends, it is the right of those who suffer from it to refuse allegiance to it, and to insist upon the institution of a new government, laying its foundation on such principles, and organizing its powers in such form, as to them shall seem most likely to effect their safety and happiness. Prudence indeed, will dictate that governments long established should not be changed for light and transient causes; and accordingly all experience hath shown that mankind are more disposed to suffer, while evils are sufferable, than to right themselves by abolishing the forms to which they were accustomed. But when a long train of abuses and usurpations, pursuing invariably the same object evinces a design to reduce them under absolute despotism, it is their duty to throw off such government, and to provide new guards for their future security. Such has been the patient sufferance of the women under this government, and such is now the necessity which constrains them to demand the equal station to which they are entitled.

The history of mankind is a history of repeated injuries and usurpations on 3 the part of man toward woman, having in direct object the establishment of an absolute tyranny over her. To prove this, let facts be submitted to a candid world.

He has never permitted her to exercise her inalienable right to the elective 4 franchise.

He has compelled her to submit to laws, in the formation of which she 5 had no voice.

He has withheld from her rights which are given to the most ignorant and 6 degraded men—both natives and foreigners.

Having deprived her of this first right of a citizen, the elective franchise, 7 thereby leaving her without representation in the halls of legislation, he has oppressed her on all sides.

He has made her, if married, in the eye of the law, civilly dead. 8

He has taken from her all right in property, even to the wages she earns. 9

He has made her, morally, an irresponsible being, as she can commit 10 many crimes with impunity, provided they be done in the presence of her hus-band. In the covenant of marriage, she is compelled to promise obedience to her husband, he becoming, to all intents and purposes, her master—the law giving him power to deprive her of her liberty, and to administer chastisement.

He has so framed the laws of divorce, as to what shall be the proper causes, 11 and in case of separation, to whom the guardianship of the children shall be given, as to be wholly regardless of the happiness of women—the law, in all cases, going upon a false supposition of the supremacy of man, and giving all power into his hands.

After depriving her of all rights as a married woman, if single, and the 12 owner of property, he has taxed her to support a government which recognizes her only when her property can be made profitable to it.

He has monopolized nearly all the profitable employments, and from those 13 she is permitted to follow, she receives but a scanty remuneration. He closes against her all the avenues to wealth and distinction which he considers most hon-orable to himself. As a teacher of theology, medicine, or law, she is not known.

He has denied her the facilities for obtaining a thorough education, all 14 colleges being closed against her.

He allows her in Church, as well as State, but a subordinate position, 15 claiming Apostolic authority for her exclusion from the ministry, and, with some exceptions, from any public participation in the affairs of the Church.

He has created a false public sentiment by giving to the world a differ- 16 ent code of morals for men and women, by which moral delinquencies which exclude women from society, are not only tolerated, but deemed of little account in man.

He has usurped the prerogative of Jehovah himself, claiming it as his right 17 to assign for her a sphere of action, when that belongs to her conscience and to her God.

He has endeavored, in every way that he could, to destroy her confidence 18 in her own powers, to lessen her self-respect, and to make her willing to lead a dependent and abject life.

Now, in view of this entire disfranchisement of one-half the people of 19 this country, their social and religious degradation—in view of the unjust laws above mentioned, and because women do feel themselves aggrieved, oppressed, and fraudulently deprived of their most sacred rights, we insist that they have immediate admission to all the rights and privileges which belong to them as citizens of the United States.

In entering upon the great work before us, we anticipate no small amount 20 of misconception, misrepresentation, and ridicule; but we shall use every instrumentality within our power to effect our object. We shall employ agents, circulate tracts, petition the State and National legislatures, and endeavor to enlist the pulpit and the press in our behalf. We hope this Convention will be followed by a series of Conventions embracing every part of the country.

⊘ READING ARGUMENTS

1. In what respects is the Declaration of Sentiments and Resolutions an argument by analogy?

2. How do Stanton's general political aims contrast with Jefferson's goals in the Declaration of Independence (p. 679)?

3. Stanton writes that men have "usurped the prerogative of Jehovah himself" and claimed the "right to assign for [women] a sphere of action" (para. 17). What do you think she means? Do you think her point is valid today?

4. According to Stanton, "The history of mankind is a history of repeated injuries and usurpations on the part of man toward woman, having in direct object the establishment of an absolute tyranny over her" (3). How does she support this generalization? Do you find her evidence convincing? Why or why not?

5. In her conclusion, Stanton summarizes how women will fulfill the goals of her declaration. What specific steps does she expect women to take?

⊘ WRITING ARGUMENTS

1. Stanton accuses male-dominated society not only of "monopoliz[ing] nearly all profitable employments" (para. 13) but also of "giving to the world a different code of morals for men and women" (16). Do you think these gender restrictions and double standards still exist today? Write an argumentative essay that takes a stand on this question.

2. In paragraph 2 of her declaration, Stanton quotes Thomas Jefferson's claim that "all experience hath shown that mankind are more disposed to suffer, while evils are sufferable, than right themselves by abolishing the forms to which they are accustomed." What view of human nature is implied here? Do you agree with this view? Do you think it is still held by people today? Explain your views in an argumentative essay.

THE CAUSE OF WAR

MARGARET SANGER

Margaret Sanger (1879–1966) was born in New York City, the sixth of eleven children. In 1910, she began working as a nurse and midwife among the immigrants of the Lower East Side of Manhattan, promoting contraception at a time when it was illegal to do so. She is credited with coining the term birth control. *In 1914, Sanger was indicted for spreading information about contraception through the mail, and she fled to England to avoid prosecution. In 1917, she founded the organization now known as Planned Parenthood. In "The Cause of War," from her 1920 book* Women and the New Race, *Sanger argues that overpopulation was the root cause of World War I.*

In every nation of militaristic tendencies we find the reactionaries demand-   1
ing a higher and still higher birth rate. Their plea is, first, that great armies are needed to *defend* the country from its possible enemies; second, that a huge population is required to assure the country its proper place among the powers of the world. At bottom the two pleas are the same.

As soon as the country becomes overpopulated, these reactionaries pro-   2
claim loudly its moral right to expand. They point to the huge population, which in the name of patriotism they have previously demanded should be brought into being. Again pleading patriotism, they declare that it is the moral right of the nation to take by force such room as it needs. Then comes war—usually against some nation supposed to be less well prepared than the aggressor.

Diplomats make it their business to conceal the facts, and politicians vio-   3
lently denounce the politicians of other countries. There is a long beating of tom-toms by the press and all other agencies for influencing public opinion. Facts are distorted and lies invented until the common people cannot get at the truth. Yet, when the war is over, if not before, we always find that "a place in the sun," "a path to the sea," "a route to India" or something of the sort is at the bottom of the trouble. These are merely other names for expansion.

The "need of expansion" is only another name for overpopulation. One   4
supreme example is sufficient to drive home this truth. That the Great War,° from the horror of which we are just beginning to emerge, had its source in overpopulation is too evident to be denied by any serious student of current history.

World War I (1914–1918), in which over 15 million people were killed

For the past one hundred years most of the nations of Europe have been   5
piling up terrific debts to humanity by the encouragement of unlimited numbers. The rulers of these nations and their militarists have constantly called upon the people to breed, breed, breed! Large populations meant more people to produce wealth, more people to pay taxes, more trade for the merchants, more soldiers to protect the wealth. But more people also meant need of greater food supplies, an urgent and natural need for expansion.

6   As shown by C. V. Drysdale's famous "War Map of Europe," the great conflict began among the high birth rate countries—Germany, with its rate of 31.7, Austria-Hungary with 33.7 and 36.7, respectively, Russia with 45.4, Serbia with 38.6. Italy with her 38.7 came in, as the world is now well informed through the publication of secret treaties by the Soviet government of Russia, upon the promise of territory held by Austria. England, owing to her small home area, is cramped with her comparatively low birth rate of 26.3. France, among the belligerents, is conspicuous for her low birth rate of 19.9, but stood in the way of expansion of high birth rate Germany. Nearly all of the persistently neutral countries—Holland, Denmark, Norway, Sweden and Switzerland have low birth rates, the average being a little over 26.

7   Owing to the part Germany played in the war, a survey of her birth statistics is decidedly illuminating. The increase in the German birth rate up to 1876 was great. Though it began to decline then, the decline was not sufficient to offset the tremendous increase of the previous years. There were more millions to produce children, so while the average number of births per thousand was somewhat smaller, the net increase in population was still huge. From 41,000,000 in 1871, the year the Empire was founded, the German population grew to approximately 67,000,000 in 1918. Meanwhile her food supply increased only a very small percent. In 1910, Russia had a birth rate even higher than Germany's had ever been—a little less than 48 per thousand. When czarist Russia wanted an outlet to the Mediterranean by way of Constantinople, she was thinking of her increasing population. Germany was thinking of her increasing population when she spoke as with one voice of a "place in the sun." . . .

8   The militaristic claim for Germany's right to new territory was simply a claim to the right of life and food for the German babies—the same right that a chick claims to burst its shell. If there had not been other millions of people claiming the same right, there would have been no war. But there *were* other millions.

9   The German rulers and leaders pointed out the fact that expansion meant more business for German merchants, more work for German workmen at better wages, and more opportunities for Germans abroad. They also pointed out that lack of expansion meant crowding and crushing at home, hard times, heavy burdens, lack of opportunity for Germans, and what not. In this way, they gave the people of the Empire a startling and true picture of what would happen from overcrowding. Once they realized the facts, the majority of Germans naturally welcomed the so-called war of defense.

10 The argument was sound. Once the German mothers had submitted to the plea for overbreeding, it was inevitable that imperialistic Germany should make war. Once the battalions of unwanted babies came into existence—babies whom the mothers did not want but which they bore as a "patriotic duty"—it was too late to avoid international conflict. The great crime of imperialistic Germany was its high birth rate.

11 It has always been so. Behind all war has been the pressure of population. "Historians," says Huxley,° "point to the greed and ambition of rulers, the reckless turbulence of the ruled, to the debasing effects of wealth and luxury,

Thomas Henry Huxley (1825–1895), an English biologist and popular advocate of Darwinian evolution

and to the devastating wars which have formed a great part of the occupation of mankind, as the causes of the decay of states and the foundering of old civilizations, and thereby point their story with a moral. But beneath all this superficial turmoil lay the deep-seated impulse given by unlimited multiplication."

Robert Thomas Malthus, formulator of the doctrine which bears his name, 12 pointed out, in the closing years of the eighteenth century, the relation of overpopulation to war. He showed that mankind tends to increase faster than the food supply. He demonstrated that were it not for the more common diseases, for plague, famine, floods and wars, human beings would crowd each other to such an extent that the misery would be even greater than it now is. These he described as "natural checks," pointing out that as long as no other checks are employed, such disasters are unavoidable. If we do not exercise sufficient judgment to regulate the birth rate, we encounter disease, starvation and war.

Charles Darwin (1809–1882), an English naturalist whose 1859 study On the Origin of Species *established evolution and natural selection as dominant scientific theories*

John Stuart Mill (1806–1873), an English philosopher and exponent of utilitarianism

Both Darwin° and John Stuart Mill° recognized, by inference at least, the 13 fact that so-called "natural checks"—and among them war—will operate if some sort of limitation is not employed. In his *Origin of Species*, Darwin says: "There is no exception to the rule that every organic being naturally increases at so high a rate, if not destroyed, that the earth would soon be covered by the progeny of a single pair." Elsewhere he observes that we do not permit helpless human beings to die off, but we create philanthropies and charities, build asylums and hospitals and keep the medical profession busy preserving those who could not otherwise survive. John Stuart Mill, supporting the views of Malthus, speaks to exactly the same effect in regard to the multiplying power of organic beings, among them humanity. In other words, let countries become overpopulated and war is inevitable. It follows as daylight follows the sunrise.

English political activists who were put on trial for publishing a book advocating the birth-control methods of American physician Charles Knowlton

When Charles Bradlaugh and Mrs. Annie Besant° were on trial in England 14 in 1877 for publishing information concerning contraceptives, Mrs. Besant put the case bluntly to the court and the jury:

I have no doubt that if natural checks were allowed to operate right through the human as they do in the animal world, a better result would follow. Among the brutes, the weaker are driven to the wall, the diseased fall out in the race of life. The old brutes, when feeble or sickly, are killed. If men insisted that those who were sickly should be allowed to die without help of medicine or science, if those who are weak were put upon one side and crushed, if those who were old and useless were killed, if those who were not capable of providing food for themselves were allowed to starve, if all this were done, the struggle for existence among men would be as real as it is among brutes and would doubtless result in the production of a higher race of men.

But are you willing to do that or to allow it to be done?

We are not willing to let it be done. Mother hearts cling to children, no 15 matter how diseased, misshapen and miserable. Sons and daughters hold fast to parents, no matter how helpless. We do not allow the weak to depart;

neither do we cease to bring more weak and helpless beings into the world. Among the dire results is war, which kills off, not the weak and the helpless, but the strong and the fit.

16   What shall be done? We have our choice of one of three policies. We may abandon our science and leave the weak and diseased to die, or kill them, as the brutes do. Or we may go on overpopulating the earth and have our famines and our wars while the earth exists. Or we can accept the third, sane, sensible, moral and practicable plan of birth control. We can refuse to bring the weak, the helpless and the unwanted children into the world. We can refuse to overcrowd families, nations and the earth. There are these ways to meet the situation, and only these three ways.

17   The world will never abandon its preventive and curative science; it may be expected to elevate and extend it beyond our present imagination. The efforts to do away with famine and the opposition to war are growing by leaps and bounds. Upon these efforts are largely based our modern social revolutions.

18   There remains only the third expedient—birth control, the real cure for war. This fact was called to the attention of the Peace Conference in Paris, in 1919, by the Malthusian League, which adopted the following resolution at its annual general meeting in London in June of that year:

> The Malthusian League desires to point out that the proposed scheme for the League of Nations has neglected to take account of the important questions of *the pressure of population*, which *causes the great international economic competition* and rivalry, and of the *increase of population*, which is put forward as a justification for *claiming increase of territory*. It, therefore, wishes to put on record its belief that the League of Nations° will only be able to fulfill its aim *when it adds a clause* to the following effect:
> "That each Nation desiring to enter into the League of Nations shall pledge itself so *to restrict its birth rate* that its people shall be able to live in comfort *in their own dominions without need* for territorial expansion, and that it shall recognize that *increase of population shall not justify* a demand either for increase of territory or for the compulsion of other Nations to admit its emigrants; so that when all Nations in the League have shown their ability to live on their own resources without international rivalry, they will be in a position to fuse into an international federation, and territorial boundaries will than have little significance."

An intergovernmental organization that existed from 1919 to 1946 and was replaced by the United Nations

19   As a matter of course, the Peace Conference paid no attention to the resolution, for as pointed out by Frank A. Vanderlip, the American financier, that conference not only ignored the economic factors of the world situation, but seemed unaware that Europe had produced more people than its fields could feed. So the resolution amounted to so much propaganda and nothing more.

20   This remedy can be applied only by woman and she will apply it. She must and will see past the call of pretended patriotism and of glory of empire and perceive what is true and what is false in these things. She will discover what base uses the militarist and the exploiter made of the idealism of peoples.

Under the clamor of the press, permeating the ravings of the jingoes, she will hear the voice of Napoleon, the archetype of the militarists of all nations, calling for "fodder for cannon."

"Woman is given to us that she may bear children," said he. "Woman is our property, we are not hers, because she produces children for us—we do not yield any to her. She is, therefore, our possession as the fruit tree is that of the gardener." 21

That is what the imperialist is *thinking* when he speaks of the glory of the empire and the prestige of the nation. Every country has its appeal—its shibboleth—ready for the lips of the imperialist. German rulers pointed to the comfort of the workers, to old-age pensions, maternal benefits and minimum wage regulations, and other material benefits, when they wished to inspire soldiers for the Fatherland. England's strongest argument, perhaps, was a certain phase of liberty which she guarantees her subjects, and the protection afforded them wherever they may go. France and the United States, too, have their appeals to the idealism of democracy—appeals which the politicians of both countries know well how to use, though the peoples of both lands are beginning to awake to the fact that their countries have been living on the glories of their revolutions and traditions, rather than the substance of freedom. Behind the boast of old-age pensions, material benefits and wage regulations, behind the bombast concerning liberty in this country and tyranny in that, behind all the slogans and shibboleths coined out of the ideals of the peoples for the uses of imperialism, woman must and will see the iron hand of that same imperialism, condemning women to breed and men to die for the will of the rulers. 22

Upon woman the burden and the horrors of war are heaviest. Her heart is the hardest wrung when the husband or the son comes home to be buried or to live a shattered wreck. Upon her devolve the extra tasks of filling out the ranks of workers in the war industries, in addition to caring for the children and replenishing the war-diminished population. Hers is the crushing weight and the sickening of soul. And it is out of her womb that those things proceed. When she sees what lies behind the glory and the horror, the boasting and the burden, and gets the vision, the human perspective, she will end war. She will kill war by the simple process of starving it to death. For she will refuse longer to produce the human food upon which the monster feeds. 23

⊘ READING ARGUMENTS

1. As the title of her essay indicates, Sanger is making a causal argument. How does she support the generalizations she makes in her opening paragraphs? What kind of evidence does she use? Is her argument convincing? Why or why not?

2. Although her essay is mainly a causal argument, Sanger uses other strategies as well. Where does she make an argument by definition? Where does she argue by analogy? In what sense is the essay a proposal argument?

3. How, according to Sanger, did German leaders convince citizens to support World War I? Does she think their argument was sound? How does Sanger's discussion of Germany support her main point?

4. Where in "The Causes of War" does Sanger use deductive reasoning?

⊃ WRITING ARGUMENTS

1. Do you think a government should have the right to legislate or impose restrictions on its citizens' reproduction—for example, by limiting the number of children people are allowed to have? Do you think governments are right to offer incentives, financial or otherwise, to encourage or limit birthrates?

2. In "The Causes of War," the writer emphasizes the role of women. How does Sanger's argument build on Elizabeth Cady Stanton's points in her Declaration of Sentiments and Resolutions?

THE OBLIGATION TO ENDURE
RACHEL CARSON

Rachel Carson (1907–1964) received a master's degree in zoology and worked as editor-in-chief of publications for the U.S. Bureau of Fisheries. Her books include Under the Sea-Wind *(1941);* The Sea around Us *(1951), a best-seller and winner of the National Book Award;* The Edge of the Sea *(1955); and* The Sense of Wonder *(published in 1965 after her death). Her most famous work is* Silent Spring *(1962), from which "The Obligation to Endure" is drawn. In this book, Carson argues that agricultural pesticides are destructive to wildlife and to the environment, an idea that predates the modern environmental movement and remains controversial.* Silent Spring, *an extremely influential work, helped lead to bans on DDT as well as other chemicals.*

The history of life on earth has been a history of interaction between living 1 things and their surroundings. To a large extent, the physical form and the habits of the earth's vegetation and its animal life have been molded by the environment. Considering the whole span of earthly time, the opposite effect, in which life actually modifies its surroundings, has been relatively slight. Only within the moment of time represented by the present century has one species—man—acquired significant power to alter the nature of his world.

During the past quarter century this power has not only increased to one 2 of disturbing magnitude but it has changed in character. The most alarming of all man's assaults upon the environment is the contamination of air, earth, rivers, and sea with dangerous and even lethal materials. This pollution is for the most part irrecoverable; the chain of evil it initiates not only in the world that must support life but in living tissues is for the most part irreversible. In this now universal contamination of the environment, chemicals are the sinister and little-recognized partners of radiation in changing the very nature of the world—the very nature of its life. Strontium 90, released through nuclear explosions into the air, comes to earth in rain or drifts down as fallout, lodges in soil, enters into the grass or corn or wheat grown there, and in time takes up its abode in the bones of a human being, there to remain until his death. Similarly, chemicals sprayed on croplands or forests or gardens lie long in soil, entering into living organisms, passing from one to another in a chain of poisoning and death. Or they pass mysteriously by underground streams until they emerge and, through the alchemy of air and sunlight, combine into new forms that kill vegetation, sicken cattle, and work unknown harm on those who drink from once pure wells. As Albert Schweitzer has said, "Man can hardly even recognize the devils of his own creation."

3   It took hundreds of millions of years to produce the life that now inhabits the earth—eons of time in which that developing and evolving and diversifying life reached a state of adjustment and balance with its surroundings. The environment, rigorously shaping and directing the life it supported, contained elements that were hostile as well as supporting. Certain rocks gave out dangerous radiation; even within the light of the sun, from which all life draws its energy, there were short-wave radiations with power to injure. Given time—time not in years but in millennia—life adjusts, and a balance has been reached. For time is the essential ingredient; but in the modern world there is no time.

4   The rapidity of change and the speed with which new situations are created follow the impetuous and heedless pace of man rather than the deliberate pace of nature. Radiation is no longer merely the background radiation of rocks, the bombardment of cosmic rays, the ultraviolet of the sun that have existed before there was any life on earth; radiation is now the unnatural creation of man's tampering with the atom. The chemicals to which life is asked to make its adjustment are no longer merely the calcium and silica and copper and all the rest of the minerals washed out of the rocks and carried in rivers to the sea; they are the synthetic creations of man's inventive mind, brewed in his laboratories, and having no counterparts in nature.

5   To adjust to these chemicals would require time on the scale that is nature's; it would require not merely the years of a man's life but the life of generations. And even this, were it by some miracle possible, would be futile, for the new chemicals come from our laboratories in an endless stream; almost five hundred annually find their way into actual use in the United States alone. The figure is staggering and its implications are not easily grasped—500 new chemicals to which the bodies of men and animals are required somehow to adapt each year, chemicals totally outside the limits of biologic experience.

6   Among them are many that are used in man's war against nature. Since the mid-1940's over 200 basic chemicals have been created for use in killing insects, weeds, rodents, and other organisms described in the modern vernacular as "pests"; and they are sold under several thousand different brand names.

7   These sprays, dusts, and aerosols are now applied almost universally to farms, gardens, forests, and homes—nonselective chemicals that have the power to kill every insect, the "good" and the "bad," to still the song of birds and the leaping of fish in the streams, to coat the leaves with a deadly film, and to linger on in soil—all this though the intended target may be only a few weeds or insects. Can anyone believe it is possible to lay down such a barrage of poisons on the surface of the earth without making it unfit for all life? They should not be called "insecticides," but "biocides."

8   The whole process of spraying seems caught up in an endless spiral. Since DDT° was released for civilian use, a process of escalation has been going on in which ever more toxic materials must be found. This has happened because insects, in a triumphant vindication of Darwin's principle of the survival of the fittest, have evolved super races immune to the particular insecticide used, hence a deadlier one has always to be developed—and then a deadlier one than that. It has happened

Dichlorodiphenyltrichloroethane, a synthetic pesticide that was used to control disease-spreading insect populations

also because, for reasons to be described later, destructive insects often undergo a "flareback," or resurgence, after spraying, in numbers greater than before. Thus the chemical war is never won, and all life is caught in its violent crossfire.

Along with the possibility of the extinction of mankind by nuclear war, 9 the central problem of our age has therefore become the contamination of man's total environment with such substances of incredible potential for harm—substances that accumulate in the tissues of plants and animals and even penetrate the germ cells to shatter or alter the very material of heredity upon which the shape of the future depends.

Some would-be architects of our future look toward a time when it will be 10 possible to alter the human germ plasm by design. But we may easily be doing so now by inadvertence, for many chemicals, like radiation, bring about gene mutations. It is ironic to think that man might determine his own future by something so seemingly trivial as the choice of an insect spray.

All this has been risked—for what? Future historians may well be amazed 11 by our distorted sense of proportion. How could intelligent beings seek to control a few unwanted species by a method that contaminated the entire environment and brought the threat of disease and death even to their own kind? Yet this is precisely what we have done. We have done it, moreover, for reasons that collapse the moment we examine them. We are told that the enormous and expanding use of pesticides is necessary to maintain farm production. Yet is our real problem not one of *overproduction*? Our farms, despite measures to remove acreages from production and to pay farmers *not* to produce, have yielded such a staggering excess of crops that the American taxpayer in 1962 is paying out more than one billion dollars a year as the total carrying cost of the surplus-food storage program. And is the situation helped when one branch of the Agriculture Department tries to reduce production while another states, as it did in 1958, "It is believed generally that reduction of crop acreages under provisions of the Soil Bank will stimulate interest in use of chemicals to obtain maximum production on the land retained in crops."

All this is not to say there is no insect problem and no need of control. I 12 am saying, rather, that control must be geared to realities, not to mythical situations, and that the methods employed must be such that they do not destroy us along with the insects.

The problem whose attempted solution has brought such a train of disas- 13 ter in its wake is an accompaniment of our modern way of life. Long before the age of man, insects inhabited the earth—a group of extraordinarily varied and adaptable beings. Over the course of time since man's advent, a small percentage of the more than half a million species of insects have come into conflict with human welfare in two principal ways: as competitors for the food supply and as carriers of human disease.

Disease-carrying insects become important where human beings are crowded 14 together, especially under conditions where sanitation is poor, as in time of natural disaster or war or in situations of extreme poverty and deprivation. Then control of some sort becomes necessary. It is a sobering fact, however, as we shall presently see, that the method of massive chemical control has had only limited success, and also threatens to worsen the very conditions it is intended to curb.

Under primitive agricultural conditions the farmer had few insect prob- 15 lems. These arose with the intensification of agriculture—the devotion of immense acreages to a single crop. Such a system set the stage for explosive increases in specific insect populations. Single-crop farming does not take advantage of the principles by which nature works; it is agriculture as an engineer might conceive it to be. Nature has introduced great variety into the landscape, but man has displayed a passion for simplifying it. Thus he undoes the built-in checks and balances by which nature holds the species within bounds. One important natural check is a limit on the amount of suitable habitat for each species. Obviously then, an insect that lives on wheat can build up its population to much higher levels on a farm devoted to wheat than on one in which wheat is intermingled with other crops to which the insect is not adapted.

The same thing happens in other situations. A generation or more ago, 16 the towns of large areas of the United States lined their streets with the noble elm tree. Now the beauty they hopefully created is threatened with complete destruction as disease sweeps through the elms, carried by a beetle that would have only limited chance to build up large populations and to spread from tree to tree if the elms were only occasional trees in a richly diversified planting.

Another factor in the modern insect problem is one that must be viewed 17 against a background of geologic and human history: the spreading of thousands of different kinds of organisms from their native homes to invade new territories. This worldwide migration has been studied and graphically described by the British ecologist Charles Elton in his recent book *The Ecology of Invasions*. During the Cretaceous Period, some hundred million years ago, flooding seas cut many land bridges between continents and living things found themselves confined in what Elton calls "colossal separate nature reserves." There, isolated from others of their kind, they developed many new species. When some of the land masses were joined again, about 15 million years ago, these species began to move out into new territories—a movement that is not only still in progress but is now receiving considerable assistance from man.

The importation of plants is the primary agent in the modern spread of 18 species, for animals have almost invariably gone along with the plants, quarantine being a comparatively recent and not completely effective innovation. The United States Office of Plant Introduction alone has introduced almost 200,000 species and varieties of plants from all over the world. Nearly half of the 180 or so major insect enemies of plants in the United States are accidental imports from abroad, and most of them have come as hitchhikers on plants.

In new territory, out of reach of the restraining hand of the natural ene- 19 mies that kept down its numbers in its native land, an invading plant or animal is able to become enormously abundant. Thus it is no accident that our most troublesome insects are introduced species.

These invasions, both the naturally occurring and those dependent on 20 human assistance, are likely to continue indefinitely. Quarantine and massive chemical campaigns are only extremely expensive ways of buying time. We are faced, according to Dr. Elton, "with a life-and-death need not just to find new technological means of suppressing this plant or that animal"; instead we need the basic knowledge of animal populations and their relations to their surroundings that will "promote an even balance and damp down the explosive power of outbreaks and new invasions."

Much of the necessary knowledge is now available but we do not use it. 21 We train ecologists in our universities and even employ them in our governmental agencies but we seldom take their advice. We allow the chemical death rain to fall as though there were no alternative, whereas in fact there are many, and our ingenuity could soon discover many more if given opportunity.

Have we fallen into a mesmerized state that makes us accept as inevitable 22 that which is inferior or detrimental, as though having lost the will or the vision to demand that which is good? Such thinking, in the words of the ecologist Paul Shepard, "idealizes life with only its head out of water, inches above the limits of toleration of the corruption of its own environment. . . . Why should we tolerate a diet of weak poisons, a home in insipid surroundings, a circle of acquaintances who are not quite our enemies, the noise of motors with just enough relief to prevent insanity? Who would want to live in a world which is just not quite fatal?"

Yet such a world is pressed upon us. The crusade to create a chemically 23 sterile, insect-free world seems to have engendered a fanatic zeal on the part of many specialists and most of the so-called control agencies. On every hand there is evidence that those engaged in spraying operations exercise a ruthless power. "The regulatory entomologists . . . function as prosecutor, judge and jury, tax assessor and collector and sheriff to enforce their own orders," said Connecticut entomologist Neely Turner. The most flagrant abuses go unchecked in both state and federal agencies.

It is not my contention that chemical insecticides must never be used. 24 I do contend that we have put poisonous and biologically potent chemicals indiscriminately into the hands of persons largely or wholly ignorant of their potentials for harm. We have subjected enormous numbers of people to contact with these poisons, without their consent and often without their knowledge. If the Bill of Rights contains no guarantee that a citizen shall be secure against lethal poisons distributed either by private individuals or by public officials, it is surely only because our forefathers, despite their considerable wisdom and foresight, could conceive of no such problem.

I contend, furthermore, that we have allowed these chemicals to be used 25 with little or no advance investigation of their effect on soil, water, wildlife, and man himself. Future generations are unlikely to condone our lack of prudent concern for the integrity of the natural world that supports all life.

There is still very limited awareness of the nature of the threat. This is an 26 era of specialists, each of whom sees his own problem and is unaware of or intolerant of the larger frame into which it fits. It is also an era dominated by industry, in which the right to make a dollar at whatever cost is seldom challenged. When the public protests, confronted with some obvious evidence of damaging results of pesticide applications, it is fed little tranquilizing pills of half truth. We urgently need an end to these false assurances, to the sugar coating of unpalatable facts. It is the public that is being asked to assume the risks that the insect controllers calculate. The public must decide whether it wishes to continue on the present road, and it can do so only when in full possession of the facts. In the words of Jean Rostand, "The obligation to endure gives us the right to know."

◎ READING ARGUMENTS

1. In her opening paragraphs, Carson makes broad and provocative claims about human beings and their place in the natural world. What evidence does she use to support these assertions? Do you find this evidence convincing?

2. According to Carson, what problem (along with the threat of nuclear war) is the greatest threat to human beings in the middle of the twentieth century?

3. In what sense is "The Obligation to Endure" an evaluation argument?

4. In paragraph 2, Carson refers to "man's assaults upon the environment." How does she characterize human beings throughout her essay? For example, how does she describe the ways in which people interact with the environment? How does her characterization of human beings support her essay's main point?

5. Where in her essay does Carson address opposing arguments? Do you think she refutes them effectively? Why or why not?

◎ WRITING ARGUMENTS

1. Carson contrasts the "heedless pace of man" with the "deliberate pace of nature" (para. 4). Is this distinction valid? Do you think her view of people and their relationship with the environment seems accurate? For example, do you think human beings are engaged in a "war against nature" (6)? Do you generally share Carson's view of scientific progress and industrial society? Write an argumentative essay that takes a stand for or against her views.

2. As a result of Carson's book, DDT was banned worldwide. Since then, some scientists have challenged this ban, blaming it for the rise of malaria, among other diseases. Write an essay arguing that the United States should reconsider its response to Carson's book.

LETTER FROM BIRMINGHAM JAIL

MARTIN LUTHER KING JR.

Martin Luther King Jr. (1929–1968), the foremost civil rights leader in America in the 1950s and 1960s, was an ordained minister and held a doctorate in theology. As head of the Southern Christian Leadership Conference, King fought against segregation through nonviolent means. At that time in the South, African Americans were forced to sit in the back of buses and were prohibited from drinking from water fountains used by whites. They also often attended segregated schools. After a protest in Birmingham, Alabama, in 1963, King was arrested. His "Letter from Birmingham Jail" is a response to a statement made by eight local clergymen who questioned his methods. In this letter, he makes the point that "Injustice anywhere is a threat to justice everywhere" (para. 4). King's efforts toward ending segregation eventually bore fruit when Congress passed the Civil Rights Act of 1965. In 1964, he was awarded the Nobel Peace Prize.

My Dear Fellow Clergymen:

While confined here in the Birmingham city jail, I came across your recent 1
statement calling my present activities "unwise and untimely." Seldom do I pause to answer criticism of my work and ideas. If I sought to answer all the criticisms that cross my desk, my secretaries would have little time for anything other than such correspondence in the course of the day, and I would have no time for constructive work. But since I feel that you are men of genuine good will and that your criticisms are sincerely set forth, I want to try to answer your statement in what I hope will be patient and reasonable terms.

I think I should indicate why I am here in Birmingham, since you have 2
been influenced by the view which argues against "outsiders coming in." I have the honor of serving as president of the Southern Christian Leadership Conference, an organization operating in every southern state, with headquarters in Atlanta, Georgia. We have some eighty-five affiliated organizations across the South, and one of them is the Alabama Christian Movement for Human Rights. Frequently we share staff, educational, and financial resources with our affiliates. Several months ago the affiliate here in Birmingham asked us to be on call to engage in a nonviolent direct-action program if such were deemed necessary. We readily consented, and when the hour came we lived up to our promise. So I, along with several members of my staff, am here because I was invited here. I am here because I have organizational ties here.

But more basically, I am in Birmingham because injustice is here. Just 3
as the prophets of the eighth century B.C. left their villages and carried their "thus saith the Lord" far beyond the boundaries of their home towns, and just

as the Apostle Paul left his village of Tarsus and carried the gospel of Jesus Christ to the far corners of the Greco-Roman world, so am I compelled to carry the gospel of freedom beyond my own home town. Like Paul, I must constantly respond to the Macedonian call for aid.

Moreover, I am cognizant of the interrelatedness of all communities and 4 states. I cannot sit idly by in Atlanta and not be concerned about what happens in Birmingham. Injustice anywhere is a threat to justice everywhere. We are caught in an inescapable network of mutuality, tied in a single garment of destiny. Whatever affects one directly, affects all indirectly. Never again can we afford to live with the narrow, provincial "outside agitator" idea. Anyone who lives inside the United States can never be considered an outsider anywhere within its bounds.

You deplore the demonstrations taking place in Birmingham. But your 5 statement, I am sorry to say, fails to express a similar concern for the conditions that brought about the demonstrations. I am sure that none of you would want to rest content with the superficial kind of social analysis that deals merely with effects and does not grapple with underlying causes. It is unfortunate that demonstrations are taking place in Birmingham, but it is even more unfortunate that the city's white power structure left the Negro community with no alternative.

In any nonviolent campaign there are four basic steps: collection of the 6 facts to determine whether injustices exist; negotiation; self-purification; and direct action. We have gone through all these steps in Birmingham. There can be no gainsaying the fact that racial injustice engulfs this community. Birmingham is probably the most thoroughly segregated city in the United States. Its ugly record of brutality is widely known. Negroes have experienced grossly unjust treatment in the courts. There have been more unsolved bombings of Negro homes and churches in Birmingham than in any other city in the nation. These are the hard, brutal facts of the case. On the basis of these conditions, Negro leaders sought to negotiate with the city fathers. But the latter consistently refused to engage in good-faith negotiation.

Then, last September, came the opportunity to talk with leaders of 7 Birmingham's economic community. In the course of the negotiations, certain promises were made by the merchants—for example, to remove the stores' humiliating racial signs. On the basis of these promises, the Reverend Fred Shuttlesworth and the leaders of the Alabama Christian Movement for Human Rights agreed to a moratorium on all demonstrations. As the weeks and months went by, we realized that we were the victims of a broken promise. A few signs, briefly removed, returned; the others remained.

As in so many past experiences, our hopes had been blasted, and the shadow 8 of deep disappointment settled upon us. We had no alternative except to prepare for direct action, whereby we would present our very bodies as a means of laying our case before the conscience of the local and the national community. Mindful of the difficulties involved, we decided to undertake a process of self-purification. We began a series of workshops on nonviolence, and we repeatedly asked ourselves: "Are you able to accept blows without retaliating?" "Are you able to endure the ordeal of jail?" We decided to schedule our direct-action program for the Easter season, realizing that except for Christmas, this is the main shopping period of the year. Knowing that a strong economic withdrawal program would be the by-product of direct action, we felt that this would be the best time to bring pressure to bear on the merchants for the needed change.

Then it occurred to us that Birmingham's mayoral election was coming 9 up in March, and we speedily decided to postpone action until after election day. When we discovered that the Commissioner of Public Safety, Eugene "Bull" Connor,° had piled up enough votes to be in the run-off, we decided again to postpone action until the day after the runoff so that the demonstrations could not be used to cloud the issues. Like many others, we wanted to see Mr. Connor defeated, and to this end we endured postponement after postponement. Having aided in this community need, we felt that our direct-action program could be delayed no longer.

Eugene "Bull" Connor (1897–1974), the public safety commissioner for the city of Birmingham, Alabama, in the 1960s. He was known for his segregationist views and violent response to civil rights marchers.

You may well ask, "Why direct action? Why sit-ins, marches, and so forth? 10 Isn't negotiation a better path?" You are quite right in calling for negotiation. Indeed, this is the very purpose of direct action. Nonviolent direct action seeks to create such a crisis and foster such a tension that a community which has constantly refused to negotiate is forced to confront the issue. It seeks so to dramatize the issue that it can no longer be ignored. My citing the creation of tension as part of the work of the nonviolent-resister may sound rather shocking. But I must confess that I am not afraid of the word "tension." I have earnestly opposed violent tension, but there is a type of constructive, nonviolent tension which is necessary for growth. Just as Socrates felt that it was necessary to create a tension in the mind so that individuals could rise from the bondage of myths and half-truths to the unfettered realm of creative analysis and objective appraisal, so must we see the need for nonviolent gadflies to create the kind of tension in society that will help men rise from the dark depths of prejudice and racism to the majestic heights of understanding and brotherhood.

The purpose of our direct-action program is to create a situation so crisis- 11 packed that it will inevitably open the door to negotiation. I therefore concur with you in your call for negotiation. Too long has our beloved Southland been bogged down in a tragic effort to live in monologue rather than dialogue.

One of the basic points in your statement is that the action that I and 12 my associates have taken in Birmingham is untimely. Some have asked: "Why didn't you give the new city administration time to act?" The only answer that I can give to this query is that the new Birmingham administration must be prodded about as much as the outgoing one, before it will act. We are sadly mistaken if we feel that the election of Albert Boutwell° as mayor will bring the millennium to Birmingham. While Mr. Boutwell is a much more gentle person than Mr. Connor, they are both segregationists, dedicated to maintenance of the status quo. I have hoped that Mr. Boutwell will be reasonable enough to see the futility of massive resistance to desegregation. But he will not see this without pressure from devotees of civil rights. My friends, I must say to

Albert Boutwell (1904–1978), the mayor of Birmingham, Alabama, from 1963 to 1967

you that we have not made a single gain in civil rights without determined legal and nonviolent pressure. Lamentably, it is an historical fact that privileged groups seldom give up their privileges voluntarily. Individuals may see the moral light and voluntarily give up their unjust posture, but, as Reinhold Niebuhr° has reminded us, groups tend to be more immoral than individuals.

Reinhold Niebuhr (1892–1971), an American Protestant theologian who focused on the relationship between Christian faith and modern politics

13   We know through painful experience that freedom is never voluntarily given by the oppressor; it must be demanded by the oppressed. Frankly, I have yet to engage in a direct-action campaign that was "well timed" in the view of those who have not suffered unduly from the disease of segregation. For years now I have heard the word "Wait!" It rings in the ear of every Negro with piercing familiarity. This "Wait" has almost always meant "Never." We must come to see, with one of our distinguished jurists, that "justice too long delayed is justice denied."

14   We have waited for more than 340 years for our constitutional and God-given rights. The nations of Asia and Africa are moving with jet-like speed toward gaining political independence, but we still creep at horse-and-buggy pace toward gaining a cup of coffee at a lunch counter. Perhaps it is easy for those who have never felt the stinging darts of segregation to say, "Wait." But when you have seen vicious mobs lynch your mothers and fathers at will and drown your sisters and brothers at whim; when you have seen hate-filled policemen curse, kick, and even kill your black brothers and sisters; when you see the vast majority of your twenty million Negro brothers smothering in an airtight cage of poverty in the midst of an affluent society; when you suddenly find your tongue twisted and your speech stammering as you seek to explain to your six-year-old daughter why she can't go to the public amusement park that has just been advertised on television, and see tears welling up in her eyes when she is told that Funtown is closed to colored children, and see ominous clouds of inferiority beginning to form in her little mental sky, and see her beginning to distort her personality by developing an unconscious bitterness toward white people; when you have to concoct an answer for a five-year-old son who is asking, "Daddy, why do white people treat colored people so mean?"; when you take a cross-country drive and find it necessary to sleep night after night in the uncomfortable corners of your automobile because no motel will accept you; when you are humiliated day in and day out by nagging signs reading "white" and "colored"; when your first name becomes "nigger," your middle name becomes "boy" (however old you are) and your last name becomes "John," and your wife and mother are never given the respected title "Mrs."; when you are harried by day and haunted by night by the fact that you are a Negro, living constantly at tiptoe stance, never quite knowing what to expect next, and are plagued with inner fears and outer resentments; when you are forever fighting a degenerating sense of "nobodiness"—then you will understand why we find it difficult to wait. There comes a time when the cup of endurance runs over, and men are no longer willing to be plunged into the abyss of despair. I hope, sirs, you can understand our legitimate and unavoidable impatience.

You express a great deal of anxiety over our willingness to break laws. This 15 is certainly a legitimate concern. Since we so diligently urge people to obey the Supreme Court's decision of 1954 outlawing segregation in the public schools, at first glance it may seem rather paradoxical for us consciously to break laws. One may well ask: "How can you advocate breaking some laws and obeying others?" The answer lies in the fact that there are two types of laws; just and unjust. I would be the first to advocate obeying just laws. One has not only a legal but a moral responsibility to obey just laws. Conversely, one has a moral responsibility to disobey unjust laws. I would agree with St. Augustine° that "an unjust law is no law at all."

Now, what is the difference between the two? How does one determine 16 whether a law is just or unjust? A just law is a man-made code that squares with the moral law or the law of God. An unjust law is a code that is out of harmony with the moral law. To put it in the terms of St. Thomas Aquinas:° An unjust law is a human law that is not rooted in eternal law and natural law. Any law that uplifts human personality is just. Any law that degrades human personality is unjust. All segregation statutes are unjust because segregation distorts the soul and damages the personality. It gives the segregator a false sense of superiority and the segregated a false sense of inferiority. Segregation, to use the terminology of the Jewish philosopher Martin Buber,° substitutes an "I-it" relationship for an "I-thou" relationship and ends up relegating persons to the status of things. Hence segregation is not only politically, economically, and sociologically unsound, it is morally wrong and sinful. Paul Tillich° has said that sin is separation. Is not segregation an existential expression of man's tragic separation, his awful estrangement, his terrible sinfulness? Thus it is that I can urge men to obey the 1954 decision of the Supreme Court° for it is morally right; and I can urge them to disobey segregation ordinances, for they are morally wrong.

Let us consider a more concrete example of just and unjust laws. An unjust 17 law is a code that a numerical or power majority group compels a minority group to obey but does not make binding on itself. This is *difference* made legal. By the same token, a just law is a code that a majority compels a minority to follow and that it is willing to follow itself. This is *sameness* made legal.

Let me give another explanation. A law is unjust if it is inflicted on a minor- 18 ity that, as a result of being denied the right to vote, had no part in enacting or devising the law. Who can say that the legislature of Alabama which set up that state's segregation laws was democratically elected? Throughout Alabama all sorts of devious methods are used to prevent Negroes from becoming registered voters, and there are some counties in which, even though Negroes constitute a majority of the population, not a single Negro is registered. Can any law enacted under such circumstances be considered democratically structured?

Sometimes a law is just on its face and unjust in its application. For 19 instance, I have been arrested on a charge of parading without a permit. Now, there is nothing wrong in having an ordinance which requires a permit for a parade. But such an ordinance becomes unjust when it is used to maintain

St. Augustine (354–430), a Catholic Church father, philosopher, theologian, and important figure in the development of European Christianity

St. Thomas Aquinas (1225– 1274), a Roman Catholic priest, theologian, and philosopher

Martin Buber (1878–1965), an Austrian-born Jewish philosopher.

Paul Tillich (1886–1965), a German American theologian and philosopher

Brown v. Board of Education of Topeka, *which declared that laws establishing separate schools for black and white students were unconstitutional*

segregation and to deny citizens the First-Amendment privilege of peaceful assembly and protest.

20   I hope you are able to see the distinction I am trying to point out. In no sense do I advocate evading or defying the law, as would the rabid segregation-ist. That would lead to anarchy. One who breaks an unjust law must do so openly, lovingly, and with a willingness to accept the penalty. I submit that an individual who breaks a law that conscience tells him is unjust, and who will-ingly accepts the penalty of imprisonment in order to arouse the conscience of the community over its injustice, is in reality expressing the highest respect for law.

21   Of course, there is nothing new about this kind of civil disobedience. It was evidenced sublimely in the refusal of Shadrach, Meshach, and Abednego° to obey the laws of Nebuchadnezzar, on the ground that a higher moral law was at stake. It was practiced superbly by the early Christians, who were willing to face hungry lions and the excruciating pain of chopping blocks rather than submit to certain unjust laws of the Roman Empire. To a degree, academic freedom is a reality today because Socrates practiced civil disobedience. In our own nation, the Boston Tea Party represented a massive act of civil disobedience.

Biblical figures who chose to be burned alive in a furnace rather than worship the Babylonian king, Nebuchadnezzar II, and survived through divine intervention

22   We should never forget that everything Adolf Hitler did in Germany was "legal" and everything the Hungarian freedom fighters did in Hungary was "illegal." It was "illegal" to aid and comfort a Jew in Hitler's Germany. Even so, I am sure that, had I lived in Germany at the time, I would have aided and comforted my Jewish brothers. If today I lived in a Communist country where certain principles dear to the Christian faith are suppressed, I would openly advocate disobeying that country's antireligious laws.

23   I must make two honest confessions to you, my Christian and Jewish brothers. First, I must confess that over the past few years I have been gravely disappointed with the white moderate. I have almost reached the regrettable conclusion that the Negro's great stumbling block in his stride toward free-dom is not the White Citizen's Counciler or the Ku Klux Klanner, but the white moderate, who is more devoted to "order" than to justice; who prefers a negative peace which is the absence of tension to a positive peace which is the presence of justice; who constantly says, "I agree with you in the goal you seek, but I cannot agree with your methods of direct action"; who paternalistically believes he can set the timetable for another man's freedom; who lives by a mythical concept of time and who constantly advises the Negro to wait for a "more convenient season." Shallow understanding from people of good will is more frustrating than absolute misunderstanding from people of ill will. Luke-warm acceptance is much more bewildering than outright rejection.

24   I had hoped that the white moderate would understand that law and order exist for the purpose of establishing justice and that when they fail in this purpose they become the dangerously structured dams that block the flow of social progress. I had hoped that the white moderate would understand that the present tension in the South is a necessary phase of the transition from an obnoxious negative peace, in which the Negro passively accepted his unjust

plight, to a substantive and positive peace, in which all men will respect the dignity and worth of human personality. Actually, we who engage in nonviolent direct action are not the creators of tension. We merely bring to the surface the hidden tension that is already alive. We bring it out in the open, where it can be seen and dealt with. Like a boil that can never be cured so long as it is covered up but must be opened with all its ugliness to the natural medicines of air and light, injustice must be exposed, with all the tension its exposure creates, to the light of human conscience and the air of national opinion, before it can be cured.

In your statement you assert that our actions, even though peaceful, must   25 be condemned because they precipitate violence. But is this a logical assertion? Isn't this like condemning a robbed man because his possession of money precipitated the evil act of robbery? Isn't this like condemning Socrates because his unswerving commitment to truth and his philosophical inquiries precipitated the act by the misguided populace in which they made him drink hemlock? Isn't this like condemning Jesus because his unique God-consciousness and never-ceasing devotion to God's will precipitated the evil act of crucifixion? We must come to see that, as the federal courts have consistently affirmed, it is wrong to urge an individual to cease his efforts to gain his basic constitutional rights because the quest may precipitate violence. Society must protect the robbed and punish the robber.

I had also hoped that the white moderate would reject the myth concern-   26 ing time in relation to the struggle for freedom. I have just received a letter from a white brother in Texas. He writes: "All Christians know that the colored people will receive equal rights eventually, but it is possible that you are in too great a religious hurry. It has taken Christianity almost two thousand years to accomplish what it has. The teachings of Christ take time to come to earth." Such an attitude stems from a tragic misconception of time, from the strangely irrational notion that there is something in the very flow of time that will inevitably cure all ills. Actually, time itself is neutral; it can be used either destructively or constructively. More and more I feel that the people of ill will have used time much more effectively than have the people of good will. We will have to repent in this generation not merely for the hateful words and actions of the bad people, but for the appalling silence of the good people. Human progress never rolls in on wheels of inevitability; it comes through the tireless efforts of men willing to be co-workers with God, and without this hard work, time itself becomes an ally of the forces of social stagnation. We must use time creatively, in the knowledge that the time is always ripe to do right. Now is the time to make real the promise of democracy and transform our pending national elegy into a creative psalm of brotherhood. Now is the time to lift our national policy from the quicksand of racial injustice to the solid rock of human dignity.

You speak of our activity in Birmingham as extreme. At first I was rather   27 disappointed that fellow clergymen would see my nonviolent efforts as those of an extremist. I began thinking about the fact that I stand in the middle of two opposing forces in the Negro community. One is a force of complacency, made up in part of Negroes who, as a result of long years of oppression, are so drained of self-respect and a sense of "somebodiness" that they have adjusted to segregation; and in part of a few middle-class Negroes who, because of a degree of academic and economic security and because in some ways they profit by segregation, have become insensitive to the problems of the masses. The other force is one of bitterness and hatred, and it comes perilously close to advocating violence. It is expressed in the various black nationalist groups that are springing up across the nation, the largest and best-known being Elijah Muhammad's Muslim movement. Nourished by the Negro's frustration over the continued existence of racial discrimination, this movement is made up of people who have lost faith in America, who have absolutely repudiated Christianity, and who have concluded that the white man is an incorrigible "devil."

I have tried to stand between these two forces, saying that we need emu-   28
late neither the "do-nothingism" of the complacent nor the hatred and despair of the black nationalist. For there is the more excellent way of love and non-violent protest. I am grateful to God that, through the influence of the Negro church, the way of nonviolence became an integral part of our struggle.

If this philosophy had not emerged, by now many streets of the South   29
would, I am convinced, be flowing with blood. And I am further convinced that if our white brothers dismiss as "rabble-rousers" and "outside agitators" those of us who employ nonviolent direct action, and if they refuse to support our nonviolent efforts, millions of Negroes will, out of frustration and despair, seek solace and security in black-nationalist ideologies—a development that would inevitably lead to a frightening racial nightmare.

Oppressed people cannot remain oppressed forever. The yearning for   30
freedom eventually manifests itself, and that is what has happened to the American Negro. Something within has reminded him of his birthright of freedom, and something without has reminded him that it can be gained. Consciously or unconsciously, he has been caught up by the *Zeitgeist*, and with his black brothers of Africa and his brown and yellow brothers of Asia, South America, and the Caribbean, the United States Negro is moving with a sense of great urgency toward the promised land of racial justice. If one recognizes this vital urge that has engulfed the Negro community, one should readily understand why public demonstrations are taking place. The Negro has many pent-up resentments and latent frustrations, and he must release them. So let him march; let him make prayer pilgrimages to the city hall; let him go on freedom rides—and try to understand why he must do so. If his repressed emotions are not released in nonviolent ways, they will seek expression through violence; this is not a threat but a fact of history. So I have not said to my people, "Get rid of your discontent." Rather, I have tried to say that this normal and healthy discontent can be channeled into the creative outlet of nonviolent direct action. And now this approach is being termed extremist.

But though I was initially disappointed at being categorized as an extrem-   31
ist, as I continued to think about the matter I gradually gained a measure of

An Old Testament prophet

Martin Luther (1483–1546), a German priest, philosopher, and primary figure in the Protestant Reformation

John Bunyan (1628–1688), an English writer and Christian preacher best known for writing The Pilgrim's Progress

satisfaction from the label. Was not Jesus an extremist for love: "Love your enemies, bless them that curse you, do good to them that hate you, and pray for them which despitefully use you, and persecute you." Was not Amos° an extremist for justice: "Let justice roll down like waters and righteousness like an ever-flowing stream." Was not Paul an extremist for the Christian gospel: "I bear in my body the marks of the Lord Jesus." Was not Martin Luther° an extremist: "Here I stand; I cannot do otherwise, so help me God." And John Bunyan:° "I will stay in jail to the end of my days before I make a butchery of my conscience." And Abraham Lincoln: "This nation cannot survive half slave and half free." And Thomas Jefferson: "We hold these truths to be self-evident, that all men are created equal. . . ." So the question is not whether we will be extremists, but what kind of extremists we will be. Will we be extremists for hate or for love? Will we be extremists for the preservation of injustice or for the extension of justice? In that dramatic scene on Calvary's hill three men were crucified. We must never forget that all three were crucified for the same crime—the crime of extremism. Two were extremists for immorality, and thus fell below their environment. The other, Jesus Christ, was an extremist for love, truth, and goodness, and thereby rose above his environment. Perhaps the South, the nation, and the world are in dire need of creative extremists.

I had hoped that the white moderate would see this need. Perhaps I was 32 too optimistic; perhaps I expected too much. I suppose I should have realized that few members of the oppressor race can understand the deep groans and passionate yearnings of the oppressed race, and still fewer have the vision to see that injustice must be rooted out by strong, persistent, and determined action. I am thankful, however, that some of our white brothers in the South have grasped the meaning of this social revolution and committed themselves to it. They are still all too few in quantity, but they are big in quality. Some—such as Ralph McGill, Lillian Smith, Harry Golden, James McBridge Dabbs, Ann Braden, and Sarah Patton Boyle—have written about our struggle in eloquent and prophetic terms. Others have marched with us down nameless streets of the South. They have languished in filthy, roach-infested jails, suffering the abuse and brutality of policemen who view them as "dirty nigger-lovers." Unlike so many of their moderate brothers and sisters, they have recognized the urgency of the moment and sensed the need for powerful "action" antidotes to combat the disease of segregation.

Let me take note of my other major disappointment. I have been so 33 greatly disappointed with the white church and its leadership. Of course, there are some notable exceptions. I am not unmindful of the fact that each of you has taken some significant stands on this issue. I commend you, Reverend Stallings,° for your Christian stand on this past Sunday, in welcoming Negroes to your worship service on a nonsegregated basis. I commend the Catholic leaders of this state for integrating Spring Hill College several years ago.

Earl Stallings, one of the eight clergymen King was responding to and pastor of the First Baptist Church in Birmingham

But despite these notable exceptions, I must honestly reiterate that I have 34 been disappointed with the church. I do not say this as one of those negative critics who can always find something wrong with the church. I say this as a minister of the gospel, who loves the church; who was nurtured in its bosom; who has been sustained by its spiritual blessings and who will remain true to it as long as the cord of life shall lengthen.

35   When I was suddenly catapulted into the leadership of the bus protest in Montgomery, Alabama, a few years ago, I felt we would be supported by the white church. I felt that the white ministers, priests, and rabbis of the South would be among our strongest allies. Instead, some have been outright opponents, refusing to understand the freedom movement and misrepresenting its leaders; all too many others have been more cautious than courageous and have remained silent behind the anesthetizing security of stained-glass windows.

36   In spite of my shattered dreams, I came to Birmingham with the hope that the white religious leadership of this community would see the justice of our cause and, with deep moral concern, would serve as the channel through which our just grievances could reach the power structure. I had hoped that each of you would understand. But again I have been disappointed.

37   I have heard numerous southern religious leaders admonish their worshipers to comply with a desegregation decision because it is the law, but I have longed to hear white ministers declare: "Follow this decree because integration is morally right and because the Negro is your brother." In the midst of blatant injustices inflicted upon the Negro, I have watched white churchmen stand on the sideline and mouth pious irrelevancies and sanctimonious trivialities. In the midst of a mighty struggle to rid our nation of racial and economic injustice, I have heard many ministers say: "Those are social issues, with which the gospel has no real concern." And I have watched many churches commit themselves to a completely otherworldly religion which makes a strange, un-Biblical distinction between body and soul, between the sacred and the secular.

38   I have traveled the length and breadth of Alabama, Mississippi, and all the other southern states. On sweltering summer days and crisp autumn mornings I have looked at the South's beautiful churches with their lofty spires pointing heavenward. I have beheld the impressive outlines of her massive religious-education buildings. Over and over I have found myself asking: "What kind of people worship here? Who is their God? Where were their voices when the lips of Governor Barnett° dripped with words of interposition and nullification? Where were they when Governor Wallace° gave a clarion call for defiance and hatred? Where were their voices of support when bruised and weary Negro men and women decided to rise from the dark dungeons of complacency to the bright hills of creative protest?"

Ross Robert Barnett (1898–1987), segregationist governor of Mississippi from 1960 to 1964

George Wallace (1919–1998), a governor of Alabama (1963–1967, 1971–1979, 1983–1987). Although a segregationist early in his political career, he abandoned that conviction later in life.

39   Yes, these questions are still in my mind. In deep disappointment I have wept over the laxity of the church. But be assured that my tears have been tears of love. There can be no deep disappointment where there is not deep love. Yes, I love the church. How could I do otherwise? I am in the rather unique position of being the son, the grandson, and the great-grandson of preachers. Yes, I see the church as the body of Christ. But, oh! How we have blemished and scarred that body through social neglect and through fear of being nonconformists.

There was a time when the church was very powerful—in the time 40
when the early Christians rejoiced at being deemed worthy to suffer for what
they believed. In those days the church was not merely a thermometer that
recorded the ideas and principles of popular opinion; it was a thermostat that
transformed the mores of society. Whenever the early Christians entered a
town, the people in power became disturbed and immediately sought to con-
vict the Christians for being "disturbers of the peace" and "outside agitators."
But the Christians pressed on, in the conviction that they were "a colony of
heaven," called to obey God rather than man. Small in number, they were big
in commitment. They were too God-intoxicated to be "astronomically intimidated." By their effort and example they brought an end to such ancient evils
as infanticide and gladiatorial contests.

Things are different now. So often the contemporary church is a weak, 41
ineffectual voice with an uncertain sound. So often it is an archdefender of the
status quo. Far from being disturbed by the presence of the church, the power
structure of the average community is consoled by the church's silent—and
often even vocal—sanction of things as they are.

But the judgment of God is upon the church as never before. If today's 42
church does not recapture the sacrificial spirit of the early church, it will lose
its authenticity, forfeit the loyalty of millions, and be dismissed as an irrelevant
social club with no meaning for the twentieth century. Every day I meet young
people whose disappointment with the church has turned into outright disgust.

Perhaps I have once again been too optimistic. Is organized religion too 43
inextricably bound to the status quo to save our nation and the world? Perhaps I must turn my faith to the inner spiritual church, the church within the
church, as the true *ekklesia*° and the hope of the world. But again I am thankful to God that some noble souls from the ranks of organized religion have
broken loose from the paralyzing chains of conformity and joined us as active
partners in the struggle for freedom. They have left their secure congregations
and walked the streets of Albany, Georgia, with us. They have gone down the
highways of the South on tortuous rides for freedom. Yes, they have gone to
jail with us. Some have been dismissed from their churches, have lost the support of their bishops and fellow ministers. But they have acted in the faith
that right defeated is stronger than evil triumphant. Their witness has been
the spiritual salt that has preserved the true meaning of the gospel in these
troubled times. They have carved a tunnel of hope through the dark mountain
of disappointment.

I hope the church as a whole will meet the challenge of this decisive 44
hour. But even if the church does not come to the aid of justice, I have no
despair about the future. I have no fear about the outcome of our struggle in
Birmingham, even if our motives are at present misunderstood. We will reach
the goal of freedom in Birmingham and all over the nation, because the goal
of America is freedom. Abused and scorned though we may be, our destiny
is tied up with America's destiny. Before the pilgrims landed at Plymouth,
we were here. Before the pen of Jefferson etched the majestic words of the

Greek for "church"

Declaration of Independence across the pages of history, we were here. For more than two centuries our forebears labored in this country without wages: they made cotton king; they built the homes of their masters while suffering gross injustice and shameful humiliation—and yet out of a bottomless vitality they continued to thrive and develop. If the inexpressible cruelties of slavery could not stop us, the opposition we now face will surely fail. We will win our freedom because the sacred heritage of our nation and the eternal will of God are embodied in our echoing demands.

45   Before closing I feel impelled to mention one other point in your statement that has troubled me profoundly. You warmly commended the Birmingham police force for keeping "order" and "preventing violence." I doubt that you would have so warmly commended the police force if you had seen its dogs sinking their teeth into unarmed, nonviolent Negroes. I doubt that you would so quickly commend the policemen if you were to observe their ugly and inhumane treatment of Negroes here in the city jail; if you were to watch them push and curse old Negro women and young Negro girls; if you were to see them slap and kick old Negro men and young boys; if you were to observe them, as they did on two occasions, refuse to give us food because we wanted to sing our grace together. I cannot join you in your praise of the Birmingham police department.

46   It is true that the police have exercised a degree of discipline in handling the demonstrators. In this sense they have conducted themselves rather "nonviolently" in public. But for what purpose? To preserve the evil system of segregation. Over the past few years I have consistently preached that nonviolence demands that the means we use must be as pure as the ends we seek. I have tried to make clear that it is wrong to use immoral means to attain moral ends. But now I must affirm that it is just as wrong, or perhaps even more so, to use moral means to preserve immoral ends. Perhaps Mr. Connor and his policemen have been rather nonviolent in public, as was Chief Pritchett° in Albany, Georgia, but they have used the moral means of nonviolence to maintain the immoral end of racial injustice. As T. S. Eliot° has said, "The last temptation is the greatest treason: To do the right deed for the wrong reason."

47   I wish you had commended the Negro sit-inners and demonstrators of Birmingham for their sublime courage, their willingness to suffer, and their amazing discipline in the midst of great provocation. One day the South will recognize its real heroes. They will be the James Merediths,° with the noble sense of purpose that enables them to face jeering and hostile mobs, and with the agonizing loneliness that characterizes the life of the pioneer. They will be old, oppressed, battered Negro women, symbolized in a seventy-two-year-old woman in Montgomery, Alabama, who rose up with a sense of dignity and with her people decided not to ride segregated buses, and who responded with ungrammatical profundity to one who inquired about her weariness: "My feets is tired, but my soul is at rest." They will be the young high school and college students, the young ministers of the gospel and a host of their elders, courageously and nonviolently sitting in at lunch counters and willingly going to jail for conscience' sake. One day the South will know that when these

Laurie Pritchett, the police chief in Albany, Georgia, during the 1961 Albany Movement, a desegregation campaign

T. S. Eliot (1888–1965), an American-born poet, playwright, and critic

James Meredith (b. 1933), in 1961 the first African American student to attend the University of Mississippi

disinherited children of God sat down at lunch counters, they were in reality standing up for what is best in the American dream and for the most sacred values in our Judaeo-Christian heritage, thereby bringing our nation back to those great wells of democracy which were dug deep by the founding fathers in their formulation of the Constitution and the Declaration of Independence.

Never before have I written so long a letter. I'm afraid it is much too long 48 to take your precious time. I can assure you that it would have been much shorter if I had been writing from a comfortable desk, but what else can one do when he is alone in a narrow jail cell, other than write long letters, think long thoughts, and pray long prayers?

If I have said anything in this letter that overstates the truth and indicates 49 an unreasonable impatience, I beg you to forgive me. If I have said anything that understates the truth and indicates my having a patience that allows me to settle for anything less than brotherhood, I beg God to forgive me.

I hope this letter finds you strong in the faith. I also hope that circum- 50 stances will soon make it possible for me to meet each of you, not as an integrationist or a civil-rights leader but as a fellow clergyman and a Christian brother. Let us all hope that the dark clouds of racial prejudice will soon pass away and the deep fog of misunderstanding will be lifted from our fear-drenched communities, and in some not too distant tomorrow the radiant stars of love and brotherhood will shine over our great nation with all their scintillating beauty.

Yours for the cause of Peace and Brotherhood,

Martin Luther King Jr.

⊘READING ARGUMENTS

1. In what sense is "Letter from Birmingham Jail" a Rogerian argument? What specific elements of Rogerian argument does King use? Why is this form of argument suited to King's overall purposes?

2. Where does King use analogies—historical and otherwise—to strengthen his arguments? Why do you think he makes these particular comparisons? How are they related to his political goals?

3. According to King, what is "direct action" (para. 6), and what is its purpose?

4. In many parts of his letter, King writes in a detached, almost scholarly style, citing philosophers and theologians. Where does he use more emotional language? What do you think he is trying to achieve with this language? Do you think this language effectively supports his argument?

5. King makes "two honest confessions" in his letter (23). What are they? Why do you think he characterizes these points as confessions?

⊘WRITING ARGUMENTS

1. According to King, people have a moral obligation to obey just laws and to disobey unjust laws. What is his standard for determining which laws are just and unjust? Is there a current law you would consider breaking for the reasons King describes? Write an argumentative essay in which you defend such a choice.

2. King agrees with the theologian Reinhold Niebuhr that "groups tend to be more immoral than individuals" (12). Do you think this statement is generally true? Take a position on the issue, and argue your case.

A

Writing Literary Arguments

When you write an essay about literature, you have a number of options. For example, you can write a **response paper** (expressing your reactions to a poem, play, or story), or you can write an **explication** (focusing on a work's individual elements, such as a poem's imagery, meter, figurative language, and diction). You can also write an **analysis** of a work's theme, a character in a play or a story, or a work's historical or cultural context. Another option, which is discussed in the pages that follow, is to write a literary argument.

What Is Literary Argument?

When you write a literary argument, you do more than just react to, explicate, or analyze a work of literature. When you develop a **literary argument**, you take a position about a literary work (or works), support that position with evidence, and refute possible opposing arguments. You might, for example, take the position that a familiar interpretation of a well-known work is limited in some way, that a work's effect today is different from its impact when it was written, or that two apparently very different works have some significant parallels.

It is important to understand that not every essay about literature is a literary argument. For example, you might use a discussion of Tillie Olsen's short story "I Stand Here Ironing," with its sympathetic portrait of a young mother in the Depression, to support an argument in favor of President Franklin D. Roosevelt's expansion of social welfare programs. Alternatively, you might use Martin Espada's poem "Why I Went to College" to explain your own decision to continue your education. But writing a literary argument involves much more than using a literary work as support for an argument or referring to a literary character to shed light on your own intellectual development or explain a choice you made. A literary argument *takes a stand* about a work (or works) of literature.

Stating an Argumentative Thesis

When you develop an argumentative thesis about literature, your goal is to state a thesis that has an edge—one that takes a stand on your topic. Like any effective thesis, the thesis of a literary argument should be clearly worded and specific; it should also be more than a statement of fact.

INEFFECTIVE THESIS (TOO GENERAL)	In "A&P," Sammy faces a difficult decision.
EFFECTIVE THESIS (MORE SPECIFIC)	Sammy's decision to quit his job reveals more about the conformist society in which "A&P" is set than about Sammy himself.
INEFFECTIVE THESIS (STATES A FACT)	The theme of *Hamlet* is often seen as an Oedipal conflict.
EFFECTIVE THESIS (TAKES A STAND)	Although many critics have identified an Oedipal conflict in *Hamlet*, Shakespeare's play is also a story of a young man who is struggling with familiar problems—love, family, and his future.

Here are some possible thesis statements that you could support in a literary argument:

- Charlotte Perkins Gilman's short story "The Yellow Wallpaper," usually seen as a feminist story, is actually a ghost story.

- August Strindberg's play *The Stronger*, whose two characters seem to be rivals for the affection of a man, are really engaged in a professional rivalry to see who gives the better performance in their confrontation.

- Although many readers might see Wilfred Owen's "Dulce et Decorum Est" as the more powerful poem because of its graphic imagery of war, Carl Sandburg's understated "Grass" is likely to have a greater impact on modern readers because they have been overexposed to violent images.

- An examination of Robert Frost's "The Road Not Taken" reveals a surprisingly complex and somewhat troubling message about the arbitrariness of our life choices and our later need to idealize those choices—a message that is not visible without close analysis.

(For more on developing a thesis statement, see Chapter 7.)

Choosing Evidence

Like any argument, a literary argument relies on evidence. Some of this evidence will come from the literary work itself. For example, to make a point about a character's antisocial behavior, you would cite specific examples of such behavior from the work. To make a point about a poet's use of Biblical allusions, you would present examples of such allusions from the poem.

> **Note:** Be careful not to rely on plot summary as evidence. For example, summarizing everything that happens to a character will not convince your readers that the character is motivated by envy. Choose only *relevant* examples—in this case, specific instances of a character's jealous behavior, including relevant quotations from the literary work.

Evidence can also come from **literary criticism**—scholarly articles by experts in the field that analyze and evaluate works of literature. If you agree with a critic's position, you can quote or paraphrase an observation and use it to support your argument. If you disagree with a critic, you can quote his or her position and argue against it. For example, to argue that a particular critical position is inaccurate, outdated, or oversimplified, you would quote some critics who take that position before you explain why you disagree with their interpretation. (For more on evaluating potential sources for your essay, see Chapter 7.)

Writing a Literary Argument

The structure of a literary argument is similar to the structure of any other argument: it includes a **thesis statement** in the introduction, supporting **evidence**, **refutation** of opposing arguments, and a strong **concluding statement**. However, unlike other arguments, literary arguments follow specific conventions for writing about literature:

- In your essay's first paragraph, include the author's full name and the title of each work you are discussing.

- Use **present tense** when discussing events in works of literature. For example, if you are discussing "I Stand Here Ironing," you would say, "The mother *worries* [not *worried*] about her ability to provide for her child." There are two exceptions to this rule. Use past tense when referring to historical events: "The Great Depression *made* things difficult for mothers like the narrator." Also use past tense to refer to events that came before the action described in the work: "The mother is particularly vulnerable because her husband *left* her alone to support her children."

- Italicize the titles of plays and novels. Put the titles of poems and short stories in quotation marks.

- When mentioning writers and literary critics in the body of your essay, use their full names ("Emily Dickinson") the first time you mention them and their last names only ("Dickinson," not "Miss Dickinson" or "Emily") after that.

- Use **MLA documentation style** in your paper, and include a works-cited list. (See Chapter 10 for information on MLA documentation.)

- In your in-text citations, cite page numbers for stories, act and scene numbers for plays, and line numbers for poems. Use the word *line* or *lines* for the first in-text citation of lines from a poem. After the first in-text citation, you may omit the word *line* or *lines*.

The following literary argument, "Confessions of a Misunderstood Poem: An Analysis of 'The Road Not Taken,'" takes a stand in favor of a particular way of interpreting poetry.

CONFESSIONS OF A MISUNDERSTOOD POEM: AN ANALYSIS OF "THE ROAD NOT TAKEN"

MEGAN McGOVERN

Introduction (identifies titles and authors of works to be discussed)

In his poem "Introduction to Poetry," Billy Collins suggests that rather than dissecting a poem to find its meaning, students should use their imaginations to help them experience poetry. According to Collins, they should "drop a mouse into a poem / and watch him probe his way out" (lines 5–6). However, Collins overstates his case when he implies that analyzing a poem to find out what it might mean is a brutal or deadly process, comparable to tying the poem to a chair and "beating

The word *lines* is omitted from the in-text citation after the first reference to lines of a poem.

it with a hose" (15). Rather than killing a poem's spirit, a careful and methodical dissection can often help the reader better appreciate its subtler meanings. In fact, with patient coaxing, a poem often has much to "confess." One such poem is the familiar but frequently misunderstood

Thesis statement

"The Road Not Taken." An examination of Robert Frost's "The

1

Road Not Taken" reveals a complex and somewhat troubling message about the arbitrariness of our life choices and our later need to idealize those choices—a message not visible without close analysis.

2   On the surface, Frost's poem seems to have a clear and fairly simple meaning. The poem's speaker talks about coming to a fork in the road and choosing the "less-traveled" path. Most readers see the fork in the road as a metaphor: the road represents life, and the fork represents an individual's choices in life. So, by following the less-traveled road, the speaker is choosing the less conventional—and supposedly more rewarding—route. At the end of the poem, the speaker indicates his satisfaction when he says his choice "made all the difference" (line 20). However, Frost himself, referring to "The Road Not Taken," advised readers "'to be careful of that one; it's a tricky poem—very tricky,'" encouraging readers not to accept the most appealing or obvious interpretation (qtd. in Savoie 7–8). Indeed, if one examines the speaker's tone and word choice carefully, the poem's message seems much darker and more complicated than one might initially assume.

Opposing argument addressed

Opposing argument refuted

3   The speaker's tone in the first three stanzas suggests indecision and regret—and, ultimately, lack of power. Rather than bravely facing the choice between one common path and one uncommon path, the speaker spends most of the poem considering two seemingly equal roads, "sorry" not to be able to "travel both" (2). Even after choosing "the other" road in line 6, the speaker continues for two more stanzas to weigh his options. The problem is that the two roads are, in fact, not all that different. As several critics have observed, "the speaker admits three times within six lines that the roads of life are the same, that they are indistinguishable: one is 'just as fair' as the other, they are 'worn really about the same,' and each 'equally lay'" (Bassett 42). So, if there is virtually no difference between the two, then why is Frost drawing our attention to this crossroads—this seemingly critical moment of choice? If Frost had wanted to dramatize a meaningful decision, the roads would be different in some significant way.

Evidence: Analysis and explication of Frost poem

Evidence: Literary criticism

4   One critic, Frank Lentricchia, argues that Frost is demonstrating "'that our life-shaping choices are irrational, that we are fundamentally out of control'" (qtd. in Savoie 13). Similarly, another critic, Sterling Eisiminger, connects "The Road Not Taken" to an essay Frost wrote years later to show that Frost was interested in "the impulsiveness and

Evidence: Literary criticism

arbitrariness with which most important decisions are made" (114).
These critical views help to explain the speaker's indecision in the
first three stanzas. The speaker impulsively chooses "the other" road

but cannot accept the arbitrariness of his choice; therefore, he cannot
stop considering the first road. He exclaims in the third stanza, "Oh,
I kept the first for another day!" (13). When, in the next two lines, he
finally gives up the possibility of following that first road, he predicts,
"Yet knowing how way leads on to way, / I doubted if I should ever
come back" (14–15). Here, the speaker further demonstrates a lack of
control over his own decisions. He describes a future guided not by his
own active, meaningful choices but rather by some arbitrary force. In
a world where "way leads on to way," he is a passive traveler, not a
decisive individualist.

Given the indecision that characterizes the previous stanzas, the   5
poem's last two lines are surprisingly decisive: "I took the one less
traveled by / And that has made all the difference" (19–20). Is Frost
contradicting himself? How has the narrator suddenly become so clear
about the rightness of his decision? In fact, the last stanza does not
make sense unless the reader perceives the irony in the speaker's tone.
The speaker is imagining himself in the future, "ages and ages hence,"
telling the story of his moment at the crossroads (17). He imagines
how he will, in hindsight, give his choice meaning and clarity that it

did not have at the time. As Eisiminger argues, Frost is showing how
"Years later, these decisions are romanticized" (114). The narrator,
rather than anticipating the satisfaction that will come from having
made the right, and braver, choice, is anticipating rewriting his own
personal history to make sense of an ultimately arbitrary chain of
events. Reading the last stanza ironically allows the reader to make
sense of the poem as a whole.

There are many possible interpretations of "The Road Not Taken,"   6
most of which can be supported with evidence from the text. However,
one can only understand these interpretations by taking the time to
take the poem apart, to look at how its parts fit together, and to reach
a thoughtful and logical conclusion. To do so, readers must go against
some of Billy Collins's well-meaning advice and be willing to tie the
poem—and themselves—to a chair: to read it carefully, ask questions,
and stay with it until it confesses.

Works Cited

Bassett, Patrick F. "Frost's 'The Road Not Taken.'" *Explicator* 39.3 (1981): 41–43. *Academic Search Premier*. Web. 14 May 2009.

Collins, Billy. "Introduction to Poetry." *Sailing Alone around the Room.* New York: Random, 1998. 16. Print.

Eisiminger, Sterling. "Robert Frost's Essay 'The Constant Symbol' and Its Relationship to 'The Road Not Taken.'" *American Notes and Queries* 19.7–8 (1981): 114–15. *Academic Search Premier*. Web. 14 May 2009.

Frost, Robert. "The Road Not Taken." *Mountain Interval.* New York: Holt, 1920. N. pag. *Bartleby.com: Great Books Online.* Web. 14 May 2009.

Savoie, John. "A Poet's Quarrel: Jamesian Pragmatism and Frost's 'The Road Not Taken.'" *New England Quarterly* 77.1 (2004): 5–24. *Academic Search Premier*. Web. 14 May 2009.

APPENDIX

B

Documenting Sources: APA

APA style was developed by the American Psychological Association and is commonly used in the social sciences. Sources are cited to help readers in the social sciences understand new ideas in the context of previous research and show them how current the sources are.*

There are several reasons to cite sources. Readers expect arguments to be well supported by evidence and want to be able to locate those sources if they decide to delve deeper. Citing sources is also important to give credit to writers and to avoid plagiarism.

Using Parenthetical References

In APA style, parenthetical references refer readers to sources in the list of references at the end of the paper. In general, parenthetical references should include the author and year of publication. You may also include page numbers if you are quoting directly from a source. Here are some more specific guidelines:

- Refer to the author's name in the text, or cite it, along with the year of publication, in parentheses: Vang asserted . . . (2004) or (Vang, 2004). When quoting words from a source, include the page number: (Vang, 2004, p. 33). Once you have cited a source, you can refer to the author a second time without the publication date so long as it is clear you are referring to the same source: Vang also found . . .

- If no author is identified, use a shortened version of the title: ("Mind," 2007).

- If you are citing multiple works by the same author or authors published in the same year, add a lowercase letter with the year: ("Peters," 2004a), ("Peters," 2004b), and so on.

---

* American Psychological Association, *Publication Manual of the American Psychological Association*, Sixth Edition (2009).

- When a work has two authors, cite both names and the year: (Tabor & Garza, 2006). For three to five authors, in the first reference, cite all authors, along with the year; for subsequent references, cite just the first author, followed by et al. When a work has six or more authors, cite just the first author, the first followed by et al. and the year: (McCarthy et al., 2010).

- Omit page numbers or dates if the source does not include them. (Try to find a .pdf version of an online source if it is an option; it will usually include page numbers.)

- If you quote a source found in another source, indicate the original author and the source in which you found it: Psychologist Gary Wells asserted . . . (as cited in Doyle, 2005, p. 122).

- Include in-text references to personal communications and interviews by providing the person's name, the phrase "personal communication," and the date: (J. Smith, personal communication, February 12, 2006). Do not include these sources in your reference list.

Parenthetical citations must be included for all sources that are not common knowledge, whether you are summarizing, paraphrasing, or quoting directly from a source. If a direct quotation is forty words or less, include it within quotation marks without separating it from the rest of the text. When quoting a passage that is more than forty words long, indent the entire block of quoted text one-half inch from the left margin, and do not enclose it in quotation marks. It should be double-spaced, like the rest of the paper.

Preparing a Reference List

Start your list of references on a separate page at the end of your paper. Center the title References at the top of the page.

- Begin each reference flush with the left margin, and indent subsequent lines one-half inch.

- List your references alphabetically by the author's last name (or by the first major word of the title if no author is identified).

- If the list includes references for two sources by the same author, alphabetize them by title.

- Italicize titles of books and periodicals. Do not italicize article titles or enclose them in quotation marks.

- For titles of books and articles, capitalize the first word of the title and subtitle as well as any proper nouns. Capitalize words in a periodical title as in the original.

When you have completed your reference list, go through your paper and make sure that every reference cited is included in the list in the correct order.

Examples of APA Citations

The following are examples of APA citations.

Periodicals

Article in a journal paginated by volume

Shah, N. A. (2006). Women's human rights in the Koran: An interpretive approach. *Human Rights Quarterly, 28,* 868–902.

Article in a journal paginated by issue

Lamb, B., & Keller, H. (2007). Understanding cultural models of parenting: The role of intracultural variation and response style. *Journal of Cross-Cultural Psychology, 38*(1), 50–57.

Magazine article

Collins, L. (2009, April 20). The vertical tourist. *The New Yorker, 85*(10), 68–79.

Newspaper article

DeParle, J. (2009, April 19). Struggling to rise in suburbs where failing means fitting in. *The New York Times,* pp. A1, A20–A21.

Books

Books by one author

Venkatesh, S. A. (2006). *Off the books: The underground economy of the urban poor.* Cambridge, MA: Harvard University Press.

Books by two to seven authors

Guerrero, L. K., & Floyd, K. (2006). *Nonverbal communication in close relationships.* Mahwah, NJ: Erlbaum.

Books by eight or more authors

Mulvaney, S. A., Mudasiru, E., Schlundt, D. G., Baughman, C. L., Fleming, M., VanderWoude, A., . . . Rothman, R. (2008). Self-management in Type 2 diabetes: The adolescent perspective. *The Diabetes Educator, 34,* 118–127.

Edited book

Brummett, B. (Ed.). (2008). *Uncovering hidden rhetorics: Social issues in disguise*. Los Angeles, CA: Sage.

Essay in an edited book

Alberts, H. C. (2006). The multiple transformations of Miami. In H. Smith & O. J. Furuseth (Eds.), *Latinos in the new south: Transformations of place* (pp. 135–51). Burlington, VT: Ashgate.

Translation

Courville, S. (2008). *Quebec: A historical geography* (R. Howard, Trans.). Vancouver, British Columbia, Canada: UBC.

Revised edition

Johnson, B., & Christensen, L. B. (2008). *Educational research: Quantitative, qualitative, and mixed approaches* (3rd ed.). Los Angeles, CA: Sage.

Internet Sources
Entire Web site

Secretariat of the Convention on Biodiversity, United Nations Biodiversity Programmes. (2005). *Convention on biological diversity.* Retrieved from http://www.biodiv.org/

Web page within a Web site

The great divide: How Westerners and Muslims view each other. (2006, July 6). In *Pew global attitudes project.* Retrieved from http://pewglobal.org/reports/display.php?ReportID=253

University program Web site

National security archive. (2009). Retrieved from George Washington University website: http://www.gwu.edu/~nsarchiv/

Journal article found on the Web with a DOI

Because Web sites change and disappear without warning, many publishers have started adding a Digital Object Identifier (DOI) to their articles. A DOI is a unique number that can be retrieved no matter where the article ends up on the Web.

To locate an article with a known DOI, go to the DOI system Web site at http://dx.doi.org/ and type in the DOI number. When citing an article that has a DOI (usually found on the first page of the article), you do not need to include a URL in your reference or the name of the database in which you may have found the article.

Geers, A. L., Wellman, J. A., & Lassiter, G. D. (2009). Dispositional optimism and engagement: The moderating influence of goal prioritization. *Journal of Personality and Social Psychology 94,* 913–932. doi:10.1037/a0014746

Journal article found on the Web without a DOI

Bendetto, M. M. (2008). Crisis on the immigration bench: An ethical perspective. *Brooklyn Law Review*, 73, 467–523. Retrieved from http://brooklaw.edu/students/journals/blr.php/

Journal article from an electronic database

The name and URL of the database are not required for citations if a DOI is available. If no DOI is available, provide the home page URL of the journal or of the book or report publisher.

Staub, E., & Pearlman, L. A. (2009) Reducing intergroup prejudice and conflict: A commentary. *Journal of Personality and Social Psychology, 11,* 3–23. Retrieved from http://www.apa.org /journals/psp/

Electronic book

Katz, R. N. (Ed.). (2008). *The tower and the cloud: Higher education in an era of cloud computing.* Retrieved from http://net .educause.edu/ir/library/pdf/PUB7202.pdf

Video blog post

Baggs, A. (2007, January 14). In my language [Video file]. Retrieved from http://www.youtube.com/watch?v=JnyIM1hI2jc

Presentation slides

Hall, M. E. (2009) *Who moved my job!? A psychology of job-loss "trauma"* [Presentation slides]. Retrieved from http://www.cew .wisc.edu/docs/WMMJ%20PwrPt-Summry2.ppt

Student Essay

The following research paper, "The High Cost of Cheap Counterfeit Goods," follows APA format as outlined in the preceding pages.

The High Cost of Cheap Counterfeit Goods

Deniz Bilgutay

Humanities 101, Section 1

Professor Fitzgerald

March 4, 2010

Abstract

The global trade in counterfeit products costs manufacturers of luxury goods millions of dollars each year. Although this illegal trade threatens the free market, employs underage labor, and may even fund terrorism, many people consider it a victimless crime. Studies show that some consumers even take pride in buying knock-off products. But a closer look at this illicit trade in counterfeit goods shows that consumers in the United States—and around the world—do not understand the ethical implications of the choices they make. Consumers should stop supporting this illegal business, and law enforcement officials should prosecute it more vigorously than they currently do. In the final analysis, this illegal practice hurts legitimate businesses and in some cases endangers the health and safety of consumers.

Keywords: counterfeiting, terrorism, ethics, crime

The High Cost of Cheap Counterfeit Goods

For those who do not want to pay for genuine designer products, a fake Louis Vuitton bag or knock-off Rolex watch might seem too good to pass up. They may even be a source of pride. According to one study, two-thirds of British consumers said they would be "proud to tell family and friends" that they bought inexpensive knock-offs (Thomas, 2007). A private firm that specializes in corporate investigation and brand protection conducted a poll in 2004 that showed that a similarly high proportion of people were willing to buy counterfeits. The trade in counterfeit goods, however, is not a victimless crime. A growing body of evidence suggests that the makers and distributers of counterfeit goods have ties to child labor, organized crime, and even terrorism. In addition, the purchase of counterfeit goods costs both legitimate companies and the United States government hundreds of billions of dollars every year in lost revenue and taxes (Kessler International, 2004). Therefore, consumers need to stop buying these products and funding the illegal activities that this activity supports.

Much of the responsibility for the trade in counterfeit goods can be placed on the manufacturers and the countries that permit the production and export of such goods. According to Lisa Movius (2002), China is the "piracy capital of the world." On assignment for *Salon.com,* Movius visited the Xiangyang market in Shanghai as well as the Silk Alley in Beijing. She found these places to be "hotbeds of pirated goods" and saw a "dizzying array of products with Western brand names . . . all available at impossibly low prices." She attributes this flourishing market to the fact that China is lax about enforcing piracy law and places less value than the West does on individualism. In other words, China is a place where antipiracy efforts would be difficult to implement under the best of

Introduction

Thesis statement

circumstances. Even if Movius's cultural explanation is perhaps unfair to the Chinese, the fact remains that as of 2002, counterfeit goods outnumbered their genuine counterparts by two to one on the Chinese market (Movius, 2002).

Aside from possible cultural explanations for the issue, there is an ethical problem associated with the production of knock-offs. As Dana Thomas (2007) has written in *The New York Times,* many of these counterfeit products are made by children—children who are "sold or sent off by their families to work in clandestine factories." To American consumers, the problem of children laboring in Chinese factories may seem remote, but it is not. If it is reasonable to place blame for this flourishing market on the countries that allow it, it is also reasonable to blame the people who buy counterfeit goods. The International Intellectual Property Alliance has determined that "46% of the pirated goods sold in America come from China" (as cited in Movius, 2002). Consequently, the simple act of buying a counterfeit Coach handbag implicates the consumer in the practice of forced child labor.

Immoral labor practices are not the only reason that the counterfeit market needs to be stopped. Organized crime is behind much of the counterfeit trade, so "every dollar spent on a knockoff Gap polo shirt or a fake Kate Spade handbag may be supporting drug trafficking, child labor, and worse" ("Editorial: The True Cost," 2007). Consumer dollars may also be supporting narcotics, weapons, and child prostitution (Thomas, 2007).

This illicit international system also helps to finance groups even more sinister than crime syndicates. American consumers of counterfeit goods should understand that profits from

Evidence:
Point 1

Evidence:
Point 2

THE HIGH COST OF CHEAP COUNTERFEIT GOODS   5

counterfeit goods support terrorist and extremist groups, including Hezbollah, paramilitary organizations in Northern Ireland, and FARC, a revolutionary armed faction in Colombia (Thomas, 2007). According to the International Anti-Counterfeiting Coalition, the sale of knock-off T-shirts may have even funded the 1993 attack on the World Trade Center. Some observers speculate that terrorists annually receive about 2% of the roughly $500 billion trade in counterfeit goods ("Editorial: The True Cost," 2007). According to Ronald K. Noble, secretary-general of the international law enforcement agency Interpol, "Intellectual property crime is becoming the preferred method of funding for a number of terrorist groups" (as cited in Langan, 2003).

    Counterfeit goods also undermine the mainstay of Western business—respect for intellectual property. In the context of a vast international market of counterfeit luxury goods, the issue of intellectual property can seem insignificant. But the creation of new products requires time, energy, and money, and "unrestrained copying robs creators of the means to profit from their works" (Sprigman, 2006). Copyright law exists to make sure that inventors and producers will be motivated to create original work and be fairly compensated for it. This principle should apply to the designers of luxury goods and fashion items as well. Christopher Sprigman (2006) disagrees, however, noting that intellectual property law does little to protect fashion designs and that this is as it should be. "Trend-driven consumption," says Sprigman, is good for the fashion industry because the industry's ability to create trends "is based on designers' relative freedom to copy." But even this argument—which addresses the influences of legitimate fashion designers

Evidence: Point 3

Evidence: Point 4

Opposing argument

Refutation

THE HIGH COST OF CHEAP COUNTERFEIT GOODS   6

and manufacturers—cannot be used to justify allowing counterfeiters to copy Prada handbags or Hugo Boss suits and pass them off as genuine branded articles. Such illicit activity creates no trends—other than perhaps increasing the market for counterfeit products, which siphons off more profits from original designers.

Evidence: Point 5

The knock-off market is not limited to fashion and luxury goods: fake products such as shoddy brake pads have directly injured many consumers. In addition, each year millions of people in the United States and abroad buy counterfeit drugs that do not work and in many cases are dangerous. Some sources estimate that the majority of drugs used to treat life-threatening diseases in Africa are counterfeit. Not coincidentally, many of the same people who are making and distributing counterfeit luxury goods are also manufacturing these drugs ("Editorial: The True Cost," 2007).

Conclusion

It is time that people realize the harm that is done by counterfeit merchandise and stop buying it. One way to combat this problem is to educate consumers about the effects of their purchases. For example, the poll conducted by Kessler International (2004) showed that people were less likely to buy counterfeit goods when they knew that the profits could support terrorism. Another way to confront the problem is for law enforcement to address this issue aggressively. Not only should local authorities do more to stop this illegal trade, but national governments should also impose sanctions on countries that refuse to honor international treaties concerning intellectual property. Only by taking this issue seriously can we ensure that this "victimless" crime does not continue to spread and claim more victims.

THE HIGH COST OF CHEAP COUNTERFEIT GOODS   7

References

Editorial: The true cost: Illegal knockoffs of name-brand products
    do widespread harm. [Editorial]. (2007, December 2). *The
    Columbus* [OH] *Dispatch*, p. 4G.

Kessler International. (2004, July 30). Counterfeiters continue to
    proliferate as consumers choose to ignore risks. *Yearbook
    of experts news release wire*. Retrieved from LexisNexis
    database.

Langan, M. (2003, July 24). Counterfeit goods make real terror-
    ism. *Pittsburgh Post-Gazette,* p. A17.

Movius, L. (2002, July 8). Imitation nation. *Salon.com.* Retrieved
    from http://dir.salon.com/story/tech/feature/2002/07/08
    /imitation_nation

Sprigman, C. (2006, August 22). The fashion industry's piracy
    paradox [Online forum comment]. Retrieved from http://
    www.publicknowledge.org/node/597

Thomas, D. (2007, August 30). Terror's purse strings. *The New
    York Times*, p. A23.

ACKNOWLEDGMENTS

Photo Credits

Page 2 Digital Vision/Getty Images/Fotosearch; **4** *Wake Up, America!* (1917) James Montgomery Flagg. Published by the Hegeman Print, New York/Library of Congress Prints and Photographs Division [LC-USZC4-3802]; **5** Creatas/JupiterImages/Fotosearch; **7** Kevin Lamarque/Reuters; **8** Scala/Ministero per i Beni e le Attività Culturali/Uffizi Gallery, Florence, Italy/Art Resource, NY; **9** US Navy/AP Images; **10** Aleksandar Jaksic/iStockphoto.com; **12** Alessandro Fucarini/AP Images; **27** Copyright © 2009 Nestle Waters. Reprinted with permission; **32, 36, 37, 38, 52** Copyright © 2009 Gerard Jones. Used with permission; **55** Rob Rogers/Copyright © The Pittsburgh Post-Gazette/Dist. by United Feature Syndicate, Inc. **58 (t)** Courtesy of EveryLifeCounts.info. Reproduced by permission; **60** Image courtesy of the Advertising Archives; **61** Copyright © 2009 by Hogbard. Reprinted with permission; **66** Sakchai Lalit/AP Images; **69** Wyatt Tee Walker/Bettmann/Corbis; **71** Hulton-Deutsch Collection/Corbis; **75** *North Carolina, 1950/* Elliott Erwitt/Magnum Photos; **88** John Harrington/AP Images; **90 (l)** Dennis Van Tine/Landov; **90 (r)** Richard Drew/AP Images; **91** *Thomas Jefferson* (undated), George Peter Alexander Healy. Oil on canvas. Musée de la cooperation franco-americaine, Blerancourt, France. Inv. MNB Dta 5; MV 4647. Photograph by Gérard Blot, Réunion des Musées Nationaux/Art Resource, NY; **96** Dave G. Houser/Corbis; **103** Krista Kennell/Zuma Press; **109** Chris Graythen/Getty Images; **115** The Granger Collection New York; **116** Used with the permission of Nick Anderson and the Washington Post Writers Group in conjunction with the Cartoonist Group. All rights reserved; **118** Maria Stenzel/Corbis; **120** Nancy Ostertag/Getty Images; **123** Mike Baldwin/www.CartoonStock.com; **144** Karl Dolenc/iStockphoto.com; **146** BloomImage/Getty Images; **147** Jose Luis Pelaez/The Image Bank/Getty Images; **148** Sheer Photo, Inc./PhotoDisc/Getty Images; **151** David Paul Morris/Getty Images; **157** Rick Bowmer/AP Images; **161** Ann Heisenfelt/AP Images; **165** Matthew S. Gunby/AP Images; **171** Ana Blazic/iStockphoto.com; **172** Courtesy of Corporation for National and Community Service. Reproduced by permission; **173 (l–r)** Roger Cracknell 01/Classic/Alamy; Steve Stock/Alamy; Ben Blankenburg/iStockphoto.com; David Cordner/The Image Bank/Getty Images; **184** Courtesy of Naugatuck Valley Community College. Reproduced by permission; **185 (l)** Andy Nelson/Christian Science Monitor/Getty Images **185 (r)** Tanya Constantine/Blend Images/Getty Images; **188** Jon Riley/Stone/Getty Images; **214** Paul M. Walsh/AP Images; **218** Jonathan Ernst/Reuters/Corbis; **221** Viorika Prikhodko/iStockphoto.com; **224 (l)** Courtesy of The Nation Magazine. Used with permission; **224 (r)** Courtesy of The American Conservative Magazine. Used with permission; **232** Steve Hix/Somos Images/Corbis; **233** Courtesy of the Office of Population Research, Princeton University. Reproduced with permission; **247** Courtesy of *The Electronic Journal of Human Sexualty*. Used with permission; **248** Nabil John Elderkin/Getty Images; **264** Yellow Dog Productions/Getty Images; **280** Copyright © 2009 iParadigms LLC. All rights reserved. Used with permission; **314** Copyright © & trademark ™ Wikimedia Foundation, Inc. All rights reserved; **317** AP Images; **318** *Writing the Declaration of Independence in 1776* (ca. 1900), Jean Leon Jerome Ferris. Oil on canvas. Lora Robins Collection of Virginia Art, Virginia Historical Society, Richmond/The Bridgeman Art Library International; **324** Everett Collection; **326 (t)** Walter Bibikow/AGE Fotostock; **326 (b)** Onne van der Wal/Nature Picture Library; **352** Copyright © 2009 Mothers Against Drunk Driving. All rights reserved; **355 (t)** © Mike Kemp/Getty Images; **355 (b)** James Leynse/Corbis; **356** US Department of Transportation, National Highway Traffic Safety Administration/Courtesy of the Ad Council; **357** Phil Schermeister/Corbis; **384 (t–b, l–r)** Yoshikazu Tsuno/AFP/Getty Images; Werner Baun/DPA/Landov; Kyodo News/AP Images; Ng Han Guan/AP Images; Heribert Proepper/AP Images; Remy de la Mauviniere/AP Images; Daniel Ochoa de Olza/AP Images; Daniel Maurer/AP Images; Daniel Ochoa de Olza/AP Images; Greg Baker/AP Images; **416** Ian Berry/Magnum; **418** Gary C. Knapp/AP Images; **419** Image courtesy of The Advertising Archives; **421** Copyright © 2009 Sunshine Week/American Society of News Editors, asne.org. All rights reserved. Reproduced with permission; **423** Dale Sparks/AP Images; **424** Courtesy of Council on the Environment of New York City (CENYC). Photo copyright © 2009 Katvan Studios, Inc. Reproduced with permission; **452** Mark Lennihan/AP Images; **471** Copyright © 2009 FindCollegeCards.com. All rights reserved. Reproduced with permission; **480** Thinkstock/Getty Images; **483** Peter Dazeley/Getty Images; **485 (t)** Bettmann/Corbis; **485 (b)** *Sign at Bus Station, Rome, Georgia* (1943), Esther Bubley/Farm Security Administration, Office of War Information Photograph Collection/Library of Congress Prints and Photographs Division [LC-USW3-037939-E]; **486** Bettmann/Corbis; **487 (t)** Rick Friedman /The New York Times/Redux; **487 (b)** Copyright © 20th Century Fox Film Corp. All rights reserved/Everett Collection; **488** Cat's Collection/Corbis; **489 (l)** Copyright © 2009 Tread Lightly!, Inc. Reproduced with permission; **489 (r)** Paul J. Richards/AFP/Getty Images; **515** Copyright © 2009 Amy Dion. Reproduced with permission; **520** John Wilkes Studio/Corbis; **530** Henny Ray Abrams/AP Images; **540** Mark Lennihan/AP Images; **550** David Alan Harvey/Magnum; **558** Rich Pedroncelli/AP Images; **572** Ty Milford/Aurora/Getty Images; **586** Debra Reid/AP Images; **604** Paul Sakuma/AP Images; **622** Peter Cade/Getty Images; **636** Kuni/AP Images; **656** *Portrait of Niccolo Machiavelli* (ca. 1560), Santi di Tito. Oil on canvas. Palazzo Vecchio (Palazzo della Signoria) Florence, Italy/The Bridgeman Art Library International; **712** Peter Marlow/Magnum; **720** Tom Leininger/The Journal and Courier/AP Images.

Text Credits

Margaret A. Miller. "The Privileges of the Parents." From *Change: The Magazine of Higher Learning* 40, January-February 2006, page 6. Reprinted by permission of the publisher, Taylor & Francis. www.informaworld.com.

Zak Moore. "Defying the Nalgene." From the *Dartmouth*, August 17, 2007. Copyright © 2007. Used with permission of The Dartmouth.

Charles Murray. "What's Wrong with Vocational School?" First published in the *Wall Street Journal*, January 17, 2007. Reprinted by permission of the author.

National Anti-Vivisection Society. "Animals in Scientific Research." Posted on www.navs.org. © 2004. Reprinted by permission.

National Immigration Law Center. FACT SHEET: "Why Denying Driver's Licenses to Undocumented Immigrants Harms Public Safety and Makes Our Communities Less Secure" Used with permission of the National Immigration Law Center. www.nile.org.

Natural Resources Defense Council. "Artic National Wildlife Refuge: Why Trash an American Treasure for a Tiny Percentage of Our Oil Needs?" Reprinted with permission from the Natural Resources Defense Council.

Naugatuck Valley Community College. "Distance Learning." Copyright © 2001–2009 Naugatuck Valley Community College. Reprinted with permission of Naugatuck Valley Community College Distance Learning Department. All rights reserved.

"Non-Issue Needs No Law." From *Contra Costa Times*, September 18, 2000. Reprinted by permission.

Linda Pastan. "Ethics." From *Waiting for My Life* by Linda Pastan. Copyright © 1981 by Linda Pastan. Used by permission of W.W. Norton & Company.

Rebecca Perl. "The Last Disenfranchised Class." Reprinted with permission from the November 24, 2003 issue of the *Nation*. For subscription information, call 1-800-333-8536. Portions of each week's *Nation* magazine can be accessed at http://www.thenation.com.

Robert T. Perry. "Real Education." First published in *Inside Higher Ed*, August 21, 2008. Used with permission of Robert T. Perry.

Pharinet. "Is College for Everyone?" From www.associatecontent.com. Copyright © 2007 by Associated Content. Reproduced with permission of Associated Content in the format Textbook via Copyright Clearance Center.

T. Boone Pickens. "My Plan to Escape the Grip of Foreign Oil." Originally published in the *Wall Street Journal*, July 9, 2008. Used by permission of the author.

Fielding Poe. "Watch Out for Stereotypes of Labor Unions." From the *Press Journal*. www.home.earthlink.net. Reprinted with permission.

Richard A. Posner. "The Truth about Plagiarism: It's Usually a Minor Offense and Can Have Social Value." Originally published in *Newsday*, May 18, 2003. Used by permission of the author.

Rajeev Ravisankar. "Sweatshop Oppression." First published in the *Lantern* (Ohio State student newspaper), April 19, 2006. Reprinted by permission of the author.

Marjorie O. Rendell. "U.S. Needs an Educated Citizenry." From the *Philadelphia Inquirer*, September 15, 2008. Copyright © 2009. Used with permission of Philadelphia Inquirer. All rights reserved.

Jessica Robbins. "Letter to the Editor: Don't Withhold Violent Games." First published in *Ka Leo O Hawaii*, October 22, 2003. Copyright © 2008 Ka Leo O Hawaii. Reprinted by permission.

Llewellyn H. Rockwell, Jr. "Legalize Drunk Driving." From *WorldNetDaily*, November 2, 2000. Copyright © 1997–2010. Reprinted with permission of the publisher, WorldNetDaily.com Inc. All rights reserved.

William Saletan. "Please Do Not Feed the Humans." From *Slate.com*, September 2, 2006. Copyright © 2006, Washingtonpost.Newsweek Interactive Company, LLC. All Rights Reserved. Used with permission.

Peter Schmidt. "At the Elite Colleges—Dim White Kids." First posted on www.boston.com. September 9, 2007. Reprinted by permission of the author.

Robert Schneider. "The Attack of the Pod People." First published in the *Chronicle Review*, December 8, 2006, page 5, vol. 53, #16. Reprinted by permission of the author.

Christine Schoefer. "Harry Potter's Girl Trouble." This article first appeared in *Salon.com*, January 12, 2000, at http://www.salon.com. An online version remains in the *Salon* archives. Reprinted with permission.

Arnold Schwarzenegger. "An Immigrant Writes." First published in the *Wall Street Journal*, April 10, 2006. Courtesy of the Office of Governer Arnold Schwarzenegger.

Carolyn Foster Segal. "Copy This." First published in *Chronicle Review*, September 15, 2006, Volume 53, Issue 4, page B5. Reprinted by permission of the author.

John Seigenthaler. "A False Wikipedia 'Biography.'" First published in *USA Today*, November 29, 2005. Reprinted by permission of the author.

Fabienne Serriere. "Teaching via iPod" by Fabienne Serriere, TWAW; a trademark of AOL LLC. From the Unofficial Apple Weblog (TUAW). Copyright © 2003–2009, Weblogs, Inc., a member of the Weblogs, Inc. Network. Used with permission. All rights reserved.

Jack Shafer. "Sidebar: Comparing the Copy." From *Slate.com*, March 5, 2008. © Copyright 2008, Washingtonpost.Newsweek Interactive Company, LLC. All rights reserved. Used with permission.

John M. Shalikashvili. "Second Thoughts on Gays in the Military." From the *New York Times*, January 2, 2007, Op-Ed. Copyright © 2007 The New York Times. Reprinted by permission. All rights reserved.

James Sherk. "Do Americans Today Still Need Labor Unions?" First posted on www.heritage.com. April 1, 2008. Reprinted by permission of the author.

Jessica Silver-Greenberg. "Majoring in Credit-Card Debt." First published in *Business Week*, September 4, 2007. Copyright 2000–2008 by The McGraw-Hill Companies Inc. Reprinted with permission. All rights reserved.

SUBJECT INDEX

accuracy of sources, evaluating, 221–23, 232–33

active reading. *See* reading arguments

ad hominem fallacy (personal attack), 114–15

advertisements, citing, MLA style, 268

afterword of book, citing, MLA style, 270

allegory, 657

allusions, considering in rhetorical analysis, 78

analogy, weak, as logical fallacy, 114

analogy, argument by, 453–79
    favorable and unfavorable comparisons in, 456
    key words in, 454
    like and *as* in, 461
    limitations of, 455
    purpose of, 454
    structure of, 457
    student writings, 457–63
    weak analogy, avoiding, 455–56

annotating
    tips for, 42–43, 43
    visual arguments, 60

anthology, citing, MLA style, 270

antithesis, 193

APA documentation, 721–33
    Digital Object Identifier (DOI), 724–25
    example of, 727–33
    Internet sources, 724–25
    parenthetical references, 721–22
    references, 722–25

appeals
    to logic/emotion/authority. *See ethos; logos; pathos*
    rhetorical analysis of, 75–76
    unfair, avoiding, 205–6
    in visual arguments, 55–59

appeal to doubtful authority fallacy, 119–20

argumentative essays, 189–216
    by analogy, 453–79
    audience, considering, 194
    authors of. *See* writers of arguments
    background information in, 201
    causal, 353–83
    credibility, establishing, 203–4
    by definition, 315–51
    editing and proofreading, 211

ethical, 481–516
evaluation, 385–413
evidence in, 194–97, 208
example of, 212–16
fairness in, 204–5
formal outline for, 202–3
induction and deduction, use of, 202
informal outline for, 192
literary, 713–19
proposal, 417–50
reading, 34–48
refutation, 197–200
revising, 208–10
source material, incorporating in, 258–61
subordination and coordination in, 495–96
taking a stand, 193
thesis statements, 193, 200–201
title for, 211
tone of, 204
topic selection, 190–93
transitional words and phrases, 207
visuals, 211

arguments. *See also* argumentative essays
    critical response to, 48–49
    debatable statements of, 5–7
    deductive, 91–102
    defined, 5
    encountering in daily life, 3
    forms of, 4–5
    inductive, 102–12
    oral arguments, 160–73
    and persuasion, 7–9
    rhetorical analysis of, 68–87
    Rogerian, 146–52
    structure and parts of, 12–14
    Toulmin logic, 153–60
    visual, 53–65

Aristotle, 7–8

Art of Rhetoric, The (Aristotle), 8

as, like, in comparisons, 461

audience
    for argumentative essay, 194
    considering in rhetorical analysis, 72–73
    and oral arguments, 162, 165

authority. *See also* sources; writers of arguments
    appeal to. *See ethos*
    appeal to doubtful authority fallacy, 119–20

background information, 201

backing, in Toulmin logic, 154–55

bandwagon appeal (*ad populum*), 122–23

begging the question, 113

beliefs, statements of, 5–6

bias
    confirmation bias, 205, 235–36
    detecting in sources, 196–97
    print sources, evaluating for, 224
    Web sites, evaluating for, 235

blog posts and comments
    citing, APA style, 725
    citing, MLA style, 272

books
    online, citing, APA style, 725
    online, citing, MLA style, 272
    print, citing, APA style, 723–24
    print, citing, MLA style, 269–71

brackets, quotations, for added or changed words, 260

brainstorming, 191–92

cartoons and comic strips, citing, MLA style, 268

casebooks, 573–655

causal arguments, 353–83
    causal chain, organizing as, 359
    comparatives and superlatives in, 392
    key words in, 360
    post hoc reasoning, avoiding, 360
    purpose of, 354
    reason is because, the, avoiding, 365
    structure of, 362
    student writings, 361–67

cause and effect, 357–62
    causal chains, 359
    contributory causes, 357–58
    immediate causes, 358–59
    main cause, identifying, 357–58
    remote causes, 359

chapters of book, citing, MLA style, 270

circular reasoning, 113–14

citation indexes, 223

claims, in Toulmin logic, 153–54

classic arguments, 657–711

common ground
    defined, 147
    establishing, 204

common knowledge, citing, 266, 284

739

foreword of book, citing, MLA style, 270

formal (dictionary) definition, 317

formal arguments, 4

formal outline, for argumentative essay, 202–3

freewriting, 191

generalization
hasty, 105, 115–16
of inductive arguments, 104–6
sweeping, 115–16

Google, writers of arguments, researching on, 70

government documents, 273

grounds, in Toulmin logic, 153–55

hanging indents, 267

hasty generalization, 105, 115–16

headnotes, considering in rhetorical analysis, 70

highlighting, 39–42
tips for, 40
visual arguments, 60

identifying tags
to indicate source information, 259–60, 288–89
verbs in, 259

immediate causes, 358–59

inductive arguments, 102–12
conclusions drawn from, 104
evidence/observations in, 102–6
example of, 110–12
inductive structure for essay, 202
inferences, 104–5
problems related to, 105–6
scientific method as, 103
structure of, 110

inferences
in inductive arguments, 104–5
inductive leap, 105

informal arguments, 4–5

informal outline, for argumentative essay, 192

instructor feedback, 209

Internet. *See also* Web sites
APA documentation, 724–25
MLA Works Cited, 271–73
and plagiarism, 283
sources, problems of, 231–32

introduction of arguments
argument by analogy, 457
argument by definition, 318
causal arguments, 362
ethical arguments, 491
evaluation arguments, 388
literary arguments, 715
proposal arguments, 427
thesis statement in, 12

introduction of book, citing, MLA style, 270

irrelevant evidence, 106

is where, is when, 321–22

journals
online, citing, APA style, 724–25
online, citing, MLA style, 272, 273
print, citing, APA style, 723
print, citing, MLA style, 267

laws, versus ethics, 484–87

legal cases, citing, MLA style, 273

letters to the editor, citing, MLA style, 268

like, as, in comparisons, 461

literary arguments, 713–19
argumentative thesis in, 713–14
citing, MLA style, 716
conventions used, 715–16
documentation style for, 716
evidence in, 714–15
plot summary, avoiding, 715
purpose of, 713
structure of, 715
student writings, 716–19

literary criticism, 715

logic
appeal to. *See logos*
and deductive reasoning, 91–102
fallacies of. *See* logical fallacies
and inductive reasoning, 102–12
logical arguments, examples of, 128–37
study of, reasons for, 90

logical fallacies, 113–23
ad hominem fallacy (personal attack), 114–15
analogy, weak, 114
appeal to doubtful authority, 119–20
bandwagon appeal (*ad populum*), 122–23
begging the question, 113

circular reasoning, 113–14

either/or fallacy (false dilemma), 116–17

equivocation, 117

generalization, hasty or sweeping, 115–16

non sequitur (it does not follow), 121–22

post hoc, ergo proper hoc (after this, therefore because of this), 121

red herring, 117–18

slippery-slope, 118–19

statistics, misuse of, 120–21

you also (*tu quoque*), 119

logos
considering in rhetorical analysis, 75
defined, 8–9
and visual arguments, 55–57

magazines
online, citing, MLA style, 273
print, citing, APA style, 723
print, citing, MLA style, 267–68

main cause, identifying, 359

major premise
enthymemes, 95
syllogisms, 91–93

metaphors, considering in rhetorical analysis, 78

middle term, 93

minor premise
enthymemes, 95
syllogisms, 91–93

MLA documentation, 265–79
example of, 274–79
for literary arguments, 716
parenthetical references, 265–66
Works Cited, 266–73
Internet sources, 271–73
print sources, 267–71

multivolume work, citing, MLA style, 271

newspapers
online, citing, MLA style, 273
print, citing, APA style, 723

non sequitur (it does not follow), 121–22

objectivity
lack of. *See* bias
print sources, evaluating for, 224
Web sites, evaluating for, 234–35

operational definitions, 318

INDEX OF TITLES AND AUTHORS